Professional Chef

LEVEL 2 DIPLOMA

Gary Hunter & Terry Tinton

DELMAR
CENGAGE Learning™

Australia • Brazil • Japan • Korea • Mexico • Singapore • Spain • United Kingdom • United States

Professional Chef Level 2 Diploma
Second edition
Gary Hunter and Terry Tinton

Publishing Director: Linden Harris

Commissioning Editor: Lucy Mills

Development Editor: Helen Green

Editorial Assistant: Claire Napoli

Project Editor: Lucy Arthy

Production Controller: Eyvett Davis

Marketing Manager: Lauren Redwood

Typesetter: MPS Limited,
 a Macmillan Company

Cover design: HCT Creative

Text design: Design Deluxe

For product information and technology assistance, contact
emea.info@cengage.com.

For permission to use material from this text or product,
and for permission queries,
email **emea.permissions@cengage.com.**

This work is adapted from *Professional Chef Level 2 Diploma* by *Gary Hunter, Terry Tinton, Patrick Carey and Steve Walpole* published by Delmar a division of Cengage Learning, Inc. © 2007.

British Library Cataloguing-in-Publication Data
A catalogue record for this book is available from the British Library.

ISBN: 978-1-4080-3909-0

Cengage Learning EMEA

Cheriton House, North Way, Andover, Hampshire, SP10 5BE
United Kingdom

Cengage Learning products are represented in Canada by Nelson Education, Ltd.

For your lifelong learning solutions, visit **www.cengage.co.uk**

Purchase your next print book, e-book or e-chapter at
www.cengagebrain.com

Printed in China by RR Donnelley
Print Number: 03   Print Year: 2014

Contents

About the authors v
Acknowledgements vi
Foreword viii
A quick reference guide to the qualification ix
About the book x
Introduction xii
CourseMate xiii

1 The hospitality industry and your role as a chef 1

1GEN4.1 Organize your own work

1GEN4.2 Support the work of your team

1GEN4.3 Contribute to your own learning and development

Unit 104 Work effectively as part of a hospitality team

Unit 201 Investigate the catering and hospitality industry

Unit 205 Catering operations, costs and menu planning

Unit 206 Applying workplace skills

2 Health, safety and food hygiene in catering and hospitality 39

Unit 1 GEN1 Maintain a safe, hygienic and secure working environment

Unit 2 GEN3 Maintain food safety when storing, preparing and cooking food

Unit 202 Food safety in catering

Unit 203 Health and safety in catering and hospitality

3 Cold food preparations, starters and salads 69

2FPC15 Prepare and present food for cold presentation

Unit 208 Prepare and cook fruit and vegetables

Unit 212 (Outcome 4) prepare and cook eggs

4 Stocks, sauces and soups 103

Unit 636 (2FPC1) Prepare, cook and finish basic hot sauces

Unit 637 (2FPC2) Prepare, cook and finish basic soups

Unit 638 (2FPC3) Make basic stocks

Unit 207 Prepare and cook stocks, soups and sauces

5 Pulses, grains, pasta and rice 184

2FPC6 Prepare, cook and finish basic pulse dishes

2FPC12 Prepare, cook and finish basic grain dishes

2FPC5 Prepare, cook and finish basic pasta dishes

2FPC4 Prepare, cook and finish basic rice dishes

Unit 212 Prepare and cook rice, pasta, grains and egg dishes

6 Eggs 243

2FPC8 Prepare, cook and finish basic egg dishes

Unit 212 Prepare and cook rice, pasta, grains and egg dishes

7   **Fish and shellfish** 257

Unit 2FPC1 Prepare, cook and finish basic fish dishes

Unit 2FPC2 Prepare, cook and finish basic shellfish dishes

Unit 211 Prepare and cook fish and shellfish

8   **Poultry** 307

Unit 2FP4 Prepare poultry for basic dishes

Unit 2FC4 Cook and finish basic poultry dishes

Unit 210 Prepare and cook poultry

9   **Game** 325

Unit 2FPC5 Cook and finish basic game dishes

Unit 209 Prepare and cook meat and offal

Unit 210 Prepare and cook poultry

10   **Meat and offal** 341

Unit 2FC3 Prepare, cook and finish meat dishes

Unit 2FPC6 Preparation and cooking of offal dishes

Unit 209 Prepare and cook meat and offal

11   **Vegetables, fruits and vegetable protein** 388

Unit 2FP7 Prepare vegetables for basic dishes

Unit 2FC7 Cook and finish basic vegetable protein dishes

Unit 208 Prepare and cook fruit and vegetables

12   **Pastes, tarts and pies** 452

Unit 2FPC10 Prepare, cook and finish basic pastry products

Unit 213 Produce paste products

13   **Breads and dough** 489

Unit 2FPC9 Prepare, cook and finish basic bread and dough products

Unit 216 Produce fermented dough products

14   **Desserts** 522

Unit 2FPC14 Prepare, cook and finish basic hot and cold desserts

Unit 213 Prepare and cook desserts and puddings

15   **Cakes, biscuits and sponges** 586

Unit 2FPC11 Prepare, cook and finish basic cakes, sponges and scones

Unit 215 Produce biscuit, cake and sponge products

16   **Healthy foods and special diets** 612

Unit 2FPC13 Prepare, cook and finish healthier dishes

Unit 204 Healthier foods and special diets

Glossary of terms 624
Index 629

About the authors

Gary Hunter *Head of Culinary Arts, Food and Beverage Service at Westminster Kingsway College*

Gary has 16 years' experience of teaching within further, higher and vocational education. He has travelled the world as a consultant for Barry Callebaut, giving seminars on chocolate, patisserie and classical cuisine. He is also an experienced international culinary competitor and judge. As a leading chef patissier in the UK, Gary has won numerous awards and competition medals and has worked with and trained many of today's successful chefs. Gary has recently helped to write the City & Guilds Diploma in Professional Cookery Qualification at Levels 1, 2 and 3 and has received an award for this work.

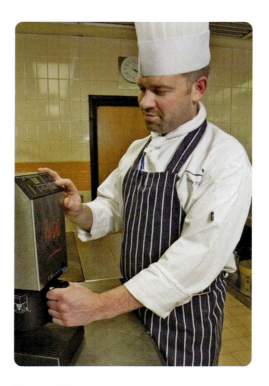

Terry Tinton *Programme Manager in Culinary Arts at Westminster Kingsway College*

Terry has seven years, experience teaching within further, higher and vocational education.

A successful professional chef with many international awards in kitchen, larder and patisserie, Terry has held senior chef positions in some of the best hotels in the world as well as Michelin-starred restaurants.

Terry holds the Advanced Hygiene Award and is an accomplished author.

Acknowledgements

The Authors would like to thank the following:

Sarah-Jane Hunter	Charlotte Hunter	
Estelle Hunter	Hilary Hunter	
Phillip Hunter	Paul Hunter	
Patricia Long	John Long	

Dom Healy, Jimmy Mair and Martin Jermy for their inspiration

Margaret Tinton	Lewis Tinton	Yvonne Hall
Terence Tinton	Kate Tinton	Liam Lane
Rosaleen Lane	Andy Tinton	Paul Lane

College acknowledgements:

Andy Wilson	Geoff Booth	Ian Wild
Barry Jones	Jose Souto	Simon Stocker
Alexandra Roberts	Javier Mercado	Vince Cottam

Contributors to the book:

Paul Jervis, Jonathan Warner, Andrew Lansdell and Allan Drummond

The Publisher wishes to thank the following for granting permission to use images:

istockphoto; Shutterstock; Dreamstime Photos; Russum's; Nisbetts.

In addition we would like to thank Nathan Allan and Laura Pinnell of Nathan Allan Photography for providing commissioned photography.

Web Address: **www.nathanallanphotography.com**

Video Content provided by Ken Franklin and Video 4 Ltd. Web Address: **www.video4.co.uk**

Photo Research and Video/Photo Project Management was provided by Jason Newman, Annalisa de Hassek, Bradley Hearn and Alexander Goldberg of Media Selectors Ltd. Web Address: **www.mediaselectors.com**

This book is endorsed by:

BRITISH CULINARY FEDERATION

National Member of the
World Association of Chefs' Societies

British Culinary Federation

Craft Guild of Chefs

The Master Chefs of Great Britain

For providing the Nutritional information for the Recipes:

KitMan

Olympus Associates specialises in providing consultancy and management services to the catering industry. With a unique kitchen management system called *The KitMan System* – the company is able to assist operations in controlling food costs and managing their food service operations more effectively.

The KitMan System is a food cost control and kitchen management system used by many leading catering establishments throughout the UK in hospitality, healthcare and education markets.

The company has a specialist version for the education sector, and has working partnerships with many catering colleges and universities throughout the United Kingdom and Ireland using the program, including the authors of this book, it is not only used for controlling their own food costs, but also as a teaching tool for the catering and hospitality students.

KitMan provides valuable detailed analysis of costs per class, per student and is ideal for use for the commercial activities of a college, including refectory and restaurant services.

We are pleased to be associated with Cengage Learning and to continue our relationships with the Hospitality & Catering departments of colleges.

For more information please visit **www.kitman.com**

Notes on Nutritional Information and recipe processing

Please note the Nutritional Information is for guidance only and may not necessarily match the final result. The sample ingredients are based on average contents. The Nutritional Information is calculated **per portion**.

The final nutritional content can be effected by any of the following factors: seasonality; storage method; storage time; brand, breed, variety; cooking method; cooking time; regeneration method. Wastage and yield may also result in the final nutritional content being lower than the results shown.

Where two alternative ingredients have been listed, the first has been used wherever possible.

If an ingredient is listed as optional it has been included if it appears in the main ingredient listing, where possible, but has not if it appears in the method or Chef's Tips part of the original recipe.

Foreword

I loved my time at Westminster College, there wasn't a day that went by without me being totally inspired by something or other.

If you're planning on becoming a professional chef, this book, along with the rest in the series, is going to become your best friend! You won't want to be without it. You'll find it an essential learning tool, whether you're just starting out or whether you're already working in a restaurant kitchen and need a catch-up. The chefs who have given their time and expertise in support of it are all superbly qualified and they've put together a concise, step-by-step guide to pretty much anything food-wise that you'll come across in most restaurant kitchens.

Becoming a chef is bloody hard work and it requires dedication, stamina and a hell of a lot of passion. But if you want to become a half-decent chef, you also need to learn the core skills to start you off on a great career journey for life. You've taken the first steps. This book will now help to provide you with a strong platform for learning how to become a talented chef.

Good luck, all the best!

Jamie Oliver

© David Loftus

A quick reference guide to the qualification

When people previously qualified as chefs there would have been a wide range of routes and options that could have been taken to achieve this. Some may have followed the NVQ curriculum and that could have been as a full-time college student, part-time college student or through an industry based apprenticeship. Others may never have followed a formal training path at all and reached the qualification by using work-based learning.

The National Vocational Qualification has provided the main curriculum route for industry and College-based training for many years. Historically, the ways in which these qualifications were structured meant that students or trainees would complete a variety of compulsory – or mandatory units and then could choose from other options or additional units in order to complete their qualification.

That has now changed. There are now two types of accredited qualification:

1   the VRQ

2   the NVQ.

The VRQ Diploma or vocationally related qualification is specifically designed for college-based delivery on either a full or part-time basis. There are a variety of qualifications designed to meet the VRQ criteria and these can provide students with practical experience and an insight to what happens in this diverse hospitality industry. The philosophy behind this Diploma is the principle that a chef needs to have a sound foundation of high quality skills and to be able to apply these skills across a wide range of kitchen activities using a broad variety of commodities.

The NVQ Diploma, as it is now called, is a qualification that provides the learner with a 'job ready' experience. That currently means that for students who want to be trained in an apprenticeship; this will be the only option available to them. However, many colleges have chosen the VRQ Diploma as the preferred route and any students enrolled on this type of programme, can expect that at least part of the course will be on a work placement out in industry.

The other main changes relate to the value or weighting of the individual units that make up the professional cookery qualification at all NVQ and VRQ Diploma levels. Now, both VRQs and NVQs are required to meet the Qualifications and Credit Framework (QCF).

The different units currently have a varying amount of credit values. In order to complete an NVQ Diploma the learner will complete all mandatory units and make up the outstanding balance of credits by choosing from optional units that will make up at least the minimum number of credits that are required to gain full certification. The VRQ Diploma requires the student to complete all units to achieve the full qualification.

People 1st, the Sector Skills Council, are the representative organization responsible for defining the standards for the hospitality industry. The National Occupational Standards (NOS) that they produce are then taken and used by awarding bodies such as City & Guilds or EDI to create the qualifications that you take part in. So in simple terms People 1st produce the standards that you work towards and the awarding bodies define the conditions and specifications against which you are assessed.

All NOS have a common structure and design. That is to say they all follow a particular format for all vocational sectors. Each vocational qualification is structured in the same way and is made up from a number of grouped components; called units and elements. The units are structured in a standard format and comprise the Unit reference number and title, which you will find aligned to each chapter in this book to help you navigate the information you need. The learning outcomes specify the practical skills and underpinning knowledge to be covered in the range, which will provide you with the detail of each learning outcome.

About the book

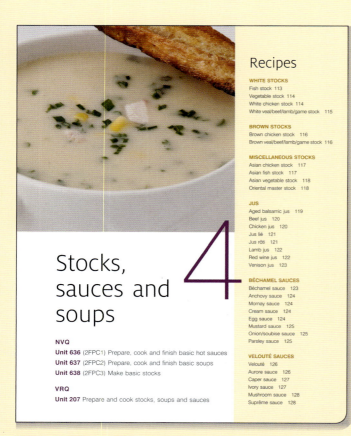

Recipes

WHITE STOCKS
Fish stock 113
Vegetable stock 114
White chicken stock 114
White veal/beef/lamb/game stock 115

BROWN STOCKS
Brown chicken stock 116
Brown veal/beef/lamb/game stock 116

MISCELLANEOUS STOCKS
Asian chicken stock 117
Asian fish stock 117
Asian vegetable stock 118
Oriental master stock 118

JUS
Aged balsamic jus 119
Beef jus 120
Chicken jus 120
Jus lié 121
Jus rôti 121
Lamb jus 122
Red wine jus 122
Venison jus 123

BÉCHAMEL SAUCES
Béchamel sauce 123
Anchovy sauce 124
Mornay sauce 124
Cream sauce 124
Egg sauce 124
Mustard sauce 125
Onion/soubise sauce 125
Parsley sauce 125

VELOUTÉ SAUCES
Velouté 126
Aurore sauce 126
Caper sauce 127
Ivory sauce 127
Mushroom sauce 128
Suprême sauce 128

Stocks, sauces and soups 4

NVQ

Unit 636 (2FPC1) Prepare, cook and finish basic hot sauces
Unit 637 (2FPC2) Prepare, cook and finish basic soups
Unit 638 (2FPC3) Make basic stocks

VRQ

Unit 207 Prepare and cook stocks, soups and sauces

Mapped to the qualification each chapter addresses a specific unit of the Level 2 Diploma in Professional Cookery qualification.

> **TASK** Research the following:
> What country does gravadlax originate from?
> Why is the salmon pressed during curing?
> As the salmon cures liquid is produced – what is this liquid called?

Task boxes provide additional tasks for you to try out.

> **HEALTH & SAFETY** Make sure the temperature in your refrigerator is 5 °C or under for best practice.

Health & Safety tip boxes draw your attention to important health and safety information.

> **SOURCING** The vegetables should be selected locally if possible and be used when in season.

Sourcing boxes give advice and tips on sourcing ingredients for recipes.

> **CHEF'S TIP** An à la Grecque salad can be made and stored in a sealed air tight jar for a week, this will allow the flavours to develop and produce a better product.

Chef's Tip boxes share author's experience in the catering industry, with helpful suggestions for how you can improve your skills.

> **HEALTHY OPTION** To produce lower fat versions try folding in low fat yoghurt into half the Caesar dressing.

Healthy Option boxes indicate where ingredients can be substituted to make a recipe healthier.

> **WEB LINK** Try using different varieties of tomatoes for this salad; try looking at the web link for ideas.
> **http://www.foodsubs.com/Tomtom.html**

Web Link boxes suggest websites to for further research and understanding of a topic.

Learning Objectives at the start of each chapter explain key skills and knowledge you need to understand by the end of the chapter.

> **LEARNING OBJECTIVES**
>
> The aim of this unit is to enable the candidate to develop skills and implement knowledge in the preparation and cookery principles of stocks, soups and sauces. This will also include materials, ingredients and equipment.
> At the end of this chapter you will be able to:
>
> - Identify a variety of stocks, soups and sauces.
> - Understand the use of relative ingredients in stocks, soups and sauce cookery.
> - State the quality points of various stock, soup and sauce commodities and their uses in a selection of dishes.
> - Prepare, cook and finish a variety of stocks, soups and sauces.
> - Identify the storage procedures of stocks, soups and sauces.
> - Be competent at preparing and cooking a range of stocks, soups and sauces.
> - Be able to state healthy options for stocks, soups and sauces
> - Describe what to do if problems with ingredients occur.
> - Describe safe and correct use of alcohol in sauces and why it is used.

TEST YOURSELF

1 Name four different types of:
   a. buffet
   b. charcuterie

2 Which salad is the odd one out and why?
   a. Waldorf, Russian, beetroot
   b. Oil, vinegar, coriander (hint: à la Grecque salad)

3 What is the ratio of oil to vinegar when making vinaigrette?

4 List three derivatives of mayonnaise.

5 Which cheese is traditionally used in croque monsieur and which herb is used when making fresh pesto?

6 Caviar is the roe of which fish and what is pumpernickel a type of?

7 What is the difference between a buck and Welsh rarebit?

8 What are the three main ingredients when curing salmon for gravadlax?

9 What meat is used in a bookmaker sandwich and what fish is used in a Caesar salad?

10 What nuts are used in:
   a. Waldorf salad
   b. Coronation chicken
   c. Satay sauce?

11 What does BLT stand for and what are terrines named after?

Test Your Knowledge questions are provided at the end of each chapter. You can use questions to test your learning and prepare for assessments.

Step-by-step: Rolling pasta

1. Carefully roll the pasta through the machine on the widest setting; this should be done twice.

2. Gradually lower the roller settings until a thin smooth sheet of pasta is formed.

3. Join the two ends of the pasta together and continue to roll the pasta, this technique will speed up the process. There is no need to keep feeding the pasta back into the top of the machine.

Step-by-step sequences illustrate each process and provide an easy-to-follow guide.

Potted duck confit

Ingredients	Makes approximately 4 portions	Makes approximately 10 portions
Duck confit (see page 322)	1 leg	2 legs
Duck fat		
Orange juice and zest	1 each	2 each
Toasted ciabatta slices	8	20
Good quality salt and pepper	To taste	To taste

energy	cal	fat	sat fat	carb	sugar	protein	fibre
3,682 kJ	881 kcal	71.8 g	22.1 g	40.6 g	3.5 g	22.2 g	3.9 g

Recipes provide examples of the different cooking processes for you to try out.

Guest Chef

Cullen skink

Chef David Keir   *Centre* Aberdeen College

The name 'Cullen skink' comes from the fishing village of Cullen, in Morayshire. 'Skink' is a soup made originally from a shin of beef. But in this recipe for a rich tasty soup, the main ingredient is Finnan haddock. It also has potatoes, onions and milk in the recipe and is finished with parsley and cream. It can either be served with oatcakes or butteries. It can be served either as a starter or as a meal in itself.

Ingredients	Makes 3–4 portions
Finnan haddock	1 large
Onion (peeled and chopped)	1 large
Potatoes (peeled and chopped)	750 g
Butter	25 g
Milk (full fat)	450 ml
To finish the soup	
Double cream	100 ml
Salt and freshly ground black pepper	To taste
Parsley chopped	To taste

METHOD OF WORK

1 Place the Finnan haddock in a stainless steel pan with enough cold water to just cover the fish.

2 Bring the water to the boil and gently simmer for 5–10 minutes until the fish is just cooked.

3 Take off the stove, cover and set aside for 20 minutes.

4 Gently take out the fish, skin the haddock and remove all the bones. Flake into large pieces, cover and set aside until the potatoes are cooked.

5 Using the same pan and cooking liquor from the fish add the onions and potatoes, cover and cook for about 15–20 minutes, until the vegetables are soft.

6 Take the pan from the stove and roughly mash the potatoes and onions with the butter. Do not mash until smooth, as you need some texture in the finished soup.

7 Add the milk and bring to the boil then simmer for a couple of minutes.

8 Add the fish and cream then reheat gently for 3–4 minutes until hot. Season lightly with salt and pepper, serve in warm bowls, sprinkle with some chopped parsley.

9 Serve with Aberdeen butteries (rowies).

Guest Chef Recipes provide examples of the different cooking processes from leading industry figures from college throughout the UK.

VIDEO CLIP A blocks man at Billingsgate fish market.

Video Clips if your college adopts Coursemate Professional Chef Level 2, will enable you to view video demonstrations of key processes online.

Introduction

The intention of this book is to guide you to the skills and introduce the foundation knowledge required to become a chef in the hospitality and catering industry.

Cooking, serving and eating food has become a major communication practice across the world. Food is prepared as a gift, as a medicine, to create friendship, to nourish, to celebrate, to generate business and to stimulate happiness. The chef now has the capacity to communicate through their food, initiate fulfilment and joy and conceive relationships.

The basic principles of being a worthy professional chef are to combine good ingredients with sound techniques, skills and basic knowledge of culinary science with attention to detail. Only then will you have the basis to show your culinary artistry and creative talents.

This book will also illustrate some of the top chefs in this country whose talent, dedication and energy have helped them achieve a high standard of excellence in the catering industry today. They share their thoughts, recipes and experience for you to learn from. It will also provide you with an important reference point to attain the professional skills and knowledge for today's classically based modern cuisine.

Enjoy learning and enjoy cooking!

Gary Hunter

CourseMate

CourseMate is a unique blended learning solution. Watch student comprehension soar as your class works with the printed textbook and the textbook-specific website. CourseMate includes: an interactive eBook; interactive teaching and learning tools including videos, games and quizzes and Engagement Tracker, a first-of-its-kind tool that monitors student engagement in the course.

Engaging, Trackable, Affordable

Professional Chef Level 2 CourseMate

Professional Chef Level 2 CourseMate brings course concepts to life with interactive learning and study tools that support the printed textbook. Professional Chef Level 2 CourseMate goes beyond the book to deliver what you need!

INTERACTIVE LEARNING TOOLS

The Professional Chef Level 2 CourseMate interactive learning tools include:

- Quizzes
- Games
- Videos demonstrations of recipes
- Flashcards
- Bonus recipes
- Interactive Food Map of the British Isles

PowerPoints, Lesson Plans, the Learner Engagement Tracker and other teaching resources are included in the Coursemate package for the instructor.

INTERACTIVE EBOOK

In addition to interactive learning tools, Professional Chef Level 2 CourseMate includes an interactive eBook. You can take notes, highlight, search and interact with embedded media specific to your book. Use it as a supplement to the printed text, or as a substitute – the choice is up to you with CourseMate.

To purchase access to CourseMate as a learner go to: www.cengagebrain.co.uk/shop/isbn/9781408048245

To purchase access to CourseMate as an instructor or institution please contact emea.fesales@cengage.com for more information.

The hospitality industry and your role as a chef

NVQ

1GEN4.1 Organize your own work

1GEN4.2 Support the work of your team

1GEN4.3 Contribute to your own learning and development

VRQ

Unit 104 Work effectively as part of a hospitality team

Unit 201 Investigate the catering and hospitality industry

Unit 205 Catering operations, costs and menu planning

Unit 206 Applying workplace skills

LEARNING OBJECTIVES

At the end of this chapter you will be able to:

- Understand the terms hospitality and catering.

- Compare the sectors and different types of operations in the industry.

- Describe the main features of establishments within the different sectors.

- Understand the key influences on the catering industry and its importance to the economy.

- Identify staffing structures and job roles in different establishments.

- Identify training opportunities, related qualifications and employment rights and responsibilities.

- List some of the associations related to professional cookery.

- Understand how a kitchen is organized.

- Plan menus and dishes for a variety of catering operations.

- Understand the costs within the catering industry.

- Apply basic calculations used in the costing of dishes and menus.

- Maintain a professional personal appearance.

- Follow recipes and instructions.

- Organize your work and your workplace, so that it is as efficient and clean as possible.

- Understand the importance of providing work on time and to the exact specifications.

- Identify your responsibility as a team member.

- Maintain good working relationships.

- Deliver clear and effective communication within the team.

- Deal with feedback in a positive manner.

- Plan a curriculum vitae.

- Create an efficient learning plan to develop your skills.

Introduction

This chapter will help you to develop the knowledge and understanding to apply the personal skills required within the workplace in the hospitality and catering industry. This industry requires you to have a high level of interpersonal skills, which must be maintained when working under pressure. You will explore the main functions, extent and range of the hospitality and catering industry, alongside purchasing commodities, menu planning and cost control concepts.

You will investigate what is an acceptable personal image and the types of behaviours associated with professionalism in the industry. It is also about making a constructive contribution to the work of a team and applying a variety of indispensable workplace skills.

Investigating the catering and hospitality industry

The hospitality, leisure, travel and tourism sector covers 15 industries. These are hotels, restaurants, pubs, bars and nightclubs, contract food service providers, hospitality services, membership clubs, events, gambling, travel services, tourist services, visitor attractions, hostels, holiday centres and self catering accommodation are all classified in this sector. The sector as a whole employs approximately 1.9 million people across the UK.

The definition of hospitality is the offer of a friendly and caring treatment to guests. The term catering refers to the offer of specific facilities to guests that includes the service of food and beverages.

The catering and hospitality industry is part of a wider spectrum which comes under the title of the catering, hospitality, leisure, travel and tourism sector.

Generally restaurants, bars, pubs, clubs and hotels are referred to as commercial businesses. Therefore, these establishments need to produce a profit. Catering services that are provided in schools, hospitals, colleges, universities, prisons and the armed services provide a food and beverage service to many people every day. Sometimes this type of catering is part of the public sector. These services do not always need to create a profit; however, many of these services are provided by profitable contract caterers.

The scope of business operations

SOLE PROPRIETORSHIP

A sole trading concern is the oldest form of commercial organization. This is usually a business carried, owned and run by one person. All the profits and loss accrue to the owner and therefore all assets and debts of the business are the proprietor's. The advantage of this type of business operation is that there is a potential reduced cost of doing business and the only official records required are those for HM Revenue and Customs (HMRC), National Insurance and VAT. The accounts are not made available to the public.

Self-employed

Self-employment is working for oneself rather than for another person or company. This is not the same as a business owner, although a self-employed person can operate as a sole proprietor and it is possible for someone to form a business that is only run part-time or while holding down a full-time job. This form of employment, while popular, does have several legal responsibilities. When working from home, clearance may sometimes be needed from the local authority to use part of your home as business premises. Other legal requirements can include the proper recording and accounting of financial transactions.

PARTNERSHIPS

A partnership is an arrangement where groups or individuals agree to collaborate to advance their business interests. Partners will share profits and losses. The partnership is similar to sole proprietorship in law in that all partners will stand for all the risks. Although, there are also silent partners or limited partners and these are partners who still share the profits and losses of the business, but who are not involved with the management or day-to-day running of the business. These partners usually provide capital investment to the business. The official records required are the same as a sole proprietorship and there may be certain tax benefits available, compared to a limited company, such as being able to pay tax at a later date and claim business expenses against tax.

COMPANIES

A company is a legal entity or group of people engaging in business. When a new company incorporates in Great Britain, it must register with an Executive Agency of the Department for Business, Innovation and Skills, usually known as Companies House.

There are different types of companies, the main ones are:

- **Private companies**
  A privately held company is a business that is owned by a relatively small number of members. It does not offer its company shares to the general public on stock market exchanges. However, the company's stock can be offered, traded or exchanged privately. Sometimes these companies are referred to as unquoted or unlisted companies. The leisure company Lego and knife producer Victorinox are both examples of some of Europe's largest private companies.

- **Limited liability businesses**
  These are businesses that are incorporated under the Companies law. They have 'Limited' or 'Ltd.' after their name. Private companies are often limited. This means that the liability of the owners, such as the amount they will have to pay if a business fails, is limited to a fixed value, most commonly the value of a person's investment or share in a business. If a business with limited liability is sued, then the people sue the business (plaintiff) and not its owners or investors. By contrast sole proprietors and general partnerships are each liable for all the debts of the business (they have unlimited liability). An example of a limited company is CH&Co Catering Ltd.

- **Public limited companies (plc)**
  These companies can be publicly traded on a stock exchange. Investors can purchase share certificates to own a percentage of the company. A public limited company must include the words 'public limited company' or 'plc' as part of its legal company name, e.g. Center Parcs plc.

FRANCHISES

Franchising is the practice of using another company's successful business model. A fee and set-up costs will be included so that the established franchisor is selling their name, standards, expertise and brand regulations. Two important payments are made to a franchisor:
  a. a royalty for the trade-mark; and
  b. reimbursement for the training and advisory services given to the franchisee.

These two fees may be combined in a single 'management' fee. A franchise usually lasts for a fixed time period (broken down into shorter periods, which each require renewal), and serves a specific 'territory' or area surrounding its location. One franchisee may manage several such locations. Agreements typically last from 5 to 30 years, with premature cancellations or terminations of most contracts bearing serious consequences for franchisees. A franchise is merely a temporary business investment, involving renting or leasing an opportunity, not buying a business for the purpose of ownership. It is classified as a wasting asset due to the finite term of the license. Examples of successful franchises are McDonald's, Burger King, Dominoes and Subway.

INDEPENDENT BUSINESSES

An independent business generally refers to privately owned companies (as opposed to those companies owned publicly through a distribution of shares on the exchange market). Independent businesses most commonly take the form of sole proprietorships. 'Independent' is frequently used to distinguish one-of-a-kind businesses from corporate chains or partnerships.

SMALL- TO MEDIUM-SIZED BUSINESS ENTERPRISES

Small- to medium-sized enterprises (SMEs) are companies whose headcount or turnover falls below certain limits. The European Union generally defines companies with fewer than ten employees as 'micro', those with fewer than 50 employees as 'small', such as Loves Restaurant in Birmingham, and those with fewer than 250 as 'medium', for example Alan Murchison Restaurant Ltd. In the UK as a whole, SMEs account for just over a half of all employment and they are usually private companies that will become 'plc' if they grow into large companies.

An international perspective

Business competition has become global. Managers and owners in the industry have to understand and adjust to changes in market demand for quality and value for money. This has meant an increased awareness of professionalism, training and profitability. Improved technology, communication, transport, socio-cultural understanding and awareness, economic development and competition throughout the world has contributed to globalization in the catering, hospitality, leisure, travel and tourism industry.

According to the World Travel and Tourism Council the annual gross output of the industry is greater than the gross national product of all countries except Japan and the United States of America. In many countries the hospitality and tourism industry plays a very important role in the national economy.

Industries are either multi-domestic or global. Multi-domestic industries have businesses that compete in a national market independently of the markets in other countries (such as pubs and restaurants). A global industry is where the same businesses compete with each other all over the world (such as hotel and cost sector catering companies). Companies such as Hilton and Compass pursue a global strategy which involves competing globally. They appreciate that to compete effectively they need a presence in almost every part of the world. The product is the same for each market and takes advantage of customer needs and requirements across international borders.

There are four main drivers which determine the extent and nature of globalization in an industry: market, cost, government policy and competition.

The catering, hospitality, leisure, travel and tourism industry in the UK

There are currently around 146 000 businesses in the hospitality, leisure, travel and tourism sector in Great Britain, operating from 206 000 outlets. The hospitality, leisure, travel and tourism sector is one of the UK's largest employers. It employs almost two million people, this equates to 7 per cent of all jobs within the UK. The sector accounts for 4.5 per cent of the UK's total economic output. The economic significance of the wider 'visitor economy', in which many sector businesses operate, is even greater. The visitor economy is estimated to contribute over 8 per cent of the UK's Gross Domestic Product (GDP), approximately £114 billion. GDP is the market value of all final goods and services made within the borders of a country in a year.

This industry benefits from expanding economic conditions. Generally as personal disposable income grows the leisure industry (of which catering and hospitality has a significant role) will expand as people broaden their leisure experiences. However, when there is a downturn in the economy, the leisure sector will suffer as people consider where they can save money.

We can further explore this industry by looking at the various activities it reaches out to. Traditionally this industry has been divided into either profit or cost sector markets. The profit sector includes restaurants, fast-food outlets, cafes, pubs, takeaway outlets and leisure and travel catering businesses. The cost sector refers to catering outlets for business and industry, education and healthcare.

TASK Each type of catering business is unique, but they all provide food and drink, employing people such as chefs, kitchen assistants, food service and bar staff. List the main industries employing the majority of these people.

Looking back to your Level 1 course or researching on the internet may help.

SIGNIFICANT INFLUENCES IMPACTING ON THE CATERING AND HOSPITALITY INDUSTRY	
Changing social trends and lifestyle choices	Corporate and global environmentalism
Cultural aspects such as celebrating occasions	Credit availability for businesses
Global recession trends (disposable income levels)	Health and well-being
Inflation	Regulation and law – tax, VAT and tourism
Global events, e.g. ash clouds, terrorism	Culinary innovation and achievements
Media influences such as TV, marketing and internet	

The hospitality services industry includes those who work in core hospitality occupations (i.e. chefs, cooks and waiting staff) and in non-hospitality industries such as schools, retail outlets and local authorities. Hospitality services are managed 'in-house'. Contract food service provision is outsourced and employees are engaged by the catering service contract employer.

Traditionally the hospitality sector is defined differently to that of the catering sector. Hospitality occupations are identified as those that provide a complete hospitality experience within a defined area such as:

- Travel (trains, planes, stations, sea travel and airports).
- Business (meetings, seminars, corporate events).
- Retail (promotions, launches, shows).
- Education (security/reception areas, events, schools).
- Healthcare (accommodation, ancillary services).
- Leisure venues (concerts, sports events, regattas, wedding and parties).
- Government and Local Authority (meetings, seminars, corporate events and launches).

Within the hospitality sector is a catering provision that directly relates to the supply and service of food and drink. This catering service can be provided in any of the above areas including restaurants, hotels, schools, hospitals, bars, nightclubs, visitor attractions and the workplace.

Identifying the products and services in hospitality

The hospitality product consists of food and beverage service, as well as other environment responsibilities such as, accommodation, atmosphere, image and concept that contribute to the overall customer experience.

The service of food and beverages is focused on the actual production, timing and delivery.

Hospitality businesses need to provide an appropriate environment within which catering and hospitality can be successfully delivered. The investment in property and equipment is substantial and will create a high fixed cost and low variable cost structure. Fixed costs are those that remain similar no matter what business is being carried out, such as bank loans, rent and salaried staff. Variable costs are those that change depending on the volume of business; such as commodities and part time staffing costs.

In general the break-even point for a hospitality business is quite high. The break-even point is the point when the whole expenditure from the business matches the income from its sales. Exceeding this level of sales will result in profit and the when the income is lower than the break-even point this will result in a loss.

CHANGES IN DEMAND FOR YOUR BUSINESS

The hospitality industry suffers from fluctuations in demand of business. This rise and fall is over a period of time and determined by your customer base. The pattern of demand is often very mixed which often makes forecasting business, outside of set calendar holidays, very difficult. This will affect the planning, resourcing and development of your business. Achieving a suitable balance between demand patterns, resource scheduling and operational capacity is a difficult task for managers in hospitality. If too many staff are on duty to cover your demand forecast, then profits will certainly suffer with too many people being paid for too little work. Being able to forecast demand in your business is a valuable skill which will play a large part in the successful continuation of your business in the hospitality industry.

DEFINING TERMS FOR BUSINESS FLUCTUATIONS	
Resourcing	Provision of food, labour, cleaning materials and equipment to undertake the job.
Demand patterns	Pattern of customer requirements, e.g. people eat out more during the weekend and holiday periods.
Scheduling	Planning and ensuring that all resources are in place when they are needed, such as commodities, staff and equipment.
Operational capacity	How much work the operation is able to cope with to deliver a consistent product at the required standard.
Fluctuation	This is the rise and flow of demand for your business due to certain elements of customer needs and situations.

The types of establishment within the industry

TASK In groups discuss the many venues people can visit in their leisure time, which require hospitality and catering services. Make a list with local examples and compare with the rest of your class.

Identify the extent of the industry by finding and listing the following businesses in each area:

- two local SME-based restaurants
- two national restaurant chains
- three multi-national contract caterers
- one independent restaurant
- one franchised food or catering operation.

The businesses you have considered offer a range of exciting jobs in hospitality, and for those with the right skills and attitude a quick career progression is on offer.

CONTRACT FOOD SERVICE

In your Level 1 course you explored the scope of the contract food service sector. Providing quality food for employees is an essential part of this sector. Contract caterers provide food and services management to customers at their place of work providing innovative and high quality services. They also provide clients with some of the finest possible executive dining facilities for boardrooms, hospitality suites and at major social and sports events. Vending is an integral part of the food and beverage operation for most modern organizations and contract caterers are developing this area to suit modern trends towards dietary requirements and ease of service.

Many industries have realized that satisfied employees work more efficiently and produce better work. So the provision of first class dining facilities and in some cases subsidized pricing so that employees can purchase food and beverages at lower prices will help to create satisfaction among employees. In some cases a 24-hour service is required for individual businesses; however the hours are more acceptable than other areas of the hospitality industry. Food and beverages are provided for all employees. The catering departments in these organizations are keen to keep and further develop their staff and therefore the potential for training and career progression is strong in this area.

Outside and event catering

When events are held at venues where there is no catering available, or where the level of catering required is more than the usual caterers can manage, then a catering company may take over the management of the event. This type of function can include art gallery launches, garden parties, parties in private houses or marquees, sporting fixtures, weddings, the opening of new buildings, military pageants and music events.

Event catering ranges from a basic lunch-box drop-off to full-service, sit down meal. When most people refer to a 'caterer', they are referring to an event caterer who serves food with waiting staff at dining tables or sets up a buffet style of service. The food may be prepared on site (for example, made completely at the event) or the caterer may choose to bring prepared food from a separate premises and present it at service point. Certain catering companies have moved toward a full-service business model commonly associated with event planners. They take charge of not only food preparation but also decorations, such as table settings, staging, technology and lighting. The trend is towards satisfying all the clients' needs with food as a focal point.

Corporate hospitality

Corporate hospitality is defined as any event for the benefit of an organization entertaining clients, staff, or prospective clients, at the organization's expense. Corporate entertaining and hospitality can be an effective way of creating networking opportunities and cementing business relationships. It is has become increasingly important in recent years to reduce the cost of keeping an existing client and building relationships with them. Hospitality plays a key role in developing and maintaining customer relationships within business.

Healthcare and hospitals

The healthcare foodservice market is one of the most demanding and sophisticated to operate. Professionalism, the highest standards of food safety and hygiene, and a detailed understanding of the nutritional needs of those being cared for, are prerequisite for this division. A unique understanding of the demands of the healthcare sector is required and various specialist services such as security and hygiene can also be provided by this diverse sector.

Many healthcare providers have an ongoing programme of professional cookery and nutrition training for chefs and dieticians. The preparation of menus which comprise fresh and seasonal foods, which are nutritious and flavoursome, are important to the overall day to day routine in a care home. They are often a major focal point of the day for residents. Hospital catering is classified as 'welfare catering'. The object is to assist the medical staff to get a patient back to health as soon as possible. To undertake this task it is necessary to provide good quality food and retain the maximum nutritional value during preparation, cooking and service.

TASK In groups discuss how a care home or hospital can make sure patients get the best diet for them in terms of nutrition and enjoyment. Look back at your Level 1 course.

The National Health Service operates approximately 1200 hospitals with about 1.7 million employees, of which there are over 300 million meals served each year to patients.

The NHS Plans for England and Wales have raised the profile of hospital catering. They have set out agendas for providing 'Better Hospital Food' by improving the range of meals available for patients, the quality of the food and its nutritional content. Trusts must give patients access to a 24-hour catering. Most hospitals also provide food for staff and visitors and raise revenue in this way. [Services provided by a catering department below].

School meals and the education sector

A formal school meals service was first introduced in 1879. The Education Act 1944 pledged that all schools should provide a main meal (lunch) to all children who wanted one. In 2006 the Government announced new guidelines for school food. They cover all food sold and served in schools ranging from breakfast, lunch and after-school meals. This also includes vending, tuck-shops, after-school clubs and mid-morning break snacks.

Research has demonstrated that pupils are more likely to concentrate in lessons if they have eaten a nutritionally balanced meal at lunchtime.

The School Food Trust has launched a web-based tool that helps catering services, pupils and parents assess whether the food and drink provided at lunchtime and at other times of the school day meets the food-based standards.

WEB LINK You can check now if your food provision at breakfast, mid-morning break, tuck shops, vending and after school clubs complies with the food based standards. This is found at **http://www.schoolfoodtrust.org.uk/**

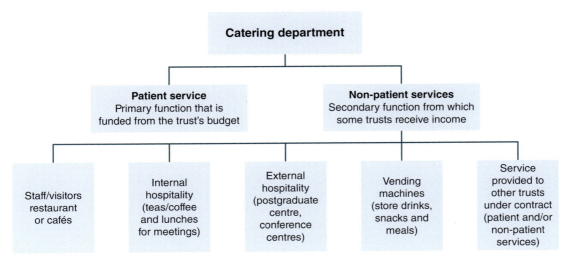

Services provided by a catering department

The eatwell plate has been designed to make healthy eating easier to understand by giving a visual representation of the types and proportions of foods people need for a healthy and well-balanced diet.

The plate is based on the five food groups:

- bread, rice, potatoes, pasta and other starchy foods
- fruit and vegetables
- milk and dairy foods
- meat, fish, eggs, beans and other non-dairy sources of protein
- foods and drinks high in fat and/or sugar.

This encourages you to choose different foods from the first four groups every day, to help ensure you obtain the wide range of nutrients your body needs to remain healthy and function properly. It is suitable for most people including people of all ethnic origins and people who are of a healthy weight or overweight. It is also suitable for vegetarians.

Residential schools and other educational establishments

These include schools, colleges, universities, hostels and children's homes where all meals are provided. It is important to consider the nutritional balance of food served in these establishments as it is the main or only food provision outlet. Many of these cater for children, teenagers and adolescents who lead active lives, so all food and beverages prepared should remain nutritious, varied and made from good quality fresh ingredients.

The armed forces

Contract caterers accounted for approximately 520 Ministry of Defence outlets, serving up to 110 million meals. Like much of contract catering, defence contract catering is no longer solely food based, with contracts commonly encompassing areas such as waste management, bakery production, cleaning and laundry management.

The vast majority of the defence catering market is currently managed by the Ministry of Defence's Catering Group, which is part of the MoD's Defence Logistics Organization. The DCG is responsible for the quality, supply and types of meals prepared in the armed forces. On the contract catering side, the main businesses tendering and providing a service to the British Armed Forces are Sodexho Defence Services, Compass Group's ESS defence, offshore and remote division and Aramark's Combined Services Division.

It should also be remembered that defence contract catering is very much a global market, with potential for growth overseas. Sodexho Defence Services, for instance, operates with NATO, UN and US forces around the world. The Navy, Army and Air Force Institute (NAAFI) began to concentrate on its overseas markets from September 2005.

This has left a potential gap in the market for contract caterers although, as a lot of what NAAFI did was leisure and retail orientated as well as catering, operators have had to look at developing new service models.

Many people want to serve their country in a very fundamental yet underappreciated way: by serving their comrades nutritious, tasty food sometimes under extreme circumstances. The armed forces provide a rewarding and incredibly diverse career and food service is one of the most vital jobs in the military.

Prison catering

Catering in prisons can be carried out by contract caterers or managed in-house by the Prison Service. The food is usually prepared by prison officers who are trained chefs and inmates. The kitchens are sometimes used to train inmates in food production so that they can obtain a recognized national qualification to help them find work when they are released. In addition to catering for the inmates there is also staff catering facilities for all prison workers such as administrative staff and prison officers.

HOTELS

> **TASK** Find out how many hotels and guest houses there are in the UK.

Hotels provide private accommodation in bedrooms with varying standards of furnishing and other services may be included such as room service, laundry bars and restaurants. There will invariably be other aspects of service ranging from a reception desk, concierge and porter assistance. There is a rating system used to help the customer identify how luxurious the hotel is. A luxury hotel will be graded with five stars with basic hotels receiving either one or two stars depending on the facilities available to the guest.

The structure of hotels is defined into the following categories:

- Budget hotels – usually located near main travel routes or destinations, directed at tourists or the business traveller.

- Bed and breakfast accommodation (guest houses) – small, privately owned establishments with owners living on the same premises.

- Consortia – a group of independent hotels with an agreement to purchase products and services together, such as marketing and international reservation systems.

- Country houses – usually stately homes or manor houses in tourist or rural areas with a good reputation for luxury service, spa or sports facilities and high standards of food and beverage service.

- Luxury – the hotels are likely to provided a full range of high class services including 24-hour room service and an à la carte restaurant.

- Business – dedicated to the business traveller with requisite facilities provided for undertaking business while travelling (internet, conference, secretarial facilities).

- Resort – intended for the tourism market and usually located in tourist areas.

- Boutique – notable for their individuality, intimacy and detail to service.

As a provider of accommodation and sometimes leisure facilities, a number of hotels will have common characteristics with other sectors of the hospitality industry such as restaurants that provide accommodation, hostels and public houses.

TASK Research the types of hotels found across the world, the range of services they provide. List the functions, apart from food and drink services, where they employ staff e.g. reception.

There is a growing trend to contract-out food and beverage services to third parties, especially in the major cities of the world. With intense competition from high street and local restaurants, the outsourcing of this facility together with its inherent costs is extremely appealing. However, this option is not as simple as it may first seem. To attract walk-in dining guests a hotel needs to be ideally located with easy outside access to the actual restaurant. The restaurant needs to fit with the clientele that the specific hotel targets. Nonetheless, more chefs seem willing to consider this option as lucrative and Gordon Ramsay, Giorgio Locatelli, Gary Rhodes and Alain Ducasse have made strong ventures from this direction.

PRIVATE MEMBERS' CLUBS AND CASINOS

To become members of private clubs people will have to pay for this privilege and sometimes they will also be required to be nominated and seconded by current members of longstanding. Private clubs are usually managed by managers or club secretaries who are also appointed by the club members or committee. London has many prestigious and historical clubs such as Boodles (founded in 1762), RAC (founded in 1897) and the Reform (founded in 1836) among many others. Members require a good food and beverage service in an old English or classic style. The food and beverage service is always of an exceptional standard and is equivalent sometimes to five-star hotels.

Casinos are open to the public as opposed to members only. Services such as bars, restaurants and leisure activities such as gaming tables are offered. Even accommodation facilities are available in some of the most exclusive casinos in the UK.

RESTAURANTS

The restaurant sector is the largest and fastest changing area in the hospitality and catering industry. This section has had a steady increase of turnover and it is estimated that there are over 65 000 restaurants currently in the UK. A high proportion of the restaurant sector is from ethnic minority groups such as Chinese and Indian origin. In your Level 1 course you learnt how restaurants can be classified by their origin of cuisine and the different segments the restaurant industry is broken down into.

Historically, the restaurant industry has been difficult to define. If we consider the function of a restaurant is to serve food and drink, therefore cafés, coffee shops and public houses can also fall within this category. Restaurants have to offer something unique to them, and this may point to the design and atmosphere of the individual restaurant. The environment of the restaurant, in turn, must reflect the type of cuisine served.

There are many restaurant and café chains spread over wide areas including town centres, shopping centres, tourist destinations and even overseas. These familiar companies have created a role in the restaurant market where moderately priced food and drink in contemporary surroundings are served to customers. Consistency of the service and product is the basis to the success of these chains, so that a customer has a regular dining experience with every different branch of a particular chain they visit.

The delicatessen, salad bar or sandwich shop can all be perceived as retail and hospitality. If you walk in to purchase a sandwich and take it away with you to eat, it is defined as retail. However, if you go in and buy your sandwich to sit at a table on the premises and eat it, it is determined as hospitality. These types of restaurant experiences are very popular due to the concept of quick, 'made-to-order' and often inexpensive food.

Fast-food restaurants offer popular foods at reasonable prices with a short waiting time. The limited menu on offer is designed so that the items are quick to cook or easy to present and then either consumed on the premises or taken away. This concept is able to serve hundreds of customers everyday and it is a model that modern Chinese and Indian take-away enterprises have developed, serving quickly cooked food to be taken away to eat. To help the customer receive food even quicker without having to even leave the confines of their own vehicle is the 'drive-thru' which has been taken directly from North America. Customers drive up to a small booth or microphone area and place their order before driving to the service window to pick up and pay for their food.

PUBLIC HOUSES, BARS AND CLUBS

A high proportion of the industry's workforce is employed on a part-time basis. This is possibly due to the nature of the industry. In this sector custom tends to be concentrated into a short number of hours (evenings and weekends) so the amount of staff needed in peak hours is considerably higher than at quieter times. Those who work part time are likely to work different hours each week and, along with their full time equivalent, tend to work unsociable hours. A relatively high proportion of this workforce describe their employment as casual, many of which may be working in the industry while studying.

TASK Make a table showing the differences between pubs, bars and night clubs.

Due to the ban on smoking in public areas and the availability of alcohol in supermarkets, many pubs have moved into providing a food offer in the form of restaurants and also providing live entertainment. There is a great variety of food served in pubs, ranging from high class restaurants with a gastro-pub style often presented by well-qualified chefs who make good use of local produce to bar-food that ranges from finger snacks such as sandwiches to fork dishes where the food is eaten at or in the bar itself as opposed to a separate restaurant area.

VISITOR ATTRACTIONS

The visitor attraction industry is small in terms of establishments, employment and turnover. However, popular visitor attractions that attract high numbers of visitors are vital to local economies.

Defining what constitutes a visitor attraction is difficult, but they tend to fall into the following categories:

- theme parks and gardens
- sporting stadia
- museums and historical sites

- holiday centres
- other attractions – including theatres, farms, health clubs and spas.

Theme parks are very popular venues for a family day out with larger parks including several different eating options ranging from fast food to chain restaurants and some fine-dining places. Theme parks can be used for corporate hospitality and can be hired by companies for conferences or other events. Some larger theme parks have their own hotels and therefore have created a tourist holiday destination.

A modern sports stadium is a place or venue for either indoor or outdoor sports, concerts, or other events and consists of a field or stage either partly or completely surrounded by a structure designed to allow spectators to stand or sit and view the event. Catering for these arenas is similar to that of theme parks and has diverse food outlets designed to give customers as much choice as possible.

THE IN-FLIGHT CATERING INDUSTRY

Flight caterers are high-volume operations. For instance, in January 2006 the Cathay Pacific flight kitchen in Hong Kong recorded its highest ever daily production output which was in excess of 74 000 meal trays. Globally there are around 630 flight kitchens with an annual output of more than one million meals each. A single flight by a long-haul Boeing 747 may require over 40 000 separate items loaded onto it. Therefore, it is very clear that flight caterers handle a considerable volume of products on a daily basis. Although referred to as 'flight kitchens', food production is only one stage in the operation. There are a number of subsequent assembly and delivery stages: dish assembly (assembling hot entrees and other dishes from their components such as meat, fish, rice and assorted vegetables), tray assembly, bar cart assembly, trolley loading and delivery to the aircraft.

Flight caterers also have to cope with a high variety of outputs. Most operators contract to supply more than just one airline, as there are few airports where a single airline has enough flights to justify the exclusive use of a kitchen, except for the 'hub' airports of major carriers. So within the flight catering business, there is a considerable variety of outputs, deriving from:

- number of airlines
- types of airline – scheduled, charter, low-cost, executive the duration of the flight (short haul, long haul)
- seat class – first, business, economy and charter flight
- type of menu – breakfast, mid-morning, lunch, mid-afternoon, dinner
- demand for special meals – 26 different types, such as kosher, halal, low-fat, low-salt and vegetarian
- menu cycles or rotations – to ensure that frequent flyers are not always served the same menu.

CRUISE SHIPS

A cruise ship or cruise liner is a passenger ship used for pleasure voyages, where the voyage itself and the ship's amenities are part of the experience, as well as the different destinations along the way. Transportation is not the prime purpose, as cruise ships operate mostly on routes that return passengers to their originating port, so the ports of call are usually in a specified region of a continent.

Dining on almost all cruise ships is included in the cruise price, except on no-frills lines. Traditionally, the ships' restaurants organize two dinner services per day and passengers are allocated a set dining time for the entire cruise, but a recent trend is to allow diners to dine whenever they want. Cunard ships maintain the class tradition of ocean liners and have separate dining rooms for different types of suites, while others have a standard dining room and upgrade specialty restaurants that require pre-booking and cover charges.

Besides the dining room, there is also a casual buffet-style eatery often open 24-hours that offers breakfast, lunch, dinner and late-night snacks. There are also numerous bars and nightclubs, where alcoholic beverages are charged extra, as most cruise lines prohibit passengers from bringing aboard and consuming their own alcohol (alcohol purchased duty-free is sealed and only returned to passengers when they disembark).

There is often a central galley responsible for serving all major restaurants aboard the ship; however specialty restaurants may have their own separate galleys. As with any vessel, adequate provisioning is crucial, especially on a cruise ship serving several thousand meals at each seating. Normally, a cruise ship stocks up at its homeport, however, they also have special arrangements with designated suppliers at ports of call if required.

SEA FERRIES

A sea ferry is a form of transportation, used to carry primarily passengers and sometimes vehicles and cargo as well, across a body of water. Most ferries operate a regular, return service such as those that operate between Dover and Calais. A passenger ferry with many stops, such as in Venice, is sometimes called a water bus or water taxi.

Ferries form a part of the public transport systems of many waterside cities and islands, allowing direct transit between points at a capital cost much lower than bridges, tunnels or airlines. Catering facilities can range from fast food to branded restaurant chains or fine dining restaurants. These can often be run by contract caterers or by the shipping company themselves. In more recent times, well-known chefs have become involved in consulting over menus and training the chefs to produce their recipes for service to customers.

RAIL TRAVEL

Since privatization, railway catering has become increasingly refined and diverse. From negative connotations of poor quality and limited choice, the offer has aligned itself more closely to that of other leisure operations. Generally situated in town centres, railway stations provide the venue for further catering opportunities, and companies are realizing that the space within the station building can be utilized in a far more valuable way.

Passenger growth is increasing year on year, and much of this is due to the investment in rail services. Operators are aiming to install a greater percentage of branded outlets on stations that customers will recognize, transferring increased consumer confidence into the rail catering offer. Today's consumer demands a higher quality and choice of product, and operators have become more aware of consumers' needs, such as the increased need for healthier food and greater variety.

On-board meals have become an important weapon in an attempt to attract greater custom. Another development is the increasing use of contracting out to caterers with many different examples of this on various main-line operators. Some operators have changed over to an 'airline' system of fixing the price so that meals and drinks are included in the First Class ticket only. This means that standard fare passengers on these services must manage with the buffet or trolley service.

WEB LINK The websites below may give you further information on the diversity of the catering and hospitality industry:
www.bha.org.uk British Hospitality Association
www.caterersearch.com Caterersearch – Hospitality news
www.catersource.com Catersource – Education, products and news for caterers
www.connexions-direct.com Connexions Direct – Information and advice for young people
www.greenhotelier.org Greenhotelier – Practical solutions for responsible tourism
www.historic-uk.com The Heritage of Britain Accommodation Guide
www.instituteofhospitality.org Institute of Hospitality – Professional body for hospitality, leisure and tourism industries
www.michelinguide.com Michelin Guide – Ratings information
www.people1st.co.uk People 1st – Sector Skills Council for Hospitality, Leisure, Travel and Tourism
www.visitbritain.com Visit Britain – Official UK Travel and Accommodation Guide

Employment in the catering and hospitality industry

The scope for employment in this industry is immense with many diverse career pathways available. The economic health of the nation is reflected by the food served in catering establishments and at home. Good employment trends, business expansion and a sense of personal well-being among the general public will encourage the hospitality and catering industry to expand too.

Catering and hospitality businesses need to have a basic structure for the staff in order for the business to run effectively. Organizations, regardless of their size will produce staffing structures, with members of the team all performing different job roles that contribute to the overall aims of the establishment. **Organizing** involves dividing tasks into jobs, specifying the appropriate department for each job, determining the optimal number of jobs in each department and delegating authority within departments.

In smaller organizations employees may have to become multi-skilled so that they can undertake multiple duties and managers may have to take on supervisory roles at times too.

Staffing structures and job roles

Organizations, regardless of their size will have a staffing structure, with members of staff performing different job roles that contribute to the overall aims of the organization.

Organizations range from individuals working by themselves to very large companies with thousands of employees. In the case of the smaller organizations, it is likely that individuals will have to perform a wide variety of roles as all operational (and management) requirements have to be completed by a few people. In larger organizations, generally, job roles are likely to be more specific as many people are working towards the aims of the organization and the breakdown of roles can be more specific.

Staffing structures can be divided into three main categories. These are as follows:

- Operational staff – Operational staff are the employees who perform the everyday practical operations. They are the staff who cook and serve the customers, clean the bedrooms and public areas, serve at a reception desk and generally provide the services that customers expect from the organization.

- Supervisory staff – Supervisory staff are generally more experienced than operational staff. They will supervise (oversee) the work and performance of operational staff and deal with any day to day (minor) issues as they arise. Supervisory staff should also provide a first point of call for

operational staff if they are uncertain about a task, have a problem that they need help with or an issue with a customer that requires a decision to be made that is out of their remit (responsibility). In the kitchen a Chef de Partie (chef of a section) may have this supervisory responsibility, but it is more likely that this will fall to the Sous Chef.

- Management staff – Depending on the size of the organization, managers often perform supervisory and operational roles. It is as organizations become larger that managers perform these tasks on a less frequent basis or perhaps never at all. Managers have an overarching responsibility for ensuring that the organization is performing well, that suitably trained staff are employed and customers receive the products and/or services they expect. Managers have many other responsibilities including planning for the future, managing finance, ensuring health and safety policies and employment laws are followed, as well as many others. An example of a manager in a kitchen would be the Head Chef.

Employment rights and responsibilities

Upon entry to employment, there are certain rights and responsibilities of both the employer and employee. The employee is protected by legislation from the Government and every employer must follow the guidelines or risk prosecution.

From the employer's perspective, they must supply a job description and contract of employment, detailing the following:

- contracted working hours

- holiday entitlement and notice period

- detailed description of the job

- provision of a healthy and safe working environment.

From the employee's perspective, they must:

- work to the conditions as described in their job description and contract of employment

- follow organizational policies and standard practices

- follow health and safety working practices, including food safety.

An employee is a person who is directly employed by a business under a contract of employment. However, there is also another role known as 'worker' or 'sub-contractor' that has been awarded a contract to deliver services but is not actually an employee of the business awarding the contract.

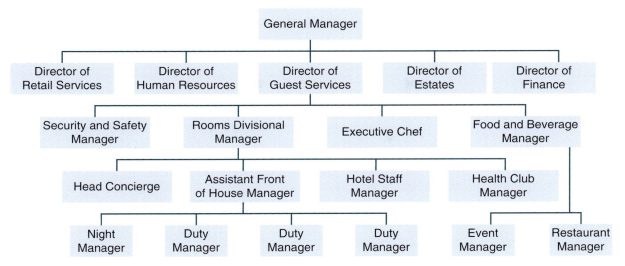

Staffing structures – large city centre hotel

The legislations designed to protect both employees and workers are as follows:

- National Minimum Wage Act 1998
- Public Interest disclosure Act 1998
- Part-time Workers (Prevention of Less Favourable Treatment) Regulations 2000
- Equality Act 2010
- Working Time Regulations 1998
- Employment Rights Act 1996
- Health and Safety Legislation
- Equal Pay Act 1970
- Disability Discrimination Act 1995.

When employers seek the recruitment and selection of new members of staff it is important that they are aware of the following additional legislation too:

- Children and Young Persons Act 1933
- Data Protection Act 1988
- Licensing Act 1964
- Human Rights Act 1998
- Sex Discrimination Act 1975
- Rehabilitation of Offenders Act 1974
- Asylum and Immigration Act 1996
- Race Relations Act 1976.

When advertising for a job it is unlawful to discriminate against job applicants on the grounds of sex, marital status, gender, colour, race, religion, nationality, disability, sexual preference or membership of political movements or trade unions.

Job application forms should always be designed with care and attention to promote inclusion for everyone. Therefore, phrases in job descriptions or titles such as 'manageress' should not be used because they indicate an intention to discriminate on the grounds of a person's gender. If sensitive information is needed such as a health record, the reason for this needs to be clearly explained and the information should always remain confidential, in line with the Data Protection Act 1998.

When candidates are informed of the date for their personal interview via a written letter they should also be notified if they need to wear protective clothing while on duty and also disclose if the company is likely to carry out any surveillance monitoring.

Job interviews

It is understandable that companies need to use a job interview to find out as much as they can about the applicant. Interviews give companies an opportunity to find out whether or not jobseekers have the skills and personal qualities that the job demands as well as allowing them to gauge whether or not an applicant would 'fit in' with the business. Likewise, potential employees also get the opportunity to ask questions of their own and interviews allow the applicants to determine, as best as they can, whether the job they are going for is likely to meet up with their own expectations.

While job interview questions tend to match a uniform pattern, sometimes you might be asked the odd awkward question. However, as an interview guide, employers need to be very careful about asking certain questions because they might contravene anti-discrimination laws. And, while jobseekers would probably be able to recognize a blatant discriminatory question, there are often 'grey' areas and questions within a job interview that may seem harmless, yet are, in fact, discriminatory and, therefore, illegal.

JOB TITLE: First Commis Chef

DEPARTMENT: Kitchen

RESPONSIBLE TO: Head Chef/Sous Chef/Chef de Partie

PRIMARY PURPOSE OF JOB:

To work as part of the kitchen team. To prepare food that conforms to company and kitchen standards and be responsible for the day-to-day running of a given section within the kitchen in the Demi Chef de Partie's absence.

Summary of duties and responsibilities:

1 To maintain the required level of hygiene standards as laid down both legally and by the company's standards manual.
2 To maintain your personal equipment used to fulfil your job, i.e. knives, shoes to the required standards as in 1.
3 On a daily basis check with the Senior Chef on duty as to the work that needs to be carried out that day.
4 To carry out all mise-en-place needed, to the standards as laid out.
5 To support colleagues at all times to ensure team-work is maintained, helping to supervise and train apprentices.
6 To ensure work area is kept to a hygienic and safe state at all times as in point 1.
7 To assist in the smooth running of the kitchen service.
8 To control a given section in the Demi Chef de Partie's absence to the standards as laid down.
9 To report any illness, open sores, diarrhoea, vomiting, nausea, to the chef in charge or the duty manager.
10 To be aware of hotel and departmental objectives and assist in achieving them.
11 To comply with and act in accordance with all company fire regulations and to adhere to the company's fire policy.
12 To act in accordance with all Health & Safety and Hygiene regulations and to adhere to the company's Health & Safety policy.
13 To attend all statutory training as and when requested.
14 To arrive at work at the correct time and in the correct uniform ensuring it is in immaculate condition.
15 To behave in a friendly and hospitable manner to all guests, customers and staff.

This job description is not exhaustive; therefore the job holder may be required, from time to time, to carry out tasks as and when requested by management.

Example of a job description for a first commis chef in a hotel

While employers are legally entitled to ask you at a job interview if you have the correct paperwork to legally work in the UK and to ask you to provide evidence of that, they are not entitled to probe into your personal history surrounding your specific place of birth. Interviewers should not make any reference to a person's marital status, children they may have or their sexual preference. All could be grounds for discrimination as companies might be deemed to view a person being married as either favourably in that they may see an applicant as being more stable or, perhaps, unfavourably in that they may see a conflict of interest between a single person having more time to devote to the job over a married person who might have family commitments to juggle with.

Other questions which interviewers cannot ask include anything related to any arrests or convictions. For certain jobs, they are entitled to run a Criminal Records Bureau (CRB) check on you prior to interview. However, any findings from that should never form part of their interview techniques. Questions about membership or affiliations with any organizations should also not be asked at interviews unless they are directly related to any problem they might foresee in terms of your time commitments and how that might affect your ability to do the job. Questions about height and weight are also discriminatory unless the job is exempt in terms of it being acceptable to have a certain minimum height requirement.

The interviewer should refrain from asking questions about religion unless, for example, aspects of the job may directly affect the beliefs of an individual such as the handling of specific meats or alcohol.

THE JOB OFFER

Once the applicant has had a successful interview an offer of employment should be made. The following checklist has been developed to provide some tips on offering a job to the successful candidate. A job offer can be made verbally but should be confirmed in writing. The job offer should outline:

- starting date, time and location
- relevant agreement
- job classification and status
- probation
- job requirements
- sick payments.

If you take time off from work due to illness, you might be entitled to sick pay. There are two types of sick pay:

- company sick pay (also called contractual or occupational sick pay)
- statutory sick pay.

If your employer runs their own sick pay scheme it is a 'company sick pay scheme' and you should be paid what you are due under that. This will depend on what is included in your employment contract. If you are not entitled to anything under a company scheme, your employer should still pay you Statutory Sick Pay (SSP) if you are eligible.

If you work for an employer under a contract of service, you are entitled to Statutory Sick Pay (SSP) if the following conditions apply:

- You are sick for at least four days in a row (including weekends and bank holidays and days that you do not normally work).

- You have average weekly earnings of at least £97 a week.

> **WEB LINK** To find out more about employment within the catering industry visit: **http://www.chefsworld.net**

WORKING TIME DIRECTIVE

The Working Time Directive applies to all workers and employees within the UK who undertake work for an employer. The 1998 Regulations are enforced by the employment tribunals and by local authority Environmental Health Officers. The Directive covers the worker's statutory right to rest breaks, rest periods and paid annual holiday.

Professional associations

A professional association (also called a professional body, professional institute, professional organization, or professional society) is a non-profit making organization seeking to further a particular profession, the interests of the individuals engaged in that profession and the overall public interest. Many professional bodies are involved in the development and monitoring of professional educational programmes and the updating of skills. This is achieved by directly working alongside colleges, universities and awarding bodies and by hosting competitions.

Some of the associations related to professional cookery are as follows:

- Academy of Culinary Arts
- Academy of Food and Wine
- Association Culinaire Française
- British Culinary Federation
- Craft Guild of Chefs
- Euro Toques

- Federation of Chefs Scotland
- Master Chefs of Great Britain
- PACE (Professional Association of Catering Education)
- Institute of Hospitality
- Welsh Culinary Association
- World Association of Chefs Societies (WACS).

Training opportunities and related qualifications

Working in the hospitality industry and particularly as a chef is a neverending learning opportunity. There is always more to learn with constant innovation from very talented chefs from around the world. The innovative ways in which to work with new commodities and applying different approaches and techniques can make working in the industry an interesting a personally rewarding experience.

As someone entering the industry without any, or very much, experience, the training opportunities are vast and varied. The following describes some of the ways in which training is provided:

- **On the job** – this refers to bite size, regular chunks, of training that is provided while at work. Occasionally, short courses (e.g. one or two days) may be provided to learn about specific aspects of the job – health and safety and food hygiene, for example.

- **College based** – most colleges in the UK offer courses and qualifications in hospitality and catering. This provides the opportunity for students to learn about the industry and develop skills in an educational environment. There are also opportunities to learn other subjects and improve other skills such as the use of language, number and IT.

- **Training providers** – work in conjunction with employers and perform the assessment of skills for apprentices in the workplace.

- **E-learning** – although it may be considered more difficult to learn skills through IT based resources, modern resources are being produced in a very interactive and personalized approach. The streaming of video based material also makes it possible for learners to review material at their own pace.

- **Work placement** – a placement provides a controlled period of time in which there is a great opportunity to observe the way in which an organization operates and performs tasks.

The organization of the professional kitchen

A well-designed kitchen organization is required so that all tasks are carried out in an efficient manner. An effective kitchen will prepare, cook and present the correct amount of high quality food within the time constraints making economical use of all the available resources.

There are distinct catering operations that serve food and drink to customers in a number of diverse ways. They are dependent on the needs and requirements of the customer. Each operation has its own workflow organization but there are certain elements that should remain constant throughout the different operations:

- effective communication between departments or sections within a kitchen

- increased efficiency of work to produce high quality food in good time

- accident prevention

- promotion of good health, safety and food safety practice

- the provision of an successful service to the customer

- high-quality end product.

Hospitals and healthcare homes

Hospital catering is usually classified as welfare catering. The service of food is of great importance to hospital patients and residents of healthcare homes because it has been documented that good quality fresh food can help to increase health and certainly creates a sense of well-being which benefits recovery from illness.

Carefully prepared, cooked and presented food can be served directly to the patient or within a restaurant area. The workflow element of this particular service is sometimes problematic because wards can be spread over a wide area in large hospitals where long distances are required for the food to travel.

Dietary constraints must be particularly adhered to and clear information about the type of food or meal to be served to individuals should be effectively communicated.

CHEF'S TIP In many hospitals a qualified dietician is responsible for designing and supervising special diets and instruction of the preparation of special dishes. They may even assist in the training of chefs and cooks with regard to food nutrition and specialist dietary products.

Hotels

Hotels will generally provide breakfast, luncheon, afternoon teas, dinners, room service, banquets and bar snacks. In large hotels there may be satellite kitchens to help prepare and serve food quickly and efficiently for banquets and room service. The careful preparation of food is essential for a busy service so that orders can be executed quickly and efficiently. With the wealth of different services required for a hotel operation the planning of work and 'mise-en-place' needs to be accurate and clearly communicated to the different teams the requirements of the day ahead.

Restaurants

There are many different types of restaurants that can be privately owned, part of a larger company (such as a hotel) or part of a chain. Therefore, restaurants will vary with the style of food that is served. They will often serve luncheon and dinner although some restaurants will open for breakfast and afternoon tea. The introduction of electronic booking, ordering and cash register systems are designed to mimic the workflow of a typical sit-down restaurant operation. This helps the restaurant plan the next service according to set timings so that the chefs will know when the busy period of service will be.

Contract catering services

The provision of staff dining rooms and corporate dining is a large part of the catering and hospitality industry. There are diverse systems of service employed to ensure the clients and customers are satisfied and therefore more productive within their own aspect of work. Staff restaurants serving breakfast, luncheon and sometimes a dinner service is required together with retail facilities, coffee shops, vending operations, banquets and conference dining. Once again the kitchen workflow system needs to be flexible enough to cope with the diversity of operations that are provided throughout the day.

School meals

Schools have traditionally provided a lunchtime meal for children up to and including the secondary school age and have been a statutory requirement of local education authorities since the early 1940s. Due to various economic changes some local education authorities have contracted out the provision and have introduced contract catering companies to provide a food and lunchtime service to schools.

Many schools now offer a multi-choice menu with an emphasis recently placed on healthy eating and health conscious choices. Other schools now offer a healthy breakfast service in addition to their luncheon service. Generally, the service style is counter service with school cooks and kitchen assistants serving the food to the students and school staff. Due to the timetabled constraints of an educational establishment a quick and efficient service is required so that the school can return to teaching and learning at a set time.

The traditional kitchen hierarchy

Many kitchens have different organizational kitchen teams with varying structures afforded them. Mainly this is due to the complexity of the menu, style of the food presented on the menu and the system which is used to prepare, cook and present the menu dishes.

Establishments that provide a limited menu are able to organize a small team to serve a large number of customers. The required standard can be produced because limited skills may be required to produce dishes on the menu. However, an organized and systematic workflow is important to the success of these businesses to ensure speed of service.

Auguste Escoffier (1846–1935) was a French chef, restaurateur and culinary writer who fashioned and updated traditional French classical cookery methods. He is a legendary figure among chefs and gourmets, and was one of the most important leaders in the development of modern French cuisine. Much of Escoffier's technique was based on that of Antoine Carême (1784–1833) the founder of French haute cuisine. Escoffier's achievement was to simplify and modernize Carême's elaborate style. Alongside the recipes he recorded and invented, another of Escoffier's contributions to cooking was to elevate it to the status of a respected profession, and to introduce discipline and structure to a kitchen brigade. He organized his kitchens using the brigade system, with each section run by a chef de partie. He also replaced the practice of service à la Française (serving all dishes at once) with service à la Russe (serving each dish in the order printed on the menu).

An example of a traditional kitchen brigade based on Escoffier's design is seen in the following diagram; this is sometimes referred to as the partie system.

Head chef (chef de cuisine)

The role of the head chef has grown in recent years in an administrative context. Sometimes known as an executive chef the role of the head chef is extensive and can incorporate more duties than those listed below:

- kitchen organization, staff work rota
- menu writing
- food and resource ordering
- cost and budget control
- training (in liaison with the HR Department)
- kitchen supervision
- implementation of food hygiene and health and safety policies
- equipment purchase and maintenance
- team management
- effective communication with guests, clients, kitchen brigade and other departments.

Second chef (sous chef)

The sous chef relieves the head chef as and when required. The primary function of this role is to supervise the work in the kitchen team that is attributed to each sous chef. In large kitchen brigades there will be sous chefs with specific responsibility for separate services such as banquets and room service. The supervision of all health and safety and food hygiene aspects, in conjunction with quality control and line managing a team of chefs is an integral part of the sous chef's role.

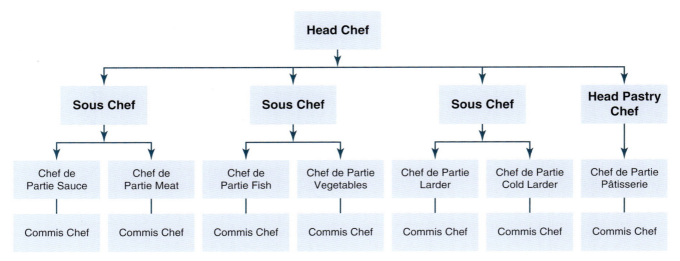

A traditional kitchen brigade

Head pastry chef (chef pâtissier)

The position of the head pastry chef is equivalent to that of the sous chef although because of the delicate and specialized nature of this department they often operate with a diverse team of specialists such as a baker (boulanger), ice cream chef (glaciér) and a decorative chef (chef décor) who specializes in chocolate, ice carving and sugar display work.

Chef de partie

The chefs de partie are in charge of their own sections within the kitchen. These can comprise the following sections:

- sauce section (saucier)
- meat section (rôtisseur)
- fish section (poissonier)
- vegetable section (l'entremettier)
- cold larder section (garde-manger)
- larder/butchery section (boucher)
- pastry section (pâtissier)
- relief chef (chef tournant).

Commis chef

These are the first chefs of the kitchen brigade. They are responsible for the set day-to-day tasks in accordance with standard operating procedures as determined by the head chef. Sometimes in large establishments there will be different levels of commis chef ranging from 1st commis, 2nd commis, commis and apprentice chef.

Other kitchen-based positions

There are many other important positions that have a significant role to play in the kitchen team. These can be as follows:

- staff cook (chef communard)
- breakfast chef (chef de petit déjeuner)
- kitchen clerk (l'aboyeur)
- kitchen porters (garcons de cuisine or plongeur)
- stores (l'economat).

A busy kitchen

The current trends in food production operations

It is essential that good communication and relationships are formed within the kitchen brigade to help the efficiency of the operation. It will also create a pleasant environment in which to work, which will in turn benefit the customer service and improve the productivity of staff.

The partie system today, nonetheless, is simpler than it was in Escoffier's time because of several historical developments:

- The introduction of machinery to do work previously done by many chefs.
- Changing public tastes toward simpler and less extravagant menus and meals.
- Economic factors that encourage the reduction of expensive labour and the simplification of recipes and service.
- The processing of food by freezing, canning and dehydration, which eliminates a great deal of basic preparation work.

The partie system will continue to experience further change as technology, computers, method study and work simplification are increasingly applied within the kitchen. Understanding the partie system will remain useful, however, because further improvements are more likely to be conveyed by those who comprehend both the traditional system and new technological breakthroughs. This ensures progress rather than haphazard changes which can hurt, or at least fail to help, productivity.

The importance of the design of the professional kitchen

Storage area

The primary area of a kitchen will include the storage section where raw foods and products are stored and cold rooms and freezers are positioned. Part of this area is also the positioning of a separate entrance for the arrival and checking of supplies. This department has to be spacious and equipped with a control office, a waste goods zone and an area for employees.

The equipment used in this department will vary according to the size of the establishment and the type of products used. Although there should be a large and small set of accurate scales, loading trolleys, stainless steel tables for the temporary placing of supplies and close access to refrigeration and freezer space.

It is in the primary area that the first check and most important check of purchased ingredients and supplies are made. This activity should be a thorough and methodical approach to checking the quality, quantity, temperature, packaging and freshness of the supplies being delivered. Ideally, an area required for unpacking is required to remove packaging and dispose of it in an environmentally acceptable manner.

The stores area should be attached to this department with enough space to allow for the correct storage of non-perishable goods. The space has to be sensibly divided in the following manner:

- general store
- drinks store (with refrigeration available)
- chemical and cleaning store.

Separate, but in an adjacent area, perishable foods such as fruit, vegetables, dairy, fish, meat and poultry products should be stored.

Shelving systems should be well divided, easily cleaned and fixed properly to avoid collapsing. Other issues to consider for the safe storage are as follows:

- Store all products away from direct sunlight to prevent condensation from building up or loss of colour in certain products.
- All products should be stored away from outside walls to avoid problems with contamination and humidity.
- Tinned foods should be stored in a dry place to avoid the formation of rust.
- All products should be maintained at an even temperature and sudden changes in temperature need to be avoided.

The areas dedicated to employees are an important factor. It is advisable to have a separate entrance to the kitchen or the food delivery zone because of possible contamination threats. It is also advisable to have separate toilets and changing areas for females and males to avoid employees using the facilities for customers.

Preparation zone

The secondary area is the preparation zone. In an ideal design, this should be situated immediately after the primary area and is the most important area because this sector has to carry out the preparation of several prime ingredient categories such as meat, poultry, vegetables, fish, dairy products and fruits. Sometimes, with large catering outlets such as hospitals, airport terminals and canteens, the space given to this area is large and all preparation zones can be installed into a line to help with the workflow.

To adhere to current regulations separate working areas are required for different ingredients such as meat, fish and vegetables. Therefore, within one area certain blocks of preparation tables and equipment should be divided for single use.

CHEF'S TIP Keep all raw meat areas separate from the main kitchen areas, this includes using separate equipment and refrigeration zones to help prevent cross contamination.

The importance of separating the preparation areas cannot be undervalued and if there is a separate bakery or pastry kitchen it is important that it should be located in an area furthest away from the cooking zone as the preparation of bakery and pastry products is always delicate and it is necessary to take into account the ambient heat, odours from the cooking area and to avoid cross contamination.

CHEF'S TIP An effective workflow will help to establish good communication between departments and improve the efficiency and quality of the end product.

The waste zone needs to be accessible from all the preparation zones, as well as from the cooking and dishwashing areas. It is important that it is positioned in a place whose access is not via the cooking area or the kitchen office.

Cooking area

The ideal position for the cooking area is immediately after the preparation section. Access to this area must be simple, without obstacles or additional sections placed in between the preparation area and the cooking area. The

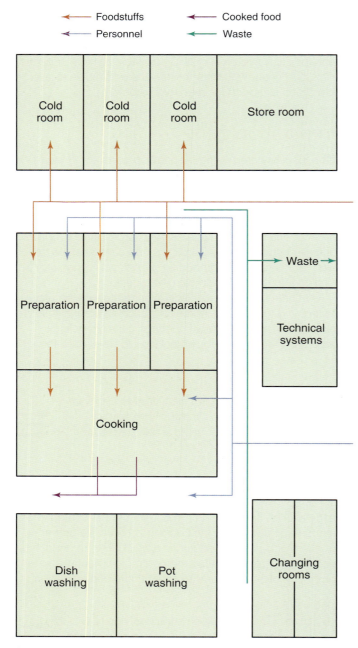

An example of a professional kitchen design layout

is required to meet the needs of the chef, the brigade and the speed of service. Particular attention should be given to the type of cooking ranges required and the choice at this stage will greatly enhance the final product of the variety of dishes to be served. Closely linked to the cooking of the prepared food is the use of blast chillers and possibly vacuum packing machines. This should be situated away from the main cooking range but still within the cooking area to facilitate workflow and the usage of these important items of machinery. Ideally, all cooked foods, blanched foods and pre-cooked foods should pass through a blast chiller, before being conserved in a refrigerator.

Service counter

Another key area is the service counter. Once cooked and presented the food has to be taken to the customer in the briefest time and in accordance with hygiene standards. The delivery methods and the equipment used depend on the type and style of food service. For waiter service a hotplate is required to help maintain the core temperature of hot dishes being passed over to a service team to serve to customers.

Hotplate in a kitchen being used for a restaurant service

equipment for this zone and its design rely heavily on the type of service to be carried out. Restaurant and large hotels generally have a personalized service for their customers with a wide range of dishes on different menus. There may also be a banqueting service available that will also influence the design of this area. The cooking area should be adjacent to the service table. In this way the different courses can be divided into separate cooking sections within the area. A functional cooking range (stove)

A self service counter system will usually have the food items portioned and presented in hot display cabinets in multi portion trays. Service staff are typically on hand to aid the customer in choice and to replenish the food on a regular basis.

Hotplate being used in a self service area

The type and size of equipment will depend on the style of the menu being produced. The equipment must be situated in the most ergonomic place and if possible the equipment should have multi-uses to help with production flow. A complete study of the technical details for each piece of equipment should be completed to help ascertain size, output and power (electricity or gas) use.

Planning a menu

The word 'menu' as it relates to food dates in French print to 1718. The Oxford English Dictionary (2nd edition) confirms the English word 'menu' was borrowed from the French. However the word 'menu' can be traced to the Latin word 'minutus' which means a detailed list.

TASK Find five different terms that are used in menu planning and briefly describe what each term means.

From the early 1770s, the use of a printed menu in restaurants allowed each customer to choose his or her own dish and marked another characteristic innovation in food service. Before the emergence of the restaurant, a menu had always been a list of all those foods to be served during a particular meal such as a banquet. Up until this point in time all the food served on a table d'hôte (table of the day) had no menu and the food arrived all together at the same time. The restaurant's role as a place for the service of food and drink, however, necessitated a new sense of the menu: the creation of a list of available items from which each customer made personal choices in sequence at the most convenient moment.

When ordering from a restaurant menu, the chef has produced a highly individualistic set of dishes, differentiating themselves from the other restaurants nearby. By the mere presence of a menu, the restaurant's style of service demanded a degree of self-definition. Restaurants had printed menus because they offered their customers a choice of unseen dishes. However, another concept was that the printed menu allowed restaurateurs to calculate costs of individual dishes and set fixed prices and dish descriptions to customers.

Today's menu is an important communication method from the caterer to the customer. It is a legal requirement for restaurants to display menus that clearly inform customers about the price and other inclusions such as the addition of VAT (Value Added Tax) and any service charges that are applied.

Types of menus

There are various types of menus that are used in restaurants, hotels, hospitals, schools and contract food service outlets.

À LA CARTE

This is a menu with individually priced dishes so that the customer can select a series of particular dishes to compile their own menu of choice. In the true sense of the term a dish from the à la carte menu should be cooked to order although with new technology and skilled chefs in today's kitchen most menus will be cooked to order.

TABLE D'HÔTE

This is a set menu with a set price. There may be a choice of dishes available for each course but it is not compulsory. Usually there are two, three or four different courses to this type of menu.

HOSPITAL MENUS

These usually consist of a limited choice written onto a card that is filled in by the patient indicating their choice on the day prior to receiving the ordered dishes. Usually the menu choice consists of two or three different courses with dietary options available. Hospitals will usually cater for special dietary requirements on the grounds of religion, vegetarianism and allergies.

HEALTHCARE MENUS

With residential healthcare homes, the dining experience has to be a pleasant, social experience to look forward to and be enjoyed by all. Menus are generally comprised of fresh and seasonal foods which are nutritious, flavoursome and balanced. The dishes need to reflect and include the likes and requests of residents and include a varied choice.

Autumn/Winter 2009/2010
Weeks Commencing 4th Sept, 25th Sept, 16th Oct, 13th Nov, 4th Dec, 8th Jan, 29th Jan, 26th Feb, 19th Mar.

Monday	Tuesday	Wednesday	Thursday	Friday
Crumb Coated Haddock Grill / Cheesy Wrap Stacks / Shepherds Pie	Home-made Red Onion & Cheddar Quiche / Pork Sausages / Home-made Chicken & Tomato Pasta	Home-made Neopolitan Pasta / Home-made Chicken Nuggets / Home-made Meat Pie	Roasted Chicken Fillet / Home-made Sweet Potato & Lentil Korma / Home-made Moussaka	Home-made Cheese & Tomato Pizza / BBQ Chicken Drumstick / Home-made Salmon & Broccoli Pasta
Potato Smiles / Mashed Potato	Home-made Potato Wedges / New Potatoes	Potato Lyonnaise / Mashed Potato	Baked Potatoes / Rice	Tri-Coloured Pasta / New Potatoes
Baked Beans / Sweetcorn	Fresh Broccoli / Fresh Cauliflower	Peas	Sweetcorn / Fresh Curly Kale / Fresh White Cabbage	Baby Carrots / Green Beans
Chocolate & Orange Sponge & Custard	Sultana Cake & Custard	Fruit Ice Smoothies	Cherry Slice & Custard	Apple & Date Flapjack & Custard

Each day a meal consists of one item from each row, i.e. a main course, potato, rice or pasta, vegetable or salad and a dessert. Fresh salad, fresh yoghurt, fresh fruit, cheese and breadstick/biscuits are also available daily. Wholemeal bread with spread is available in addition to these items are for those children with larger appetites. This meal aims to give the balance of nutrients required by your child but due to the nature of the items written in red the potato row may be substituted with additional vegetables or salad if your child wishes.

A Junior school menu

LUNCH MENU
Wednesday 6th September 2011

CÊP — Roasted cêps with cauliflower cassonade, cêp ravioli and cauliflower purée

Or

COCO BEAN — Chilled coco bean soup with poached chicken and coco bean mousse

SEA BASS — Roasted fillet of sea bass, celeriac fondant puy lentils, bacon and langoustine emulsion

Or

PORK — Roasted loin of pork with black pudding, glazed pork belly and rosemary sauce

APPLE — Poached apple with vanilla tapioca and apple granité

Or

CHEESE — From our lunch selection of French cheeses

COFFEE AND PETIT FOURS — A selection of tea, coffee and tisanes

LUNCH MENU £29.00 inclusive of VAT
Optional 12.5% service charge will be added to your bill

A table d'hôte lunch menu

SCHOOL MENUS

In recent times, due to an array of public opinion the emphasis on healthy eating has been firmly placed onto the school menu agenda. All menus written have to be nutritionally balanced and offer suitably sized portions to give each student a healthy and nutritious lunch every day. Choices are offered and catering for vegetarianism and religious diets are commonplace. Investing in good quality food and a balanced diet is a primary function for school caterers so that school children will benefit from the social experience of eating with others, developing a taste for different foods, and gaining confidence to make the right food choices.

CONTRACT CATERING MENUS

Generally these are menus that are served to people at their place of work and sometimes at a subsidized price to the customer. Providing quality food for employees is an essential part of keeping them happy and motivated. Contract catering companies strive to provide innovative and high quality solutions, developing and delivering original food and service in the workplace, schools, colleges, hospitals, leisure centres and stadia, airlines or in remote environments for specialist functions. Clients are increasingly seeking more specialized answers to their needs, and operating in different regions and cultural environments means that menus have to be adapted to suit the locality. Executive dining menus are also catered for with the finest possible executive dining facilities for boardrooms, hospitality suites and at major social events.

BREAKFAST MENUS

These are written to meet the different needs of the customer, based on the amount of time they may have in the morning and the type of establishment that serves the breakfast. Breakfast can be served as an à la carte, table d'hôte, buffet or continental. As large choice as possible should be offered to maintain a practical and economic selection which meets the customer's expectations.

AFTERNOON TEA MENUS

These menus will vary depending on the type of establishment and may typically include the following aspects; assorted sandwiches, scones, assorted pastries and cakes, selection of teas and tisanes and toasted teacakes.

DESSERT MENUS

This type of menu has expanded somewhat in terms of meeting the latest trends of light, delicate and flavoursome selection of desserts that do not overindulge the customer. Sometimes the desserts can be a list of varied dishes that are priced individually or based on a set price. The desserts should be carefully selected to meet seasonal requirements and match against the rest of the menu that your customers have previously chosen from.

FUNCTION MENUS

When composing function menus the chef must consider the volume of customers that could attend a function so that each course can be dressed and finished as quickly as possible. Chefs occasionally reflect on the amount of movements or actions that it takes to present a dish. This means how many times you add a finished commodity to the plate to complete the dish. This in turn reflects the amount of time it takes a chef or team of chefs to present the dish. A luncheon menu usually consists of between two to four courses and should reflect lightness to the type of dishes served unless the event has a specific theme to it (such as Christmas). A dinner function menu generally consists of three to five courses, again depending on the occasion.

> **LEARNER SUPPORT** Examples of all of the above menus can be found on the *Professional Chef Level 2 CourseMate*.

Factors to consider when planning a menu

When providing menu choices to customers, whether this is in a school, restaurant, hotel or hospital it is important to plan menus adequately. This planning will not only ensure that they are attractive and acceptable to target customers but also that other aspects receive due consideration. Effective planning and control will result in accurate and timely purchasing, the reduction of waste, a more productive operation, and better customer satisfaction through consistent quality and better service.

A series of factors need to be considered before writing a menu, these include the following:

TYPE OF CUSTOMER

Writing menus to a certain style will attract different customers but may deter others from potentially becoming a new customer. Customer demand must be considered and traditional dishes and modern food trends need to be taken into account.

TYPE OF ESTABLISHMENT

As mentioned earlier in the chapter, there are a significant variety of different menus available for distinct establishments. This requires careful consideration alongside other issues such as location of the premises.

PRICING POLICY

Pricing needs to be seen as fair or considered good value if repeat custom is developed.

AVAILABILITY OF COMMODITIES

If the restaurant will be aimed at a specialist market, certain commodities will need to be available throughout the year and be of a high quality. Storage may also be a factor and this will also have a direct effect on the pricing of the menu.

EQUIPMENT AND SPACE AVAILABLE

The correct kitchen resource should be available to be able to prepare and cook the menu effectively. The chef should be aware of potential equipment deficiencies or lack of space that may make certain dishes difficult to produce.

STAFFING

Training is important to establish a good team of kitchen and front of house staff to deliver the requirements of the menu skilfully and efficiently.

COMPETITION FROM COMPETITORS

It is important to be aware of the locality and what is offered by the competition which should include price monitoring and their quality.

SEASONALITY

Local foods in season will usually be in good supply and reasonable in price. The temperature and time of year should also be considered because certain dishes suitable for cold weather will prove unpopular during the summer. Special dishes for different festivals can be considered such as St. Valentines Day, Christmas and Shrove Tuesday.

BALANCED MENU

Avoid repetition of ingredients, flavours, colours and textures. Create a menu with variety.

The use of cyclic menus

A cyclic menu is where the chef will compile set menus to cover a certain period of time. They are usually seen in the cost sector establishments such as staff canteens, cafeterias, hospitals or schools. At the end of each period the menus are then used again. This overcomes the need to constantly write new menus and the length of the cycle is usually determined by management policy and seasonality. This style of menu is monitored carefully to take into account customer preferences, changes of customer requirements, fluctuations in commodity prices and seasonal change that might result in a change of demand for specific dishes.

The disadvantages for using cyclic menus are that the chef or manager cannot take advantage of price friendly commodities offered by suppliers on a one-off basis if they are not used as part of the menu. Also, when this style of menu is used to serve a captive clientele, the cycle needs to be lengthy enough for the customers not to become jaded with the duplication of the dishes contained within the menus.

However, the advantages are that cyclic menus can create greater efficiency with time and labour costs and that you can reduce the amount of commodities held for long periods in stock, thus reducing storage requirements within your kitchen plan.

Basic cost control

It is essential to understand the exact cost of every dish produced. To undertake this, a reliable system of cost analysis and cost information is required. The advantages of an efficient costing system will include:

- The effective calculation of net profit made by each dish, department and the business. Preparation and cooking losses can be calculated alongside wastage percentages.

- The disclosure of potential savings or economic measures that can result in greater cost effectiveness.

- Information necessary to form a sound pricing policy.

- Facilitates the head chef to maintain budget control.

- Maintenance of costing records for future reference or to supply quotations for special events.

- The effective monitoring of commodity prices and potential fluctuation.

- The calculation of the total cost of a specific dish involves identifying the total cost of all items that combine to make up the dish.

- Food or material cost: These are known as variable costs because the actual cost will vary according to the volume of business, quality of food purchased, control of wastage and accurate weighing, measuring and portion control.

- Labour: All labour costs are divided into direct and indirect costs. Direct labour costs are attributed to the wages paid to chefs, waiters, bar staff and kitchen assistants where the cost can be directly related to the income from food and drink sales. Indirect labour costs are credited to the wages paid to managers, office staff and maintenance personnel who work for all departments and therefore their costs are spread over the number of departments that have a direct income.

- Cleaning materials: This is an area that is sometimes overlooked so it is important to understand and recognize the costs of these materials can be expensive but also necessary. It is important to ensure that an allowance is made for them in this section.

- Overheads (gas, electricity, rates, servicing, advertising, rent and equipment): It is important to factor the costs of overheads into every dish because these are the 'unseen' aspects of the serving of an individual dish.

- Gross and net profit.

To enable the caterer to control the element of profits it is usual to express this in terms of a percentage of the selling price of a dish. There are two terms of profit that must be distinguished.

Gross profit is the difference between the cost of the food to prepare the dish and the selling price of the dish.

Selling price − Food cost = Gross profit

Net profit is the difference between the selling price of the dish and the total cost of the dish (labour, overheads and cost of food).

Selling price − Total cost = Net profit

The table below describes an example of a crème caramel as the dish in question and how it relates to costing and profit analysis.

Selling price for a crème caramel	£4.50
Food cost for a crème caramel	£1.00
Addition of labour and overheads	£1.50
Total cost of the crème caramel	£2.50
Gross profit	£3.50
Net profit	£2.00

To determine the percentage gross profit of the crème caramel the following calculation needs to be used:

$$\frac{\text{Gross profit}}{\text{Sales}} \times 100 =$$

(or)

3.50 (gross profit) × 100 ÷ 4.50 (selling price)

= 77% (percentage gross profit)

To determine the percentage net profit of the crème caramel the following calculation needs to be used:

$$\frac{\text{Net profit}}{\text{Sales}} \times 100 =$$

(or)

2.00 (net profit) × 100 ÷ 4.50 (selling price)

$$= 44\% \text{ (percentage net profit)}$$

A rule that can be applied to effectively calculate the food cost price of a dish is to let the food cost of the dish equal 35% and fix the selling price at 100%.

For example:

Cost of the crème caramel = 100p = 35%

$$\text{Selling price} = \frac{100 \times 100}{35} = \text{£2.85}$$

Selling the crème caramel at £2.85 makes 65% gross profit above the 35% cost price

Fundamentals to controlling food costs

Ensure that you are charging the correct price for everything on your menu.

Remember to include a 40–50 per cent total dish cost when calculating each dish. Determining the cost of sauces and accompaniments such as salt, pepper and garnishes is very important in this process.

The average cost for commodities can rise by approximately 3–5 per cent per year. If the menu is not reviewed every three to six months, dishes may increase in cost which will shorten the profit margins. Seasonal ingredients will certainly fluctuate in price heavily due to quality and availability.

> **TASK**
>
> 1 If a dish costs £4.45, to calculate the selling price on the basis of 65 per cent gross profit, what would the final selling price be?
> 2 Using the latest market prices calculate the full dish cost per portion for a cream of celery soup.

COMPLETE WEEKLY STOCK TAKES AND FOOD COST CALCULATION

A weekly food cost calculation should be completed. An example of this is the stock take. This method is used to find out and value the amount of ingredients and commodities you currently have in storage. The stock takes can be divided into a number of different categories (dairy, meat, vegetables, fruit, dry commodities).

A food stock take spreadsheet is used for a more accurate stock take result. The use of a spreadsheet allows you to record weekly food deliveries and also count your stock at the end of the week. By counting your stock weekly you have a better chance to act on arising problems.

> **LEARNER SUPPORT** Download a stocktake spreadsheet from CourseMate.

PREVENT THEFT

The back door is still a key area where ingredients and commodities can disappear. To help prevent this there should be an alarm fitted on this door and no employee should be allowed to exit through this door without a manager present to turn off the alarm.

Employee purses, bags and coats should be kept out of the food production area and this will help to lessen the chances of food or other products potentially being taken.

CONTROLLING KITCHEN WASTE

Undertake rubbish-bin inspections on a regular basis. At the end of a service or production session, taking a few minutes to check through discarded food from the kitchen will help to emphasize to the team the importance of reducing food wastage through their preparation techniques or through portion control.

PORTION CONTROL

Continuously check portion sizes during service. Setting dish specifications for each menu item containing the precise quantities and quality points, with the sequence of preparation and service will enable the establishment to have greater control over costs and quality. The objective for a standard dish specification is to determine the number of portions a recipe should make and also describe the quality of the ingredients to be used. Ensure that the correct portion control equipment is available for the team to use.

IDENTIFY PRICE VARIATIONS ON INGREDIENTS

Always try to purchase ingredients at the best price that will ensure the specified quality will also meet your profit margins. The cheapest ingredient you purchase may prove to be the most expensive if most of it is wasted due to poor quality.

Learn about all the commodities to be purchased and keep up to date with new ingredients on the market and seasonal availability. Being aware of the different grading and classifications of fresh fruit, vegetables, meat and fish is also important to identify quality.

Compare prices with other suppliers and visit your suppliers on a regular basis if possible to build a strong and trusting relationship and monitor their reliability.

PURCHASING INGREDIENTS AND COMMODITIES

Part of planning a menu involves fully understanding the cost of each dish and how much the commodities used for each dish actually costs. Efficient purchasing of quality ingredients and commodities will help to ensure that your menu is cost effective and there are six important steps to consider when purchasing ingredients and commodities:

1   Clearly define the purchase needs.

2   Know the market.

3   Design a robust purchase procedure.

4   Always receive and check your purchases for quality control.

5   Establish and use specification sheets.

6   Continually evaluate and monitor the purchasing procedure.

Purchasing process encompasses the purchase of foods and beverages for an establishment, the receiving of the goods, storage and issuing of all commodities as well as being involved with the purpose for which the items are purchased and the final use for them. In many organizations this role may come under the heading of procurement and be a function for a different department such as finance or stores section. However, the chef needs to have a strong knowledge of the purchasing process because they deal directly with suppliers in most cases and with the actual raw commodity.

The purchasing function chart as illustrated below is vitally important to control the purchase system. Should this system not be managed efficiently it will create problems with unsatisfactory costs and profit for the establishment and potentially dissatisfied customers.

The purchasing function will vary between establishments, but however this role is maintained, the following aspects will usually need to be considered:

- Responsibility for the management of purchasing and maintaining purchasing records, recording the receiving and correct storage of goods.

- The purchase of all commodities within their responsibility.

- Ensuring the stability of supply of those items to the different sections within the kitchen.

- Find cheaper, but for the same quality, and more efficient sources of supply of selected commodities.

- Keeping up to date with markets being dealt with and evaluating new products.

- Research into products, markets, price trends and ethical purchasing.

- Co-ordinating with the whole kitchen to help standardize commodities and help to reduce stock levels.

PURCHASING POINT	FUNCTION
Management policies	This establishes the market sector aim, target pricing for certain commodities, the quality standards and the price to be charged to customers. They also set standard operating procedures (SOPs) to regulate the purchasing function.
Menu	Determines the selection of items available to customers.
Dish specification	Sets quality points and volumes for each dish on the menu.
Volume forecasting	Ascertains the quantity to be purchased.
Requisition	Indicates the precise requirements against the dish specification.
Purchasing	Selects and contacts suppliers, sets contracts with minimum and maximum delivery quantities. Ensures adequate temperature controlled storage is available and ensures continuity of supply.
Receiving	Inspects for quality and quantity – reports any discrepancies, checks compliance with required temperature laws and maintains records for HACCP. May check delivery vehicle temperatures as set in SOPs.
Storing	Correct storage for each item, ensures that all temperature sensitive items are stored quickly and correctly and ensures that freezers and refrigeration are not overloaded.
Production	Preparation of all items purchased with minimal wastage factor.
Selling	Provision of the finished menu products at the correct selling price and set quality level.
Control	The measurement of performance of all the outlets involved with adherence to company policy and SOPs. Provide feedback to the team and management.

- Liaising with all specific departments involved with the purchasing function such as; the kitchen, restaurant, accounts, marketing and management.

THE SELECTION OF A SUPPLIER

With competitive pricing and expanding global markets the selection of a supplier should be given prudent consideration. Seeking a new supplier requires care and detailed enquiries need to be made. Sometimes, larger establishments will carry out routine checks on a potential supplier which include credit reference checks and visits to the supplier's premises to check aspects of quality and adherence to HACCP regulations. Other points which require scrutiny are:

- Full details of the company and the range of items they are selling.

- A copy of recent price lists.

- Details of trading terms.

- Details of other customers (with whom you should consult).

- Samples of products.

- Selected suppliers will be added to an approved suppliers list and will be periodically evaluated for their performance using operational criteria established for each range of commodity; typically this will include price, quality and delivery.

- Purchase specifications for food.

A purchase specification is a concise description of the quality, size, grade and weight for a particular item. Other information can include the variety, maturity, colour and shape.

The reasoning behind the development of purchase specifications is to establish a buying standard of a commodity for the operation so that a standard product is available for the kitchen and restaurant to prepare for the customer. It also helps to inform the supplier precisely what is required and it assists the supplier in being competitive with pricing.

Introduction to applying workplace skills

Working within a team environment involves many process skills, interpersonal skills and personal qualities. These skills are important to the effectiveness of the team when undertaking various projects (e.g. preparing for a large buffet). Once again it includes co-operation with your employer, owner or manager to ensure that health and safety procedures are always followed.

Chefs' team planning meeting

One of the most vital skills any employer will seek is the ability to become a valued member of a team. Therefore, the skills shown below are essential in the contribution to the effectiveness of a team and its overall performance.

PURCHASE SPECIFICATION FOR A LOIN OF PORK	
Definition:	Taken from a rare breed (Gloucester Old Spot) and from organic Suffolk based farm. Eight (8) Rib End (Rack), Centre-cut. The tenderloin shall remain intact.
Weight range:	Between 6 and 8 kg.
Surface fat:	Surface fat shall be trimmed to an average of ¼–inch (6 mm) in depth.
Chine bone:	Off.
Other boning specifications:	All boning to be done so that no bone fragments remain and no knife cuts are deeper than 12 mm.
Packaging:	Wrapped in wax paper with quality tag.
Delivery:	Day following the order date.

- Process skills:
  - target setting
  - planning
  - clarifying roles and responsibilities
  - organizing
  - obtaining resources
  - reviewing the work.
- Interpersonal skills:
  - teamwork and supporting co-workers
  - communicating ideas and needs
  - listening to others
  - showing assertiveness
  - negotiating support
  - asking for help and feedback
  - handling disagreement and conflict.
- Personal qualities:
  - reliable
  - confident
  - empathetic
  - self aware
  - open to feedback
  - willing to learn from experience
  - persistent.

Effective teamwork is an essential ingredient in all successful organizations. The traditional kitchen brigade has always been a strong team that is usually made up of smaller groups with specific tasks and roles. Nowadays these traditional hierarchies have given way to flatter structures and chefs are more multi-skilled. Some teams can be relatively permanent, and repetitive tasks and familiar work mean that each team member has a fixed role. Experience shows that team working increases creativity, makes the most of a range of skills and knowledge, improves understanding, communication and a sense of shared purpose and overall it will improve efficiency.

'Changes in working methods and technology have had a profound effect on work. People who work well in groups, are well organized and can solve their problems are the people who get on best at work and get promoted.'

Employment Policy Institute (2003)

CHEF'S TIP When working in a kitchen, regardless whether it is a large company chain or small independent restaurant, you are an important member of the team. You will be working with other people that you do not know, and yet will have to develop an instant working relationship. As an integral part of the team you will need to quickly establish who the other members of the team are, who is responsible for different things and to whom you need to go to for any help and guidance.

Professional presentation

Presentation includes your appearance and conduct. You should promote a high standard of cleanliness and professionalism. How you dress and your personal hygiene are a vital part of this; see pages 51–54 for more information. Your conduct includes your attitude, initiative, punctuality, dependability, organization, communication and time-management.

Organizing your own work

Forecasting is the ability to plan ahead and trying to predict possible changes in terms of the amount of covers a restaurant will serve in the days ahead. This requires experience, previous knowledge and good judgement.

Planning is a crucial part of work in a kitchen and in the workplace generally. In order to complete a task effectively and on time planning is always involved. Larger tasks will need to be broken down into smaller sized, more manageable tasks, with 'milestones' along the way. Planning needs to be undertaken to:

- Identify what needs to be done, when and by whom.
- Help to foresee any potential problems so plans can be developed on how to tackle them.
- Provide a method for monitoring and controlling work, helping to ensure that things are done to the correct standard and on time.

CHEF'S TIP A 'milestone' is a significant point where you can stop to review what has been achieved on your way to the overall completion of the actual task.

ACTION PLANS

Action plans will vary in detail depending on the level of task that needs to be completed. At every level, the first stage is to identify the steps that need to be taken to get the task done. It is often helpful to begin by brainstorming a list of tasks and then sketching a rough diagram, using boxes and arrows, rather than by trying to list the steps in order from the start. Sometimes this is referred to as a 'work-flow diagram'.

It can be difficult to estimate how much time is required to carry out a task. It is always helpful to check recipes and cooking times in order for a reasonable idea of how long a task will take can be assumed. Other activities will also need to be thought about, such as, assembling the ingredients and tools, preparing pans and baking sheets, pre-heating ovens and ensuring that all tools and equipment are clean and hygienic. These activities are essential to the successful completion of a specific task and are collectively referred to as mise-en-place. This is a French term that means 'getting everything ready and in its place'. There are six basic organizational skills needed before actual preparation and cooking can take place. The flow-chart below illustrates these skills and how a flow-chart is produced:

Read the recipe carefully

↓

Identify tools and equipment needed

↓

Gather all necessary ingredients, tools and equipment close to the work area

↓

Prepare all the equipment and tools for use

↓

Measure the ingredients accurately

↓

Practice good sanitation

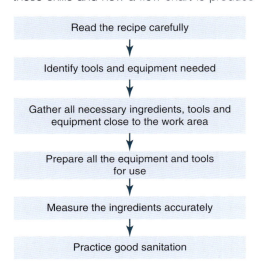

Chef reading a recipe

READING THE RECIPE CAREFULLY

Reading the recipe carefully is the first skill of a successful chef. As tedious as this may appear, many people scan the recipe too quickly and miss the specific information, methods, ingredients or tools required to complete the task. If it is read unsystematically, the recipe may not turn out as expected because the chef did not have the necessary

ingredients, tools or skills to prepare it. Recipes are specific ingredients in exact quantities and some professional pastry chefs refer to these as formulas.

Selection of tools and equipment on a rack

IDENTIFYING TOOLS AND EQUIPMENT NEEDED

As a recipe is studied, the chef should be making a note as to which tools and equipment will be needed. If a specific tool is not available, can another be substituted without jeopardizing the recipe? For example, if a chicken mousseline recipe is being prepared and a food blender is needed but unavailable, what could be used instead? Maybe a fine mincing attachment to a food mixer can be used before combining all the required ingredients in a bowl on the mixer. Some chefs try to make substitutions that do not work. For example, if a sponge cake recipe that relies on the aeration of eggs states to fold the egg whites into a batter with a spatula but a whisk is used instead, what is the end result? The sponge may not rise because air was lost when the egg was folded in too roughly with an inappropriate tool and technique.

Selection of tools to prepare a dish on a work station

GATHERING THE NECESSARY INGREDIENTS, TOOLS AND EQUIPMENT CLOSE TO THE WORK AREA

Once the chef is ready to commence, all the ingredients, tools and equipment must be gathered and brought close to the work area. If these items are not gathered beforehand, then too much time will be spent running around the kitchen to obtain the ingredients and tools, thus wasting valuable time and energy. One piece of equipment that must be prepared if being used is the oven. Pre-heating the oven should be done at least 10–15 minutes before it will be used.

Chef preparing a baking sheet with melted butter

PREPARING THE EQUIPMENT AND TOOLS FOR USE

Before the actual preparation of food commences, all equipment and tools need to be checked to ensure that they are clean and in good repair. Certain equipment such as baking sheets will need to be prepared which could include; lining with baking parchment, greasing or greasing and flouring.

Chef measuring flour using digital scales

MEASURING THE INGREDIENTS ACCURATELY

Measuring ingredients properly is the foundation of success. Recipes in cookbooks have already been tested with specific amounts of ingredients. It is important to accurately measure each ingredient so that the recipe consistently works every time it is used. The use of digital scales is easier to use, faster and more accurate than many of its predecessors. There are different ways to measure ingredients: by volume (litres and millilitres) and by weight (kilograms and grams).

Chef sanitizing a work station and knives

PRACTISING GOOD SANITATION

It is critical for any person preparing food in a kitchen to keep ingredients sanitary and to practise good hygiene. Sanitation refers to the various practices used to reduce the number of micro organisms that can lead to food contamination and food borne illnesses. It is important to wash your hands before commencing food preparation, also during the preparation sequence and immediately after. Avoid cross contamination or spreading bacteria from one surface to another by washing your hands, tools and work surfaces before commencing each new task.

Skills required to work with colleagues and customers

ORGANIZING

The skill of organization in the kitchen refers to ensuring that the equipment, ingredients, chefs and information that are required is at hand. For the head chef or the manager, organization involves the production of cleaning schedules, ordering of supplies, managing duty rotas and training programmes.

COMMANDING

Being able to command effectively means giving instructions to the team. This is especially required during the service time where orders need to be clearly communicated, timings adhered to and discipline maintained under pressure.

CO-ORDINATION

This skill is similar to that of organizing whereby the skill is to get the team to work together and synchronize the work of each section. This is an essential area for the success of any hospitality operation.

CONTROLLING

The control of products, team members, implementing systems and monitoring quality to consistently improve performance is paramount. Possessing a professional attitude and developing a professional organization boosts morale and potentially gains the confidence of customers in the establishment. Controlling all aspects of the kitchen such as equipment, maintenance, hygiene standards, cleaning, quality standards of food and wastage are very important functions for a chef.

WORKING TO DEADLINES

Working to realistic deadlines is an important factor for a chef, especially during a busy luncheon or dinner service. Doing this effectively depends on the prior skills of estimating how long the task is and being able to prioritize individual jobs. Once that is achieved, it may be helpful to set intermediate deadlines related to relatively short and defined cookery or food preparation based tasks.

CHEF'S TIP Find out which tasks take priority over others. Some jobs are more important or urgent than others and will need to be done first. Remember, that if you have to leave a task halfway through, make sure that you get back to complete it at the earliest convenient moment.

Time management is an important skill for chefs working in the hospitality industry. In order to manage your time more effectively, you must have a realistic assessment of all the tasks required (as mentioned earlier in the chapter) and then plan the workload accordingly.

The ability to set shared targets and make plans is decisive to successful teamwork. If chefs do not know what they are aiming to achieve, they cannot determine what has been achieved. Summarily, if there is no real planning, progression cannot be properly monitored to review how well things are going and to be able to learn from the experience. It is during these stages that team members can support each other and provide help where necessary to achieve the end result.

SUPPORT THE WORK OF YOUR TEAM

Teams often have to agree targets and plans when preparing a luncheon, special function or dinner. The most effective plans have SMART targets that clearly set out what needs to be done to achieve the targets. The acronym SMART is often used to describe an effective target.

SMART TARGETS	
Specific	Outlining exactly what the group aims to do, rather than expressing vague general aims.
Measurable	Outlining how the group will know it has met the targets and what evidence will show this.
Achievable	Challenging for the group, but not too difficult.
Realistic	The opportunities and resources should be available.
Time-bound	There should be both interim and final deadlines.
TARGETS CAN BE EVEN SMARTER. THEY CAN BE:	
Enjoyable	
Rewarding	

It is important that during this early stage job roles are clearly defined and set to specific employees. Each job role should be considered to strategically meet the requirements of the organization and to successfully contribute to the effectiveness of the team.

COMMUNICATION SKILLS

To become effective in communication such as speaking and listening, you should have an understanding of non-verbal communication (NVC), or body language.

NVC can take many forms:

- touch: greetings, agreements, apologies, goodbyes
- posture: sitting or standing straight, leaning forward or back
- proximity: distance between people, personal territory
- dress: clothes, hair, appearance
- eye contact: indicates interest and attention or the opposite
- hand gestures: agreement, disagreement, impatience, welcome
- facial expression: shows emotions and provides feedback.

Asking questions or making a point during discussions is an essential element to effective communication. Many people will want to ask questions but some will not do so because they lack the confidence to put their thoughts across at the right moment. It is a key sign of support if you can ask questions in a positive manner.

- Briefly express your appreciation of the speaker, e.g. 'That was a really interesting point'.
- Briefly summarize the point made by the speaker, e.g. 'I was particularly interested in what you said about …'
- Ask your question, if you need to, write it down and read it out and try to make it clear, concise, relevant, informed and non-aggressive.

Listening skills are crucial for effective communication and teamwork. They ensure that we obtain the right information from the right people, help us understand what information or support other people need and help to work more effectively as a group.

Other forms of communication are the telephone and via a written format (e.g. email, memorandum, fax or letter). The telephone is a fast and effective way of communicating specific requirements or orders to a supplier or to communicate events from another location that may affect the overall outcome of a specific task. It should be noted that when using the telephone, your face cannot be seen and it is important to consider your tone of voice and to speak clearly.

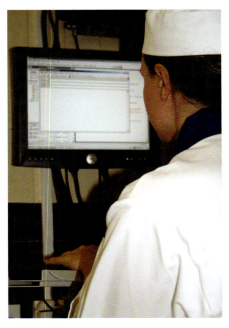
Chef using the email system on a PC

With the advent of information technology and the email system it is now easier than ever to record conversations and attach relevant documents. Suppliers can now usually accept orders electronically via an email system which makes it easier to see potential mistakes in the order or gives a greater sense of clarity to the order. Staff training in areas of communication and especially IT awareness is imperative if the organization is to develop and succeed.

Preparing for a job application

The curriculum vitae

A curriculum vitae (CV) is a Latin term meaning 'the story of your life'. It should be a maximum length of two sides of A4 paper. This may require a selective approach so that you do not include too much detail and should only literally include the highlights of your education, experience and career.

Your CV is a marketing document; therefore it should include everything that reflects you in the most positive light for a specific position with a particular company. One of the main purposes of the CV is to obtain an interview, so it needs to persuade the recruiter that they want to meet you in person to discuss your qualities.

Before beginning to write a CV the first task is to try brainstorming all you have to offer an employer on to a piece of paper. Focus on getting all your details on paper.

It is essential that you do your research before applying for a position. Find out as much as you can about the company, the industry sector and the specific position. It is more productive to spend time undertaking a lot of preparation and applying for fewer posts that you have researched thoroughly, than to send out lots of CVs across the board.

When focusing on the positions and companies that you are interested in, it is important to consider the following:

● What are the company's needs?

● How and what can you contribute to this organization?

● What are the main requirements for the post?

● Are there any general or specific skills that are required?

● What are the specific qualifications needed?

It is important to try to match your details in your brainstormed paper to the requirements of the job. Rather than merely listing your skills, think of an example as evidence of how you have gained, developed or used a specific skill. On your brainstorm paper write the evidence beside each item.

APPEARANCE AND STYLE

First impressions really do count. Research has shown that recruiters initially spend only 30 seconds scanning a CV to see if the qualifications match and the potential applicant show qualities that are needed by the company. This means that appearance and presentation of the CV are very important.

When writing a CV, you do not have to use sentences. Short, concise phrases that get straight to the point with positive words to describe any roles you have performed are fine. Use bullet points to help to emphasize this impression.

Always keep a copy for your records and to take with you to the interview. Use an A4 envelope to avoid folding your CV.

The following points should be considered when producing the CV:

● Use bold fonts where necessary, apply the font size and lower/upper case to make the section headings and key points stand out.

● Be consistent and logical in the use of bold and plain fonts, underline and font size.

● Centre it on the page with top and bottom margins of equal size, as well as left and right margins.

● Use good white or cream paper only.

● Print on one side only using a printer which gives a good quality printout.

● Get someone to proof read, check spelling, grammar and punctuation.

● Size 12 and Times New Roman or Arial font are usually acceptable because they tend to be easier on the reader's eye.

There may be some aspects of your life that are difficult to tackle on a CV. An example of this could be a disability or gaps in your education and employment due to ill health. How you choose to approach this will be a personal evaluation that you may feel strongly about. However, there are methods of disclosing information positively so that it does not look too negative in the CV. Alternatively you can choose not to disclose this information at all. There are no quick answers to this dilemma and the decision is ultimately a personal choice. But you may find it beneficial to discuss this with a careers adviser.

THE CONTENT OF A CV

While there is no existent standard format to a CV, there are some general expectations of what it should contain. The key areas are the following:

Personal details

Always include your name, address, telephone number, mobile telephone number and email address at the beginning.

Use your name as an overall heading rather than the words 'Curriculum Vitae'.

It is not necessary to include your nationality, sex or marital status. If you are a mature graduate and you fear ageism, you may wish to exclude your date of birth or state it at the end. It may be advantageous to put 'no work permit needed' or 'permanent UK resident', but only if there is anything on your CV to suggest otherwise.

Education and qualifications

These should be listed in reverse order, starting with the most recent. State your qualifications, schools, colleges and university with the appropriate dates.

It is not necessary to give the full address of your, college, university or school and it is not necessary to go further back than secondary school.

If you have studied overseas, list each qualification and state its equivalence to UK qualification. It may be helpful to provide further information but do not include grades that an employer may not understand. You do not have to list any examinations you may have failed. Emphasize only your successes.

Work history

Once again, this needs to be listed in reverse order, starting with the most recent and working in reverse. You can include details of full and part-time paid work. You should also include work experience or placements.

State the job title first, then the name and location of the organization, the dates and a brief description of responsibilities and duties of the position. It is not necessary to give the full address of every employer.

Explain the overall purpose of the job, in its context, rather than simply listing all the tasks. Describe the most demanding or responsible aspects of the job and highlight any special achievements obtained during this time.

Highlight the skills that you developed which are relevant to the post you are applying for.

If you have a long work history, you may need to make some firm decisions about what to include or leave out. Do not leave any gaps which cannot be accounted for. Most recruiters expect you to account for your time. If there are long periods of time unaccounted for, they may imagine the worst.

Interests or achievements

In this section you might include sports, voluntary work, travel, membership of clubs and societies, positions of responsibility and competition work, which have developed team-working skills or other important personal qualities.

Quality is more important than quantity. One or two interests that you have developed to a high level, or shown long term commitment to, are better than a long list. Culinary Competition work, in which you have performed well or undertake regularly, look better than a long list of sports events of which you are just a spectator or have not played since school.

References

Include at least two references; preferably an academic reference and one from a recent employer.

State the name, address, telephone number and occupation of the referee and how they know you. Always ask referees first if they are happy to be used.

Keep them informed about the type of position you are looking for and the result of the applications. Give them a copy of your CV and always thank them – especially when you are successful! If there is a particular reason why you do not wish to give details of references at this stage, then you can state 'references available on request'.

Your key skills

Under this heading you can list the skills that are most relevant to the post, for example, communication, teamwork, attention to detail and problem-solving. Always offer an example of something you have done as evidence that you possess the skills you are claiming.

Exhibitions, awards, prizes and achievements

For chefs this may be one of the most important aspects of the CV.

Personal profile

This can provide a useful summary at the top of the CV which draws together your career goals with the highlights of your CV.

Languages

List languages spoken, or written and level of fluency. For example; German (fluent), French (read and understand), Spanish (basic).

In addition to the above sections, there are a number of others which might be included. You will need to decide on these, according to what works best for you. Start by listing everything you wish to include, and then decide how to organize it.

> **TASK** Using the information given in this book, prepare a curriculum vitae detailing your education and work experience to date.

COVERING LETTERS

A CV should always be accompanied by a covering letter. It should explain why you are sending your CV and it must grab the attention and lead the reader into wanting to look at your CV.

The covering letter is where you can make your case for being the right person for that post in that particular organization. The letter should be well presented with perfect spelling and grammar that demonstrates your ability to express yourself correctly in good business English. This applies even if you are applying for a post where writing skills are not critical.

The style should be positive, convincing and convey enthusiasm. 'I would welcome' surpasses 'I am willing to'. 'I am especially enthusiastic about ...' is more positive than 'I am quite interested in'.

This should not sound like a standard letter and can be tailored to the individual position and to the organization you are addressing. If possible, address it to a named person.

The letter should be no longer than one side of A4, and set out as a formal business letter. Always be concise and to the point. It would normally be word-processed; however some employers do ask for hand-written letters.

The interview

Your application form, CV and covering letter were successful and you been invited to interview. Interviewing is an expensive process for any employer, so you must have met most, if not all, of the requirements of the job for the employer to want to meet you. Having got so far, how can you ensure that you excel at the interview?

You should always research the job description and company you are having your interview with, practising answering questions out loud is also a good way of refining your interview technique.

While you should not learn your answers off by heart, practising with friends or family will help develop your confidence and mean you will be equipped for the most general questions.

Although many employers use sophisticated recruitment methods, especially for senior positions, the interview still forms a vital part of the process.

The employer will want to quiz you on certain aspects of your application form/CV, make a judgement as to how well you will do the job and assess how you will cope in different situations. They will be asking, 'Will your skills and personality complement those of others in the team? Will you get on with other people? Will you identify with the aims of the organization?'

On your side the interview gives you the chance to meet future colleagues, ask any questions you may have about the post or the company, and try to get a feeling for the culture of the organization and possibly see where you will be working. You will be asking yourself, 'Can I see myself working here? Will I be successful? Is the job likely to give me what I am looking for?'

Sometimes an employer may ask you to commence a work trial for a limited time so that they can see you in their environment. This is also a good tool for you to understand the background to the organization and meet your potential team members.

Many factors are outside your control, such as the format of the interview, the personalities of the interviewer(s) and the quality of the other candidates. However, many factors that contribute to a successful interview are within your control. The key area for this is preparation.

MAKING A GOOD IMPRESSION

If the company has a brochure or web page, look to see what people are wearing in any photos – that can often give you a indication of the company philosophy.

If you feel you ought to buy something new to wear to the interview, make sure it feels comfortable. If in doubt wear a suit and tie, or smart skirt/trousers, and a jacket. Do not wear jeans or exceed the wearing of jewellery or scent. Always

look clean and tidy. Rightly or wrongly, interviewers will always draw conclusions about you from your appearance.

Plan your route, double checking train or bus times and parking arrangements if driving. Aim to arrive 15 minutes early. It is better to sit and reread your application, than to arrive in a panic. If possible, do a 'dummy run' to the place of interview the day before.

Read the brochure and web site again, together with any job description, person specification, copies of menus and restaurant reviews. Read the Annual Report (if available) and any other information you can find about the employer.

Check that you know:

- something of the company background
- its products, services, menus and accolades
- the approximate number of employees
- the mission statement of the company.

It is very important to consider and list questions you want to ask about the post and the organization.

CURRENT ISSUES

In the days and weeks before your interview, read the business sections of the quality press and specialist hospitality and catering journals to find out everything you can about the organization, its rivals and the marketplace in which it operates. Use the internet to gather information. You will be expected to show at the interview that you are aware of current issues affecting the organization and your specific job.

Dealing with questions can be the most daunting part of the interview process. It helps to understand the nature of questioning and what different types of questions are commonly used and how to respond effectively.

TYPES OF QUESTIONS USED IN INTERVIEWS

- Open – 'Tell me about your qualifications' This question is often used at the start of an interview to allow you to relax and talk freely.

- Technical – 'What types of menu are you familiar with?' Used to find out how much you know and assess your level of competence in relation to the job description.

- Hypothetical – 'What would you do if ...?' This is used to test out your ability to think on your feet and to check your skills in problem solving and prioritizing.

- Leading – 'I see you changed your course, couldn't you cope?' A more insinuating way of challenging you and making you justify a decision/action you have made.

- Reflective – 'Am I right in thinking from what you say that ...?' By repeating what you have said to encourage you to expand your thoughts.

GOLDEN RULES WHEN ANSWERING QUESTIONS IN INTERVIEWS

- Look the interviewer in the eye.

- If it is a panel interview, look at other members of the panel from time to time to 'include' them in the conversation.

- Speak clearly and confidently. Try not to speak too fast or too quietly.

- If you don't understand the question ask for it to be repeated or clarified.

- There is not always a right or wrong answer. The interviewer is sometimes looking more at how you respond to the question or hypothetical situation.

WHAT EMPLOYERS LIKE TO SEE AT THE INTERVIEW

- Genuine interest in the post and organization.

- Saying what they want to hear – demonstrate that you have what they are looking for.

- An open and frank approach.

- A willing attitude.

- An interest in developing yourself and being trained.

- Motivation towards job rather than money.

- Appearance and attitude matching the organization's image.

WHAT EMPLOYERS DO NOT LIKE TO SEE

- Lack of openness.

- Blaming other people for any problems you have had.

- Little effort made to find out about the organization or post.

- Inappropriate dress and appearance.

- Too many questions about pay, pensions and holidays.

- Arrogance or a negative attitude.

- Being over familiar, e.g. using the interviewers first name.

- Smoking, chewing gum, eating or drinking (unless offered refreshments).

EVALUATING THE INTERVIEW

If you do not achieve the result you wanted and do not get the post, it is important to evaluate and try to work out what, if anything, went wrong. Consider asking the company to give you feedback. Many will do this and it could help you to be successful at your next interview.

REMEMBER: there might have been nothing wrong with you or the way you performed. It could simply be that on the day there was a stronger candidate. Try not to think of it as a failure, but as a learning experience that can be used to perform even better at the next interview.

If you continue to get interviews but they do not result in job offers do not get despondent and arrange to talk it over with a careers adviser to see how you can improve your interview technique.

Contribute to your own development of skills

Appraisal or progress reviews are an important method of communication, where one member of staff looks at the way another employee/member of staff is performing in their job role. It is usual for an employee to receive an appraisal from their line manager.

CHEF'S TIP   Continuing Professional Development (CPD) is a term used by professionals who constantly update their skills. Every opportunity should be explored to continue to update and learn new skills, techniques and knowledge wherever possible.

Appraisals provide an opportunity to review individuals' performance against targets set. Each team member will have their own strengths and weaknesses and it is important to utilize those strengths and action plan to build upon and improve the weaknesses with appropriate personal goals.

Performance appraisal will identify:

- results achieved against pre-set targets

- any additional accomplishments and contributions.

This may seem overwhelming, but it is an important and useful process. It can also be used to one's own advantage.

- Identify with your line manager the tasks you see that need to be accomplished, and how these will be met.

- Identify training needs. This will provide you with a greater range of skills and expertise and will ultimately improve your opportunities for promotion, giving you increased responsibilities.

- Identify obstructions which are affecting your progress.

- Identify and amend any changes to your current job role.

- Identify what additional responsibilities you would like.

- Identify and focus on your achievements to date against the targets set.

- Update your action plan, which will help you achieve your targets.

If personal targets are not being met it is important to identify the problem. Following this, new performance targets should be put in place to resolve any difficulties. At the next appraisal the agreed objectives and targets set for the previous period will be reviewed.

In order to develop personally and to improve your skills professionally, it is important to have personal targets against which you can measure your achievement. If these are confidential, the workplace policy on confidentiality should be observed. As mentioned earlier in the chapter all targets set should be SMART.

To an employer it is important that you are consistent. You must always perform your skills to the highest standard and present and promote a positive image of the industry and the business you represent.

CHEF'S TIP Internal promotion may require an employee to put in extra work, take on more responsibility or come up with new ideas.

The development of skills by entering culinary competitions, will give you the chance to meet and compete against other chefs and give you the opportunity to see new techniques and exchange ideas. This is an immense learning strategy personally and will also give a positive reputation to both yourself and your place of work. There are many different competitions both on a local and national basis with categories for both junior chefs and senior chefs.

Student chef competing at a competition

Chefs can also learn and develop through the membership of professional associations. Developing a network of associates, friends and peers is very important for business and learning. Chefs, employers, suppliers, training providers and managers are able to exchange ideas and to discuss

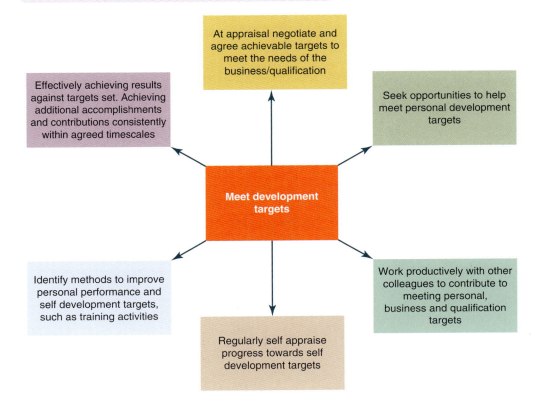

At appraisal negotiate and agree achievable targets to meet the needs of the business/qualification

Effectively achieving results against targets set. Achieving additional accomplishments and contributions consistently within agreed timescales

Seek opportunities to help meet personal development targets

Meet development targets

Identify methods to improve personal performance and self development targets, such as training activities

Regularly self appraise progress towards self development targets

Work productively with other colleagues to contribute to meeting personal, business and qualification targets

ways to help meet industry targets such as training, profitability and links to other industries across the world.

The continuation of learning is essential to succeed in this industry and the prospect of continuing to acquire knowledge and further develop skills to advance your career is a very real incentive. Colleges have diverse courses of study to help match your development plan. They assess the future skills that the industry requires in order for your job to be carried out effectively and for your progress in your profession.

CHEF'S TIP   In quieter periods observe colleagues who have more advanced qualifications and experience. Practice your skills at every opportunity! The more you practice the more skilled and efficient you will become.

Your individual learning plan can be based on the following chart below. It is imperative that you can revisit the chart on a regular basis to review your progress and match your aims and objectives against this.

TEST YOURSELF

To test your level of knowledge and understanding, answer the following short questions. These will help to prepare you for your summative (final) assessment.

1   Identify three ways of maintaining good working relationships with other team members and list three examples of effective team work.

2   Explain the French term 'mise-en-place'.

3   Feedback on your job role performance may not always be positive and may identify areas for improvement:

   a. State the importance in responding positively to such feedback.
   b. Explain how this information improves your performance in the future.

4   State how you would consider which important personal activities you would add to the CV.

5   State the purpose of an appraisal or performance review.

6   Explain the importance of a good workflow in a kitchen.

7   Describe the traditional kitchen hierarchy, using a diagram.

8   Explain the importance of a menu, stating the three main aspects a menu should communicate to a customer.

9   State three factors that need to be considered in the planning of menus. Design a luncheon menu for a Contract Catering Service which serves 1000 meals per lunch in a large factory.

10   The cost of the food is important.

   a. Explain why.
   b. Describe two factors which must be monitored to control food costs.
   c. Describe one factor which must be monitored to control net profit.
   d. Explain the term net profit and gross profit.

2

Health, safety and food hygiene in catering and hospitality

NVQ

Unit 1 GEN1 Maintain a safe, hygienic and secure working environment

Unit 2 GEN3 Maintain food safety when storing, preparing and cooking food

VRQ

Unit 202 Food safety in catering

Unit 203 Health and safety in catering and hospitality

LEARNING OBJECTIVES

The aim of this chapter is to enable the reader to develop proficiency and put into practice their knowledge of the health, safety and hygienic practices within the workplace. It discusses the health and safety requirements and policies that you will need to use if you are to work safely and responsibly in the professional kitchen. This will also include information on resources at the disposal of the chef to implement any government and industry sector guidelines and legislation.

At the end of this chapter you will be able to:

- Identify the correct attire for the chef in the workplace.

- Understand the implications and responsibility in the workplace for personal health and hygiene.

- Be able to report illnesses and minor accidents.

- Recognize the importance of security in the workplace and how to enforce emergency procedures.

- Indicate potential hazards in the workplace and how to effectively deal with them.

- Identify the legislation and action enabling the reduction of hazards and risks at work Identify the correct attire for the chef in the workplace.

- Be aware of your responsibility for personal cleanliness during food preparation and cooking in the workplace and for unsafe behaviour.

- Maintain clean and hygienic work surfaces and equipment.

- Check food into the premises and identify specific labels.

- Understand the correct use of storage control, the stock rotation system and keeping records.

- Know how to safely defrost food and thoroughly wash food.

- Know the regulations for the safe cooking, the safe holding and the safe reheating of food.

- Chill and freeze cooked food that is not for immediate consumption.

Introduction to safety in the professional kitchen

Chef working in a clean and tidy kitchen

Whatever job role you have in the hospitality industry, everyone is required to behave safely and professionally. Reasonable care must be taken to safeguard the health and safety of yourself and others who may be affected by what you do. You must always be responsible for your own behaviour and ensure that your actions do not cause a health and safety risk to yourself, others that you work with or customers. This includes co-operation with your employer, owner or manager to ensure that health and safety procedures are followed.

TASK Make a list of the people you think have a direct interest and involvement in health and safety? Compare your list with the rest of your group.

Legal responsibilities for health and safety

All employees and employers must take reasonable care of their own safety and the safety of others. In this respect, employees must inform their line manager if they see anything they deem to be unsafe and might cause an accident. Under the Health and Safety at Work Act an employer must also ensure that all staff are safe while at work. This includes the regular training of staff in safe practices and of dangerous equipment.

HEALTH & SAFETY Aspects that will help to minimize the risk of accidents are:

- wearing protective clothing
- up to date training schemes in health, safety and food hygiene
- continued monitoring and updated health and safety practices
- good lighting throughout the work premises
- provision of safe and regularly maintained equipment
- adequate storage of chemicals.

If you affect harm to a customer, or place them at risk of harm, you will personally be held responsible and could be liable to criminal prosecution under current law. There are many legislative directives relating to health and safety and the details are widely available. It is your duty to become aware of your own accountability and responsibilities towards this.

The potential costs of health and safety

Tackling health and safety should not be thought of as a regulatory burden: it offers significant opportunities. The benefits can include:

- reduced costs to the employer
- reduced risks to the employee
- lower employee absence and turnover rates
- fewer accidents in the workplace
- lessened threat of legal action
- improved standing among suppliers and partners
- better reputation for corporate responsibility among investors, customers and communities
- increased productivity, because employees are healthier, happier and better motivated.

Health and Safety Executive (HSE) statistics reveal the human and financial cost of failing to address health and safety, such as: more than 150 people are killed at work in the United Kingdom each year. In 2009, 38.5 million working days were lost in the UK due to occupational ill health and injury, imposing an annual cost to society of about £30bn (more than three per cent of GDP). Surveys have shown that about two million people suffer from an illness that they believe to be caused or made worse by work. Organizations can incur further costs – such as uninsured losses and loss of reputation.

Reporting of Injuries, Diseases and Dangerous Occurrences Regulations (RIDDOR) (1996)

All injuries must be reported to the member of staff responsible for health and safety: this includes injuries involving guests, visitors and staff. An accident book must be completed with basic personal details of the person or persons involved, together with a detailed description of the incident. Each accident report book should comply with the recent Data Protection Act 2003.

The Act's key message is that you must report:

- any fatal accidents
- injuries sustained such as electric shocks or burns that lead to unconsciousness and/or send the person to hospital for more than 24 hours
- work-related diseases such as asthma attacks, dermatitis, skin cancer, hepatitis, tetanus and tuberculosis
- major injuries sustained while at work that lead to hospitalization, unconsciousness, fractures, dislocations, loss of sight or amputation
- any potentially dangerous event that takes place at work
- accidents causing more than three days' absence from work.

Always ensure that the accident report book is in an accessible place for everyone to use and that everybody is trained in the documentation of accidents. It is important that the report book is checked to monitor for regular occurrences.

The Health and Safety at Work Act (1974)

The Health and Safety at Work Act (1974) covers employees, employers, the self-employed, customers and visitors. It describes the minimum standards of health, safety and welfare required in each area of the workplace. The Act's key message is that when working in a kitchen you must maintain a safe and healthy working environment at all times.

Health and Safety (Information for Employees) Regulations (1989)

These Regulations require the employer to provide employees with health and safety information in the form of posters, notices and leaflets. The Health and Safety Executive provides relevant publications.

Regular health and safety checks should be made to ensure that safe practices are being used. Employees must co-operate with their employer to provide a safe and healthy workplace. As soon as any hazard is observed, it must be reported to the designated authority or line manager so that the problem can be rectified. Hazards can include:

- obstructions to corridors, stairways and fire exits
- spillages and breakages
- faulty electrical machinery.

Hazard warning symbols

The Workplace (Health, Safety and Welfare) Regulations (1992)

This Act provides a set of benchmarks to cover the legal requirements necessary in a working environment such as ventilation, indoor temperature, lighting and staff facilities. The Act's key message is that when working in the hospitality industry you must maintain a safe and healthy working environment. Another subject covered is the maintenance of the workplace and equipment, cleanliness and the safe and correct handling of waste materials.

The Control of Substances Hazardous to Health (COSHH) Regulations (1999)

The COSHH Regulations are a workplace policy that is relevant to everyday working practices. Toxic chemicals such as detergents are hazardous and present a high risk. They must be stored, handled, used and disposed of correctly in accordance with COSHH. Essentially these Regulations state that an employer must not continue any work that could expose employees to any substances that are hazardous to health, unless the employer has correctly assessed the risks of this work to employees.

Hazardous substances are usually identified through the use of identified symbols, examples of which are shown here.

Any substance in the workplace that is hazardous to health must be identified on the packaging and stored and handled correctly.

Hazardous substances can enter the body via:

- the skin
- the eyes
- the mouth (ingestion)
- the nose (inhalation).

The COSHH Regulations were consolidated (updated) in 2002 and employers are held responsible for assessing the risks from hazardous substances and for controlling exposure to them to prevent ill health. Any hazardous substances identified should be formally recorded in writing and given a risk rating.

HAZARDOUS SUBSTANCES FOUND IN THE CATERING INDUSTRY
Cleaning chemicals for heavy equipment
Detergents
Sanitizers
Descalers
Pest control substances
Polishes
Methylated spirits
Glass washing detergent
Beer-line cleaning agent

THE REQUIREMENTS OF COSHH

To act in accordance with the COSHH Regulations employers need to abide by the following eight steps:

Step 1 **Assess the risks** to health from hazardous substances used in or created by the workplace activities.

Step 2 **Decide what precautions are needed.** Employees must not carry out work which could expose anyone to hazardous substances without first considering the risks and the necessary precautions. Where possible, high-risk products should be replaced with lower-risk products.

Step 3 **Prevent or adequately control exposure** to hazardous substances. Where preventing exposure is not reasonably practicable, then they must adequately control it.

Step 4 **Ensure that control measures are used and maintained** correctly and that safety procedures are followed at all times.

Step 5 **Monitor the exposure** of employees to hazardous substances, if necessary.

Step 6 **Carry out appropriate health surveillance** where your assessment has shown this is necessary or where COSHH sets specific requirements.

Step 7 **Prepare plans and procedures to deal with accidents, incidents and emergencies** involving hazardous substances, where necessary.

Step 8 **Ensure employees are properly informed, trained and supervised.** Employers should provide their employees with suitable and sufficient information, instruction and training.

Although the eight steps only mention the employee the Regulations also cover anyone who works in the premises, in the case of the kitchen this includes, for example, students, contractors and suppliers.

The Regulations place a legal duty on any employee to make full and proper use of any control measures, e.g. wearing protective clothing, and to report any defects immediately.

Substances covered by the COSHH Regulations are as follows:

a. Those classified as dangerous to health under the Chemicals (Hazard Information and Packaging for Supply) Regulations 2002 (CHIP), i.e. substances classified as very toxic, toxic, harmful, corrosive or irritant.

b. Substances with a Workplace Exposure Limit (WEL).

c. Any biological agent if it is directly connected to the work.

d. Dust, if its average concentration in the air exceeds the levels specified in COSHH.

e. Any substance not mentioned above that creates a risk to health but which for technical reasons is not covered by CHIP including asphyxiates, pesticides, medicines and cosmetics.

WORKPLACE EXPOSURE LIMITS (WEL)

Before the risk assessment can be carried out it is necessary to check whether the substances you are using have been assigned a WEL. These are listed in a table (search for table 'EH40') on the HSE website. This publication is updated regularly so it is important to check the latest version in case the limits have been reduced.

WEB LINK Check the latest version of the Workplace Exposure Limits (WEL) for yourself. Search on the website **www.hse.gov.uk**

TASK Carry out a COSHH assessment on the following products. Consider the hazard, the risk, who is at risk, the degree of the risk and the action to be taken to reduce the risk.

a. heavy duty oven cleaner
b. washing detergent.

Hazards and risks

The Health and Safety Act protects all full-time and part-time employees and unpaid workers (such as students in work placements). Everyone needs to be aware of their legal duties for health and safety in the workplace as required by the Health and Safety at Work Act 1974.

HEALTH & SAFETY All hazardous substances must be identified when completing the risk assessment. This includes cleaning agents, gels and some preservatives. Where possible, high risk products should be replaced with lower risk products. COSHH assessments should be reviewed on a regular basis and updated with the inclusion of any new products.

The Health and Safety Executive (HSE) is the body appointed to support and enforce health and safety in the workplace. They have defined the two concepts for hazards and risk:

1   a **hazard** is something with the potential to cause harm

2   a **risk** is the likelihood of the hazard's potential being realized.

A hazard has the potential to cause harm and everyone must identify working practices within the kitchen environment which could harm people. All employees are required to ensure that the kitchen equipment and the workplace in general is well maintained and safe to use.

Two examples of this are:

● A light bulb that requires replacing is a hazard. If it is one out of several it presents a very small risk, but if it is the only light within a 'walk-in' refrigerator, it poses a high risk.

● A pot of boiling hot oil on a trolley top is a potential hazard that can fall off, causing spillage onto clothes, causing burns and creating a slippery floor surface unless cleared away immediately. Therefore it is high in risk.

Common causes of accidents

The majority of industrial accidents in kitchen and restaurant areas are directly through people slipping, tripping and falling over. Consequently, floor surfaces are required to be of a suitable composition to help reduce the risk. A key reason for the high incident rate of this type of accident is that water and grease are more likely to be spilt and the mixture of these substances is dangerous and will make the floor surface extremely slippery. For this reason, any spillage must be cleaned immediately and floor warning notices put in place to alert people of a wet floor and highlighting the risk of slipping.

Fire is another common cause and all employees should be vigilant to the potential signs and causes of fire.

● Electricity – neglect and misuse of wiring and electrical appliances.

● Refuse/rubbish – accumulating in work/storage areas.

● Smoking – discarded cigarettes and matches.

● Heaters – portable heaters can be knocked over, poorly sited or inadequately guarded. All heaters could overheat if obstructed.

● Hazardous goods – includes materials such as guéridon trolley fuel, acids or other cleaning chemicals.

● Arson – by mischievous children and adult fire raisers, facilitated by ineffectively secured buildings.

● Specific hazards – machinery and equipment in dusty environments, heated equipment (e.g. ovens and deep fryers), blow torches, salamanders, and flammable liquids.

Other common areas are manual handling, electrical accidents, working with equipment and machinery and traffic accidents (with supplier vehicles).

Electricity at Work Regulations (1989)

With the often heavy use of electrical equipment in kitchens these Regulations are particularly important. They state that every item of electrical equipment in the workplace must be tested every 12 months by a qualified electrician.

Slippery trip hazard warning sign

Electrical equipment in kitchen

In addition to this annual testing, a trained member of staff or qualified electrician should regularly check all electrical equipment for safety. This is recommended every three months but generally most employers undertake this annually.

A quick visual inspection by the chef before using an electrical item on a daily basis is a good method of reducing potential accidents or breakdowns. Records must be kept of the check.

General checks should be undertaken and reported for potential hazards, such as exposed wires in flexes, cracked plugs or broken sockets, worn cables and overloaded sockets.

Any electrical equipment that appears faulty must be immediately checked and repaired before use. It should also be labelled or have the plug removed to ensure that it is not used by accident before repairing.

The Manual Handling Operations Regulations (1992)

These apply where manual lifting occurs. The employer is required to carry out a risk assessment of all activities undertaken which involve manual lifting. The Regulations provide guidelines on how to protect oneself when lifting heavy objects.

When unpacking a delivery, always ensure the product packaging is undamaged to help avoid possible personal injury from broken goods.

TASK Using an electrical hand blender is a hazard. What is the possibility of it causing harm? How can you assess the risk?

Stand with your feet apart

Your weight should be evenly spread over both feet

Bend your knees slowly keeping your back straight

Squat with your feet apart

Tuck your chin in towards your chest

Get a good grip on the base of the box

Bring the box to your waist height keeping the lift as smooth as possible

Keep the box close to your body

Proceed carefully making sure that you can see where you are going

Lower the box, reversing the lifting procedure

HEALTH & SAFETY When unpacking a delivery always ensure the product packaging is undamaged to help avoid possible personal injury from broken goods that may be inside.

If moving packages, equipment or goods on trolleys or alternative wheeled vehicles you must ensure that you carefully load them so that the vehicle is not unbalanced or overloaded. Also, it is important to load them so that your view is not obscured at all.

When moving large pots of liquid, especially if the liquid is hot, two people should be used to move it. Always ensure that the liquid is not overflowing as a result of the pot being overfilled. Use a warning sign to identify that the pot is hot; traditionally the sprinkling of some flour onto the part that is hot is used as a sign in the kitchen not to touch the object without protection.

Warning signs in the kitchen

Safety instruction sign

Safety signs are used in the kitchen and surrounding areas to help identify hazards, obligatory actions and prohibited actions for all staff, customers and visitors. Usually these signs are clearly displayed and should be made in laminated plastic. All signage should comply with the relevant health and safety regulations and different colours signify different actions.

- Yellow – warning signs to alert people to various dangers such as slippery floors and hot water.

Yellow warning signs

- Blue – mandatory signs to inform everyone what they must do in order to progress safely through a certain area. Usually this would indicate the need to wear protective clothing.

Blue warning signs

- Red – prohibition signs are designed to stop persons from certain tasks in a hazardous area, such as no smoking or no access.

Red warning signs

- Green – escape route signs, designed to show fire and emergency exits to staff, visitors and customers.

Green warning signs

The local authority Environmental Health Department enforces the Health and Safety at Work Act, and an environmental health officer will visit and inspect local business premises on a regular basis. The inspector identifies any area of danger and will issue an improvement notice. It is the responsibility of the employee to remove this danger within a designated period of time. Failure to comply with the notice will lead to prosecution. The inspector also has the authority to close a business until they are satisfied that all danger to employees and the public has been removed.

Fire Precautions Act 1971

The **Fire Precautions Act 1971** declares that all employees must be aware of and trained in fire and emergency evacuation procedures for their workplace. The emergency exit route will be the easiest route by which all staff, customers and visitors can leave the building safely. Fire action plans should be prominently displayed to show the emergency exit route.

The fire evacuation procedure should be carried out at least once a year and should be reviewed regularly to account for personnel changes or physical changes to the building in which you work.

The Fire Precautions (Workplace) Regulations 1997

This requires that every employer must carry out a risk assessment for the premises under the Management of Health and Safety Regulations 1999.

- Any obstacles that may hinder fire evacuation should be identified as a hazard and be dealt with.
- Suitable fire detection equipment should be in place.
- All escape routes should be clearly marked and free from obstacles.
- Fire alarm systems should be tested on a weekly basis to ensure they are in full operational condition.

Fire fighting equipment should be easily accessed in a specified area of every kitchen. This should only be used when the cause of the fire has been identified: the use of a wrong fire extinguisher can make the fire worse. Only use fire fighting equipment when correctly trained to do so.

Fire extinguishers are available to tackle different types of fire. It is important that these are checked and maintained as required.

TASK Think of several potential causes of fire in the kitchen. How could each of these be prevented?

Fire fighting equipment

CAUSE OF FIRE AND CHOICE OF EXTINGUISHER

CAUSE	EXTINGUISHER	LABEL COLOUR
Electrical fire	Carbon dioxide (CO_2)	Black
Flammable liquids	Foam	Cream/yellow
Solid material fire	Water	Red
Vaporizing liquids	Dry powder	Green
		Blue

Fire blankets are used to smother small, localized fires such as a hot fat fire or burning caramel.

Fire can only occur when three factors are present:

1 fuel
2 air (oxygen)
3 heat.

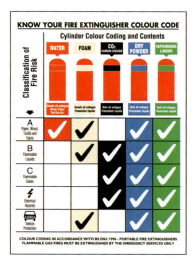
Fire extinguishers

Three factors of fire

Should any one of these factors be removed, ignition cannot take place; therefore it is essential that flammable materials are stored safely and securely in a locked fireproof cupboard. Gas canisters must be stored away from direct sunlight and any other direct heat source.

In the event of a fire it is essential that no-one is placed at risk and that the emergency alarm is operated as soon as possible to alert others. The emergency services should also be contacted immediately. Fires can spread quickly and easily – so it is important to leave the building at once, closing doors to prevent the spread of fire, and report at the identified fire assembly point.

Fire risk assessment

The employer must manage any fire risk on your premises, and to do this they need to carry out a fire risk assessment.

The recommended way to carry out a risk assessment is to follow a step-by-step process.

- *Identification of the hazards*
  Hazards include:

  – Anything that can start a *fire*, such as naked flames, heaters or commercial processes such as ovens and stoves.

  – Anything that can *burn* in a fire, including piles of waste, display materials, textiles or other flammable products such as ingredients.

  – Oxygen sources such as air conditioning, medical products or commercial oxygen supplies which might *intensify* a fire.

- *Identify people at risk*
  These include:

  – People who work close to or with fire hazards.

  – People who work alone, or in isolated areas such as storerooms.

  – Children or parents with babies.

  – Elderly people.

  – Disabled people.

- *Evaluate, remove or reduce the risk*
  You should:

  – Where possible, get rid of the fire hazards you identified, e.g. remove build-ups of waste and reduce any hazards you cannot remove entirely.

  – Replace highly flammable materials with less flammable ones.

Fire alarm red with glass front that you break

– Keep anything that can start a fire away from flammable materials.

– Have a safe-smoking policy for employees or customers who want to smoke in a designated area near your premises.

Once you have reduced the risk as is far as practical, you need to look at any risk that cannot be removed and decide what fire safety measures to provide.

EXAMPLE OF A FIRE RISK ASSESSMENT

The fire risk assessment process should cover five key steps:

- Identifying fire hazards – including areas where ignition, fuel and oxygen sources are close together.

- Identifying people who are at risk – including people in and around the premises and people who are especially at risk.

- Evaluating, removing or reducing, and protecting from risk – evaluate the risk of a fire starting, the risk to people from fire, remove or reduce fire hazards and risks to people from a fire, and protect people by providing fire precautions.

- Recording, planning, informing, instructing and training – record any major findings and action you have taken, discuss and work with other responsible persons if necessary, prepare an emergency plan, and inform and instruct relevant people and provide training.

- Reviewing your fire risk-assessment regularly – make changes where necessary.

Frying pan fire

First aid kit

A fire drill should be carried out at least once a year. It is good practice not to announce fire drills in advance so you can obtain a realistic idea of how effective the fire evacuation plans are. Everyone must participate in the fire drill. A record of the result of each fire drill in a fire log book is necessary.

All employees must be trained so that they know what to do in the event of a fire. Everyone must know:

- how to raise the alarm if they discover a fire
- how to contact the fire brigade
- how to use the fire-fighting equipment
- How and where to evacuate the building
- where to assemble and who to report to.

First aid

Employers must have appropriate and adequate first aid arrangements in the event of an accident or illness occurring. All employees should be informed of the first aid procedures including:

- where to locate the first aid box
- who is responsible for the maintenance of the first aid box
- which member of staff should be informed in the event of an accident or illness occurring
- the staff member to inform in the event of an accident or an emergency.

The Health and Safety (First Aid) Regulations 1981 state that workplaces must have first aid provision. The Health and Safety Executive (HSE) have recommended a minimum standard of first aid kits for use in food production areas. This should contain a minimum level of first aid equipment as set out in the table opposite, although this is by no means a restricted list.

NUMBER OF EMPLOYEES	1–10	11–50
First aid guidance notes	1	1
Triangular bandage	4	8
Sterile eye pad	2	6
Sterile dressings – large	3	5
Sterile dressings – medium	5	11
Blue detectable plasters	20	60
Blue fingerstalls	2	12
Blue detectable tape	1	1
Blue disposable polythene gloves	1 pair	3 pairs
Moist wipes	6	20
Safety pins	6	12
Burn gel sachets	3	3

Cuts

All cuts should be covered with a waterproof dressing after the cut has been cleaned and dried. When there is substantial bleeding it should be slowed as much as possible before transferring the person to professional medical care. The bleeding may be reduced by applying direct pressure, or by the use of a firm bandage attached to the wound.

Burns and scalds

Types of burns:

- dry – caused by flames, hot metal and friction
- scalds – caused by steam, hot water and hot fat
- electrical – caused by domestic current, high voltage and lightning
- cold – caused by freezing metal or liquid nitrogen.

- chemical – caused by industrial and domestic chemicals

- radiation – caused by exposure to the sun or extreme heat in an oven.

As soon as possible place the injury under slowly running cold water or place an ice pack on top of it for a minimum of ten minutes. If the burn or scald is serious the wound should be dressed with a sterile dressing and professional medical help sought immediately. It is important that adhesive dressings, lotions or kitchen cloths do not come into contact with the injury.

Sometimes the person may go into a state of shock due to the significance of the burn or scald. The signs are clammy skin with a pale face, faintness, lethargic characteristics and sometimes vomiting. The person in shock should be treated by keeping them comfortable at all times, lay them down in the recovery position and keep them warm with a light blanket.

For an electric shock, switch off the current immediately if possible. Any burns should be dealt with as above and professional medical advice should be sought once the person is comfortable.

- First aid should only be given by a qualified first-aider.

- A first aid certificate is only valid for three years. After this period, it must be renewed with additional first aid training.

- Know what action you can take within your responsibility in the event of an accident occurring.

Security and other emergencies

The security of the workplace is a fundamental concern and is associated with:

- protection of personal and customer property

- correct locked storage of flammable materials

- workplace security procedures.

The workplace should have a clearly defined set of security procedures for every employee, visitor and customer to follow. It is essential that employees are fully aware of these measures in order to help identify potential breaches of security. Specific areas that are of concern are listed below.

1   **Arson:** deliberate attempt to set fire to property.

2   **Assault:** violent attacks or clashes between employees or sometimes on staff by customers.

3   **Burglary:** when a burglar trespasses into the premises and steals property belonging to the employer, employee, supplier or customer.

4   **Theft:** where employers', employees' or customers' property has been stolen, such as food, drink, equipment and money.

5   **Robbery:** usually theft with assault.

6   **Fraud:** the use of stolen credit cards or counterfeit money when paying for services or goods.

7   **Terrorism:** bombs which may have been dropped in unsuspecting packages.

8   **Vagrancy and undesirable persons:** having drug dealers or gangs on the premises.

9   **Vandalism:** deliberate damage to property.

Security lock and card key

Ordinarily there is a set of useful telephone numbers in the kitchen office or by the kitchen phone such as local plumbers, gas engineers, electricians, emergency services and local maintenance persons. In the event of possible threats to security, such as a bomb alert, all employees must be trained in the appropriate emergency procedures. This will involve the recognition of a suspect package, how to deal with a bomb threat, evacuation of staff and customers and contacting the emergency services. Your local Crime Prevention Officer can advise on bomb security and the security of the premises in general.

The Health and Safety at Work Act requires employers to conduct a risk assessment regarding the safety of staff in the working environment. The prevention of crime is always the first consideration when assessing the risk.

Security concerns should be taken into consideration to prevent loss of stock through theft. These are some measures that can be taken:

1 The restaurant/service/public area should be designed to be in full view of employees and with a security camera placed for additional security if needed.

2 Stock should be kept in a secure area, accessed only by those with authority to do so.

3 Reception and front of house staff should be trained to recognize suspicious individuals.

4 All contract workers should be registered and given security passes so that they can be restricted from entering certain areas.

5 Employees who process money should be trained in anti-fraud measures such as checking bank notes and inspecting names and signatures on credit cards.

6 CCTV (closed circuit television) cameras can be used as a deterrent against crime and can be linked to a video system recording and saving images of people entering the premises.

> **TASK** Find out where or what to do with the following:
> Where the fire assembly point is.
> How to raise the fire alarm.
> What is the procedure in the event of a fire.
> If a bank note offered by a customer is counterfeit.

Appearance and hygiene in the workplace

The appearance of a chef or food handler should promote a high standard of cleanliness and professionalism. Employees in the workplace should always reflect the desired image of the profession that they work in.

Personal appearance

A chef's uniform is both traditional and functional. It is a compelling design that is thought to have initially originated from Napoleon, who wanted his favourite cooks in a military-style uniform; it has now evolved into a functional outfit.

CHEF JACKET

This is designed to protect the food from the chef and the chef from the physical dangers of the kitchen. Originally made of cotton and linen, the materials have evolved into modern, lightweight textiles. It is double-breasted to protect the chest and stomach from the heat from ovens and stoves, burns and scalds. It acts as a barrier and gives a few vital extra seconds to protect its wearer if there is a spillage of hot liquid onto the upper body. The sleeves should be worn to the wrist to give the arms protection from burns.

Chef jacket

TROUSERS

These are generally made of lightweight cotton or mixed material and Teflon-coated fabric. They should not be worn tight-fitting to the leg as this creates a hazard if a spillage occurs and will also be uncomfortable during work in a kitchen.

Trousers

NECKTIE

The original use of the necktie was to mop the brow – due to the lack of adequate ventilation and the intense heat generated by solid fuel stoves. In the current kitchen the necktie is largely traditional, but in larger organizations such as the armed forces, contract caterers, hotels and most catering colleges, a system of coloured neckties allows for recognition of department or seniority within the workplace.

A toque

FOOTWEAR

Shoes should be of a hard-wearing design with non-slip soles and steel toecaps. It is important that the footwear is comfortable and will give support to the chef, who will be on their feet for many hours.

The wearing of trainers and non-specialist shoes should be prohibited. They give no protection to the feet, the soles are not invariably non-slip, which is dangerous, and they will not give sufficient protection from hot spillages.

Necktie

CHEF'S HATS (TOQUES)

The tall hat has always epitomized the stature of the chef. Traditionally an apprentice cook would wear a skull cap and graduate to a toque when they reached a position of Chef de Partie. Nowadays even some head chefs prefer the skullcap. The main function of the hat is to stop loose hair falling into the food and help absorb perspiration on the forehead. However, when the hair is worn beyond collar length it cannot be contained in a hat. In this case a hairnet should be worn.

Shoes

APRONS

This item is probably the only article of chef's clothing that has remained unchanged over the years. It is one of the most important items of protection and must be worn at full length to protect the legs (always to below the knee). If a spillage of hot liquid occurs it is the first line of protection. It should be tied at the front to allow for quick release. Aprons are sometimes different in colour depending on the work the chef is engaged in.

Uniforms must be changed on a shift-by-shift basis. It is good practice to change uniforms when a spillage takes place, although this cannot always be achieved. The clothing should be of an easily washable material. Generally all chefs' attire is white so that it shows when clothing has been soiled and thus when it needs to be changed.

A skull cap

Apron

Two students fully dressed in chef uniform

Maintaining personal hygiene

It is essential that the chef maintains a high standard of personal hygiene. Bodily cleanliness is achieved through daily showering or bathing. A deodorant may be applied to the underarm area to reduce perspiration and thus the smell of sweat. Clean underwear should be worn each day.

HANDS

Hands and everything that has been touched are covered with bacteria, and although most of these are harmless, some can cause ill health. Hands must be washed regularly and frequently, particularly after visiting a toilet, before commencing the preparation of food and during the handling of food. They should be washed using hot water with the aid of a nailbrush and an antibacterial gel or liquid. The frequent use of sanitizing wipes to disinfect hands is convenient for the killing of a wide range of bacteria and is efficient on a day-to-day basis.

To ensure good health and safety practice some employers insist on the use of plastic disposable gloves when preparing food items. When wearing these, remember that the gloves should be changed with every task to prevent cross-contamination.

Fingernails should always be kept clean and short. Nails should be cleaned with a nailbrush and nail varnish should not be worn. Dirt can easily accumulate under the nails and will then be introduced into food.

Wash your hands with a liquid gel from a sealed dispenser. Soap should be discouraged because bar soap can accumulate germs when passed from hand to hand.

HAIR

Hair should be clean, washed regularly and kept tidy. It should be cut and maintained on a frequent basis. If hair is worn long it should be covered within a hairnet and tied back. The hair should never be scratched or touched while preparing food as bacteria can be transferred to the food.

FEET

Feet should be kept fresh and healthy by washing them daily and drying thoroughly. Deodorizing foot powder can be applied and toenails should be short and clean.

MOUTH AND TEETH

There are many germs within and around the area of the mouth, and it is essential that the mouth does not come into contact with utensils or hands that will come into contact with food. Cooking utensils and fingers should *not* be used for tasting food as bacteria will be transferred to food quickly. A clean disposable spoon should be used for tasting and thrown away afterwards. Coughing over foods and working areas is to be avoided at all costs to prevent the spreading of bacteria from illness.

SMOKING

Smoking must never take place near food preparation areas: when a cigarette is taken from the mouth using the fingers, bacteria from the mouth can be transferred onto the fingers and therefore onto food. Any ash found on food is unacceptable and it is an offence to smoke while preparation of food is taking place.

When handling or preparing food, blue plasters should be used so that they are easily identifiable when lost. These dressings can feature an internal metal strip that allows them to be detected by electromagnetic equipment and metal detectors in large food production units.

Safeguarding of personal health

The safeguarding of personal health is important to prevent the introduction of germs and bacteria into food preparation areas. To maintain physical fitness sufficient rest, good exercise and a nutritious diet are essential.

The Workplace (Health, Safety and Welfare) Regulations 1992 cover a wide range of basic health, safety and welfare issues and apply to most workplaces. Employers have a general duty under the Health and Safety at Work Act 1974 to ensure, so far as is reasonably practicable, the health, safety and welfare of their employees at work. These Regulations aim to ensure that workplaces meet the health, safety and welfare needs of all members of a workforce, including people with disabilities.

VENTILATION

Workplaces and especially kitchens need to be adequately ventilated. Fresh, clean air should be drawn from a source outside the workplace, uncontaminated by discharges from flues, chimneys or other process outlets, and be circulated through the area.

Ventilation should also remove and dilute warm, humid air and provide air movement which gives a sense of freshness without causing a draught.

LIGHTING

Lighting should be sufficient to enable people to work and move about safely. If necessary, local lighting should be provided at individual workstations and at places of particular risk such as crossing points on traffic routes. Lighting and light fittings should not create any hazard.

Automatic emergency lighting, powered by an independent source, should be provided where sudden loss of light would create a risk.

SANITARY CONVENIENCES AND WASHING FACILITIES

Suitable and sufficient sanitary conveniences and washing facilities should be provided at readily accessible places. They and the rooms containing them should be kept clean and be adequately ventilated and lit. Washing facilities should have running hot and cold or warm water, soap and clean towels or other means of cleaning or drying. If required by the type of work, showers should also be provided. Men

and women should have separate facilities unless each facility is in a separate room with a lockable door and is for use by only one person at a time.

DRINKING WATER

An adequate supply of high-quality drinking water, with an upward drinking jet or suitable cups, should be provided. Water should only be provided in refillable enclosed containers where it cannot be obtained directly from a mains supply. Bottled water/water dispensing systems may still be provided as a secondary source of drinking water.

ACCOMMODATION FOR CLOTHING AND FACILITIES FOR CHANGING

Adequate, suitable and secure space should be provided to store workers' own clothing and work clothing. As far as is reasonably practicable the facilities should allow for drying clothing. Changing facilities should also be provided for workers who change into chef whites. The facilities should be readily accessible from the kitchen area and washing and eating facilities, and should ensure the privacy of the user, be of sufficient capacity, and be provided with seating.

> **TASK** Evidence is important when creating your portfolio. Within your own work role, provide some detailed examples on how you have taken steps to reduce those health and safety risks, which you may come into contact within the kitchen.

Food safety in catering

Fresh dirty white onions

The chef must be particularly conscious of the need for hygiene: many commodities have to be handled and prepared for the customer without any type of heat treatment. High standards of hygiene are essential to prevent food poisoning, food spoilage, loss of productivity, pest infestation and potential criminal prosecution for malpractice.

Food safety implies more than just the sanitation of work areas. It includes all practices, precautions and legal responsibilities involved in the following:

1   Protecting food from risk of contamination.

2   Preventing organisms from multiplying to an extent which would pose a health risk to customers and employees.

3   Destroying any harmful bacteria in food by thorough heat treatment or other techniques.

The Food Hygiene (England) Regulations 2006 provide the framework for the EU legislation to be enforced in England. There are similar Regulations in Wales, Scotland and Northern Ireland. The Food Safety (General Food Hygiene) Regulations 1995 and the Food Safety (Temperature Control) Regulations 1995 no longer apply. Many of the requirements of these Regulations are included in the new EU legislation, so what businesses need to do from day to day have not changed very much.

Consuming contaminated food can potentially cause ill health and in a few cases, even death. Food poisoning is an sickness of the human digestive system that is the result of eating foods contaminated with pathogenic bacteria and toxins. Certain groups of high-risk people are particularly vulnerable to illness from food borne bacteria:

● babies and infants

● pregnant women

● elderly people

● people who are already unwell

● people who have a repressed immune system.

Food poisoning may also be caused by eating poisonous plants, fungi, fish and foods contaminated with chemicals. The symptoms of food poisoning may vary but can include:

● diarrhoea

● dehydration

● fever

● nausea

● vomiting.

The requirement to have 'food safety management procedures' and keep up to date records of these is an important characteristic to help ensure food safety. Disposal of waste is an additional Hazard Analysis Critical Control Points (HACCP) matter (see pages 62–63 for more information). Bacteria and pathogens can multiply at an alarming rate in waste disposal areas. In ideal circumstances the areas for cleaning crockery and pots should be separate from each other and from the food preparation area. Waste bins in the kitchen should be emptied at regular intervals and be kept clean. Food waste can be safely disposed of in a waste disposal unit. Oil should only be disposed of by a specialist oil clearance company and must not be placed in a sink or waste disposal unit.

How does food become contaminated?

Food may become contaminated as it is produced, or as it is prepared.

ANIMALS

Many food borne microbes are present in healthy animals (usually in their intestines) raised for food. Meat and poultry can become contaminated during slaughter by contact with small amounts of intestinal contents. Fresh fruits and vegetables can be contaminated if washed or irrigated with water contaminated by animal manure or human sewage.

FOOD HANDLING

During food processing, food borne microbes can be introduced by infected humans handling the food or by cross contamination with other raw agricultural products. For example, *Shigella* (bacterium) and Norwalk virus (Norovirus) can be introduced by an infected food handler's unwashed hands.

FOOD PREPARATION

In the kitchen, microbes can be transferred from one food to another by using the same knife, cutting board, or other utensil without washing in-between. Fully cooked foods can become re-contaminated if they touch other raw foods that contain pathogens.

FOOD STORAGE

Many bacterial microbes need to multiply to larger numbers in food in order to cause disease. Under warm and moist conditions, for instance, slightly contaminated food left out overnight can become highly infectious as bacterial microbes multiply. Prompt refrigeration or freezing prevents most bacteria on food from multiplying. High salt, sugar, or acid levels also keep bacteria from growing.

HEATING FOOD

Microbes are killed by heat. If food is heated to an internal temperature above 160 °F (78 °C), even for a few seconds, this is enough to kill most bacteria, viruses, or parasites. Toxins produced by bacteria vary in their sensitivity to heat. For instance, the toxin that causes botulism is inactivated by boiling, whereas the staphylococcal toxin is not.

CHEMICALS

Chemicals can accidentally contaminate food through poor storage and these deserve a special mention. Disinfectants, pesticides, insecticides, cleaning chemicals and machine oils can find their way into the food system if not stored or used correctly.

ALLERGENS

These can cause allergic reactions when a person's immune system reacts to a specific food. Allergic reactions can appear as swelling, skin irritation, rashes on the skin, breathlessness and even anaphylactic shock. *Food intolerance* is different because it does not affect the immune system, but the food still can cause a reaction. Foods usually associated with allergies and intolerances are dairy products, eggs, nuts, seafood and wheat based products (gluten).

HEALTH & SAFETY Anaphylactic shock is a serious reaction often causing swelling of the throat and mouth that prevents breathing.

Types of bacteria that cause food poisoning

SALMONELLA

There are approximately over 2000 types of salmonella; the commonest varieties are *Salmonella enteriditis* and *Salmonella typhimurium*. These organisms survive in the intestine and can cause food poisoning by releasing a toxin on the death of the cell. The primary source of salmonella is the intestinal tract of animals and poultry. It will therefore be found in:

- human and animal excreta
- excreta from rats, mice, flies and cockroaches
- raw meat and poultry
- some animal feed.

STAPHYLOCOCCUS AUREUS

About 40–50 per cent of adults carry this organism in their nose, mouth, throat, ears and hands. If present in food, *Staphylococcus aureus* will produce a toxin which may survive boiling for 30 minutes or more. The majority of outbreaks are caused by poor hygiene practices which result in direct contamination of the food from sneezing or uncovered septic cuts and abrasions. Frequently, the cooked food has been handled while still slightly warm, and these storage conditions have encouraged the organism to produce its toxin.

CLOSTRIDIUM PERFRINGENS

This is commonly found in human and animal faeces and is present in raw meat and poultry. This organism forms spores which may survive boiling temperatures for several hours. Outbreaks can involve stews and large joints of meat which have been allowed to cool down slowly in a warm kitchen and either eaten cold or inadequately reheated the following day.

BACILLUS CEREUS

This is a spore-forming organism. The spores survive normal cooking and rapid growth will occur if the food has not cooled quickly and refrigerated. These bacteria will induce nausea and vomiting within five hours of ingestion.

OTHER BACTERIA

Food borne pathogens do not multiply in food but will use food as a carrier into the human stomach where they will then multiply. These pathogens include:

- *E coli 0157:H7* which is present in the intestines and faeces of animals and humans. It is also found in raw meat and vegetables.
- *Campylobacter* is found in raw poultry and meat, sewage, animals, insects and birds.
- *Norovirus* is found in raw oysters, shellfish, water and ice and salads and can also be passed from person to person.
- *Shigella* is found in raw vegetables, salads, dairy products and poultry.
- *Listeria* can multiply slowly at refrigeration temperatures and is linked to products such as unpasteurized cheeses, pâté, salads and cook/chill meals.

Hygiene routines

It is a necessity that good hygiene routines are adhered to by all food handlers. Personal hygiene is discussed in depth on pages 51–54.

A chef washing her hands using a nail brush

Chef tasting food with a spoon

THE IMPORTANCE OF HAND WASHING

Frequent hand washing is a necessity for the chef, and in all aspects of a chef's working day.

Hand washing must be undertaken:

- Before commencing work (to wash away general bacteria accumulated from the outside environment).
- After using the toilet or contact with faeces.
- After breaks.
- Between touching raw food and cooked food.
- Before and after handling raw food.
- After disposing of waste materials.
- After cleaning down the workspace.
- After administering any first aid or dressing changes.
- After touching the face, nose, mouth or blowing your nose.
- Hand washing and sanitation should take place at every possible opportunity.

TASTING FOOD WHILE COOKING

Whereas it is good practice for a chef to constantly taste food during cooking, you must use a spoon that is washed between tastings to prevent the possible contamination of the food from your mouth. A disposable plastic spoon that is discarded after each tasting is the best practice to follow if possible.

Personal hygiene

HAIR

This should be cleaned regularly and kept covered. If hair is at shoulder length it must be tied up and placed inside a hairnet. To maintain food hygiene standards there are now many types of hat available from suppliers, many of which are disposable. They also present a professional image in serving and kitchen areas that are visible to the public and customers.

Hair tied back

CUTS, BOILS AND SEPTIC WOUNDS

Food handlers should always cover cuts, grazes, boils and septic wounds with the appropriate dressing or with brightly coloured blue waterproof plasters. Cuts on fingers may need extra protection with waterproof fingerstalls or latex disposable gloves.

SMOKING

This is prohibited where food is being prepared because of:

- The danger of contaminating food by *Staphylococci* on the fingers which may touch the lips and from saliva from the cigarette end.
- It also encourages coughing.
- Ash and smoke can get into the food.

JEWELLERY AND COSMETICS

Food handlers and chefs should not wear earrings, watches, rings or other piercings because they can harbour dirt and bacteria. Plain weddings bands are permitted, but these can still harbour significant levels of bacteria. Strong-smelling perfume may cause food to be tainted and make-up should be used minimally.

Tatoos are not acceptable to some employers, especially in food service. Tatoos should be concealed from view while you are at work.

PROTECTIVE CLOTHING

Every person handling food must wear protective clothing which should be lightweight, washable and strong. White clothing has the advantage of showing up dirt more easily (see page 52).

A clean and hygienic work area

The use of premises which are clean and can be correctly maintained is essential for the preparation, cooking and service of food. Cross-contamination risks should be minimized by the provision of separate preparation areas for the various raw and cooked foods.

The table below describes the various fittings and fixtures that need to be considered in a kitchen before the main equipment is planned.

FIXTURES AND FITTINGS	RECOMMENDATIONS
Ceilings	White in colour to reflect the light. Smooth-textured, without cracks or peeled paint/plaster. Usually panelled to hide the ventilation system.
Floors	Should have a durable, non-slip and non-permeable material. They can be tiled but polyurethane screeds are now used extensively in food processing areas. This type of screed is fast to install, offers good levels of chemical resistance even to the most aggressive acids and fats, and can be installed to withstand steam cleaning. It is a slip-resistant surface (equally important), designed to give a textured finish.
Lighting	Good lighting is essential to avoid eye strain. Natural light is best but where artificial lighting is used some thought should be given to the type used.
Ventilation	The requirements of a high-performance kitchen ventilation system for the modern kitchen. The extracted air should be free from grease and odours, and be discharged up single or multiple chimney stacks. A canopy system should be built around the existing structure of the kitchen to cover at least all cookery areas. The incorporation of a balancing system to ensure equal extract along the whole cook line is very important. Replacement air is introduced into the kitchen through low-velocity diffusers mounted in the front face of the canopy and spot cooling nozzles can also provide a cooler air temperature in the kitchen. These are a potential source of dirt, grease and dust and should be cleaned on a very regular basis.
Walls	Ceramic wall tiles were considered the best surface for areas where liquids splash a wall surface, potentially overcoming a damp or hygiene problem. Many such areas still exist in industrial and commercial hygiene-sensitive areas. Their durability, long-term appearance and cost of maintenance can be questionable and today there is a viable alternative to consider. Modern alternatives to ceramic wall tiles include PVC wall cladding systems, resin wall coatings and screed mortars. They offer a hygienic finish capable of withstanding heavy-impact use.

The reporting of maintenance issues

The preparation of food for cookery must take place on surfaces that are hygienic and suitable for use. Work surfaces, walls and floors can become damaged, and they too can be a source of contamination and danger to customers and staff alike. This should be reported to your line manager. A maintenance reporting system can easily be designed to suit each establishment and each section in that kitchen. Areas for attention are:

- cracks in walls
- damage to tables and workbenches
- cooking equipment such as pots, pans and utensils
- windows, sanitary systems and lights
- flooring an any other structural issues
- electrical equipment relating to that particular operation.

Controlling cross-contamination

Cross-contamination takes place when bacteria are transferred from contaminated food, equipment or surfaces onto food just about to be served. Instances of cross-contamination can be raw food touching cooked food (e.g. raw and cooked meat), soil from dirty vegetables coming into contact with high risk foods such as dairy products and hands touching raw meat and then cooked food without being washed in-between tasks.

Fly on food

To avoid cross-contamination separate storage, preparation and cooking areas are recommended. If this is not possible you should ensure that the foods are stored separately from each other. Vegetables must be washed before preparation and peeling and then washed again subsequently. Leafy vegetables may need to be washed in several changes of fresh water to ensure that all the insects, grit, sand and soil are removed from them.

Good personal hygiene practices are very important in controlling cross contamination and the consistent washing of hands is essential in the prevention of pathogens transferring from hands onto food. The use of colour coded chopping boards, knives, cloths, service equipment, storage trays and sometimes staff uniforms are an effective way to keep food preparation areas separate from cooking areas (i.e. preventing raw and cooked food from coming into contact). Kitchen cloths are a perfect habitat for growing bacteria. Using disposable kitchen towels is the most hygienic way to clean down food areas.

> **TASK** A piece of beef fillet is cooked at 75 °C and left in the kitchen uncovered to cool down. When it leaves the oven there are no bacteria present on the beef.
>
> However, the chef uses a dirty cloth, contaminated from a previously prepared raw chicken, to move the fillet onto a storage tray. A minimum of 6000 pathogenic bacteria may now be present. Bacteria double in numbers every 20 minutes in warm conditions, like a kitchen. Calculate how many bacteria will be present after two hours.
>
> Food poisoning can be created by 1.5 million pathogenic bacteria, in this case would people eating the beef get food poisoning?

Cleaning and maintaining equipment

A high standard of cleanliness and regular disinfection is essential to ensure that food is protected from physical and microbial contamination and to prevent the accumulation of material which would attract pests. Hygienic and clean food areas perform an important role in the production of safe food and the team must be responsible for planning, recording and monitoring all cleaning using a cleaning schedule. A cleaning schedule is aimed at monitoring the effectiveness of routine cleaning and staff should still maintain the practice of 'cleaning as they go'. Cleaning schedules are a method of supporting this practice, not replacing it.

Any proposed schedule should be discussed with team members and then confirmed in written format so that the team can refer to this as necessary. The schedule will specify:

1 What is to be cleaned – for example, floors, walls, ceilings, doors, ventilation canopies, work surfaces (including sinks, taps and crockery drying racks),

equipment (including chopping boards, refrigerators, food blenders, pots), utensils and laundry (including drying up cloths and overalls).

2   When it is to be cleaned – for example, monthly, weekly, daily, between shifts or after each use.

3   How it is to be cleaned – for example, the chemicals (e.g. bactericidal detergent, disinfectant) and their dilutions, materials (e.g. scrubbing brush, scourers, dishcloth) and equipment to be used (e.g. steam cleaner, floor cleaning machine) and how equipment is to be dismantled.

4   The precautions to be taken – for example, disconnect equipment from its electrical supply, use cleaning materials according to manufacturer's instructions and wear protective equipment (e.g. rubber gloves, overalls, eye protection).

5   Who is to clean it either by name or position.

6   Who will be responsible for ensuring that cleaning tasks have been completed?

7   Where cleaning materials and protective equipment are stored and who to report to when stocks are running low.

Sanitizing a work surface

You may find that your supplier of cleaning chemicals/materials may be able to assist you in the provision of a card index system specifying procedures and precautions. Checklists can also be used to ensure the work has been carried out to the correct standard and proper frequency. They may also be essential in establishing a due diligence defence in the event of a complaint.

Work surfaces and equipment for the preparation, cooking and service of food should be impervious and easy to clean. Equipment should be constructed from materials which are non-toxic, corrosion resistant, smooth and free from cracks. Apparatus such as a *bain-marie* should be able to store hot food for up to two hours at an ambient temperature of 63 °C and regular temperature checks should be taken. The surfaces should be easy to clean even when hot and should allow the food to be presented in an attractive manner.

Chefs chopping on different coloured boards

WORKTOPS AND CHOPPING BOARDS

It is very important to keep all worktops and chopping boards clean because they touch the food your customers are going to eat. If they are not properly clean, bacteria could spread to food and make your customers ill.

● Always wash worktops before you start preparing food.

● Wipe up any spilt food straight away.

● Always wash worktops thoroughly after they have been touched by raw meat, including poultry, or raw eggs.

● Never put ready-to-eat food, such as tomatoes or fruit, on a worktop or chopping board that has been touched by raw meat, unless you have washed it thoroughly first.

If you possess a dishwasher, this is a very effective way to clean plastic chopping boards. Dishwashers can wash at a very high temperature, which kills bacteria. Otherwise, wash chopping boards thoroughly with hot water and washing-up liquid.

If at all possible, it is standard practice to have separate chopping boards for raw meat and for other foods. There are systems of coloured boards and knife handles which help to minimize cross-contamination. The system below is widely used:

- red – raw meat and poultry
- yellow – cooked meat and poultry
- blue – raw fish (in this book, white and wooden backgrounds may be used for photographic purposes)
- brown – vegetables
- green – fruit and salads
- white – dairy and pastry items.

There is also a French version, which is used by some establishments. So you need to check the code used in your establishment and stick to it.

These boards must be cleaned between use, ideally with sanitizer and clean cotton, non-woven fabric or specialized paper cleaning cloths. They should be soaked overnight in a sterilizing solution on a regular basis. The boards are stored in racks and should not be touching each other.

Colour coded chopping boards

If boards become damaged they should be discarded. Bacteria can multiply in cracks and blemishes, and be the cause of contamination.

KITCHEN CLOTHS

Dirty, damp cloths are the perfect breeding ground for bacteria. It is very important to wash kitchen cloths and other cleaning cloths, sponges and abrasive materials regularly and leave them to dry before using them again.

Pile of tea towels

If possible, try to keep different coloured cloths for different jobs. For example, use one cloth to wipe worktops and another to wash dishes. This helps to stop bacteria spreading and helps to prevent cross contamination. The safest option is the use of disposable kitchen towels to wipe worktops and chopping boards. This is because you throw the kitchen towel away after using it once, so it is less likely to spread bacteria than cloths you use again.

Tea towels can also spread bacteria, so it's important to wash them regularly and be careful how you use them. Remember, if you wipe your hands on a tea towel after you have touched raw meat, this will spread bacteria to the towel. Then, if you use the tea towel to dry a plate, the bacteria will spread to the plate.

KNIVES, SPOONS AND OTHER UTENSILS

It is important to keep knives, wooden spoons, spatulas, tongs and other utensils clean to help stop bacteria spreading to food. It is especially important to wash them thoroughly after using them with raw meat, or else they can spread bacteria to other food.

Set of knives

Once again, a dishwasher is a very effective way to clean knives and other utensils because dishwashers can wash at a very high temperature, which kills bacteria. Otherwise, wash them thoroughly with hot water and washing-up liquid.

WEB LINK   The European food hygiene regulations changed on 1 January 2006, so the Food Standards Agency issued new guidance on temperature control legislation in England, Wales and Northern Ireland. The guidance contains advice on the types of foods that are required to be held under temperature control and on the circumstances in which some flexibility from the temperature control requirements is allowed.

Find out more by searching at:

http://www.food.gov.uk

Look on the 'Safety and hygiene' page.

CLEANING PRODUCTS

There are numerous diverse cleaning products that are designed for different tasks.

Detergents	are intended to remove grease and grime build up. It is produced as a powder, liquid, gel or foam and requires dilution with hot water to use. Detergents do not kill pathogenic bacteria and they usually work well in conjunction with other products such a disinfectant.
Disinfectants	are designed to wipe out bacteria and kitchen based products must be applied to cleaned and grease-free surfaces for a required amount of contact time to be rendered effective.
Sanitizers	clean and disinfect surfaces and they are usually found in a liquid form with spray attachments. This form of cleaning is very useful for work surfaces and equipment, especially when cleaning between jobs.
Heat	can also be used to disinfect surfaces and equipment. The use of steam cleaners and dishwashers are helpful to both clean and disinfect appropriately.

PEST CONTROL IN THE KITCHEN

Good food, well presented and served in an attractive environment is the recipe to attract customers and provide a commercial success.

However, this can all be put at risk if pest infestation occurs. Pests are a serious source of contamination and disease and having them near food is against the law. The apparent risks are as follows:

- Rodent control is not put in place.
- Insects annoy customers and foul both in the preparation kitchen and dining areas.
- Waste food can cause hazards in the rear yard if not dealt with appropriately and quickly.
- Waste cooking oil can be left to be removed (you will need to find licensed companies to dispose of this).
- The drains may be blocked by congealed grease.
- The structure of the kitchen may be defective with broken tiles or damaged refrigeration.
- Cleaning may not be done regularly enough.
- Extractor systems may be blocked or poorly serviced.
- Fly-control systems are not audited and upgraded.

CHEF'S TIP   Good pest control means:
- Keeping pests out
- Keeping the kitchen and rubbish area clean
- Checking for signs of pests
- Removing access to food and water
- Covering all food
- Fixing dripping taps
- Removing rubbish from the kitchen
- Storing dry foods in containers.

Hazard Analysis Critical Control Points

Hazard Analysis Critical Control Points (HACCP) are an internationally recognized and recommended system of food safety management. They focus on identifying the critical points in a process where food safety problems (or hazards) could arise and putting steps in place to prevent things going wrong. This is sometimes referred to as controlling hazards. Keeping records is also an important part of HACCP systems.

HACCP involves the following seven steps.

1   Identify what could go wrong (the hazards).

2   Identify the most important points where things can go wrong (the critical control points – CCPs).

3   Set critical limits at each CCP (e.g. cooking temperature/time).

4   Set up checks at CCPs to prevent problems occurring (monitoring).

5   Decide what to do if something goes wrong (corrective action).

6   Prove that your HACCP plan is working (verification).

7   Keep records of all of the above (documentation).

Your HACCP plan must be kept up to date and you will need to review it from time to time, especially whenever something in your food operation changes such as menu changes or new cooking equipment is purchased. You may also wish to ask your local Environmental Health Officer for advice. Remember that even with a HACCP plan in place, you must comply with all of the requirements of current food safety legislation. The chart below details the processes involved and the possible hazards for each process, alongside the control.

> **TASK**   Carry out a HACCP assessment on the following products. Consider the hazard, the critical control point and the action to be taken.
>
> a.   fresh raw poultry
> b.   fresh fruit and vegetables.

STEP	HAZARD	CONTROL
Receipt of goods	• Contaminated high-risk foods • Damaged or decomposed goods • Incorrect specifications • Growth of pathogens between the time of receipt and storage	• All deliveries inspected and checked by a staff member • Appropriate labelling • Prompt and correct storage
Storage	• Contamination of high-risk foods • Contamination through poor handling • Contamination by pests • Spoilage of food by decomposition	• Correct usage of refrigeration regimes • Foods must be suitably stored in the correct packaging or receptacles • Materials that are in direct contact with food must be of food-grade quality • A contract for a pest control service must be in place • Correct stock rotation • Out of date and unfit food stuffs must be segregated from other foods and removed from the premises
Preparation	• Contamination of high-risk foods • Contamination through poor handling • Growth of pathogens and toxins	• Keep raw and cooked foods separate • Use pasteurized eggs for raw and lightly cooked egg dishes • All food contact surfaces must be fit for purpose • Food handlers must be trained in hygienic food handling techniques • Keep the exposure of fresh foods at ambient temperatures to a minimum • Label all food that is to be used more than one day in advance of production with its description and use by date
Cooking	• Survival of pathogens and spores	• Cook all foods to the minimum recommended temperature
Chilling	• Growth of pathogens, spores = toxin production • Contamination	• Cool foods as quickly as possible, to 8 °C in 90 minutes • Keep food that is chilling loosely covered • Use only clean equipment
Hot hold	• Growth of pathogens and toxin production • Contamination by staff and customers, especially in self-service operations	• Maintain food at 63 °C and discard after two hours • Keep containers covered when not in service • Use sneeze screens • Supervise self-service
Cold hold	• Growth of pathogens and toxin production • Contamination by staff and customers especially in self-service operations	• Keep food at 5 °C and discard after four hours • Keep containers covered when not in service • Use sneeze screens • Supervise self-service

Controlling food safety by temperature control

Good temperature control is essential to keep certain foods safe. Products such as prepared foods, cooked foods, smoked meat or fish and certain dairy products must by law be kept hot or chilled until they are served to the customer. If this basic regulation is not followed harmful bacteria could grow or toxins could form in the food and create potential food poisoning.

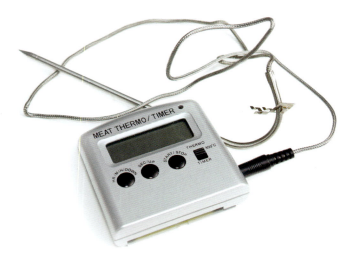

Electronic temperature probe

It is essential to cool hot foods quickly and when cooking, reheating and hot holding to ensure that food reaches sufficient core temperatures to destroy food poisoning bacteria. Temperatures between 5 °C and 63 °C are noted as the danger zone because it is possible for bacteria to multiply within the temperature range. The most rapid multiplication occurs at a temperature of 37 °C.

Electronic temperature probes are very useful to measure the temperature of the centre of both hot and cold food.

They can also be used to record the temperatures of deliveries and to check air temperatures in both refrigerators and freezers. Ensure that the probe device is disinfected before each use and regularly calibrate the probe to check accuracy at high and low temperatures.

Chilling temperatures

It is a legal requirement to ensure perishable foods are maintained at 8 °C or below. To enable this specific air temperature, the temperature your thermometer records, should be between 0 °C and 5 °C. Food requiring refrigeration can be held at higher temperature for no longer than four hours. At the end of that time the food temperature must be lowered to below 8 °C until sold or discarded. A system should be developed so that products are not displayed for more than four hours out of refrigeration (e.g. documentation to indicate a time the product was brought out and the time it was disposed of or returned to the refrigerator).

It is strongly recommended to monitor and record refrigerator temperatures daily to demonstrate compliance with this requirement. Refrigerated food deliveries should also be checked to ensure they are at an acceptable temperature. If you are not satisfied do not accept the consignment. It is recommended you maintain record of refrigerated deliveries and that freezer temperatures are maintained at −18 °C or below; it is good practice to record freezer temperatures on a daily basis.

Hot holding

It is a legal obligation to maintain hot-held food at 63 °C or above. It is strongly advisable to monitor and record the core temperature of food held hot to enable you to prove you are complying with this requirement. If cooked food is being cooled to serve cold or to reheat at a later time, it must be protected from contamination and cooled quickly to 8 °C within 90 minutes of being cooked. The best method to achieve this is through the use of a blast chiller. A system should be planned to enable you to demonstrate that products are not displayed for more than two hours below 63 °C.

Cooking and reheating

It is a legal obligation to identify food safety hazards involved in your business. One obvious hazard is the survival of food poisoning bacteria in insufficiently cooked and reheated foods. High-risk food such as poultry and food containing egg should reach a core temperature of 75 °C or above. At this temperature food poisoning bacteria will be destroyed but some toxins and spores may not be killed. Other heat treatments are used to destroy bacteria such as:

- Canning – very high temperatures are employed to ensure that the food is safe from all micro-organisms, toxins and spores. A typical temperature of 121 °C is maintained for approximately three minutes.

- Pasteurization – this involves heating food to a temperature similar to cooking temperatures. Milk is the most obvious commodity that undergoes this process and it is heated to 72 °C for 15 seconds before rapidly cooling.

- Sterilization – this process destroys all micro-organisms as it involves heating the food to 100 °C for 15–30 minutes by applying steam and pressure as its method of cooking.

- Ultra heat treatment (UHT) – this gives dairy products such as milk and cream a long shelf life without the need to refrigerate the product until opened. The food is heated under pressure to around 135 °C and cooled rapidly.

Cooling of foods

It is a legal requirement to cool food after cooking as quickly as possible. It is good practice to cool hot food and place within the refrigerator within 90 minutes from cooking. To facilitate quick cooling you should implement the following measures:

1 Food should be transferred from hot pans or trays to cool ones.

2 Cut large joints of meat into smaller joints.

3 Divide liquids such as soup into smaller dishes.

4 Stand pans or containers in sinks filled with cold water and ice, and stir regularly.

5 Always allow the movement of air around food and food containers when cooling to increase the speed of cooling the food.

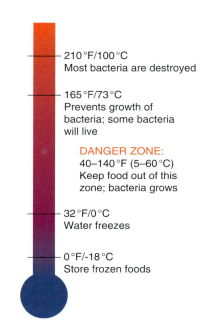

210 °F/100 °C
Most bacteria are destroyed

165 °F/73 °C
Prevents growth of bacteria; some bacteria will live

DANGER ZONE:
40–140 °F (5–60 °C)
Keep food out of this zone; bacteria grows

32 °F/0 °C
Water freezes

0 °F/-18 °C
Store frozen foods

Safe food deliveries and storage

A HACCP food management system will examine the point of food delivery and storage. It should cover the receiving of goods where the core temperatures and condition of the delivery is thoroughly checked. Fresh meat that has been delivered should have a core temperature of a maximum of 8 °C.

All fresh produce should be delivered in unbroken, clean packaging and in clean delivery vehicles that are appropriately refrigerated. If you suspect a delivery has not met the requirements of your HACCP it should be refused

Chef's name _____

Production area _____

Goods received checklist

DATE	TIME	SUPPLIER	ORDER CORRECT	DELIVERY NOTE/ INVOICE NUMBER	FAULT (IDENTIFY PRODUCT)	ACTION	TEMPERATURE READING	SIGNATURE

and returned immediately to the supplier. A goods inwards sheet showing the company, invoice number, core temperature, any problems and how they were dealt with allows received goods to be monitored.

Goods received checklist

After the commodity has been received it needs to be correctly stored. Raw meat and fish should be stored, covered, in separate refrigerators at 4 °C. If there is not enough capacity for two separate refrigeration systems, *cooked products must be stored above fresh meat.* Fish should be stored as low in the refrigerator as possible. This is the coldest part of the refrigerator and a layer of crushed ice placed on top of the fish will help to keep the temperature down. This method helps to eliminate cross contamination from storage and optimizes quality. All foods should be labelled with the date of delivery/production, a description of the contents and the recommended use by date.

Food storage and temperatures

Raw meat, poultry, game and charcuterie: 4 °C or below.

Store away from cooked meat and cooked meat products to avoid any risk of cross-contamination.

Cooked meat: 4 °C or below.

Keep away from raw meat and meat products.

Uncooked fish: 4 °C or below.

Hold in separate compartments or in plastic fish trays with lids if possible, and away from other foods which may become tainted.

Frozen food: −18 °C or below.

Thaw only immediately prior to using the commodity.

Fish (smoked or cured): 8 °C.

Keep in chilled storage away from other foods, which may become tainted.

Fruit (fresh and dried).

Store in a cool, dry, well-ventilated area, away from other food, at least 15cm from the ground. Discard at the first sign of mould growth. Do not overstock.

Pasta, rice and cereals – Store in self-closing tightly lidded containers in dry cool storeroom or cupboard.

Eggs – Refrigerate at 8 °C or below.

Use strictly in rotation and ensure the shells are clean.

Fats, butter, dairy and non-dairy spreads: 8 °C or below.

Keep covered and away from highly flavoured food, which may taint.

Milk and cream: 8 °C or below.

In a separate dairy refrigerator that is used for no other purpose and in strict rotation.

Canned and bottled goods – Cool, dry, well-ventilated storage area. Blown, rusty or split tins must not be used.

Root vegetables – Store in sacks or nets as delivered in cool, well-ventilated area.

Leaf and green vegetables: 8 °C. Use on day of delivery.

Freezers, whether upright or chest freezers, must be maintained at a maximum temperature of −18 °C. All food should be covered to prevent freezer burn and labelled with the date of production and a use by date.

Ambient stores should be clean and well ventilated, with mesh over windows and doors to help with pest control. All foodstuffs must be stored away from the floor and be rotated on a first in and first out basis.

'First in first out' method

This term is used to describe stock rotation and should be consistently applied to all types of food and commodity. Essentially it prescribes that foods already in storage are used before new deliveries so long as the stock is still within the recommended dates and in good condition. Food deliveries must be labelled with the delivery date and preferably the date by which they should be used.

CHEF'S TIP The correct measurement of temperature should be monitored by the use of an accurate digital food thermometer. The probe is inserted into the centre of meat joints or placed onto the surface of other ingredients to give a temperature reading within a few seconds. Alcohol-based sanitizer wipes should be used to clean the stainless steel probe after every use to prevent cross-contamination.

Food labelling

SATURDAY
MM Sabado - Samedi

Item: _____

Prep
Date:_____ Time:_____ ☐ AM ☐ PM

Shelf
Life:_____ ☐ Shifts ☐ Fresh Daily

Use
By:_____ ☐ 4 PM ☐ Close Emp:_____

Food label

The correct labelling of all perishable food products can help you rotate frozen, chilled, fresh and dried food stored for a later use. Rotation is essential in serving the best product possible and preventing food-borne illness. Accurate date and time labelling indicates the safe shelf life of perishable food and health inspectors look for evidence of how knowledgeable employees are about the food that is being reserved hot and cold for any length of time.

The safest way to label food and containers is to use labels made especially for this purpose. Some labelling systems are biodegradable and will dissolve in under 30 seconds – leaving no sticky residue after washing the container. All labels should adhere to hard plastics and stainless steel containers. Look for labels that are FSA approved for indirect food contact.

Using masking tape and a marker is not considered safe or consistent. Masking tape leaves behind a sticky residue and it can harbour bacteria.

CHEF'S TIP Require your team to initial the label they produce and this will help the employee take greater pride in their product. You can also use this for training purposes when you see the work is not done to your standards.

The Day Dots System has *SmartDot* labels that develop food rotation by accurately indicating the combined effects of time and temperature on stored items. By utilizing the patented TT Sensor technology from Avery Dennison, this label system provides a visual colour indication of freshness. The clear activator label commences an irreversible colour change at different temperatures which notifies the chef about the surface temperature range of a specific product.

Food safety legislation

New food hygiene laws have applied in the UK since 1 January 2006. They affect all food businesses, including caterers, primary producers (such as farmers), manufacturers, distributors and retailers.

The legislation makes it an offence for anyone to sell (or keep for sale) food that is unfit for people to eat or cause food to be dangerous to health, sell food that is not what the customer is entitled to expect, in terms of content or quality or describe or present food in a way that is false or misleading.

They also place an obligation on businesses to ensure that their activities are carried out in a hygienic way. As an employer and employee, you are responsible for checking specifically what you need to do to comply with the law. Failure to do this could lead to formal action being taken, which could result in financial penalties and accompanying adverse publicity.

The Regulations also set out the basic hygiene principles that food businesses must follow in relation to staff, premises and food handling. Under the Regulations, there must be effective controls necessary to avoid contamination, to ensure that food is produced safely and that the health of your customers is not put at risk.

The controls include:

1 Premises are clean and in a good state of repair.

2 Good drainage, lighting and ventilation.

3 Sufficient waste disposal facilities.

4 Toilet facilities for staff.

5 Equipment is in good condition and kept clean.

6 Permanent arrangements for pest control which guard against infestation by rats, mice, flies, cockroaches and other insects.

7 An effective cleaning routine.

8 Staff who are appropriately clothed and trained and have good personal hygiene habits.

9 Arrangements for ensuring that all foods received into the premises are in good condition.

10 Handling, storage and transport practices which meet temperature control requirements and avoid contamination.

11 You must identify potential hazards associated with your business and introduce routines which will control the risks and ensure food safety.

The Food Hygiene (England) Regulations 2006 require certain foods to be held at temperatures that will prevent the growth of harmful bacteria. It is an offence to allow food to be kept at temperatures that would cause a risk to health, so you must make sure foods that need temperature control are kept at the right temperature.

● Foods that need to be kept hot should be kept at 63 °C or above.

● Foods that need to be kept cold should be kept at 8 °C or below (preferably at 5 °C or below).

● Foods that need to be kept frozen should be kept between –18 °C and –24 °C.

Enforcement and the serving of notices

The day to day enforcement is in the main responsibility of local authorities. Environmental health officers (EHOs) check on food safety and hygiene. They carry out routine inspections, how often depends on the potential risk posed by the type of business and the history of that business. Food law affords that officers can:

● Enter food premises to investigate possible offences.

● Inspect food to see if it is safe.

● Detain suspect food or seize and ask a Justice of the Peace to condemn it.

- Environmental health officers do not have to make an appointment. At any reasonable time and if the food business is open an environmental health officer can call.

To carry out their duties, authorized EHOs must be able to enter the premises to observe what is happening there. They are empowered to enter (at any reasonable time) and inspect food premises, processes and records and may seize or copy any relevant records and take samples of food for analysis. Officers will identify unsafe practices and investigate food complaints and incidents of food poisoning. If entry is refused officers can apply to a magistrate's court for a warrant.

Depending on what officers find at the time of the inspection will depend on the varying action that may be taken:

- Failure to comply with food hygiene regulations may result in the service of an improvement notice specifying the contraventions, measures necessary to secure compliance and the time allowed for compliance. Prior to serving an improvement notice a minded to notice must be served giving at least 14 days notice there is intention of serving an improvement notice. Failure to comply with an improvement notice is an offence.

- If the inspecting officer considers that there is an imminent risk to public health the officer may issue and emergency prohibition notice which may require the immediate closure of part or the whole of the business. The matter must also be taken to court within three days of serving the notice to apply for an emergency prohibition order. A prohibition may also be served on the proprietor or manager of a food business, which would prevent that person from owning a food business.

- Businesses may be taken to court even though their business has not been closed. The courts have powers to impose fines of up to £20 000 and prison sentences of up to six months. The officer may write informally asking you to put right any problems they find. Verbal advice may be given at the time of the visit. In any case, the feed back of the inspection must be given by the officer. Any hazards identified and what you must do to comply with the law must be discussed.

- Due diligence can be an important defence under the food safety legislation. This means that if there is proof that a business took all reasonable care and undertook all it could to prevent food safety problems, legal action may be avoided. Proof would need to be provided in the form of accurate written documentation such as fridge temperature records, staff training records and HACCP system implementation.

TEST YOURSELF

To test your level of knowledge and understanding, answer the following short questions. These will help to prepare you for your summative (final) assessment.

1   State the food safety hazards that wearing jewellery can cause.

2   State three reasons why work surfaces and chopping boards should be clean and hygienic.

   i) _____

   ii) _____

   iii) _____

3   Explain the reason for regular maintenance checks.

4   Explain the importance of storing food at the correct temperature.

5   Describe the term 'stock rotation'.

6   State the main responsibilities under the Health and Safety at Work Act 1974.

7   Explain the word *risk*.

8   Explain the word *hazard*.

9   Identify the importance of reporting illnesses quickly and the significance of stomach illnesses.

10 State the procedure for dealing with an accident in the workplace.

Cold food preparations, starters and salads

3

NVQ

2FPC15 Prepare and present food for cold presentation

VRQ

Unit 208 Prepare and cook fruit and vegetables

Unit 212 (Outcome 4) prepare and cook eggs

Recipes

SALADS

À la Grecque 80

Beetroot salad 80

Caesar salad 81

Chicory and orange 81

Coronation chicken 82

Couscous salad 82

French bean salad 83

Coleslaw 83

French salad 83

Fruit platter 84

Green salad 84

Mixed bean salad 85

Mixed salad 85

Moroccan bulgur wheat salad 86

Niçoise salad 86

Potato salad 87

Russian salad 87

Tomato, basil and mozzarella 88

Tomato, cucumber and herb
  vinaigrette 88

Tropical fruit platter 89

Waldorf salad 89

MEAT AND POULTRY STARTERS

Chicken and roasted red pepper
  terrine 90

Chicken liver parfait 91

Pork satay 92

Potted duck confit 92

Teriyaki beef 93

VEGETARIAN STARTERS

Avocado salad and sun blushed
  tomato bruschetta 93

Baked Camembert with garlic ciabatta
  and red onion marmalade 94

Mozzarella and red onion tartlet 94

Halloumi and grilled vegetables 95

FISH AND SHELLFISH STARTERS

Crayfish cocktail 95

Gravadlax 96

Seafood terrine 96

Smoked mackerel with pickled
cucumber 97

Smoked salmon with classic
garnish 97

CANAPÉS AND SANDWICHES

BLT 98

Bookmaker sandwich 98

Pumpernickel and smoked
salmon 99

Welsh and buck rarebit 99

Club sandwich 100

Croque Monsieur 100

Selection of canapés and bowl
food 101

LEARNING OBJECTIVES

At the end of this chapter you will be able to:

- Identify each type of salad and how they are composed.

- Understand the use of relative ingredients and their quality points.

- Understand the quality points in the presentation of cooked, cured and prepared foods.

- Identify the storage and holding procedures of cold salads, starters and buffet items.

- Identify the correct tools and equipment to utilize during the production and presentation of cooked, cured and prepared foods.

- Recognize the healthy eating options when preparing and presenting cold foods for presentation.

This chapter will enable you to develop skills and apply knowledge in the principles of producing a range of cold larder items that include salads, cold starters, **buffet** items, cold sauces and dressings. The chapter will also introduce the use of relevant materials, ingredients and equipment.

Hors d'oeuvres, appetisers and starters

Although they are a relatively minor element in a full menu the set of first courses are significant. They are also the most likely dishes that require cold preparation. Great care and attention needs to be initiated because the quality will give an indication of the menu to follow. The service of canapés is similar because these represent the tone of a meal and tempt the palette before a meal commences. The first rule is to keep canapés and starters simple, not too overpowering in taste or have too many contrasting flavours. Dishes are usually chosen for the menu in order to complement and balance the main course.

However, the starter selection should be balanced to offer all dietary requirements such as vegetarian, religious and various allergies.

HEALTH & SAFETY For the safety of customers, always be aware of what ingredients are present within dishes in case of allergies.

HEALTH & SAFETY Make sure the temperature in your refrigerator is 5 °C or under for best practice.

HEALTH & SAFETY When preparing cold products, processes should be carried out as efficiently and quickly as possible to minimize the risk of food contamination and poisoning. When handling ready to eat high protein items such as pâté its is advisable to wear disposable gloves; changing them as hygienically required.

A platter of pastry hors d'oeuvres

There are generally two main kinds of hors d'oeuvre.

Hors d'oeuvres varieties

These can be classed as a starter, main course or extended further into a buffet selection. It is a traditional and standard title for defining a selection of **hors d'oeuvre**. There will be a good choice of salads, eggs, vegetables, fruits, meats, fish, game and poultry items to select from. These dishes should always be presented in small portions, replenished frequently and should be **diced** or cut into small strips or pieces for ease of service.

Single hors d'oeuvres

As the name implies, these dishes usually consist of a single item, but can also consist of two or more compatible items. Classically, the service of hors d'oeuvres was on a hors d'oeuvre trolley. Similar to a **canapé** tray or cheese board, there would be a selection of different items on the trolley. A restaurant service team would fetch over the trolley and

suggest a selection and serve to the guest or let the customer choose for themselves.

TASK Your menu has a main course of braised herdwick lamb shank (see page 242), suggest a range of three hors d'oeuvres to complement this dish.

Commodities used and quality points

Caviar

This is the roe of the sturgeon fish which has been removed, salted and packed into tins. The best known types are *Beluga* (a large grain with a light colour), *Sevruga* (a small grain with a darker colour) and *Osetra* (a small grain and darker colour).

Sevruga caviar and quails egg canapé

Caviar should be stored at 1–2 °C and should always have a bright, almost shiny appearance. The best quality caviar is usually served direct from the tin, which sits on an ice **socle** (making a mount for the caviar by moulding ice into required shape) or crushed ice, and is served with blinis.

Oysters – huîtres

English oysters are in season from September to April each year. During the remaining summer months they are breeding and should not be eaten.

British oysters are termed as 'natives', with the best known being from Colchester, Whitstable, Poole and Shannon. The most recognized imported varieties are Belon from France and these are purchased in graded sizes whereby number 1 is the largest and number 4 is the smallest.

Fresh oysters

WEB LINK Below is a link for a small respected oyster distributor in Colchester, a family run business since 1792 specializing in quality products
http://www.richardhawardsoysters.co.uk

It is important that oysters are alive, which can easily be established by their tightly closed shells. Furthermore it is imperative that they are stored in a cool damp room and kept in the wooden containers that they were delivered in.

Charcuterie

Charcuterie consists of a wide range of cured meats and sausages such as bratwurst, mortadella, salamis and Parma ham which should be cut into thin slices or carved in front of the guest.

Parma ham, salamis and mortadella hanging in a delicatessen

Smoked and cured fish

Examples of these are smoked salmon, mackerel, herring (kippers), haddock, trout and eel. Gravadlax (originating from Scandinavia) is cured in a liquid brine with fresh dill.

Fruits

Citrus fruits are popular for turning into cocktails, with oranges and grapefruit being the most accepted. They can be mixed with other fruits such as pineapple, grapes, nectarines, melons and mangoes. The natural sharpness of these fruits is an ideal balance within a selection of hors d'oeuvres or as a starter.

CHEF'S TIP Ensure that all fruits are fresh, without bruising or blemishes, and are not over-ripe.

Grapefruit, pink-grapefruit, lemon and lime

Vegetables

Before preparation, all vegetables should be thoroughly washed and dried. The natural colours of fresh vegetables greatly enhance any starter or hors d'oeuvre display. Vegetables should therefore be carefully cut in their raw state and never overcooked if cooking is required.

Vegetables should be carefully prepared; they can be used to enhance a dish when cut and presented correctly as shown at top of next page.

white mirepoix   mirepoix

finely chopped   julienne   brinoise   paysanne

jardinière   macedoine   chiffonade

Crudités are raw vegetables that have been cut into bite-sized shapes and are presented on a serving plate with a selection of dressings and sauces. Other vegetable preparations can be pickled onions, cucumber, celery or red cabbage.

Selection of crudités

A range of cooked vegetable hors d'oeuvres are presented within the following techniques

● **À la Grecque** – (see page 80).

● **Portugaise** – a stew is made with olive oil, garlic, shallots, bay leaves, tomato puree and fresh pulp, then the main commodity, such as mushrooms, is added.

When checking for the quality points of fresh vegetables it is important to ensure that they are ripe, not bruised, have a good colour and aroma and that they have no infestation by insects.

Herbs and micro herbs

The use of fresh herbs within cooking will always add aroma, colour and flavour to any presented dish. Some aromatic herbs such as tarragon, fennel and basil are excellent to infuse in oils and vinaigrettes. Others such as dill, chervil, chives, mint and parsley add colour and flavour to salads.

Micro herbs are grown in a minimum of dirt to make their use simpler for the chef: they are grown in a mixture of sand and small stone so the herbs can be picked and then sprayed with water.

WEB LINK Find out more about herbs or salad leaves harvested at seed or first leaf stage. **http://www.wowmicroleaf.co.uk/**

Micro herbs come in a range of colours, sizes and flavours such as bull's blood chard, mizuna, baby rocket, rock chives and lemon cress.

The flavours are used to complement dishes such as rock chives with a garlic, citrus hint is especially good with smoked salmon.

Living micro herbs

It is best to purchase fresh herbs in smaller quantities as and when required and prior to use it is important to remove any bruised or damaged leaves.

CHEF'S TIP Keep herbs fresh for a few days by wrapping in damp kitchen paper and placing into a plastic bag before storing in a refrigerator.

Terrines

These are named after the mould they are made in. **Terrines** are produced in different sizes and can be made from meat, game, fish, poultry, **pâté** and vegetables.

There are many varieties of a terrine, all of which will provide the chef with the opportunity to use different colours, textures and flavours in a creative fashion.

Terrines can be cooked or can be cold set **mousses**, coarse pâtés, fine smooth **parfaits**, meat jellies or cooked layered ingredients that have been cold pressed. The terrine mould is usually lined with either bacon, seaweed, vegetables or fat because these help to hold the terrine together for presentation and cutting. Lining with fats can keep it moist as well.

Varying terrine moulds

Butler's tray of open sandwiches

CHEF'S TIP Gelatine is widely used in the setting of terrines. As gelatine is made from boiled beef bones, remember to replace it with agar agar, which is made from seaweed, when creating vegetarian dishes.

Pâtés and parfaits

Generally made of offal, meat, fish, vegetable or game products, pâtés are usually served coarse and parfaits are fine, smooth pastes that are rich in flavour and have a consistency of whipped cream or butter.

Mousses

Similar to both parfaits and terrines, these can be either raw or cooked. Mousses tend to be of a lighter texture because they have the addition of cream but are not as rich in flavour as pâtés or terrines and therefore a little more versatile to use.

Preparation of sandwiches

Open or Scandinavian sandwiches

These are ideal buffet and reception items. An **open sandwich** is one layer of any variety bread with a filling decorated on top and garnished in an attractive way to display the sandwich and its contents. This type of sandwich

is considered more appealing to guests than a closed sandwich.

However, the time required to prepare open sandwiches is usually longer due to the decorative sequence and preparation. Classically these types of sandwiches were part of a buffet, although it is thought that the open sandwich originates from Russia when they were used as an item of food for drinks receptions and parties. The various breads that can be used are French, Vienna, rye, wholemeal, pumpernickel and small bread rolls. The principle of a sandwich menu is that it should be balanced, consisting of a selection of meat fillings, fish fillings, vegetarian fillings, dairy fillings and egg fillings.

HEALTH & SAFETY When you are using a knife, do not cut towards you or your fingers. Pay particular attention to where the edge of your sharp blade is pointing and make sure it cannot harm you or others if you slip.

Closed sandwiches

These varieties are also sometimes referred to as tea sandwiches, buffet sandwiches, conventional sandwiches and reception sandwiches. Closed sandwiches are less sophisticated and far easier to prepare, present and eat because of the filling being enclosed. Furthermore, they will keep slightly longer if prepared in advance and stored, covered by plastic film in a refrigerator.

The 4th Earl of Sandwich was reputed to have invented the sandwich because he required something to eat while

Butler's tray of closed sandwiches

spending his time (and money) gambling. Perhaps this was the forerunner to the 'fast food' fashion of today. The afternoon tea sandwich is a light and delicate presentation and is usually cut into finger shapes or smaller triangles. Currently, club sandwiches, modern wraps or tortillas are popular as they can be easily cut and are visually effective.

TASK A business client has ordered a range of ten sandwiches for a working lunch. Produce a menu that details the sandwiches you plan to provide.

A selection of meat, fish, poultry and vegetarian options are required.

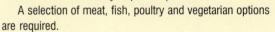

SANDWICH IDEAS – ALL VARIETIES		
DISH	**INGREDIENTS**	**SERVED IN/ON**
Egg mayonnaise with watercress	Eggs, mayonnaise, picked and chopped watercress	Brown bread or wholemeal French stick
Sliced roast beef with basil pesto	Roasted beef, basil, olive oil, parmesan cheese, pine nuts	White sliced loaf or granary bap
Smoked salmon with horseradish cream	Smoked salmon, lemon, dill, cream, fresh horseradish	Wholemeal bread or blinis
Cheddar cheese with sweet pickle	Grated or sliced cheddar cheese, homemade or pre-made pickle	White bread or French stick
Waldorf salad	Apples, celery, crème fraiche, walnuts, grapes	Walnut bread or loaf
Egg with curried yoghurt and coriander	Eggs, curry powder, natural yoghurt, chopped coriander	White bread or naan bread
Cajun chicken with lime mayonnaise	Cajun spice, mayonnaise, olive oil, limes, chicken breast	Tortilla wrap or soda bread
Prawn Marie rose	Prawns, tomato puree, sherry, mayonnaise, lemon juice	Brown bread or toasted bagel
Goats cheese with olive tapanade	Goats cheese, cream, olives, olive oil, anchovy, parsley	Ciabatta or multi-grain bloomer
Aubergine with red pepper salsa	Aubergine, garlic, yoghurt, olive oil, red peppers, red onion	White loaf or pita
Egg mayonnaise with sorrel and baby spinach	Eggs, mayonnaise, sorrel, baby spinach, seasoning	Onion bread or wholemeal baguette
Maple syrup roasted pork or ham with grain mustard and apple puree	Loin of pork or ham, maple syrup, brown sugar, butter, cooking apples, grain mustard	French stick or white crusty loaf

SANDWICH IDEAS – ALL VARIETIES		
DISH	**INGREDIENTS**	**SERVED IN/ON**
Avocado and crab sticks with seafood dressing	Avocado pear, seafood or crab sticks, mayonnaise, diced red pepper, tomato ketchup, sherry, cayenne pepper, lemon juice	White bread or baguette
Cottage cheese with chives and spring onion	Cottage cheese, chopped chives and sliced spring onion	Wholemeal loaf or baguette
Roasted Mediterranean vegetables with balsamic syrup	Reduced balsamic vinegar, peppers, courgette, aubergine, red onion, mixed leaves	Brown bloomer or focaccia
Egg with grain mustard and cress	Eggs, grain mustard, cress	White or granary bread
Turkey with orange and cranberry chutney	Roasted breast of turkey, onions, honey, orange zest and juice, fresh or frozen cranberries, cinnamon stick, cloves, mixed leaves	White sliced or baguette
Tuna with sweet corn and parsley crème fraiche	Tinned or fresh cooked and flaked tuna, sweet corn fresh cooked, tinned or frozen, crème fraiche, chopped parsley	Brown bread or bloomer
Brie with grape and port compote	Brie sliced, grapes, red onion, sugar, honey, port	French stick or bagel
Humus with grilled courgette	Chick peas, olive oil, garlic, tahini paste, ground cumin, turmeric and coriander, courgette	Pita bread or flat bread
Egg with sausage and bacon	Chopped egg, chopped sausage, diced bacon, tomato ketchup	Brown bread or tomato bread
Coronation chicken with apple	Curry mayonnaise or yoghurt, chicken breast cooked, diced apple, sultanas	White bread or poppadom
Mackerel pate with pickled cucumber	Brown soft breadcrumbs, white wine vinegar, salt sugar, cucumber	Pumpernickel or brown bread
Stilton with red wine poached pear	Stilton cheese crumbled and beaten with cream, pears, peeled and cored, red wine, stock syrup	Walnut bread or rye bread
Plum tomato red onion with rocket pesto	Blanched skinned plum tomatoes, sliced red onion, rocket leaves, pine nuts toasted, basil leaves, olive oil, parmesan cheese grated	Rosemary scented bread or French stick

The different types of buffets

Full cold buffet

When producing different sections for a full cold buffet it is critical to present food that is eye catching and easily served. The buffet should always be well presented, even after the 150th guest has been served. Usually a team of service staff are on hand to help the flow of service and to clearly communicate and explain the broad range of food on show.

A full cold buffet is usually produced for weddings, state or official banquets and celebration ceremonies; therefore a full table service is maintained with the exception that guests are required to be served at the buffet table. To help select the dishes and presentation of the food certain criteria must be followed to ensure a successful service:

1 Refrigeration should be used to display food where possible. If this is not available, food should only be presented to guests at the last possible moment directly from a storage refrigerator.

2 Ensure that all accompaniments, dressings, sauces and **garnishes** are served next to the appropriate buffet item.

3 Make certain that serving equipment is always available for service staff and guests to use.

4 Create a centrepiece (usually an ice carving, fat carving, or the most superior dish available) and build the other items around this.

5   When planning the display, ensure that guests have a natural route to negotiate access to the whole buffet table in as quick a time as possible.

6   Make use of different styles of presentations such as small dishes, shot glasses, soup spoons, different shaped platters and ornate butler's trays.

HEALTH & SAFETY Always remember that steam will rise out of a boiling pot of water when you take off the cover. Remove the cover far side first so that the steam does not scald your hand.

HEALTH & SAFETY Chopping boards, equipment, containers and hands should be washed before and immediately after use.

Fork buffet

This is a type of buffet that should be served to guests where there is limited space to sit down and eat.

Normally guests will stand and eat from the buffet table: this is a style of service most suited for large business functions and luncheons where conversation and interaction between guests is of equal importance. The items of food on display must therefore be small and easy to serve. Some hot food selections may also be provided.

HEALTH & SAFETY Store food correctly. Never store raw meats or fish above cooked. All items should be labelled and dated correctly.

Finger buffet

This is the least formal of all buffets and will usually be at a reception where the main aspect of the assembly is to meet in a social capacity or as a business function. This is not regarded as a full meal and there is no cutlery used to consume the food, hence its name. The food should be bite sized and not difficult to eat but still well presented and flavoured.

HEALTH & SAFETY Refrigerator and freezer temperatures should be recorded regularly to comply with health and safety regulations.

Breakfast buffet

The breakfast buffet should have a varied display of foods. Consequently, a choice of hot and cold food items should be available with choices offered such as cured meats, kippers, vegetarian options, cereals and bakery items. A fresh selection of fruit juices, smoothies, fruit and yoghurts should also be provided.

Speciality buffets

These can vary, from buffets with certain religious directions to modern and trendy ways of serving foods. It is becoming increasingly popular and necessary in hospitality to be aware of every type of eating trend, habits and allergies. Focus is now far more customer oriented and the whole experience should therefore be a memorable one.

In this style the chef and the service team can be more extravagant in the presentation and service of the food and follow themes and directions in connection to the customer's wishes (e.g. product launches or sporting themes).

TASK Make a list of speciality buffets, choose one of them and create a menu for it. Present your themed buffet to the rest of your group. Mention minimum and maximum covers, price, food trends and use of meat, fish, poultry and vegetarian options.

Utilizing individual, open, food presentation tables around a room and with each serving a different style of food or course is a good way of organizing a buffet. This is because guests can move freely between different sections at their desire, making the event more relaxed and sociable. Another benefit is that it can distribute the work load evenly around the sections as guests will not all follow the same service route.

HEALTH & SAFETY Always use a sanitizer after the surface has been cleaned with soapy water.

HEALTH & SAFETY Spillages should be cleaned immediately and an appropriate sign put in place to make other staff aware and help prevent accidents.

Salads

Salads are a presentation of raw, cooked, cold or warm food items that are usually dressed and seasoned, with their purpose being to offer an alternative within the menu or as an accompaniment to another dish. They are a lighter and usually healthier option.

The range of different styles of salads has grown over the past 20 years, especially with the ease of long distance travel more people are being exposed to different styles of cuisine. Below are some varieties of salad items.

Salad counter

Simple salads

A **simple salad** consists of one basic ingredient served with a dressing or sauce and further sometimes a garnish can be added for decoration. Examples include cucumber salad, tomato salad, beetroot salad.

Compound salads

Compound salads are salads that are composed of more than two ingredients and dressed appropriately. They can be a mixture of leaves, vegetables, fruit, meats or fish. Examples might be Florida salad, Mimosa salad, Waldorf salad and Russian salad.

American salads

American salads usually accompany a roast dish such as turkey or duck. In North America during a banquet or function the sauce would also be served with a salad rather than vegetables; for example, orange salad with duck.

Salade tiède

Tiède means warm. This type of salad is usually made from ordinary salad vegetables and dressed with a hot dressing in place of the usual cold ones. In many instances this salad is a means for a small item of hot meat such as foie gras or chicken livers to be served, where the fat and juices of the pan are used to make the hot dressing. **Salad tiède** are utilized for starters or main courses rather than a side accompaniment. They have to be quickly prepared to order and served immediately due to the hot elements and dressing wilting the cold ingredients such as lettuce. Examples include *salade tiède bergère*.

Cooked served cold salads

These originated during the time when there was no form of refrigeration to preserve food and therefore these salads would have a longer shelf life as they were pickled, lightly cooked or placed in a sauce. À la Grecque is a classic example because in translation it means 'to be cooked in a Greek style'; this process is cooking in a vinegar and oil solution with aromatic spice. These salads can be meat and fish based but are generally vegetable.

HEALTH & SAFETY High-risk foods such as raw meat, fish and eggs should be stored and cooked as quickly as possible to reduce the risk of food poisoning.

Tools and equipment

A set of preserving jars

Tools and equipment are essential for the preparation and final decorative work required to prepare and present cold food. The list below shows a basic selection of the equipment and tools needed:

- canale knife
- turning knife
- tomato knife
- small and medium sized palette knives
- parisienne cutters; large and small
- serrated and scalloped carving knives
- selection of piping bags and different size tubes
- stainless steel bowls

- wire balloon whisks
- stainless steel or plastic tongs and spoons
- electric food mixer
- food processor and a food blender
- colour coded chopping boards.

HEALTH & SAFETY It is important that the selection of equipment used is thoroughly cleaned before and after each use. The potential for cross-contamination is high with the type and styles of preparation in this chapter so excellent standards of hygiene must be observed at all times.

CHEF'S TIP When freezing items, the flatter and thinner things are, the quicker they will freeze and likewise the quicker they will defrost. Sliced items should be wrapped individually so they can be separated better.

Storage procedures

The use of refrigeration and freezing facilities is essential and these must be maintained at the appropriate temperature zone at all times. Any rise in temperature must be immediately reported and suitable action taken.

Freezer organization must at all times ensure that food which is to be frozen is correctly sealed in a moisture free material such as being vacuum packed, if at all possible. Frozen food, once defrosted, should never be re-frozen under any circumstances.

All foods that are to be refrigerated must be appropriately wrapped or sealed and labelled with the date, name of the product, quantity of the product and preferably the name of the person who is storing the item.

Stock rotation is essential in the reduction of wastage and the 'first-in, first-out' method of usage must be applied at all times. Any deterioration of stored foods should be immediately reported and constant monitoring of 'shelf life' dates on packaging is standard practice.

TASK You have just been given the responsibility of ensuring that the refrigerator is used in a safe and hygienic manner. Write a set of procedures for using the refrigerator, that can be inserted into a 'Kitchen manual'.

Before service, even if the buffet item, cold starter or hors d'oeuvre is refrigerated correctly, it should be remembered that the incubation time of 20 minutes for bacterial growth is still applicable.

Buffets should have a 'rolling service' whereby the food is replaced in small amounts to cut down on wastage and making sure no items are left out for too long. This practice is not necessarily what is required in legislation but is a good practice to follow when planning buffets and displays. Low risk items should be incorporated into the menus to lessen the pressure of maintaining the high risk elements of the buffet.

TEST YOURSELF

1 Name four different types of:
   a. buffet
   b. charcuterie

2 Which salad is the odd one out and why?
   a. Waldorf, Russian, beetroot
   b. Oil, vinegar, coriander (hint: à la Grecque salad)

3 What is the ratio of oil to vinegar when making vinaigrette?

4 List three derivatives of mayonnaise.

5 Which cheese is traditionally used in Croque Monsieur and which herb is used when making fresh pesto?

6 Caviar is the roe of which fish and what is pumpernickel a type of?

7 What is the difference between a buck and Welsh rarebit?

8 What are the three main ingredients when curing salmon for gravadlax?

9 What meat is used in a bookmaker sandwich and what fish is used in a Caesar salad?

10 What nuts are used in:
   a. Waldorf salad
   b. Coronation chicken
   c. Satay sauce?

11 What does BLT stand for and what are terrines named after?

Salads

À la Grecque
(mushroom, cauliflower and fennel)

Ingredients	Makes approximately 4 portions	Makes approximately 10 portions
Mushrooms, cauliflower or fennel	400 g	1 kg
Olive oil	¼ litre	½ litre
Peppercorns	2	4–5
Parsley stalks	10 g	25 g
Bayleaf	½	1
White wine vinegar	⅛ litre	½ litre
Lemon juice	1	3
Coriander seeds	2	4–5
Thyme	1 sprig	3 sprigs
Garlic	1 clove	2 cloves
Good quality salt and pepper	To taste	To taste

energy	cal	fat	sat fat	carb	sugar	protein	fibre
3002 kJ	730 kcal	78.7 g	10.4 g	1.4 g	0.5 g	2.8 g	2.4 g

METHOD OF WORK

1 If using cauliflower cut into florets, Use baby fennel or cut into quarters or eighths depending on the size, quarter the mushrooms.
2 Mix all the remaining ingredients together in a pan and bring to the boil.
3 Add the main ingredient and slowly cook until tender.
4 Remove the pan from the heat and allow the mixture to cool naturally to infuse the spices.

CHEF'S TIP An à la Grecque salad can be made and stored in a sealed air tight jar for a week, this will allow the flavours to develop and produce a better product.

SOURCING The vegetables should be selected locally if possible and be used when in season.

Beetroot salad

Ingredients	Makes approximately 4 portions	Makes approximately 10 portions
Sliced cooked beetroot	200 g	500 g
French dressing (see page 149)	20 ml	50 ml
Finely chopped chives	2 tsp	5 tsp
Good quality salt and pepper	To taste	To taste

energy	cal	fat	sat fat	carb	sugar	protein	fibre
174 kJ	42 kcal	2.0 g	0.3 g	4.9 g	4.5 g	1.3 g	1.0 g

METHOD OF WORK

1 Combine the dressing with the chives and season to taste.
2 Spoon carefully over the beetroot and arrange on a plate.
3 Garnish as required.

CHEF'S TIP The beetroot can be purchased raw, pre-cooked or in baby form – this will allow different presentation and flavour combinations.
The dish also works well with aged balsamic vinegar.

Caesar salad

Ingredients	Makes approximately 4 portions	Makes approximately 10 portions
Cos lettuce	1	2
Croutons	25 g	50 g
Parmesan	50 g	100 g
Olive oil	100 ml	200 ml
Garlic	1 ½	3
Baby gem lettuce	1	2
Anchovy fillets	½ tin	1 tin
Egg yolks	2	4
Lemons	1	2
Good quality salt and pepper	To taste	To taste

energy	cal	fat	sat fat	carb	sugar	protein	fibre
1491 kJ	361 kcal	32.9 g	7.0 g	7.0 g	1.9 g	9.4 g	1.5 g

METHOD OF WORK

1   Wash and pick the leaves off the lettuces.
2   Grate the Parmesan cheese.
3   Make the dressing by placing the garlic, half the anchovies, the zest and juice of the lemon and the egg yolks into a blender and blending to a paste, then incorporating the oil slowly to form an emulsion. Season and stir in the parmesan.
4   Toss the salad leaves with anchovy fillets and the dressing. Serve.

CHEF'S TIP Caesar salad can be served with char grilled salmon, chicken or steak.
  Care should be taken to combine the dressing with the leaves at the last minute to prevent them becoming wilted and soggy.

HEALTHY OPTION To produce lower fat versions try folding in low fat yoghurt into half the Caesar dressing.

Chicory and orange

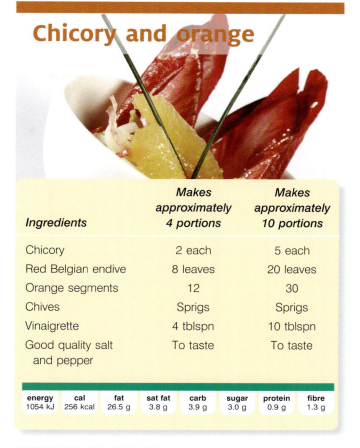

Ingredients	Makes approximately 4 portions	Makes approximately 10 portions
Chicory	2 each	5 each
Red Belgian endive	8 leaves	20 leaves
Orange segments	12	30
Chives	Sprigs	Sprigs
Vinaigrette	4 tblspn	10 tblspn
Good quality salt and pepper	To taste	To taste

energy	cal	fat	sat fat	carb	sugar	protein	fibre
1054 kJ	256 kcal	26.5 g	3.8 g	3.9 g	3.0 g	0.9 g	1.3 g

METHOD OF WORK

1   Cut the chicory in half length ways, remove the core and chiffonade.
2   Dress with the vinaigrette and season to taste.
3   Arrange in a bowl with orange segments, red Belgian endive and chives.

CHEF'S TIP Try using blood oranges for a different effect, the juice can be added to the vinaigrette to increase the flavour.

Coronation chicken

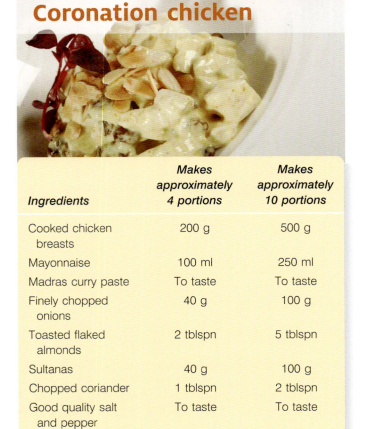

Ingredients	Makes approximately 4 portions	Makes approximately 10 portions
Cooked chicken breasts	200 g	500 g
Mayonnaise	100 ml	250 ml
Madras curry paste	To taste	To taste
Finely chopped onions	40 g	100 g
Toasted flaked almonds	2 tblspn	5 tblspn
Sultanas	40 g	100 g
Chopped coriander	1 tblspn	2 tblspn
Good quality salt and pepper	To taste	To taste

energy	cal	fat	sat fat	carb	sugar	protein	fibre
1355 kJ	326 kcal	24.5 g	3.6 g	8.5 g	7.9 g	18.4 g	1.2 g

METHOD OF WORK

1 Dice the cooked chicken, combine with the mayonnaise, onion, sultanas and coriander.

2 Add enough curry paste to taste.

3 Season and finish with the flaked almonds.

Couscous salad

Ingredients	Makes approximately 4 portions	Makes approximately 10 portions
Couscous	½ box	1 box
Boiling water	Enough to just cover the couscous	Enough to just cover the couscous
Chillies red	1	2
Spring onions	¼ bunch	½ bunch
Honey	25 ml	50 ml
Ground coriander	12 g	25 g
Ground cumin	12 g	25 g
Garlic	1 clove	2 cloves
Mint	¼ bunch	½ bunch
Turmeric	12 g	25 g
Olive oil	50 ml	100 ml
Baby red and yellow cherry tomatoes	40 g	100 g
Good quality salt and pepper	To taste	To taste

energy	cal	fat	sat fat	carb	sugar	protein	fibre
975 kJ	234 kcal	14.4 g	2.0 g	24.4 g	7.5 g	3.2 g	3.2 g

METHOD OF WORK

1 Crush the garlic and finely chop the chillies.

2 Sweat off the garlic and chillies before adding the dried spices and cooking out.

3 Add to sultanas.

4 Place the couscous into a bowl and bring the water to the boil before pouring over the couscous. Cover in cling film and allow to steam for a few minutes before mixing the previous ingredients and spices with a fork and refrigerating.

5 Mix in the chopped mint, coriander, spring onions and tomatoes. Add the honey and season.

CHEF'S TIP Couscous can be bland and dry, ensure there is enough dressing and additional flavours to complement the dish such as citrus fruits, garlic, tomatoes, sultanas, cumin, coriander and chilli.

French bean salad

Ingredients	Makes approximately 4 portions	Makes approximately 10 portions
French Beans	200 g	500 g
Vinaigrette (see page 149)		
Good quality salt and pepper	To taste	To taste

energy	cal	fat	sat fat	carb	sugar	protein	fibre
1690 kJ	411 kcal	44.1 g	6.4 g	2.2 g	1.3 g	1.1 g	1.5 g

METHOD OF WORK

1 Top the French beans before placing them into a large saucepan of boiling salted water and cook until the French beans are soft but still retain their vibrant green colour. Refresh immediately in iced cold water and drain.

2 Toss with enough vinaigrette to coat evenly and season to taste.

3 Garnish as required.

Coleslaw

Ingredients	Makes approximately 4 portions	Makes approximately 10 portions
Mayonnaise	100 ml	250 ml
White cabbage	200 g	500 g
Carrot	50 g	125 g
Onions	25 g	60 g
Good quality salt and pepper	To taste	To taste

energy	cal	fat	sat fat	carb	sugar	protein	fibre
791 kJ	192 kcal	19.2 g	2.9 g	3.7 g	3.3 g	1.3 g	1.5 g

METHOD OF WORK

1 Trim the outer leaves of the cabbage, cut into quarters and remove core.

2 Wash and then chiffonade the cabbage.

3 Combine with a julienne of carrot and finely sliced onion.

4 Gradually add the mayonnaise until the desired consistency is achieved; season to taste.

CHEF'S TIP An alternative to this dish would be using Savoy cabbage and instead of mayonnaise heat a low fat vinaigrette and steep the cabbage until it is tender; finish with finely sliced shallots and bacon lardons.

French salad

Ingredients	Makes approximately 4 portions	Makes approximately 10 portions
Blanched French beans	100 g	250 g
Vinaigrette emulsified French (see page 149)	100 ml	250 ml
Tomberry tomatoes	50 g	125 g
Curly endive, water-cress and shiso cress	100 g	250 g
Tomatoes, blanched peeled, deseeded and cut into julienne	50 g	125 g
Good quality salt and pepper	To taste	To taste

energy	cal	fat	sat fat	carb	sugar	protein	fibre
1888 kJ	458 kcal	45.1 g	6.4 g	10.2 g	7.8 g	5.0 g	3.1 g

METHOD OF WORK

1 Combine all ingredients, dress and season to taste.

2 Neatly arrange on a serving dish or plate.

WEB LINK Try using different varieties of tomatoes for this salad; try looking at the web link for ideas.
http://www.foodsubs.com/Tomtom.html

Fruit platter

Ingredients	Makes approximately 4 portions	Makes approximately 10 portions
Pears, halved, cored and sliced	1 each	2 each
Apples, peeled, halved and sliced	1 each	2 each
Strawberries, halved	8 each	20 each
Raspberries, halved	8 each	20 each
Blackberries, halved	8 each	20 each
Grapes, halved	8 each	20 each
Picked basil leaves	Sprigs	Sprigs

energy	cal	fat	sat fat	carb	sugar	protein	fibre
311 kJ	73 kcal	0.4 g	0.1 g	17.2 g	17.1 g	1.3 g	3.7 g

METHOD OF WORK

1   Wash and neatly arrange the fruits on a plate or platter.
2   The basil may be placed in a pestle and mortar with a little sugar; ground together and sprinkled over the fruit.

CHEF'S TIP   When using apples or pears place them in acidulated water (water with a little lemon juice in); this will stop them oxidizing and turning brown before use.

Green salad

Ingredients	Makes approximately 4 portions	Makes approximately 10 portions
Curly endive	20 g	50 g
Lollo Bionde lettuce	20 g	50 g
Baby gems	20 g	50 g
Cucumber	20 g	50 g
Blanched green beans, split lengthways	20 g	50 g
Watercress	20 g	50 g
Vinaigrette (see page 149)		

energy	cal	fat	sat fat	carb	sugar	protein	fibre
1659 kJ	404 kcal	43.9 g	6.3 g	1.1 g	0.5 g	0.6 g	0.8 g

METHOD OF WORK

1   Wash all the ingredients and drain well.
2   Mix with vinaigrette and season to taste.
3   Arrange neatly and serve.

WEB LINK   The web link shows a comprehensive range of salad leaves; try to create your own green salad using different varieties.
http://www.foodsubs.com/Greensld.html

Mixed bean salad

Ingredients	Makes approximately 4 portions	Makes approximately 10 portions
Cooked red kidney beans	20 g	50 g
Cooked haricot beans	20 g	50 g
Cooked butter beans	20 g	50 g
Cooked flageolet beans	20 g	50 g
Chiffonade of flat leaf parsley	1 tblspn	2 tblspn
Vinaigrette (see page 149)		

energy	cal	fat	sat fat	carb	sugar	protein	fibre
1034 kJ	251 kcal	26.2 g	5.8 g	2.7 g	0.4 g	1.1 g	1.1 g

METHOD OF WORK

1 Drain all the beans, wash well.
2 Mix with vinaigrette and season to taste.
3 Combine with the parsley.
4 Arrange neatly and serve.

HEALTHY OPTION Pulses are an excellent source of fibre, try using this salad to complement a main course dish such as grilled sea bass fillets.

CHEF'S TIP Tinned beans work just as well as dried beans for this recipe. If using dried ensure they are adequately soaked, washed and cooked correctly.

Mixed salad

Ingredients	Makes approximately 4 portions	Makes approximately 10 portions
Assorted picked lettuce leaves	40 g	100 g
Sun blushed tomatoes	20 g	50 g
Tomberry tomatoes	20 g	50 g
Finely shredded shallots	20 g	50 g
Peeled, cored and finely sliced cucumber	20 g	50 g
Chiffonade of flat leaf parsley	1 tblspn	2 tblspn
Vinaigrette (see page 149)		

energy	cal	fat	sat fat	carb	sugar	protein	fibre
940 kJ	228 kcal	24.6 g	3.5 g	1.1 g	0.6 g	0.6 g	0.9 g

METHOD OF WORK

1 Wash all the vegetables and salad, drain well.
2 Mix with vinaigrette and season to taste.
3 Combine with the parsley.
4 Arrange neatly and serve.

Moroccan bulgur wheat salad

Ingredients	Makes approximately 4 portions	Makes approximately 10 portions
Bulgur wheat	40 g	100 g
Chickpeas, tinned	25 g	50 g
Chillies red	1	2
Coriander	¼ bunch	½ bunch
Honey	25 ml	50 ml
Ground coriander	12 g	25 g
Ground cumin	12 g	25 g
Mixed pepper	1 of each	3 of each
Garlic	1 clove	2 cloves
Mint	¼ bunch	½ bunch
Turmeric	12 g	25 g
Olive oil	50 ml	100 ml
Micro herbs		
Good quality salt and pepper	To taste	To taste

energy	cal	fat	sat fat	carb	sugar	protein	fibre
1055 kJ	253 kcal	15.0 g	2.1 g	26.4 g	12.8 g	4.7 g	5.1 g

METHOD OF WORK

1   Crush the garlic and finely chop the chillies.
2   Sweat off the garlic and chillies before adding the dried spices and cooking out.
3   Place the bulgur wheat into a bowl and bring the water to the boil before pouring over the bulgur wheat. Cover with cling film and allow to steam for a few minutes before mixing the previous ingredients, spices and chickpeas with a fork and refrigerating.
4   Mix in the chopped mint and coriander. Add the honey and season.
5   Serve in a bowl and garnish with micro herbs.

CHEF'S TIP   Bulgur wheat has a nutty texture and taste, it works exceptionally well with lamb served with a cool minted yoghurt such as a raita (see page 145).

Niçoise salad

Ingredients	Makes approximately 4 portions	Makes approximately 10 portions
New potatoes	8	20
Fine green beans	50 g	125 g
Mixed leaves	50 g	100 g
Tomberry tomatoes	12	30
Anchovy fillets	8	20
Hard boiled eggs	2	5
Pitted black olives	8	20
Finely chopped red onion	40 g	100 g
Vinaigrette (see page 149)		

energy	cal	fat	sat fat	carb	sugar	protein	fibre
1083 kJ	261 kcal	15.5 g	2.6 g	23.0 g	2.7 g	8.1 g	2.9 g

METHOD OF WORK

1   Boil the new potatoes in salted water, then refresh and cut into wedges.
2   Boil the green beans in salted water, refresh and cut into 3cm pieces.
3   Cut the anchovies into neat thin strips.
4   Peel, and cut the eggs into quarters.
5   Combine all the remaining ingredients, season to taste and serve.

CHEF'S TIP   Niçoise salad has a history connected to the south of France. In some versions of this salad it is combined with Tuna. Try serving it with soft poached quail eggs for another twist.

SOURCING   The olives and anchovies play a crucial part in this dish, the salt content combines well with the other ingredients. When selecting these commodities try to source good quality options: they may be more expensive but less are required due to their depth of flavour.

Potato salad

Ingredients	Makes approximately 4 portions	Makes approximately 10 portions
New potatoes (Jersey Royals when in season)	400 g	1 kg
Chives	½ bunch	1 bunch
Mayonnaise		
Finely chopped shallots	1 tblspn	2 tblspn
Good quality salt and pepper	To taste	To taste

energy	cal	fat	sat fat	carb	sugar	protein	fibre
732 kJ	176 kcal	9.6 g	1.5 g	20.6 g	1.4 g	2.3 g	2.2 g

METHOD OF WORK

1   Wash and scrub the potatoes then place into boiling salted water and cook until tender before draining and chilling.
2   Cut the cooked potatoes into an even dice. (The skin can be removed or left on with this being down to preference and personal taste.)
3   Finely chop the chives.
4   Bind the potatoes, shallots and chives with enough mayonnaise to form the potato salad.
5   season to taste and garnish.

CHEF'S TIP When producing potato salad use waxy varieties such as Charlotte as they maintain their shape once cooked, dry floury potatoes will simply disintegrate in the bowl.

SOURCING Use the link to research detailed information regarding Jersey Royal potatoes: http://www.jerseyroyals.co.uk

Russian salad

Ingredients	Makes approximately 4 portions	Makes approximately 10 portions
Macédoine of carrot, turnip, swede and celery	200 g	500 g
Green beans, 1 cm lengths	50 g	125 g
Mayonnaise		
Peas	50 g	125 g
Good quality salt and pepper	To taste	To taste

energy	cal	fat	sat fat	carb	sugar	protein	fibre
168 kJ	41 kcal	2.7 g	0.4 g	3.0 g	1.6 g	1.4 g	1.8 g

METHOD OF WORK

1   Wash the macédoine of vegetables, then place in cold salted water and bring to the boil; remove once tender then drain and refresh.
2   Blanch the beans and peas in boiling salted water, once tender drain and refresh.
3   Bind the ingredients with mayonnaise.
4   Season to taste and garnish.

Tomato, basil and mozzarella

Ingredients	Makes approximately 4 portions	Makes approximately 10 portions
Cherry tomatoes	200 g	500 g
Tomberry tomatoes	50 g	125 g
Mozzarella balls (small)	16	40
Picked basil leaves	50 g	125 g
Herb oil or pesto (optional)		
Good quality sea salt and pepper	To taste	To taste

energy	cal	fat	sat fat	carb	sugar	protein	fibre
711 kJ	172 kcal	14.6 g	6.1 g	1.9 g	1.2 g	8.2 g	0.5 g

METHOD OF WORK

1   Carefully de-eye the tomatoes, cut the larger ones in half.
2   Neatly arrange the tomatoes, mozzarella and basil in a chilled dish.
3   Season to taste with sea salt, pepper and dress with either basil oil or pesto.

CHEF'S TIP   The mozzarella can be marinated in advance; for example in basil oil (see page 150). Small mozzarella balls are called 'Bocconcini'.

Tomato, cucumber and herb vinaigrette

Ingredients	Makes approximately 4 portions	Makes approximately 10 portions
Plum tomatoes (on the vine if possible)	100 g	250 g
Cucumber	100 g	250 g
Finely chopped chives	2 tblspn	5 tblspn
Vinaigrette (see page 149)		
Good quality sea salt and pepper	To taste	To taste

energy	cal	fat	sat fat	carb	sugar	protein	fibre
858 kJ	209 kcal	22.1 g	3.2 g	1.7 g	1.4 g	0.7 g	0.9 g

METHOD OF WORK

1   Carefully de-eye the tomatoes, slice thinly.
2   Peel and thinly slice the cucumber.
3   Arrange as shown in a chilled dish.
4   Combine the chives with the vinaigrette, season to taste.
5   Spoon the vinaigrette over the tomatoes and cucumber.
6   Garnish as required.

CHEF'S TIP   In addition try using sun blushed tomatoes in the salad, sundried tomatoes can also be chopped finely and mixed through the dressing for additional flavour and colour. The tomatoes may be blanched, refreshed in ice water and sliced.

Tropical fruit platter

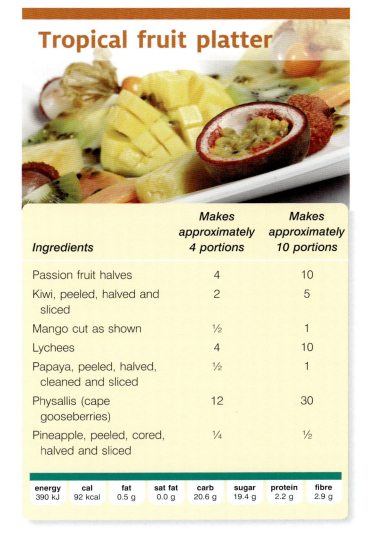

Ingredients	Makes approximately 4 portions	Makes approximately 10 portions
Passion fruit halves	4	10
Kiwi, peeled, halved and sliced	2	5
Mango cut as shown	½	1
Lychees	4	10
Papaya, peeled, halved, cleaned and sliced	½	1
Physallis (cape gooseberries)	12	30
Pineapple, peeled, cored, halved and sliced	¼	½

energy	cal	fat	sat fat	carb	sugar	protein	fibre
390 kJ	92 kcal	0.5 g	0.0 g	20.6 g	19.4 g	2.2 g	2.9 g

METHOD OF WORK

1   Neatly arrange the fruit on a chilled plate or platter.
2   As an addition combine a little sugar with mint and grind to a powder, sprinkle over the fruit.

CHEF'S TIP When selecting pineapples for this salad try to remove the central leaves; if they come away easily this is a good indication of ripeness.

For the mango; leave the skin on and cut a slice as close to the stone as possible, with the flesh upwards make vertical and horizontal cuts taking care not to pierce the skin.

Cut a grid pattern as shown:

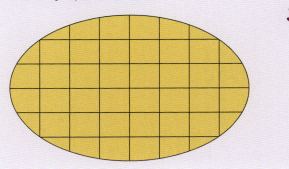

Waldorf salad

Ingredients	Makes approximately 4 portions	Makes approximately 10 portions
Celeriac	½	1
Granny Smith apples	1	2
Red dessert apples	1	2
Greek yoghurt or mayonnaise	100 ml	200 ml
Walnuts	40 g	100 g
Celery peeled	2 sticks	5 sticks

energy	cal	fat	sat fat	carb	sugar	protein	fibre
669 kJ	162 kcal	10.0 g	2.4 g	13.4 g	12.6 g	4.9 g	6.7 g

METHOD OF WORK

1   Peel and finely slice the celeriac, cutting into julienne or a brunoise.
2   Peel and finely slice the red dessert and Granny Smith apples and cut into julienne or a brunoise.
3   Peel and cut the celery into julienne or a brunoise.
4   Blanch the walnuts in boiling water, drain and rub with a clean cloth: this will remove the skin. Chop to desired size.
5   Mix all the ingredients together before adding the yoghurt/mayonnaise, and seasoning. Garnish as required.

Meat and poultry starters

Chicken and roasted red pepper terrine

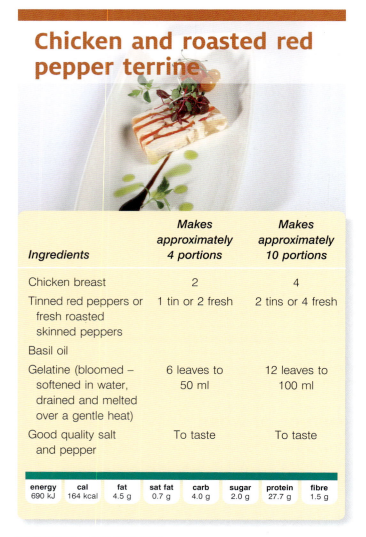

Ingredients	Makes approximately 4 portions	Makes approximately 10 portions
Chicken breast	2	4
Tinned red peppers or fresh roasted skinned peppers	1 tin or 2 fresh	2 tins or 4 fresh
Basil oil		
Gelatine (bloomed – softened in water, drained and melted over a gentle heat)	6 leaves to 50 ml	12 leaves to 100 ml
Good quality salt and pepper	To taste	To taste

energy	cal	fat	sat fat	carb	sugar	protein	fibre
690 kJ	164 kcal	4.5 g	0.7 g	4.0 g	2.0 g	27.7 g	1.5 g

METHOD OF WORK

1   Place the chicken breast onto a chopping board between a vac pac bag then bat out the chicken breast with a meat bat or rolling pin until it forms a fairly even square shape.

2   Season the breast, then quickly pan fry until cooked.

3   Line a terrine mould with cling film then place a layer of chicken in the mould, brush with the gelatine mixture.

4   Add a layer of red pepper, then brush with the gelatine mixture.

5   Continue this layering until the mould is full.

6   Cover with cling film and press with another terrine mould preferably overnight.

7   Slice when chilled, arrange on the plate and garnish as required.

SOURCING   Use the web link to investigate how to trace chickens which may be used in this dish:
http://www.redtractor.org.uk

CHEF'S TIP   The peppers can be skinned by either cutting into quarters, marinating in oil, seasoning, garlic and thyme then roasted, placed into a bowl and covered. This will allow the steam to blister the skin and allow easy removal.

Alternatively the peppers can be held directly over a naked flame until the skin blackens, and then placed into a bowl and the same process applied to remove the skin.

Note:
Agar agar has stronger setting properties than gelatine and sets at room temperature after about an hour. Gelatine requires refrigeration to set. It is advisable to store dishes gelled with agar agar in the fridge as it is a high protein food.

The gelling ability of agar agar is affected by the acidity or alkalinity of the ingredients it is mixed with, also by factors such as the season of the seaweed harvest.

More acidic foods, such as citrus fruits and strawberries, may require higher amounts of agar agar. Some ingredients will not set with it at all such as kiwi fruit (too acidic), pineapple, fresh figs, paw paw/papaya, mango and peaches. They contain enzymes which break down the gelling ability, although cooked fruit seems to lose this effect.

Chicken liver parfait

Ingredients	Makes approximately 4 portions	Makes approximately 10 portions
Shallots	60 g	150 g
Chicken livers (clean and trim)	200 g	500 g
Butter for terrine	80 g	200 g
Butter for whipping	100 g	250 g
Garlic	2	3–4
Brandy	20 ml	50 ml
Double cream	160 ml	300 ml
Spiced tomato chutney (see recipe online)	4 tblspn	10 tblspn
Sliced white bread	2 slices	5 slices
Good quality salt and pepper	To taste	To taste

energy	cal	fat	sat fat	carb	sugar	protein	fibre
2935 kJ	709 kcal	63.4 g	37.9 g	18.7 g	9.8 g	14.1 g	1.1 g

METHOD OF WORK

1 Melt the butter and fry-off the onion and garlic in butter and oil.

2 In a hot pan sear the chicken livers and flambé with the liquor.

3 In a food processor blend the shallots and the chicken livers before adding the melted butter and cream.

4 Line a terrine mould with cling film and pour the parfait mixture in before folding the cling film over. Chill and press lightly.

5 Whip the butter until light and almost white in colour, de-mould the terrine and carefully spread the butter onto the outside surfaces. Chill again until set.

6 To make the melba toast, toast the bread on both sides; remove the crusts. Carefully slice the bread laterally leaving two identical pieces with one side toasted and one not. Rub the untoasted side together to remove excess bread then gently toast to finish.

7 To serve, place a slice of parfait on the plate with melba toast, spiced tomato chutney and garnish as required.

CHEF'S TIP When slicing the terrine submerge the blade of an long non serrated knife in boiling water, this will allow the terrine to be cut smoothly and cleanly. Duck livers can also be used for this recipe.

Pork satay

Ingredients	Makes approximately 4 portions	Makes approximately 10 portions
Loin of pork trimmed and boned	500 g	1 kg
Vegetable oil	240 ml	500 ml
Red chillies	1	2
Peanut oil	75 ml	150 ml
Coriander	¼ bunch	½ bunch
Garlic	1 clove	3 cloves
Ginger	40 g	100 g
Soy sauce	10 ml	30 ml
Peanut butter	300 g	600 g
Shallot	100 g	200 g
Ground cumin	5 g	10 g
Ground coriander	5 g	10 g
Ground turmeric	5 g	10 g
Cream	100 ml	200 ml
Good quality salt and pepper	To taste	To taste

energy	cal	fat	sat fat	carb	sugar	protein	fibre
3740 kJ	900 kcal	65.8 g	14.9 g	16.2 g	6.4 g	58.6 g	7.4 g

METHOD OF WORK

1 Cut the pork loin into strips and place onto skewers, with three pieces per portion.
2 Mix together both oils, chopped chilli, garlic, coriander, ginger and soy sauce and place skewers into this marinade, leaving for 24 hours.
3 Warm peanut butter so it will easily come out of the jar.
4 Dice shallots and sweat in a pan with some of the peanut oil then add the dried spices followed by the peanut butter. Once this has infused add the cream to thin it down. The sauce should be kept warm for service.
5 Skewers should be sealed off in a pan with a small amount of the marinade oil.
6 To serve, place the sauce into a small dish and serve with some mixed leaves and a few skewers.

Potted duck confit

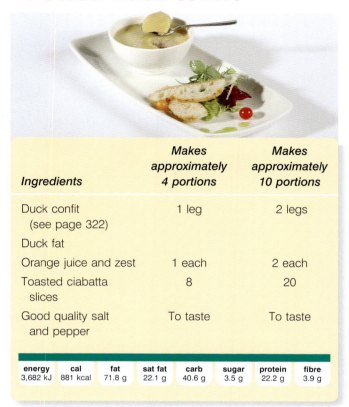

Ingredients	Makes approximately 4 portions	Makes approximately 10 portions
Duck confit (see page 322)	1 leg	2 legs
Duck fat		
Orange juice and zest	1 each	2 each
Toasted ciabatta slices	8	20
Good quality salt and pepper	To taste	To taste

energy	cal	fat	sat fat	carb	sugar	protein	fibre
3,682 kJ	881 kcal	71.8 g	22.1 g	40.6 g	3.5 g	22.2 g	3.9 g

METHOD OF WORK

1 Warm the duck leg confit in enough fat to cover.
2 Once warm remove the legs, pick the meat into a clean bowl and keep warm.
3 Bring the orange juice and zest to the boil; then pour over the duck.
4 Season to taste and then spoon into suitable dishes.
5 Spoon enough fat over to form a skin.
6 Chill until required.
7 Garnish as required.

CHEF'S TIP This dish works exceptionally well replacing the duck with slow cooked belly of pork; simply marinade the pork belly with aromatics, garlic, thyme etc. and then cook the pork belly in fat in an oven at 160 °C using a dish covered with foil. This will take at least four hours, once cooked and warm flake the meat and store as for the duck.

Vegetarian starters

Teriyaki beef

Ingredients	Makes approximately 4 portions	Makes approximately 10 portions
Beef fillet or skirt steaks cut into strips	200 g	500 g
Soy sauce	2 tblspn	5 tblspn
Honey	2 tblspn	5 tblspn
Good quality salt and pepper	To taste	To taste

energy	cal	fat	sat fat	carb	sugar	protein	fibre
503 kJ	119 kcal	4.0 g	1.8 g	6.4 g	6.3 g	14.8 g	0.1 g

METHOD OF WORK

1 Warm the honey gently then add the soy and mix well.
2 Allow to cool then add the beef, marinate for at least an hour.
3 Meanwhile take some wooden skewers and place in water – this will stop them burning during cooking.
4 Take the beef and skewer neatly allowing a quarter of skewer to remain visible – this will enable them to be picked up during cooking and eating.
5 Place the beef on a hot char grill to give a light smoky flavour, cook until medium.
6 Garnish as required.

Avocado salad and sun blushed tomato bruschetta

Ingredients	Makes approximately 4 portions	Makes approximately 10 portions
Ciabatta slices	8	20
Garlic oil (see page 151)	2 tblspn	4 tblspn
Sun blushed tomatoes halves	8	20
Haas avocado	½	1 ½
Wild rocket leaves	80 g	200 g
Finely sliced shallots	50 g	125 g
Sun-dried tomato pesto (see page 145)	15 ml	25 ml
Good quality salt and pepper	To taste	To taste

energy	cal	fat	sat fat	carb	sugar	protein	fibre
2366 kJ	568 kcal	42.0 g	5.5 g	42.0 g	2.9 g	8.4 g	7.6 g

METHOD OF WORK

1 Brush the ciabatta slices with garlic oil then grill until golden brown on both sides.
2 In a bowl combine the shallots with the pesto and rocket.
3 Remove the avocado skin, stone then cut into neat slices.
4 Spoon the shallot mixture over the ciabatta, then lay the avocado and sun blushed tomatoes on top.
5 Garnish as required.

CHEF'S TIP Ensure the avocado is ripe but not too soft, once prepared dress immediately or use a little acidulated water to prevent oxidation (going brown).

Baked Camembert with garlic ciabatta and red onion marmalade

Ingredients	Makes approximately 4 portions	Makes approximately 10 portions
Onion and rosemary bread (see page 504)	6 slices (cut in half)	15 slices (cut in half)
Small Camembert in the box	4	10
Red onion marmalade (see opposite)	8	20
Walnut oil	4 tsp	10 tsp

energy	cal	fat	sat fat	carb	sugar	protein	fibre
4395 kJ	1053 kcal	62.1 g	36.0 g	60.7 g	56.2 g	56.0 g	4.1 g

METHOD OF WORK

1. Make small fork holes in the top of the Camembert cheese, spoon over the walnut oil then bake at 180 °C until the cheese is piping hot.
2. Warm the bread through or toast if preferred.
3. Serve with chilled red onion marmalade.

WEB LINK The following link is a comprehensive source of cheese, sourcing, equipment and taste tests: **http://www.houseofcheese.co.uk**

Mozzarella and red onion tartlet

Ingredients	Makes approximately 4 portions	Makes approximately 10 portions
Mozzarella	150 g	300 g
Reduced balsamic vinegar	2 tblspn	4 tblspn
Puff pastry rectangles 3 cm x 1 cm x ¼ cm	4	10
Egg wash (equal egg yolk and water)	2 yolks	5 yolks
Finely sliced red onion	1	2 ½
Redcurrant jelly	50 g	125 g
Cassis	15 ml	25 ml
Good quality salt and pepper	To taste	To taste

energy	cal	fat	sat fat	carb	sugar	protein	fibre
853 kJ	237 kcal	16.5 g	6.7 g	18.8 g	10.8 g	9.2 g	1.5 g

METHOD OF WORK

1. Prepare the red onion marmalade by placing the onion, jelly and cassis in a saucepan, simmer for approximately 20 minutes until thick and glossy. Place the marmalade into a clean bowl and keep warm.
2. Brush the puff pastry with egg wash, then lay onto a sheet of silicone paper and bake at 180 °C until cooked and golden brown.
3. Remove the pastry and spoon over a little marmalade, lay the mozzarella slices over the marmalade and return to the oven.
4. Once the mozzarella is starting to melt remove and serve with the balsamic glaze and appropriate garnish.

Halloumi and grilled vegetables

Ingredients	Makes approximately 4 portions	Makes approximately 10 portions
Halloumi cheese	12 slices	30 slices
Herb oil	2 tblspn	4 tblspn
Red, yellow peppers	1	2 ½
Courgettes	1	2 ½
Aubergines	½	1
Good quality salt and pepper	To taste	To taste

energy	cal	fat	sat fat	carb	sugar	protein	fibre
3163 kJ	763 kcal	64.3 g	27.2 g	10.9 g	10.3 g	34.9 g	2.9 g

METHOD OF WORK

1 Prepare the peppers by cutting them in quarters and de-seeding them.
2 Slice the courgettes and aubergines into ½ cm slices.
3 Lightly coat and season the vegetables and char grill until tender.
4 Lightly brush the cheese and char grill to form a neat quadrillage pattern as shown.
5 Arrange neatly in bowl and spoon over the herb oil.

HEALTHY OPTION Halloumi cheese in an excellent source of protein; however, like most cheeses it contains a high fat content. Use in moderation as part of a healthy balanced diet.
See the chart below for 100 g serving:

Calories	316
Protein	20.8
Carbohydrates	1.6
Fat	24.7
Fibre	0

Fish and shellfish starts

Fish and shellfish starters

Crayfish cocktail

Ingredients	Makes approximately 4 portions	Makes approximately 10 portions
Cooked and prepared crayfish tails	100 g	250 g
Marie Rose sauce (see page 144)	100 ml	250 ml
Lemon wedges	4	10
Lettuce		
Cayenne pepper	½ tsp	1 tsp
Good quality salt	To taste	To taste

energy	cal	fat	sat fat	carb	sugar	protein	fibre
1070 kJ	259 kcal	26.4 g	2.1 g	1.3 g	0.9 g	4.6 g	0.7 g

METHOD OF WORK

1 Wash, drain and pick over the lettuce.
2 Place into a suitable chilled bowl or glass.
3 Mix the crayfish with the Marie Rose sauce, season with cayenne and salt.
4 Finish with lemon wedges.

WEB LINK Use the web link, type in 'crayfish' and investigate how crayfish are caught and where:
http://www.environment-agency.gov.uk

Gravadlax

Ingredients	Makes approximately 4 portions	Makes approximately 10 portions
Fresh salmon, pin boned with skin on	500 g	1.25 kg
Lemons	2	3
Oranges	2	3
Sugar	400 g	1 kg
Salt	200 g	500 g
Dill (chopped – including stalks)	2 bunches	5 bunches
Cracked black pepper	2 tblspn	5 tblspn

energy	cal	fat	sat fat	carb	sugar	protein	fibre
2897 kJ	685 kcal	14.6 g	2.5 g	119.2 g	110.9 g	28.6 g	4.4 g

METHOD OF WORK

1   Zest and juice the lemons and oranges.
2   Combine with the salt, sugar, pepper and ¾ of the chopped dill.
3   Place a layer onto a tray then top with the salmon, cover with more salt and sugar mixture.
4   Ensure the salmon is completely covered and packed tightly.
5   Gently press with another tray to help push out the water.
6   Cover and refrigerate; turn the salmon over after 12 hours. Leave for a further 12 hours.
7   Remove the salmon from the mixture, rinse clean and pat dry.
8   Pack a neat layer of dill over the flesh side, slice thinly taking care to leave the skin behind.

TASK   Research the following:
What country does gravadlax originate from?
Why is the salmon pressed during curing?
As the salmon cures liquid is produced – what is this liquid called?

Seafood terrine

Ingredients	Makes approximately 4 portions	Makes approximately 10 portions
Sliced smoked salmon	100 g	250 g
Cooked peeled prawns	100 g	250 g
Cream cheese	200 g	500 g
White crab meat	50 g	125 g
Blanched green beans, baby carrots and baby fennel	50 g	125 g
Good quality salt and pepper	To taste	To taste
Lemon juice and zest	½ lemon	1 lemon

energy	cal	fat	sat fat	carb	sugar	protein	fibre
1237 kJ	299 kcal	25.8 g	15.2 g	0.6 g	0.4 g	16.2 g	0.7 g

METHOD OF WORK

1   Line a terrine mould with cling film and then neat slices of smoked salmon.
2   Roughly chop the prawns and mix with the cream cheese, crab and lemon, season to taste.
3   Pipe a layer into the bottom of the mould then layer with the vegetables until the mould is filled.
4   Cover with the smoked salmon and cling film.
5   Place in the freezer and allow to semi freeze.
6   Remove and then slice to desired thickness.
7   Allow to defrost on the plate, garnish as required.

Smoked mackerel with pickled cucumber

Ingredients	Makes approximately 4 portions	Makes approximately 10 portions
Smoked mackerel with crushed peppercorns	2 fillets	5 fillets
Cucumber	½	1 ½
Rice wine vinegar	50 ml	125 ml
Sugar	20 g	50 g
Lemon juice	½ lemon	1 lemon
Oyster sauce	1 tblspn	2 ½ tblspn
Soy sauce	2 tblspn	5 tblspn
Good quality salt and pepper	To taste	To taste

energy	cal	fat	sat fat	carb	sugar	protein	fibre
730 kJ	176 kcal	11.4 g	3.0 g	7.4 g	6.6 g	10.6 g	0.4 g

METHOD OF WORK

1 Cut two thin slices of cucumber at an angle and reserve.
2 With the remaining cucumber, peel and core neatly then make 1 cm thick slices – note make a flat cut at the bottom so the cucumber will stand unaided.
3 In a bowl mix the vinegar, lemon juice, oyster sauce and half the sugar, mix well.
4 Steep the cucumber discs in the marinade for a minimum of 2 hours.
5 Mix soy with the remaining sugar, boil and reduce.
6 On a plate arrange two slices of mackerel cut at an angle, garnish with the pickled cucumber rings, cucumber twist and the soy glaze.

CHEF'S TIP Pre-prepared smoked mackerel can be used as it is very good quality, alternatively fresh fillets can be hot smoked over the following mixture: hickory chips (approx. 100g); jasmine tea bags (approx. 3); long grain rice, raw (approx. 70g) and sugar (approx. 80g).
 Place all the smoking ingredients into a frying pan or tray, heat over a flame until they begin to smoke.
 Transfer this to the bottom shelf of an oven, lay the mackerel fillets on a wire rack above them and cook for 2–3 minutes at 190 °C.

Smoked salmon with classic garnish

Ingredients	Makes approximately 4 portions	Makes approximately 10 portions
Sliced smoked salmon pack	400 g	1 kg
Lemons	2	3
Horseradish	10 g	20 g
Capers	40 g	100 g
Shallots	40 g	100 g
Cream	40 ml	100 ml
Brown bread and butter, crusts off	2 slices – cut into triangles	5 slices – cut into triangles
Good quality salt and pepper	To taste	To taste

energy	cal	fat	sat fat	carb	sugar	protein	fibre
1045 kJ	249 kcal	11.1 g	4.7 g	10.2 g	1.7 g	28.1 g	2.7 g

METHOD OF WORK

1 Finely chop the shallots.
2 Grate the horseradish, semi whip the cream and mix together.
3 Cut the lemons into wedges.
4 Place the slices of smoked salmon on the plate in a square pattern.
5 To serve, garnish the plate with the shallots, capers, a lemon wedge, a little horseradish and brown bread and butter.

WEB LINK When producing this dish try to source the best possible ingredients; a family run business such as Forman's is ideal: http://www.formans.co.uk

Canapés and sandwiches

BLT

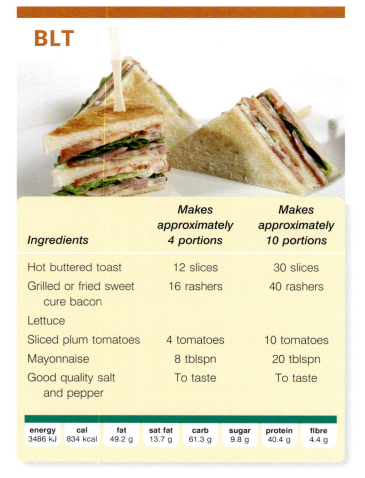

Ingredients	Makes approximately 4 portions	Makes approximately 10 portions
Hot buttered toast	12 slices	30 slices
Grilled or fried sweet cure bacon	16 rashers	40 rashers
Lettuce		
Sliced plum tomatoes	4 tomatoes	10 tomatoes
Mayonnaise	8 tblspn	20 tblspn
Good quality salt and pepper	To taste	To taste

energy	cal	fat	sat fat	carb	sugar	protein	fibre
3486 kJ	834 kcal	49.2 g	13.7 g	61.3 g	9.8 g	40.4 g	4.4 g

METHOD OF WORK

1 Spread an even layer of mayonnaise onto the toast.
2 Arrange the bacon, lettuce and tomatoes onto two slices.
3 Season to taste.
4 Finish with the third slice of toast.
5 Remove the crusts, cut into triangles and secure with wooden skewers.

Bookmaker sandwich

Ingredients	Makes approximately 4 portions	Makes approximately 10 portions
Hot buttered toast	8 slices	20 slices
Minute steak (80–100 g)	4 rashers	8 rashers
Lettuce garnish		
Good quality salt and pepper	To taste	To taste

energy	cal	fat	sat fat	carb	sugar	protein	fibre
1388 kJ	329 kcal	8.8 g	3.7 g	37.8 g	2.9 g	27.0 g	2.4 g

METHOD OF WORK

1 Season then fry, grill or griddle the minute steaks medium rare.
2 Arrange on to hot buttered toast.
3 Cut into triangles.
4 Garnish as required.

WEB LINK Use this web link to investigate how beef is transported and how it is traced from farm to the professional kitchen: **http://ww2.defra.gov.uk**

Pumpernickel and smoked salmon

Ingredients	Makes approximately 4 portions	Makes approximately 10 portions
Pumpernickel	4 slices	10 slices
Smoked salmon	4 slices	10 slices
Crème fraiche	4 tblspn	10 tblspn
Rock chives		
Cherry tomatoes	4	10
Hot garlic and herb oil		

energy	cal	fat	sat fat	carb	sugar	protein	fibre
639 kJ	152 kcal	5.0 g	1.9 g	12.0 g	0.2 g	15.0 g	1.9 g

Pumpernickel is a type of very heavy, slightly sweet rye bread traditionally made with coarsely ground rye. It is now often made with a combination of rye flour and whole rye berries.

METHOD OF WORK

1 Cut neat squares of pumpernickel, top with rosettes of smoked salmon, crème fraiche and garnish with rock chives.

2 For colour and flavour contrast serve cherry tomatoes steeped in hot garlic and herb oil until tender.

Welsh and buck rarebit

Ingredients	Makes approximately 4 portions	Makes approximately 10 portions
Butter or margarine	50 g	125 g
Flour	20 g	50 g
Milk	250 ml	600 ml
Cheddar cheese, grated	200 g	500 g
Egg yolks	2	5
Beer	100 ml	225 ml
Worcester sauce	To taste	To taste
English mustard	To taste	To taste
Hot buttered toast		
Good quality salt and pepper	To taste	To taste
For buck rarebit (Fried eggs)	To taste	To taste

energy	cal	fat	sat fat	carb	sugar	protein	fibre
3209 kJ	769 kcal	48.6 g	27.1 g	54.1 g	7.4 g	31.1 g	2.7 g

Buck rarebit

METHOD OF WORK

1 Melt the butter then add the flour, cook gently for 2 minutes.

2 Gradually add the milk and mix to a smooth paste, simmer for a few minutes.

3 Add the cheese and melt over a gentle heat, add the yolks and remove from the heat.

4 In a separate pan boil the beer until it has reduced to 1/10 the amount (100 ml to 10 ml).

5 Add the beer to the mixture with the remaining ingredients.

6 Allow the mixture to cool, then spread over the toast.

7 Place under the salamander until lightly coloured, serve.

8 For the buck rarebit serve with a fried egg.

Club sandwich

Ingredients	Makes approximately 4 portions	Makes approximately 10 portions
Hot buttered toast	12 slices	30 slices
Grilled or fried sweet cure bacon	8 rashers	20 rashers
Sliced boiled eggs	2	5
Sliced cooked chicken breast	1	2 ½
Mayonnaise	8 tblspn	20 tblspn
Lettuce		
Good quality salt and pepper	To taste	To taste

energy	cal	fat	sat fat	carb	sugar	protein	fibre
3139 kJ	750 kcal	41.4 g	10.5 g	57.2 g	5.7 g	40.7 g	3.1 g

METHOD OF WORK

1 Spread an even layer of mayonnaise onto the toast.
2 Arrange the bacon, lettuce, egg and chicken onto two slices.
3 Season to taste.
4 Finish with the third slice of toast.
5 Remove the crusts, cut into triangles and secure with wooden skewers.

Croque Monsieur

Ingredients	Makes approximately 4 portions	Makes Approximately 10 Portions
Hot buttered toast	8 slices	20 slices
Sliced gruyere cheese	8	20
Sliced cooked ham	4	8
Clarified butter or oil	50 g	125 g

energy	cal	fat	sat fat	carb	sugar	protein	fibre
2088 kJ	499 kcal	28.5 g	16.8 g	37.2 g	3.0 g	25.8 g	2.0 g

METHOD OF WORK

1 Place a slice of ham between two slices of cheese, then between two slices of toast.
2 Fry in clarified butter or oil.
3 Cut into triangles and serve.

CHEF'S TIP A Croque Madame is essentially the same as a Croque Monsieur with the addition of a fried egg and béchamel sauce served on top.

Selection of canapés and bowl food

Canapés come in many different shapes and sizes, hot, cold, warm, and frozen.

Examples may come in the form of cold canapés such as:

- Meat – liver parfait with red pepper chutney, salt beef and mustard mini bagels.

- Poultry – smoked chicken and mango, quail eggs with caviar.

- Fish and shellfish – smoked salmon or gravadlax, grain mustard dressing, sushi.

- Vegetarian based – ratatouille with parmesan crisps, asparagus with cream cheese, chilled minted pea veloute with white truffle oil.

Examples of hot canapés are:

- chicken satay

- curried lamb samosas

- smoked bacon and risotto croquettes

- parma ham and mozzarella mini pizzas

- spiced meatballs with sun blushed tomato sauce

- crab and spring onion beignets.

To accompany canapés, dips may be provided such as:

- sweet chilli dressing

- garlic mayonnaise

- mint raita

- apple and golden raisin chutney

- spiced tomato chutney

- pear and ginger chutney

In addition modern events often cater using bowl food, this is small bowls, plates, cups or cones used to serve guests while standing or sitting informally.

The food is served to guests in individual small bowls, ramekins or suitable service ideas such as fish and chip cones.

A typical menu may look as follows:

MENU

Bowl Food Menu
Demi Tasse of Pumpkin Soup with a Cheddar and Cauliflower Foam Toasted
Hazelnut dust
Mini Bowl of Penne Arabiatta
Mini Bowl of Sausage and Sage Derby Mash, Onion Gravy
Mini Cottage Pie in Demi Tasse
Lamb Koftas, Taboullah Salad
Smoked Haddock Fishcakes Green Herb Sauce
King Prawns Tempura, Sweet Chilli Dip
Seared Sea Bream on Niçoise Salad
Battered Skate Knobs, Mini Chips in Cone
Chicken Satay Sticks, Satay Sauce
Stir Fried Vegetables Quorn and Cashews
Mini Caesar Salad (No Anchovy Vegetarian)
Shot-glass Tiramisu
Mini Lemon Tarts

Guest Chef

Bath chap terrine

Chef Scott Lucas   **Centre** City of Bristol College

This recipe is based upon a 'Bath chap' which is a boned and rolled pig's head wrapped around its own tongue and is a local West Country delicacy. It is done here as a terrine because it is easier to make, portion and serve.

Ingredients	Makes 1 terrine or 16 portions
Pig's head – cut in half (pour boiling water in the pig's ears to wash out any ear wax)	1
Ham hock	1
Pig's tongue	1 extra
Pig's trotters	4
Mirepoix of:	
Onions	3 large
Carrots	4 large
Leeks	2
Celery	3 sticks
Garlic (cut in half)	1 head
Bay leaves	2
Cloves	5
Star Anise	1
Black peppercorns	1 tblspn
Parsley stalks	small handful
Lemon juice	½ a lemon
Parsley	1 tblspn
Thyme	1 tblspn
Salt and freshly milled black pepper	To taste

METHOD OF WORK

1. Wash all the meats and soak overnight in plenty of cold water mixed with salt (brine = 300 g salt to 1 litre of water).

2. Lift out the meats and place into a large pan of unsalted cold water to cover. Add the mirepoix vegetables, garlic, bay leaves, peppercorns, parsley stalks, star anise and cloves. Bring to the boil, reduce the heat and simmer for 4 hours, skimming often.

3. When the meats are soft, remove and set aside to cool until you are able to handle them.

4. Reduce the cooking juices by at least half. Strain through a chinois and discard the vegetables.

5. Pick over the meats, chopping the fat and skin into small pieces. Cut the larger pieces of meats, peeled tongue, and the hock meat into small chunks.

6. Add the parsley, thyme and a good amount of seasoning to the mixed meats, mix in the lemon juice and then add a little of the reduced cooking liquor. Mix well.

7. Ladle into a lined terrine dish and put to one side until it is cooled enough to place in the fridge overnight to set. Weigh the terrine down to compress it.

8. Remove from fridge next day, slice and serve with some crusty bread, micro fennel salad, allumette (match stick) apple and sauce gribiche.

Stocks, sauces and soups

4

NVQ

Unit 636 (2FPC1) Prepare, cook and finish basic hot sauces

Unit 637 (2FPC2) Prepare, cook and finish basic soups

Unit 638 (2FPC3) Make basic stocks

VRQ

Unit 207 Prepare and cook stocks, soups and sauces

Recipes

WHITE STOCKS

Fish stock 113

Vegetable stock 114

White chicken stock 114

White veal/beef/lamb/game stock 115

BROWN STOCKS

Brown chicken stock 116

Brown veal/beef/lamb/game stock 116

MISCELLANEOUS STOCKS

Asian chicken stock 117

Asian fish stock 117

Asian vegetable stock 118

Oriental master stock 118

JUS

Aged balsamic jus 119

Beef jus 120

Chicken jus 120

Jus lié 121

Jus rôti 121

Lamb jus 122

Red wine jus 122

Venison jus 123

BÉCHAMEL SAUCES

Béchamel sauce 123

Anchovy sauce 124

Mornay sauce 124

Cream sauce 124

Egg sauce 124

Mustard sauce 125

Onion/soubise sauce 125

Parsley sauce 125

VELOUTÉ SAUCES

Velouté 126

Aurore sauce 126

Caper sauce 127

Ivory sauce 127

Mushroom sauce 128

Suprême sauce 128

SAUCES

Brown onion sauce   129

Brown sauce   129

Chasseur sauce   130

Demi glace   130

Reform sauce   131

Madeira/sherry/port wine/red
wine sauce   131

Devilled sauce   132

Italian sauce   132

Robert sauce   132

MISCELLANEOUS SAUCES

Roasted bell pepper sauce   133

Madras curry sauce   133

Peppercorn sauce   134

Plum tomato coulis   134

Bread sauce   134

Thai green curry paste   135

Tomato sauce   135

HOT AND WARM BUTTER SAUCES

Hollandaise sauce   136

Béarnaise sauce   136

Black butter   137

Melted butter   137

Nut brown butter   137

COMPOUND BUTTERS

Anchovy compound butter   138

Café de Paris compound butter   138

Garlic compound butter   138

Herb compound butter   139

Lobster compound butter   139

Mustard compound butter   139

Parsley, cayenne and lemon juice   139

Shrimp compound butter   139

**COLD SAUCES, SALSAS, PASTES,
SPREADS AND INTERNATIONAL
SAUCES**

Aïoli   140

Apple sauce   140

Gribiche sauce   141

LEARNING OBJECTIVES

The aim of this unit is to enable the candidate to develop skills and implement knowledge in the preparation and cookery principles of stocks, soups and sauces. This will also include materials, ingredients and equipment.

At the end of this chapter you will be able to:

- Identify a variety of stocks, soups and sauces.

- Understand the use of relative ingredients in stocks, soups and sauce cookery.

- State the quality points of various stock, soup and sauce commodities and their uses in a selection of dishes.

- Prepare, cook and finish a variety of stocks, soups and sauces.

- Identify the storage procedures of stocks, soups and sauces.

- Be competent at preparing and cooking a range of stocks, soups and sauces.

- Be able to state healthy options for stocks, soups and sauces

- Describe what to do if problems with ingredients occur.

- Describe safe and correct use of alcohol in sauces and why it is used.

Basic stocks

Stocks are the foundation of many soups, sauces, and **jus**.

They are an essential part of the modern day professional kitchen and if made correctly will enhance any dish.

The base stock is the building block required to produce a first class sauce or soup. Attention to detail at the beginning will allow the sauce or stock to be pure, highly flavoured and without faults.

They are created by extracting the flavour (essence) from a base ingredient or ingredients and transforming them into a liquid. Stocks are obtained by gentle simmering of bones/carcasses with vegetables and aromatics (**bouquet garni**). Fresh cold water provides a neutral base for all stocks.

All stocks whether white or brown should be clear and grease free. The process of making stocks goes through numerous stages to achieve a good quality.

CHEF'S TIP   When deglazing a pan ensure the majority of fat has been removed. This will prevent a cloudy stock being formed.

Deglazing

This is the process of allowing the caramelized pan or tray juices and sediment to be released into the liquid with the use of water, stock, wine, etc. when making a brown stock.

The second stage is to pour off any excess fat and then add the bones to a pan and add liquid.

CHEF'S TIP Skim a stock regularly to help prevent the stock turning cloudy and becoming bitter.

Skimming

This process is one of the most important a chef must master. A well skimmed stock will have clarity and clear flavour which will be ruined if left unattended. The use of a perforated spoon or small ladle to remove the scum and foam will prevent the stock from becoming cloudy and bitter.

An excess of oil can be removed with dish papers dragged across the top of the liquid until crystal clear. A brown stock can be chilled, the solidified fat removed and then it can be finished on the stove.

It is important to skim stock

Straining and passing

By pouring a liquid through a conical strainer, **chinois** or muslin will ensure that the finished stock will be sediment free. Removing the fat can be done in a number of ways: spooning off the excess, removing once cold or pouring over ice.

Guacamole   141

Honey and mustard dressing   141

Houmous   142

Papaya and black bean salsa   142

Mango and lime salsa   143

Pickled ginger salsa   143

Tomato, shallot and cucumber salsa   144

Mayonnaise and Marie Rose sauce   144

Mint raita   145

Pesto   145

Sun-dried tomato pesto   145

Raw tomato coulis   146

Remoulade sauce   146

Thousand island sauce   146

Salsa verde   147

Tapenade   147

Tartare sauce   148

Thai dressing   148

Vert sauce   148

Vinaigrette   149

Tomato vinaigrette   149

Vinaigrette emulsified   149

Balsamic split vinaigrette   149

FLAVOURED OILS

Basil oil   150

Chilli oil   150

Chorizo oil   150

Curry oil   151

Garlic oil   151

Herb oil   151

Lemon oil   151

Roasted hazelnut oil   152

Sun-dried tomato oil   152

Vanilla oil   152

Walnut oil   152

PURÉE SOUPS

Butternut squash and coriander soup 157

Mushroom soup   158

Potato soup   159

Red lentil soup   160

Tomato and basil soup   161

Vegetable soup   162

Vegetable soup (Recipe 2)   162

VELOUTÉS

Mushroom velouté   163

Pea velouté   163

POTAGES

Green pea soup   164

Potage paysanne   164

CREAM SOUPS

Cream of chicken soup   165

Cream of spinach soup   166

CHOWDERS

Chicken and sweetcorn chowder   166

Clam chowder   167

BROTHS

Chicken broth   168

Mutton broth   168

Scotch broth   169

CONSOMMÉS (CLEAR SOUPS)

Beef consommé   170

Consommé brunoise   171

Consommé celestine   171

Consommé julienne   171

Consommé royale   171

Consommé vermicelli   171

Chicken consommé   172

BISQUES

Crab bisque   173

Lobster bisque   174

Prawn bisque   175

FOREIGN AND MISCELLANEOUS

Chicken noodle soup with spiced
    dumplings   176

Cock a leekie   177

French onion soup   177

Gazpacho   178

Minestrone soup   179

Roasted mediterranean
    vegetable soup   180

Pass the stock through muslin

Reducing

By reducing the liquid over a fierce heat a more intensified flavour is achieved; however, the volume is reduced and this must be taken into account when preparing a dish.

This is the general process used for brown stocks; the cooking times vary according to the bones used; but as a guide:

- **brown beef/veal** – stock 6–8 hours

- **brown chicken** – stock 3–4 hours

- **brown game** – stock 4–6 hours (depending on the bone size and finished strength required).

A white stock (except fish) is prepared by bringing the bones to the **boil** then removing them from the liquid and thoroughly washing them. This will remove all the scum and help the finished stock stay **clarified**.

Fish stock, however, does not require the bones to be washed due to the short cooking time which would result in a loss of flavour.

The general rule is:

- **white beef/veal** – stock 6–8 hours
- **white chicken** – stock 3–4 hours
- **fish** – stock 20 minutes.

TASK The recipe for Asian vegetable stock is on page 118. Produce three dishes suitable to be cooked using Asian vegetable stock.

Quality of materials

Due to the nature of the materials, it is imperative that the bones/carcasses and vegetables be of the highest quality as old, stale or mouldy commodities will taint the colour and flavour of the stock.

Finishing and storage

Once stock has been cooked it should be strained and chilled/reduced otherwise the stock will become sour.

Stocks in general are protein based and as such require careful temperature control and hygienic practices at all times as they are normally present in most finished dishes.

HEALTH & SAFETY Stocks should be kept below 8 °C or frozen below −18 °C. Chilling will slow down the growth of pathogenic bacteria and freezing will make them dormant (sleeping).

Stocks, soups and sauces should be chilled below 8 °C within 90 minutes to slow the multiplication of bacteria, this can be done in a blast chiller or an iced water bath with cold running water. Care must be taken to ensure the entire liquid is cold and there are no hot spots.

Glazes

Stocks can be reduced to form a **glaze**; this process requires the stock to evaporate until a sticky consistency is achieved. These bases can be chilled and added to stocks/sauces which lack flavour.

A glaze is produced by taking a stock and reducing the water content by boiling, the end result is a stronger concentration of flavour and the end product will become jellified.

Meat stocks contain collagen which is naturally occurring in the tendons, connective tissue and bones. As stocks are heated especially boiling more collagen is extracted and the thicker the end product will become. As the thickening process takes place care must be taken as further reduction will result in burning.

Lower temperature reduction of stocks will result in less collagen being released and so more flavour released.

Thai chicken soup   181

Vichyssoise   182

ONLINE RECIPES

LEARNER SUPPORT
Mint sauce
Tomato chutney
Chutneys
Picalilli
Breaking spaghetti

A glaze should be used to improve a sauce or stock and used with caution as the salt content will be higher than normal.

Pre-prepared stocks

Pre-prepared stocks are manufactured products created by boiling the stock until it is totally dry (powder) or mixed into a paste (**bouillon**). These bases are common place within the industry and are either used to completely make a stock or to improve the flavour of a home made version.

Although the standard is improving year by year the basic formula still contains colouring and a relatively high salt content so caution must be used if these bases are to be worked with.

Points to consider

- No salt should be added to stocks.
- Fat should be skimmed regularly to prevent it tasting greasy.
- Scum should be removed to prevent the stock becoming bitter and cloudy.
- Poor quality or old bones and vegetables will result in a poor stock.
- Stocks should simmer gently to extract the maximum flavour otherwise they evaporate too quickly and become bitter and cloudy.
- When making white meat or poultry stock it is advisable to soak the bones first to remove any excess blood or waste residue.

Hot sauces

A sauce is most accurately described as a flavoured liquid which in essence is a base that has been thickened in one way or another.

Sauces are normally classified according to their preparation method as follows:

- roux sauces
- starch thickened sauces
- egg based sauces
- meat, vegetable and poultry roasting gravies.

In addition there are other sauces used in the professional kitchen, such as reduction or foams; these are not traditionally classified but use some of the original versions in preparation. For example a reduction sauce may use a good quality chicken stock and double cream which is reduced to a good consistency and flavour; it may require thickening using a product such as **fécule.**

Thickened

Roux

The most well known of all thickening agents in the kitchen the basic **roux** is a combination of equal quantities of melted butter and flour mixed over the heat until the mix comes away from the pan sides.

Top to Bottom – Brown, blonde and white roux

There are three types of roux. A white roux is generally used with milk to achieve a béchamel. A blonde roux is achieved by cooking the mix for slightly longer until a light sandy colour develops, white stock is added which creates a **velouté**.

The final roux is a brown roux which uses flour browned in the oven and then made with dripping or oil, brown stock (**estouffade**) is added which makes a brown sauce (**espagnole**).

When cooking a roux keep it moving in the pan so to ensure even cooking.

The liquid must be slowly added to ensure the sauce becomes smooth and glossy; if the sauce is not cooked out correctly the sauce will lose the shine.

The sauce will thicken due to the starch molecules exploding when cooked; this needs to be cooked further or the sauce will taste of flour.

Never use an aluminium pan when making sauces as it will taint the colour and give a metallic flavour.

The sauce can be covered with a greaseproof paper circle called a **cartouche** (see next page).

A cartouche is used to produce a covering – skin – on top of a stock or sauce, this will prevent heat loss, over reduction and excessive loss of moisture.

Top to Bottom – The process of cooking a roux

Beurre manié

Beurre manié is a combination of equal quantities of flour and butter which makes a paste, this cold uncooked mix is whisked into hot liquid and cooked out until the desired thickness is achieved.

If a tomato soup is slightly too thin this mixture could be slowly added to enable the soup to thicken to the desired consistency.

Breadcrumbs/rice

These are used in a raw state and added to a hot sauce, the cooking process makes the starch in the products explode which creates a natural thickening agent.

Rice is a traditional thickener of bisque as well as mulligatawny soup.

Butter (monte au beurre)

This process is achieved by whisking or hand blending small cubes of chilled unsalted butter into a hot sauce this will give

Step-by-step: Making a cartouche

1. Take a square piece of silicone or greaseproof paper and fold in half.

2. Turn the paper and fold in half again.

3. Fold the corner over so the middle of the paper becomes the point.

4. Fold the corner over again; notice the middle of the paper is still in the same position – the point. Make a final corner fold, this is the third time.

5. To produce a circle, hold the point over the centre of the saucepan; place your finger where the edge of the saucepan would be then cut just above it with scissors.

6. Open the paper to reveal a circular cartouche.

a glossy rich texture; however, the sauce must not be re-boiled as the butter will split.

Powdered starch thickening agents

These come in numerous forms such as cornflour, arrowroot and fécule. To use these products a little powder should be mixed with cold liquid until a paste is formed, this mix is added to hot liquid which will instantly thicken. The paste must be smooth and gradually added because lumps will form in the sauce.

Arrowroot once added to sauce becomes transparent and is therefore used when thickening **coulis**, fruit sauces, etc., when clarity is required.

As a rule arrowroot is generally reserved for sweet applications.

Egg yolks and cream (liaison)

A **liaison** is achieved by whisking yolks, cream and a little hot sauce together and then return to the pan. The sauce must not boil again as it will curdle. This sauce thickening agent is classically used when using velouté sauces.

As a guide use 40 ml of double cream to one egg yolk.

CHEF'S TIP Ensure the liaison is not poured directly into the sauce; it will split instantly and render the sauce useless.

Purée thickened sauces use the natural commodity where possible to thicken, e.g. roasted peppers (liquidized to give body to the sauce).

BASIC SAUCES AND THEIR DERIVATIVES

Béchamel

Anchovy (anchovy essence)	sauce anchois
Egg (diced hardboiled egg)	sauce aux oeufs
Cheese (grated cheese and egg yolk)	sauce Mornay
Onion (sweated chopped onion)	sauce aux oignons
Soubise (passed onion sauce)	sauce Soubise
Parsley (chopped parsley)	sauce persil
Cream (cream, milk or yoghurt)	sauce crème
Mustard (mustard)	sauce moutarde

Velouté

Caper sauce (capers)	sauce aux câpres
Suprême sauce (mushroom trimmings, cream, egg yolk, lemon juice)	sauce suprême
Aurore sauce (suprême and tomato purée)	sauce aurore
Mushroom sauce (suprême, sliced mushroom, cream, egg yolk)	sauce aux champignons
Ivory sauce (suprême sauce, meat glaze)	sauce ivoire

Purée based

Apple sauce	sauce aux pommes
Tomato sauce	sauce tomate
Smitaine sauce	sauce Smitaine

Demi glace (equal quantities espagnole (brown sauce) and estouffade (brown stock) reduced by half)

Demi glace (espagnole based)

Bordelaise sauce (red wine, shallots, bone marrow)	sauce bordelaise
Chasseur sauce (tarragon, white wine)	sauce chasseur
Devilled sauce (cayenne pepper)	sauce diable
Pepper sauce (crushed peppercorns)	sauce poivrade
Italian sauce (mushrooms, tomato, ham)	sauce italienne
Brown onion sauce (sliced onions, white wine)	sauce lyonnaise
Madeira sauce (Madeira wine)	sauce madère
Sherry sauce (sherry)	sauce Xérès
Port wine sauce (port wine)	sauce Porto
Piquant sauce (gerkins, capers, herbs)	sauce piquante
Robert sauce (white wine, mustard)	sauce Robert
Charcutière sauce (gerkin, white wine)	sauce charcutière
Reform sauce (ham, tongue, beetroot, truffle)	sauce réforme

Jus

Roast gravy	jus rôti
Thickened gravy	jus lié

However, when using green leaves to colour a sauce they should be added at the last minute as the sauce will generally turn brown.

HEALTHY OPTION   Using fresh organic spinach leaves added to a fresh vegetable stock and blended will produce a smooth soup or sauce with no fat content.

TASK   Research and compile one recipe specification for each main item:

- Grilled lamb cutlets
- Pan fried salmon escalopes
- Pork chops
- Venison sausages.

Cold sauces

The word sauce comes from the Latin word *salus* which means 'salted' as salt has always been a condiment served with food.

The function of a sauce is to add flavour, moisture and additional texture to a particular dish and complement the combined ingredients. Classical sauces have names derived from regions, countries and cities and they generally denote a speciality of the area or a certain technique attributed. Sauces Cambridge, Albert and Cumberland are all traditional English sauces, whereas sauce L'italienne is an Italian based sauce. Other sauces often allude to their content within the name, such as sauce Diable, which translated means 'a devil' sauce and as such is a highly spiced sauce. Other sauces and garnishes are attributed to its creator or to a person's influence such as sauce Vincent and sauce Mornay.

Modern trends have tended to try and re-define the classic French names and terms of cookery and the finished item no longer bares the true resemblance to the classic dish. An example of this is *sauce tartare* which is commonly thought of as mayonnaise with chopped parsley, capers, gherkin and onion. However, classically it should be chopped spring onion, chopped chives and chopped chervil with mayonnaise.

TEST YOURSELF

1 Name the three different types of roux.

2 How long should a fish stock be cooked for?

3 Which of the following stocks take 6–8 hours to cook?

   Brown beef, brown chicken, white chicken.

4 What happens to a stock if it is not skimmed during cooking?

5 Name three derivatives of béchamel.

6 Name three derivatives of velouté.

7 What are the two ingredients used to produce a demi glace?

8 Name three derivatives of demi glace.

9 What is jus rôti?

10 What is jus lié?

11 Name three derivatives of mayonnaise.

Recipes
White stocks

Fish stock *(fumet de poisson)*

Ingredients	Makes approximately 2 litres
White fish bones, no heads, gills or roe	5 kg
Onions finely sliced	3 medium
Leeks finely sliced	3
Celery sticks finely sliced	3
Fennel bulbs finely sliced	1
Dry white wine	400 ml
Parsley stalks	12
Bay leaf	1
Thyme sprigs	3
White peppercorns	10
Lemons finely sliced	1

energy	cal	fat	sat fat	carb	sugar	protein	fibre
133 kJ	32 kcal	0.4 g	0.1 g	3.1 g	2.5 g	1.0 g	1.8 g

METHOD OF WORK

1 Wash the bones until completely clean from any impurities.

2 Melt the butter in a thick bottomed pan then add the vegetables and sweat without colour for 4 minutes.

3 Add the fish bones and continue to sweat for a further 4 minutes.

4 Add the wine and enough water to just cover then bring to the boil and skim well.

5 Reduce the heat to a light simmer.

6 Continue to cook for 20 minutes.

7 Remove from the heat and allow to stand for a further 20 minutes.

8 Pass into a clean pan and reduce by half to intensify the flavour.

CHEF'S TIP Remove all gills, scales and unwanted parts of the fish before making the stock as these will taint the flavour and cause cloudiness.

TASK Create a chart indicating which fish are suitable for making stocks, paying attention to species, sustainability and region.

Vegetable stock *(fond de légumes)*

Ingredients	Makes approximately 3 litres
Onion	1 each
Garlic	1 clove
Fennel	½ each
Leek	1 each
White mushroom trimmings	30 g
Water	3 litres
Unsalted butter	25 g
Veg oil	25 ml
Tarragon	2 sprigs
Coriander	2 sprigs

energy	cal	fat	sat fat	carb	sugar	protein	fibre
78 kJ	19 kcal	1.8 g	0.5 g	0.6 g	0.4 g	0.2 g	0.4 g

METHOD OF WORK

1 Wash all the vegetables well, then drain.

2 Finely chop all vegetables and sweat in butter and oil for 2–3 minutes in a saucepan without letting the vegetables colour.

3 Add 500 ml of water and bring to the boil then simmer for 15 minutes.

4 Add chopped herbs and cook for a further 5 minutes.

5 Pass, season, chill and use as required.

CHEF'S TIP The vegetables can be left in the stock to infuse and then chilled, the stock can be passed when required.

White chicken stock
(fond blanc de volaille)

Ingredients	Makes approximately 3 litres
Chicken carcass	5 kg
Shallots	4 peeled
Leek	1 each
Celery	2 sticks
Garlic	2 cloves crushed
White wine	100 ml
Water	6 litres
Bay leaf	1
Thyme	1 sprig
White peppercorns	10

energy	cal	fat	sat fat	carb	sugar	protein	fibre
22 kJ	5 kcal	0.1 g	0.0 g	0.5 g	0.4 g	0.2 g	0.3 g

METHOD OF WORK

1 Remove any excess fat from the chicken and wash thoroughly.

2 Cut the vegetables into large mirepoix then wash well and then drain.

3 Place the bones into a sauce pan with the vegetables then add the wine and reduce until wine as evaporated.

4 Add the water then bring to the boil.

5 Skim well.

6 Reduce the heat; this will allow the ingredients to settle and reduce the risk of cloudiness.

7 Simmer slowly for 3 hours, skimming as required.

8 Pass, chill and use as required.

Note: The stock may be cooked for extended periods of time to increase the flavour; however care must be taken to ensure the vegetables and bones do not turn the stock cloudy and bitter.

CHEF'S TIP A boiling fowl can be used to enhance the chicken flavour.

CHEF'S TIP Chicken can be fatty so ensure any fat is poured away once roasted and before making the stock.

White veal/beef/lamb/game stock *(fond blanc de veau, boeuf, mutton, gibier)*

Ingredients	Makes approximately 4 litres
Veal/beef or lamb bones	1 ½ kg
Large white mirepoix	500 g
Water	5 litres
Bouquet garni (onion, celery, bay, thyme, rosemary, peppercorns)	1
White peppercorns	6

energy 9 kJ	cal 2 kcal	fat 0.1 g	sat fat 0.0 g	carb 0.4 g	sugar 0.3 g	protein 0.1 g	fibre 0.2 g

METHOD OF WORK

1 Chop the bones into small pieces, remove any fat and marrow.

2 Wash the bones in cold water until no blood or waste is visible.

3 Wash all the vegetables well and then drain.

4 Place the bones in water and bring to the boil.

5 Remove the bones and wash thoroughly to remove all the scum.

6 Discard the liquid and return the bones to the washed pot.

7 Add the vegetables, bouquet garni, peppercorns and water.

8 Bring to the boil and skim.

9 Reduce the heat and simmer for 6–8 hours skimming occasionally.

10 Season, pass and chill or reduce as required.

CHEF'S TIP The bones must be boiled and washed thoroughly before use, this will remove any excess scum in preparation for the end stock.

CHEF'S TIP As game is a strong flavour, use a sharp piquant flavour when making the sauce to balance the dish.

SOURCING When purchasing bones for stocks ask the butcher for a list of locally reared and slaughtered animals.

Left to Right – White vegetable, fish, veal and chicken stock

Brown stocks

Left to Right – Brown veal and brown chicken stock

Brown chicken stock *(fond brun de volaille)*

Ingredients	Makes approximately 3 litres
Chicken carcase	2 ½ kg
Mushrooms	200 g
Carrots	500 g
Onions	2 peeled and ¼
Leek	1 each
Celery	2 sticks
Garlic	4 cloves
White wine	100 ml
Water	4 litres
Bouquet garni	1
Tomato purée	50 g
White peppercorns	6

energy	cal	fat	sat fat	carb	sugar	protein	fibre
95 kJ	23 kcal	1.2 g	0.1 g	2.0 g	1.7 g	0.6 g	0.8 g

METHOD OF WORK

1 Wash the vegetables well, drain and roughly cut into **mirepoix**.

2 Roughly chop the bones then roast until brown, drain any fat, and then place the bones into a sauce pan.

3 Deglaze the pan with tomato purée and wine; pour this onto the bones.

4 Fry the vegetables in a little oil until brown, remove the fat and add the vegetables to the bones.

5 Add the water, bouquet garni and peppercorns then bring to the boil.

6 Simmer slowly over a low heat for 3 hours, skimming as required.

7 Pass, chill and use as required.

Brown veal/beef/lamb/game stock *(fond brun de veau, estouffade, fond brun de mouton, fond brun de gibier)*

Ingredients	Makes approximately 3 litres
Veal/beef/lamb/game Bones	2 ½ kg
Large mirepoix of vegetables	500 g
Tomato purée	50 g
Water	4 ltr
Bouquet garni (onion, celery, bay, thyme, rosemary, peppercorns) (juniper for game)	1

energy	cal	fat	sat fat	carb	sugar	protein	fibre
18 kJ	4 kcal	0.1 g	0.0 g	0.8 g	0.7 g	0.2 g	0.3 g

METHOD OF WORK

1 Wash the vegetables well, drain and roughly cut into mirepoix.

2 Roughly chop the bones then roast until brown, drain any fat, and then place the bones into a sauce pan.

3 Deglaze the pan with tomato purée and wine; pour this onto the bones.

4 Fry the vegetables in a little oil until brown, remove the fat and add the vegetables to the bones.

5 Add the water, bouquet garni and peppercorns then bring to the boil.

6 Simmer slowly over a low heat for 6–8 hours, skimming as required.

7 Pass, chill and use as required.

Miscellaneous stocks

Left: Asian chicken stock, Bottom: Asian vegetable stock, Right: Oriental master stock, Top: Asian fish stock

Asian chicken stock

Ingredients	Makes approximately 1ltr
Water	400 ml
Soy sauce	50 ml
Mirin	50 ml
Sugar	120 g
Garlic	3 cloves sliced
Ginger	3 cm sliced
White chicken stock	400 ml
Star anise	6
Szechuan pepper corns	20
Cloves	4
Red chilli	2 sliced
Coriander fresh	1 bunch

energy	cal	fat	sat fat	carb	sugar	protein	fibre
311 kJ	73 kcal	0.2 g	0.1 g	17.9 g	13.5 g	0.7 g	0.6 g

METHOD OF WORK

1 Combine all the ingredients except the coriander in a saucepan and bring to the boil.

2 Reduce the heat and simmer for 10 minutes.

3 Remove from the heat and add the bunch of washed coriander.

4 Allow to cool and store overnight until required.

Asian fish stock

Ingredients	Makes approximately 1ltr
Water	400 ml
Soy sauce	50 ml
Mirin	50 ml
Sugar	120 g
Garlic	3 cloves sliced
Ginger	3 cm sliced
Fish stock	400 ml
Star anise	6
Fish sauce	50 ml
Red chilli	2 sliced
Coriander fresh	1 bunch

energy	cal	fat	sat fat	carb	sugar	protein	fibre
340 kJ	80 kcal	0.5 g	0.1 g	17.9 g	13.6 g	1.8 g	0.4 g

METHOD OF WORK

1 Combine all the ingredients except the coriander in a saucepan and bring to the boil.

2 Reduce the heat and simmer for 10 minutes.

3 Remove from the heat and add the bunch of washed coriander.

4 Allow to cool and store overnight until required.

Asian vegetable stock

Ingredients	Makes approximately 1ltr
Water	400 ml
Soy sauce	50 ml
Mirin	50 ml
Sugar	120 g
Garlic	3 cloves sliced
Ginger	3 cm sliced
Vegetable stock	400 ml
Cinnamon stick	1
Red chilli	2 sliced
Coriander fresh	1 bunch
Szechuan pepper corns	20
Cloves	4

energy	cal	fat	sat fat	carb	sugar	protein	fibre
329 kJ	78 kcal	0.8 g	0.3 g	17.8 g	13.5 g	0.7 g	0.6 g

METHOD OF WORK

1 Combine all the ingredients except the coriander in a saucepan and bring to the boil.

2 Reduce the heat and simmer for 10 minutes.

3 Remove from the heat and add the bunch of washed coriander.

4 Allow to cool and store overnight until required.

Oriental master stock

Ingredients	Makes approximately 1ltr
Water	700 ml
Light Soy sauce	200 ml
Shaosang rice wine	150 ml
Rock sugar	120 g
Garlic	3 cloves sliced
Ginger	3 cm sliced
Red chilli	2 sliced
Coriander seeds	10
Szechuan pepper corns	20
Dried mandarin peel	4
Star anise	3
Shallots sliced	5

energy	cal	fat	sat fat	carb	sugar	protein	fibre
344 kJ	81 kcal	0.1 g	0.0 g	16.6 g	15.7 g	1.2 g	0.6 g

METHOD OF WORK

1 Combine all the ingredients in a saucepan and bring to the boil.

2 Simmer for 20 minutes, remove from the heat and store for use.

Note: This stock is used to slowly cook/braise dishes such as belly of pork, the flavour and consistency will become more gelatinous when used.

Jus

Left to Right – Chicken, beef and aged balsamic jus

Aged balsamic jus

Ingredients	Makes approximately 1ltr
Sliced shallots	100 g
Butter	50 g
Garlic sliced	1
Aged balsamic vinegar	200 ml
Chicken stock	300 ml
Beef or lamb jus	200 ml
Bay leaves	1
Thyme sprigs	1

energy	cal	fat	sat fat	carb	sugar	protein	fibre
335 kJ	81 kcal	6.2 g	3.7 g	0.9 g	0.8 g	2.6 g	0.4 g

METHOD OF WORK

1 Cook the shallots in butter until golden and caramelized, then add the garlic.

2 Add the balsamic and deglaze the pan.

3 Pass this through a chinois into a clean pan.

4 Reduce the stock and jus by half and add to the balsamic.

5 Simmer for 25 minutes with the bay and thyme.

6 Pass through muslin and use as required.

CHEF'S TIP Place the muslin in cold water and then squeeze the excess water out. This will prevent the sauce from being absorbed into the cloth instead of passing through.

CHEF'S TIP This jus could be used with lamb, beef or duck.

Beef jus

Ingredients	Makes approximately 1½ litres
Beef trimmings	400 g
Sliced shallots	400 g
Butter	100 g
Garlic sliced	3
Red wine	800 ml
Chicken stock	400 ml
Beef or lamb jus	1 litre
Bay leaves	1
Thyme sprigs	1

energy	cal	fat	sat fat	carb	sugar	protein	fibre
756 kJ	182 kcal	10.5 g	5.4 g	1.4 g	1.2 g	11.4 g	0.6 g

METHOD OF WORK

1 Cook the shallots in butter until golden and caramelized, then add the garlic.

2 Fry the beef trimmings until caramelized, then add the red wine and deglaze the pan, reduce by half.

3 Pass this through a chinois into a clean pan and add the shallots and garlic.

4 Add the stock, jus, bay leaf and thyme; reduce until a sauce consistency is achieved.

5 Pass through muslin and store until required.

CHEF'S TIP Ensure the beef trimmings are fat free, this will make the end sauce cleaner and will require less work to produce a clear finish (removing excess fat).

Chicken jus

Ingredients	Makes approximately 1 litre
Chicken stock	2 litres
Chicken carcass cut into small pieces	600 g
Sliced shallots	4
Butter	100 g
Garlic sliced	3
Olive oil	25 ml
Red wine	100 ml
Roasted ½ tomatoes	3
White wine vinegar	50 ml
Bay leaves	1
Chervil stalks	5 g

energy	cal	fat	sat fat	carb	sugar	protein	fibre
482 kJ	117 kcal	10.9 g	5.8 g	2.2 g	1.7 g	0.8 g	1.0 g

METHOD OF WORK

1 Cook the shallots in butter until golden and caramelized, then add the garlic.

2 Blanch, deseed the tomatoes then add the shallots.

3 Roast with a little oil for 20 minutes at 180 °C.

4 Roast the chicken carcasses until caramelized and golden brown.

5 Remove the chicken from the tray, remove the fat, deglaze with the vinegar.

6 Reduce the wine by half.

7 Reduce the stock by half.

8 In a saucepan add all the ingredients and reduce to a sauce consistency.

9 Pass through a chinois then muslin.

10 Use as required.

Jus lié *(thickened gravy)*

Ingredients	Makes approximately 500 ml
Jus rôti (roast gravy)	500 ml
Tomato purée	1 tblspn
Mushroom trimmings	50 g
Thyme	Sprig
Arrowroot or cornflour	As required

energy	cal	fat	sat fat	carb	sugar	protein	fibre
382 kJ	91 kcal	6.6 g	2.1 g	3.8 g	1.4 g	4.2 g	1.1 g

METHOD OF WORK

1 Simmer the jus rôti with the tomato purée, thyme and mushroom trimmings for 20 minutes.

2 Thicken with a slurry made with either cornflour or arrowroot.

3 A slurry is achieved by diluting the cornflour or arrowroot in a little cold water.

4 Once the jus lié thickens adequately pass through a chinois then muslin.

CHEF'S TIP Add the slurry of cornflour or arrowroot slowly to ensure the sauce does not become to thick.

Jus rôti *(roast gravy)*

Ingredients	Makes approximately 500 ml
Bones (chicken, beef, lamb, veal)	200 g
Brown stock	500 ml
Large mirepoix	150 g

energy	cal	fat	sat fat	carb	sugar	protein	fibre
273 kJ	65 kcal	5.0 g	2.0 g	1.2 g	1.0 g	3.8 g	0.6 g

METHOD OF WORK

1 Brown the bones and mirepoix in a pan or a hot oven.

2 Drain any fat off.

3 Bring the bones, stock and mirepoix to the boil and skim.

4 Simmer for 2 hours and regularly skim.

5 Once the roast joint is cooked remove from the tray and rest.

6 Strain off the fat.

7 Place the tray on the stove and deglaze with the stock.

8 Simmer for 5 minutes.

9 Re-season and pass through muslin.

CHEF'S TIP The addition of garlic or ginger can improve a sauce's flavour as long as it suits the dish and is used correctly.

Lamb jus

Ingredients	Makes approximately 2 litre
Lamb stock	2 litres
Lamb trimmings cut into small pieces	2 kg
Red wine	500 ml
Large mirepoix	1 kg
Garlic bulbs	3
Tomato purée	4 tblspn

energy	cal	fat	sat fat	carb	sugar	protein	fibre
1404 kJ	336 kcal	19.8 g	8.5 g	2.3 g	1.9 g	32.8 g	2.0 g

METHOD OF WORK

1 Place the trimmings, garlic and mirepoix into an oven at 180 °C and roast until all the components have caramelized.

2 Remove the ingredients and place in a saucepan, drain the oil and deglaze with the wine and purée, reduce by half.

3 Poor the wine into the saucepan.

4 Add the stock and simmer very gently for 2 hours.

5 Pass through a conical strainer, then increase the heat and reduce until a sauce consistency is achieved.

6 Pass through a chinois then muslin.

7 Use as required.

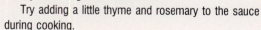

SOURCING Growing fresh herbs will not only save money but will give a better flavour.

Try adding a little thyme and rosemary to the sauce during cooking.

Red wine jus

Ingredients	Makes approximately 1 litre
Sliced shallots	200 g
Butter	50 g
Garlic crushed	3
Red wine vinegar	50 ml
Red wine	300 ml
Chicken stock	400 ml
Beef or lamb jus	300 ml
Bay leaves	1
Thyme sprigs	1

energy	cal	fat	sat fat	carb	sugar	protein	fibre
493 kJ	119 kcal	7.3 g	4.2 g	1.5 g	1.2 g	3.9 g	0.7 g

METHOD OF WORK

1 Cook the shallots in butter until golden and caramelized, then add the garlic.

2 Add the red wine and vinegar then deglaze the pan, reduce by half.

3 Pour into a saucepan.

4 Reduce the stock and jus by half.

5 Add the stock, jus, bay leaf and thyme into the saucepan: reduce until a sauce consistency is achieved.

6 Pass through muslin and store until required.

CHEF'S TIP Adding the wine at the beginning and reducing will prevent the sauce being tainted with a bitter after taste.

Venison jus

Ingredients	Makes approximately 1 litre
Mirepoix of vegetables	200 g
Venison trimmings cut into small pieces	400 g
Chicken jus	400 ml
Venison stock	600 ml
Red wine vinegar	50 ml
Red wine	100 ml
Gin	50 ml
Bay leaf	1
Juniper berries	4

energy	cal	fat	sat fat	carb	sugar	protein	fibre
581 kJ	139 kcal	5.5 g	2.8 g	2.1 g	1.6 g	14.9 g	0.9 g

METHOD OF WORK

1 Roast the mirepoix of vegetables until caramelized.

2 Add the stock and reduce by half.

3 Roast the trimmings until caramelized, drain the fat and add the vinegar and gin, reduce until dry.

4 Add all ingredients to the saucepan, simmer for 45 minutes.

5 Pass though a chinois then reduce again until a sauce consistency is achieved.

6 Pass through muslin.

7 Use as required.

CHEF'S TIP **Alcohol** should be reduced until dry or burnt off using a naked flame as it will turn a sauce bitter if present.

Béchamel sauces

Béchamel sauce

Ingredients	Makes approximately 4 portions	Makes approximately 10 portions
Butter	20 g	50 g
Flour	20 g	50 g
Milk	200 ml	500 ml
Cloute (onion studded with cloves)	½	1
Good quality salt	To taste	To taste
White pepper	To taste	To taste

energy	cal	fat	sat fat	carb	sugar	protein	fibre
343 kJ	82 kcal	5.1 g	3.2 g	7.3 g	3.1 g	2.4 g	0.6 g

METHOD OF WORK

1 Melt the butter in a saucepan (stainless steel if possible).

2 Add the flour and mix well.

3 Cook the mixture gently without colouring.

4 Remove from the heat and allow the roux to cool slightly.

5 Meanwhile heat the milk with the cloute then slowly add to the roux stirring continuously until the mix is smooth.

6 Gently simmer for at least 20 minutes.

7 Pass the sauce through a conical strainer.

8 Season and use as required. The consistency will depend on the particular usage, i.e. sauce or binding agent.

CHEF'S TIP To make a healthier sauce a low-fat spread can be substituted for butter; however, the flavour can be slightly distorted.

Anchovy sauce

Ingredients	Makes approximately 4 portions	Makes approximately 10 portions
Béchamel sauce	200 ml	500 ml
Anchovy essence	½ tblspn	1 tblspn
Good quality salt	To taste	To taste
White pepper	To taste	To taste

energy	cal	fat	sat fat	carb	sugar	protein	fibre
292 kJ	70 kcal	4.2 g	2.6 g	6.3 g	2.7 g	2.2 g	0.5 g

METHOD OF WORK

1 Just before service whisk the anchovy essence into the béchamel sauce.

Note: This sauce is classically served with fish.

CHEF'S TIP Using finely chopped fresh anchovies in oil gives a more Mediterranean flavour.

Mornay sauce

Ingredients	Makes approximately 4 portions	Makes approximately 10 portions
Béchamel sauce	200 ml	500 ml
Grated cheese	40 g	100 g
Egg yolks	1	2
Good quality salt	To taste	To taste
White pepper	To taste	To taste

energy	cal	fat	sat fat	carb	sugar	protein	fibre
520 kJ	125 kcal	9.0 g	5.2 g	6.2 g	2.6 g	5.3 g	0.5 g

METHOD OF WORK

1 Just before service whisk the cheese and egg yolk into the simmering béchamel.

2 Do not allow this sauce to re-boil.

Note: This sauce is classically used to coat fish, meat and vegetables and is usually gratinated.

CHEF'S TIP Add a small amount of hot sauce to cream before returning to the main pan to prevent splitting.

Cream sauce

Ingredients	Makes approximately 4 portions	Makes approximately 10 portions
Béchamel sauce	200 ml	500 ml
Cream or yoghurt (healthier option)	50 ml	125 ml
Good quality salt	To taste	To taste
White pepper	To taste	To taste

energy	cal	fat	sat fat	carb	sugar	protein	fibre
480 kJ	115 kcal	9.1 g	5.7 g	6.6 g	3.0 g	2.3 g	0.5 g

METHOD OF WORK

1 Just before service add the cream and bring back to the boil.

2 Simmer, re-season and use as required.

Note: This sauce is classically served with fish and vegetables.

CHEF'S TIP Use a low-fat yoghurt to create a low-fat version of this sauce.

Egg sauce

Ingredients	Makes approximately 4 portions	Makes approximately 10 portions
Béchamel sauce	200 ml	500 ml
Hard boiled eggs, diced in small pieces	1 each	2 each
Good quality salt	To taste	To taste
White pepper	To taste	To taste

energy	cal	fat	sat fat	carb	sugar	protein	fibre
435 kJ	104 kcal	6.8 g	3.4 g	6.2 g	2.6 g	5.1 g	0.5 g

METHOD OF WORK

1 Just before service stir the diced egg into the béchamel sauce carefully to prevent them breaking up too much.

Note: This sauce is classically served with fish.

CHEF'S TIP Carefully stir in the egg to avoid the pieces becoming smashed and destroying the appearance required.

Mustard sauce

Ingredients	Makes approximately 4 portions	Makes approximately 10 portions
Béchamel sauce	200 ml	500 ml
English mustard (grain mustard can also be used for appearance)	To taste	To taste
Good quality salt	To taste	To taste
White pepper	To taste	To taste

energy	cal	fat	sat fat	carb	sugar	protein	fibre
302 kJ	72 kcal	4.4 g	2.6 g	6.4 g	2.8 g	2.2 g	0.6 g

METHOD OF WORK

1 Just before service add the mustard.

2 Simmer, re-season and use as required.

3 This sauce should have enough mustard to give a hot taste.

Note: This sauce is classically served with grilled fish (especially herrings).

CHEF'S TIP The predominant flavour in this sauce is mustard so use a high-quality one such as Pommery grain mustard.

Onion/soubise sauce

Ingredients	Makes approximately 4 portions	Makes approximately 10 portions
Béchamel sauce	200 ml	500 ml
Finely diced onion	40 g	100 g
butter	20 g	50 g
Good quality salt	To taste	To taste
White pepper	To taste	To taste

energy	cal	fat	sat fat	carb	sugar	protein	fibre
448 kJ	108 kcal	8.3 g	5.2 g	6.6 g	2.9 g	2.1 g	0.6 g

METHOD OF WORK

1 Melt the butter in a saucepan then add the onions and sweat without colour.

2 Add the mixture to the béchamel, re-season and use as required.

3 For soubise sauces pass through a chinois and serve.

Note: This sauce is classically served with mutton.

CHEF'S TIP Small onions give a sweeter flavour to the sauce.

Parsley sauce

Ingredients	Makes approximately 4 portions	Makes approximately 10 portions
Béchamel sauce	200 ml	500 ml
Chopped parsley	½ tblspn	1 tblspn
Good quality salt	To taste	To taste
White pepper	To taste	To taste

energy	cal	fat	sat fat	carb	sugar	protein	fibre
290 kJ	69 kcal	4.3 g	2.7 g	6.2 g	2.6 g	2.1 g	0.6 g

METHOD OF WORK

1 Just before service add the chopped parsley to the béchamel.

2 Re-season and use as required.

Note: This sauce is classically served with fish and vegetables.

CHEF'S TIP Add the chopped parsley at the last minute to ensure the sauce stays green.

Velouté sauces

Velouté

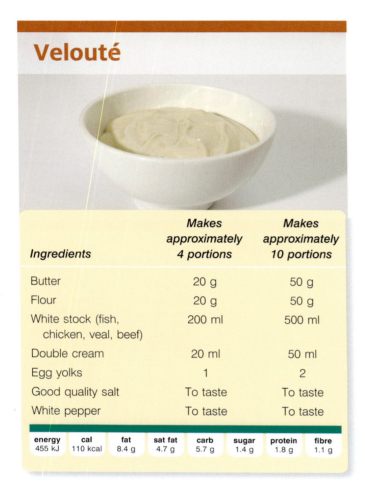

Ingredients	Makes approximately 4 portions	Makes approximately 10 portions
Butter	20 g	50 g
Flour	20 g	50 g
White stock (fish, chicken, veal, beef)	200 ml	500 ml
Double cream	20 ml	50 ml
Egg yolks	1	2
Good quality salt	To taste	To taste
White pepper	To taste	To taste

energy	cal	fat	sat fat	carb	sugar	protein	fibre
455 kJ	110 kcal	8.4 g	4.7 g	5.7 g	1.4 g	1.8 g	1.1 g

METHOD OF WORK

1 Melt the butter in a saucepan (stainless steel if possible).

2 Add the flour and mix well.

3 Cook the roux gently until a very light golden colour is achieved (blonde roux).

4 Remove from the heat and cool slightly.

5 Meanwhile bring the stock to the boil.

6 Slowly add the stock to the roux mixing continuously until smooth.

7 Simmer gently for at least 50 minutes.

8 Season and pass through a conical strainer.

Note: The sauce can be enriched with the cream and egg yolk but should not be re-boiled.

HEALTH & SAFETY Sauces are high-risk foods so must be stored at below 8 °C in the refrigerator and −18 °C in the freezer.

Aurore sauce

Ingredients	Makes approximately 4 portions	Makes approximately 10 portions
Velouté sauce (chicken)	200 ml	500 ml
Button mushroom trimmings	20 g	50 g
Double cream	40 ml	100 ml
Egg yolks	1	2
Lemon juice	¼ lemon	½ lemon
Tomato purée (fresh tomato sauce if possible)	To taste and colour	To taste and colour
Good quality salt	To taste	To taste
White pepper	To taste	To taste

energy	cal	fat	sat fat	carb	sugar	protein	fibre
697 kJ	168 kcal	14.6 g	8.0 g	6.0 g	2.9 g	2.4 g	1.2 g

METHOD OF WORK

1 Simmer the velouté and add the mushroom trimmings which have been well washed.

2 Pass the sauce through a chinois.

3 Make a liaison by whisking the egg yolks with the cream.

4 Add a little hot sauce to this mix then return it to the velouté.

5 Do not re-boil the sauce again.

6 Add the lemon juice to taste and the tomato purée then re-season.

7 The sauce should have a pale red colour.

Note: The sauce is classically served with chicken and chaud froid sauce.

CHEF'S TIP Hot sauces should be kept in a bain-marie during service to prevent over-reducing. This will allow them to maintain the correct temperature without the risk of burning.

Caper sauce

Ingredients	Makes approximately 4 portions	Makes approximately 10 portions
Velouté sauce (mutton, lamb)	200 ml	500 ml
Capers	1 tblspn	2 tblspn
Good quality salt	To taste	To taste
White pepper	To taste	To taste

energy	cal	fat	sat fat	carb	sugar	protein	fibre
330 kJ	80 kcal	6.0 g	3.4 g	4.3 g	1.1 g	1.4 g	0.9 g

METHOD OF WORK

1 Just before service add the capers to the simmering velouté.

Note: The sauce is classically served with mutton.

CHEF'S TIP Thoroughly wash the capers before use as they are very salty and will ruin the sauce.

Ivory sauce

Ingredients	Makes approximately 4 portions	Makes approximately 10 portions
Velouté sauce (veal)	200 ml	500 ml
Button mushroom trimmings	20 g	50 g
Double cream	40 ml	100 ml
Egg yolks	1	2
Lemon juice	¼ lemon	½ lemon
Reduced brown chicken stock (glaze)	To taste and to give an ivory colour	To taste and to give an ivory colour
Good quality salt	To taste	To taste
White pepper	To taste	To taste

energy	cal	fat	sat fat	carb	sugar	protein	fibre
623 kJ	151 kcal	13.5 g	7.1 g	4.4 g	1.2 g	2.2 g	0.9 g

METHOD OF WORK

1 Simmer the velouté and add the mushroom trimmings which have been well washed.

2 Pass the sauce through a chinois.

3 Make a liaison by whisking the egg yolks with the cream.

4 Add a little hot sauce to this mix then return it to the velouté.

5 Do not re-boil the sauce again.

6 Add the lemon juice to taste and then re-season.

7 Add the meat glaze to achieve an ivory colour.

Note: This sauce is classically used with a blanquette of veal.

CHEF'S TIP Using a pre-made glaze will speed up the preparation of this sauce.

Mushroom sauce

Ingredients	Makes approximately 4 portions	Makes approximately 10 portions
Velouté sauce (chicken)	200 ml	500 ml
Button mushroom trimmings	20 g	50 g
Double cream	40 ml	100 ml
Egg yolks	1	2
Lemon juice	¼ lemon	½ lemon
Sliced button mushrooms	40 g	100 g
Butter	20 g	50 g

energy	cal	fat	sat fat	carb	sugar	protein	fibre
839 kJ	203 kcal	19.2 g	9.9 g	4.3 g	1.3 g	2.5 g	1.1 g

METHOD OF WORK

1 Simmer the velouté and add the mushroom trimmings which have been well washed.

2 Pass the sauce through a chinois.

3 Make a liaison by whisking the egg yolks with the cream.

4 Add a little hot sauce to this mix then return it to the velouté.

5 Do not re-boil the sauce again.

6 Add the lemon juice to taste and then re-season.

7 In a separate pan melt the butter and sweat the sliced mushrooms without colour then add to the sauce.

Note: The sauce is classically served with chicken.

SOURCING   Use only the freshest mushrooms available as they are not only visible but are the main flavouring.

WEB LINK   http://www.wildharvestuk.com
This website has an excellent reputation for sourcing and sustainability regarding produce.

Suprême sauce

Ingredients	Makes approximately 4 portions	Makes approximately 10 portions
Velouté sauce (chicken)	200 ml	500 ml
Button mushroom trimmings	20 g	50 g
Double cream	40 ml	100 ml
Egg yolks	1	2
Lemon juice	¼ lemon	½ lemon
Good quality salt	To taste	To taste
White pepper	To taste	To taste

energy	cal	fat	sat fat	carb	sugar	protein	fibre
623 kJ	151 kcal	13.5 g	7.1 g	4.4 g	1.2 g	2.2 g	0.9 g

METHOD OF WORK

1 Simmer the velouté and add the mushroom trimmings which have been well washed.

2 Pass the sauce through a chinois.

3 Make a liaison by whisking the egg yolks with the cream.

4 Add a little hot sauce to this mix then return it to the velouté.

5 Do not re-boil the sauce again.

6 Add the lemon juice to taste and re-season.

Note: The sauce is classically served with chicken.

CHEF'S TIP   Thoroughly wash the mushroom trimmings or the dirt and grit will discolour and flavour the sauce.

Sauces

Brown onion sauce

Ingredients	Makes approximately 4 portions	Makes approximately 10 portions
Butter	20 g	50 g
Finely sliced onions	80 g	200 g
Red wine vinegar	2 tblspn	5 tblspn
Demi glace	200 ml	500 ml
Good quality salt	To taste	To taste
White pepper	To taste	To taste

energy	cal	fat	sat fat	carb	sugar	protein	fibre
333 kJ	80 kcal	7.0 g	3.5 g	2.3 g	0.9 g	1.8 g	0.6 g

METHOD OF WORK

1 Melt the butter and sweat the onions until very soft.

2 Add the vinegar and reduce.

3 Add the demi glace then simmer for 5 minutes.

4 Skim if required then re-season.

CHEF'S TIP If the sauce appears slightly bitter at the end add a little sugar: this will transform the end product.

Brown sauce *(espagnole)*

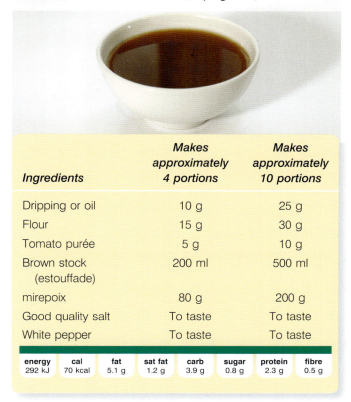

Ingredients	Makes approximately 4 portions	Makes approximately 10 portions
Dripping or oil	10 g	25 g
Flour	15 g	30 g
Tomato purée	5 g	10 g
Brown stock (estouffade)	200 ml	500 ml
mirepoix	80 g	200 g
Good quality salt	To taste	To taste
White pepper	To taste	To taste

energy	cal	fat	sat fat	carb	sugar	protein	fibre
292 kJ	70 kcal	5.1 g	1.2 g	3.9 g	0.8 g	2.3 g	0.5 g

METHOD OF WORK

1 Heat the dripping/oil in a saucepan (stainless steel if possible).

2 Add the flour and mix well.

3 Cook the roux until a light brown colour is achieved (brown roux).

4 Cool slightly and add the tomato purée.

5 Meanwhile boil the stock then slowly add to the roux stirring continuously until smooth.

6 Brown the vegetables in a frying pan or hot oven, drain any excess fat then add to the sauce.

7 Simmer the sauce for a minimum of 4 hours.

8 Regularly skim the sauce.

9 Pass through a conical strainer then re-season as required.

CHEF'S TIP This sauce will enhance the flavour of the original stock; it is therefore important that the original stock is of the highest quality.

Chasseur sauce

Ingredients	Makes approximately 4 portions	Makes approximately 10 portions
Butter	20 g	40 g
Finely diced shallots	10 g	20 g
Sliced button mushrooms	50 g	100 g
White wine	50 ml	100 ml
Tomato concassée	90 g	180 g
Demi glace	200 ml	500 ml
Chopped tarragon	1 tblspn	2 tblspn
Chopped parsley	½ tblspn	1 tblspn
Good quality salt	To taste	To taste
White pepper	To taste	To taste

energy	cal	fat	sat fat	carb	sugar	protein	fibre
462 kJ	112 kcal	9.1 g	3.9 g	3.1 g	1.7 g	2.4 g	1.0 g

METHOD OF WORK

1 Melt the butter in a saucepan (stainless steel if possible).

2 Add the shallots and sweat without colour.

3 Add the mushrooms and sweat without colour then deglaze with white wine.

4 Reduce by half then add the tomato and demi glace.

5 Simmer, add herbs and correct seasoning.

CHEF'S TIP Acidic sauces are best served with fatty foods as together they aid digestion: for example, chasseur with chicken.

Demi glace

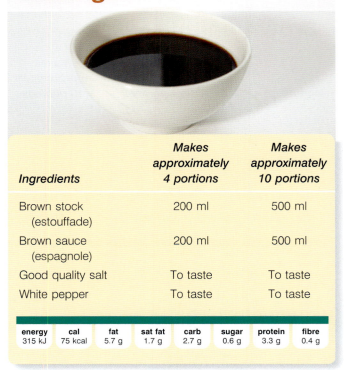

Ingredients	Makes approximately 4 portions	Makes approximately 10 portions
Brown stock (estouffade)	200 ml	500 ml
Brown sauce (espagnole)	200 ml	500 ml
Good quality salt	To taste	To taste
White pepper	To taste	To taste

energy	cal	fat	sat fat	carb	sugar	protein	fibre
315 kJ	75 kcal	5.7 g	1.7 g	2.7 g	0.6 g	3.3 g	0.4 g

METHOD OF WORK

1 Simmer the stock and sauce together in a saucepan (stainless steel if possible).

2 Reduce by half.

3 Skim regularly.

4 Pass through a chinois and re-season.

CHEF'S TIP This sauce can be made and chilled then used as required which will save time and effort.

Reform sauce

Ingredients	Makes approximately 4 portions	Makes approximately 10 portions
Mirepoix small cut	30 g	80 g
Butter	15 g	30 g
Peppercorns	½ tsp	1 tsp
Red wine vinegar	½ tblspn	1 tblspn
Red currant jelly	½ tblspn	1 tblspn
Demi glace	200 ml	500 ml
Julienne of cooked egg white, cooked beetroot, tongue, truffle, gherkin and mushroom	50 g	120 g
Good quality salt	To taste	To taste
White pepper	To taste	To taste

energy	cal	fat	sat fat	carb	sugar	protein	fibre
365 kJ	88 kcal	7.0 g	2.9 g	3.7 g	2.1 g	2.7 g	0.7 g

METHOD OF WORK

1 Melt the butter and brown the mirepoix, drain the fat and add the peppercorns and vinegar.

2 Reduce by half.

3 Add the demi glace and simmer for 20 minutes.

4 Skim regularly.

5 Add the jelly and simmer for a further 5 minutes.

6 Pass through a fine chinois and re-season.

7 Garnish the sauce with the julienne.

CHEF'S TIP The julienne needs to be very neat as it is the main focal point.

Madeira/sherry/port wine/ red wine sauce

Ingredients	Makes approximately 4 portions	Makes approximately 10 portions
Alcohol as above	10 ml	25 ml
Demi glace	200 ml	500 ml
Chilled diced butter	20 g	50 g
Good quality salt	To taste	To taste
White pepper	To taste	To taste

energy	cal	fat	sat fat	carb	sugar	protein	fibre
328 kJ	79 kcal	7.0 g	3.5 g	1.8 g	0.7 g	1.7 g	0.3 g

METHOD OF WORK

1 Bring the demi glace to the boil then add the alcohol and re-boil for 5 minutes.

2 Whisk the diced butter into the sauce, re-season and serve.

CHEF'S TIP When using alcohol in sauces it is important to reduce or burn it off first, otherwise the sauce will taste bitter.

Devilled sauce

Ingredients	Makes approximately 4 portions	Makes approximately 10 portions
Finely diced shallots	40 g	100 g
Mignonette pepper	Pinch	Pinch
White wine	5 ml	20 ml
White wine vinegar	5 ml	20 ml
Cayenne pepper	To taste	To taste
Demi glace	200 ml	500 ml
Good quality salt	To taste	To taste
White pepper	To taste	To taste

energy	cal	fat	sat fat	carb	sugar	protein	fibre
197 kJ	47 kcal	3.0 g	0.9 g	3.0 g	0.8 g	2.0 g	1.0 g

METHOD OF WORK

1   Make a reduction of shallots, pepper, wine, vinegar and cayenne.

2   Reduce by half.

3   Add the demi glace and simmer for 5 minutes.

4   Pass through a fine chinois and re-season with extra cayenne.

Italian sauce

Ingredients	Makes approximately 4 portions	Makes approximately 10 portions
Butter	20 g	50 g
Finely diced shallots	8 g	20 g
Finely chopped button mushrooms	30 g	80 g
Demi glace	200 ml	500 ml
Finely chopped cooked ham	15 g	40 g
Tomato concasse	70 g	180 g
Chopped tarragon, parsley, chervil	1 tblspn	2 tblspn
Good quality salt	To taste	To taste
White pepper	To taste	To taste

energy	cal	fat	sat fat	carb	sugar	protein	fibre
414 kJ	100 kcal	8.5 g	3.9 g	2.9 g	1.1 g	3.2 g	0.9 g

METHOD OF WORK

1   Melt the butter and sweat the shallots without colour then add the mushrooms and cook for a further 2 minutes.

2   Add the demi glace, tomatoes and ham, simmer for 5 minutes.

3   Re-season and add the herbs.

Robert sauce

Ingredients	Makes approximately 4 portions	Makes approximately 10 portions
Butter	10 g	20 g
Onions finely diced	50 g	100 g
Red wine vinegar	50 ml	100 ml
Demi glace	200 ml	500 ml
English mustard	1 tblspn	2 tblspn
Sugar	¼ tblspn	½ tblspn
Good quality salt	To taste	To taste
White pepper	To taste	To taste

energy	cal	fat	sat fat	carb	sugar	protein	fibre
293 kJ	70 kcal	5.2 g	2.2 g	3.4 g	2.0 g	2.1 g	0.5 g

METHOD OF WORK

1   Melt the butter and sweat the onions until transparent.

2   Add the vinegar and reduce completely.

3   Add the demi glace and simmer for 5 minutes.

4   Mix the sugar, mustard with a little warm water and add to the sauce.

5   Simmer for 5 minutes, re-season.

Note: Add gherkin julienne to the finished sauce and it becomes charcutière sauce.

CHEF'S TIP Ensure the mustard is mixed with water before adding to the sauce: this will allow emulsification and prevent tiny mustard lumps forming.

Miscellaneous sauces

Roasted bell pepper sauce

Ingredients	Makes approximately 4 portions	Makes approximately 10 portions
Onions sliced	1 each	2 each
Garlic chopped	1 cloves	3 cloves
Olive oil	20 ml	50 ml
Bell peppers, peeled and deseeded	400 g	1 kg
Red wine	40 ml	100 ml
Thyme	Sprigs	Sprigs
Good quality salt	To taste	To taste
White pepper	To taste	To taste

energy	cal	fat	sat fat	carb	sugar	protein	fibre
335 kJ	81 kcal	5.6 g	0.8 g	5.0 g	3.6 g	1.4 g	2.1 g

METHOD OF WORK

1 Sweat the onions and garlic in the oil for 10 minutes without colour.

2 Roast the peppers with the thyme for 10 minutes.

3 Add to the onions.

4 Add the wine and reduce until almost evaporated.

5 Cover with a tight fitting lid.

6 Cook on a very low heat for 15 minutes.

7 Liquidize, correct the seasoning and use as required.

CHEF'S TIP Use ripe peppers which have a delicate sweetness to the flesh.

Madras curry sauce

Ingredients	Makes approximately 4 portions	Makes approximately 10 portions
Ground nut oil	4 tblspn	10 tblspn
Cardamom pods	4	10
Cinnamon stick	5cm piece	2 x 5 cm piece
Onion sliced	2	5
Green chilli chopped	2	5
Garlic cloves sliced	4	10
Turmeric	½ tsp	1 ½ tsp
Salt	½ tsp	1 ½ tsp
Ground cumin	1 tsp	2 ½ tsp
Ground coriander	1 tsp	2 ½ tsp
Tomato purée	2 tsp	5 tsp
Grated ginger	½ tsp	1 ½ tsp
Garam masala	½ tsp	1 ½ tsp
Coriander leaves	60 g	150 g
Boiling water	300 ml	1 litre

energy	cal	fat	sat fat	carb	sugar	protein	fibre
750 kJ	181 kcal	16.0 g	3.1 g	7.7 g	3.8 g	2.2 g	2.9 g

METHOD OF WORK

1 Heat the oil in a large pan, then add the cardamoms and cinnamon and fry for 1 minute.

2 Add the onion and fry for 4 minutes.

3 Add the chilli, garlic and fry for 4 minutes.

4 Then add the salt, turmeric, cumin and coriander.

5 Add the tomato purée to the boiling water and add to the pan.

6 Cook for 3 minutes.

7 Add the ginger, garam masala and then the coriander.

CHEF'S TIP If possible grind the spices freshly; this will give a much cleaner, more fragrant and aromatic flavour.

Peppercorn sauce

Ingredients	Makes approximately 4 portions	Makes approximately 10 portions
Pink, whole white or crushed black peppercorns	As required, approximately 1 flat tsp per portion	As required, approximately 1 flat tsp per portion
Brandy	10 ml	25 ml
Double cream	100 ml	250 ml
Demi glace	100 ml	250 ml
Good quality salt	To taste	To taste

energy	cal	fat	sat fat	carb	sugar	protein	fibre
666 kJ	161 kcal	15.0 g	8.8 g	4.4 g	0.6 g	1.8 g	1.4 g

METHOD OF WORK

1   Heat a thick bottomed saucepan then add the peppercorns and then the brandy, allow this to ignite.

2   Once the flame has burnt away add the demi glace and allow this to boil.

3   Add enough cream to create the desired colour.

4   Add salt as required.

Plum tomato coulis

Ingredients	Makes approximately 4 portions	Makes approximately 10 portions
Onions sliced	1 each	2 each
Garlic chopped	1 cloves	3 cloves
Olive oil	20 ml	50 ml
Plum tomatoes, peeled and quartered	400 g	1 kg
White wine	60 ml	150 ml
Basil	½ bunch	bunch

energy	cal	fat	sat fat	carb	sugar	protein	fibre
364 kJ	87 kcal	5.5 g	0.9 g	6.1 g	4.9 g	1.5 g	2.2 g

METHOD OF WORK

1   Sweat the onions and garlic in the oil for 10 minutes without colour.

2   Add the tomatoes and cook for a further 10 minutes.

3   Add the wine and reduce until almost evaporated.

4   Add the basil and cover with a tight fitting lid.

5   Cook on a very low heat for 1 hour.

6   Liquidize, correct the seasoning and use as required.

CHEF'S TIP Once liquidized this sauce should not be reboiled as it will split.

Bread sauce

Ingredients	Makes approximately 4 portions	Makes approximately 10 portions
Fresh milk	400 ml	1100 ml
Onion studded with 2 cloves and a bay leaf	½ each	1 each
White breadcrumbs (fresh is best)	Approx 40 g	Approx 70 g
Butter	10 g	25 g
Good quality salt	To taste	To taste
White pepper	To taste	To taste

energy	cal	fat	sat fat	carb	sugar	protein	fibre
444 kJ	105 kcal	4.0 g	2.4 g	13.5 g	5.6 g	4.9 g	0.7 g

METHOD OF WORK

1   Bring the milk to the boil with the studded onion and simmer for 10 minutes to allow the flavours to infuse.

2   Remove the onion and add the breadcrumbs gradually, then simmer for a further 3 minutes.

3   Season to taste and add the butter to the top to prevent a skin from forming.

4   Stir well and ensure the temperature is correct before serving.

Thai green curry paste

Ingredients	Makes approximately 4 portions	Makes approximately 10 portions
Green chillies	10	25
Lemon grass	2 tblspn	5 tblspn
Coriander root	1 tsp	2 ½ tsp
Chopped shallots	1 tblspn	2 ½ tblspn
Chopped garlic	1 tblspn	2 ½ tblspn
Galangal grated	1 tsp	2 ½ tsp
Ground coriander	1 tsp	2 ½ tsp
Caraway seeds	1 tsp	2 ½ tsp
White pepper	2.5 g	6 g
Salt	1 tsp	2 ½ tsp
Shrimp paste	1 tsp	2 ½ tsp

energy	cal	fat	sat fat	carb	sugar	protein	fibre
171 kJ	41 kcal	1.1 g	0.1 g	5.7 g	0.7 g	2.6 g	2.6 g

METHOD OF WORK

1 Heat a large pan, then dry fry all the ingredients except the shrimp paste.

2 Pour all the ingredients into a blender with shrimp paste and a little water to slacken the mixture if required.

Tomato sauce

Ingredients	Makes approximately 4 portions	Makes approximately 10 portions
Unsalted butter	40 g	100 g
Chopped shallots	1 ½	4
Chopped thyme	½ tsp	1 tsp
Bay leaf	½	1
Chopped garlic	2	4 cloves
Chopped ripe plum tomatoes	300 g	800 g
Tomato purée	10 g	25 g
Sugar	30 g	75 g
Tomato juice	60 ml	150 ml
Basil stalks	¼ bunch	½ bunch

energy	cal	fat	sat fat	carb	sugar	protein	fibre
544 kJ	131 kcal	8.6 g	6.1 g	12.6 g	11.9 g	1.5 g	1.9 g

METHOD OF WORK

1 Sweat the shallots, thyme, bay and garlic in butter.

2 Add the tomato, purée, sugar, juice and stalks.

3 Simmer for 45 minutes.

4 Blend until smooth then pass through a chinois.

5 Season and serve.

Hot and warm butter sauces

Left to Right – Béarnaise and hollandaise sauce

Hollandaise sauce

Ingredients	4 portions	10 portions
White wine vinegar	1 tblspn	2 tblspn
Water	1 tblspn	2 tblspn
Crushed peppercorns	½ tblspn	1 tblspn
Egg yolks	2	4
Clarified butter	125 g	250 g
Lemon juice	¼ lemon	½ lemon
Good quality salt and cayenne pepper	To taste	To taste

energy	cal	fat	sat fat	carb	sugar	protein	fibre
1087 kJ	264 kcal	28.3 g	17.0 g	0.7 g	0.3 g	1.7 g	0.2 g

METHOD OF WORK

1 Place the vinegar, water and peppercorns in a saucepan and reduce by half.

2 Strain the liquid and allow to cool.

3 Whisk the egg yolks with the reduction over a bain-marie until the ribbon stage is achieved, ensure the egg does not overcook as this will give a scrambled egg appearance.

4 Slowly drizzle the warm clarified butter into the egg mixture, whisking constantly until the sauce is thick and glossy. Add the lemon juice and seasoning to taste.

5 Keep warm until ready for service.

Béarnaise sauce

Ingredients	4 portions	10 portions
White wine vinegar	1 tblspn	2 tblspn
Water	1 tblspn	2 tblspn
Crushed peppercorns	½ tblspn	1 tblspn
Egg yolks	2	4
Clarified butter	125 g	250 g
Lemon juice	¼ lemon	½ lemon
Tarragon		
Chervil		
Finely sliced shallots	1 tblspn	2 tblspn
Good quality salt and cayenne pepper	To taste	To taste

energy	cal	fat	sat fat	carb	sugar	protein	fibre
1094 kJ	266 kcal	28.3 g	17.0 g	1.0 g	0.4 g	1.8 g	0.3 g

METHOD OF WORK

1 Place the vinegar, water, peppercorns, shallots and half the chervil and tarragon in a saucepan and reduce by half.

2 Strain the liquid and allow to cool.

3 Whisk the egg yolks with the reduction over a bain-marie until the ribbon stage is achieved, ensure the egg does not overcook as this will give a scrambled egg appearance.

4 Slowly drizzle the warm clarified butter in to the egg mixture, whisking constantly until the sauce is thick and glossy. Add the lemon juice, chopped tarragon, chervil and seasoning to taste.

5 Keep warm until ready for service.

Black butter

Top to Bottom – Melted butter, nut brown butter and black butter

Ingredients	Makes approx 100 g
Salted butter	100 g
Lemon juice	¼ lemon
Chopped parsley (optional)	2 tsp

energy	cal	fat	sat fat	carb	sugar	protein	fibre
769 kJ	187 kcal	20.6 g	13.0 g	0.3 g	0.3 g	0.2 g	0.1 g

METHOD OF WORK

1 Heat a pan until very hot.

2 Add the butter and allow it to foam, it will turn dark brown.

3 Squeeze in the lemon juice, this will stop the cooking.

4 Add the chopped parsley and use as required.

5 This is traditionally used for skate wings or brains.

Melted butter (beurre fondu)

Ingredients	Makes approx 100 g
Salted butter	100 g
Water	100 ml

energy	cal	fat	sat fat	carb	sugar	protein	fibre
765 kJ	186 kcal	20.6 g	13.0 g	0.2 g	0.2 g	0.2 g	0.0 g

METHOD OF WORK

1 Heat the water in a thick bottomed pan until it boils.

2 Slowly add the chilled diced butter, whisking constantly to form an emulsion.

3 Do not add the butter too quickly or stop whisking as this will split the sauce.

4 This is used for glazing vegetables.

Nut brown butter (beurre noisette)

Ingredients	Makes approx 100 g
Salted butter	100 g
Lemon juice	¼ lemon
Chopped parsley	2 tsp

energy	cal	fat	sat fat	carb	sugar	protein	fibre
769 kJ	187 kcal	20.6 g	13.0 g	0.3 g	0.3 g	0.2 g	0.1 g

METHOD OF WORK

1 Heat a pan until very hot.

2 Add the butter and allow it to foam, it will turn golden brown.

3 Squeeze in the lemon juice, this will stop the cooking.

4 Add the chopped parsley and use as required.

5 This is traditionally used for shallow fried fish, meat and poultry dishes.

6 Toasted flaked almonds can be added to this if serving dishes such as trout meuniere.

Compound butters

Left to Right – Mustard, herb, anchovy, Café de Paris, maitre d'hôtel and garlic compound butters

CHEF'S TIP The butters can be piped into neat shapes and chilled or frozen until required.

Anchovy compound butter

Ingredients	Makes 500 g
Unsalted butter, soft	500 g
Anchovy fillets	100 g
Lemon	1

energy	cal	fat	sat fat	carb	sugar	protein	fibre
805 kJ	196 kcal	21.1 g	13.1 g	0.2 g	0.2 g	1.4 g	0.0 g

METHOD OF WORK

1 Place the anchovy and lemon zest in a food processor and pulse until minced.

2 Mix the butter and anchovy in a bowl until well blended.

3 Form into a log shape in wet greaseproof paper, wrap in cling film and chill until required.

Café de Paris compound butter

Ingredients	Makes 500 g
Unsalted butter, soft	400 g
Shallot	25 g
Parsley	25 g
Dijon mustard	1 tsp
Anchovy fillets	15 g
Coriander	10 g
Capers	10 g
Cayenne	5 g
Curry powder	5 g
Salt and pepper	As required

energy	cal	fat	sat fat	carb	sugar	protein	fibre
629 kJ	153 kcal	16.6 g	10.5 g	0.5 g	0.3 g	0.5 g	0.3 g

METHOD OF WORK

1 Finely dice the shallot and sweat until soft. Add the spices and continue to cook. Allow to cool.

2 Finely chop the herbs, capers and anchovy fillets.

3 Combine all the ingredients together with the soft butter, season and shape into a log in wet greaseproof paper.

4 Wrap in cling film and refrigerate until firm.

Garlic compound butter

Ingredients	Makes 500 g
Unsalted butter, soft	500 g
Garlic	4 cloves
Salt and pepper	As required

energy	cal	fat	sat fat	carb	sugar	protein	fibre
767 kJ	187 kcal	20.6 g	13.0 g	0.3 g	0.2 g	0.2 g	0.0 g

METHOD OF WORK

1 Crush the garlic with a little salt until smooth.

2 Combine with the softened butter, correct the seasoning and shape into a log in wet greaseproof paper.

3 Wrap in cling film and refrigerate until firm.

Herb compound butter

Ingredients	Makes 500 g
Unsalted butter, soft	500 g
Parsley	25 g
Chives	25 g
Tarragon	25 g
Salt and pepper	As required

energy	cal	fat	sat fat	carb	sugar	protein	fibre
771 kJ	187 kcal	20.6 g	13.0 g	0.3 g	0.2 g	0.3 g	0.1 g

METHOD OF WORK

1 Finely chop the herbs and combine with the softened butter.

2 Correct the seasoning and shape into a log in wet greaseproof paper.

3 Wrap in cling film and refrigerate until firm.

Lobster compound butter

Ingredients	Makes 500 g
Unsalted butter, soft	500 g
Lobster coral	50 g
Salt and pepper	As required

energy	cal	fat	sat fat	carb	sugar	protein	fibre
769 kJ	187 kcal	20.6 g	13.0 g	0.2 g	0.2 g	0.4 g	0.0 g

METHOD OF WORK

1 Cook the green lobster coral until it turns pink and then pass through a drum sieve.

2 Cool and combine with the softened butter, season and shape into a log in wet greaseproof paper.

3 Wrap in cling film and refrigerate until firm.

Mustard compound butter

Ingredients	Makes 500 g
Unsalted butter, soft	500 g
Grain mustard	50 g
Salt and pepper	As required

energy	cal	fat	sat fat	carb	sugar	protein	fibre
780 kJ	190 kcal	20.8 g	13.0 g	0.3 g	0.3 g	0.4 g	0.1 g

METHOD OF WORK

1 Combine the mustard with the softened butter, season and shape into a log in wet greaseproof paper.

Parsley, cayenne and lemon juice (maitre d'hôtel compound butter)

Ingredients	Makes 500 g
Unsalted butter, soft	500 g
Parsley	25 g
Cayenne pepper	5 g
Lemon juice	1 lemon
Salt and pepper	As required

METHOD OF WORK

1 Chop the parsley, and combine the remaining ingredients with the softened butter.

2 Shape in to a log in wet greaseproof paper. Wrap in cling film and refrigerate until firm.

Shrimp compound butter

Ingredients	Makes 500 g
Unsalted butter, soft	500 g
Cooked shrimps	50 g
Salt and pepper	As required

energy	cal	fat	sat fat	carb	sugar	protein	fibre
778 kJ	189 kcal	20.6 g	13.0 g	0.2 g	0.2 g	0.8 g	0.0 g

METHOD OF WORK

1 Mince the shrimps until they form a paste.

2 Combine with the softened butter, season and shape into a log in wet greaseproof paper.

3 Wrap in cling film and refrigerate until firm.

Cold sauces, salsas, pastes, spreads and international sauces

Aïoli

A Provençale mayonnaise-based sauce. Its name comes from the word 'ail' which means garlic and 'oli' which means oil.

Ingredients	Makes approx 450 ml
Chopped fresh garlic	30 g
Egg yolks	3
Olive oil	450 ml
Lemon juice	2 tblspn
Warm water	2 tblspn
Salt and pepper	As required

energy	cal	fat	sat fat	carb	sugar	protein	fibre
874 kJ	213 kcal	23.3 g	3.4 g	0.3 g	0.0 g	0.5 g	0.1 g

METHOD OF WORK

1 Pound the chopped garlic with a little salt until a purée is formed.

2 Mix together with the egg yolks and slowly drizzle in the oil (as for mayonnaise).

3 Finish with the lemon juice and enough warm water to adjust the consistency.

4 Season as required.

Apple sauce

Ingredients	Makes approx 450 ml
Peeled, quartered and cored apples (granny smith, cooking, gala as required)	500 g
Caster sugar	150 g (250 g if using cooking apples)
Unsalted butter	50 g
Lemon juice	2 tblspn
Warm water	2 tblspn
Cinnamon	Optional 2 cm
Star anise	1

energy	cal	fat	sat fat	carb	sugar	protein	fibre
242 kJ	57 kcal	2.1 g	1.3 g	10.2 g	10.1 g	0.1 g	0.4 g

METHOD OF WORK

1 Place the butter into a thick bottomed pan and melt, add the apples and sweat for approximately 3 minutes.

2 Add the lemon, water, cinnamon/star anise and sugar.

3 Cover with a lid and cook gently until the apples have broken down.

4 Remove the star anise and cinnamon.

5 Pass through a drum sieve, liquidize, mash or leave a rough consistency as required.

Gribiche sauce

This is a classic French sauce named after Napoleon's favourite general in his army. As a debt of gratitude, Napoleon's chef was asked to create a sauce in his honour. Sauce gribiche is served with cold fish and meats.

Ingredients	Makes approx 1 litre
French mustard	1 tsp
White wine vinegar	200 ml
Vegetable oil	650 ml
Chopped gherkins	50 g
Chopped capers	50 g
Chopped fresh herbs	25 g
Sieved hard boiled eggs	3
Good quality salt and pepper	To taste

energy	cal	fat	sat fat	carb	sugar	protein	fibre
1263 kJ	307 kcal	33.3 g	2.5 g	0.4 g	0.2 g	1.1 g	0.2 g

METHOD OF WORK

1 Mix the mustard, sieved yolks and vinegar together.

2 Slowly drizzle in the oil.

3 Mix well then add the remaining ingredients and season to taste.

Guacamole

Ingredients	Makes 1 kg
Avocados	10
Lime juice	2 limes
Tomato concassée	200g
Jalapeno chilli	1
Red onion	50 g
Coriander	10 g
Salt and pepper	As required

energy	cal	fat	sat fat	carb	sugar	protein	fibre
1201 kJ	291 kcal	29.4 g	5.3 g	3.6 g	1.3 g	3.4 g	5.4 g

METHOD OF WORK

1 Halve the avocado, remove the stone and scrape out the flesh.

2 Chop the flesh roughly and combine with the lime juice.

3 Chop the red onion finely and chop the coriander.

4 Combine the ingredients together and season as required.

5 Cover the guacamole tightly and refrigerate until needed.

6 The guacamole should be prepared on the day required.

Honey and mustard dressing

Ingredients	Makes 100 ml
Vinaigrette	100 ml
Grain mustard	To taste
Honey	To taste
Salt and pepper	As required

energy	cal	fat	sat fat	carb	sugar	protein	fibre
667 kJ	162 kcal	17.6 g	2.5 g	0.7 g	0.5 g	0.1 g	0.2 g

METHOD OF WORK

1 Combine all the ingredients and adjust the seasoning to taste.

Houmous

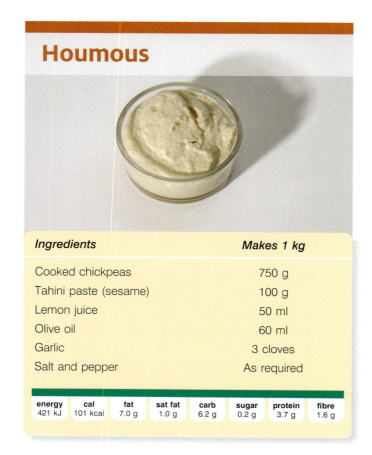

Ingredients	Makes 1 kg
Cooked chickpeas	750 g
Tahini paste (sesame)	100 g
Lemon juice	50 ml
Olive oil	60 ml
Garlic	3 cloves
Salt and pepper	As required

energy	cal	fat	sat fat	carb	sugar	protein	fibre
421 kJ	101 kcal	7.0 g	1.0 g	6.2 g	0.2 g	3.7 g	1.6 g

METHOD OF WORK

1 Crush the garlic with a little salt.

2 Place all ingredients into a food processor and blend, adding a little water if mixture becomes too thick.

3 Adjust the seasoning as required.

4 Cover and refrigerate until required.

Papaya and black bean salsa

Top Left – Pickled ginger salsa, Top Right – Papaya and black bean salsa, Bottom Left – Mango and lime salsa, Bottom Right – Tomato, cucumber and shallot salsa

Ingredients	Makes 1 kg
Cooked black beans	200 g
Lime juice	2 limes
Papaya	1
Red pepper	1
Red onion	100 g
Coriander	10 g
Olive oil	50 ml
Red chilli	1
Salt and pepper	As required

energy	cal	fat	sat fat	carb	sugar	protein	fibre
184 kJ	44 kcal	2.6 g	0.4 g	4.0 g	1.6 g	1.2 g	1.4 g

METHOD OF WORK

1 Peel the papaya and remove the black seeds. Cut into small dice.

2 Finely dice the red onion and chop the coriander.

3 Deseed and dice the red pepper.

4 Combine all the ingredients in a bowl and season to taste.

5 Allow ingredients to infuse for at least an hour before using.

6 Cover and refrigerate until required.

Mango and lime salsa

Ingredients	Makes 1 kg
Mango	3
Lime juice and zest	3 limes
Jalapeno chilli	1
Red onion	100 g
Coriander	10 g
Salt and pepper	As required

energy	cal	fat	sat fat	carb	sugar	protein	fibre
89 kJ	21 kcal	0.1 g	0.0 g	5.0 g	4.8 g	0.4 g	1.0 g

METHOD OF WORK

1 Peel the mango and remove the flesh from the stone.

2 Cut into small dice and combine with the lime juice and zest.

3 Finely dice the red onion and chop the coriander.

4 Remove the seeds from the chilli and finely chop.

5 Combine all ingredients and season as required.

6 Allow ingredients to infuse for at least an hour before using.

7 Cover and refrigerate until required.

Pickled ginger salsa

Ingredients	Makes 1 kg
Pickled ginger	200 g
Cucumber	1
Red onion	200 g
Water chestnuts	150 g
Mirin	50 ml
Olive oil	50 ml
Limes, juiced	3
Rice wine vinegar	50 ml
Salt and pepper	As required

energy	cal	fat	sat fat	carb	sugar	protein	fibre
307 kJ	74 kcal	3.1 g	0.6 g	10.7 g	1.6 g	1.3 g	1.7 g

METHOD OF WORK

1 Shred the pickled ginger and place into a bowl.

2 Split the cucumber lengthways and remove the seeds.

3 Cut into small dice and add to the ginger.

4 Finely dice the red onion and dice the water chestnuts.

5 Combine all the remaining ingredients together and season as required.

6 Allow ingredients to infuse for at least an hour before using.

7 Cover and refrigerate until required.

Tomato, shallot and cucumber salsa

Ingredients	Makes 1 kg
Tomato concassée	700 g
Cucumber	2
Shallot	150 g
Basil	50 g
Parsley	50 g
Olive oil	50 ml
Salt and pepper	As required

energy	cal	fat	sat fat	carb	sugar	protein	fibre
148 kJ	36 kcal	2.7 g	0.4 g	2.1 g	1.9 g	0.8 g	0.9 g

METHOD OF WORK

1   Finely chop the shallot and place into a bowl.

2   Split the cucumber lengthways and remove the seeds. Cut into a small dice and combine with the shallots.

3   Chop the herbs and add to the bowl with the olive oil.

4   Combine the tomato concassée gently and season as required.

5   Cover and refrigerate until required.

Mayonnaise and Marie Rose sauce

This is suitable for serving with hors d'oeuvre, cold meats and is a major base component in many salads and dressings.

Ingredients	Makes approx 400 ml
Egg yolks	3
White wine vinegar	10 g
Mustard powder	½ tsp
Vegetable, sunflower or olive oil	400 ml
Salt and pepper	As required

energy	cal	fat	sat fat	carb	sugar	protein	fibre
973 kJ	237 kcal	26.0 g	2.0 g	0.1 g	0.0 g	0.6 g	0.0 g

METHOD OF WORK

1   Whisk together the egg yolks, vinegar, mustard and seasoning.

2   While whisking continuously slowly drizzle in the oil in a slow steady stream.

3   An emulsion should take place between the egg yolks and the oil.

4   Adjust seasoning and consistency with a little warm water if necessary.

Note: Marie rose sauce is mayonnaise with the addition of tomato ketchup, cognac (brandy) and cayenne pepper to taste – this is also known as cocktail sauce.

Mint raita

Ingredients	Makes 200 ml
Yoghurt, Greek, full fat or low fat	150 ml
Cucumber	1
Picked mint	4 tblspn
Chopped garlic	1 tblspn
Salt and pepper	As required

	energy	cal	fat	sat fat	carb	sugar	protein	fibre
	123 kJ	30 kcal	1.6 g	1.0 g	2.5 g	1.2 g	1.5 g	0.8 g

METHOD OF WORK

1 Peel, quarter, deseed and grate the cucumber.

2 Place in a colander with a little salt and leave for at least 10 minutes.

3 Squeeze the cucumber gently to remove any excess liquid.

4 Place the yoghurt, cucumber, garlic and mint into a bowl and mix well.

5 Season as required.

Pesto

Left to Right – Pesto and sun-dried tomato pesto

Pesto is an Italian sauce and is quite coarse in texture but highly flavoured.

Ingredients	Makes approx 100 ml
Toasted pine nuts	100 g
Olive oil	100 ml
Grated parmesan cheese	30 g
Chopped clove of garlic	1
Basil	¼ bunch
Salt and pepper	As required

energy	cal	fat	sat fat	carb	sugar	protein	fibre
7120 kJ	1727 kcal	177.7 g	24.8 g	6.6 g	4.3 g	25.9 g	2.7 g

METHOD OF WORK

1 Pick the basil leaves and blanch them in boiling water, remove and place into iced water.

2 Squeeze gently to remove any excess water.

3 Place all ingredients into a liquidizer and blend until the desired consistency is achieved.

Sun-dried tomato pesto

Ingredients	Makes 200 g
Fresh pesto	100 g
Sun-dried tomatoes	100 g
Salt and pepper	As required

energy	cal	fat	sat fat	carb	sugar	protein	fibre
177 kJ	43 kcal	4.3 g	0.7 g	0.7 g	0.4 g	0.4 g	0.4 g

METHOD OF WORK

1 Combine the ingredients together and season as required.

2 The sun-dried tomatoes can be blended with the pesto, finely chopped, cut into brunoise or julienne strips and folded through.

Raw tomato coulis

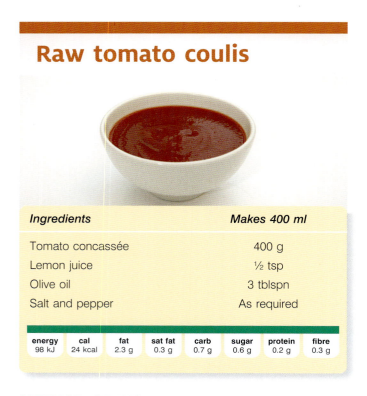

Ingredients	Makes 400 ml
Tomato concassée	400 g
Lemon juice	½ tsp
Olive oil	3 tblspn
Salt and pepper	As required

energy	cal	fat	sat fat	carb	sugar	protein	fibre
98 kJ	24 kcal	2.3 g	0.3 g	0.7 g	0.6 g	0.2 g	0.3 g

METHOD OF WORK

1 Place all the ingredients into a liquidizer and blend until smooth.

2 Place the purée into a fine sieve or chinois and pass the liquid through.

3 Correct the seasoning.

Remoulade sauce

This originates from the Picardy word meaning black radish because the finished sauce has a taste and looks similar to that of black radish.

Ingredients	Makes approx 900 g
Mayonnaise	900 g
Chopped capers	25 g
Chopped gherkins	50 g
Chopped fresh parsley, tarragon and chervil	10 g
Anchovy essence	2 tblspn
Salt and pepper	As required

energy	cal	fat	sat fat	carb	sugar	protein	fibre
1289 kJ	313 kcal	34.1 g	5.1 g	1.1 g	0.7 g	0.7 g	0.1 g

METHOD OF WORK

1 Combine the ingredients together and season as required.

Thousand island sauce

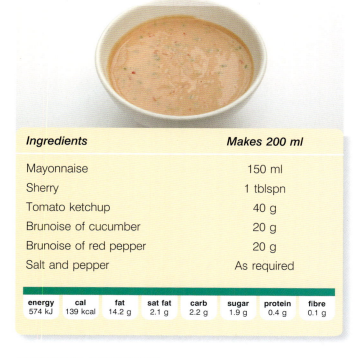

Ingredients	Makes 200 ml
Mayonnaise	150 ml
Sherry	1 tblspn
Tomato ketchup	40 g
Brunoise of cucumber	20 g
Brunoise of red pepper	20 g
Salt and pepper	As required

energy	cal	fat	sat fat	carb	sugar	protein	fibre
574 kJ	139 kcal	14.2 g	2.1 g	2.2 g	1.9 g	0.4 g	0.1 g

METHOD OF WORK

1 Combine the ingredients together and season as required.

2 Additional tomato ketchup can be added to darken the colour if preferred.

Salsa verde

Ingredients	Makes 1 kg
Parsley	150 g
Mint	50 g
Capers	100 g
Garlic	3 clove
Dijon mustard	50 ml
Lemons, juiced	2
Olive oil	250 ml
Salt and pepper	As required

energy	cal	fat	sat fat	carb	sugar	protein	fibre
201 kJ	49 kcal	5.1 g	0.8 g	0.5 g	0.2 g	0.3 g	0.3 g

METHOD OF WORK

1 Wash and pick the mint and parsley.

2 Chop and place into a bowl.

3 Chop the capers and crush the garlic and add to the herbs.

4 Add the remaining ingredients and season as required.

Tapenade

Ingredients	Makes 1 kg
Black olives	650 g
Anchovy fillets	100 g
Capers	100 g
Garlic	2 cloves
Lemon juice	2
Parsley, chopped	50 g
Olive oil	50 ml
Salt and pepper	As required

energy	cal	fat	sat fat	carb	sugar	protein	fibre
300 kJ	72 kcal	6.6 g	0.9 g	2.5 g	0.1 g	1.8 g	1.4 g

METHOD OF WORK

1 Place the olives, anchovies, capers and garlic into a food processor and blend while incorporating the lemon juice and olive oil.

2 Blend until a chunky paste is formed which should be easy to spread. Do not over mix.

3 Adjust the seasoning as required and add the chopped parsley to finish.

4 Cover and refrigerate until required.

SOURCING Careful selection of olives should be addressed when producing tapenade, a cheap poor quality olive will be over salty.

Tartare sauce *(modern version)*

Ingredients	Makes 500 g
Mayonnaise	500 g
Chopped capers	50 g
Chopped gherkins	50 g
Finely chopped parsley	2 tblspn
Lemon juice	To taste
Salt and pepper	As required

energy	cal	fat	sat fat	carb	sugar	protein	fibre
1435 kJ	349 kcal	37.9 g	5.8 g	1.4 g	0.9 g	0.8 g	0.4 g

METHOD OF WORK

1   Combine the ingredients together and season as required.

Thai dressing

Ingredients	Makes approx 200 ml
Vinaigrette	150 ml
Brunoise red and green chilli	20 g
Brunoise garlic	10 g
Brunoise ginger	10 g
Coriander finely chopped	2 tblspn
Cracked black pepper	2 tsp
Salt	As required
Lime juice and zest	1 tblspn

energy	cal	fat	sat fat	carb	sugar	protein	fibre
1007 kJ	245 kcal	26.4 g	3.8 g	1.4 g	0.3 g	0.5 g	0.7 g

METHOD OF WORK

1   Combine the ingredients together and season as required.

2   This is best left for a few days to allow the flavours to infuse

3   It can then be used straight away or passed to remove the brunoise.

Vert sauce *(Sauce verte)*

Ingredients	Makes 200 ml
Mayonnaise	150 ml
Picked chervil	2 tblspn
Picked tarragon	2 tblspn
Chopped chives	2 tblspn
Spinach leaves	50 g
Salt and pepper	As required

energy	cal	fat	sat fat	carb	sugar	protein	fibre
588 kJ	143 kcal	14.4 g	2.2 g	2.6 g	0.4 g	1.5 g	0.7 g

METHOD OF WORK

1   Blanch the spinach and herbs, then refresh in ice water.

2   Squeeze gently to remove any excess water.

3   Combine the ingredients together and liquidize.

4   Season as required.

Vinaigrette

This is a non-protein based emulsion. It was made as an accompaniment for cured fish, salads or cold meats to aid digestion. Another name widely used for this dressing is *sauce ravigote*.

Ingredients	Makes 400 ml
White wine vinegar	100 ml
Olive oil	300 ml
Finely chopped shallots	30 g
Finely chopped capers	20 g
Finely chopped aromatic herbs	10 g
Salt and pepper	As required

energy	cal	fat	sat fat	carb	sugar	protein	fibre
1642 kJ	399 kcal	43.8 g	6.3 g	0.7 g	0.2 g	0.2 g	0.4 g

METHOD OF WORK

1 Combine the ingredients together and whisk thoroughly, season as required.

Tomato vinaigrette

Ingredients	Makes 200 ml
Vinaigrette	150 ml
Tomato juice	50 ml
Tomato concassée	50 g
Salt and pepper	As required

energy	cal	fat	sat fat	carb	sugar	protein	fibre
1242 kJ	302 kcal	32.9 g	4.7 g	1.0 g	0.5 g	0.3 g	0.5 g

METHOD OF WORK

1 Combine the ingredients together and season as required.

Vinaigrette emulsified
(French)

Ingredients	Makes 100 ml
White wine vinegar	25 ml
Olive or vegetable oil	75 ml
Dijon mustard	1 tblspn
Salt and pepper	As required

energy	cal	fat	sat fat	carb	sugar	protein	fibre
362 kJ	88 kcal	9.5 g	1.4 g	0.3 g	0.2 g	0.2 g	0.1 g

METHOD OF WORK

1 In a bowl whisk the seasoning, mustard and vinegar together.

2 Slowly add the oil, adjust seasoning.

Balsamic split vinaigrette

Ingredients	Makes approx 100 ml
Good quality balsamic vinegar	30 ml
Sunflower or olive oil (or 50% of each)	60 ml
Salt and pepper	As required

energy	cal	fat	sat fat	carb	sugar	protein	fibre
226 kJ	55 kcal	6.0 g	0.7 g	0.1 g	0.0 g	0.0 g	0.0 g

METHOD OF WORK

1 Combine all the ingredients and shake or whisk together.

2 This will produce a vinaigrette with small dark spots: care must be taken to not over mix as this will form an emulsified dark brown liquid.

Flavoured oils

Back row Left to Right – Tomato, chilli and lemon oil
Middle row Left to Right – Walnut, chorizo and herb oil
Front row Left to Right – Basil, vanilla and garlic

Basil oil

Ingredients	Makes 500 ml
Vegetable oil	500 ml
Basil	200 g

energy	cal	fat	sat fat	carb	sugar	protein	fibre
376 kJ	92 kcal	10.0 g	0.7 g	0.2 g	0.0 g	0.1 g	0.1 g

METHOD OF WORK

1   Pick the basil and blanch for a few seconds and refresh. Allow to dry thoroughly.

2   Heat the oil to 55 °C.

3   Add the basil and allow to infuse for 30 minutes.

4   Blend the ingredients and again allow to stand.

5   Pass through a muslin cloth and cool.

Chilli oil

Ingredients	Makes 500 ml
Vegetable oil	500 ml
Dried chillies	150 g

energy	cal	fat	sat fat	carb	sugar	protein	fibre
410 kJ	100 kcal	10.5 g	0.8 g	0.9 g	0.3 g	0.4 g	0.8 g

METHOD OF WORK

1   Place the chillies and oil into a pan and heat to 55 °C.

2   Allow at least 30 minutes to infuse.

3   The chillies can be retained in the oil to allow further infusion.

CHEF'S TIP   The oils can be stored in a cool environment until required; alternatively they can be refrigerated and warmed through when required.

Chorizo oil

Ingredients	Makes 500 ml
Vegetable oil	450 ml
Chorizo	250 g

energy	cal	fat	sat fat	carb	sugar	protein	fibre
393 kJ	95 kcal	10.2 g	1.1 g	0.2 g	0.1 g	0.9 g	0.0 g

METHOD OF WORK

1   Dice the chorizo and place into a pan over a medium heat.

2   Cook the chorizo to render the natural fats from the sausage.

3   Add the remaining oil and maintain a temperature of 55 °C for at least 30 minutes to infuse.

4   Pass through a muslin cloth and allow to cool.

Curry oil

Ingredients	Makes 500 ml
Vegetable oil	500 ml
Ground cumin	5 g
Ground coriander	5 g
Curry powder	5 g
Turmeric	5 g
Shallots	10 g

energy	cal	fat	sat fat	carb	sugar	protein	fibre
376 kJ	91 kcal	10.1 g	0.7 g	0.2 g	0.1 g	0.1 g	0.1 g

METHOD OF WORK

1 Sweat the shallots in a little of the oil.

2 Add the spices and cook out over a medium heat.

3 Add the remaining oil to pan.

4 Gently heat the oil to 55 °C.

5 Remove from the heat and infuse for at least 30 minutes.

6 Pass through a muslin cloth and allow to cool.

Garlic oil

Ingredients	Makes 500 ml
Vegetable oil	500 ml
Garlic	1 bulb

energy	cal	fat	sat fat	carb	sugar	protein	fibre
370 kJ	90 kcal	10.0 g	0.7 g	0.0 g	0.0 g	0.0 g	0.0 g

METHOD OF WORK

1 Heat the oil to 55 °C.

2 Add the garlic and allow to infuse for 30 minutes.

3 Blend the ingredients and allow to stand.

4 Pass through a muslin cloth and cool.

Herb oil

Ingredients	Makes 500 ml
Vegetable oil	500 ml
Parsley	100 g
Basil	50 g
Tarragon	25 g

energy	cal	fat	sat fat	carb	sugar	protein	fibre
375 kJ	91 kcal	10.0 g	0.7 g	0.1 g	0.1 g	0.1 g	0.1 g

METHOD OF WORK

1 Pick the herbs and blanch for a few seconds and refresh. Allow them to dry thoroughly.

2 Heat the oil to 55 °C.

3 Add the herbs and allow to infuse for 30 minutes.

4 Blend the ingredients and again allow to stand.

5 Pass through a muslin cloth and cool.

Lemon oil

Ingredients	Makes 500 ml
Vegetable oil	500 ml
Lemon, rind	4 lemon
Lemongrass, split lengthways	1 stick

energy	cal	fat	sat fat	carb	sugar	protein	fibre
375 kJ	91 kcal	10.0 g	0.7 g	0.4 g	0.1 g	0.0 g	0.2 g

METHOD OF WORK

1 Pare the rind from the lemon and remove any white pith.

2 Add the rind and lemongrass to the oil and gently heat to 55 °C.

3 Remove from the heat and allow to infuse for 30 minutes.

4 This oil is stored with the rind still present to continue the infusion over time.

Roasted hazelnut oil

Ingredients	Makes 500 ml
Vegetable oil	500 ml
Hazelnuts	250 g

energy	cal	fat	sat fat	carb	sugar	protein	fibre
497 kJ	121 kcal	12.8 g	0.9 g	0.4 g	0.2 g	1.1 g	0.4 g

METHOD OF WORK

1   Roast the hazelnuts in an oven set at 190 °C for 5 minutes.

2   Remove and place onto a clean cloth.

3   Rub the hazelnuts in the cloth to remove the skin.

4   Place the hazelnuts in a pestle and mortar and press to remove some natural oils present in the nuts.

5   Place the nuts into a pan with the oil and gently heat to 55 °C.

6   Remove from the heat and allow to infuse.

7   Blend the oil and pass through a muslin cloth and allow to cool.

Sun-dried tomato oil

Ingredients	Makes 500 ml
Vegetable oil	500 ml
Sun-dried tomato	200 g
Garlic	2 cloves

energy	cal	fat	sat fat	carb	sugar	protein	fibre
452 kJ	110 kcal	12.1 g	1.0 g	0.2 g	0.1 g	0.1 g	0.3 g

METHOD OF WORK

1   Place the tomatoes and garlic into the oil and heat gently to 55 °C.

2   Allow to infuse for at least 30 minutes.

3   Blend the oil and pass through a muslin cloth.

4   Allow to cool.

Vanilla oil

Ingredients	Makes 500 ml
Vegetable oil	500 ml
Vanilla pod	2

energy	cal	fat	sat fat	carb	sugar	protein	fibre
370 kJ	90 kcal	10.0 g	0.7 g	0.0 g	0.0 g	0.0 g	0.0 g

METHOD OF WORK

1   Split the vanilla pod lengthways and scrape the seeds out.

2   Place both the seeds and pod with the oil into a pan.

3   Gently heat to 55 °C and remove from the heat.

4   Store with the pod retained for stronger flavour.

Walnut oil

Ingredients	Makes 500 ml
Vegetable oil	500 ml
Walnuts	250 g

energy	cal	fat	sat fat	carb	sugar	protein	fibre
511 kJ	124 kcal	13.4 g	1.1 g	0.2 g	0.1 g	0.7 g	0.2 g

METHOD OF WORK

1   Blanch the walnuts in boiling water and remove onto a clean cloth.

2   Rub the walnuts in the cloth to remove the skin.

3   Place the walnuts in a pestle and mortar and press to remove some natural oils present in the nuts.

4   Place the nuts into a pan with the oil and gently heat to 55 °C.

5   Remove from the heat and allow to infuse.

6   Blend the oil, pass through a muslin cloth and allow to cool.

Introduction to soup

Soup has long been the foundation of menus across the world and a general source of nutrition for the vast majority of the population. From the hearty main course soup of minestrone served with focaccia bread drizzled in olive oil, to the most delicate of consommés accompanied by the lightest profiteroles; both the contemporary chef and the humblest of family cooks need a deep understanding of the preparation and finishing of soups.

It is widely thought that the first recorded soup recipe was of a barley soup from a Roman cook book. Originally, in France the *soupe* was the actual slice of bread on which was poured the contents of a cooking pot (potage), the contents were usually gruel, boiled water with vegetables and grains. Later, the emergence of the stockpot came about, where cooks would add mutton, beef or other bones to a big cooking pot, that would endlessly simmer away and be replenished when required, hence the word *pot-au-feu*.

Soups are easily digested and have been prescribed for illness since ancient times. The modern restaurant industry is said to be based on soup. *Restoratifs* (where the word 'restaurant' originates) were some of the first items served in public restaurants in 18th century Paris. Broth (*Pot-au-feu*), bouillon, and consommé started at this point. French classic cuisine has produced many of the soups we recognize today.

> **CHEF'S TIP** On the modern menu, a soup can be served as a first course in a shot glass or small bowl where its function is to stimulate the appetite. Soups should be a delicate flavour and a natural colour. Thick soups should not be too heavy in consistency.

Advancements in science enabled soups to take many forms, such as portable, canned, dehydrated and micro-wave-ready. 'Pocket soup' was carried by colonial travellers, as it could easily be reconstituted with a little hot water. Canned and dehydrated soups were available from the turn of the 19th century. These initially supplied the military and eventually the home pantry. Advances in science also permitted the adjustment of nutrients to fit specific dietary needs such as low in salt, high fibre diets and gluten free diets.

A brief history of canning

During the early Revolutionary Wars, the French government offered a cash award of 12 000 Francs to any inventor who could invent a cheap and effective method of preserving great quantities of food. The massive armies of the time needed regular supplies of food, and so preservation became a necessity. In 1809, a French confectioner called Nicolas Appert developed a method of vacuum-sealing food inside glass jars. However, glass containers were unsuitable for transportation, and soon they had been replaced with steel cans. Soup was an ideal food used in these early preservation tests.

Based on Appert's methods of food preservation, the packaging of food in sealed airtight tin cans was first patented by an Englishman, Peter Durand, in 1810. Initially, the canning process was slow and labour-intensive, making the tinned food too expensive for ordinary people to buy.

A number of inventions and improvements followed, and by the 1860s, the time to process food in a can reduced from 6 hours to 30 minutes. Urban populations in Victorian era Britain demanded ever-increasing quantities of cheap, varied, good-quality food that they could keep on the shelves at home. Demand for tinned food hugely increased during the First World War, as military commanders searched for cheap, high-calorie food which could be transported safely and would survive trench warfare conditions.

Soup classification

Soups can be categorized as follows:

Purée A soup named after or thickened by its main ingredient such as mushroom, potato and leek or tomato. Dried vegetables cooked with stock can also be used.

Cream A purée soup with the addition of cream, thin béchamel, crème frâiche or a liaison of egg yolks and cream. Cream of mushroom, cream of potato and leek, cream of tomato and cream of vegetable are all variations. It is essential that these soups have a smooth consistency and have been passed or strained.

Velouté A cream soup to which a liaison of cream and egg yolk is added. These soups are prepared from a base roux with the addition of an appropriately flavoured stock. Mushroom velouté, velouté of potato and leek are examples.

Broth A soup that is comprised of a strongly flavoured stock and accompanied by a named garnish, such as mutton. This is a soup that is not passed and the vegetables are cut in varying shapes according to the recipe requirement. Examples include mutton broth and Scotch broth. Potages also come under this type of soup.

Consommé These are clear soups that are prepared from stock flavoured with various meats and vegetables. They are clarified and should be clear when finished. Bouillons also come under this category but are not clarified to the same level. Examples can be consommé julienne (with julienne of vegetables), consommé madrilène (with brunoise of deseeded tomato; tomato and celery flavour) and consommé royale (with egg custard).

Bisque Taken from the French term 'bi cuit' (biscuit), it is a soup made from crustaceans and is traditionally served with water biscuits. It is thickened with rice and the shell of the crustacean used and finished with cream. Examples are lobster and prawn bisque.

Chowder This is generally a seafood soup, based upon molluscs that can have the addition of smoked white fish. It is usually associated with New England. The most popular form is clam chowder. The term may also describe a buttery, hearty soup made with corn and chicken. The origins of the word 'chowder' may derive from the French word for a large cauldron, *chaudiere*, in which Breton fishermen threw their catch to make a communal fish stew. Examples can be clam, cockle or chicken and sweetcorn chowder.

Foreign Also known as miscellaneous soups: these are all soups of a traditional, modern and national nature that do not fall into any other category, such as the simple Jewish chicken soup, and the gumbos made from okra, chicken, seafood or meat, of the American South. India has many types of lentil soups: Middle Eastern Muslims break their Ramadan fast with harira, made from lentils, chickpeas, and lamb. Japan is famous for soups based on miso (fermented soybean paste).

Eastern Europe possesses goulash (a beef and paprika stew that started life as soup) and borsch (beetroot and meat soup). Spanish gazpacho is always in vogue; the Greek avgolemono is an egg and lemon soup; and Italy has numerous bean and pasta soups, such as minestrone. Scotland is renowned for Cullen skink (smoked haddock soup) and Scotch broth (mutton and barley soup).

The skills required to create an outstanding soup are the same as that needed to make a delicate sauce. The modern chef has a wider variety of ingredients at their disposal to meet the requirements of today's more perceptive customer. The balance of flavours, seasoning, consistency, texture and temperature needs to be understood to create a well-flavoured and satisfying soup.

> **TASK** Research and select soups for the following occasions:
>
> - summer dinner party
> - bonfire night
> - lunch with sandwiches
> - supper.
>
> Explain your selection.

Use of tools and equipment

In the past, all chopping and blending was done by hand, making soup production at the upper end of the market, very labour intensive. However, with the introduction of the stick blenders and larger blending machines the making of fresh soups is almost as easy as using convenience soups.

The use of heavy-bottomed saucepans is recommended for soups that require a long simmering time. This is suggested because of the ability to consistently transfer even heat distribution to the soup and reduces the risk of scalding or burning the contents of the pan.

The exact weighing and measuring of the ingredients is important to determine the correct consistency and flavour to each soup. Also accurate measuring will result in the right amount of portions produced for service and will result in less wastage.

When passing or straining a soup a conical strainer (chinois) is often used to great effect. It is used to strain out lumps and to create a smooth consistency to the soup. Alternatives are to use fine graded sieves or muslin cloth to produce a velvety smooth or crystal clear finish to soups and consommés.

> **CHEF'S TIP** When passing soup through a chinois, use a sauce ladle and gently bounce it in the bottom of the strainer. This creates a vacuum effect and forces the soup through much faster.
>
>

The quality points for ingredients

It is imperative to use unblemished, fresh ingredients when making soups. Always check that the ingredients meet the dish requirements by using correct 'mise-en-place' methods and weighing each ingredient prior to preparation.

Checking the quality of ingredients

- **Carrots** No apparent blemishes and crisp in texture.
- **Onions** Firm to the touch, no mould and no brown flesh when cut in half.
- **Meat** Should be fat free and fresh with a pleasant smell and not sticky to the touch.
- **Celery** Light coloured, no blemishes and aromatic smell.

- **Herbs** Not wilted. Bright and aromatic when touched.
- **Stocks** Freshly made, not greasy or cloudy.

When in doubt about the quality and freshness of ingredients bring it to the attention of the chef or line manager who will identify your concerns and communicate to the supplier.

HEALTHY OPTIONS There are always alternatives you can use to make a soup healthier. The addition of yoghurt or single cream instead of double cream and the use of unsaturated oils instead of butter reduce fat and cholesterol intake. But, in general, soups are a healthy part of our diet, especially lightly cooked broths that are nutritious and easily digested. During this chapter each recipe will have variations attached. The list is not restricted. It is only limited to the imagination and skills of the chef.

Garnishes and accompaniments

Most soups are accompanied by bread, usually in the form of bread rolls or sliced baguettes. However, croûtons, sippets and toasted flutes are served at the table. In modern times croûtons are sometimes more rustic, with larger pieces of bread drizzled with olive oil and baked in the oven until crisp.

Croûtons

Small cubes of white crustless bread (1 x 1 cm) that are pan fried in clarified butter. Heat the butter in a pan and add the diced bread, constantly shaking the pan so that the croûtons colour evenly. Spoon out onto kitchen paper and pat dry.

Sippets

Triangles of bread cut from the corners of pan loaves, thinly sliced and toasted in an oven. To add flavour garlic can be rubbed onto the bread before turning over to toast the other side.

Croûtes de flûte (toasted flutes)

Slices, taken from a thin baguette. They can be either toasted on both sides or brushed in melted butter and crisped in the oven.

Vegetable garnishes

Used as a light garnish for consommés, broths or purée based soups. Careful cutting into neat, even and standardized shapes is important to the finished result.

- **Brunoise:** Cut equal amounts of carrot, turnip, leek and celery into 2 mm dice for consommés and slightly larger for broths.

- **Julienne:** Cut equal amounts of carrot, turnip, leek and celery into thin strips up to 35 mm in length.

● **Paysanne:** Cut equal amounts of turnips, carrots, swede, potato, leek and celery into 1 cm squares.

● **Concassée:** Blanched, quartered, deseeded and diced flesh of tomatoes.

Serving temperatures and quantities

Hot soups require serving very hot and any accompanying garnishes should be added when serving. The Food Hygiene (England) Regulations 2006 state that hot food needs to be kept at or above 63 °C in order to control the growth of pathogenic micro-organisms or the formation of toxins. The soup should not be kept for service or on display for sale for a period of more than two hours.

Cold soups should be served chilled at below 5 °C and not at room temperature.

When chilling the soups they must reach below 8 °C within 90 minutes to slow the rate of bacterial growth.

This can be achieved with a blast chiller or in an iced bath of water.

When calculating the required amount of a soup for a given number of portions it should be estimated on the basis of the following points:

● Dependant on the size and style of the menu and the amount of courses that follow.

● That the recipe is followed correctly.

● That each ingredient is accurately measured for the recipe.

● No more than between 200 and 250 ml per portion should be served.

Recipes
Purée soups

Butternut squash and coriander soup

Ingredients	Makes approximately 4 portions	Makes approximately 10 portions
Butternut squash	400 g	1000 g
Onion	40 g	100 g
Celery	40 g	100 g
White of leek	40 g	100 g
Cumin powder	10 g	20 g
Good quality salt	To taste	To taste
White pepper	To taste	To taste
Nutmeg	To taste	To taste
Butter	40 g	100 g
Fresh coriander	50 g	120 g
White vegetable stock	1500 ml	3250 ml
Bouquet garni	1 small	1 medium

energy	cal	fat	sat fat	carb	sugar	protein	fibre
820 kJ	198 kcal	15.8 g	7.4 g	11.8 g	7.0 g	2.9 g	2.8 g

METHOD OF WORK

1 Wash and cut the butternut squash in half, peel and dice into 2 cm cubes. Repeat the process with the onion, celery and leek.

2 Melt the butter in a large saucepan and add the cumin powder. Gently sweat for about 2 minutes to release the full flavour of the spice.

3 Add all the chopped vegetables and sweat for 5 minutes or until they are translucent.

4 Add the white vegetable stock, bouquet garni, season well with the salt, pepper and a little grated nutmeg and simmer until all the vegetables are cooked, this may take approximately 45 minutes. Skim the surface as necessary.

5 Remove the bouquet garni. Liquidize the soup using a blender and correct the seasoning and consistency of the soup.

6 Wash and remove the coriander leaves from the stalks. Cut the coriander into a chiffonade and add to the soup after it has been brought back to the boil.

7 Cook for a further 2 minutes to infuse the coriander flavour and then serve immediately.

CHEF'S TIP Butternut squash is a winter vegetable and needs to be peeled before use. Pumpkin can substitute the main ingredient in this recipe if required.

Mushroom soup *(purée de champignon)*

Ingredients	Makes approximately 4 portions	Makes approximately 10 portions
White button mushrooms	200 g	500 g
Caps of chestnut mushrooms	40 g	100 g
Onion	40 g	100 g
White of leek	40 g	100 g
Butter	40 g	100 g
Good quality salt	To taste	To taste
White pepper	To taste	To taste
White flour	40 g	100 g
White stock (vegetable or chicken)	1000 ml	2500 ml
White wine	40 ml	100 ml
Bouquet garni	1 small	1 medium

energy	cal	fat	sat fat	carb	sugar	protein	fibre
1083 kJ	262 kcal	22.6 g	7.4 g	10.5 g	2.0 g	3.2 g	2.7 g

METHOD OF WORK

1 Wash the vegetables and carefully clean the mushrooms before cutting them into macédoine. Melt the butter in a saucepan.

2 Add the vegetables and mushrooms and sweat.

3 Add the white wine and reduce the quantity by half.

4 Add the flour to make a loose roux, without colouring.

5 Remove from the heat to cool slightly before adding the hot stock, the bouquet garni and bringing to the boil.

6 Simmer for 45 minutes, skimming when required.

7 Remove the bouquet garni, liquidize and return to a clean pan, reboil.

8 Correct the seasoning and consistency.

9 Thinly slice the chestnut mushroom caps and lightly cook in a little stock or clarified butter and serve as a garnish on top of the soup.

CHEF'S TIP Wild mushrooms can be used instead of or in addition to the cultivated varieties. The addition of tarragon, thyme or Pernod can enhance the flavour of the mushrooms.

HEALTHY OPTION Cream may be added to the mushroom soup to give a smooth and richer consistency. However, skimmed milk, soya milk, non-dairy cream or yoghurt could be used instead.

Potato soup *(purée parmentier)*

Ingredients	Makes approximately 4 portions	Makes approximately 10 portions
Potatoes	400 g	1000 g
Onion	80 g	500 g
White stock (vegetable or chicken)	1000 ml	2500 ml
Butter	40 g	100 g
Bouquet garni	1 small	1 medium
Good quality salt	To taste	To taste
White pepper	To taste	To taste
Chopped fresh flat leaf parsley	15 g	30 g
Croûtons	25 g	60 g

energy	cal	fat	sat fat	carb	sugar	protein	fibre
990 kJ	238 kcal	13.2 g	6.7 g	27.1 g	2.5 g	3.4 g	3.5 g

METHOD OF WORK

1 Peel, wash and thinly slice the onions, melt the butter and sweat the onions in the butter until soft and translucent.

2 Wash, peel, re-wash and chop the potatoes into a 1 cm dice.

3 Add the potatoes, hot stock and bouquet garni to the saucepan with the onions.

4 Lightly season and bring to the boil. Allow to simmer for approximately 45 minutes, skimming when necessary.

5 When the potato has completely dissolved and amalgamated into the liquid remove the bouquet garni.

6 Liquidize the soup and pass through a fine sieve into a clean pan.

7 Bring back to the boil, correct the seasoning and consistency.

8 Serve with croûtons and the chopped flat leaf parsley.

CHEF'S TIP Gradual sweating of vegetables brings out their flavour. A floury potato such as desiree, maris piper or pentland dell will give a smoother and creamier texture to this soup.

Variations of potato soup

This basic soup has many variations with the simple addition of another ingredient:

Sweet potato soup	Substitute sweet potato for potatoes in the basic recipe
Potato and bacon soup	Add 25 g of cooked pancetta lardons
Potato and chive soup	Add 15 g of chopped chives per portion of soup
Potato and chorizo soup	25 g per portion. Gently fry small cubes of chorizo and use the oil to drizzle over the soup just before service
Potato and leek soup	Add 50 g of white of leek per portion and sweat with the onions. Garnish with julienne of leek
Potato and watercress soup	Add 25 g of blanched watercress to the soup 5 minutes before puréeing (note: less white pepper will be required in this recipe)

Red lentil soup

Ingredients	Makes approximately 4 portions	Makes approximately 10 portions
Red lentils	200 g	500 g
Butter or sunflower oil	40 g	100 g
Carrot	40 g	100 g
Leek	30 g	80 g
Onion	40 g	100 g
Good quality salt	To taste	To taste
White pepper	To taste	To taste
Dry cured bacon	50 g	125 g
White stock (vegetable)	1500 ml	3500 ml
Ripe tomatoes	50 g	125 g
Croûtons	25 g	75 g
Bouquet garni	1 small	1 medium

energy	cal	fat	sat fat	carb	sugar	protein	fibre
1088 kJ	262 kcal	17.6 g	8.2 g	17.2 g	3.3 g	9.4 g	4.9 g

METHOD OF WORK

1 Wash the lentils in several changes of cold water.

2 Place in a saucepan, cover with cold stock, bring to the boil and skim. At this stage refrain from adding any seasoning.

3 Wash, peel and chop the remainder of the ingredients but leave the bacon whole. Sweat them off with the butter or oil and then add to the lentils.

4 Add the remainder of the ingredients including the bouquet garni and simmer gently, continue to skim and allow to simmer until tender (approximately 45 minutes).

5 Remove the bacon and bouquet garni, liquidize and pass through a chinois.

6 Re-boil, check the seasoning and adjust the consistency.

7 Serve with the croûtons.

CHEF'S TIP   Red lentils are used a great deal in Indian cuisine; they are mildly spiced to accompany meat dishes. They are often called dhal, which is a general Hindi term for split lentils.

CHEF'S TIP   This soup can be made from any dried lentil or pulse. For example, yellow split peas, puy lentils, or green and brown lentils. Some of the pulses will need to be soaked prior to cooking.

Tomato and basil soup

Ingredients	Makes approximately 4 portions	Makes approximately 10 portions
Ripe plum tomatoes	400 g	1000 g
White stock (vegetable or chicken)	1000 ml	2500 ml
Onion	80 g	200 g
Leeks	80 g	200 g
Celery	80 g	200 g
Good quality salt	To taste	To taste
White pepper	To taste	To taste
Garlic	1 clove	3 cloves
Olive oil	40 ml	100 ml
Granulated sugar	20 g	50 g
Red wine vinegar	20 ml	50 ml
Smoked bacon rind	40 g	50 ml
Fresh basil leaves and stalks	20 g	50 g

energy	cal	fat	sat fat	carb	sugar	protein	fibre
1095 kJ	265 kcal	23.1 g	7.1 g	12.1 g	10.9 g	2.6 g	3.7 g

METHOD OF WORK

1 Wash, peel, re-wash and roughly chop the vegetables. Place into a saucepan with the olive oil and sweat with the lid firmly placed on the pan.

2 Add the granulated sugar and red wine vinegar, allow to reduce to a light syrup, forming a 'gastrique'.

3 Wash and roughly chop the tomatoes and add them with the basil stalks and allow cooking for 10 minutes before adding the hot white stock.

4 Bring to the boil while stirring occasionally. Add the bacon rind and allow the soup to simmer for 30 minutes, skimming when necessary.

5 Remove the bacon rind, liquidize the soup and pass through a fine chinois.

6 Return to the pan and reboil, add the chopped basil and correct the seasoning and consistency.

7 Serve garnished with a chiffonade of basil and croûtons

CHEF'S TIP When making a gastrique for flavouring tomato soup you can tell if the vinegar has evaporated by waving a hand over the pan and smelling the vapour. Boiling vinegar has a rather acidic smell. The addition of this will sweeten and draw out the flavour of the tomato.

CHEF'S TIP Some of the chopped tomato flesh can be reserved and added after liquidizing to make a more rustic soup. A focaccia croûte placed on the top of the soup and sprinkled with Parmesan makes a hearty lunchtime indulgence.

Vegetable soup
(purée de légumes)

Ingredients	Makes approximately 4 portions	Makes approximately 10 portions
Carrots	80 g	200 g
Onion	80 g	200 g
Leeks	80 g	200 g
Celery	80 g	200 g
Turnip	40 g	100 g
White vegetable stock	1000 ml	2500 ml
Good quality salt	To taste	To taste
White pepper	To taste	To taste
Bouquet garni	1 small	1 medium
Butter	40 g	100 g
White or wholemeal flour	40 g	100 g

energy	cal	fat	sat fat	carb	sugar	protein	fibre
713 kJ	172 kcal	13.1 g	6.6 g	12.0 g	3.4 g	2.3 g	2.7 g

METHOD OF WORK

1 Wash, peel and rewash the vegetables.

2 Roughly chop all the vegetables and sweat them in the butter until soft and translucent.

3 Add the flour to make a loose roux, again without colour being added during the cooking process and allow to cool slightly.

4 Add the hot white vegetable stock and bring to the boil.

5 Add the bouquet garni and allow to simmer for 45 minutes, skim when necessary.

6 Remove the bouquet garni and using a stick blender, liquidize the soup until it is smooth.

7 Pass the soup through a fine chinois.

8 Return to a clean saucepan and bring back to the boil, adjust the seasoning and consistency.

9 Serve with croûtons.

CHEF'S TIP   This soup can be enriched with cream or a liaison of cream and egg yolks to give a cream finish. Alternatively replace half the quantity of the white vegetable stock with a béchamel sauce.

Vegetable soup (Recipe 2)
(purée de légumes)

Ingredients	Makes approximately 4 portions	Makes approximately 10 portions
Named vegetable (e.g. cauliflower, carrot)	200 g	500 g
Onion	50 g	200 g
White of leek	50 g	200 g
Celery	50 g	200 g
White vegetable stock	1000 ml	2500 ml
Good quality salt	To taste	To taste
White pepper	To taste	To taste
Bouquet garni	1 small	1 medium
Butter	40 g	100 g
Potato	80 g	250 g

energy	cal	fat	sat fat	carb	sugar	protein	fibre
659 kJ	159 kcal	13.2 g	6.6 g	7.6 g	2.8 g	2.8 g	2.7 g

METHOD OF WORK

1 Peel, wash and slice all the vegetables except the potatoes. Sweat the vegetables in the butter without colouring.

2 Add the hot stock, sliced potatoes, bouquet garni and allow to simmer for 45 minutes until all ingredients are fully cooked.

3 Remove the bouquet garni and liquidize. Pass the soup through a chinois.

4 Return to a clean pan and bring back to the boil.

5 Adjust the seasoning and consistency and serve with croûtons.

Veloutés

Mushroom velouté

Ingredients	Makes approximately 4 portions	Makes approximately 10 portions
Button mushrooms	400 g	1 kg
Vegetable stock	100 ml	250 ml
Sunflower oil	2 tblspn	5 tblspn
Sliced shallots	1	3
Double cream	200 ml	500 ml
Milk	50 ml	125 ml
Butter	50 g	125 g
Good quality salt	To taste	To taste
White pepper	To taste	To taste

energy	cal	fat	sat fat	carb	sugar	protein	fibre
2379 kJ	578 kcal	61.5 g	25.8 g	2.4 g	2.0 g	3.9 g	2.1 g

METHOD OF WORK

1 Sweat the shallots and mushrooms in oil with no colour until soft.

2 Add the stock and reduce by half.

3 Add the milk and continue to cook for 5 minutes.

4 Place the ingredients into a liquidizer or use a stick blender to achieve a smooth mixture.

5 Add the cream, butter and seasoning to taste.

SOURCING Using the freshest produce will result in a higher quality soup, use the web link below to research seasonal vegetables and produce list of soups that should be produced in:

- spring
- summer
- autumn
- winter.

http://eatseasonably.co.uk

Pea velouté

Ingredients	Makes approximately 4 portions	Makes approximately 10 portions
Frozen peas	400 g	1 kg
Sunflower oil	2 tblspn	5 tblspn
Sliced shallots	1	3
Double cream	200 ml	500 ml
Milk	50 ml	125ml
Butter	50 g	125 g
Good quality salt	To taste	To taste
White pepper	To taste	To taste

energy	cal	fat	sat fat	carb	sugar	protein	fibre
2006 kJ	486 kcal	45.8 g	24.4 g	11.6 g	4.5 g	7.5 g	5.7 g

METHOD OF WORK

1 Blanch the peas in boiling water for 4 minutes then drain well.

2 Sweat the shallots in oil until soft with no colour, then add the peas.

3 Add the milk and continue to cook for 5 minutes.

4 Place the ingredients into a liquidizer or use a stick blender to achieve a smooth mixture.

5 Add the cream, butter and seasoning to taste.

Potages

Green pea soup
(potage saint germain)

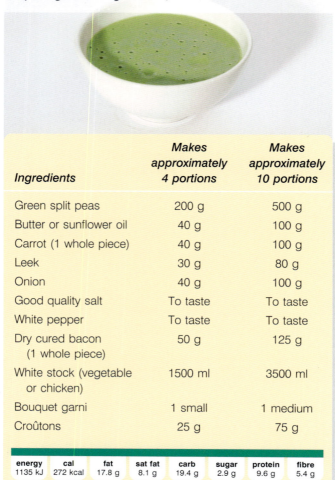

Ingredients	Makes approximately 4 portions	Makes approximately 10 portions
Green split peas	200 g	500 g
Butter or sunflower oil	40 g	100 g
Carrot (1 whole piece)	40 g	100 g
Leek	30 g	80 g
Onion	40 g	100 g
Good quality salt	To taste	To taste
White pepper	To taste	To taste
Dry cured bacon (1 whole piece)	50 g	125 g
White stock (vegetable or chicken)	1500 ml	3500 ml
Bouquet garni	1 small	1 medium
Croûtons	25 g	75 g

energy	cal	fat	sat fat	carb	sugar	protein	fibre
1135 kJ	272 kcal	17.8 g	8.1 g	19.4 g	2.9 g	9.6 g	5.4 g

METHOD OF WORK

1 Wash the peas in several changes of cold water.

2 Place in a deep saucepan, cover with cold stock and bring to the boil. Skim when necessary.

3 Wash, peel and chop the onion and leek and place them into a pan with the fat to sweat them with the whole washed and peeled carrot.

4 Add all the ingredients to the peas, season and simmer gently. As scum forms, skim the surface as required. Allow to simmer until the peas are tender (approximately 1 hour).

5 Remove the bacon, carrot and the bouquet garni. Liquidize the soup and pass through a chinois.

6 Re-boil in a clean pan, season, and correct the consistency of the soup.

7 Serve with croutons to accompany.

Potage paysanne

Ingredients	Makes approximately 4 portions	Makes approximately 10 portions
Unsalted butter	50 g	125 g
Vegetable stock	500 ml	1.25 ltr
Paysanne of celery, onion, turnip, carrot, leek and potatoes	400 g	1 kg
Good quality salt	To taste	To taste
White pepper	To taste	To taste

energy	cal	fat	sat fat	carb	sugar	protein	fibre
587 kJ	142 kcal	12.8 g	7.2 g	6.0 g	2.5 g	1.2 g	2.0 g

METHOD OF WORK

1 Wash the vegetables and drain well.

2 In a thick bottomed pan melt the butter then sweat the paysanne of vegetables for approximately 5 minutes without colour.

3 Add the hot stock and simmer for around 30 minutes.

4 Season to taste and serve with finely chopped parsley.

CHEF'S TIP There are various derived potages made from this green pea soup:

- *Potage lamballe* – As for the green pea soup recipe and garnished with boiled tapioca seed.
- *Potage longchamps* – As for the green pea soup recipe and garnished with broken, cooked vermicelli, chopped sorrel and fresh chervil.
- *Other potages* – Use haricot beans, lentils, red beans and yellow split peas as a replacement for the green split peas.

Cream soups

Cream of chicken soup *(crème de volaille)*

Ingredients	Makes approximately 4 portions	Makes approximately 10 portions
Butter	50 g	125 g
Flour	50 g	125 g
Onion	40 g	100 g
Celery	40 g	100 g
White of leek	40 g	100 g
Good quality salt	To taste	To taste
White pepper	To taste	To taste
White chicken stock	800 ml	2000 ml
Cooked white chicken meat (garnish)	45 g	110 g
Single cream	200 ml	550 ml
Bouquet garni	1 small	1 medium

energy	cal	fat	sat fat	carb	sugar	protein	fibre
1101 kJ	265 kcal	20.7 g	12.8 g	12.7 g	2.6 g	6.9 g	1.4 g

METHOD OF WORK

1 Wash and chop the vegetables into a mirepoix. Sweat the chopped vegetables in melted butter in a large saucepan without colour.

2 Add the flour, stirring and cooking over a moderate heat to make a roux without colour and then allow to cool slightly.

3 Gradually add the hot chicken stock, stir and bring to the boil.

4 Season well with the salt and pepper and add the bouquet garni.

5 Simmer for 45 minutes, skimming the surface of the soup when necessary.

6 Remove the bouquet garni and liquidize the soup with a blender. Pass through a fine strainer into a clean pan and re-boil.

7 Add the single cream and correct the seasoning and the consistency.

8 Dice the cooked chicken meat and add to the soup. Serve immediately.

CHEF'S TIP Cooked leg and thigh meat adds more flavour as a garnish than white meat. It can also be more cost-effective to use than breast meat. This can be used as an alternative to create a hearty soup.

Cream of spinach soup
(crème d'epinard)

Ingredients	Makes approximately 4 portions	Makes approximately 10 portions
Spinach	300 g	750 g
Butter	40 g	100 g
Onion	40 g	100 g
Potato	80 g	200 g
Leek	40 g	100 g
Good quality salt	To taste	To taste
White pepper	To taste	To taste
White stock (chicken or vegetable)	1000 ml	2500 ml
Grated nutmeg	To taste	To taste
Single cream	200 ml	550 ml
Bouquet garni	1 small	1 medium

energy	cal	fat	sat fat	carb	sugar	protein	fibre
876 kJ	212 kcal	18.7 g	11.5 g	7.3 g	3.0 g	4.1 g	2.6 g

METHOD OF WORK

1   Wash, peel and finely dice the onion, leek and potatoes into brunoise. Wash the spinach well in several changes of water to remove any sand, grit and dirt pockets.

2   Melt the butter in a large heavy based saucepan and add the brunoise of vegetables. Sweat gently for 10 minutes.

3   Prepare a large saucepan of boiling water and plunge the spinach into the water to blanch for a few seconds. Drain immediately in a colander and refresh the spinach in iced water while the remainder of the ingredients are sweating.

4   Add the hot white stock and bouquet garni to the vegetables and simmer for a further 15 minutes.

5   Next add the spinach and the grated nutmeg.

6   Simmer for another 5 minutes and remove from the heat.

7   Take out the bouquet garni and liquidize the soup until smooth.

8   Pass the soup through a chinois, and re-boil and add the cream. Correct the seasoning and consistency.

9   Serve garnished with a julienne of cooked spinach a generous portion of croûtons.

Chowders

Chicken and sweetcorn chowder

Ingredients	Makes approximately 4 portions	Makes approximately 10 portions
Diced lean raw chicken	80 g	200 g
Onion	60 g	150 g
Celery	40 g	100 g
White of leek	40 g	100 g
Sweetcorn (fresh, frozen or tinned)	80 g	200 g
Potato	100 g	250 g
White chicken stock	1000 ml	2500 ml
White wine	40 ml	100 ml
Butter	40 g	100 g
Salted water biscuits	20 g	50 g
Good quality salt	To taste	To taste
White pepper	To taste	To taste

energy	cal	fat	sat fat	carb	sugar	protein	fibre
821 kJ	197 kcal	10.4 g	5.7 g	15.2 g	2.7 g	8.6 g	2.4 g

METHOD OF WORK

1   Wash, peel, re-wash and chop all the vegetables and sweat in the butter for 5 minutes without colour.

2   Add the pieces of chicken and continue to cook for a further 4–5 minutes.

3   Add the white wine, white chicken stock and sweetcorn. Bring to the boil.

4   Simmer for 30 minutes.

5   Using a stick blender, lightly purée the soup, to allow for an uneven texture (with some chicken pieces and sweetcorn still remaining).

6   Correct the seasoning and consistency.

7   Serve with crushed salted water biscuits liberally strewn on top of the chowder. Chopped parsley is optional.

CHEF'S TIP   Chowders were originally made by the early settlers in America. The differed from other soups because they used salt pork and ship's biscuits. Today most chowders do not include biscuits, but generally have crackers sprinkled on top.

Clam chowder

Ingredients	Makes approximately 4 portions	Makes approximately 10 portions
Fresh clams	400 g	1000 g
Pancetta	80 g	200 g
Onion	40 g	100 g
Butter	20 g	50 g
Leek	40 g	100 g
Celery	40 g	40 g
Potato	200 g	500 g
Good quality salt	To taste	To taste
White pepper	To taste	To taste
Fish stock	1000 ml	2500 ml
Double cream	100 ml	250 ml
Bouquet garni	1 small	1 medium

energy	cal	fat	sat fat	carb	sugar	protein	fibre
2035 kJ	490 kcal	30.3 g	15.3 g	16.6 g	1.5 g	35.7 g	1.4 g

METHOD OF WORK

1 Wash the clams well to purge all grit and sand in several water changes.

2 Place the clams into a saucepan with the fish stock and placing a lid over the pan cook the clams until their shells open.

3 Carefully remove the clams and remove from the shells. Trim and chop the clams and retain to one side. Let the remaining fish stock stand for 10 minutes to let any grit and sand from the clams settle at the bottom. Strain very carefully and reserve for later use.

4 Remove the rind from the pancetta and cut into lardons. Melt the butter and cook the lardons slowly until a light golden brown colour has been achieved.

5 Add the washed and finely diced vegetables and sweat with the lardons.

6 Wash, peel and cut the potatoes into 4 mm dice and add to the vegetables in the pan, season lightly.

7 Add the stock and bouquet garni, bring to the boil and simmer for 30 minutes.

8 Add the clams and simmer for a further 5 minutes.

9 Finish by adding the cream and correcting the seasoning. Serve with crushed salted water biscuits, chopped parsley and a sprinkling of paprika if desired.

CHEF'S TIP Clams can be stored overnight and have some of the sand purged by covering in cold water and adding some oat flakes to the water. This feeds them, helps to remove further sandy deposits and can plump them up a little.

CHEF'S TIP The addition of poached and flaked smoked haddock at stage 7 gives a very different finish and flavour to the chowder. The addition of 40 g per portion of tomato concassée at the same stage will enhance the appearance.

Broths

Chicken broth

Ingredients	Makes approximately 4 portions	Makes approximately 10 portions
Boiling fowl	400 g (¼)	800 g (½)
Carrot	50 g	125 g
Onion	50 g	125 g
Turnip	50 g	125 g
Leek	50 g	125 g
Celery	50 g	125 g
Long grain rice (Basmati)	20 g	50 g
Good quality salt	To taste	To taste
White pepper	To taste	To taste
White chicken stock	1250 ml	3250 ml
Bouquet garni	1 small	1 medium
Fresh chopped parsley	For garnish	For garnish

energy	cal	fat	sat fat	carb	sugar	protein	fibre
1065 kJ	254 kcal	11.7 g	3.1 g	7.3 g	2.6 g	26.8 g	2.0 g

METHOD OF WORK

1   Ensure the boiling fowl is cleaned and place into a saucepan and cover with the chicken stock. Simmer the boiling fowl and bouquet garni in the stock for approximately 1 hour until a rich, aromatic stock has been formed. Skim as required.

2   Wash, peel, re-wash and cut the vegetables into paysanne.

3   Remove the chicken and bouquet garni.

4   Add the vegetables and rice and simmer until cooked. This may take about 20 minutes.

5   Remove the meat from the chicken and cut into small dice and add to the broth.

6   Re-boil and skim, season and add the chopped, washed parsley.

7   This can be served with sippets as a garnish.

CHEF'S TIP The use of a boiling fowl on the bone when cooking the stock will enhance the chicken flavour of this broth.

Mutton broth

Ingredients	Makes approximately 4 portions	Makes approximately 10 portions
Scrag end of mutton	200 g	500 g
Carrot	50 g	125 g
Onion	50 g	125 g
Turnip	50 g	125 g
Leek	50 g	125 g
Celery	50 g	125 g
Pearl barley	20 g	50 g
Good quality salt	To taste	To taste
White pepper	To taste	To taste
White mutton or lamb stock	1250 ml	3250 ml
Bouquet garni	1 small	1 medium
Fresh chopped parsley	For garnish	For garnish

energy	cal	fat	sat fat	carb	sugar	protein	fibre
1616 kJ	387 kcal	30.4 g	13.4 g	4.1 g	2.1 g	23.9 g	1.6 g

METHOD OF WORK

1   Place the mutton into a saucepan and cover with cold water.

2   Bring to the boil and immediately remove from the heat and wash under running cold water.

3   Place the mutton into a clean pan, cover with the cold stock and bring to the boil once again and skim as necessary.

4   Wash the pearl barley and add to the simmering mutton broth and continue to simmer for 1 hour.

5   Wash and dice the vegetables into a 2 mm brunoise and add to the broth.

6   Add the bouquet garni and season well, allow to simmer for a further 20 minutes, skimming when necessary.

7   Remove the meat, cool and remove the fat, and cut the meat into a small dice, and return to the broth.

8   Correct the seasoning and add the washed and chopped parsley and serve.

Scotch broth

Ingredients	Makes approximately 4 portions	Makes approximately 10 portions
Turnip	40 g	100 g
Carrot	40 g	100 g
Leek	40 g	100 g
Celery	40 g	40 g
Pearl barley	20 g	50 g
Good quality salt	To taste	To taste
White pepper	To taste	To taste
White stock (vegetable or chicken)	1250 ml	3250 ml
Bouquet garni	1 small	1 medium
Fresh chopped parsley	For garnish	For garnish

energy	cal	fat	sat fat	carb	sugar	protein	fibre
301 kJ	73 kcal	5.7 g	1.7 g	4.4 g	2.2 g	1.2 g	2.1 g

METHOD OF WORK

1 Wash the barley and place in a large saucepan. Add the stock, bring to the boil and simmer for 1 hour, skimming occasionally.

2 Cut the vegetables into a 3 mm brunoise and add to the broth, season and skim when necessary.

3 Simmer for approximately 30 minutes, once again skimming when necessary.

4 Adjust the seasoning and serve with chopped parsley.

CHEF'S TIP Traditionally a white vegetable stock is used for this recipe, but to add further flavour some recipes call for a white chicken or beef stock instead.

Consommés (clear soups)

Beef consommé

Ingredients	Makes approximately 4 portions	Makes approximately 10 portions
Minced shin of beef	200 g	2500 g
Carrot	40 g	100 g
Onion	40 g	100 g
Celery	40 g	100 g
Leek	40 g	100 g
Bay leaf	1	2
Fresh thyme	1 sprig	2 sprigs
Good quality salt	To taste	To taste
Black peppercorns	4	4
Cold brown beef stock	200 ml	500 ml
Egg whites	2	5
Hot brown beef stock	1000 ml	2500 ml

energy	cal	fat	sat fat	carb	sugar	protein	fibre
1197 kJ	286 kcal	20.1 g	8.1 g	2.6 g	1.8 g	22.5 g	1.2 g

METHOD OF WORK

1 Wash, peel and chop all of the vegetables into macédoine.

2 Thoroughly mix all of the minced beef shin, vegetables, herbs, egg whites, cold stock and seasonings together (this is called the clarification) and place in a refrigerator for 30 minutes.

3 Place the hot stock in a large saucepan or preferably a stock pot with a tap at the base.

4 Mix the clarification well with the hot stock and bring to the boil as quickly as possible. Stir one more time while boiling and lower the heat so that the consommé is simmering gently. Avoid disturbing the clarification.

5 As this sets on top this is called a float.

6 Allow to simmer gently for 2½ hours.

7 Make a small hole in the centre so the consommé can be removed with a ladle.

8 Strain through a dampened, folded muslin cloth. Remove all fat deposits using kitchen paper placed on the surface of the consommé to soak it up.

9 Adjust the seasoning with only salt and check the colour of the consommé, which should be done by placing a small amount of the soup onto a clean, white plate. It should be a delicate amber colour without any traces of fat.

10 Degrease again if required. Bring to the boil.

11 Serve in a warm consommé cup plain or with a named garnish.

CHEF'S TIP A consommé should be crystal clear and light amber in colour. The clarification process is produced by the coagulation of the minced raw meat and the egg white (albumen), which rises to the top of the hot liquid, attaching itself to other solids to clear the liquid beneath the coagulated surface.

CHEF'S TIP Cloudiness in a consommé is due to:
- Greasy and poor quality stock.
- Imperfect coagulation of the clarification.
- Not allowing the soup to settle before straining.
- Saucepan or muslin cloth not clean.
- Traces of grease or starch deposits in the pan or on utensils.
- Impurities have been mixed with the liquid through whisking during simmering.

Step-by-step: Making a consommé

1. Adding the clarification (minced chicken, vegetables and egg whites) to the base stock.

2. Whisking the clarification into the stock and allowing it to gently come to the boil.

3. Making one final stir before reducing the heat to a gentle simmer, this will allow the liquid to clarify and the protein to form a float – removing the sediment.

4. A float on top of the stock, gently simmering which will produce a crystal clear consommé.

Consommé garnishes

Consommé is named on the menu after its garnishes. The following are a selection of the more common garnishes:

Consommé brunoise: A fine brunoise of cooked carrot, onion, celery and leek. Add to the soup at the last minute: use approximately 20 g per portion.

Consommé celestine: Savoury pancake cut into fine julienne. Add at the last minute approximately 10 g per portion.

Consommé julienne: Fine julienne of cooked carrot, onion celery and leek. Add to the soup at the last minute using approximately 20 g per portion.

Consommé royale: Savoury egg custard cooked gently in a bain-marie and cut into neat shapes served at approximately 20 g per portion.

Consommé vermicelli: Cooked broken vermicelli pasta served at approximately 10 g per portion.

Chicken consommé

Left to Right – Brunoise, paysanne, vermicelli, celestine and julienne

Ingredients	Makes approximately 4 portions	Makes approximately 10 portions
Minced chicken	200 g	2500 g
Carrot	40 g	100 g
Onion	40 g	100 g
Celery	40 g	100 g
Leek	40 g	100 g
Bay leaf	1	2
Fresh thyme	1 sprig	2 sprigs
Good quality salt	To taste	To taste
Black peppercorns	4	4
Cold brown chicken stock	200 ml	500 ml
Egg whites	2	5
Hot brown chicken stock	1000 ml	2500 ml

energy	cal	fat	sat fat	carb	sugar	protein	fibre
638 kJ	152 kcal	5.1 g	0.8 g	6.7 g	5.3 g	18.8 g	3.0 g

METHOD OF WORK

1 Wash, peel and chop all of the vegetables into macédoine.

2 Thoroughly mix all of the minced chicken, vegetables, herbs, egg whites, cold stock and seasonings together (this is called the clarification) and place in a refrigerator for 30 minutes.

3 Place the hot stock in a large saucepan or preferably a stock pot with a tap at the base.

4 Mix the clarification well with the hot stock and bring to the boil as quickly as possible. Stir one more time while boiling and lower the heat so that the consommé is simmering gently. Avoid disturbing the clarification.

5 As this sets on top this is called a float.

6 Allow to simmer gently for 2½ hours.

7 Make a small hole in the centre so the consommé can be removed with a ladle.

8 Strain through a dampened, folded muslin cloth. Remove all fat deposits using kitchen paper placed on the surface of the consommé to soak it up.

9 Adjust the seasoning with only salt and check the colour of the consommé, which should be done by placing a small amount of the soup onto a clean, white plate. It should be a delicate amber colour without any traces of fat.

10 Degrease again if required. Bring to the boil.

11 Serve in a warm consommé cup plain or with a named garnish.

Bisques

Crab bisque *(bisque de crebbe)*

Ingredients	Makes approximately 4 portions	Makes approximately 10 portions
Raw crab (breakers – broken claws, etc.)	500 g	900 g
Butter	40 g	250 g
Carrot	40 g	250 g
Onion	40 g	250 g
Celery	40 g	250 g
Leek	40 g	250 g
Long grain rice	50 g	125 g
Tomato purée	20 g	50 g
Brandy	50 ml	125 ml
Fresh thyme	1 sprig	2 sprigs
Good quality salt	To taste	To taste
White peppercorns	4	10
Fish stock	1000 ml	2500 ml
Dry white wine	80 ml	200 ml
Bouquet garni	1 small	1 medium
Cayenne pepper	To taste	To taste
Unsalted butter	80 g	200 g
Double cream	40 ml	100 ml

energy	cal	fat	sat fat	carb	sugar	protein	fibre
1838 kJ	444 kcal	34.7 g	19.8 g	6.9 g	2.7 g	15.5 g	1.0 g

METHOD OF WORK

1 Take the crabs and smash into small pieces, reserving any liquid.

2 Peel, wash and dice the vegetables. Sweat in the half the unsalted butter in a large saucepan.

3 Add the lobster and cook at a slightly higher temperature.

4 Raise the heat and add the brandy. Shake the pan and flambé until the flames disappear.

5 Add the tomato purée and cayenne pepper.

6 Add the fish stock, rice, bouquet garni, fresh thyme and wine. Bring to the boil and simmer, skimming when necessary, for 45 minutes.

7 Remove the bouquet garni and liquidize the soup. Pass through a chinois into a clean pan and adjust the seasoning and consistency.

8 Re-boil and add the rest of the unsalted butter and double cream. Check the consistency.

9 Serve with crushed water biscuits.

Lobster bisque *(bisque de homard)*

Ingredients	Makes approximately 4 portions	Makes approximately 10 portions
Raw lobster (breakers – broken claws, etc.)	500 g	900 g
Butter	40 g	250 g
Carrot	40 g	250 g
Onion	40 g	250 g
Celery	40 g	250 g
Leek	40 g	250 g
Long grain rice	50 g	125 g
Tomato purée	20 g	50 g
Brandy	50 ml	125 ml
Fresh thyme	1 sprig	2 sprigs
Good quality salt	To taste	To taste
White peppercorns	4	10
Fish stock	1000 ml	2500 ml
Dry white wine	80 ml	200 ml
Bouquet garni	1 small	1 medium
Cayenne pepper	To taste	To taste
Unsalted butter	80 g	200 g
Double cream	40 ml	100 ml

energy	cal	fat	sat fat	carb	sugar	protein	fibre
1801 kJ	434 kcal	33.1 g	19.6 g	6.9 g	2.7 g	17.0 g	1.0 g

METHOD OF WORK

1 Take the lobster and smash into small pieces, reserving any liquid.

2 Peel, wash and dice the vegetables. Sweat in half the unsalted butter in a large saucepan.

3 Add the lobster and cook at a slightly higher temperature.

4 Raise the heat and add the brandy. Shake the pan and flambé until the flames disappear.

5 Add the tomato purée and cayenne pepper.

6 Add the fish stock, rice, bouquet garni, fresh thyme and wine. Bring to the boil and simmer, skimming when necessary, for 45 minutes.

7 Remove the bouquet garni and liquidize the soup. Pass through a chinois into a clean pan and adjust the seasoning and consistency.

8 Re-boil and add the rest of the unsalted butter and double cream. Check the consistency.

9 Serve with crushed water biscuits.

Prawn bisque (bisque de crevettes)

Ingredients	Makes approximately 4 portions	Makes approximately 10 portions
Shell-on prawns (crevettes roses)	300 g	750 g
Butter	40 g	250 g
Carrot	40 g	250 g
Onion	40 g	250 g
Celery	40 g	250 g
Leek	40 g	250 g
Long grain rice	50 g	125 g
Tomato purée	20 g	50 g
Brandy	50 ml	125 ml
Fresh thyme	1 sprig	2 sprigs
Good quality salt	To taste	To taste
White peppercorns	4	10
Fish stock	1000 ml	2500 ml
Dry white wine	80 ml	200 ml
Bouquet garni	1 small	1 medium
Cayenne pepper	To taste	To taste
Unsalted butter	80 g	200 g
Double cream	40 ml	100 ml

energy	cal	fat	sat fat	carb	sugar	protein	fibre
1724 kJ	416 kcal	32.5 g	19.6 g	6.9 g	2.7 g	13.4 g	1.3 g

METHOD OF WORK

1 Peel, wash and dice the vegetables. Sweat in half the unsalted butter in a large saucepan.

2 Add the prawns and cook at a slightly higher temperature.

3 Raise the heat and add the brandy. Shake the pan and flambé until the flames disappear.

4 Add the tomato purée and cayenne pepper.

5 Add the fish stock, rice, bouquet garni, fresh thyme and wine. Bring to the boil and simmer, skimming when necessary, for 45 minutes.

6 Remove the bouquet garni and liquidize the soup. Pass through a chinois into a clean pan and adjust the seasoning and consistency.

7 Re-boil and add the rest of the unsalted butter and double cream. Check the consistency.

8 Serve with crushed water biscuits.

CHEF'S TIP The addition of a few strands of saffron during the simmering will give this soup a rich golden-tinged colour.

Foreign and miscellaneous

Chicken noodle soup with spiced dumplings

Ingredients	Makes approximately 4 portions	Makes approximately 10 portions
Grated fresh ginger	20 g	50 g
Finely sliced peppers	1	2–3
Good quality salt	5 g	10 g
White pepper	To taste	To taste
Brown chicken stock	1000 ml	2500 ml
Egg noodles	80 g	200 g
Finely sliced red chilli pepper	1	2
Dark soy sauce	1 tblspn	2 tblspn
Spiced dumpling Ingredients		
Minced chicken	100 g	250 g
Pork sausage meat	100 g	250 g
Crushed garlic	1 clove	2–3 cloves
Szechwan pepper	pinch	2 pinches
Salt and pepper to taste	To taste	To taste

energy 811 kJ	cal 194 kcal	fat 9.9 g	sat fat 2.6 g	carb 12.2 g	sugar 5.9 g	protein 13.8 g	fibre 3.3 g

METHOD OF WORK

1 Mix all the ingredients together to make the dumplings and season well. Form into small round dumplings of 10 g each. Place on a tray and cover with plastic film before resting in the refrigerator for 1 hour to allow the spice to infuse with the chicken.

2 Bring a large pan of water to the boil. Take the pan off the heat and put the noodles into the hot water to soak for 15 minutes.

3 Prepare the ingredients for the soup mix them together in a saucepan, bring to the boil and simmer for 10 minutes, skimming occasionally.

4 Add the dumplings and simmer gently until they are cooked, this should take approximately 8 minutes.

5 Heat the noodles and place a portion in each soup bowl for service.

6 Pour over the soup making sure to distribute the dumplings evenly and serve immediately.

CHEF'S TIP This clear soup can be thickened to give it more body. Arrowroot, cornflour or kuzu (which is of Japanese origin) can be used, but kuzu will thicken almost like gelatine, giving body to clear and hot soup.

Cock a leekie

Ingredients	Makes approximately 4 portions	Makes approximately 10 portions
Boiling fowl	400 g (¼)	800 g (½)
White stock (chicken or veal)	1250 ml	3250 ml
Bouquet garni	1 small	1 medium
Onion	50 g	100 g
Butter	40 g	100 g
Leek	150 g	400 g
Good quality salt	To taste	To taste
White pepper	To taste	To taste
Cooked and stoned prunes	4	10

energy	cal	fat	sat fat	carb	sugar	protein	fibre
1512 kJ	367 kcal	20.0 g	8.3 g	18.2 g	17.5 g	26.7 g	3.3 g

METHOD OF WORK

1 Simmer the boiling fowl and bouquet garni in the stock for 1 hour until a rich, aromatic stock has been formed. Skim when required.

2 Carefully remove the chicken and set aside to cool.

3 Cut the leek into a julienne and the onion into a fine dice and sweat in the butter.

4 Add the stock and simmer until the leek and onion are cooked and tender.

5 Remove the meat from the chicken and cut into julienne. Cut the prunes into a julienne and add both to the broth.

6 Re-boil and skim, season and serve.

CHEF'S TIP Care must be taken not to over boil the soup just before serving. This will cause the clear soup to become cloudy and discolour. Also ensure that the fat from the boiling fowl has been drained before cutting it into julienne and adding to the soup.

French onion soup
(soupe à l'oignon)

Ingredients	Makes approximately 4 portions	Makes approximately 10 portions
Butter	40 g	100 g
Onion	800 g	2000 g
Garlic (optional)	1 clove	2 cloves
Good quality salt	To taste	To taste
White pepper	To taste	To taste
Brown stock	1000 ml	2500 ml
Gruyere cheese	50 g	125 g
Parmesan cheese	40 g	100 g
Bread flute	1 small	1 medium

energy	cal	fat	sat fat	carb	sugar	protein	fibre
1630 kJ	390 kcal	27.9 g	14.7 g	16.6 g	6.3 g	18.5 g	3.7 g

METHOD OF WORK

1 Peel, halve and finely slice the onions.

2 Melt the butter in a thick based pan, add the sliced onions and cook over a gentle heat until soft and slightly caramelized.

3 Add the brown stock and bring to the boil simmer for 10 minutes.

4 Slice and toast the flutes.

5 Finely grate and mix the two cheeses together.

6 Correct the seasoning of the soup and pour into oven proof earthenware cups or marmites.

7 Layer the top with the toasted flutes. Sprinkle liberally with the cheese and gratinate under a salamander until bubbling and brown.

8 Serve immediately on a dish.

Note: The flutes can be added after if preferred.

CHEF'S TIP Onions are rich in sulphur and vitamin C. The substance that makes the eyes water when cutting an onion is called allyl sulphide and it disappears on cooking. To peel onions in relative comfort, place them in a freezer 10 minutes prior to peeling them.

Gazpacho

Ingredients	Makes approximately 4 portions	Makes approximately 10 portions
Chives, fresh	5 g	15 g
Chervil, fresh	5 g	15 g
Parsley, fresh	5 g	15 g
Basil, fresh	5 g	15 g
Garlic clove	2	4
Red pepper	½	1
Green pepper	½	1
Bread crumbs	40 g	100 g
Plum tomatos	3	8
Olive oil	80 ml	200 ml
lemon	1	2 ½
Water or white vegetable stock	500 ml	1250 ml
Onion	20 g	55 g
Cucumber; diced	80 g	200 g
Sea salt, mill pepper	To taste	To taste
Garnish		
Olives	40 g	100 g
Green peppers	40 g	100 g
Tomato concassée	40 g	100 g
Shallots	40 g	100 g
Croutons	40 g	100 g
Red wine vinegar	40 ml	100 ml

energy	cal	fat	sat fat	carb	sugar	protein	fibre
1277 kJ	307 kcal	22.5 g	3.3 g	22.7 g	6.1 g	4.4 g	3.9 g

METHOD OF WORK

1. Wash and chop the herbs, then blend thoroughly with the garlic.

2. Peel and deseed the tomatoes and cut roughly, deseed and chop the peppers in the same way.

3. Liquidize the blended herbs, peppers and tomatoes in a food processor, adding the oil very slowly, and the lemon juice. Add the cold water or white vegetables stock.

4. Peel, wash and cut the onion as finely as possible. Peel, deseed and dice the cucumber and add to the soup.

5. Season and mix in the breadcrumbs. Chill for at least 4 hours before serving.

6. Serve accompanied by small bowls of chopped olives, shallots, green peppers, tomato concassée, croutons and red wine vinegar.

Minestrone soup

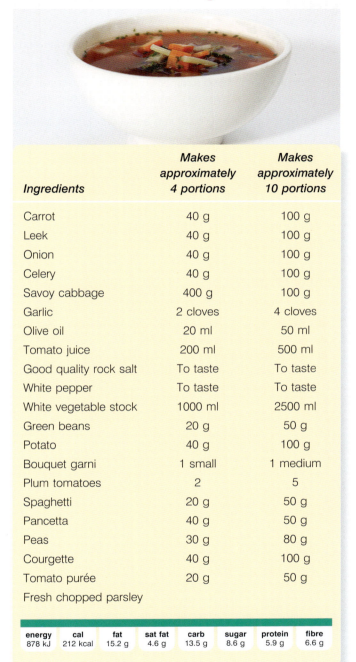

Ingredients	Makes approximately 4 portions	Makes approximately 10 portions
Carrot	40 g	100 g
Leek	40 g	100 g
Onion	40 g	100 g
Celery	40 g	100 g
Savoy cabbage	400 g	100 g
Garlic	2 cloves	4 cloves
Olive oil	20 ml	50 ml
Tomato juice	200 ml	500 ml
Good quality rock salt	To taste	To taste
White pepper	To taste	To taste
White vegetable stock	1000 ml	2500 ml
Green beans	20 g	50 g
Potato	40 g	100 g
Bouquet garni	1 small	1 medium
Plum tomatoes	2	5
Spaghetti	20 g	50 g
Pancetta	40 g	50 g
Peas	30 g	80 g
Courgette	40 g	100 g
Tomato purée	20 g	50 g
Fresh chopped parsley		

energy	cal	fat	sat fat	carb	sugar	protein	fibre
878 kJ	212 kcal	15.2 g	4.6 g	13.5 g	8.6 g	5.9 g	6.6 g

METHOD OF WORK

1 Wash and peel the vegetables with half of the garlic and cut into paysanne.

2 Sweat the vegetables without colour in the olive oil in a saucepan with a lid placed on top.

3 Add the white stock, bouquet garni, season well and simmer for approx 25 minutes, skimming occasionally.

4 Break the spaghetti into 2 cm lengths, wash and peel and cut the potatoes in paysanne. Add to the soup.

5 Create a concassée with the plum tomatoes. Add to the soup and simmer gently until the vegetables almost cooked.

6 Add the tomato purée.

7 Add the washed green beans cut into diamonds, the washed courgette in paysanne and the peas and simmer for a further 8 minutes.

8 Meanwhile, mince the pancetta, parsley and the rest of the garlic and form into a paste.

9 Mould the paste into tablets the size of a marble and drop into the simmering soup.

10 Remove the bouquet garni and correct the seasoning. Serve with shaved parmesan and toasted flutes.

CHEF'S TIP There are as many variations to minestrone soup as there are regions, towns, villages and households in Italy. Some use rice, potatoes or different pastas according to where you are geographically in Italy. Others use aubergine and more courgette and some use more or less tomatoes or garlic. Minestrone is a hearty soup that is traditionally used as a main course and lends itself to interpretation.

Roasted mediterranean vegetable soup

Ingredients	Makes approximately 4 portions	Makes approximately 10 portions
Pepper (red, yellow and green)	1 whole	5 whole
Courgette	100 g	250 g
Red onion	100 g	250 g
Plum tomatoes	2 in number	5 in number
Aubergines	100 g	250 g
Garlic	1 clove	3 cloves
Clear honey	40 g	80 g
Tomato juice	200 ml	500 ml
Good quality rock salt	To taste	To taste
White pepper	To taste	To taste
White vegetable stock	2000 ml	5000 ml
Bouquet garni	1 small	1 medium
Fresh basil	20 g	100 g
Focaccia bread	160 g	400 g
Olive oil	40 ml	100 ml
Pecorino cheese	40 g	100 g

energy	cal	fat	sat fat	carb	sugar	protein	fibre
3137 kJ	748 kcal	42.6 g	8.3 g	81.7 g	23.3 g	14.0 g	11.1 g

METHOD OF WORK

1 Pre-heat an oven to 230 °C.

2 Wash and chop the peppers, courgettes, aubergines, garlic and onions into a macedoine.

3 Mix with the honey and half of the washed and chopped basil. Pour over half the olive oil, season well with the salt and pepper, and place in the oven to roast for approximately 10 minutes or until all the ingredients are golden in colour.

4 Place the roasted vegetables in a large saucepan and add the stock and tomato juice.

5 Bring to the boil and simmer until all the vegetables are just cooked, this will take approximately 15 minutes.

6 Chop the remaining basil into a chiffonade and add to the soup.

7 Meanwhile, break the focaccia into chunky pieces of about 2 cm, drizzle with olive oil, lightly season with the rock salt and pepper and bake in the oven until golden and crisp.

8 Serve the soup topped with shaved pecorino cheese and the chunky croûtons or julienne of peppers.

CHEF'S TIP The variations of this soup are limited only to the chef's imagination. For example:

- Add toasted pine nuts to vary the flavour and texture.
- Add fennel to the roasted vegetables.
- Add seasonal squashes.
- Add a selection of cooked beans such as borlotti, Lima or broad beans.

Thai chicken soup

Ingredients	Makes approximately 4 portions	Makes approximately 10 portions
Galangal	200 g	500 g
Lemongrass stalks	4	9
Lime leaves	4	9
Chicken leg	1 whole	3 whole
Cold water	500 ml	1500 ml
Small red chillies	2	5
Coconut milk	1000 ml	2600 ml
Nam pla	1 tblspn	4 tblspn
Limes	3	7
Spring onions	2	6
Good quality salt	5 g	10 g
White pepper	Pinch	Pinch
Fresh coriander	20 g	55 g

energy	cal	fat	sat fat	carb	sugar	protein	fibre
2489 kJ	602 kcal	49.5 g	36.9 g	25.5 g	8.6 g	15.4 g	4.6 g

METHOD OF WORK

1 Peel, wash and dice the galangal. Cut the lemongrass into 1 cm lengths. Wash the lime leaves and finely chop the spring onions. Run the back of a heavy knife against the lime leaves and the lemon grass to help obtain a good infusi during cooking.

2 Place the galangal, lemon grass, lime leaves, chicken and water into a large saucepan and bring to the boil. Simmer for 30 minutes, skimming occasionally if required.

3 Once the chicken has cooked, remove it from the cooking liquor, cool and then cut the meat into small dice. Reserve to one side.

4 Add the chillies and then add the coconut milk. Heat slowly but do not let the soup reach boiling point. This will begin to infuse flavours and the heat should be maintained for 3–4 minutes.

5 Pass the soup into a clean pan, retain the chillies and cut into a fine julienne. Add the nam pla, lime juice from the limes, spring onions, chopped coriander and chicken.

6 Check the seasoning and consistency and serve with the chilli julienne as garnish.

CHEF'S TIP Coconut milk will separate if it is heated for too long and will rise to the top of the surface of the soup when cooled. If this happens, place the liquid into a blender with some of the chicken and blend until it becomes homogenous.

Vichyssoise

Ingredients	Makes approximately 4 portions	Makes approximately 10 portions
Butter	10 g	50 g
Potatoes	400 g	1000 g
White of leek	100 g	250 g
Onion	80 g	200 g
White stock (chicken or vegetable)	500 ml	1250 ml
Fresh milk	200 ml	500 ml
Bouquet garni	1 small	1 medium
Double cream	40 ml	100 ml
Good quality salt	To taste	To taste
Ground white pepper	To taste	To taste
Fresh chives	10 g	30 g

energy	cal	fat	sat fat	carb	sugar	protein	fibre
788 kJ	189 kcal	8.6 g	5.2 g	24.5 g	4.7 g	4.2 g	2.8 g

METHOD OF WORK

1 Peel and wash the onion and chop into a macédoine with the washed leek.

2 Melt the butter in a large saucepan and sweat the onion and leek in the butter until soft and translucent.

3 Meanwhile, peel, wash and chop the potatoes into a 1 cm dice.

4 Add the potatoes, hot stock, milk and bouquet garni to the leeks and onion.

5 Season well and bring to the boil. Allowing to simmer for approximately 45 minutes or until the potato is completely cooked. Skim the surface of the soup as required.

6 Remove the bouquet garni and liquidize the soup with a stick blender until smooth. Pass through a fine chinois.

7 Allow to chill completely, and then correct the seasoning. Use the cream to correct the consistency. Serve well chilled with the chopped fresh chives.

Guest Chef

Cullen skink

Chef *David Keir* **Centre** *Aberdeen College*

The name 'Cullen skink' comes from the fishing village of Cullen, in Morayshire. 'Skink' is a soup made originally from a shin of beef. But in this recipe for a rich tasty soup, the main ingredient is Finnan haddock. It also has potatoes, onions and milk in the recipe and is finished with parsley and cream. It can either be served with oatcakes or butteries. It can be served either as a starter or as a meal in itself.

Ingredients	Makes 3–4 portions
Finnan haddock	1 large
Onion (peeled and chopped)	1 large
Potatoes (peeled and chopped)	750 g
Butter	25 g
Milk (full fat)	450 ml
To finish the soup	
Double cream	100 ml
Salt and freshly ground black pepper	To taste
Parsley chopped	To taste

METHOD OF WORK

1 Place the Finnan haddock in a stainless steel pan with enough cold water to just cover the fish.

2 Bring the water to the boil and gently simmer for 5–10 minutes until the fish is just cooked.

3 Take off the stove, cover and set aside for 20 minutes.

4 Gently take out the fish, skin the haddock and remove all the bones. Flake into large pieces, cover and set aside until the potatoes are cooked.

5 Using the same pan and cooking liquor from the fish add the onions and potatoes, cover and cook for about 15–20 minutes, until the vegetables are soft.

6 Take the pan from the stove and roughly mash the potatoes and onions with the butter. Do not mash until smooth, as you need some texture in the finished soup.

7 Add the milk and bring to the boil then simmer for a couple of minutes.

8 Add the fish and cream then reheat gently for 3–4 minutes until hot. Season lightly with salt and pepper, serve in warm bowls, sprinkle with some chopped parsley.

9 Serve with Aberdeen butteries (rowies).

Recipes

PULSES

Black eyed peas and red lentil
   curry   189
Steamed lemon rice with borlotti
   beans   190
Broad bean bruschetta with tomato
   and oregano   190
Cassoulet   191
Chickpea stew with red onion
   and chilli peppers   192
Mushy peas   193
Stuffed plum tomatoes with rice
   and peas   193
Sweet potato and chick pea falafel with
   a mint and lime dip   194

GRAINS

Cornbread   199
Leek and mushroom pearl barley
   risotto, parmesan crisps and black
   truffle oil   200
Wholegrain and dill blinis with smoked
   salmon, crème fraîche, bitter leaves
   and salmon caviar   201
Curried millet and spinach cake,
   pimento and leek with a poached
   egg and minted yoghurt   202
Parmesan and thyme polenta with
   Mediterranean vegetables with
   pesto dressing   203
Tian of Moroccan spiced quinoa,
   bulgur wheat and chick peas with
   roasted peppers, wild rocket and
   spiced chutney   204
Couscous   205
Aubergine and roasted vegetable
   cannelloni   205
Polenta gnocchi romaine, parmesan
   crisp and basil oil   206

5 Pulses, grains, pasta and rice

NVQ

2FPC6   Prepare, cook and finish basic pulse dishes
2FPC12 Prepare, cook and finish basic grain dishes
2FPC5   Prepare, cook and finish basic pasta dishes
2FPC4   Prepare, cook and finish basic rice dishes

VRQ

Unit 212 Prepare and cook rice, pasta, grains and egg dishes

LEARNING OBJECTIVES

The aim of this unit is to enable the candidate to develop skills and implement knowledge in the preparation and cookery principles of pulses, grains, pasta and rice. This will also include materials, ingredients and equipment.

At the end of this chapter you will be able to:

● Identify each pulse, grain, pasta and rice variety and finished dish.

● Understand the use of relative ingredients in pulse, grain, pasta and rice cookery.

● State the quality points of various pulse, grain, pasta and rice commodities and dishes.

● Prepare, cook, finish and hold each type of pulse, grain, pasta and rice variety.

● Identify the storage procedures of pulse, grain, pasta and rice.

● Have an understanding of preparing and cooking a range of pulse, grain, pasta and rice based dishes.

● Recognize value of pulses, grains and rice, and the healthy eating options of pulse, grain, pasta and rice recipes.

Pulses

Peas, beans and lentils are collectively known as pulses. There are many varieties with a wide range of flavours and textures. They originate from the légume family, which are pods full of seeds. Generally speaking the seeds are removed and dried, which we then call pulses. With approximately 13 000 species, the légume family is the second largest in the plant kingdom.

All pulses are formed in two halves, encased in an outer shell or skin. They can be bought separated, e.g. yellow split peas. The advantage of using pulses in the modern day professional kitchen is they add volume to dishes, combine well with other ingredients and are relatively cheap to use, which increases the potential profit margins.

PASTA

Egg pasta dough   214

Linguine with smoked salmon   214

Butternut squash ravioli with thyme, tomato and red onion butter sauce   215

Crab and coconut cannelloni with lobster bisque   216

Farfalle with pancetta and oyster mushrooms   217

Fusilli arrabiatta   217

Gnocchi parisienne   218

Gnocchi piedmontaise   218

Lasagne   219

Macaroni with blue cheese and leeks   220

Spaghetti bolognaise   221

Tortellini filled with ratatouille on wilted spinach with tomato coulis   222

RICE

Braised rice (pilaff)   228

Steamed basmati rice   228

Pesto rice with sun-dried tomatoes   229

Lemon and mustard seed braised rice   229

Chilli bean rice with sour cream   230

Risotto   230

Chinese crab cakes with mango and lime salsa   231

Deep fried risotto balls   232

Egg fried rice with ham, prawns and vegetables   233

Jambalaya   234

Kedgeree   235

Lamb biryani   236

Lemon grass risotto cakes with burnt chilli and crème fraîche   237

Paella   238

Risotto of pea and mint with goat's cheese   239

Teriyaki beef and wild rice filo parcels with pickled cucumber   240

Tiger prawn and coconut rice   241

WEB LINK   The following web page link for the vegetarian society will give additional information regarding sourcing, storage, possible toxins and correct storage for pulses:
http://www.vegsoc.org

Pulses work well in soups and stews and are an important source of fibre, protein, vitamin B and iron for vegetarians. Dried pulses store well for long periods, if kept in dry conditions, in an airtight container and away from the light. But it is best to eat them as soon as possible, as they toughen on storage, especially if over one year old and will take longer to cook. Split pulses take less time to cook as they are more exposed to the cooking medium; however, they do not retain their shape as well and can turn to mush if left unattended to overcook.

Origins of pulses

Pulses have been used as food for thousands of years. The lentil was probably one of the first plants that early humans harvested.

Most pulses prefer warm climates to grow but there are a few species which can grow in lower temperatures.

They can be eaten fresh or dried and come in a number of varieties with a range of colours, flavours, and textures.

PEAS	BEANS	LENTILS
Whole green	Lima	Cream/beige
Split green	Black	Red
Split yellow	Aduki	Yellow
Chick peas	Red kidney	Puy
Marrowfat	Haricot	
	Pinto	
	Flageolet	
	Cannellini	
	Broad	
	Soya	
	Black eyed	
	Mung	

Preparation

Pulses need to be thoroughly washed several times if possible to remove dust, dirt and grit.

Allow approximately 55 g dried weight per portion – once soaked and cooked they will at least double in weight.

Most dried pulses need soaking for a minimum of eight hours, but 12 hours is more usual before they can be cooked. It is often most convenient to soak them overnight. Exceptions are all lentils and green and yellow split peas.

Always discard the soaking water, then rinse well and cook in fresh water without any salt, which causes the skins to toughen and makes for longer cooking. Regularly skim the top of the cooking liquid to remove any scum which is naturally produced. Vegetables, herbs, spices and aromatics can be added to the pulses once cooked and either served with the dish or removed and discarded. Canned pulses are already cooked and need to be drained, rinsed and then used as required.

CHEF'S TIP   Pulses can be dry and bland to eat. Careful selection of flavoursome commodities is essential. Suitable combinations include: garlic, cumin, coriander, vine ripened tomatoes, buttered spinach.

Storage

Pulses are now readily available and are of very high quality. Try to purchase them from a supplier who has a good turnover as pulses deteriorate after one year. Pulses should have a good colour and not be wrinkled as this is a sign of age. Keep in a cool, dark, dry and well ventilated area in sealed containers. Keep a date stamp when purchased on the containers so good rotation can be introduced.

Once cooked, keep pulses well covered in the refrigerator for up to three days.

Lentils

- Originated from the Eastern Mediterranean but are now extensively used in the Middle East and India.

- They are available whole or split.

- Varying in size and colour, the red lentils are tasteless, cream/beige have a slightly stronger flavour and puy lentils have a very distinctive flavour and are excellent when cooked as they hold their shape well.

- Red and yellow lentils cook down well, can be puréed and are used a great deal in Indian cooking to create dishes such as tarka dhal, which is the cooked lentil garnished with a 'tarka' of fried garlic and spiced oil.

Beans

- Aduki beans are small, round, dark red and rich in protein. They are extensively used in the Far East, especially in Japan, and are often used to make flour.

- Black eyed beans are cream coloured with a black strip which is where they were joined to the pod. They work well in rice dishes, stews and salads.

- Black beans have a shiny black shell and are pure white inside. They are used extensively in Latin America.

- Borlotti beans are Italian beans with a mild flavour. They are used in rice dishes, stews and soups.

- Broad beans are a larger green coloured bean which was once extensively used in Europe. However, some people can become ill from eating broad beans through an allergic-like reaction.

- Cannellini beans are similar to haricot beans and are used a lot in Italian cookery.

- Flageolet beans are pale green in colour, have a subtle flavour and are used extensively in Italian and French cookery.

- Haricot beans are possibly the best known of all beans and are commonly used in tinned baked beans.

- Lima beans are white and small with a sweet flavour. They originate from America.

- Mung beans originated from Asia and are one of the most widely used pulses. The seeds are used as a vegetable and they are also used as a bean sprout.

- Pinto beans are very similar to borlotti beans, once cooked they turn pink in colour.

- Red kidney beans are normally dark red-brown. This kidney-shaped bean holds its shape and colour. They are most famously used in the dish chilli con carne.

- Soya beans are full of protein, making them ideal for vegetarian food. Fairly bland in taste, they need a dish with plenty of distinctive flavours. They can be puréed and added to soups and casseroles. They are most commonly found in soya based products including TVP (textured vegetable protein), tempeh, tofu, miso and soy sauces.

Peas

- Chick peas have a nutty flavour and are available tinned or dried. Chickpeas are ideal for hot and cold dishes and are the main ingredient in the dish hoummus which is a Greek dip usually served with pitta bread and olives.

- Whole peas are normally cooked from fresh, frozen or tinned but are also available dried.

- Split green/yellow peas are great in sauces or stews as they break slightly and give the dish a little extra volume.

- Marrowfat peas have a sweet flavour, with a tough skin and floury texture once cooked. They are commonly used in the dish mushy peas.

Soaking and cooking times of pulses

The times shown in the table below are all approximate and will vary depending on the age and quality of the pulses being used. The first ten minutes of cooking (except split peas and lentils) should be continuous boiling to kill the toxins present in most beans. The exception to the rule is the soya bean, which should be boiled for one hour to kill the toxins. Soya and red kidney beans contain the most toxins.

Alternatively, many of the above pulses are available in cans. The quality of these is very good and they can be used without pre-soaking and cooking, saving a lot of time.

PULSE	SOAKING TIME	COOKING TIME (APPROX)
Aduki beans	8–12 hours	45 minutes
Black eyed beans	8–12 hours	45 minutes
Black beans	8–12 hours	1 hour
Borlotti beans	8–12 hours	50 minutes
Broad beans	8–12 hours	1½ hour
Cannellini beans	8–12 hours	50 minutes
Flageolets	8–12 hours	50 minutes
Haricot beans	8–12 hours	1 hour
Lima beans	8–12 hours	1½ hours
Mung beans	8–12 hours	40 minutes
Pinto beans	8–12 hours	1 hour 20 minutes
Red kidney beans	8–12 hours	50 minutes

PULSE	SOAKING TIME	COOKING TIME (APPROX)
Soya beans	8–12 hours	2½ hours
Chick peas	8–12 hours	75 minutes
Whole green peas	8–12 hours	75 minutes
Split peas	Steeped in boiling water for 30 minutes	40 minutes
Whole lentils	Steeped in boiling water for 30 minutes	40 minutes
Split lentils	Steeped in boiling water for 30 minutes	25 minutes

NUTRITIONAL INFORMATION

Pulses are an excellent source of carbohydrates and protein – this will help provide energy to the body.

They are high in fibre, iron and vitamin B. Pulses, with the exception of soya beans, contain no fat.

VIDEO CLIP Preparing and cooking pulses.

TEST YOURSELF

1 Identify three types of beans.

2 Identify three types of peas.

3 The majority of pulses should be soaked for how long?

4 Borlotti beans originate from which country?

5 Humous is produced using which pulse?

6 Approximately how many grams of dried weight pulses per person should be allowed?

7 Once cooked pulses can be kept refrigerated for how long?

8 Approximately how many species of légume are there?

9 Which of the below is the odd one out:

- black beans
- haricot beans
- soya beans.

10 Pulses are a good source of which vitamin: A, B or C?

Recipes

Black eyed peas and red lentil curry

Ingredients	Makes approximately 4 portions	Makes approximately 10 portions
Black eyed peas	200 g	450 g
Red lentils	200 g	450 g
Finely chopped onions	150 g	375 g
Garam masala	2 tblspn	5 tblspn
Turmeric	2 tblspn	5 tblspn
Ground coriander	2 tblspn	5 tblspn
Ground cumin	2 tblspn	5 tblspn
Chilli powder	To taste	To taste
Vegetable stock	400 ml	1000 ml
Chopped fresh coriander	⅛ bunch	¼ bunch
Good quality salt and pepper	To taste	To taste
Leaf spinach, picked and washed	100 g	220 g
Red, green and yellow peppers macedoine	50 g	100 g

energy	cal	fat	sat fat	carb	sugar	protein	fibre
1121 kJ	266 kcal	7.8 g	1.1 g	37.4 g	6.4 g	13.8 g	13.9 g

METHOD OF WORK

1. Soak the black eyed peas and lentils separately for a minimum of 8 hours.
2. Place the peas and lentils into separate pans of cold water and bring to the boil, cook until just tender then drain.
3. Heat a little oil in a saucepan and sweat the finely chopped onions, peppers and spices in the hot oil for 4 minutes with colour. Then add the pulses and continue to cook for a further 2 minutes.
4. Add the stock, bring to the boil and simmer for 10 minutes.
5. Add the leaf spinach and season the curry well. Check the consistency and finish with chopped coriander.

CHEF'S TIP The curry can be finished with half a chilli for additional spice, for a softer effect burn the chilli over a naked flame until blackened then peel the skin.
  Cut the chilli in half and remove the seeds; this will reduce the level of spice.

Steamed lemon rice with borlotti beans

Ingredients	Makes approximately 4 portions	Makes approximately 10 portions
Basmati rice	200 g	500 g
Lemon juice and zest	2 lemons	4½ lemons
Tinned or soaked and boiled cooked borlotti beans	200 g	500 g
Finely chopped onion	75 g	150 g
Finely chopped garlic	½ clove	2 cloves
Picked oregano	3 tblspn	5 tblspn
Vegetable stock	400 ml	1000 ml
White wine	50 ml	125 ml
Good quality salt	To taste	To taste
White pepper	To taste	To taste

energy	cal	fat	sat fat	carb	sugar	protein	fibre
1092 kJ	259 kcal	2.8 g	0.7 g	47.9 g	1.9 g	8.6 g	5.0 g

METHOD OF WORK

1 Wash the basmati rice and set into a deep steaming tray. Add the grated lemon zest, juice and a few slices of lemon on top.

2 Pour over a little hot stock, seasoning and place in the steamer to cook.

3 Heat a little oil in a saucepan and add the onion and garlic to sweat for 3 minutes add the borlotti beans and the white wine and allow the liquid to reduce.

4 Add the oregano at the end.

5 When the rice is cooked, separate grains with a fork.

6 Combine the rice with the beans and serve.

CHEF'S TIP Wild rice added to this dish will give a good colour contrast and a nuttier flavour. The borlotti beans complement the rice because of the size and their bittersweet flavour.

Broad bean bruschetta with tomato and oregano

Ingredients	Makes approximately 4 portions	Makes approximately 10 portions
Shelled broad beans	300 g	750 g
Finely chopped shallots	4	10
Tomato concassée	200 g	500 g
Olive oil	4 tblspn	10 tblspn
Chopped garlic	2 cloves	5 cloves
Shredded flat leaf parsley	4 tblspn	10 tblspn
Chopped red chilli peppers	1	2
Oregano	1 tblspn	2 tblspn
Bruschetta bread	4 × 2 cm thick slices	10 × 2 cm thick slices
Garlic oil	4 tblspn	10 tblspn
Good quality salt	To taste	To taste
White pepper	To taste	To taste

energy	cal	fat	sat fat	carb	sugar	protein	fibre
1804 kJ	434 kcal	33.0 g	4.2 g	27.4 g	4.6 g	8.5 g	8.7 g

METHOD OF WORK

1 Heat a saucepan with some olive oil and add the garlic, shallots, chillies and beans. Sweat for 5 minutes without colour.

2 Add the tomato **concassée**, shredded parsley and oregano, remove from the heat, season well and allow to cool.

3 Drizzle the garlic oil over the sliced bruschetta and lightly grill under a salamander until golden in colour.

4 Spoon the salsa on top of the bruschetta and garnish.

CHEF'S TIP Parsley oil can be used in this recipe instead of garlic oil. It is simply a good-quality olive oil blended together with some blanched flat leaf parsley. This can be made well in advance and has a good shelf life if kept in a plastic container and refrigerated. The garlic oil uses a similar process.

Cassoulet

Ingredients	Makes approximately 4 portions	Makes approximately 10 portions
Haricot or cannellini beans	200 g	500 g
Diced carrot	50 g	125 g
Diced onion	50 g	125 g
White chicken stock	300 ml	750 ml
Tomato concassée	100 g	250 g
Diced raw chicken	100 g	250 g
Toulouse sausage cut into 1 cm thick slices	100 g	250 g
Diced shoulder of pork	100 g	250 g
Tomato purée	2 tblspn	5 tblspn
Bouquet garni	1 small	1 small
Butter	100 g	250 g
Good quality salt	To taste	To taste
White pepper	To taste	To taste

energy	cal	fat	sat fat	carb	sugar	protein	fibre
1722 kJ	414 kcal	29.4 g	16.3 g	14.7 g	4.0 g	23.1 g	5.2 g

4 Sweat the chopped onion, carrot and bouquet garni in a saucepan with butter for 4 minutes without colour.

5 Add the diced chicken, pork and tomato purée and continue cooking for 4 minutes.

6 Add the stock and beans. Bring to the boil and simmer for 30 minutes.

7 Fry the sausage in a separate pan quickly on both sides and add to the cassoulet of beans.

8 Cover the pan and simmer for a further 30 minutes.

9 Check the seasoning and serve.

CHEF'S TIP The term cassoulet refers to the dish (casserole) it is cooked in, it comes from the Languedoc region in France but has strong links with Spain (Catalonia). This quick **cassoulet** is a modern variation on the classical dish, which can use duck, goose and offal according to the regional adaptation to give its distinct flavour. A modern twist is the crust of fine breadcrumbs, gratinated under a salamander. Never use smoked sausages, smoked meat or mutton.

METHOD OF WORK

1 Soak the beans for a minimum of 8 hours.

2 Drain and wash well.

3 Boil the beans in plenty of boiling water until just cooked and refresh in cold running water.

Chickpea stew with red onion and chilli peppers

Ingredients	Makes approximately 4 portions	Makes approximately 10 portions
Tinned chickpeas	400 g	1000 g
Diced red onion	100 g	250 g
Finely chopped red chilli peppers	2	5
Chopped garlic	2 cloves	4 cloves
Tomato concassée	300 g	750 g
Vegetable stock	150 ml	375 ml
Butter	50 g	125 g
Diced courgettes	100 g	250 g
Diced carrots	100 g	250 g
Good quality salt	To taste	To taste
White pepper	To taste	To taste

energy	cal	fat	sat fat	carb	sugar	protein	fibre
1086 kJ	260 kcal	15.4 g	8.0 g	22.5 g	6.1 g	9.2 g	6.7 g

METHOD OF WORK

1. Open the tinned chickpeas and drain in a colander. Wash well under clean water and leave to drain.

2. In a saucepan, sweat the prepared onion, garlic and red chilli peppers in butter for 3 minutes without colour.

3. Add the diced carrot and sweat for a further 3 minutes.

4. Add the tinned chickpeas and diced courgettes and sweat for a further 3 minutes.

5. Put the tomato concassée and the vegetable stock into the saucepan to combine all the ingredients. Simmer for 25 minutes.

6. Thicken slightly if required with some beurre manié (equal quantities of flour and butter mixed together to a paste) by dropping tiny pieces into the stew, stirring and cooking out.

7. Correct the seasoning and serve as required.

CHEF'S TIP Tinned chickpeas require draining and rinsing well only. If using dried chickpeas, soak overnight and boil separately until tender, refresh in cold water and then continue the recipe as shown.

VIDEO CLIP Making pulse stews.

Mushy peas

Ingredients	Makes approximately 4 portions	Makes approximately 10 portions
Marrowfat peas soaked for 8 hours	220 g	550 g
Butter	40 g	100 g
Good quality salt	To taste	To taste
White pepper	To taste	To taste

energy	cal	fat	sat fat	carb	sugar	protein	fibre
563 kJ	135 kcal	8.7 g	5.4 g	11.1 g	0.6 g	3.9 g	3.1 g

METHOD OF WORK

1 Drain and wash the peas well.
2 Place the peas into a saucepan of cold water so the peas are just covered and then bring to the boil.
3 Add some salt and allow the peas to simmer until cooked. Skim regularly to remove any scum that forms on the surface.
4 The peas will eventually begin to break up.
5 Once cooked remove from the heat add the butter and season well.

CHEF'S TIP Do not use too much salt when boiling as it can toughen the skin of the peas and increase the cooking time. Pulses create a natural scum when boiling so always skim during cooking.

VIDEO CLIP Mushy peas.

Stuffed plum tomatoes with rice and peas

Ingredients	Makes approximately 4 portions	Makes approximately 10 portions
Plum tomatoes	8 each	20 each
Chopped garlic	2 cloves	5 cloves
Mixed beans, tinned or pre soaked and cooked	100 g	250 g
Chickpeas, tinned or pre soaked and cooked	100 g	250 g
Onion, cut into brunoise	4 tblspn	10 tblspn
Coconut shavings	4 tblspn	10 tblspn
Basmati rice, cooked	100 g	250 g
Lemon and lime juice and zest	¼ of each	½ of each
Chopped fresh coriander	3 tblspn	6 tblspn
Good quality salt	To taste	To taste
White pepper	To taste	To taste

energy	cal	fat	sat fat	carb	sugar	protein	fibre
1333 kJ	319 kcal	15.7 g	14.3 g	36.3 g	9.7 g	8.6 g	6.5 g

METHOD OF WORK

1 Blanch the plum tomatoes and peel.
2 Remove the top and deseed.
3 Fry the onion, garlic, beans and peas together.
4 Add the basmati rice, lemon and lime juice and zest.
5 Season and fold the coconut shavings through.
6 Transfer to a baking sheet and heat through in the oven, taking care not to overcook the tomatoes.

Sweet potato and chick pea falafel with a mint and lime dip

Ingredients	Makes approximately 4 portions	Makes approximately 10 portions
Tinned chickpeas	300 g	700 g
Sweet potato purée	100 g	250 g
Fresh white breadcrumbs	180 g	400 g
Curry paste	2 tblspn	5 tblspn
Chopped coriander	3 tblspn	6 tblspn
Whole eggs	1	2
Garlic	1 clove	2 cloves
Lime juice and zest	2 limes	5 limes
Chopped fresh mint	3 tblspn	6 tblspn
Greek yoghurt	200 ml	500 ml
Good quality salt	To taste	To taste
White pepper	To taste	To taste

energy	cal	fat	sat fat	carb	sugar	protein	fibre
1616 kJ	383 kcal	11.3 g	4.3 g	57.7 g	7.6 g	16.5 g	6.5 g

METHOD OF WORK

1   Place the drained and washed chickpeas into a food blender with the breadcrumbs, curry paste, garlic, eggs, fresh coriander and sweet potato. Blend until a course paste is formed.

2   Season to taste with salt and pepper and blend for a few seconds further.

3   Roll the balls into shape and place onto a tray. Cover with plastic film and chill for 30 minutes in a refrigerator.

4   **Deep fry** at 170 °C until golden in colour and then drain well on kitchen paper.

5   Serve with the dip made from the yoghurt, lime juice and grated zest and chopped mint mixed together.

CHEF'S TIP   This is the Middle Eastern version, the Egyptian version of falafel contains fava beans.

Grains

Cereals are among the oldest farmed products in the world. Cereals are grasses producing edible starchy seeds or grains. The cereals most commonly grown are wheat, rice, rye, oats, barley, corn (maize) and sorghum. The name cereal is derived from *Ceres*, the Roman goddess of grain, and grains were seen as so important that each type of grain was thought to be a gift from the gods.

Grains form a staple part of many diets across the globe because they are inexpensive and sustainable. Only in wealthy countries has meat and fish begun to replace cereals and grains as the primary food. Grains can be utilized in many different foods ranging from breads and salads to risottos and stews. It has also become a notable way for vegetarians to increase the variety in food products.

Whole grains are made of all three parts of a grain kernel: the bran, endosperm and germ.

Bran is the coarse, outer layer of the kernel that includes concentrated amounts of several nutrients, including:

- fibre
- B vitamins (thiamine, riboflavin, niacin and folic acid)
- minerals (zinc, copper, iron)
- protein
- phytochemicals (beneficial chemical compounds from plants).

CHEF'S TIP Grains are a very good way of improving the overall healthy eating aspect of dishes because of their nutritional value.

The endosperm is the middle layer and is the biggest section of the whole grain. It acts as the main energy supply for the living plant. It contains:

- carbohydrates
- protein
- small amounts of B vitamins.

The germ is the smallest part of the grain, but is crammed with nutrients. It develops into a new plant, so it will hold plentiful supplies of the following nutrients:

- minerals
- B vitamins
- vitamin E
- phytochemicals (beneficial chemical compounds).

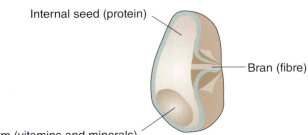

Internal seed (protein)

Bran (fibre)

Germ (vitamins and minerals)

Anatomy of a whole grain

CHEF'S TIP A processed grain has been broken down into flakes, nibs or ground into finer particles. Because it has been processed it will cook quicker than the hardened whole grain.

Grain is a starch-based commodity so it is able to absorb a lot of water. This is why it is easier to boil or steam grains, as they will then become swollen and eventually softer in texture. Whole grains will take longer to cook than processed grains. Grains can be cooked dry without any pre-soaking, except for whole wheat, barley, rye and brown rice.

Barley

Barley is available in two forms. Processed barley is known as pearled; unprocessed is known as unhulled and contains more vitamins, minerals and fibre. This is because it is unrefined and contains the germ and endosperm making it more nutritious to eat, although once cooked it tends to be quite chewy. Barley makes up approximately seven per cent of the world's total grain production and has been used in cooking for thousands of years.

CHEF'S TIP Barley and quinoa can be used as alternative thickening agents for soups or stews. Barley can also be used instead of rice for risotto.

VIDEO CLIP Cooking barley.

Buckwheat

Buckwheat is also available in different forms:

- raw (whole)
- roasted
- cracked
- hulled (processed).

The raw stage is a fruit seed which is reddish-brown in colour, is free from gluten and therefore is not classified as wheat. Once cooked it has a soft texture and can be combined with quinoa to create appealing salads.

Roasted buckwheat is known as kasha and is stronger in flavour and drier than the raw form of buckwheat. Buckwheat is more commonly known and used in catering today as buckwheat flour, and is used for lightly textured Russian pancakes known as blinis. It is also found as an additional ingredient in bread, breakfast cereals and stuffing for poultry.

Corn/maize

Corn is probably the most widely used grain and grows on a cob. It is also ground down into cornmeal, which is then used to make breads and tortillas and used for animal feed. In the United States it is one of the largest crops grown.

It is more popularly known for polenta, which can be substituted for rice and pasta and will accompany fish, meat and game dishes very well. Polenta is a classic dish from Italy, mainly from the northern regions. It is versatile and can be made into soft or firm pastes that can also be cut, shaped and grilled or baked. Polenta can also combine well with additional flavours such as fresh herbs, Parmesan cheese or garlic. Sometimes polenta can substitute flour in various pasta recipes.

Oats

The history of oats dates back to Germany in 1000 BC, but their popularity did not extend across Europe quickly. This was due in part to the bland flavour and the commonly held view that it was a food more suited for animal feed. By the mid 1980s, the popularity of oats was boosted to health food status by some research suggesting that it helped to prevent heart disease. Oats are the edible seeds of a cereal grass, which is available in two forms, raw (groats) and rolled (flaked). Oat flakes are used in porridge and other breakfast dishes such as muesli. Fine oatmeal can also be made into bannocks (Scottish griddle cakes).

CHEF'S TIP Never mix old and new grains together because the older grains can take longer to cook. The longer they are stored, even in correct conditions, the drier they will become.

Millet

Millet is thought to be one of the first grains cultivated. The first recorded comments regarding millet date back to

5500 BC in China. Millet may have been domesticated in Africa hundreds or even thousands of years before, where it still grows wild. It was an extremely important grain whose popularity diminished somewhat with the arrival of maize and rice. The variety of this grain, sold in Europe and North America for human consumption, is called pearl millet. It is produced in grain form and in flakes which can be used like other grain flakes as a thickening agent for stews and soups.

Wheat (bulgur, semolina, couscous)

The first evidence of wheat was discovered in an ancient civilization in what is now Iraq, dating back to at least 6700 BC. Wheat made its way to England around the twelfth century and is classified as either spring or winter wheat, depending on the time of year it is planted and grown. It is a plant which has many uses today such as bulgur wheat, couscous, durum wheat, cracked wheat and various flours including strong glutinous flours used for bread making or semolina.

Bulgur wheat is made by boiling wheat grains until they crack. As a result, this grain only has to be soaked or simmered in water. It is a staple commodity in the Middle East where it is combined with lamb to make kibbeh. It is also the main ingredient of the Lebanese salad called tabbouleh, which is usually served as a starter.

Couscous is a mixture of coarse grains of semolina that are mixed with finer grains of semolina until they coat each larger grain. Because traditional couscous takes a long time to cook the most commonly available is precooked, so the cooking time is dramatically reduced. Read the labels carefully to check that the couscous is of the correct type. Widely found in North Africa where it is cooked in a special tagine dish or a couscousière which allows it to be steamed in a pot above stewing vegetables.

Semolina is the ground endosperm from durum wheat. It is found as a fine powder or in a granular form that is primarily used to make fresh pasta. Semolina pasta is firmer than that made from other wheat-based flours and has a strong yellow colour. Semolina can be used to produce a dessert milk pudding, breads, cakes and gnocchi.

WEB LINK   Search this website for valuable information regarding grains and cereals; their nutritional content, storage and uses:
http://www.healthysupplies.co.uk

Quinoa

Quinoa is not a member of the grass family, but its seeds are eaten like grains. It has been grown for 5000 years in South America, in and around the Andes Mountains. The Incas called quinoa 'the Mother Grain' because eating this food tended to give long life. Quinoa contains 50 per cent more protein than wheat and is full of nutrition. It is a small disc-shaped seed with a very light flavour which can be prepared in dishes such as salads, stews and soups. Its cooking time is also very short. Not only is this grain healthy, due to its nutritional value, but it is also gluten free.

Rye

This is a cereal grass similar to wheat. It has long been a staple grain in northern Europe and Russia. It is milled to produce rye flour and rye flakes to create rye bread (sometimes referred to as black bread). It produces a dark-coloured flour but it does have a lower gluten content than wheat-based flours. For this reason it is best to combine a strong flour with rye flour when making rye bread.

The preparation of grains

The preparation of grains for cooking is quite simple. The focal detail for preparing them is the washing process, as they can have surface dust, which may be harmless but should be removed under running cold water in a colander. Sometimes infestation may be present, so it is important to identify any alien dark specs or insects within the grain before use. Although grain products are dried, very rarely do they need to be soaked. This is the same with oats and barley, although

soaking will speed up the cooking process. The majority of grains can be cooked from dry within a reasonable time limit.

As grains are starch-based the best methods of cooking are boiling, stewing, steaming and braising because the apparent moisture in each cooking process will help the starch cells to swell and burst. They begin to cook at between 60 and 70 °C, depending on the type of grain. These methods will ensure the grain will cook evenly. However, couscous, bulgur wheat and millet should have a boiling liquid poured over and be left to cool. As long as the mixture is stirred occasionally to stop the product sticking then the grain should never overcook.

This method of cooking grains is ideal if no further cooking is required or the items are for salads. Another method to consider in the preparation and cooking grains is baking. Items like porridge oats, polenta and cornmeal can be soaked and flavoured or par-cooked and then poured into a lined or greased baking tin and placed into the oven to bake. The dry heat from the oven will heat the grain mixture, the water mixed with the grain will cook the product and eventually the moisture will evaporate in the heat. Due to the way water is absorbed steaming is also another good and healthy way to cook grain either over water, stock or any flavoured and scented liquid.

CHEF'S TIP   If boiling or cooking grains in a saucepan: first line the pan with a touch of oil before heating, the grain will not stick against the sides of the pan and potentially burn.

Storage

Grains in whole seed form will have the longest shelf-life span of any food group. When stored in a dry cool place within airtight plastic containers, grains retain their excellent nutritional and flavour characteristics over time unlike other food groups. This shelf life is greatly reduced the more refined the product becomes. Milled flours from grain will not last longer than a year if kept in the right storage condition compared to the numerous years which whole grains can last. This is because the hard outer skin or husk that stops the oxidization of the grain has been removed from flours, thus shortening their shelf life. When preparing to store grains the use of a vacuum pack machine is valuable. The vacuum bags are very strong and durable, and they prolong shelf life further because the air is removed during the sealing of the bags. The vacuum will also compact the grain into a smaller size so it is easier to store and will take up less room on the shelf.

CHEF'S TIP   Store grain in small amounts rather than in large batches. The quality will not deteriorate as quickly when you open one smaller batch and then another, rather than one large batch.

AVERAGE COOKING TIMES FOR GRAINS

GRAIN	LIQUID TO GRAIN RATIO	COOKING TIME (APPROXIMATE MINUTES)
Barley hulled/whole	3 : 1	90
Barley pearled	3 : 1	45
Millet	2½ : 1	25
Oats, whole	3 : 1	60
Oats, rolled	2 : 1	15

GRAIN	LIQUID TO GRAIN RATIO	COOKING TIME (APPROXIMATE MINUTES)
Buckwheat groats	2 : 1	15
Quinoa	2 : 1	20
Corn grits	3 : 1	20
Bulgur	2 : 1	15
Couscous	2 : 1	1

TEST YOURSELF

1 Wholegrain is broken down into which three parts?

2 Barley is available in which two forms?

3 List four types of buckwheat.

4 Polenta is a classical dish relating to which country?

5 Which country does tabbouleh originate from?

6 Grains begin to cook between which two temperatures?

7 What is the approximate cooking time for millet?

8 Quinoa is which of the following:

   a grain, a seed, a pulse?

9 Couscous is a mixture of coarse grain from which of the following:

   Bulgur wheat, semolina, rye?

10 The liquid to grain ratio for pearl barley is:

   3:1, 2:1, 1:1?

Recipes

Cornbread

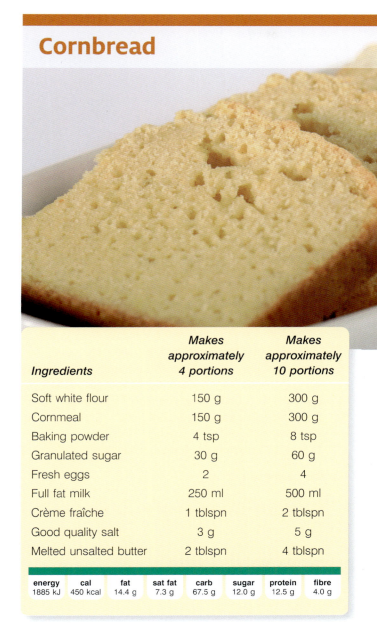

Ingredients	Makes approximately 4 portions	Makes approximately 10 portions
Soft white flour	150 g	300 g
Cornmeal	150 g	300 g
Baking powder	4 tsp	8 tsp
Granulated sugar	30 g	60 g
Fresh eggs	2	4
Full fat milk	250 ml	500 ml
Crème fraîche	1 tblspn	2 tblspn
Good quality salt	3 g	5 g
Melted unsalted butter	2 tblspn	4 tblspn

energy	cal	fat	sat fat	carb	sugar	protein	fibre
1885 kJ	450 kcal	14.4 g	7.3 g	67.5 g	12.0 g	12.5 g	4.0 g

METHOD OF WORK

1 Preheat an oven to 190 °C.

2 Mix the flour, cornmeal, baking powder, salt and sugar together in a bowl.

3 Pour in the beaten eggs, milk, crème fraîche and melted butter.

4 Mix well to create a smooth batter.

5 Pour the mixture in a greased and silicone paper lined square cake tin. Bake in the oven for approximately 30 minutes.

6 Leave to cool for five minutes in the cake tin before turning out onto a chopping board and cutting into squared shaped portions. Serve the bread warm.

Leek and mushroom pearl barley risotto, parmesan crisps and black truffle oil

Ingredients	Makes approximately 4 portions	Makes approximately 10 portions
Washed pearl barley	125 g	300 g
Chiffonade of leeks	100 g	250 g
Finely chopped shallot	70 g	140 g
Finely chopped garlic	1 clove	2 cloves
Button mushrooms	100 g	250 g
Dry white wine	50 ml	100 ml
Vegetable stock	200 ml	500 ml
Double cream	100 ml	250 ml
Finely grated parmesan cheese	100 g	250 g
Fresh parsley, chopped	1 tblspn	2 tblspn
Unsalted butter	50 g	125 g
Good quality salt and pepper	To taste	To taste
Black truffle oil		

energy	cal	fat	sat fat	carb	sugar	protein	fibre
1784 kJ	431 kcal	36.9 g	20.4 g	11.6 g	2.5 g	11.8 g	2.8 g

METHOD OF WORK

1   Wash the pearl barley under cold running water.

2   Melt the butter in a saucepan and add the chopped shallots, leeks and garlic. Sweat gently for 2 minutes until they have slightly softened.

3   Add the pearl barley and sliced button mushrooms then continue to sweat for another 2 minutes. Pour in the white wine and reduce by half with the pearl barley.

4   Add half of the vegetable stock and bring to simmering point. Continue to add more stock as required, little by little, until the pearl barley is sufficiently cooked.

5   Add the double cream and cook until a creamy texture has been achieved.

6   Serve with a parmesan crisp and black truffle oil to taste

For the parmesan crisp

1   Sprinkle grated parmesan onto silicone paper or a silpat mat.

2   Place in an oven at 180 °C or under the salamander until melted and slightly coloured.

3   Remove and allow to cool and go crisp.

CHEF'S TIP   The parmesan can be trimmed into a neat rectangle and bent around a mould, once cool this will form a band which can be filled with the risotto if preferred

Wholegrain and dill blinis with smoked salmon, crème fraîche, bitter leaves and salmon caviar

Ingredients	Makes approximately 4 portions	Makes approximately 10 portions
Cracked buckwheat	50 g	125 g
Buckwheat flour	100 g	300 g
Soft white flour	100 g	300 g
Fresh milk	200 ml	600 ml
Egg yolks	2	6
Egg whites	2	6
Fresh yeast	½ tsp	1 tsp
Butter	50 g	120 g
Smoked salmon	4	10
Bitter salad leaves e.g. rocket	100 g	300 g
Fresh dill, chopped	1 tsp	1 tblspn
Crème fraîche	100 ml	250 ml
Good quality salt and pepper	To taste	To taste
Salmon caviar	To taste	To taste

energy	cal	fat	sat fat	carb	sugar	protein	fibre
2793 kJ	668 kcal	32.7 g	16.3 g	51.1 g	4.2 g	46.0 g	5.5 g

METHOD OF WORK

1   Wash the cracked buckwheat under cold water to wash off any dust.

2   Following the ratio – 2 parts water: 1 part cracked buckwheat, bring the cracked buckwheat to the boil and simmer for approximately 15 minutes.

3   Immediately refresh under cold running water and allow to cool down.

4   Sieve the two flours and the baking powder together then add the chopped dill.

5   Combine the egg yolks and milk to a smooth paste.

6   Season with salt and pepper.

7   Aerate the egg whites with a pinch of salt to stiff peaks and carefully fold into the batter, one-third at a time.

8   Melt the butter in a non-stick frying pan and add two tablespoons of the mixture separately, fry lightly until golden on each side.

9   Serve the blinis, smoked salmon, crème fraîche and caviar.

CHEF'S TIP   If the buckwheat flour flavour is too strong then reduce the amount by half and make up the difference with white flour.

Curried millet and spinach cake, pimento and leek with a poached egg and minted yoghurt

Ingredients	Makes approximately 4 portions	Makes approximately 10 portions
Millet grain	100 g	250 g
Vegetable or chicken stock	250 ml	625 ml
Curry paste	20 g	50 g
Butter	50 g	125 g
Fresh eggs	4	10
Pimentos, tinned	50 g	125 g
Leeks, chiffonade	50 g	125 g
Egg yolks	2	4
Spinach, washed and stalks removed and chiffonade	250 g	600 g
Greek yoghurt	350 ml	700 ml
Grated parmesan cheese	20 g	50 g
Soft white flour	20 g	50 g
Good quality salt and pepper	To taste	To taste
Mint	1 tsp	2 tsp

energy	cal	fat	sat fat	carb	sugar	protein	fibre
1981 kJ	477 kcal	32.1 g	16.4 g	30.4 g	5.7 g	20.2 g	3.1 g

METHOD OF WORK

1 Preheat an oven to 170 °C.

2 Wash and drain the millet. Bring the stock to the boil in a saucepan with the curry paste.

3 Place the millet into a large based shallow pan and cover with the hot stock adding small pieces of the butter. Soak for 2 minutes.

4 Cover with a cartouche, and slowly bring to the boil.

5 Place into the oven and allow to bake for approximately 20 minutes until all the stock has been absorbed.

6 Using a fork stir the millet, add the spinach and then cover with clean, dry kitchen cloth and allow to cool down completely.

7 Poach the eggs gently in simmering water for 2–3 minutes until lightly set.

8 Refresh immediately in iced water, trim each egg and retain in the iced water for service.

9 Season the millet and add the egg yolks to bind.

10 Take the millet and mould into shallow round cakes approximately 5 cm in diameter and 1 cm thick, season again and coat lightly in flour.

11 Heat a little sunflower or vegetable oil in a shallow pan and add the millet cakes.

12 Cook on both sides for about 2 minutes until golden in colour.

13 Heat a sauteuse pan until very hot and add a tablespoon of water and a little butter then add the leeks until soft and then stir in the pimentos and season well.

14 To serve top the millet cake with leek and pimento, hot poached eggs and serve with the minted yoghurt dressing.

Parmesan and thyme polenta with Mediterranean vegetables with pesto dressing

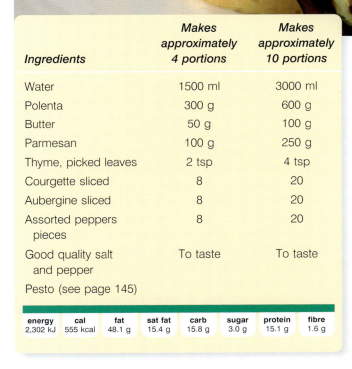

Ingredients	Makes approximately 4 portions	Makes approximately 10 portions
Water	1500 ml	3000 ml
Polenta	300 g	600 g
Butter	50 g	100 g
Parmesan	100 g	250 g
Thyme, picked leaves	2 tsp	4 tsp
Courgette sliced	8	20
Aubergine sliced	8	20
Assorted peppers pieces	8	20
Good quality salt and pepper	To taste	To taste
Pesto (see page 145)		

energy	cal	fat	sat fat	carb	sugar	protein	fibre
2,302 kJ	555 kcal	48.1 g	15.4 g	15.8 g	3.0 g	15.1 g	1.6 g

METHOD OF WORK

1 Pour the water, thyme and salt into a large heavy based saucepan. Bring to the boil.

2 Gradually stir in the polenta, whisking continuously to ensure no lumps form.

3 Reduce to a very low heat and cook for 35 minutes, or until thick and creamy in texture. Whisk occasionally to prevent a skin from forming and then stir in the parmesan and butter.

4 Pour into an oiled baking tray and spread out evenly to a thickness of 1.5 cm. Leave to cool and then set in a refrigerator.

5 Turn the sheet of set polenta out and cut as required, then brush with oil and char grill for 3–4 minutes on each side.

6 Oil, season and char grill all prepared vegetables.

7 Serve the polenta with the vegetables and pesto.

CHEF'S TIP A soft polenta can be produced and served with the grilled vegetables instead. Simply add 100 g parmesan cheese to the cooking polenta and serve it while still creamy and hot. Alternatively the polenta can be mixed with mashed potato for a different texture.

VIDEO CLIP Grilled polenta.

Tian of Moroccan spiced quinoa, bulgur wheat and chick peas with roasted peppers, wild rocket and spiced chutney

Ingredients	Makes approximately 4 portions	Makes approximately 10 portions
Quinoa	100 g	250 g
Bulgur wheat	100 g	250 g
Chick peas, tinned	100 g	250 g
Garam masala	2 tblspn	4 tblspn
Vegetable stock	300 ml	750 ml
Chopped shallot	1	2
Butter	50 g	125 g
Green pepper	1	3
Yellow pepper	1	3
Red peppers	2	5
Olive oil	100 ml	250 ml
Garlic	1 clove	3 cloves
Fresh thyme	3 sprigs	6 sprigs
Good quality salt and pepper	To taste	To taste
Balsamic vinegar	To taste	To taste
Spiced chutney, e.g. tomato chutney		
Wild rocket		

energy	cal	fat	sat fat	carb	sugar	protein	fibre
2774 kJ	665 kcal	41.0 g	10.9 g	65.2 g	24.5 g	11.9 g	6.8 g

METHOD OF WORK

1 Preheat an oven to 190 °C.

2 Wash the quinoa and bulgur wheat well in cold water and drain.

3 Heat the butter in a saucepan and gently sweat the chopped shallot until it softens.

4 Add the quinoa, bulgur wheat, chick peas, garam masala powder and cook out for 2 minutes before adding the vegetable stock and simmering until all liquid has been absorbed.

5 Cover the pan tightly with plastic film and set aside to keep warm.

6 Wash, cut the peppers in half and deseed.

7 Heat a roasting tray in the oven before adding a little olive oil, the peppers, thyme and crushed garlic.

8 Gently roast for approximately 20 minutes until the pepper skins blister then peel peppers.

9 Season and stir the warm quinoa mix and pack into a round stainless steel mould before topping with slices of the different coloured roasted peppers.

10 De-mould on the plate and serve with wild rocket and spiced chutney.

CHEF'S TIP This dish can be served hot or cold. The tian tastes better if made the day before; allowing the flavours to infuse and develop.

Couscous *mint, garlic, olives, tomatoes and cucumber with grilled halloumi cheese*

Ingredients	Makes approximately 4 portions	Makes approximately 10 portions
Couscous	150 g	450 g
Vegetable stock	300 ml	900 ml
Cherry tomatoes	40 g	100 g
Black olives brunoise	40 g	25 g
Cucumber brunoise	40 g	25 g
Chopped garlic	1 clove	2 cloves
Chiffonade of mint	2 tsp	5 tsp
Sliced halloumi cheese	200 g	500 g
Good quality salt and pepper	To taste	To taste

energy	cal	fat	sat fat	carb	sugar	protein	fibre
1154 kJ	278 kcal	15.8 g	8.7 g	21.7 g	2.2 g	13.2 g	1.3 g

METHOD OF WORK

1   Slice and char grill the halloumi cheese, then keep warm.

2   Bring the vegetable stock to the boil in a saucepan.

3   Place the couscous in a large bowl and pour the hot stock over it. Cover the bowl with plastic film and allow the couscous to absorb the stock for a few minutes until all the liquid has been taken in.

4   Allow couscous to cool down and then mix in all the additional ingredients.

5   Season to taste.

6   Serve as an accompaniment to a lunch, buffet or eat as a salad.

CHEF'S TIP Add 1 tsp of saffron or ground coriander before adding the hot stock to give a different colour and flavour to the overall dish. Olive oil may also be added if the couscous is a little too dry for service.

Aubergine and roasted vegetable cannelloni *on tomato and basil bulgur wheat with pesto*

Ingredients	Makes approximately 4 portions	Makes approximately 10 portions
Aubergine, sliced lengthways	12 slices	30 slices
Assorted peppers	¼ of each	½ each
Courgettes	50 g	125 g
Plum tomatoes, concassée	2 each	5 each
Bulgur wheat	100 g	250 g
Vegetable stock	300 ml	750 ml
Basil	¼ bunch	½ bunch
Pesto (see page 145)		
Olive oil		
Good quality salt and pepper	To taste	To taste

energy	cal	fat	sat fat	carb	sugar	protein	fibre
3992 kJ	959 kcal	89.7 g	12.6 g	29.7 g	9.5 g	9.4 g	6.9 g

METHOD OF WORK

1   Bring the vegetable stock to the boil in a saucepan.

2   Add the bulgur wheat and simmer until just cooked.

3   Cover and then mix in the basil and tomatoes concassée.

4   Char grill the aubergines and reserve.

5   Slice, oil, season and roast the peppers and courgettes then julienne.

6   Lay the julienne on the aubergines and roll like cannelloni.

7   Place the aubergine rolls on a tray and heat through an oven.

8   To serve spoon the bulgur wheat onto a plate and lay three aubergine rolls on top, finish with pesto.

Polenta gnocchi romaine, parmesan crisp and basil oil

Ingredients	Makes approximately 4 portions	Makes approximately 10 portions
Polenta	150 g	400 g
Water and milk	300 ml	800 ml
Fresh milk	300 ml	800 ml
Parmesan cheese	200 g	500 g
Egg yolk	1	3
Good quality salt	To taste	To taste
White pepper	To taste	To taste
Grated nutmeg	To taste	To taste
Butter	100 g	300 g
Basil oil (see page 150)		
Parmesan crisp (see page 200 – leek and mushroom pearl barley risotto)		
Tomato sauce (see page 135)	200 ml	500 ml

energy	cal	fat	sat fat	carb	sugar	protein	fibre
2850 kJ	685 kcal	53.4 g	32.6 g	19.0 g	12.6 g	33.4 g	1.2 g

METHOD OF WORK

1   Bring the milk and water to the boil and add the polenta. Continuously stir with a whisk until it thickens avoiding lumps.

2   Season with salt, pepper and nutmeg.

3   Remove from the heat and add most of the grated parmesan leaving approximately ¼ aside for later and the egg yolk.

4   Mix well and then pour into a deep tray which has been lightly buttered. Spread to a thickness of approximately 1.5 cm.

5   Allow to cool and set. (Alternatively allow to semi set and roll into neat shapes.)

6   Once cold, cut out as required and place into a buttered earthenware dish. Add any trimmings on the bottom to form a base for the discs to sit on.

7   Brush some melted butter on top of the polenta gnocchi and sprinkle generously with the remaining parmesan cheese.

8   Gratinate under the salamander and serve accompanied with parmesan crisps, tomato sauce and basil oil.

Pasta

Pasta is a generic term used to describe many products made from semolina or flour which has been milled from the hardest of all wheat, durum wheat.

The secret to creating good pasta dough is to use the strongest, hardest flour which contains a high gluten content. Using softer wheat when making pasta paste gives a texture and colour which does not lend itself to the requirements of good paste. This gives the product a floury appearance when cooking in water and the end result is very soft and flavourless.

When making pasta dough you should ideally use only the best and freshest ingredients as this will ensure the end product will be of the highest quality both in appearance and flavour. Pasta dough, like most pastes, is affected by temperature both in the preparation and cooking stages.

The traditional way of making pasta dough is to prepare and create the mixture on a large unvarnished wooden table, which keeps the temperature and humidity constant. Modern methods include the use of stainless steel for hygiene reasons.

The method, whereby you create a flour mound with a well in the centre for the eggs, oil and salt and then bring in the flour to form a dough slowly, then **knead**, is still used in classical training. The modern method now commonly implemented is to place all the ingredients into a food processor and blend for approximately 10–20 seconds until a loose ball is formed.

> **CHEF'S TIP** Durum wheat or semolina flour is best used for pasta as it has the highest gluten content of all flours. It is this gluten that holds the pasta together and gives it its springiness. If you cannot find either of these, try using a good bread flour as this will also have a relatively high gluten content.

> **CHEF'S TIP** DO NOT overwork the dough or add too much excess flour when kneading or the dough will dry out and crack. If, once rested, the dough is still a little slack or sticky then rub a little extra flour in to absorb any excess moisture from the outside of the dough.

When using either method, the paste should feel just firm to the touch and not be sticky.

The finished paste should be wrapped in a plastic film and rested for a minimum of 30 minutes (overnight if possible), which will allow the gluten to relax and prevent shrinkage when rolling out the paste.

Step-by-step: Making fresh egg pasta

1. Adding eggs and oil to the flour well.

2. Carefully incorporate the flour into the centre; ensure the liquid does not spill out of the sides.

3. Continue to mix in the flour until the dough begins to form.

4. Bring the dough together and begin to knead until a smooth ball has been produced.

5. Wrap the smooth dough in cling film and then refrigerate for a minimum of 30 minutes.

Step-by-step: Rolling pasta

1. Carefully roll the pasta through the machine on the widest setting; this should be done twice.

2. Gradually lower the roller settings until a thin smooth sheet of pasta is formed.

3. Join the two ends of the pasta together and continue to roll the pasta, this technique will speed up the process. There is no need to keep feeding the pasta back into the top of the machine.

4. Once the desired thickness has been achieved cut the pasta along the top edge as shown; the pasta can then be removed

5. The rolled pasta can then be placed onto a floured work surface ready to be used as required.

VIDEO CLIP Rolling pasta.

The dough can now be rolled out with a rolling pin or formed using a pasta machine, with the latter allowing large quantities to be rolled out to an exact thickness and with greater speed.

Once the pasta has been rolled out, numerous processes can be implemented, including cutting, shaping, filling, cooking or drying.

CHEF'S TIP As pasta is a paste it is very delicate. The best results are gained by resting after every movement of the product, i.e. after kneading, rolling or moulding.

TASK Using the plain egg pasta dough as a recipe guide: research and develop your own recipe using different flavour combinations, e.g. sun-dried tomato and basil pasta dough.

Equipment needed in pasta making

This equipment is required for creating pasta at Level 2. It is quite straightforward as general equipment is necessary and will include items from the list below.

Spoons

Slotted spoons

Tongs

Conical strainer

Bowls

Metal spider

Fish slice

At a higher level, you will need further items:

Pasta machine

Wooden chopping board for shaping

If required, small rolling pins and ravioli tray

Palette knives

Fluted cutter or roller

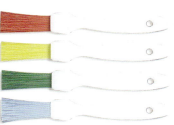

Pastry brushes

IMAGES COURTESY OF RUSSUMS.CO.UK

CHEF'S TIP When making fresh long length pasta for service, it is always best to leave it to hang and dry slightly over a wooden handle or raised rolling pin. This will help the pasta not to stick when cooked as the strands will not tend to group together.

Fresh or dried pasta

Many people assume dried pasta is just fresh pasta that has been set out to dry and, although this can be the case, dried pasta does have a recipe of its own.

Fresh pasta, which is traditionally made in northern and central Italy, is almost always made with eggs, which are highly perishable. Fresh pasta must be eaten within a few days of its preparation.

Dried pasta, a southern Italian trademark, almost never contains eggs. Its main ingredients are usually semolina flour, water and salt, meaning that dried pasta can last almost indefinitely without refrigeration.

Fresh pasta can be made with a wide variety of flours, including semolina flour (a derivative of durum wheat), chestnut flour and wheat flour. It is most often made with the more delicate bread flour, which is easier to roll and shape by hand. Dried pasta, on the other hand, almost exclusively relies on semolina flour.

Left to right — Rice noodles and egg noodles

Stuffed pasta

This can be in the form of dried or fresh pasta and either open with a filling, such as cannelloni, or closed, such as ravioli. Pasta that is stuffed for items such as ravioli or tortellini has to be as thin as possible so that when the filling is added the product is not too hard to eat or cook.

Step-by-step: Making tortellinis

1. Using a round cutter cut out a neat disc of pasta.

2. Place a neat ball of filling into the centre of the pasta disc.

3. Wet the inner edges with a little water; then fold the pasta over to create a semi circle.

4. Squeeze the two thinnest parts together and gently roll back the top as shown.

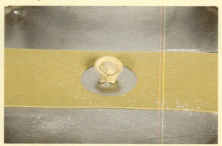

5. A finished tortellini.

VIDEO CLIP Tortellini.

WEB LINK See the web page for products created using wheat (durum). The site gives detailed nutritional information as well as uses, production notes and quality points to look for.
http://www.wheatfoods.org

The stuffing should be a pleasant marriage of flavours, neither too overpowering nor overpowered by the accompanying sauce or garnishes. The main difficulty and fault that occurs when stuffing pasta is poor sealing of the edges and failing to make them look neat. The same care has to be taken with pasta work as with pastry items.

CHEF'S TIP Ensure that stuffed pasta is not overfilled as it becomes hard to seal and will break when blanched causing the filling to leak out into the water.

TASK Produce a chart identifying suitable fillings for tortellinis and raviolis.

HEALTH & SAFETY All products not for immediate use should be stored correctly and be clearly labelled.

Step-by-step: Making ravioli

1. Brush the pasta sheet with a little water.

2. Arrange neat balls of filling as shown (alternatively the filling may be piped into position).

3. Carefully lay another sheet of pasta over the filling.

4. Using the reverse end of a pastry cutter carefully press down to expel any excess air: this will make a neat seal and prevent the filling from escaping during cooking.

5. Using a slightly larger cutter begin to cut out the raviolis.

6. An example of ravioli. This may also be produced as triangles or squares. The edge can also be marked using a fork for decorative effect.

VIDEO CLIP Filling pasta.

VIDEO CLIP Shaping ravioli.

Quality points

- Dried pasta has come a long way in recent years and the quality of these products has greatly improved in both variety and taste.

- When choosing dried pasta, the box or container should not be opened or damaged. The pasta itself should not be broken or damaged: even though the product is dry, it will need to last for a long time. Furthermore a reasonable use by date should be applied to the packaging.

- Dry pasta should be completely dry and not damp in any way, and must be even in colour and not discoloured or speckled.

- With fresh pasta a lot more consideration has to be given to quality. Fresh pasta should be received at a temperature below 5 °C and be evenly coloured, not mottled and not greying in colour.

- The pasta should not be ripped, torn, dried or damaged in any way.

- If stuffed, the pasta should not open at the seams or be uneven in shape.

- Ensure when receiving pasta that it has not stuck together which could mean that moisture has found its way into the packaging.

Preparation and cooking methods

Blanching – this technique is used to speed up the cooking process and shorten service time. It can be utilized with both dried and fresh pasta using boiling salted water then ice cold water to refresh.

Straining – pasta is a delicate commodity, and a colander or spider should be used for straining. Pasta should be cooked and refreshed in more water than is necessary, thus ensuring that it has enough room to move, and that you are then able to remove it easily.

Mixing – for this method a larger container is required so that the items can be evenly mixed or bound together. Large spoons are best, using large, gentle stirring movements which will help to prevent damage to the end product.

Boiling – a large deep saucepan with plenty of water is required for boiling pasta. Pasta is a starch-based product and has a tendency to absorb water: to help prevent it sticking together during the cooking process a large amount of boiling water is needed. Ensuring that there is more than enough liquid means the water is less likely to thicken and you will have plenty to actually cook the pasta.

When boiling batches of pasta for service the water needs to be changed at regular intervals so that the best end result can be achieved. Adding salt to the water can raise the temperature so that the water will maintain boiling or stay at a high temperature for longer. This also helps with the flavouring in general and will bring out the taste of the pasta.

Baking – this tends to be used for dishes that have already been made up or require no further preparation. Care must be taken so that the dish cooks evenly and has a nice all-over colour. Items that are baked should be cleaned up before and after cooking so that a more presentable dish can be achieved.

When baking, check at regular intervals to monitor quality. A probe should be used to check the core temperature so that when the product seems cooked and the correct colour is achieved you can ensure that it is also at a safe temperature for service.

Combination cooking – general boiling, poaching or deep frying will be the starting block for most pastas and sauces, closely followed by either baking or simmering.

A perfect example of this would be using fresh pasta. The pasta has to be blanched, the filling has to be cooked, and finally the dish has to be baked.

> **CHEF'S TIP** Filled pasta items should always be produced thinner than required as they will contract slightly on cooking and if they are too thick they will be heavy to eat.

> **CHEF'S TIP** When making stuffed pasta, work as quickly as possible to prevent the pasta dough from drying out and becoming too difficult to work with. This will also prevent problems occurring with the pasta sealing properly.

> **CHEF'S TIP** For best results with stuffed pasta, they should be blanched first in boiling salted water then placed onto a tray with a damp, clean cloth or paper towel to take off excess water.

Issues with cooking, holding and storage

With the storage of dried pasta, the same rules apply to this that would with any dry or dried product, namely airtight containers that are clearly labelled, dated and stored in a cool dry place. Dried pasta can be stored for a few months in this way and generally tends to not lose its quality.

If the pasta is dried in flat form, i.e. pasta sheet, tagliatelle or noodles, then this should be stored in a large square container with greaseproof paper in between layers so that they do not stick.

When cooking and holding dried pasta for service, the pasta should be blanched, dried and then lightly coated in oil in order to prevent it from sticking. This rule applies to almost all shaped pasta but excludes sheets like lasagne or cannelloni which should be made dry and then baked in order to cook the pasta.

CHEF'S TIP When cooking pasta you do not need oil in the water to stop it sticking. This is purely a myth as the oil sits on the top and does not mix with the water or pasta.

For service and holding, use only what is required as pasta can tend to overcook very easily. As the pasta has been blanched its cooking time is greatly reduced and it should therefore only take minutes to reheat. The holding temperature should be maintained at about 65 °C.

For fresh pasta the ruling is different. Fresh pasta is generally made with fresh or pasteurized eggs and so the shelf life is immediately reduced. When storing fresh pasta it should be wrapped tightly in plastic film with no holes or openings and placed into a refrigerator to avoid the paste

from oxidizing and turning grey. This should then be clearly labelled, including the date of production.

When pasta has been shaped it should be stored in a large container with semolina to prevent it from getting sticky and again, similar to dried flat pasta, inbetween layers of greaseproof paper in an airtight container.

Fresh pasta that has been stuffed or is in small shapes should be blanched, drained and frozen or chilled in small amounts so that it can be easily separated. The frozen pasta will keep for between one and three months.

For service, fresh pasta that is shaped can be cooked to order as the cooking time is short. Fresh pasta can be blanched but does not hold as well as dried pasta. The exception to this rule is stuffed fresh pastas such as ravioli or flat shapes such as lasagne which can be blanched and refreshed and will hold quite well.

In its raw form, fresh and blanched pasta should be stored in a fridge below 5 °C. If it is for service then it should be held at 65 °C.

TEST YOURSELF

1 Name four pasta shapes.

2 Which of the below are not used in the production of fresh pasta: butter, eggs, flour?

3 Name three varieties of dried pasta.

4 Name three accompaniments to pasta.

5 Finished fresh pasta should be rested for a minimum of how long?

6 What two flours are suitable for pasta making?

7 What cheese is traditionally served with carbonara?

8 Pasta is famous from which country?

9 What is the name of the dish consisting of pasta sheets, béchamel and mince?

10 Name four pasta sauces.

Recipes

Egg pasta dough

Ingredients	Makes approximately 4 portions	Makes approximately 10 portions
OO Grade flour	72 g	180 g
Eggs	1	2
Egg yolks	1	3
Olive oil	5 ml	12 ml
Good quality salt and pepper	To taste	To taste

energy	cal	fat	sat fat	carb	sugar	protein	fibre
442 kJ	105 kcal	4.1 g	1.0 g	14.1 g	0.3 g	3.9 g	0.6 g

METHOD OF WORK

1   In a large bowl or on a clean work surface, sieve the flour and using your hands create a well by pushing the flour out to create a ring.

2   In a bowl beat the eggs, yolks and oil together.

3   Slowly add the egg mixture to the middle of the flour before slowly incorporating the two sets of ingredients to form a paste.

4   On the work surface, knead the dough until smooth.

5   Cover with plastic film and refrigerate for at least 15 minutes. Before rolling out use a little flour or semolina to dust the work surface so that the dough does not stick.

VIDEO CLIP Fresh basic pasta.

Linguine with smoked salmon *cucumber ribbons and crème fraîche*

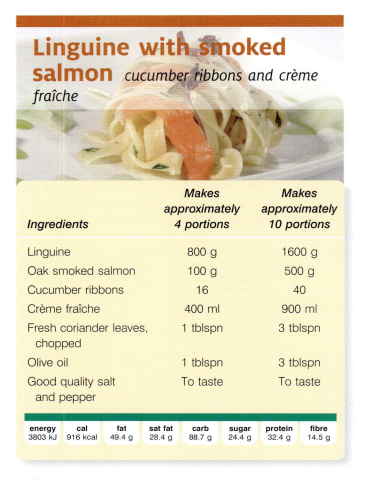

Ingredients	Makes approximately 4 portions	Makes approximately 10 portions
Linguine	800 g	1600 g
Oak smoked salmon	100 g	500 g
Cucumber ribbons	16	40
Crème fraîche	400 ml	900 ml
Fresh coriander leaves, chopped	1 tblspn	3 tblspn
Olive oil	1 tblspn	3 tblspn
Good quality salt and pepper	To taste	To taste

energy	cal	fat	sat fat	carb	sugar	protein	fibre
3803 kJ	916 kcal	49.4 g	28.4 g	88.7 g	24.4 g	32.4 g	14.5 g

METHOD OF WORK

1   Blanch the linguine in a large saucepan of boiling salted water for the time stated on the packaging.

2   Over a high heat sauté the stripped salmon in the olive oil before adding the cooked and drained linguine.

3   Fold in the cucumber ribbons. Keep the pan on the heat for about 3 minutes to fully warm through the salmon and the cucumber. Season well.

4   Remove the pan from the heat and stir in the crème fraîche so that it does not split.

5   Stir in the coriander, check the seasoning and serve immediately.

Butternut squash ravioli with thyme, tomato and red onion butter sauce

Ingredients	Makes approximately 4 portions	Makes approximately 10 portions
Egg pasta dough (see recipe)		
Filling		
Butternut squash, peeled and deseeded	1000 g	2500 g
Fresh thyme (leaves only)	1 tblspn	2 tblspn
Red onion, finely chopped	2	4
Unsalted butter	150 g	300 g
Tomatoes, chopped	3	6
Garlic clove, finely chopped	1	2
Good quality salt and pepper	To taste	To taste

energy	cal	fat	sat fat	carb	sugar	protein	fibre
2064 kJ	495 kcal	35.5 g	21.1 g	39.3 g	14.6 g	7.6 g	3.9 g

METHOD OF WORK

1 Make the pasta paste using the method on page 207.

2 Using one tablespoon of the butter, sweat the onion, garlic and thyme leaves. Leave for approximately 5 minutes or until all the ingredients have softened.

3 Add the tomatoes and continue to simmer for a further 5 minutes before removing from the heat and blast chilling.

4 Cut the butternut squash into large even pieces and in a saucepan cover them with vegetable stock. Bring the squash to the boil and simmer for approximately 15 minutes until tender. Place the squash onto a tray and allow the cooked squash to dry out in a moderate oven before gently mashing with a fork and seasoning.

5 Using a pasta machine, roll out the paste to a thickness at 'level 3' ensuring the pasta is kept covered and floured as much as possible.

6 Using an appropriately sized cutter, cut out pieces from the pasta sheets and set a spoonful of the butternut squash mixture into the centre. Use a little water around the edges of the pasta pieces before placing another piece of pasta over the top and sealing with your fingers or a fork. Leave the pasta to rest for 15 minutes.

7 Blanch the pasta in a large pan of boiling salted water.

8 Warm the tomato and red onion sauce until boiling. When the sauce is boiling, remove from the heat and whisk the rest of the cold butter into the sauce.

9 Add the drained pasta to the sauce, coat, garnish and serve.

Crab and coconut cannelloni with lobster bisque

Ingredients	Makes approximately 4 portions	Makes approximately 10 portions
Egg pasta dough (see recipe)		
Filling:		
White crab meat	400 g	1000 g
Minced white fish	100 g	250 g
Coconut milk	1 tblspn	2 tblspn
Finely chopped shallots	2	4
Unsalted butter	50 g	125 g
Single cream	50 ml	125 ml
Eggs	1	2
Good quality salt and pepper	To taste	To taste
Lobster bisque (see page 174)		

energy	cal	fat	sat fat	carb	sugar	protein	fibre
2571 kJ	618 kcal	41.2 g	20.5 g	18.6 g	2.7 g	38.9 g	2.0 g

METHOD OF WORK

1 Make the pasta paste using the method in on page 207.

2 Roll the pasta into thin sheets and cut into rectangles (this will form the base of the cannelloni).

3 Using one tablespoon of the butter, sweat the shallots for approximately 5 minutes or until they have softened.

4 Take a food processor bowl and place in the freezer for 15 minutes.

5 Remove the bowl and add the crab meat, white fish, coconut and shallots: then blend well.

6 Add the butter and egg and blend until totally incorporated.

7 Slowly add enough cream to form a smooth consistency, season and test a little by spooning a small piece into boiling water (this will check the setting properties: taste and adjust the seasoning.

8 Pipe the filling onto the pasta sheets, roll in cling film and steam until the pasta is cooked.

9 Serve with the bisque and garnish as required.

Farfalle with pancetta and oyster mushrooms

Ingredients	Makes approximately 4 portions	Makes approximately 10 portions
Farfalle pasta	600 g	1200 g
Pancetta lardons	200 g	400 g
Oyster mushrooms	320 g	650 g
Double cream	200 ml	400 ml
Vegetable stock	200 ml	400 ml
Butter	½ tblspn	1 tblspn
Garlic, finely chopped	1 clove	2 cloves
Parsley, finely chopped	1 tblspn	3 tblspn
Good quality salt and pepper	To taste	To taste

energy	cal	fat	sat fat	carb	sugar	protein	fibre
3100 kJ	744 kcal	53.3 g	27.4 g	49.4 g	2.3 g	19.7 g	5.2 g

METHOD OF WORK

1 Blanch the pasta bows in a large saucepan of boiling salted water. Refresh in iced water.

2 In a saucepan melt the butter and sweat the garlic and pancetta; fry until golden then remove from the pan.

3 In the same pan add the mushrooms and fry for approximately 2 minutes until the mushrooms have softened.

4 Add the stock and reduce the mixture by half.

5 Add the cream and also reduce by half or until the sauce has reached a consistency capable of coating the back of a spoon. Season well and add the fresh chopped parsley, pancetta and the drained cooked pasta before serving.

SOURCING Try to use locally sourced, in season mushrooms for this dish, for example:
Pied de mouton are at their best in January and February whereas European ceps have better depths of flavour in September and October.

Fusilli arrabiatta

Ingredients	Makes approximately 4 portions	Makes approximately 10 portions
Fusilli pasta	600 g	1500 g
Olive oil	2 tblspn	5 tblspn
Garlic, finely chopped	3 cloves	5 cloves
Onion, finely chopped	80 g	240 g
Red chilli, brunoise	1	3
White wine	200 ml	500 ml
Concassée of plum tomatoes	200 g	450 g
Fresh oregano leaves	1 tblspn	3 tblspn
Good quality salt and pepper	To taste	To taste
Focaccia bread		

energy	cal	fat	sat fat	carb	sugar	protein	fibre
3099 kJ	735 kcal	23.0 g	3.9 g	111.2 g	7.1 g	20.1 g	10.6 g

METHOD OF WORK

1 Cook the pasta twists in a large saucepan of boiling salted water following the guidelines on the packaging. Refresh immediately in iced cold water.

2 Gently heat the oil before adding the prepared onion, garlic, chilli and oregano. Sweat for 5 minutes or until softened.

3 Add the white wine and reduce until just a little liquid is left.

4 Add the concassée of plum tomatoes and leave to simmer for approximately 15 minutes or until all excess liquid has been evaporated.

5 Reheat the pasta and coat in the spicy tomato sauce. Serve immediately.

CHEF'S TIP Fresh or dried pasta can be used in this dish. Try adding other Italian-derived ingredients such as olives or capers to add a different flavour.

Gnocchi parisienne
(choux paste-based)

Ingredients	Makes approximately 4 portions	Makes approximately 10 portions
Water	125 ml	300 ml
Butter unsalted	50 g	125 g
Salt		
White plain flour	60 g	150 g
Eggs	2	5
Grated cheese	50 g	125 g
Béchamel	250 ml	625 ml
Good quality salt and pepper	To taste	To taste

energy	cal	fat	sat fat	carb	sugar	protein	fibre
1322 kJ	317 kcal	22.7 g	13.3 g	19.4 g	3.6 g	10.2 g	1.1 g

METHOD OF WORK

1. Heat the water, butter and salt in a saucepan until the butter melts and the salt has dissolved, then remove from the heat.
2. Mix in the flour and place back on the heat, continue until the mixture leaves the sides.
3. Cool slightly then gradually add the beaten egg.
4. Mix in ¾ of the cheese.
5. Place the mixture into a piping bag with a ½ cm plain tube.
6. Pipe out 1 cm lengths into a shallow pan of simmering water.
7. Do not boil.
8. Once cooked between 8–10 minutes, drain and combine with the béchamel.
9. Pour into a dish, sprinkle with cheese and colour under the salamander.

Gnocchi piedmontaise
(potato-based)

Ingredients	Makes approximately 4 portions	Makes approximately 10 portions
Dry mashed potato	200 g	500 g
Butter unsalted	20 g	50 g
Eggs	1	2
Egg yolks	1	3
Butter for sauté	40 g	100 g
Good quality salt and pepper	To taste	To taste
Strong flour	60 g	150 g
Sun blushed tomatoes		
Sage leaves		

energy	cal	fat	sat fat	carb	sugar	protein	fibre
1378 kJ	331 kcal	22.1 g	10.8 g	26.9 g	1.0 g	7.5 g	2.5 g

METHOD OF WORK

1. Add the butter, eggs and flour to the hot potato and mix well.
2. Season to taste.
3. Using a little flour shape the gnocchi into small rounds, then use a fork and press down slightly to flatten.
4. Place in boiling salted water then simmer for 5 minutes until cooked.
5. Drain well then in a non stick pan sauté the gnocchi in butter for colour, add the sage and sun blushed tomatoes to finish.

Note: Piedmontaise is usually served with tomato sauce – here the dish uses sun blushed tomatoes as an alternative.

Lasagne

Ingredients	Makes approximately 4 portions	Makes approximately 10 portions
Lasagne	200 g	500 g
Olive oil	1 tblspn	3 tblspn
Lardons of bacon	50 g	125 g
Onion, diced	170 g	350 g
Celery, diced	100 g	200 g
Carrot, diced	150 g	300 g
Minced beef	200 g	550 g
Tomato purée	50 g	125 g
Beef stock	400 ml	1 litre
Garlic, finely chopped	3 cloves	5 cloves
Fresh marjoram, leaves	1 tblspn	2 tblspn
Button mushrooms, sliced	100 g	250 g
Béchamel sauce	250 ml	600 ml
Cheddar cheese, grated	50 g	150 g
Butter for greasing	½ tsp	1 tsp
Good quality salt and pepper	To taste	To taste

energy	cal	fat	sat fat	carb	sugar	protein	fibre
1816 kJ	435 kcal	26.0 g	10.2 g	26.8 g	9.0 g	25.3 g	4.4 g

METHOD OF WORK

1. Preheat an oven to 190 °C.
2. If using lasagne sheets that require pre-cooking, cook as per the packaging guidelines and refresh immediately in iced cold water.
3. Butter a suitable oven-proof dish before covering with a layer of the meat sauce followed by a layer of cooked lasagne sheets. Repeat this process two more times.

Cover the complete layers with béchamel sauce (see page 123) and top with the cheese before covering the dish with foil and baking for 20 minutes in the pre-heated oven. After this time, remove the foil and continue to bake for a further 15 minutes to **gratinate** the cheese.

CHEF'S TIP For a vegetarian option simply exchange the beef mince for quorn, vegetable stock for beef stock and remove the bacon.

For different approach select seasonal vegetables, cut into **macédoine**: finish with a little tomato sauce and continue as normal.

Macaroni with blue cheese and leeks

Ingredients	Makes approximately 4 portions	Makes approximately 10 portions
Macaroni	200 g	1000 g
Fresh milk	1000 ml	2500 ml
Butter	150 g	375 g
Flour	150 g	375 g
Blue cheese (Stilton)	200 g	500 g
Leek	200 g	500 g
Freshly chopped parsley	1 tsp	3 tsp
Unsalted butter	1 tsp	3 tsp
Good quality salt and pepper	To taste	To taste

energy	cal	fat	sat fat	carb	sugar	protein	fibre
3295 kJ	790 kcal	54.7 g	34.6 g	51.8 g	13.8 g	26.5 g	3.2 g

METHOD OF WORK

1   Preheat an oven to 190 °C.

2   Cook the macaroni in a large pan of boiling salted water for the time stated on the packaging. Refresh immediately in iced cold water.

3   In a medium sized saucepan melt the butter and stir in the flour. Cook out the rawness of the flour over a medium heat for 1 minute before slowly starting to add the milk, one ladle at a time.

4   Continue adding a ladle of the milk at intervals, but only when the previous ladle has been mixed in and absorbed, the sauce is boiling and there are no lumps present within the sauce.

5   Continue to cook the flour out of the sauce by allowing the sauce to gently simmer over a very low heat for approximately 45 minutes. Season well.

6   Gently sweat the leek for 5 minutes in the butter.

7   Add the cooked leek and half the cheese to the béchamel, ensuring the cheese has completely melted. Add the cooked macaroni.

8   Pour into a suitable oven-proof dish and sprinkle with the remaining cheese before baking for about 20 minutes or until golden brown on top. Sprinkle with parsley and serve.

SOURCING Try using different cheeses to change the dish's appearance and flavour: see the website for a list of specialities from UK regions:
www.britishcheese.com

Spaghetti bolognaise

Ingredients	Makes approximately 4 portions	Makes approximately 10 portions
Spaghetti	600 g	1500 g
Oil	1 tblspn	3 tblspn
Bacon lardons	50 g	125 g
Onion, diced	120 g	270 g
Celery, diced	75 g	180 g
Carrot, diced	100 g	200 g
Minced beef	200 g	500 g
Tomato purée	50 g	125 g
Beef stock	400 ml	1000 ml
Garlic, finely chopped	3 cloves	6 cloves
Marjoram leaves	2 tblspn	5 tblspn
Mushroom, sliced	100 g	250 g
Béchamel sauce	250 ml	600 ml
Cheddar cheese, grated	25 g	125 g
Concassée of tomatoes	200 g	450 g
Good quality salt and pepper	To taste	To taste

energy	cal	fat	sat fat	carb	sugar	protein	fibre
2200 kJ	525 kcal	24.4 g	9.0 g	51.3 g	10.3 g	28.3 g	6.5 g

METHOD OF WORK

1 If using spaghetti that requires pre-cooking, cook as per the packaging guidelines and refresh immediately in iced cold water.

2 In a large saucepan heat 1 tablespoon of the oil and fry the lardons for 3 minutes.

3 Add the prepared onion, carrot and celery to the lardons, place a lid onto the pan and sweat for a further 5 minutes until the vegetables have softened.

4 Remove the lid and add the mince. Over a high heat brown the mince stirring continuously.

5 Once the mince is completely browned, remove the pan from the heat and stir in the tomato purée, garlic and marjoram.

6 Return to the heat for two minutes to cook out the bitterness from the tomato purée before adding the stock and the tomato concassé. Bring the pan to the boil, season well and simmer for 15 minutes.

7 Mix in the prepared mushrooms and cook for a further 5 minutes before reheating the spaghetti and serving.

CHEF'S TIP Try enriching the sauce with a tablespoon of balsamic vinegar or a dash of red wine and reduce to thicken.

CHEF'S TIP A vegetarian option can be made by using minced quorn instead of beef mince, vegetable stock instead of beef stock and removing the bacon.

Tortellini filled with ratatouille on wilted spinach with tomato coulis

Ingredients	Makes approximately 4 portions	Makes approximately 10 portions
Plain egg pasta dough		
Brunoise of peppers, courgettes, aubergines, onions	50 g of each	125 g of each
Tomato juice	50 ml	125 ml
Garlic crushed	1	2
Olive oil		
Good quality salt and pepper	To taste	To taste
White wine	25 ml	60 ml
Baby spinach	100 g	250 g
Unsalted butter	25 g	60 g
Raw tomato coulis (see page 146)		

energy	cal	fat	sat fat	carb	sugar	protein	fibre
3387 kJ	803 kcal	27.4 g	7.7 g	119.4 g	4.7 g	26.3 g	6.1 g

METHOD OF WORK

1 Sweat the brunoise of vegetables and garlic in the olive oil until just cooked but still with bite.

2 Add the white wine and reduce until dry.

3 Add the tomato juice and reduce by half.

4 Chill until required.

5 Roll the pasta dough as shown when making tortellini (see page 210).

6 Fill with the ratatouille, reserving a little for garnish.

7 Add enough coulis to the ratatouille to produce a sauce.

8 Blanch the tortellini for 4–5 minutes then drain well.

9 Sweat the baby spinach in butter until just cooked and season to taste.

10 Arrange the spinach on the plate with the tortellini and warmed ratatouille.

Rice

Rice descended from wild grasses, and is a staple food in South Asia. Historians believe that it was first produced and harvested in the area covering the foothills of the eastern Himalayas, and stretching through Burma, Thailand, Laos, Vietnam and southern China. Remains of early produced rice were found in the Yangtze valley dating to about 8500 BC. The commodity soon spread in all directions and was adapted by humans to create numerous varieties.

What is rice?

Rice is a type of short-lived plant related to grass. The normal lifespan of a rice plant is 3–7 months depending on variety and climate. Rice is not a water plant but needs a large amount of irrigation to grow well.

Rice is harvested from a field sometimes called a paddy field. A complete seed of rice is called a paddy. One grain of paddy contains one rice kernel. Each paddy consists of many layers. The outermost layer of the rice shell is called a husk. A husk consists of two interlocked half-shells, each protecting one side of the paddy. The husk consists mostly of silica and cellulose.

The next layers are all called bran layers. Each is made up of very thin bran film. Bran is mainly fibre, vitamin B, protein and fat, the most nutritious part of rice.

At the base of each grain is the embryo which will grow and produce a new plant.

The central part is the rice kernel (endosperm), consisting mainly of two types of starch: amylose and amylopectin. Mixtures of these two starches determine the cooking texture of rice.

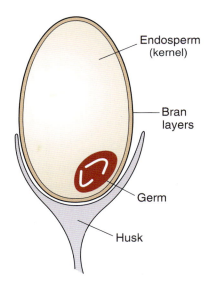

A cross-section of a rice grain

> **CHEF'S TIP** Rice is an excellent source of fibre and can be used to balance a meal; using brown rice instead of bleached white will also increase the nutritional value.

Rice is a very nutritious grain, especially brown rice. It has a high fibre content, vitamin B, carbohydrate and protein, but has no gluten, so is safe to eat for sufferers of coeliac disease and those with gluten allergies.

There are three main varieties of rice in the world, Indica (long grain), Japonica (round grain) and Javanica (medium grain).

Indica rice concentrates in a warm climate belt, from Indochina, Thailand, India, Pakistan, Brazil and the southern US. Japonica is grown in mostly temperate climate countries, Japan, Korea, northern China and California. Javanica is grown only in Indonesia.

Types of rice

There are more than 40 000 varieties of cultivated rice produced today, the exact figure is uncertain. Over 90 000 samples of cultivated rice and wild species are stored at the International Rice Gene Bank and are used by researchers all over the world.

The rice varieties can be divided into two basic groups, long grain/all purpose and speciality.

LONG GRAIN/ALL PURPOSE

All-purpose long grain rice is imported mainly from the US, Italy, Spain, Guyana and Thailand, and can be used for all styles of cooking. Long grain rice was once exported from

India and was called Patna after the district in which it grew. Today most of the long grain rice is imported into the UK from America. Long grain rice is a slim grain which is 4–5 times as long as it is wide. When harvested it is known as 'rough' or 'paddy' rice. It undergoes different milling techniques to give different types of rice.

LONG GRAIN WHITE RICE (MOST COMMON)

This is one of the most popular types of rice because it has a subtle flavour, which perfectly complements both rich and delicate sauces. Milled to remove the husk and bran layer, on cooking the grains separate to give an attractive fluffy effect. Extremely versatile, it is used extensively in Chinese cooking.

EASY-COOK LONG GRAIN WHITE RICE (PARBOILED/CONVERTED/PRE-FLUFFED)

This variety has a slightly rounded flavour. Unlike regular white rice which is milled direct from the field, it is steamed under pressure before milling. This process hardens the grain, reducing the possibility of overcooking. It also helps to retain much of the natural vitamin and mineral content present in the milled layers.

When raw the rice has a golden colour, but turns white upon cooking. This rice can be used in the same way as the common rice above. It works particularly well in salads.

BROWN LONG GRAIN RICE (WHOLEGRAIN RICE)

This rice has a distinctly nutty flavour. Brown rice undergoes only minimal milling, which removes the husk but retains the bran layer. Because of this the rice retains more vitamins, minerals and fibre content than the common or easy-cook white rice. The grains remain separate when cooked, like long grain white, but take longer to soften. The cooked grains have a chewy texture, which many people enjoy. It is also available in easy-cook form.

CHEF'S TIP Rice works exceptionally well in salads. However, care must be taken when cooking and refreshing the rice, as once chilled the grains harden slightly giving a somewhat raw texture.

SPECIALITY

These include the aromatics, risotto, glutinous and pudding rice which are particularly suited to ethnic cuisines. These are often grown, cooked and eaten in the same location. This is partly due to the climate in which the rice needs to grow.

Arborio rice is the classic risotto rice from the north Italian region of Piedmont; a medium to long grain rice, it absorbs a lot of cooking liquid yet still retains a good bite in texture, known as **al dente**.

CHEF'S TIP Arborio rice is cooked using stock; ensure only the best quality ingredients are used to guarantee a quality end product is achieved.

THE AROMATICS

The first class of speciality rice is aromatic rice. These contain a natural ingredient which is responsible for their fragrant taste and aroma. The fragrance quality of aromatic rice can differ from one year's harvest to the next, due to weather changes. The finest aromatic rice is aged to bring out a stronger aroma in the same way that wine is.

BASMATI RICE

This is a very long, slender-grained aromatic rice grown mainly around the Himalayas in India and Pakistan. Sometimes described as the Prince of Rice, it has a fragrant flavour and aroma and is used in Indian dishes. The grains are separate and fluffy when cooked. In Indian recipes it is often cooked with spices to enhance the grain's aromatic properties. Easy-cook basmati and brown rice basmati are also available. Brown basmati rice has higher fibre content and an even stronger aroma than white basmati. Aged basmati rice is a better quality, but is more expensive to buy.

JASMINE RICE (THAI FRAGRANT RICE)

This is another aromatic rice, although its flavour is slightly less pronounced than basmati. It originates from Thailand. The length and shape of the grains look as though they should remain separate on cooking but instead it has a soft and slightly sticky texture when cooked. Good with Chinese and South East Asian food.

CHEF'S TIP Jasmine rice is ideal for sushi as it sticks together well and has a distinctive flavour.

CHEF'S TIP Rice wine is excellent for flavouring sushi: when the rice is cooked drizzle the rice wine into the hot rice and allow it to be absorbed.

AMERICAN AROMATICS

The American rice industry has developed varieties of aromatic rice which are very similar to both basmati and jasmine rice. These varieties are not usually available in the UK except in specialist shops.

JAPONICA RICE

This short and medium grain rice is grown mainly in California. It comes in a variety of colours including red, brown and black. This type of rice is used in Japanese and Caribbean cookery due to its tacky, moist and firm nature when cooked.

WILD RICE

This is not rice, but in fact an aquatic grass. Wild rice is extremely difficult to harvest. It is expensive but this is acceptable as the colour, a purplish black, and its subtly

nutty flavour combine well with other dishes. It is a good colour enhancer for a special dish or rice salad and it can be mixed economically with other rice (but may need pre-cooking as it takes 45 to 50 minutes to cook, using one part grain to three parts of water).

SUMMARY

White rice has had the bran and germ removed which makes the end product more delicate and gives it a softer flavour. Brown rice is chewier and nuttier due to the bran being left on the rice kernel. It is also more nutritious.

Other products made from rice

GROUND RICE

Made from rice grains which are ground up and then used for milk-based desserts.

RICE FLOUR

This is rice which is finely milled to produce flour and is then used to thicken some soups.

RICE PAPER

This is paper made from milled rice and is mainly used in pastry kitchens.

LIQUID

Rice wines (also known as rice beer) because the fermentation process is undertaken with rice (beer-based) as opposed to fruit (grapes for wine).

Mirin is a sweet rice wine used to flavour sauces and cooked rice dishes (this particular wine is not usually drunk). Sake is the most famous of Japanese rice wines and is served warm. It does not keep well and unlike normal wine should be consumed within one year of bottling. Shaoxing wine is the Chinese variety of the Japanese sake.

COOKED PRODUCTS

Rice cakes are circular cooked cakes which have very little flavour and fat. Rice crackers are a Japanese snack now served in bars and restaurants.

VIDEO CLIP Rice noodles.

NOODLES

Rice noodles are made with rice flour, are available dried and require **soaking** in hot water until transparent then used as required.

Laksa noodles are used to make the dish laksa which is an Indonesian and Malaysian speciality. They resemble white spaghetti.

Rice flake noodles resemble tortilla chips and are dried. Soak in hot water and use as required.

Rice sticks – thin, medium or wide varieties are available. Thin sticks are used in soups and salads, medium for the majority of dishes and wide for braised dishes or stir fry.

The preparation and cooking of rice

The washing and soaking of rice removes any excess starch which when cooked could cloud the cooking medium and cause the rice to become 'gloopy'. By washing the rice any debris, dirt or impurities will be removed. It ensures the grains are clean and as such is recommended as good working practice.

When cooking rice the factors to be taken into account are the liquid used and the quantity, which vary depending on the dish being cooked and the variety of rice grain.

A general rule is:

- 1½ times liquid to rice for sushi
- 2 times liquid to rice for braised rice dishes
- 3 times liquid to rice for risotto
- 3 times liquid to rice for wild rice
- 3–4 times liquid to rice for boiled
- 4 times liquid to rice for paella.

These amounts are approximate and will of course vary depending on the grains used.

When cooking sushi, risotto and paella the idea is to allow the grains to burst and release starch which will act as a natural thickening agent. This process is caused by the size and shape of the grain.

Rice can be an extremely versatile commodity and is used extensively in international cooking for both sweet and savoury dishes.

HEALTH & SAFETY The bacteria commonly found in rice is *Bacillus cereus*, which will multiply effectively if the rice is not kept above 75 °C or below 4 °C (best practice) in its cooked state.

CHEF'S TIP The liquid is a very important part of rice cookery: the rice will absorb any flavour added during cooking so quality, freshness and attention to detail are essential.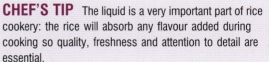

Rice can be used as a starter, main course accompaniment and can be cost-effective as left over food can be reused or made into salads. Rice lends itself well to a large selection of cooking methods:

- boiling
- frying
- stewing
- braising

- steaming
- microwaving.

The grains are porous and as such absorb large amounts of liquid. Flavours added before, during or after cooking will be taken on by the rice.

Most rice should be cooked **al dente**: this is an Italian phrase denoting the texture of rice as tender or soft on the outside but still firm to the bite within: its exact translation is 'to the tooth'.

If rice (boiled) is cooked in large quantities of liquid it will be necessary to drain the rice. This will dry the rice slightly and prevent the grains from over-cooking in the liquid.

Rice can be moulded when hot or cold; this practice does, however, require the rice to be perfectly cooked. Too little cooking and it will not stay in shape, too much and the rice will be stodgy and full of water. The best way to use a mould is by warming it slightly and brushing with melted butter to stop the rice sticking.

PLAIN BOILED

The rice should be washed then poured into a large amount of boiling salted water. Stir regularly to prevent sticking to the bottom of the pan and burning. Once cooked al dente the rice should be drained and served or refreshed and refrigerated immediately.

BRAISED

This method of cookery requires the rice to be cooked in the oven with a **cartouche** on top so the liquid is absorbed and the grains become light and fluffy.

STEWING

This method is used for risotto and requires the rice to be cooked on the stove top. The rice absorbs all of the liquid causing the grains to swell.

STIR FRYING

This is a finishing method and the rice must be steamed or boiled in advance. The rice is tossed in hot fat with numerous flavours: this is a very quick method of reheating.

VIDEO CLIP Stir frying rice.

TEXTURE

The texture and flavour of cooked rice depends on the time, temperature and amount of liquid used. Undercooked rice is gritty, tasteless and hard whereas overcooked rice is stodgy and unpleasant. Where possible use the guidelines of liquid to rice as this will help prevent poor cooking methods.

STORAGE

Rice must be stored carefully once cooked as it can harbour the pathogenic bacteria *Bacillus cereus* which can cause vomiting and diarrhoea. The risk can be minimized by storing the rice below 4 °C in a covered container in a well-aerated refrigerator for no longer than four days and reheating to above 75 °C. Dried rice can be stored in a sealed airtight container for as long as the use by date, usually approximately six to nine months. The type of container is important as rice is porous and can be tainted by strong-smelling foods or moisture. Rice will deteriorate over time and signs of poor/out of date rice are:

1 split grains

2 dust

3 musty smell.

HEALTH & SAFETY If possible only purchase the required amount of rice and ensure good stock rotation at all times.

TEST YOURSELF

1 What are the three main categories of rice?

2 Name the bacteria associated with rice.

3 What is the ratio of liquid to rice when making risotto?

4 Where should braised rice be cooked:

  stove, microwave, oven?

5 Name the four layers of a rice grain.

6 What is the Italian phrase for perfectly cooked rice?

7 What is the traditional Spanish rice dish called?

8 What temperature should rice reach when reheating?

9 Why is brown rice nuttier in flavour than white rice?

10 What are rice noodles made from?

Recipes

Braised rice (pilaff)

Back – Braised rice, Front – pesto rice with sun-dried tomatoes, Right – Lemon and mustard seed braised rice

Ingredients	Makes approximately 4 portions	Makes approximately 10 portions
Butter	50 g	125 g
Finely diced onion	40 g	100 g
Long grain rice	125 g	300 g
White chicken stock or vegetable stock	250 ml	600 ml
Good quality salt	To taste	To taste
White pepper	To taste	To taste

energy	cal	fat	sat fat	carb	sugar	protein	fibre
575 kJ	139 kcal	10.4 g	6.5 g	9.6 g	0.6 g	1.1 g	0.5 g

METHOD OF WORK

1 Preheat an oven to 200 °C.
2 In a saucepan/**sauteuse** melt the butter and sweat the onions until they are translucent.
3 Add the pre-washed rice and cook for a further minute stirring until all the grains are coated.
4 Add the stock and bring to the boil.
5 Remove from the heat and cover with a cartouche.
6 Place in the oven to **braise** until tender for approximately 15 minutes.
7 Remove from the oven, discard the cartouche and season.

Note: the rice can be flavoured with cardamom, cinnamon, garlic or any aromatic required to give a distinct flavour and aroma.

CHEF'S TIP This method of cookery involves the absorption of liquid into the rice, this is to maximize the flavour and delicacy. Adding cardamom pods, cinnamon sticks or star anise will add another dimension to the dish.

Steamed basmati rice

Ingredients	Makes approximately 4 portions	Makes approximately 10 portions
Basmati rice	125 g	300 g
Optional flavours added after cooking		
Lemon juice and zest	1	2½
Herbs	⅛ bunch	¼ bunch
Butter	50 g	125 g
Oils (basil, curry, chilli)	Drizzle	Drizzle
Cooked vegetables – peppers, carrots, onions, courgettes, etc., cut into brunoise	50 g	125 g
Diced cooked fish, meat, etc.	50 g	125 g
Good quality salt and white pepper	To taste	To taste

METHOD OF WORK

1 Wash the rice and drain well.
2 Place the rice into a **gastronorm** tray and just cover with cold water.
3 Place the gastronorm into the steamer for 25 minutes.
4 Remove, check the rice is cooked, season and stir glently to help the grains separate.
5 If required add the additional ingreadients.
6 Mould, serve or chill as required.

VIDEO CLIP Braised rice.

Pesto rice with sun-dried tomatoes

Ingredients	Makes approximately 4 portions	Makes approximately 10 portions
Long grain rice (boiled)	400 g	1 kg
Basil	½ bunch	1 bunch
Pine nuts roasted	100 g	250 g
Garlic	4 cloves	10 cloves
Olive oil	100 ml	250 ml
Grated parmesan	8 tblspn	20 tblspn
Sun-dried tomatoes	4 tblspn	10 tblspn
Good quality salt	To taste	To taste
White pepper	To taste	To taste

energy	cal	fat	sat fat	carb	sugar	protein	fibre
3036 kJ	733 kcal	59.1 g	11.7 g	31.4 g	1.8 g	18.1 g	2.1 g

METHOD OF WORK

1 Blend half the basil with the grated parmesan, garlic, pine nuts until smooth while drizzling in the oil.

2 Mix the pesto with the hot rice: season well and place into a warm bowl.

3 Garnish with a few toasted pine nuts and sun-dried tomatoes.

Lemon and mustard seed braised rice

Ingredients	Makes approximately 4 portions	Makes approximately 10 portions
Long grain rice	200 g	500 g
Finely diced onion	50 g	125 g
Butter	50 g	125 g
Vegetable stock	350 ml	750 ml
Lemon zest and juice	1	2 ½
Mustard seeds	2 tsp	5 tsp
Flat leaf parsley (chopped)	¼ bunch	½ bunch
Olive oil	4 tblspn	10 tblspn
Good quality salt	To taste	To taste
White pepper	To taste	To taste

energy	cal	fat	sat fat	carb	sugar	protein	fibre
1349 kJ	326 kcal	27.8 g	9.2 g	16.4 g	1.3 g	2.6 g	1.4 g

METHOD OF WORK

1 Melt the butter in a saucepan and sweat the onions until translucent.

2 Add the rice and stir until all the grains are coated.

3 Add the stock and bring to the boil.

4 Remove from the heat, cover with a cartouche and place in the oven at 180 °C.

5 Cook for approximately 15 minutes or until the liquid has evaporated and the rice is tender.

6 Take the pan out of the oven and leave to rest.

7 Toast the mustard seeds until they pop then mix into the rice.

8 Mix the lemon, oil and parsley into the rice, season well and serve.

CHEF'S TIP For a deeper flavour steep the lemon zest in the oil for at least a week prior to cooking with it.

Chilli bean rice with sour cream

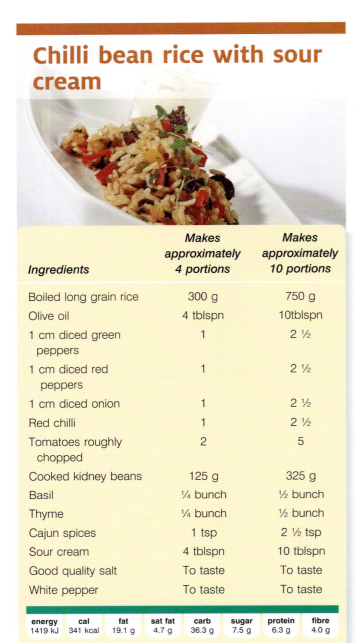

Ingredients	Makes approximately 4 portions	Makes approximately 10 portions
Boiled long grain rice	300 g	750 g
Olive oil	4 tblspn	10tblspn
1 cm diced green peppers	1	2 ½
1 cm diced red peppers	1	2 ½
1 cm diced onion	1	2 ½
Red chilli	1	2 ½
Tomatoes roughly chopped	2	5
Cooked kidney beans	125 g	325 g
Basil	¼ bunch	½ bunch
Thyme	¼ bunch	½ bunch
Cajun spices	1 tsp	2 ½ tsp
Sour cream	4 tblspn	10 tblspn
Good quality salt	To taste	To taste
White pepper	To taste	To taste

energy	cal	fat	sat fat	carb	sugar	protein	fibre
1419 kJ	341 kcal	19.1 g	4.7 g	36.3 g	7.5 g	6.3 g	4.0 g

METHOD OF WORK

1 Sauté the peppers and onions until slightly softened.
2 Add the chillies and tomatoes then cook for a further 2 minutes.
3 Add rice, kidney beans, chopped herbs and Cajun spices. Cook until the dish begins to thicken naturally.
4 Serve with a glass of sour cream.

Risotto

Ingredients	Makes approximately 4 portions	Makes approximately 10 portions
Butter	50 g	125 g
Finely diced onions	40 g	100 g
Garlic chopped	2 cloves	5 cloves
White wine	50 ml	125 ml
Arborio risotto rice	125 g	300 g
White chicken stock, vegetable stock	200 ml	500 ml
Grated and shaved parmesan	2 tblspn of each	5 tblspn of each
Good quality salt	To taste	To taste
White pepper	To taste	To taste

energy	cal	fat	sat fat	carb	sugar	protein	fibre
1166 kJ	280 kcal	14.9 g	9.5 g	26.0 g	1.2 g	8.1 g	0.7 g

METHOD OF WORK

1 Melt half the butter and sweat the onions and garlic until translucent.
2 Add the rice and cook for 2 minutes until all the grains are coated.
3 Add the wine and reduce until the mixture begins to dry out.
4 Gradually add the hot stock, stirring regularly until the liquid is absorbed and the rice is al dente.
5 At the last minute season, stir in the butter and grated parmesan.
6 Finish with the parmesan shavings.
7 Note: Do not allow the risotto to re-boil once the cheese and butter have been added.

CHEF'S TIP Arborio rice is ideal for making risotto as the grains contain enough starch to thicken the dish and are hard enough to prevent overcooking.
  Using long grain rice or pudding rice will not give the correct consistency or appearance.

VIDEO CLIP Risotto.

Chinese crab cakes with mango and lime salsa

Ingredients	Makes approximately 4 portions	Makes approximately 10 portions
Brown rice	400 g	1 kg
Chicken stock	750 ml	2 litres
Spring onion	1 bunch	2 ½ bunch
Cooked white crab meat	175 g	400 g
Raw minced white fish	175 g	400 g
Ground rice	25 g	65 g
Eggs	1	3
Chinese five spice	2 tsp	5 tsp
Olive oil	2 tblspn	5 tblspn
Soy sauce	1 tblspn	2 ½ tblspn
Mango	½	1 ½
Lime	1	1 ½
Coriander	¼ bunch	½ bunch
Red onion	½	1 ½
Good quality salt	To taste	To taste
White pepper	To taste	To taste

energy	cal	fat	sat fat	carb	sugar	protein	fibre
1497 kJ	358 kcal	13.5 g	2.2 g	37.4 g	7.0 g	22.5 g	4.7 g

METHOD OF WORK

1 Place the rice in a pan with the boiling stock and simmer until tender.

2 Drain any excess liquid off and leave the rice to chill.

3 Roughly chop the spring onions.

4 Place the crab, fish, spring onion, ground rice, egg, soy and five spices in the food processor and pulse until the ingredients cohere to each other.

5 Remove the ingredients from the food processor and mix with the rice; season well.

6 Divide the mixture into patties: 3 to a portion.

7 Take the patties and chill well.

8 Make the salsa by dicing the mango, red onion then mix with lime juice, zest and chopped coriander.

9 Pan fry the cakes (finish in the oven if necessary) and serve with the cold salsa.

SOURCING Ensure all the fish and shellfish are sustainable and on the approved MSC list.

Deep fried risotto balls

Ingredients	Makes approximately 4 portions	Makes approximately 10 portions
Toasted pine nuts	25 g	75 g
Cooked plain risotto (see recipe page 230)	500 g	1.25 kg
Pasteurized eggs	50 ml	125 ml
Diced fried smoked bacon	40 g	100 g
Diced mozzarella	75 g	225 g
Breadcrumbs	75 g	225 g
Olive oil	2 tblspn	5 tblspn
Basil	½ bunch	1 bunch
Endive	50 g	125 g
Shishu cress	¼ punnet	½ punnet
Good quality salt	To taste	To taste
White pepper	To taste	To taste
Baby cherry tomatoes		

energy	cal	fat	sat fat	carb	sugar	protein	fibre
2455 kJ	589 kcal	35.1 g	15.1 g	46.6 g	4.5 g	21.0 g	2.4 g

METHOD OF WORK

1 Mix the rice, egg, chopped basil and chopped pine nuts together.

2 Shape into small balls.

3 Make a hole in the centre of the rice and insert a piece of bacon and mozzarella then reshape the balls.

4 Roll in breadcrumbs and chill well.

5 Deep fry at 190 °C moving the balls regularly for even colour.

6 Liquidize the basil with the oil and season.

7 Lightly dress the shishu and endive and place on the plate with the tomatoes.

8 Drain the balls well and serve.

SOURCING   The smoked bacon used in this recipe should ideally be home smoked and locally sourced.

This website locates the nearest sustainable breeder, butcher, abattoir and retailer.

http://www.localpork.co.uk

Egg fried rice with ham, prawns and vegetables

Ingredients	Makes approximately 4 portions	Makes approximately 10 portions
Sunflower oil	100 ml	250 ml
Boiled long grain rice	400 g	1 kg
Eggs	2	5
Diced peppers	1 of each	2 of each
Diced courgettes	1	2
Diced red onion	1	2
Blanched peas	80 g	200 g
Quartered button mushrooms	160 g	400 g
Diced honey roast ham	160 g	400 g
Cooked prawns	120 g	300 g
Lemon juice and zest	1 ½	3
Chopped parsley	¼ bunch	½ bunch
Good quality salt	To taste	To taste
White pepper	To taste	To taste

energy	cal	fat	sat fat	carb	sugar	protein	fibre
2495 kJ	601 kcal	39.6 g	5.5 g	35.1 g	4.2 g	25.5 g	4.4 g

METHOD OF WORK

1 Take a wok and heat with a little oil then drizzle in the beaten egg, toss quickly then remove.

2 Fry the vegetables and season well then remove and mix with the egg.

3 Fry the ham quickly then remove and add to the egg mix.

4 Fry the rice with the prawns until hot then add the egg mix, lemon and parsley.

5 Re-season and serve.

CHEF'S TIP Before stir frying food it is important to ensure the wok is spotlessly cleaned and proved – in the same way as an omelette pan is done:

● Heat the wok to a very high heat and add salt: this will act as a natural abrasive and remove any sediment and dirt.

● Discard the salt and wipe the wok clean: apply a thin layer of oil with a cloth: paying attention to the hot surface.

The wok is now ready for use.

Jambalaya

Ingredients	Makes approximately 4 portions	Makes approximately 10 portions
Corn oil	2 tblspn	5 tblspn
Pork (shoulder or leg) cut into 2 cm dice	300 g	750 g
Chicken 2 cm dice	200 g	500 g
Sliced onion	1	3
Chopped garlic	3 cloves	8 cloves
Diced green peppers	1	3
Chillies diced	2 green	5 green
Chopped plum tomatoes	400 g	1 kg
Long grain rice	300 g	750 g
Chicken stock	600 ml	1.5 kg
Raw tiger prawns (shelled)	8	20
Sliced celery	2 sticks	5 sticks
Chopped flat leaf parsley	¼ bunch	½ bunch
Good quality salt	To taste	To taste
White pepper	To taste	To taste

energy	cal	fat	sat fat	carb	sugar	protein	fibre
2136 kJ	510 kcal	17.0 g	5.1 g	28.6 g	6.4 g	60.1 g	4.5 g

METHOD OF WORK

1 In a frying pan sauté the chicken and pork until brown.
2 Remove the chicken and pork from the pan then add the celery, onion, garlic, peppers and chillies.
3 Add the tomato, rice and stock then simmer for 10 minutes.
4 Add the meat and prawns; cook for a further 5 minutes.
5 Season, serve and garnish with chopped parsley.

CHEF'S TIP   This is a classic Louisiana dish full of varying ingredients with a strong meat element. The meat can be substituted with different fish and shellfish (try monkfish for the meatiness) and razor clams.

Kedgeree

Ingredients	Makes approximately 4 portions	Makes approximately 10 portions
Smoked haddock	500 g	1.25 kg
Butter	50 g	125 g
Red onions	2	5
Garlic	3 cloves	7 cloves
Boiled basmati rice	250 g	625 g
Eggs	2	5
Crème fraîche	100 ml	250 ml
Finely sliced red chillies	½	1 ½
Dill	Sprigs	Sprigs
Milk	125 ml	300 ml
Saffron	Pinch	Pinch
Good quality salt	To taste	To taste
White pepper	To taste	To taste

energy	cal	fat	sat fat	carb	sugar	protein	fibre
2706 kJ	647 kcal	31.8 g	19.1 g	56.2 g	6.3 g	34.3 g	2.7 g

METHOD OF WORK

1   Poach the haddock in milk until it flakes into little pieces.
2   Sauté the onions, garlic and saffron in butter.
3   Add the fish and the cooked rice.
4   Add a little cooking liquor and cook gently until hot.
5   Add the seasoning, crème fraîche and chillies.
6   Peel and quarter the eggs.
7   Arrange the rice with wedges of egg.

CHEF'S TIP Ensure you use natural smoked haddock and not the dyed variety: this will give a much gentler flavour and a more subtle appearance.

SOURCING In addition use either organic or free range eggs which are locally sourced.

WEB LINK This link will tell you more about organic ingredients:
http://www.aboutorganics.co.uk

Lamb biryani

Ingredients	Makes approximately 4 portions	Makes approximately 10 portions
Sunflower oil	100 ml	250 ml
Steamed basmati rice (see page 228)	200 g	600 g
Diced leg of lamb	300 g	800 g
Finely diced onion	80 g	200 g
Chopped garlic	3 cloves	8 cloves
Grated ginger	1 tblspn	3 tblspn
Ground cumin	1 tblspn	3 tblspn
Ground coriander	1 tblspn	3 tblspn
Turmeric	1 tblspn	3 tblspn
Garam masala	1 tblspn	3 tblspn
Brown lamb stock	400ml	1ltr
Sliced red chillies	1 ½	4
Sliced lemons	1 ½	4
Sliced tomatoes	3	8
Chopped mint	¼ bunch	½ bunch
Chopped coriander	¼ bunch	½ bunch
Mustard seeds	1 tblspn	3 tblspn
Crème fraîche	4 dessert spoons	10 dessert spoons
Good quality salt	To taste	To taste
White pepper	To taste	To taste

energy	cal	fat	sat fat	carb	sugar	protein	fibre
3022 kJ	725 kcal	43.2 g	10.2 g	53.4 g	5.8 g	31.3 g	6.7 g

METHOD OF WORK

1   Marinate the lamb with the onion, garlic, ginger and spices for 24 hours.

2   Fry the meat until golden brown then add the stock and simmer for 2 hours until tender.

3   Using a gastronorm, place a 2 cm layer of rice on the bottom, lay on some lemon, tomato, mustard seeds, chillies and chopped herbs.

4   Place a layer of lamb on top.

5   Continue the layering so there is 3 layers of rice mix and 2 layers of lamb.

6   Cover the trays with tin foil and bake in the oven for 40 minutes at 160 °C.

7   Remove the tray from the oven, mix the biryani slightly and arrange in a bowl.

8   Finish with crème fraîche and mint.

CHEF'S TIP   This dish works well with normal long grain rice as the grains keep separate and absorb the curry flavours. The lamb can be substituted with chicken or beef.

Lemon grass risotto cakes with burnt chilli and crème fraîche

Ingredients	Makes approximately 4 portions	Makes approximately 10 portions
Saffron risotto cooked with lemongrass (use the base risotto recipe on page 230)	600 g	1.5 kg
polenta	50 g	125 g
Red chillies	4	10
Olive oil	4 tblspn	10 tblspn
Crème fraîche	4 tblspn	10 tblspn
Rocket leaves	40 g	100 g
Curly endive	40 g	100 g
Lime juice	1 lime	3 limes
Balsamic reduction	4 tsp	10 tsp
Good quality salt	To taste	To taste
White pepper	To taste	To taste

energy	cal	fat	sat fat	carb	sugar	protein	fibre
2037 kJ	491 kcal	36.0 g	15.7 g	30.0 g	2.6 g	9.3 g	1.3 g

METHOD OF WORK

1 Prepare a basic risotto: adding saffron and 1 lemon grass stick when adding the liquid for every 4 people.

2 Pour the risotto into a tray and chill.

3 Then divide the risotto into cakes (2 per person), roll in polenta and shape making criss-cross marks on top.

4 Take the chillies and hold over a flame until the skin starts bubbling and turning black.

5 Pan fry the cakes until golden.

6 Dress the curly endive and rocket with a little oil and lime juice then arrange on the plate.

7 Place the cakes on top.

8 Finish with the crème fraîche, balsamic and chilli.

CHEF'S TIP   These cakes (made half the size) work well with pan-fried red mullet fillets as a fish course. For extra spice use scotch bonnet chillies instead, but be careful to balance the dish correctly.

Paella

Ingredients	Makes approximately 4 portions	Makes approximately 10 portions
Squid cut into rings	1	2 each
Live mussels	400 g	1 kg
Diced chicken breast	200 g	500 g
Uncooked tiger prawns (shelled)	8	20
Butter	130 g	300 g
Short grain rice (bomba or calasparra if possible)	225 g	600 g
Sliced onions	1 ½	3
Chopped garlic	2	6 cloves
Diced mixed peppers	1 of each	3 of each
Fresh tomato sauce	80 ml	200 ml
Saffron	Pinch	Pinch
Fish stock	400 ml	1 litre
Good quality salt	To taste	To taste
White pepper	To taste	To taste

energy	cal	fat	sat fat	carb	sugar	protein	fibre
3583 kJ	857 kcal	44.1 g	20.9 g	39.3 g	10.2 g	75.0 g	3.8 g

METHOD OF WORK

1 Heat a sauteuse then add the mussels, add the white wine then remove once the shells have opened (place the mussels in a bowl) and save the liquid.

2 Quickly fry the squid and prawns in a large flat pan with the garlic.

3 Remove the squid and prawns from the pan and add the chicken. Fry the chicken until golden coloured on all sides.

4 Then add the peppers, onion, rice, tomato, mussel liquor and saffron.

5 Add the stock and simmer until the rice is cooked.

6 Season well then add the seafood, heat through and serve.

CHEF'S TIP Bomba and calasparra rice are well known for their paella cooking qualities in Spain.

The calasparra especially is used extensively in traditional Spanish restaurants. Its grain composition requires extra liquid to cook but it can hold its shape and flavour over a longer period.

The use of round, short grain rice is acceptable but will never give the same qualities as bomba or calasparra.

Risotto of pea and mint with goat's cheese

Ingredients	Makes approximately 4 portions	Makes approximately 10 portions
Risotto	200 g	500 g
Peas (fresh)	4 tblspn	10 tblspn
Mint	Sprigs	Sprigs
Goat's cheese	100 g	250 g
Good quality salt	To taste	To taste
White pepper	To taste	To taste

energy	cal	fat	sat fat	carb	sugar	protein	fibre
1124 kJ	268 kcal	6.9 g	4.6 g	41.2 g	0.6 g	10.0 g	1.5 g

METHOD OF WORK

1 Place the mint into boiling salted water, add the peas and blanch until just cooked.

2 Fold the goats cheese through the risotto and finish with the drained peas.

3 Garnish and serve.

SOURCING This dish works well as the peas are seasonal and require little or no cooking; they are sweet and delicate.

When out of season exchange them with butternut squash in Autumn for example, diced and roasted.

Teriyaki beef and wild rice filo parcels with pickled cucumber

Ingredients	Makes approximately 4 portions	Makes approximately 10 portions
Beef fillet cut into strips	200 g	500 g
Soy	2 tblspn	5 tblspn
Honey	2 tblspn	5 tblspn
Sesame seeds	½ tblspn	2 tblspn
Filo pastry sheets	8 × 5 cm squares	20 × 5 cm squares
Butter	100 g	250 g
Boiled wild rice	40 g	100 g
Boiled basmati rice	120 g	300 g
Cucumber julienne	1½	3
Red onion finely sliced	1	2
Coriander	¼ bunch	½ bunch
Sake rice wine	2 tblspn	5 tblspn
Rice wine vinegar	3 tblspn	8 tblspn
Good quality salt	To taste	To taste
White pepper	To taste	To taste

energy	cal	fat	sat fat	carb	sugar	protein	fibre
3037 kJ	724 kcal	29.0 g	15.3 g	86.0 g	12.0 g	26.7 g	4.8 g

METHOD OF WORK

1   Marinate the beef for 1 hour in soy, honey and toasted sesame seeds.

2   Mix the cucumber with the red onion, chopped coriander (reserve some leaves for garnish), sake and rice wine vinegar and leave to marinate.

3   Quickly pan fry the beef then mix with the rices and season well.

4   Brush the filo with butter then divide the beef mix between them.

5   Fold the corners in and turn over to form a parcel.

6   Lay the filo parcels on silicone paper and brush with butter.

7   Bake for 15 minutes 180 °C until golden.

8   Arrange the parcels on the plate and finish with the cucumber mix and a few coriander leaves.

CHEF'S TIP   The filo pastry can be exchanged for pâte dé brique, or even very thinly rolled puff pastry which can be egg washed, decorated and baked in a similar way to a pithivier.

Tiger prawn and coconut rice

Ingredients	Makes approximately 4 portions	Makes approximately 10 portions
Finely diced onion	½	1 ½
Chopped garlic	1 clove	3 cloves
Grated ginger	1 tblspn	2½ tblspn
Chopped green chilli	1	2½
Ground cumin	¼ tsp	½ tsp
Ground coriander	¼ tsp	½ tsp
Coconut milk	2 tblspn	5 tblspn
Tiger prawns peeled and de-veined	12	30
Shredded chicory	100 g	250 g
Double cream	200 ml	500 ml
Lime juice	2 tblspn	5 tblspn
Grated coconut	2 tblspn	5 tblspn
Wild rice (boiled)	100 g	250 g
Basmati rice (boiled)	300 g	750 g
Picked coriander	Sprigs	Sprigs
Good quality salt	To taste	To taste
White pepper	To taste	To taste

energy	cal	fat	sat fat	carb	sugar	protein	fibre
3135 kJ	751 kcal	37.2 g	24.1 g	67.5 g	3.2 g	36.7 g	3.3 g

METHOD OF WORK

1 Sauté the onion, garlic, ginger, chilli and spices.
2 Add the prawns, chicory and rice.
3 Add the coconut milk and cream then reduce by half.
4 Season well then serve in a warm bowl.
5 Finish with grated coconut, coriander and lime juice.

CHEF'S TIP In this dish the coconut can be used in a number of ways such as:

- Grated
- Shaved and dried for decoration
- Coconut milk/cream to enrich the rice.

Guest Chef

Braised Herdwick lamb shank with carlings, bacon and rosemary, finished with a lemon, garlic and parsley crust

Chef Andrew Stacey MCGB
Centre Carlisle College, Cumbria

On the Sunday before Mother's Day, it is the custom to eat a type of pea called a carling (normally these are pigeon food). The peas are soaked overnight and brought to the boil and simmered with bacon for at least one hour. Some pubs and clubs still supply the food free on that day.

Ingredients	Makes approximately 4 portions
Herdwick lamb shanks	4 small
Olive oil	2 tblspn
Onion (finely diced)	100 g
Carrot (finly diced)	75 g
Celery stick (strung and finely diced)	1
Cloves garlic (finely chopped)	2
Rosemary (picked and finely chopped)	1 sprig
Carlings (soaked overnight and drained)	200 g
Smoked back bacon (fat removed and cut into 1 cm squares)	4 rashers
Lamb stock	150 ml
Veal jus (thickened)	500 ml
Bouquet garni	1
Plum tomatoes (blanched, refreshed, skinned, deseeded and concassed)	200 g
Tomato purée	1 tblspn
Red chilli (finely diced)	¼
Light muscovado sugar	½ tblspn
Salt and freshly ground black pepper	To taste
Pak choi (cut in half, blanched, refreshed and drained)	2
For the crust	
Lemon (finely grated zest)	1
Garlic (crushed)	2 cloves
Parsley (chopped, washed and dried)	4 tblspn

METHOD OF WORK

1 Preheat oven to 180°C, 350°F or gas mark 4.

2 Collect all ingredients, equipment and utensils.

3 Ensure all equipment, utensils and work surfaces to be used are clean and in a good, safe working order.

4 Trim the lamb shanks and season. Heat oil and brown all over in a sauteuse before transferring to a deep casserole dish.

5 Add onion, carrot and celery to the sauteuse.

6 Over a medium heat, cook until tender and lightly coloured. Add garlic and cook for further minute, then drain and place vegetables into the casserole along with the carlings and bouquet garni.

7 Tip excess fat out of sauteuse, pour in lamb stock, add the rosemary, bring to the boil and stir to deglaze. Pour this liquid over the lamb, cover and transfer to the oven. Cook for approximately 1 hour.

8 Remove the casserole from the oven with care, stir in tomato purée, bacon, chilli and sugar. Season. Cover casserole and return to the oven for a further 1½ hours.

9 Pour off liquid into a saucepan (cover lamb shank etc. and keep hot).

10 Over a medium heat, reduce liquid by half and add thickened veal jus. Add the tomato concassé, bring back to the boil and simmer for 5 minutes.

11 Taste and adjust the seasoning.

For the crust

1 Mix together the lemon rind, crushed garlic and parsley. Chop very finely. Dry out slightly.

2 Heat the pak choi through in boiling, salted water and drain well on a cloth.

3 Sprinkle the crust over the lamb shanks, flash under the salamander and serve immediately with the pak choi.

Eggs

Recipes

EGGS

Boiled eggs   247

Eggs en cocotte   247

Eggs en cocotte Alsace style   248

Eggs en cocotte with asparagus   248

Egg en cocotte with chicken   249

Eggs sur le plat   249

Fried eggs   250

Omelettes (basic recipe)   250

Omelette with cheese   251

Omelette with tomato   251

Omelette with ham   251

Poached eggs   252

Poached eggs benedict   252

Poached eggs dauphinoise   253

Poached eggs florentine   253

Scrambled eggs   254

Scrambled eggs with herbs   254

Scrambled eggs with smoked salmon   255

Spanish omelette (tortilla)   255

6

NVQ

2FPC8 Prepare, cook and finish basic egg dishes

VRQ

Unit 212 Prepare and cook rice, pasta, grains and egg dishes

LEARNING OBJECTIVES

The aim of this unit is to enable the candidate to develop skills and implement knowledge in the preparation and cookery principles of eggs. This will also include materials, ingredients and equipment.

Eggs are without doubt the most versatile of foods used by the chef. They feature on the menu from the hors d'oeuvres through to the dessert.

By the end of this chapter you will be able to:

● Demonstrate techniques with the cooking, storage and quality points of eggs.

● Demonstrate a range of cookery methods.

● Be able to prepare, cook and finish omelettes, boiled, poached and scrambled egg dishes.

● Identify and rectify problems when cooking and finishing egg dishes.

● State the correct cooking and holding and storage requirements for fresh egg dishes.

Nutritional information

Eggs are referred to as nature's functional food due to the fact that they contain so many nutrients. They are relatively low in saturated fats and contain about 80 kcals, depending on size.

They contain the following vitamins, minerals and elements.

● A: Essential for normal growth and development.

● B: Vitamins that are involved in many bodily functions.

● D: For mineral absorption and good bone health.

● E: Gives some protection against heart disease and certain cancers.

They also contain minerals and trace elements.

● Iodine: For the production of thyroid hormones.

● Phosphorous: For healthy teeth and bones.

● Zinc: For improved immunity.

● Iron: For red blood cell production.

TASK Find out what the current healthy eating advice is for eggs, using the internet, and produce a leaflet.

Types of egg

Although the vast majority of eggs that we eat are chicken eggs almost any egg can be eaten. Thousands of years ago humans lived as hunter gathers and the eggs of all animals were an essential part of the diet. Types of eggs used by the professional chef today are:

● chicken

● goose

● duck

● quail.

SOURCING Find out where you can source goose, duck and quail eggs in your locality and the provenance of the eggs. You could ask local restaurants where they source theirs or use the internet.

Egg sizes

When a recipe is constructed using eggs, the size of egg is a very important factor to consider. As recipes are scaled up for larger portions the difference becomes greater. The chef should have a plus or minus factor built in their mind and generally err on the side of caution. In this chapter all recipes are for medium eggs (size three eggs). For mass production recipes using eggs, you should usually use egg quantities by weight and not by unit.

Eggs are now sold in four different sizes: small, medium, large and very large (these replace the old sizes 0 to 7). If you see a recipe with egg numbers instead of sizes. This guide will help with conversion.

NEW SIZE	WEIGHT	OLD SIZE
Very large	73 g and over	Size 0
		Size 1
Large	63–73 g	Size 1
		Size 2
		Size 3
Medium	53–63 g	Size 3
		Size 4
		Size 5
Small	53 g and under	Size 5
		Size 6
		Size 7

Quality

There are three grades of eggs.

Grade A Shell eggs that are clean and internally perfect with an air sac that is no more than 6 mm deep.

Grade B These eggs are removed from the shells and pasteurized.

Industrial Rejected eggs that are used in the production of soaps and shampoos.

Below are the quality points you should consider.

- Look for a quality mark on the egg shell and egg box such as the Red Lion, it shows that the eggs have been produced to the highest standards of food safety. This includes the hens having a programme of vaccination against *Salmonella enteritidis*. Quality symbols are subject to rigorous audits by an independent monitoring agency to ensure they are meeting the standards of the Code of Practice.

- Buy eggs from a reputable retailer where they will have been transported and stored at the correct temperature (below 20 °C).

- Keep eggs in the fridge in their box after purchase at no more than 10 °C.

- Store eggs separately from other foods.

- Make sure you use eggs by the 'best before' date shown on the egg or box.

- Wash hands before and after handling eggs.

- Discard dirty or cracked egg.

- Eat cooked egg dishes as soon as possible after cooking.

> **WEB LINK**
>
> Go to **http://www.lioneggfarms.co.uk** to trace Lion quality eggs and understand more about the British Lion quality.

How to test for freshness

Because egg shells are porous they take in a small amount of air each day. There are two simple methods to test freshness.

1 Put some water in a jug or tumbler and place the egg into the tumbler. A day old egg will lie almost flat on the bottom. A week old egg will be more upright. As the egg ages it will become more upright, until after about three weeks it will start to float. At this point the egg should be discarded.

2 As an egg ages the proteins in the white and yolk change and their integrity is reduced. A new laid egg has a proud yolk and compact white. As the egg ages you will see that the yolk flattens and the white will spread.

Purchasing

In the UK more than 10 billion eggs are used annually. And approximately 20 per cent of those are used by the catering industry. Because of the vast quantities used it is important that a professional chef should have an understanding of production and specifications.

How the hens are kept

There are four main types of production that can affect flavour appearance and quality.

1 *Laying cages* These are the most common method of commercial egg production in the UK – representing around two thirds of egg production. Typically a laying cage system consists of a series of at least three tiers of cages. The cages have sloping mesh floors so that the eggs roll forward out of the reach of the birds to await collection. Droppings pass through the mesh floors onto boards, belts, the floors of the house, or into a pit to await removal. This system allows for very little movement of the hens and a poor quality of life.

2 *Barn system* Around seven per cent of UK eggs are produced in this manner. In the barn system the hen house has a series of perches and feeders at different levels. The Welfare of Laying Hens Directive stipulates a maximum stocking density of nine hens per square metre of useable floor space. This system allows for some movement of the bird and a better quality of life.

3 *Free range system* This system accounts for around 27 per cent of all eggs produced in the UK. The Welfare of Laying Hens Directive stipulates that for eggs to be termed 'free range', hens must have continuous daytime access to runs, which are mainly covered with vegetation and with a maximum stocking density of 2500 birds per hectare. The hen house conditions for free range hens must comply with the regulations for birds kept in barn systems, or deep litter stocked at seven birds per square metre when no perches are provided. Free-range eggs are more flavourful than battery eggs.

4 *Organic system* Hens producing organic eggs are always free range. In addition, hens must be fed an organically produced diet and ranged on organic land. Organic eggs are produced in the UK according to criteria set by the Advisory Committee on Organic Standards (ACOS), which sets basic standards for organic production in the UK, in line with EU legislation. Members of ACOS include the Soil Association, Organic Farmers and Growers and Organic Food

Federation. They all adhere to ACOS' basic standards, but may introduce higher standards in certain areas for their members.

WEB LINK   Use this link to the British Egg Information Service to enhance your knowledge of eggs, products, hens and their lifestyle:
http://www.britegg.co.uk

The diet of laying hens is similar across all production systems. The hen's diet is calculated using a computer formula which takes into account their nutritional needs at different ages.

A hen's diet is usually made up as follows:

- wheat 60 per cent
- soya bean meal 20 per cent
- limestone 10 per cent (this is required for shell formation)
- sunflower meal 5 per cent
- soya oil 5 per cent.

If the hens and eggs are organic then all of the ingredients have also been grown in an organic environment.

Types of egg products

There are many egg products available to chefs and food manufacturers. For example, eggs are available in the following forms.

1   Liquid.

2   Frozen.

3   Dried.

4   Fried, poached, boiled, scrambled eggs and omelettes are available cooked and ready to serve.

5   Extended shelf life egg. In the past, liquid egg would only have a life of around one week. Now, as in the dairy industry, it is possible to pasteurize the egg at higher temperatures for a short time. This type of egg will typically have a shelf life of about 30 days, provided it is refrigerated.

Cooking and holding temperatures

The protein in the white of an egg and the yolk start to cook at different temperatures and this enables the chef to have a varied degree of 'firmness'.

White (albumen)

The white contains up to 67 per cent of the liquid weight of an egg. Fresh egg whites **coagulate** at a temperature range of 62–64 °C but this can decrease in older eggs. If the egg white is set and the yolk has started to cook it is safe to eat as the killing temperature of 60 °C for salmonella has been passed.

TASK   Using egg white without the yolk is a healthy eating option as it contains protein, but no fat. Using the internet, research some recipes which use egg whites only.

Yolk

The yolk (yellow portion) makes up about 33 per cent of the liquid weight of the egg. It contains all of the fat in the egg and slightly less than half of the protein. Coagulation occurs in the range 65–70 °C.

Awareness of these temperatures prevents the yolk temperature getting too high (about 70 °C). Above this temperature hydrogen sulphide, generated by the white, reacts with iron in the yolk, causing a (harmless) grey-green film of ferrous sulphide to form on the surface of the yolk.

All egg dishes should be served as soon as possible after cooking and kept at a minimum temperature of 63 °C.

TEST YOURSELF

1   List three quality points to look for when receiving eggs.

2   What are the main bacteria associated with eggs?

3   What are the four sizes of eggs?

4   Name four ways of cooking eggs.

5   How should the centre of an omelette be cooked (the French term)?

6   Which of the below is not an omelette dish:

- Spanish
- cheese
- cocotte?

7   What ingredient is used to prove an omelette pan?

8   List three animals that produce eggs.

9   List three vitamins associated with eggs.

10   What is the white of the egg called?

Recipes

Boiled eggs

Ingredients	4 portions	10 portions
Medium eggs	4–8	10–20

energy	cal	fat	sat fat	carb	sugar	protein	fibre
441 kJ	106 kcal	7.7 g	2.2 g	0.0 g	0.0 g	9.1 g	0.0 g

METHOD OF WORK

1 Place the eggs into boiling salted water.
2 Allow to simmer for approximately:
   soft boiled eggs – 4 minutes
   medium boiled eggs – 6 minutes
   hard boiled eggs – 10–12 minutes.
3 Either serve immediately in an egg cup or refresh, peel and use as required.

CHEF'S TIP If the eggs are at room temperature before they are placed in water they are less likely to crack.

Eggs en cocotte

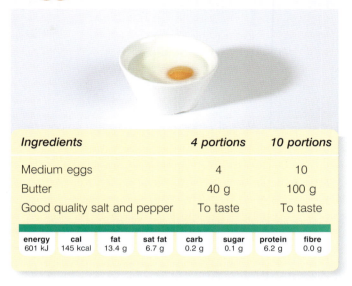

Ingredients	4 portions	10 portions
Medium eggs	4	10
Butter	40 g	100 g
Good quality salt and pepper	To taste	To taste

energy	cal	fat	sat fat	carb	sugar	protein	fibre
601 kJ	145 kcal	13.4 g	6.7 g	0.2 g	0.1 g	6.2 g	0.0 g

METHOD OF WORK

1 Butter and season a ramekin or cocotte dish.
2 Break and egg into the dish and cook in a bain-marie for 5–6 minutes until the white is just set.
3 Serve in the dish.

CHEF'S TIP The bain-marie creates a barrier around the dish and allows the sides to cook without colour.

Eggs en cocotte Alsace style

Left to Right – Alsace, asparagus and chicken en cocotte

Ingredients	4 portions	10 portions
Medium eggs	4	10
Butter	40 g	100 g
Sauerkraut	80 g	200 g
Garlic sausage		
Good quality salt and pepper	To taste	To taste

energy	cal	fat	sat fat	carb	sugar	protein	fibre
1002 kJ	242 kcal	21.0 g	9.5 g	0.9 g	0.4 g	12.4 g	0.5 g

METHOD OF WORK

1   Butter and season a ramekin or cocotte dish.
2   Place 20 g of sauerkraut into the bottom of each ramekin.
3   Break an egg into the dish and cook in a bain-marie until just set.
4   Garnish with either a sautéed julienne or pan fried slice of garlic sausage.
5   Serve in the dish.

Eggs en cocotte with asparagus

Ingredients	4 portions	10 portions
Medium eggs	4	10
Butter	40 g	100 g
Asparagus spears	8	20
Cream sauce (see page 124)	100 ml	250 ml
Double cream	40 ml	100 ml
Good quality salt and pepper	To taste	To taste

energy	cal	fat	sat fat	carb	sugar	protein	fibre
1041 kJ	251 kcal	22.7 g	12.4 g	3.5 g	2.0 g	8.6 g	0.9 g

METHOD OF WORK

1   Peel and slice the asparagus taking care to keep the heads intact for garnish.
2   Gently cook the asparagus in the butter, season and cover with half the sauce.
3   Divide the asparagus equally into the bottom of each ramekin or cocotte.
4   Reak and egg into the dish and cook in a bain-marie until just set.
5   Warm the sauce and add the cream.
6   Garnish with the asparagus heads and cream sauce.
7   Serve in the dish with a twist of milled pepper.

CHEF'S TIP   The sauce can be varied by using a jus, demi-glace or tomato sauce.

HEALTHY OPTION   For a healthier option steam the asparagus.
   The cream sauce can be replaced with a béchamel sauce (see page 123), but the milk should be skimmed and the butter replaced with a low fat option.

Egg en cocotte with chicken

Ingredients	4 portions	10 portions
Medium eggs	4	10
Butter	40 g	100 g
Cooked chicken supreme	100 g	250 g
Chicken velouté	100 ml	250 ml
Tarragon	10 g	25 g
Double cream	40 ml	100 ml
Good quality salt and pepper	To taste	To taste

energy	cal	fat	sat fat	carb	sugar	protein	fibre
1130 kJ	272 kcal	22.3 g	11.9 g	2.5 g	0.8 g	15.0 g	0.4 g

METHOD OF WORK

1 Dice the chicken and gently cook in the butter, season, add the chopped tarragon and cover with half the sauce.
2 Divide equally into the bottom of each dish.
3 Break an egg into the dish and cook on the side of the stove or in a hot oven until just set.
4 Heat the remainder of the sauce, add the cream and drizzle over the top of the egg.
5 Garnish with slices of sautéed chicken.

Eggs sur le plat *(eggs cooked in a sur le plat dish)*

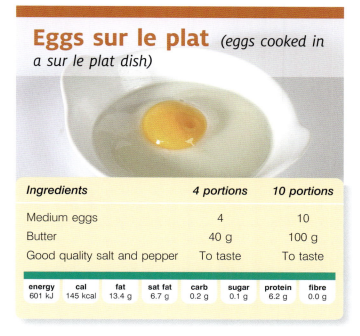

Ingredients	4 portions	10 portions
Medium eggs	4	10
Butter	40 g	100 g
Good quality salt and pepper	To taste	To taste

energy	cal	fat	sat fat	carb	sugar	protein	fibre
601 kJ	145 kcal	13.4 g	6.7 g	0.2 g	0.1 g	6.2 g	0.0 g

METHOD OF WORK

1 Butter and season an egg dish.
2 Break the egg into the sur le plat dish and cook on the side of the stove (on a solid top – try to find a cooler place as the centre of the stove will overcook the egg) or in the oven until just set.
3 Serve in the dish.

VIDEO CLIP Eggs sur la plat.

Fried eggs

Ingredients	4 portions	10 portions
Medium eggs	4–8	10–20
Butter	80 g	200 g
Vegetable oil		
Good quality salt and pepper	To taste	To taste

energy	cal	fat	sat fat	carb	sugar	protein	fibre
1516 kJ	367 kcal	36.7 g	13.5 g	0.2 g	0.1 g	9.3 g	0.0 g

METHOD OF WORK (1)

1 Add a thin layer of oil to a thick bottomed frying pan.
2 When slightly hot add half the butter.
3 Break an egg into a shallow dish and slide into the pan.
4 Allow to cook gently until the white has set and the yolk is still runny.
5 Add the remainder of the butter and allow to melt.
6 Season the eggs, remove from the pan and place on a plate.
7 Quickly allow the butter to foam without colour.
8 Pour a little of the butter onto each egg.

METHOD OF WORK (2)

1 Add a thin layer of oil to a hot frying pan or onto a medium temperature griddle.
2 Break the required amount of eggs into either the pan or the griddle.
3 Allow to cook gently until the required degree of doneness is achieved.
4 Season and serve.

HEALTH & SAFETY Crack the eggs into a dish to ensure that there will be no splashing of hot oil.

VIDEO CLIP Frying an egg.

Omelettes (basic recipe)

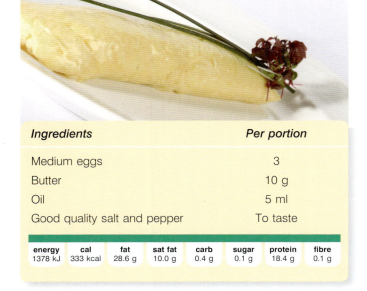

Ingredients	Per portion
Medium eggs	3
Butter	10 g
Oil	5 ml
Good quality salt and pepper	To taste

energy	cal	fat	sat fat	carb	sugar	protein	fibre
1378 kJ	333 kcal	28.6 g	10.0 g	0.4 g	0.1 g	18.4 g	0.1 g

METHOD OF WORK

1 Break the eggs into a basin, season and **beat** lightly with a fork.
2 Heat a seasoned omelette pan, add the butter and oil, continue to heat until foaming but not brown (the oil helps prevent burning).
3 Double cream can be added to the egg mixture at this stage to enrich the omelette.
4 Add the eggs and cook quickly. Moving the eggs with a fork do not let them settle in one part of the pan as this can cause excess browning.
5 Remove from the heat and fold the omelette using the fork.
6 Tap the handle of the pan with your palm to bring the other side of the omelette up.
7 Turn the pan over the service dish or plate and allow falling in a neat oval.
8 Neaten the shape and serve.

HEALTH & SAFETY Extreme care should be taken when seasoning an omelette pan as the temperature of the pan can be very high with no visual evidence of heat such as steam.

VIDEO CLIP Making an omelette.

Omelette with cheese

Ingredients	Per portion
Medium eggs	3
Butter	10 g
Oil	5 ml
Grated cheese	60 g
Good quality salt and pepper	To taste

energy	cal	fat	sat fat	carb	sugar	protein	fibre
2413 kJ	582 kcal	49.6 g	23.0 g	0.5 g	0.1 g	33.6 g	0.1 g

METHOD OF WORK

1   Add the cheese to the omelette just before you start the folding process.

CHEF'S TIP   Almost any type of cheese can be used in an omelette. This gives great range on the menu.

Omelette with tomato

Ingredients	Per portion
Medium eggs	3
Butter	10 g
Oil	5 ml
Tomato concassée	50 g
Good quality salt and pepper	To taste

energy	cal	fat	sat fat	carb	sugar	protein	fibre
1420 kJ	343 kcal	28.8 g	10.6 g	2.2 g	1.8 g	18.8 g	1.0 g

METHOD OF WORK

1   Heat the tomato concassée in a little butter and keep warm.
2   Make a plain omelette and turn it out onto a service dish and neaten the shape.
3   Cut an incision in the top of the omelette and spoon in the warm tomato concassé.

Omelette with ham

Ingredients	Per portion
Medium eggs	3
Butter	20 g
Oil	5 ml
Cooked ham	50 g
Chopped shallots	25 g
Good quality salt and pepper	To taste

energy	cal	fat	sat fat	carb	sugar	protein	fibre
1983 kJ	478 kcal	39.4 g	16.1 g	1.5 g	1.2 g	29.4 g	0.6 g

METHOD OF WORK

1   Sweat the shallots in a little of the butter.
2   Dice the ham and add to the shallots.
3   Add the ham and shallots to the omelette pan at the same time as the eggs and proceed as for a plain omelette.

CHEF'S TIP   This dish can be served as a breakfast item using smoked or unsmoked ham to add a different taste to the end dish.

Poached eggs

Ingredients	4 portions	10 portions
Medium eggs	4	10
White wine vinegar	10 ml	10 ml
Salt		

energy	cal	fat	sat fat	carb	sugar	protein	fibre
296 kJ	71 kcal	5.1 g	1.5 g	0.0 g	0.0 g	6.1 g	0.0 g

METHOD OF WORK

1 Three quarters fill a pan approximately 10 cm deep with **acidulated** (add vinegar), seasoned water.

2 Bring to a gentle rolling boil.

3 Add the eggs one at a time and allow to gently poach until the whites are set with the yolks still soft.

4 If for immediate use trim the eggs.

5 If for storage the poached eggs can be placed into iced water and refreshed. They must be kept at 4 °C and used within 48 hrs.

VIDEO CLIP Poaching an egg.

Poached eggs benedict

Ingredients	4 portions	10 portions
Poached eggs	8	20
Sliced ox tongue	200 g	500 g
English muffins	4	10
Hollandaise sauce (see page 136)	200 ml	500 ml
Butter	40 g	100 g
Good quality salt and pepper	To taste	To taste

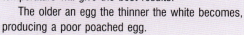

energy	cal	fat	sat fat	carb	sugar	protein	fibre
3320 kJ	799 kcal	62.5 g	28.5 g	30.6 g	2.6 g	30.5 g	2.1 g

METHOD OF WORK

1 Cut the muffins in half and toast until a light golden brown and butter lightly.

2 Place a slice of tongue on top and place a warmed egg on top of each half.

3 Season, coat with hollandaise and glaze under a salamander or serve unglazed and garnished as required.

CHEF'S TIP Using the freshest eggs at room temperature will give the best results.

The older an egg the thinner the white becomes, producing a poor poached egg.

Poached eggs dauphinoise

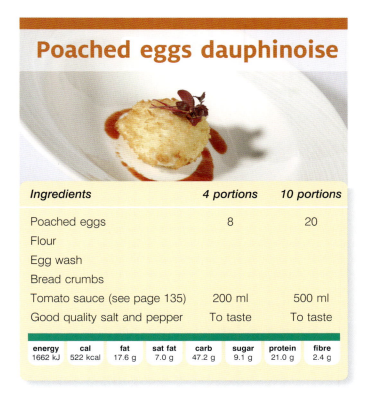

Ingredients	4 portions	10 portions
Poached eggs	8	20
Flour		
Egg wash		
Bread crumbs		
Tomato sauce (see page 135)	200 ml	500 ml
Good quality salt and pepper	To taste	To taste

energy	cal	fat	sat fat	carb	sugar	protein	fibre
1662 kJ	522 kcal	17.6 g	7.0 g	47.2 g	9.1 g	21.0 g	2.4 g

METHOD OF WORK

1   **Pané** the poached egg in flour, egg wash and breadcrumbs.
2   Deep fry until golden brown.
3   Serve with the tomato sauce.

CHEF'S TIP Make sure the eggs are well chilled and dry when they are **dusted** with flour during the pané process.

HEALTH & SAFETY Care should be taken when deep frying the eggs. Always allow the eggs to fall into the oil away from you.

Poached eggs florentine

Ingredients	4 portions	10 portions
Poached eggs	4	10
Mornay sauce (see page 124)	200 ml	500 ml
Grated parmesan	80 g	200 g
Spinach	400 g	2 kg
Butter	20 g	50 g
Grated nutmeg		
Mill pepper and good quality salt	To taste	To taste

energy	cal	fat	sat fat	carb	sugar	protein	fibre
1294 kJ	311 kcal	23.3 g	12.2 g	6.2 g	3.2 g	19.8 g	2.5 g

METHOD OF WORK

1   Blanch and refresh the spinach.
2   Allow to drain thoroughly.
3   Season with salt, pepper and nutmeg and gently reheat in the butter.
4   Place the spinach in a buttered oven proof dish and place the poached eggs on top.
5   Coat with the mornay sauce.
6   Sprinkle with finely grated parmesan and glaze under a salamander or in a hot oven.
7   Serve immediately.

Scrambled eggs

Ingredients	4 portions	10 portions
Medium eggs	4–8	10–20
Butter	80 g	200 g
Cream	40–80 ml	100–200 ml
Good quality salt and pepper	To taste	To taste

energy	cal	fat	sat fat	carb	sugar	protein	fibre
1174 kJ	284 kcal	27.0 g	14.5 g	0.5 g	0.5 g	9.8 g	0.0 g

METHOD OF WORK

1 Melt the butter in a thick bottomed sauté pan.
2 Beat the eggs in a basin and season.
3 Add to the pan and cook very gently.
4 When they begin to set, add the cream, remove from the heat and continue to stir until lightly set (baveuse).
5 Serve immediately.

HEALTHY OPTION Use unsalted butter and low sodium salt. Reducing sodium in the diet helps to reduce high blood pressure and fluid retention.

SOURCING When producing egg dishes look for local suppliers and farms which can offer the freshest eggs possible. This allows provenance on the menu and support of local business.

Scrambled eggs with herbs

Ingredients	4 portions	10 portions
Medium eggs	4–8	10–20
Butter	40–80 g	100–200 g
Cream	40–80 ml	100–200 mll
Shallots	40–80 g	100–200 g
Garlic	1–2 cloves	2–4 cloves
Parsley	10–20 g	25–50 g
Sage	10–20 g	25–50 g
Good quality salt and pepper	To taste	To taste

energy	cal	fat	sat fat	carb	sugar	protein	fibre
1062 kJ	257 kcal	23.2 g	12.0 g	1.8 g	1.0 g	10.3 g	0.5 g

METHOD OF WORK

1 Chop the shallots and garlic.
2 Finely chop the herbs.
3 Melt the butter in a thick bottomed sauté pan.
4 Add the shallots and garlic and allow to sweat.
5 Beat the eggs in a basin and season.
6 Add to the pan and cook very gently.
7 When they begin to set, add the herbs and the cream, remove from the heat and continue to stir until lightly set (baveuse).
8 Serve immediately.

VIDEO CLIP Scrambling eggs.

Scrambled eggs with smoked salmon

Scrambled egg with smoked salmon, scrambled egg and scrambled egg with herbs

Ingredients	4 portions	10 portions
Medium eggs	4–8	10–20
Butter	40–80 g	100–200 g
Smoked salmon	80–160 g	100–200 g
Cream	40–80 ml	100–200 ml
Good quality salt and pepper	To taste	To taste

energy	cal	fat	sat fat	carb	sugar	protein	fibre
1200 kJ	289 kcal	24.3 g	12.1 g	0.5 g	0.4 g	17.4 g	0.2 g

METHOD OF WORK

1 Cut the smoked salmon into fine julienne.
2 Melt the butter in a thick bottomed sauté pan.
3 Beat the eggs in a basin and season.
4 Add to the pan and cook very gently.
5 When they begin to set, add the salmon and the cream, remove from the heat and continue to stir until lightly set (baveuse).
6 Serve immediately.

CHEF'S TIP Use smoked trout or smoked eel to replace the salmon.

Spanish omelette (tortilla)

Ingredients	4 portions	10 portions
Medium eggs	12	30
Olive oil	100 ml	250 ml
Peeled potatoes	400 g	1 kg
Peppers	2	5
Chopped onions	200 g	500 g
Good quality salt and pepper	To taste	To taste

energy	cal	fat	sat fat	carb	sugar	protein	fibre
2255 kJ	543 kcal	40.9 g	8.1 g	23.7 g	3.7 g	21.0 g	3.3 g

METHOD OF WORK

1 Slice the potatoes and gently fry in the oil. Do not allow to over brown.
2 Dice the peppers and add to the potatoes allow to cook until tender.
3 Beat the eggs and add to the pan, stir gently, cover with a lid and allow to cook very gently until set (approximately 10 minutes).
4 Turn the omelette using a plate or the lid.
5 Slide onto a service dish and serve.

Guest Chef

Smoked haddock on parsley mash with quail's egg, caper and lemon sauce

Chef: *Steve Thorpe MCGB*
Centre: *City College, Norwich*

We use fresh smoked haddock from Cley smokehouse on the Norfolk coast, this gives a really deep flavour to the dish.

Ingredients	Makes 10 portions
Smoked haddock	1 kg
Lemon	1
Sauce	
Butter (to sweat shallots)	20 g
Shallots (chopped)	100 g
Capers	25 g
Stock	250 ml
White wine	200 ml
Cream	200 ml
Butter (to finish)	200 g
The quail's eggs	
Quail's eggs	10
Red wine	300 ml
To serve	
Mashed potato	500 g
Butter	25 g
Chopped parsley	25 g
Cream	100 ml

METHOD OF WORK

1 Skin and trim haddock to 80 g portions.
2 Use any left over haddock to infuse flavour into stock.
3 Sweat the shallots in butter.
4 Add stock, and wine and reduce by half.
5 Add cream and reduce by half.
6 Add the capers and lemon.
7 Finish with butter.
8 Cook and mash the potatoes adding the parsley, butter and cream. Keep warm.
9 Lightly cook the quail's eggs in the red wine and keep warm.
10 Poach haddock to set.
11 Serve haddock as soon as cooked on a bed of mashed potato which has been piped onto the plate.
12 Place a poached quail's egg on top.
13 Spoon sauce around the fish.

Fish and shellfish

NVQ

Unit 2FPC1 Prepare, cook and finish basic fish dishes

Unit 2FPC2 Prepare, cook and finish basic shellfish dishes

VRQ

Unit 211 Prepare and cook fish and shellfish

Recipes

FLAT WHITE FISH

Grilled Dover sole with parsley butter   273

Paupiettes of lemon sole   274

Halibut with lobster mousse, pappardelle, English asparagus and sauce vin blanc   275

Goujons of lemon sole with lemon in muslin and aioli   276

ROUND WHITE FISH

Baked whiting with herb crust and a cream sauce   277

Deep fried haddock and thick cut chips   278

Fish pie   279

Grilled sea bream with a modern minted pea velouté   280

Roasted pollack with vegetable julienne and mouclade   281

Steamed pollack, Marquis potato, bacon lardons, curly kale and dill cream sauce   282

OILY FISH

Hot smoked jasmine and green tea salmon with ribbons of vegetables   283

Pan fried salmon with asparagus, broad beans, Biarritz potatoes and chive cream sauce   284

Salmon fish cakes with pea shoots and tartar sauce   285

Sesame tuna with hoi sin and pak choy   286

FRESHWATER FISH

Poached trout with carrots and shallots   287

MISCELLANEOUS FISH

Bouillabaisse Marseille   288

Monkfish wrapped in pancetta with salsa verde   289

Pan fried red mullet with ratatouille
and sauce vierge 290

Skate with capers and black
butter 290

SHELLFISH

Moules mariniére 298

Deep fried clams 299

Thai green curry tiger prawns 299

Scallops served in the shell with
vegetable brunoise and lemon
oil 300

Langoustines en papillotte 300

Oysters cooked three ways: deep
fried beignet, grilled with a herb
crumb and with a champagne
jelly 301

Crab and prawn cakes with
mango salsa 302

Tempura of crayfish with basil
mayonnaise 303

Lobster thermidor 304

Razor clams and chorizo, butter bean
and tomato stew 305

ONLINE RECIPES

LEARNER SUPPORT

Step-by-step tronçon of large
flat fish

Baked brown trout with wilted
spinach and chilli butter

LEARNING OBJECTIVES

The aim of this unit is to enable the candidate to develop skills and apply knowledge in the preparation and cookery principles of fish and shellfish. This will also include materials, ingredients and equipment.

At the end of this chapter you will be able to:

● Identify each fish and shellfish variety.

● Understand the use of relative ingredients in fish and shellfish cookery and their quality points.

● State the quality points of various fish and shellfish commodities.

● Prepare and cook each type of fish and shellfish variety.

● Identify the storage procedures for fish and shellfish.

● Identify the correct tools and equipment to utilize during the preparation and cooking of fish and shellfish.

● Recognize potential alternative healthy eating options.

● Show competence at preparing and cooking a range of fish and shellfish-based dishes.

Introduction to fish

Fish has become a major feature on the majority of menus across the world, as professional chefs find new and appealing ways to cook and present it. Its versatility makes fish a healthy, flavoursome and colourful choice for any menu. Fish is considered a delicate commodity requiring expertise and great care in its preparation. It is essential to have a lightness of touch at all stages of preparation to help ensure that the natural flavour and quality of the fish is not overwhelmed with heavy and incompatible garnishes.

Usually fish is featured on the menu as part of the main course selection. Its honourable place is as an intermediate course directly before the main course of meat or poultry. Alternatively, fish is used in other sections of the menu such as canapés, starters, hors d'oeuvre, garnishes for pasta and rice, salads and savouries.

Fish fall into five categories:

1 flat white

2 round white

3 oily

4 freshwater

5 miscellaneous.

These different categories are formed due to the derivative of the species, environment where they live, shape and size of the fish, as seen in the table overleaf.

FLAT WHITE FISH	ROUND WHITE FISH	OILY FISH	MISCELLANEOUS	FRESHWATER FISH
Sole	Whiting	Salmon	Grouper	Zander
Plaice	Cod	Trout	Swordfish	Perch
Turbot	Grey mullet	Mackerel	Shark	Rainbow trout
Flounder	Pollack	Sardines	Skate	Pike
Halibut	Hake	Sprats	Monkfish	Carp
Brill	Haddock	Herrings	Red snapper	Eel
Megrim	Sea bass	Tuna	John Dory	Tilapia

> **CHEF'S TIP** Fresh fish should be purchased on a daily basis if at all possible. A really fresh fish should retain its natural colouring and be bright in its appearance. The colours fade as the fish loses its freshness.

Quality points

When buying fresh fish it is important to consider a range of quality points to help determine absolute freshness and good condition.

SMELL

Fresh – there should be a delicate, pleasant odour reminiscent of the sea.
Not fresh – unpleasant, fishy and strong smell, sometimes a sour and ammonia smell will be apparent.

APPEARANCE

Fresh – shiny, slippery, moist, glistening skin and the presence of sea slime.
Not fresh – dull, colourless, dry appearance.

SCALES

Fresh – strong, attached, shiny in appearance.
Not fresh – loose, easy to remove or partially removed.

SKIN

Fresh – taut, colourful, glistening and adhered to fish.
Not fresh – puckered, dry and easily damaged.

EYES

Fresh – clear, bright, transparent and protruding eyes.
Not fresh – flat, glassy, opaque, sunken and dry.

GILLS

Fresh – moist, shiny, deep red flush with aerated blood.
Not fresh – dry, grey and indistinct.

FLESH

Fresh – firm flesh, translucent, white or pink with a gleaming brightness.
Not fresh – separates into large chunks, very soft, red or brown flecks, dry fillets at the edges and limp.

Yields of fish

Accepting cheap and poor quality fish will only give the chef an unsatisfactory end result, regardless of what masking takes place when cooking and finishing the dish.

The wastage obtained from cutting fillets is approximately 60 per cent for round fish and 50 per cent loss on flat fish. This can be reduced slightly by using whole fish to cook where possible, cutting **tronçons** of large flat fish and **darnes** of round fish. Fish wastage means the amount of fish that is inedible when being prepared, such as the head, bones, intestines, tail and fins.

PERCENTAGES OF USABLE FLESH IN FISH (%)

Cod	45
Monkfish	30
Whiting	55
Sole	50
Salmon	45
Pike	45
Turbot	50
Trout	60

It is unusual to have over 60 per cent of usable flesh when preparing filleted fish. If serving round fish for grilling there will be an approximate 5 per cent weight loss from the discarding of the trimmed fins and the gutting, with a further 10 per cent if the head is removed.

To estimate the weight loss of fish, the calculation below should be applied:

$$\frac{\text{Total waste weight}}{\text{Total original fish weight}} \times 100 = \%\text{wastage}$$

The percentage of weight loss should be taken into account when pricing dishes.

Ethical fishing

The consumption of fish has increased steadily over the past few years. This is generally due to increased customer awareness of the healthy benefits afforded from fish and its growing appreciation as an international delicacy. This popularity has had the consequence of improving the vast array of fish available throughout the year. Modern transport is quick and efficient and the use of air transport now provides us with the ability to purchase quality fish from all over the world such as swordfish and grouper.

Tropical fish

Flat fish

Oily fish

Because the UK is an island it is seen as having abundant supplies of fish. Nonetheless, pollution and overfishing are starting to have a damaging effect on the stock of certain fish. The contamination in some sea areas and rivers has affected the supply and fitness of certain fish and shellfish for human consumption. This is one of the reasons that the chef should be attentive in checking the quality of the fish they purchase and should also be concerned with the origin of the fish. Fish farms have been established to contribute to the demand of the customer. Stocks of wild salmon, cod and haddock are on a steady decline largely due to over-fishing. Although these farms are a welcome addition to the food supply chain (especially those that are organic and responsible to the environment), it is important that the chef is sensitive to this issue and looks at purchasing lesser known fish such as pollack and hake.

TASK When purchasing fish you should make sure that it comes from an ethical source. In groups research the guidelines for ethical fishing and present your findings to the rest of your class. Your presentation should either support or oppose ethical fishing and give examples.

Nutrition

Fish is an excellent source of easily digestible protein. White fish is very low in fat content and the fat itself is unsaturated. Oily fish contains a higher fat content and is not as easily digested as white fish. However, it is an excellent source of vitamins A and D and contains the essential fatty acids omega 3 and 6 which can help fight heart disease. Cod liver also has these attributes. The edible bones of whitebait and sardines can provide additional calcium. Generally fish is a good provision for building immune systems.

SEASONALITY OF FISH

	JAN	FEB	MAR	APR	MAY	JUN	JUL	AUG	SEP	OCT	NOV	DEC
BREAM					S/R	S/R	S/R					
BRILL			S/R	S/R	S/R							
COD			S/R	S/R								
EEL												
GREY MULLET			S/R	S/R								
GURNARD												
HADDOCK												
HAKE			S/R	S/R	S/R							
HALIBUT				S/R	S/R							
HERRING												
JOHN DORY												
MACKEREL												
MONKFISH												
PLAICE			S/R	S/R								
RED MULLET												
SALMON FARMED												
SALMON WILD												
SARDINES												
SEA BASS				S/R	S/R							
SEA TROUT								S/R	S/R	S/R	S/R	
SKATE												
SQUID												
SOLE (DOVER)												
SOLE (LEMON)												
TROUT												
TUNA												
TURBOT				S/R	S/R	S/R						
WHITING												

Key

	Fish at their best
	Available
S/R	Fish are spawning and roeing, poor flesh yield and nutrient content
	Not available

HEALTHY OPTION Oily fish contain a large amount of polyunsaturated fatty acids which may help to fight against heart disease.

Preparation techniques

In this section we explore the preparation techniques that lead to a choice of cooking methods. Such techniques use skills which are compatible when handling round or flat fish. For example, most round or flat fish are filleted using similar techniques.

Round white fish have delicately flavoured flesh that requires simple and fast cookery methods. Fish such as cod and haddock have been intensely fished to the point that natural stocks are being depleted. The modern chef should take these facts into consideration when planning menus and look to include under-used fish such as ling, whiting, pollock and coley.

Top left – Pavé of salmon, supreme of salmon, darne of salmon, goujons of sole
Bottom left – Supreme of whiting, en tresse, stuffed paupiettes, tronçon of halibut

CHEF'S TIP If you need to keep the fish intact while gutting, you can remove the guts from the gill slits, although this is quite an advanced and time-consuming technique. It is used for fish that is to be poached whole because it retains the natural shape of the fish.

VIDEO CLIP Trimming and gutting round fish.

Preparation of round white fish

1 Cut through the stomach of the fish by making a shallow incision along the underside of the fish. Remove the guts (viscera) and then cut off the gills. Rinse the cavity under cold running water to remove any remaining blood and guts.

Step-by-step: Filleting round fish

1. Removing fins from a whiting.

2. Removing the head of the whiting.

3. Running a knife along the backbone to remove the top fillet.

4. Trimming and removing bones from the belly side.

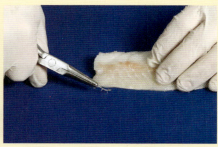

5. Removing the pin bones with fish tweezers.

6. Neatly trimmed and pin boned fillets of whiting.

2 De-scale the skin with the back of a knife and trim the fish of any fins. Using a filleting knife, cut into the fish at the head just behind the gills until the backbone is reached.

3 Cut the fish down the length of the back, cutting along the top side of the backbone, and working from head to tail continue cutting over the bone to remove the fillet completely.

4 Turn over the fish and remove the second fillet in the same way. Trim both fillets to the required shape and size.

5 Skin the fillet by inserting the filleting knife near the tail end cutting through the flesh to the skin. Run the blade along the skin pulling the flesh away from it as the cut is made.

VIDEO CLIP Skinning white round fish.

SUPRÊME OF WHITE ROUND FISH

1 Using a sharp and semi-flexible knife cut along the backbone until you reach the ribs.

2 Stand the fish on its belly and continue to cut down until the fillet is removed.

3 Cut the pin bones from the fillet into a V shape.

4 Remove the thicker suprêmes (also known as **pavé**) and then the flatter suprêmes. Average weight should be 150 g.

CHEF'S TIP Always ensure knives are clean and sharp when filleting to prevent tearing the flesh.

VIDEO CLIP Cutting a supreme from a round fish.

Preparation of flat white fish

Because of their flatness, these fish are usually fried, poached or grilled. They cook very quickly and are very unforgiving because they can change from succulent to dry in a very short time during the cooking process. Examples are Dover sole, lemon sole, plaice, megrim, witch sole (or Torbay sole) and dabs. The exceptions to this are brill, turbot and the largest of the true flat fish, halibut. Because they are such large flat fish they can be prepared into tronçons and suprêmes.

Step-by-step: Single filleting flat fish

1. Cut down the lateral line as carefully as possible.

2. Continue to remove the single fillets by running the knife flat along the bones.

3. Repeat the process on the other side of the fish.

4. Holding the tail firmly carefully start to remove the skin from the fillet.

5. Continue to remove the skin, ensure the knife stays flat to the board.

6. Trim the fillets neatly and use as required.

CROSS-CUT FILLETING

A blocks-man is a professional fishmonger who fillets and prepares fish commercially. Economically, a blocks-man would not have the time to fillet fish in the same fashion as a chef. They have to balance the waste against the time it takes to fillet the fish, although they are generally highly skilled people and usually have little or no waste.

> **VIDEO CLIP** A blocks man at Billingsgate fish market.

Step-by-step: Cross-cut filleting

1. Cut an incision just behind the head and slide the knife along the bone.

2. Continue to slide the knife forwards along the bones towards the tail.

3. Lift the first side of the plaice up and continue to cut over the backbone and across the other side.

4. Run the knife over the bones and carefully remove the double fillet.

5. The completed double fillet.

Step-by-step: Fillet of plaice en tresse (plait)

1. Skin the fillet.
2. Being careful not to cut along the entire fillet make an incision 1 cm from thickest end of the fillet. Repeat this until you have three equal strips.

3. Plait the strips until they come to a point at the end of the fillet. Fish prepared en tresse can be steamed or breaded and deep fried.

4. A completed plait 'en tresse'.

GOUJONS OF FLAT FISH

1 Cut the fillets into strips approximately 6 cm × 0.5 cm.

2 Pass through seasoned flour, beaten egg and bread-crumbs (pané) and roll.

Step-by-step: Preparing goujons of flat fish

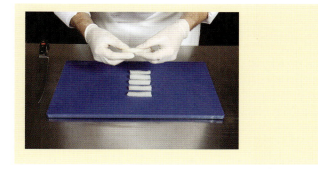

 VIDEO CLIP Goujons of plaice.

Step-by-step: Preparing a Dover sole

PAUPIETTES OF SOLE

Paupiettes are a rolled fillet of flat fish, however in modern cuisine they are usually filled with mousseline or fine **forcemeat**.

Paupiettes can also be prepared with four fillets wrapped and filled with a mousseline to create a sausage shape.

 CHEF'S TIP Paupiettes can be produced individually using single fillets of fish such as sole, plaice or megrim.

 VIDEO CLIP Skinning Dover sole.

1. Remove the fins with a pair of scissors.

2. Carefully make a knife incision at the tail end of the sole and begin to pull the skin towards the head.

3. Remove the skin in one piece by gently pulling towards the head.

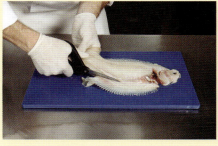

4. Trim the sole after the skin has been removed from both sides.

5. Finally remove the eyes and wash the finished Dover sole.

6. The trimmed Dover sole.

Step-by-step: Preparing paupiettes of sole

1. Lay the fillets on top of the plastic film with the presentation side down. Use a sprinkling of water to stop the fish flesh sticking to the bat or another piece of cling film then lightly bat out the fillets.

2. Pipe or spread a mousse or forcemeat (in this case a crab and salmon mousse) onto the fillet, ensuring the presentation side is facing downwards.

3. Use the cling film to help roll the fillets.

4. Remove the cling film then reposition the fillets and re roll to help secure the shape.

5. Roll the fillet tightly in the cling film: this will secure the shape during cooking.

6. The finished paupiette.

DÉLICE OF SOLE

As with paupiettes, traditionally a délice is a folded fillet of flat fish. However, this is folded into two or three with the seam facing down. In modern cookery these are almost always stuffed with a mousseline or fine **farce**.

1   Lightly bat out and lay the fillets as you would with a paupiette but ensure the pointed end of the fillet is facing away from you.

2   Pipe a filling from the halfway point, starting with a deep fill and tapering to a shallow fill. Fold the thin end over to the middle and then the thicker end should be folded into the middle before ensuring that the sides are neat.

Step-by-step: Preparing délice of sole

1. Piping a mousseline into the centre of the fillet.

2. Carefully folding over one side and then the other.

3. The completed stuffed délice.

Preparation of oily fish

SUPRÊME OF SALMON

1   Gut, wash, de-scale and remove the head, trim the fins.

2   Cut just above the backbone so that the knife rests on the bone, insert the knife over the bone structure below the anal vent and allow the knife to follow the contours of the fish until it removes the bottom end of the fillet.

3   Remove the rib bones and any cartilage by cutting along each side and underneath until all the central backbone is clear.

4   Remove the pin bones using a pair of sterile fish pliers.

5   There are two accepted techniques associated with suprêmes of salmon:

●   The modern method where the suprêmes are cut at a straight angle with the skin still attached.

●   The traditional method where the fillet is skinned and the suprême is cut at 45° angle.

HEALTH & SAFETY   The use of correctly colour-coded chopping boards for preparing raw fish and different ones for cutting cooked fish is imperative to help prevent **cross-contamination**. Wash the boards frequently with hot water and a detergent and use disposable alcohol wipes to help disinfect them.

WEB LINK   Use this link to discover what different fishing methods are used to catch fish:
    http://www.fishonline.org

Step-by-step: Preparing suprême of salmon

1. Removing the fins with scissors.

2. Removing the head of the salmon.

3. Running the knife along the back bone to clear the fillet from the rib bones of the salmon.

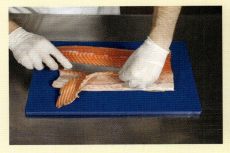

4. Removing the bones located on the belly.

5. Trimming the top of the salmon.

6. Removing the pin bones.

DARNE OF SALMON AND VARIATIONS

1   Scale, wash, gut and remove the head.

2   Cutting from the top of the fish, slice darnes at the required weight (usually 180–225 g).

3   Pinch the belly until a natural round shape is formed and cut off the surplus belly.

4   Tie with a gentle knot, ensuring that there is sufficient string to allow a slipknot to be tied. This allows for a

smooth service because the string doesn't need to be cut away and cause potential damage to the darne.

● Method 2 is to tie at the natural round line.

● Method 3 is to remove the bone and stuff the darne with a fish farce before tying up.

> **CHEF'S TIP**   Certain fish such as grouper, snapper, weaver and sea bass have sharp, spiny fins or spines and care should be taken when preparing these fish.
>
>

Step-by-step: Preparing darne of salmon

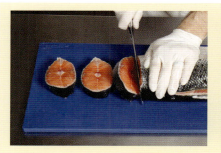

VIDEO CLIP   Cutting darnes.

Cutting a darne from a salmon.

Different end products; natural and using a farce.

Preparation of small oily fish

Fish such as sardines, mackerel, trout and herrings that are small enough to be served whole can be prepared in the following fashion.

1   Gut the fish by inserting the knife into the anal cavity and cutting through the skin up to the head. Pull out the intestines and any blood lying next to the back bone and wash the cavity well with clean water.

2   Trim off the fins and remove the head. If the head is to be retained, the gills and eyes should be removed.

3   Place the fish onto a chopping board and press along the backbone until you feel the bone separating from the flesh. Turnover and gently remove the entire backbone.

4   Make sure that all bones are removed. The fish is now ready for cooking. It can be stuffed or just **scored** on the skin with a sharp knife, seasoned, brushed with oil and simply grilled.

1. Removing the guts of the trout.

2. Pressing down backbone of trout to loosen it from flesh for removal.

3. Removing bones from the trout.

4. Trout with head and bones removed.

BUTTERFLY FILLETING

If a fish is small enough to be used as a single portion it may be **butterfly** filleted without removing the guts.

1   Cut along the fish just above the ribs and inside, along the backbone until you reach the back skin: be careful not to pierce the skin. Turn the fish over and repeat the operation.

2   Holding the fish, cut under the hand and remove the bones with the guts still intact. This yields a butterfly fillet that can be used as any other fillet or stuffed and folded.

Storing and preserving fish

Fresh fish should be used on the day of purchase where possible, although this may not always be practical so care should be taken when storing fresh fish. Fish should be stored at 1 °C in a refrigerator that is only used to store fish and shellfish. It should be kept covered with a clean, damp cloth and under crushed ice. The cloth barrier is to maintain the low temperature and prevent the flesh from drying out for as long as possible. It is important that under these conditions the fish is used quickly and is checked on a day by day basis to ensure its freshness. Ideally fish should be bought whole and on the bone, this way the freshness can easily be determined and the cost can be reduced by preparing the fish yourself.

Frozen fish is usually frozen at sea in long-range fish processing trawlers that can stay out fishing for long periods of time. It is always best to freeze fresh fish as quickly as possible with the use of a blast freezer to help prevent spoilage and deterioration of the flesh. This rapid process ensures that the ice crystals within the flesh are tiny, which allows for minimum water absorption and deterioration of the flesh. If freezing fresh fish in the kitchen, certain aspects will need to be observed by the chef. All frozen fish whether prepared whole, in fillets or darnes should be evenly coated with a thin layer of clean ice. Vacuum packing individual portions before freezing will help to prevent dehydration and **freezer burn**. As mentioned earlier, the rapid freezing of the flesh will also help maintain the fish in a good condition. Frozen fish must be stored at a maximum of –18 °C in a deep freeze cabinet. Although in order to produce sashimi, the Japanese freeze yellow tail tuna to temperatures of

about –60 °C. This helps to maintain the delicate colour of the fish but will also kill off parasites which would usually hibernate when frozen under normal conditions and will help the chef when cutting very fine slices of the fish. Defrosted fish should *never* be refrozen as this can be a significant health hazard. When the frozen fish is required it should be defrosted in a refrigerator and not come into contact with any other ingredients.

Curing

Most methods for **curing** seafood are usually to incorporate flavour to the fish rather than to maximize the storage. There are different methods for curing fish that reveal a diversity of textures, flavours and overall end results.

● *Ceviche*. This technique derives from Mexico and it involves the **marinating** of fish in fresh lemon or lime juice with the addition of herbs and aromatic vegetables. Fish and shellfish such as salmon, turbot and scallops are ideal for this method because they can be thinly sliced before marinating takes place.

● *Escabeche*. This is a popular way of curing used by South American countries and the Mediterranean regions. Fish is filleted and then **shallow fried** before being marinated with aromatic vegetables, fresh herbs and lemon juice or vinegar.

● *Pickling*. Herrings and shellfish such as whelks, prawns and cockles can be pickled in vinegar. Usually white vinegar is used with the addition of peppercorns and aromatic vegetables. The seafood must be cleaned before pickling commences and sealed jars are utilized to help the preservation process. Herrings that have been cleaned, filleted and rolled up are pickled in vinegar and called rollmops.

● *Salting*. This is primarily used for white, round fish such as cod. The fish is covered with a good quality sea salt to draw out the moisture. It is then dried to preserve it. The fish is always soaked in water to reconstitute it before cooking. Salted cod is the main ingredient in brandade. Caviar is also slightly salted and comes from the roe of the sturgeon. It is carefully processed, tinned and refrigerated before being served on crushed ice with buckwheat cakes called **blinis**.

- *Smoking*. Fish that is smoked can be prepared and gutted or left whole. After soaking in a solution of salt and other additional ingredients to help the flavour, it is then drained and washed before being hung on racks and placed into a smoking chamber. Hot smoking fish is cured at between 70–80 °C and it cooks the fish as it is being smoked. As it is only partially preserved it can only be kept for a few days in refrigeration. Cold smoking takes place at temperatures of no more than 33 °C and will cure the fish over a period of time (usually 5–6 hours). This process has a drying characteristic to aid preservation.

- *Canning*. Oily fish such as sardines, tuna, anchovies, herring and salmon are usually canned. The fish is preserved in its own juices, oil, **brine** or a sauce (such as tomato). This process is documented in greater detail in Chapter 4 in this book (in relation to canned soup).

TASK Find out which fish are traditionally smoked, the methods and why this was important. Explain why smoked fish should be stored in a separate refrigerator.

HEALTH & SAFETY To help avoid the risk of cross-contamination fish should always be stored in a separate refrigerator and away from other foods. Cooked fish and raw fish should always be stored separately.

Cooking methods for fish

Boiling

Whole fish such as salmon and turbot are suitable for this method of cookery. Whole fish should be placed into a cold cooking liquid which can be water, milk, or a **court bouillon**. Cuts of fish on the bone should be placed into simmering liquid. This will help to prevent the juices from escaping and coagulating into a white coating on the surface of the fish. The fish should be completely immersed in the cooking liquid. It is not recommended that fish be boiled rapidly as this will damage the texture and may eventually break up the shape of the fish. The cooking liquid should barely move and retain the heat at 90–95 °C. On occasion a fish kettle may be employed.

CHEF'S TIP Poaching fish in a court bouillon or white wine and fish stock improves the overall flavour of the fish.

Poaching

Fish may be poached in shallow or deep liquid. With shallow poaching the cooking liquid is usually retained for the sauce. The fish can be barely covered with the liquid and buttered baking parchment and then cooked in a moderately heated oven. The cooking liquid used for shallow poaching can be fish stock, with addition of a little white wine.

CHEF'S TIP Aromatic vegetables are used to present flavour to fish dishes, court bouillons and sauces. These include onions, carrots, shallots, fennel and celery.

Fish that is suitable for boiling and poaching may also be cooked by steaming. The preparation techniques are the same as for poaching and the fish is placed onto a buttered tray, seasoned lightly and covered with buttered baking parchment. It is an easy method of cooking and is accepted as a good method of cookery for large-scale operations such as banquets. Cooking by steam is rapid and will therefore help to retain flavour, nutrients and colour.

CHEF'S TIP When poaching or boiling whole fish do not allow the liquid to boil as it will cause the fish to break.

CHEF'S TIP Poach fish for approximately 5–7 minutes for a thickness of 2.5 cm starting in hot liquid (or until the core temperature of the fish is 63 °C). Reserving the poaching liquid and turning it into a sauce to accompany the halibut will add another element to this dish.

Baking

Whole, filleted or portioned fish can be baked in an oven. Care must be taken to ensure that the direct heat does not overcook or burn the fish. Whole fish may be stuffed with a mousseline or forcemeat and brushed with oil or butter before baking. In Portugal whole fish is covered with sea salt and baked to help retain flavour and moisture. Another way of protecting the fish during baking is to wrap it in pastry such as puff pastry or filo pastry. Portions of fish can be baked in buttered dishes and basted frequently or herb crusts can be made to cover the fish portions.

CHEF'S TIP Oily fish are ideal for baking because they remain moist while in the oven. Lean whole fish will require **basting** during cooking to prevent them from drying out in the heat of the oven.

CHEF'S TIP Thin fillets of fish will only require approximately two minutes of cooking per side. It is important not to overcook the fish otherwise nutrients and the flavour and texture of the fish will be lost.

Grilling

Whole small fish and most cuts and types of fish are suitable for grilling. They need to be seasoned, passed lightly through flour, brushed with oil and scored before being grilled on both sides under a salamander or cooked over heat on the bars of a chargrill.

Stewing

The usual method is to cook a variety of fish and shellfish with vegetables, aromatic herbs, fish stock and wine. The best known type of stewed fish dish is bouillabaisse.

Shallow frying

Whole small fish, a variety of cuts and fillets are suitable for shallow frying. The term 'meuniere' can be used to indicate fish cooked by shallow frying. The fish is passed through seasoned flour and then shallow fried presentation side first in clarified butter before turning over to complete the cooking process. The cooked fish is then served with nut-brown butter flavoured with a little lemon juice and freshly chopped parsley.

VIDEO CLIP Searing and pan frying fish.

EXAMPLES OF SUITABLE COOKING METHODS

	BAKING	BOILING	DEEP FRYING	GRILLING	POACHING	ROASTING	SHALLOW FRYING	STEAMING	STIR FRYING
Bream	✓			✓			✓		
Cod	✓	✓	✓	✓	✓	✓	✓	✓	
Coley		✓	✓				✓		
Dover sole			✓	✓	✓		✓	✓	
Grouper				✓		✓			
Haddock	✓			✓	✓		✓		
Hake	✓			✓	✓		✓	✓	
Halibut	✓			✓	✓		✓	✓	✓
Herring				✓			✓		
Huss			✓				✓		
John dory					✓		✓	✓	
Lemon sole			✓	✓	✓		✓	✓	
Mackerel				✓			✓		
Marlin	✓						✓		
Monkfish	✓					✓	✓		✓
Plaice			✓	✓			✓	✓	
Red mullet				✓		✓	✓		
Red snapper				✓		✓	✓		
Salmon	✓	✓	✓	✓	✓		✓	✓	✓
Sardines				✓			✓		
Sea bass	✓			✓	✓		✓	✓	
Shark	✓			✓		✓	✓	✓	✓
Skate wings		✓	✓		✓				

	BAKING	BOILING	DEEP FRYING	GRILLING	POACHING	ROASTING	SHALLOW FRYING	STEAMING	STIR FRYING
Swordfish	■			■			■		■
Trout	■			■			■		
Tuna				■	■		■		■
Turbot	■	■	■	■	■	■	■		
Whitebait			■						

Deep frying

Whole small round and flat fish, fillets and goujons are suitable for deep frying. The fish must be coated before frying with one of the following combinations:

- seasoned flour, beaten egg and breadcrumbs
- milk and flour
- seasoned flour and batter
- seasoned flour and beaten egg.

The coating forms a protective layer to prevent the fish absorbing too much fat from the deep frying process. Deep fried fish is usually served with deep fried fresh sprigs of parsley, a quarter of a lemon and a suitable sauce (e.g. sauce tartare or sauce remoulade).

Roasting

Thick cuts of fish such as sea bass and cod are suitable for roasting. The fish is usually portioned and the skin is left on before being lightly seared on both sides in a hot pan with oil. It is then roasted in the oven for a few minutes. Finely chopped vegetables and herbs may be placed under the fish on the roasting tray so that after the fish has been cooked any residual flavour in the bottom of the tray can be deglazed to help form the basis of a sauce.

TEST YOURSELF

1 List three variaties of flat white fish.

2 List three variaties of round white fish.

3 List three variaties of oily fish.

4 List three variaties of fresh water fish.

5 List five quality points when purchasing fresh fish.

6 Which fish is the odd one out:

   cod, haddock or mackerel?

7 What is the cut called when cutting across a round fish?

8 What is the cut called when cutting across a flat fish?

9 What term is used when removing small bones with tweezers from a round fish?

10 In which direction is skin removed from a Dover sole?

Recipes
Flat white fish

Grilled Dover sole with parsley butter

Ingredients	Makes approximately 4 portions	Makes approximately 10 portions
Skinned, trimmed Dover sole	4 × 500 g	10 × 500 g
Unsalted butter	200 g	500 g
Plain flour	100 g	250 g
Sliced fennel	200 g	500 g
Chopped fresh parsley	2 tblspn	5 tblspn
Fresh lemon	1 lemon	3 lemons
Good quality salt	To taste	To taste
White pepper	To taste	To taste
Lemon juice and finely grated zest	1 lemon	2 lemons
Lemon muslin halves	4	10
Watercress		

energy	cal	fat	sat fat	carb	sugar	protein	fibre
3850 kJ	925 kcal	51.3 g	27.6 g	21.2 g	1.9 g	95.8 g	2.7 g

4 Place in a refrigerator for a few minutes to chill.

5 Meanwhile, beat the unsalted butter and add the lemon juice, finely grated zest and chopped parsley mixing well until all the ingredients have been incorporated.

6 Transfer the butter onto silicone paper and roll into a cylindrical shape, chill until required.

7 Prepare the lemon by cutting in half and removing any seeds and trimming any white pith then wrapping in muslin.

8 Heat an iron bar, metal skewer or solid griddle pan until it is very hot. Carefully mark the Dover soles in a quadrilateral pattern.

9 Lay the sliced fennel onto a greased baking tray, rest the Dover sole on top and place under the salamander to begin grilling for a few minutes, until the flesh begins to slightly colour.

10 Place the Dover sole into the oven and continue to cook for approximately 12 minutes.

11 Serve either on or off the bone with the parsley butter, lemon muslin and watercress.

METHOD OF WORK

1 Preheat the oven to 180 °C.

2 Prepare the Dover sole for grilling by trimming the fins and skinning the fish on both sides.

3 Lightly season and flour the sole, then brush with melted butter.

CHEF'S TIP When bar marking the sole on a contact surface ensure the bars are spotlessly clean, red hot and lightly oiled; this will prevent sticking.

Paupiettes of lemon sole
with baby leek confit and sauce Dugléré

Ingredients	Makes approximately 4 portions	Makes approximately 10 portions
Prepared lemon sole paupiettes	8 paupiettes	20 paupiettes
Dry white wine	50 ml	125 ml
Finely chopped shallots	20 g	45 g
White pepper	To taste	To taste
Good quality salt	To taste	To taste
Tomato concassée	200 g	500 g
Double cream	200 ml	400 ml
Butter	45 g	100 g
Fish stock	100 ml	200 ml
Lemon juice	¼ lemon	½ lemon
Chopped flat leaf parsley	2 tblspn	6 tblspn
Baby leeks	8 each	20 each
Olive oil	4 tsp	9 tsp
Lime juice	½ lime	1 lime

energy	cal	fat	sat fat	carb	sugar	protein	fibre
2474 kJ	596 kcal	43.7 g	24.2 g	4.8 g	4.4 g	43.9 g	1.7 g

METHOD OF WORK

1 Preheat an oven to 180 °C.
2 Prepare the paupiettes of sole as mentioned on page 266 in this chapter.
3 Lightly butter a poaching pan or tray and sprinkle the chopped shallots over. Place the paupiettes on top with three-quarters of the tomato concassée and half of the chopped flat leaf parsley. Season well.
4 Add the white wine and the fish stock and cover with a buttered piece of baking parchment.

5 To prepare the confit of leek, carefully cut the leek into lozenges and place into a baking tin with the olive oil and lime juice. Season well and place in the oven to cook to a confit for approximately 45 minutes. Remove from the oven and add the rest of the chopped flat leaf parsley and drain the leek oil from the confit. Retain the confit and the oil separately in a warm place.
6 Place the paupiettes into the oven to poach for approximately 10 minutes.
7 Remove the paupiettes, drain and reserve in a warm place covered with the buttered baking parchment.
8 Pass the cooking liquor into a small pan and reduce by two-thirds.
9 Add the double cream and once again reduce the liquid to a smooth coating consistency. Incorporate the butter by whisking in off the direct heat (monter au beurre) until completely blended into the sauce. Correct the consistency and seasoning. Add any remaining fresh chopped parsley to the sauce at this point.
10 To serve, arrange the ingredients neatly on the plate, speed is important as fish cools quickly.

CHEF'S TIP for paupiette of lemon sole, leek confit and sauce Dugléré Any white fish can be used for this recipe although consideration must be taken when poaching larger cuts. There are numerous classical poached sole dishes available:

- *Fillet of sole Bercy* – poached as for this recipe without the tomato concassée. The cooking liquor used as part of the sauce in the same way but adding a fish velouté sauce, lemon juice, freshly chopped parsley and cayenne pepper and making a sabayon with the addition of some egg yolks. The sauce should be glazed under a salamander.
- *Fillet of sole bonne femme* – poached as for this recipe with the cooking liquor used as part of the sauce using sliced button mushroom instead of the tomato concassé. The sauce is a fish velouté made from the reduced cooking liquor, cream, and egg yolks, used to produce a sabayon with the addition of butter and cayenne pepper; it is then glazed under the salamander for service.
- *Fillet of sole mornay* – poached as for this recipe without the tomato concassée. The cooking liquor is reduced and then added to a béchamel sauce along with grated cheese, cayenne pepper, butter and egg yolks to create a sabayon before the dish is glazed under a salamander to serve.

Halibut with lobster mousse, pappardelle, English asparagus and sauce vin blanc

Ingredients	Makes approximately 4 portions	Makes approximately 10 portions
Halibut supreme	4 × 120 g	10 × 120 g
Reduced brown chicken stock	80 ml	200 ml
Beurre noisette	40 ml	100 ml
Fish mousse	120 g	300 g
Diced lobster	120 g	300 g
truffle	4 g	10 g
Fines herb	2 g	5 g
Cayenne pepper	To taste	To taste
lemon juice	To taste	To taste
Pappadellle uncooked	200 g	500 g
Fish veloute	280 ml	700 ml
Fish stock	200 ml	500 ml
Asparagus medium	20 spears	50 spears
Unsalted butter		
Good quality salt	To taste	To taste
White pepper	To taste	To taste

energy	cal	fat	sat fat	carb	sugar	protein	fibre
3391 kJ	812 kcal	47.3 g	25.5 g	26.6 g	6.0 g	70.2 g	4.6 g

METHOD OF WORK

1. Mix the lobster, fish mousse and fines herb together, season and add cayenne pepper and lemon juice.
2. Poach a small amount to check consistency and flavour.
3. Spread mousse evenly over the halibut and season well, place into a shallow pan and add fish stock.
4. Bring to a simmer and place in a 180 °C oven until cooked.
5. Reduce cooking liquor and add to fish velouté cooking liquor.
6. Mix reduced chicken stock and beurre noisette together, use to glaze the cooked halibut.
7. Cook asparagus in boiling water and glaze with butter.
8. Cook pasta as normal.

SOURCING Asparagus is not seasonally available all year. Selecting seasonal vegetables to complement this dish will give an enhanced flavour and maintain cost effectiveness. See the eat seasonably website at:
http://eatseasonably.co.uk

Goujons of lemon sole with lemon in muslin and aioli

Ingredients	Makes approximately 4 portions	Makes approximately 10 portions
Lemon sole goujons	8 fillets	20 fillets
Pasteurized egg	100 g	200 g
Plain flour	100 g	250 g
White breadcrumbs	100 g	250 g
Aioli (see page 140)	4 tblspn	10 tblspn
Lemon muslin halves	4	10
Good quality salt	To taste	To taste
White pepper	To taste	To taste

energy	cal	fat	sat fat	carb	sugar	protein	fibre
2564 kJ	610 kcal	19.8 g	2.8 g	39.2 g	1.2 g	70.4 g	1.5 g

METHOD OF WORK

1. To prepare the goujons, cut each fillet of lemon sole into strips, approximately 6 cm by 0.5 cm.

2. Prepare to pané by setting up trays of seasoned flour, beaten egg and breadcrumbs.

3. Pass the goujons of sole through each tray in the same order as step 2 (above).

4. Once sufficiently coated lay the goujons flat on a cling filmed tray and place into a freezer.

5. Deep fry the goujons at 180 °C for approximately 3 minutes until golden in colour. Drain well and present on a serving plate with the aioli and the lemon muslin.

CHEF'S TIP This dish works well during the summer served with a tossed salad and a sun-dried tomato coulis instead of aioli.

Round white fish

Baked whiting with herb crust and a cream sauce

Ingredients	Makes approximately 4 portions	Makes approximately 10 portions
Whiting fillets, skinned and pin boned	4 × 120 g fillets	10 × 120 g fillets
Mashed potato	8 tblspn	20 tblspn
Egg yolks	2	4
Unsalted butter	100 g	250 g
Fresh parsley	10 g	20 g
Fresh dill	10 g	20 g
Fresh chervil	10 g	20 g
Fresh mint	5 g	10 g
Breadcrumbs	100 g	250 g
Finely grated lemon zest	1 lemon	2 lemons
Fish cream sauce (see page 279)	150 ml	375 ml
Tomato concassée	40 g	100 g
Good quality salt	To taste	To taste
White pepper	To taste	To taste

energy	cal	fat	sat fat	carb	sugar	protein	fibre
2736 kJ	658 kcal	47.4 g	27.9 g	27.4 g	2.2 g	32.4 g	1.8 g

METHOD OF WORK

1 Preheat an oven to 180 °C.

2 Place the washed and dried herbs, breadcrumbs and finely grated lemon zest into a food processor and blend until a fine green coloured crumb has been produced.

3 Add the unsalted butter and blend until totally smooth and amalgamated.

4 Place this mix in between two sheets of plastic film and roll out to 5 mm thick. Chill in a refrigerator until hardened.

5 Prepare the whiting fillets, season and lay onto a baking tray brushed with a little oil.

6 Bake the whiting in the preheated oven until tender to the touch (approximately 8 minutes) and then place on top a square of herb crust.

7 Set under a salamander until the crust begins to bubble and colour slightly. Reserve to one side to rest, keeping the fish hot.

8 Heat the fish cream sauce and add the tomato concassée to it. Season well and adjust the consistency.

9 Heat the mashed potato either in a microwave oven or in a saucepan constantly stirring to prevent burning. Remove from the heat and beat in the egg yolks. Season well and transfer the potato into a piping bag with an 8 mm plain tube.

10 Quickly pipe the potato mash onto the presentation plate.

11 Position the whiting and finish with the fish cream sauce around the plate. Serve immediately.

Deep fried haddock and thick cut chips

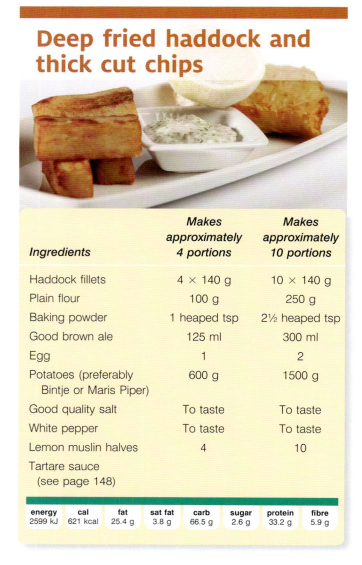

Ingredients	Makes approximately 4 portions	Makes approximately 10 portions
Haddock fillets	4 × 140 g	10 × 140 g
Plain flour	100 g	250 g
Baking powder	1 heaped tsp	2½ heaped tsp
Good brown ale	125 ml	300 ml
Egg	1	2
Potatoes (preferably Bintje or Maris Piper)	600 g	1500 g
Good quality salt	To taste	To taste
White pepper	To taste	To taste
Lemon muslin halves	4	10
Tartare sauce (see page 148)		

energy	cal	fat	sat fat	carb	sugar	protein	fibre
2599 kJ	621 kcal	25.4 g	3.8 g	66.5 g	2.6 g	33.2 g	5.9 g

METHOD OF WORK

1   To make the batter for the fish, mix the flour, baking powder, egg and the beer using a whisk until a smooth consistency has been obtained. Season with salt and allow to rest for at least 1 hour before using.

2   Peel, wash and cut the potatoes into straight sided batons approximately 6 cm long and 2 cm thick. Wash and dry well.

3   Place into frying baskets and blanch in cool oil at 160 °C without colour until cooked through and soft. Drain on kitchen paper on trays until required.

4   Prepare the fish by removing the fillets and trimming. Wash well and dry before seasoning with salt and pepper and passing through flour and then the batter.

5   Carefully place the fish into the deep fryer and fry at 180 °C until golden and cooked through which will take approximately 5 minutes. Drain the fried fillet well on kitchen paper.

6   Place the blanched potatoes into a frying basket and cook at 180 °C until crisp and golden brown in colour. Drain well on kitchen paper, season lightly with a little salt.

7   Serve the fish with the chipped potatoes, tartare sauce (page 148) and lemon muslin.

CHEF'S TIP   When deep frying always place the fish into the oil away from you so as to prevent splashes of hot oil.

HEALTHY OPTION   The use of chipped potatoes on menus is popular. However, this dish has become a benchmark for poor dietary control in recent years. The Potato Marketing Board has stated guidelines on the cooking of chips such as:

- Using high polyunsaturated oils to cook with.
- Cooking chipped potatoes quickly will prevent the potato from absorbing more fat.
- Cooking in small batches will help to achieve this.
- Refrain from overheating the oil: temperatures above 198 °C will induce the quick breakdown of fat.
- Do not overfill the fryer with fat as this becomes a hazard when frying and spillages of hot fat may occur.

VIDEO CLIP   Deep frying fish in batter.

Fish pie

Ingredients	Makes approximately 4 portions	Makes approximately 10 portions
Fish fillet, skinned, pin boned (use sustainable varieties)	400 g	1 kg
Fish cream sauce (50% fish stock, 50% double cream reduced by half))	200 ml	500 ml
Fresh dill	¼ small bunch	½ small bunch
Baby spinach	100 g	250 g
Butter	100 g	250 g
Shallots (thinly sliced into rings)	4 shallots	10 shallots
Mashed potato	400 g	1 kg
Egg yolks	2	5
Good quality salt	To taste	To taste
White pepper	To taste	To taste
Fresh milk (infused with bay leaf, parsley stalks and white peppercorns)	300 ml	750 ml

energy	cal	fat	sat fat	carb	sugar	protein	fibre
3114 kJ	752 kcal	60.9 g	36.1 g	24.0 g	7.5 g	27.9 g	3.1 g

METHOD OF WORK

1   Preheat an oven to 160 °C.

2   Warm the milk **infusion** in a saucepan and add the prepared fish. Simmer for six minutes and remove the fish, leaving to drain on a tray. Break the fish into 2 cm pieces, season with some salt and pepper and place into a stainless steel bowl.

3   Melt half of the butter in a saucepan and add the sliced shallots. Sweat until tender and then add the washed and dried baby spinach and continue cooking lightly until the spinach has wilted.

4   Chop the fresh dill and add to the fish with the baby spinach and then carefully fold in the fish cream sauce, season to taste.

5   Transfer the fish mixture into individual pie dishes and place in a refrigerator to chill.

6   Warm the mashed potato either in a microwave oven or in a saucepan constantly stirring to prevent burning. Remove from the heat and beat in the egg yolks. Season well and transfer the potato into a piping bag with a 8 mm star tube.

7   **Pipe** the potato on top of the fish mixture in the pie dishes and then brush the top with melted butter.

8   Place in the oven and bake for approximately 12 minutes or until the centre has reached a minimum of 63 °C.

9   Finish the fish pie under a salamander to colour the surface a light golden finish if required just before serving.

CHEF'S TIP Instead of finishing the pie with piped potato an alternative is to cover the top with puff pastry, egg wash and bake this through the oven at 180 °C until the pastry has a golden brown colour.

Grilled sea bream with a modern minted pea velouté

Ingredients	Makes approximately 4 portions	Makes approximately 10 portions
Sea bream fillets	4 × 120 g fillets	10 × 120 g fillets
Frozen or fresh green peas	200 g	500 g
Chopped shallots	2	5
Fresh mint leaves	10 leaves	20 leaves
Butter	50 g	125 g
Plain flour	50 g	125 g
Fish stock	100 ml	250 ml
Sunflower oil	50 ml	125 ml
Good quality salt	To taste	To taste
White pepper	To taste	To taste
Watercress		

energy	cal	fat	sat fat	carb	sugar	protein	fibre
2034 kJ	488 kcal	31.7 g	11.0 g	15.6 g	2.3 g	36.0 g	3.9 g

METHOD OF WORK

1   Prepare the sea bream by filleting and trimming it ready to be grilled.

2   Place the fish stock into a saucepan and bring to the boil.

3   Then add the peas and chopped shallots.

4   Add the fresh mint 2 minutes before cooking is complete and then place into a liquidizer.

5   Blend until smooth. Season to taste.

6   Lightly season and flour the fish fillets. Brush with melted butter and a little sunflower oil.

7   Place under a preheated salamander and cook the sea bream on both sides until slightly golden in colour and tender to the touch.

8   Serve the sea bream with the velouté and watercress.

Note: The velouté used in this dish is not the classical version, it is a modern twist designed to add a different texture and flavour using modern terminology.

CHEF'S TIP   The velouté can be replaced with crushed peas cooked in a similar way but with a quarter of the stock. If the mixture is too wet slowly heat it in a saucepan so the extra liquid can evaporate.

SOURCING   The chef should always try to source fresh green peas during the season as these will always give a better result to the finished dish.

Roasted pollack with vegetable julienne and mouclade

Ingredients	Makes approximately 4 portions	Makes approximately 10 portions
Pollack 140 g	4	10
Julienne of carrot	50 g	125 g
Julienne of mouli	50 g	125 g
Julienne of leek	50 g	125 g
Julienne of courgette	50 g	125 g
Fish velouté	100 ml	250 ml
Double cream	25 ml	75 ml
Mussels	100 g	250 g
White wine	50 ml	125 ml
Curry powder	1 tblspn	3 tblspn
Butter	100 g	250 g
Good quality salt	To taste	To taste
White pepper	To taste	To taste

energy	cal	fat	sat fat	carb	sugar	protein	fibre
1999 kJ	482 kcal	30.5 g	17.3 g	5.9 g	2.7 g	41.0 g	2.6 g

METHOD OF WORK

1 Heat a thick bottomed pan until very hot then add the cleaned mussels and white wine.

2 Once the mussels are cooked and open, remove the flesh and discard the shells, reserve the liquor.

3 Melt the butter in a small saucepan and the vegetables cut into julienne. Cook the vegetables without colour, aiming to keep a little firmness to the texture of the vegetables. Drain and keep aside to remain warm.

4 Lightly flour the pollack then place into a hot pan, place in the oven at 170 °C until the pollack is cooked.

5 Drain the mussel cooking liquor into a saucepan and add the fish velouté, curry powder and the heated double cream.

6 Bring to the boil and then pass through a fine chinois, at the last minute add the mussels and warm through.

7 Serve the pollack on top of the vegetables and with the mouclade (mussels and curry sauce).

CHEF'S TIP Pollack is from the cod family and is sometimes known as greenfish or lythe. It is recognized by its slender green-brown body and can weigh up to 9 kg whole. Coley is another alternative fish which is also from the cod family and can be known as pollack or coalfish. Its flavour is not as pronounced as cod but as a cheaper and more conservation-friendly option it certainly has its value.

Steamed pollack, Marquis potato, bacon lardons, curly kale and dill cream sauce

Ingredients	Makes approximately 4 portions	Makes approximately 10 portions
Pollack	4 × 160 grams	10 × 160 grams
Marquis potato (see page 436)	4	10
Chopped dill	1 tblspn	2.5 tblspn
Curly kale	100 g	250 g
Bacon lardons	100 g	250 g
Cream sauce (see page 124)	400 ml	1000 ml
Good quality salt	To taste	To taste
White pepper	To taste	To taste

energy	cal	fat	sat fat	carb	sugar	protein	fibre
3228 kJ	775 kcal	39.8 g	22.1 g	44.6 g	12.1 g	58.6 g	7.3 g

METHOD OF WORK

1   Season pollack and brush with olive oil. Season well and leave to come up to room temperature.

2   Steam for 6 minutes, drain and season again.

3   Blanch the kale in boiling water, drain and toss in butter and season.

4   Heat the cream sauce and finish with the dill.

5   Fry the bacon lardons in a dry pan until crispy, then mix with the curly kale.

6   Heat the marquis potatoes and serve.

CHEF'S TIP   Steaming is a gentle way of cooking fish. Any fish that is suitable for poaching can be cooked by steaming too.

Some shellfish is also suitable for steaming, such as clams, mussels, lobster and crab.

WEB LINK   Use this web link to establish what fish should be avoided to maintain sustainability:
http://www.fishonline.org/advice/avoid

Oily fish

Hot smoked jasmine and green tea salmon with ribbons of vegetables

Ingredients	Makes approximately 4 portions	Makes approximately 10 portions
Salmon fillets with the skin left intact	4 × 140 g	10 × 140 g
Jasmine tea	10 g	30 g
Green tea leaves	10 g	30 g
Long grain rice	100 g	250 g
Granulated sugar	50 g	125 g
Carrot, courgette and asparagus ribbons	100 g	250 g
Butter	50 g	125 g
Good quality salt	To taste	To taste
White pepper	To taste	To taste
Herb oil (see page 151)		

energy	cal	fat	sat fat	carb	sugar	protein	fibre
2140 kJ	513 kcal	33.7 g	9.8 g	21.2 g	14.0 g	31.9 g	0.5 g

METHOD OF WORK

1   Prepare the salmon by cutting into suprêmes, trimming, washing and drying well.

2   Place the rice, both loose teas and sugar into the bottom of a roasting tray and mix well, put into a hot oven at 200 °C and bake until smoke begins to form.

3   Rest a cooling rack over the top of the tray and place the prepared salmon onto it and cover loosely with tin foil.

4   Lower the oven heat to 165 °C and cook for approximately 12 minutes.

5   Melt the butter then add the ribbons of vegetables, **sauté** until just cooked but still slightly crunchy.

6   To serve: place the vegetables in the centre of the plate and rest the salmon on top.

7   Spoon around some herb oil.

CHEF'S TIP   The smoking process gives a subtle flavour to the salmon.

Other teas can be used such as Earl Grey, Keemun and various black teas. Oils, essences and spices can be added to the mix to give a deeper flavour. Sometimes the salmon can be marinated for 12 hours before smoking to create a stronger flavour and colour.

Pan fried salmon with asparagus, broad beans, Biarritz potatoes and chive cream sauce

Ingredients	Makes approximately 4 portions	Makes approximately 10 portions
Salmon supreme	4 × 160 g	10 × 160 g
Broad beans, shelled	50 g	125 g
Unsalted butter	60 g	150 g
Cooked asparagus spears	12	30
Biarritz potatoes (see page 434)	4 portions	10 portions
Fish cream sauce (see page 279)	100 ml	250 ml
Finely chopped chives	1 tblspn	2.5 tblspn
Good quality salt	To taste	To taste
White pepper	To taste	To taste

energy	cal	fat	sat fat	carb	sugar	protein	fibre
3716 kJ	896 kcal	66.2 g	32.1 g	28.1 g	3.9 g	47.7 g	4.7 g

METHOD OF WORK

1 Blanch the broad beans in boiling salted water then drain.

2 Pan fry the salmon skin side down until coloured and crisp, turn over and cook until pink, remove and rest.

3 Reheat the broad beans and asparagus in butter and season.

4 Warm the fish cream sauce and finish with chopped chives.

5 Quenelle the Biarritz potatoes onto the plate, add the salmon, vegetable garnish and sauce.

Salmon fish cakes with pea shoots and tartar sauce

Ingredients	Makes approximately 4 portions	Makes approximately 10 portions
Salmon trimmings	300 g	750 g
Mashed potato	150 g	375 g
Finely diced shallots	50 g	125 g
Grated cheddar cheese	50 g	125 g
Lime juice and zest	1 lime	3 limes
Pasteurized egg	80 g	200 g
Plain flour	100 g	250 g
White breadcrumbs	100 g	250 g
Finely grated zest and juice of lemon	1 lemon	3 lemons
Tartar sauce	50 ml	125 ml
Pea shoots		
Vinaigrette (see page 149)	2 tblspn	5 tblspn
Good quality salt	To taste	To taste
White pepper	To taste	To taste

energy	cal	fat	sat fat	carb	sugar	protein	fibre
2787 kJ	668 kcal	40.9 g	9.7 g	46.9 g	2.8 g	30.4 g	2.7 g

METHOD OF WORK

1 Using the salmon trimmings, ensure that all the skin and bone have been removed.

2 Place the salmon trimmings into a steamer with the lime juice and zest for 8 minutes to completely cook through.

3 Take out of the steamer and leave to cool.

4 Flake the salmon flesh into a bowl and add the mashed potato, chopped shallots and grated cheese. Combine these ingredients well, season and leave to rest covered in plastic film in a refrigerator.

5 Using a round 6 cm pastry cutter as a mould, fill the salmon mixture inside to form a large cake.

6 Pass the salmon cake through seasoned flour, beaten egg and then the breadcrumbs. Utilizing a palette knife press the crumbs into the cake and redefine the circular shape if required. Leave in a refrigerator to rest for 15 minutes.

7 Wash the pea shoots well and carefully pat dry. Dress with the vinaigrette and set aside.

8 Deep fry each salmon cake at 180 °C until golden brown. Drain the cakes on kitchen paper and then serve with the pea shoots and tartar sauce.

CHEF'S TIP Alternatives for serving are:

- The cakes can be made smaller (using a 2 cm ring) and used for serving as canapés accompanied with sauce tartare.
- Using different fish such as haddock, cod and crab.
- Coat with seasoned flour and shallow fry instead of deep fry.
- Serve with a tomato sauce or beurre blanc.
- These fish cakes can be made in advance and cooked from frozen.

Sesame tuna with hoi sin and pak choy

Ingredients	Makes approximately 4 portions	Makes approximately 10 portions
Tuna fish, prepared into cylindrical lengths	4 × 120 g circular slices	10 × 120 g circular slices
Sesame seeds	4 tsp	10 tsp
Hoi sin sauce	4 tblspn	10 tblspn
Pak choy	200 g	500 g
Finely chopped garlic	1 clove	3 cloves
Grated fresh ginger	1 tsp	3 tsp
Dark soy sauce	2 tblspn	5 tblspn
Finely chopped red chilli	¼ chilli	½ chilli
Finely sliced spring onions	2 onions	5 onions
Groundnut oil	4 tblspn	10 tblspn
Good quality salt	To taste	To taste
Black pepper	To taste	To taste

energy	cal	fat	sat fat	carb	sugar	protein	fibre
1832 kJ	440 kcal	26.1 g	5.4 g	10.5 g	6.6 g	38.7 g	2.1 g

METHOD OF WORK

1 Brush the sides of the tuna steaks with a little of the hoi sin sauce and then roll the sides into the sesame seeds to give a coating around the edges.

2 Place in a refrigerator to chill for 30 minutes.

3 Using a wok or a steep sided pan for stir frying heat the groundnut oil spreading it evenly throughout the pan.

4 When the oil is very hot add the spring onions, red chilli, ginger and garlic. Quickly toss these ingredients to prevent burning.

5 Add the pak choy and move the ingredients from the centre of the pan to the sides continuously. Quickly add the soy sauce and a few drops of water and cover the pan for a minute to complete the cooking. This final steaming of the food, combined with the initial stir frying will finish the process perfectly.

6 Brush any remaining hoi sin sauce decoratively on service plates, as a presentation option.

7 Sear the tuna for approximately 2 minutes on each side to ensure that the tuna steak maintains a pink centre (the tuna can be cooked for longer if preferred).

8 Arrange the pak choy, neat slices of tuna, hoi sin and garnish as required.

CHEF'S TIP The tuna can be replaced with swordfish or salmon. Ensure the tuna is extremely fresh as this gives a better flavour and colour and reduces the risk of bacterial poisoning.

Freshwater fish

Poached trout with carrots and shallots

Ingredients	Makes approximately 4 portions	Makes approximately 10 portions
Sea trout fillets	8 × 50 g	20 × 50 g
White wine	50 ml	125 ml
Carrot slices	50 g	125 g
Finely sliced shallots	50 g	125 g
Chiffonade of flat leaf parsley	1 tblspn	2 tblspn
White wine vinegar	30 ml	75 ml
Water	30 ml	75 ml
White peppercorns	4	10
Good quality salt	To taste	To taste

energy	cal	fat	sat fat	carb	sugar	protein	fibre
630 kJ	151 kcal	4.8 g	1.3 g	1.6 g	1.5 g	21.9 g	0.6 g

METHOD OF WORK

1 Place the water, wine, vinegar and peppercorns into a saucepan and bring to the boil.

2 Add the carrots and shallots and simmer for 2 minutes.

3 Carefully add the trout and poach until pink.

4 Finish with the parsley and serve.

CHEF'S TIP   The dish can be made using small whole sea bass or fillets of different fish such as red mullet.

Miscellaneous fish

Bouillabaisse Marseille

Ingredients	Makes approximately 4 portions	Makes approximately 10 portions
Monkfish	100 g	250 g
Weaver fish	100 g	250 g
John Dory	100 g	250 g
Red mullet	100 g	250 g
Julienne of carrot	20 g	50 g
Julienne of leek	20 g	50 g
Julienne of celery	20 g	50 g
Soup		
Small mirepoix	100 g	250 g
Fish stock	600 ml	1500 ml
Tomato flesh	100 g	250 g
Saffron	1 small pinch	1 large pinch
Pernod	10 ml	25 ml
White wine	50 ml	125 ml
Bouquet garni	1 small	1 large
Star anise	1	2.5
Olive oil	50 ml	125 ml
Good quality salt	To taste	To taste
White pepper	To taste	To taste

energy	cal	fat	sat fat	carb	sugar	protein	fibre
1264 kJ	305 kcal	20.0 g	2.9 g	2.8 g	2.3 g	24.6 g	1.1 g

METHOD OF WORK

1 Clean fish, the cut into neat pieces as required then set to one side.

2 Sweat the mirepoix in olive oil, until soft without colour, deglaze the pan with pernod and white wine and reduce by half.

3 Add the tomatoes, stock, saffron, star anise and bouquet garni.

4 Simmer for 30 minutes, then pass through a fine chinois.

5 Cook the julienne of vegetables in the soup and remove, keep warm.

6 Then add the fish and gently poach until cooked.

7 Place the fish in bowls and pour over soup, garnish with julienne and fresh herbs.

Monkfish wrapped in pancetta with salsa verde

Ingredients	*Makes approximately 4 portions*	*Makes approximately 10 portions*
Monkfish tail fillets	4 × 120 g fillets	10 × 120 g fillets
Thinly sliced unsmoked pancetta	12 slices	30 slices
Tuned vegetables		
Good quality salt	To taste	To taste
White pepper	To taste	To taste
Chateau or cocotte potatoes (see page 444)		
Salsa verde (see page 147)	4 tblspn	10 tblspn
Olive oil	100 ml	250 ml

energy	cal	fat	sat fat	carb	sugar	protein	fibre
3019 kJ	728 kcal	53.3 g	10.5 g	28.4 g	3.1 g	34.5 g	3.8 g

METHOD OF WORK

1 Prepare the monkfish tail into fillets by removing the bone and trimming each fillet, ensuring the weight of 120 g per portion is maintained.

2 Lay the pancetta onto a sheet of plastic film, slightly overlapping, and then place the monkfish on top. Season the monkfish with salt and pepper.

3 Fold over the pancetta and the plastic film to encase the monkfish fillet inside.

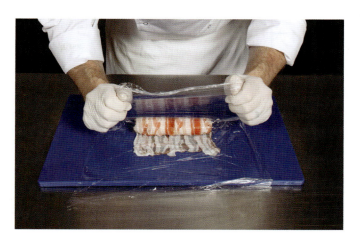

4 Continue to roll the fillet into a sausage shape, then use a roll of cling film to tighten: then place in a refrigerator to chill for at least 30 minutes.

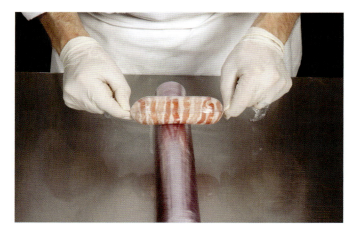

5 Place the wrapped monkfish into a steamer and cook for 7 minutes. Remove and rest for 2 minutes still inside the plastic film.

6 Heat some olive oil in pan. Remove the plastic film then fry the monkfish to crisp the pancetta on all sides and to add colour.

7 Serve the sliced monkfish with the salsa verde and turned vegetables.

CHEF'S TIP The salsa verde is best made 30 minutes before service to give the most vibrant colour and flavours possible. Always ensure that the fresh herbs are washed carefully in plenty of cold water. Dry them by gently shaking the water off and patting dry with a cloth.

Pan fried red mullet with ratatouille and sauce vierge

Ingredients	Makes approximately 4 portions	Makes approximately 10 portions
Red mullet fillets	4 × 80 g fillets	10 × 80 g fillets
Fine ratatouille (see page 430)	1 tblspn	2 tblspn
Olive oil	50 ml	125 ml
Basil leaves deep fried	4	10
Good quality salt	To taste	To taste
White pepper	To taste	To taste
Sauce vierge (see recipe online)	2 tblspn	5 tblspn

energy	cal	fat	sat fat	carb	sugar	protein	fibre
981 kJ	236 kcal	18.6 g	3.4 g	0.6 g	0.3 g	16.5 g	0.3 g

METHOD OF WORK

1   Scale, remove the fins and cut the fillets off the red mullet. Trim and remove any pin bones as necessary. Run the back of a knife over the skin to ensure that all scales are removed.

2   Heat some oil in a shallow pan and season the fillets of red mullet before cooking the fillets skin side down for 2 minutes. Turn over each fillet and finish the cooking process.

3   Spoon the warm ratatouille onto the serving plate and then lay the fillet on top.

4   Finish with sauce vierge and crispy basil leaves.

CHEF'S TIP To test if the red mullet is cooked correctly, insert a thin-bladed knife into the centre of the fish. Then touch the tip of the knife with your thumb or forefinger. If the knife tip is warm, the fish is ready.

Skate with capers and black butter

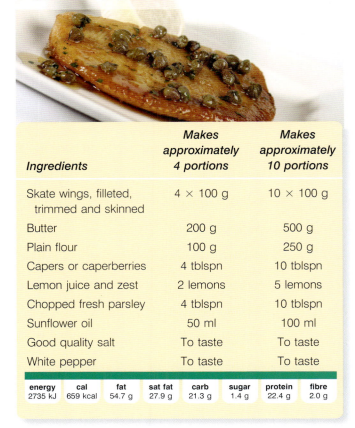

Ingredients	Makes approximately 4 portions	Makes approximately 10 portions
Skate wings, filleted, trimmed and skinned	4 × 100 g	10 × 100 g
Butter	200 g	500 g
Plain flour	100 g	250 g
Capers or caperberries	4 tblspn	10 tblspn
Lemon juice and zest	2 lemons	5 lemons
Chopped fresh parsley	4 tblspn	10 tblspn
Sunflower oil	50 ml	100 ml
Good quality salt	To taste	To taste
White pepper	To taste	To taste

energy	cal	fat	sat fat	carb	sugar	protein	fibre
2735 kJ	659 kcal	54.7 g	27.9 g	21.3 g	1.4 g	22.4 g	2.0 g

METHOD OF WORK

1   To prepare the skate: cut fillets from the wings and remove the skin, trimming as required. Cut into equal sized portions.

2   Lightly flour and season the skate and then in a frying pan heat the oil and a little butter.

3   Shallow fry the skate, presentation side down first until golden, before turning over to cook the other side.

4   Remove from the pan and allow to drain briefly on absorbent paper before keeping in a warm place for service.

5   Wipe the pan clean then add the remaining butter over the heat and allow to melt and begin to foam.

6   Continue to cook until a dark brown colour is achieved then add the capers, lemon zest and juice and then the chopped parsley.

7   Place a fillet of the skate onto a serving plate before spooning the butter and the capers on top. Serve with some additional fresh lemon.

CHEF'S TIP An alternative way of cooking skate is to poach the prepared wings in a court bouillon and drain well before making the caper and black butter sauce to spoon over the finished dish.

Shellfish

Shellfish is a collective term for crustacean, mollusc and other types of seafood such as sea urchin. Each category has its own variations and consequently they will have differing methods of preparation. Shellfish are usually cooked by boiling, poaching and steaming. However, some crustaceans can also be grilled and many molluscs are served raw. Shellfish are suitable for lunch and dinner service and can be utilized as a main course in its own right, as an intermediate course or as a garnishing role for starters, hors d'oeuvre, salads, fish dishes and meat and poultry dishes.

- Molluscs — Can have a single shell (univalve)
  Can have a pair of shells (bivalve)
  Can have no shell (cephalopods)

- Crustaceans — Have an external skeleton (shell) and jointed limbs.

CLASSIFICATION OF SHELLFISH

GASTROPODS	BIVALVE	CRUSTACEAN	CEPHALOPODS
Limpets	Cockles	Lobsters	Octopus
Whelks	Mussels	Crabs	Cuttlefish
Winkles	Razor	Crayfish	Squid
Abalone	shell		
	clams		
Conch	Scallops	Prawns	
	Oysters	Shrimps	
	Clams	Langoustine	
		Crawfish	

Quality points

- All shellfish are best if purchased live. This will help to ensure that they are of maximum freshness and that there can be no possibility of contamination from pollutants that the shellfish may have absorbed. It is accepted that shellfish items such as prawns are usually purchased in a frozen or a cook-chilled format.

- On delivery, lobsters, crabs, crayfish and crawfish should be evidently alive and they should feel heavy in relation to their size. It is important to touch and handle these crustaceans to check this. Also check for signs of damage such as claws that are missing and that they are generally of a good size.

- Bivalve molluscs should have shells that are tightly closed, mostly free of barnacles and mud. They should feel heavy in relation to their size and any shells that remain open after being moved or slightly tapped should be immediately discarded. Any signs of a foul smell, rather than a fresh, sweet, seawater smell, should also be rejected. If any of the shells have broken it is also important to discard these too.

- All shellfish will deteriorate quickly, raw and cooked, and so should be purchased for immediate consumption.

KEY

▨	Shellfish at their best
▨	Available
	Not available

SEASONALITY OF SHELLFISH

	JAN	FEB	MAR	APR	MAY	JUN	JUL	AUG	SEP	OCT	NOV	DEC
Crab (brown cock)	Available	Available	Available	Available	Available	Available	Available	Best	Best	Best	Best	
Crab (spider)	Best	Best	Available	Available	Available	Available	Available	Best	Best	Best	Best	Best
Crab (brown hen)	Best	Best	Available	Available	Available	Available	Available	Best	Best	Best	Best	Best
Clams	Best	Best	Available	Available	Available	Available	Available	Best	Best	Best	Best	
Cockles	Best	Best	Best	Best	Best	Best	Available	Best	Best	Best	Best	Best
Crayfish				Available	Available	Available	Available	Best	Best			
Lobster	Available	Available	Available	Available	Best	Best	Best	Best	Best	Best	Best	Available
Langoustines			Available	Available	Available	Available	Available	Available	Available	Available		
Mussels	Best	Best	Available	Available					Best	Best	Best	Best
Oysters (rock)	Best	Best	Best	Best	Best	Best	Best	Best	Best	Best	Best	Best
Oysters (native)	Best	Best	Best	Best					Best	Best	Best	Best
Prawns						Available	Available	Available	Best	Best	Best	Best
Scallops	Best	Available	Available	Available	Available	Available	Available	Available	Best	Best	Best	Best

3. Ensure that all shellfish remain moist.

4. Molluscs should be kept in a container embedded in ice. The round side of the shell should face downwards to help collect and retain the natural juices.

5. Check regularly to make sure that they are still alive. Reject any dead or dying specimens.

Follow these guidelines when storing cooked shellfish:

1. The shells of cooked shellfish should be intact with no cracks.

2. The shells should not release copious amounts of liquid when shaken.

3. The cooked product should exhibit no signs of discolouration and there should be no odours indicative of spoilage.

4. Freshly cooked prawns and shrimps should be firm to the touch and should be chilled immediately.

Transportation and storage

The best transportation and storage for live crustaceans is to use a seawater or freshwater tank. For shellfish to be transported in these conditions the following points should be observed:

- Controlled water temperature within the tanks.

- Good aeration of the water.

- Suitable water quality depending on the type of crustacean or mollusc.

- Species should be separated into independent tanks.

However, this method is costly and only catering establishments that specialize in serving shellfish will have this facility. Fish and shellfish suppliers will also have this facility on their own premises, but generally when making deliveries crustaceans such as lobster, crabs and crayfish will be packed in cases (usually polystyrene), covered with wet cloths and kept in a refrigerated environment.

Follow these guidelines when storing fresh shellfish:

1. Keep the shellfish at a temperature of between 2 °C and 8 °C.

2. Keep shellfish in its packaging until preparation, this is to avoid moisture loss.

Shellfish allergy

Since November 2005, prepacked food sold in Europe must show clearly on the label if it contains crustaceans including lobster, crab, prawns and langoustines. However, other groups of shellfish, such as bivalve molluscs (including mussels, scallops and oysters), cephalopods (squid and octopus) or gastropods (whelks and snails) do not need to be labelled individually.

Allergy to shellfish is quite common and people who are sensitive can react to a number of different types of shellfish, such as shrimps, prawns, lobsters, crabs, crayfish, oysters, scallops, mussels and clams.

People who are allergic to one type of shellfish often react to others. Shellfish allergy can often cause severe reactions, and some people can react to the vapours from shellfish that is being cooked.

When these reactions occur, the cause could be the shellfish themselves, or from associated bacteria, viruses or naturally occurring toxins. It is therefore crucial that people who believe they have a food allergy get confirmatory diagnostic tests done so the right food is avoided in the future. The only treatment for seafood allergies is avoidance of the known food which induces the symptoms.

Gastropod shellfish

Whelks

Whelks resemble pointed snails when fresh, and are usually sold already cooked and without their shell. After scrubbing only keep the good whelks and discard any damaged or dead ones. They can also be purged by placing into a large bowl with clean water and some polenta and then left to soak overnight in a refrigerator. (The shellfish will eat the polenta and expel any sand and grit.) These can be served as part of a seafood platter with other shellfish or cooked in the shell by simmering in salted water or a court bouillon. They can be used to garnish soups or fish stews.

Winkles

Winkles are known as 'black sea snails' and are served as appetisers. They are usually sold cooked without their shells. They should be steamed in white wine for a couple of minutes and then served simply seasoned with fresh parsley. If purchased in shells the meat is easily removed with a pin from the shells once cooked and should taste salty, slightly chewy and juicy.

Bivalve shellfish

If these crustaceans are purchased live, ensure the shells are intact and not broken. Remove any mud and grit by washing thoroughly in fresh water several times. Discard any dead bivalves before cooking by tapping the open shells with your finger until they close: if they stay open they should be discarded at once. There is a connective hair-like substance which hangs out of many shells, especially mussels, which is called the **beard**. This also should be removed prior to cooking, along with any barnacles, by scraping with the back of a knife and then rinsing in cold water. Place the cleaned mussels in a bowl of cold water then remove any that float to the top. After cooking, any shells that remain closed should also be discarded.

Clams

Clams are well known for the classical dish clam chowder, associated mainly with the east coast of America. All clams should be well scrubbed and they may need to be purged too. They can be opened and eaten raw (if very fresh) or cooked by boiling or steaming.

Step-by-step: Preparation of scallops

1. Hold the scallop shell firmly in hand with the flat shell uppermost.

2. Place a thick knife between the shells by the hinge and push up to break the connection.

3. Slide the knife along the inside of the flat shell, remove the flat shell and discard.

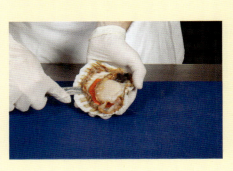

4. Work the knife under the skirt (frilly gills) and then under the white and coral to separate from the shell. Take care not to pierce the scallop meat.
Discard the skirt or save for making a stock.
Separate the white from the coral and gently wash both in clean water, store in a refrigerator until required.

Cockles

Cockles are not readily available in fishmongers and usually require a little notice when ordering from the suppliers. They are a salty and juicy shellfish which can often be found preserved in vinegar or brine. They have a pink and yellow-beige-coloured shell and are quite uniform in shape and size. Cockles should be purged in the same way as whelks.

> **WEB LINK** Using the following link identify the shellfish that can be farmed and the shellfish that are caught wild:
> **http://www.fishonline.org**

Scallops

Scallops are highly regarded and expensive. The shells are rounded and fan-shaped; varying in size from the smaller queen scallop (7 cm across) to the larger great scallop (up to 18 cm across). The edible part is the round whitish muscle and the orange roe (called the coral). The frilly gills and mantle can be used for soup and stocks. Scallops can be opened by separating the shells with a knife. This can be done relatively easily once the basic techniques have been mastered. Because the scallop lives on the sea bed they will have grit and dirt inside the shells and will need to be purged or cleaned thoroughly upon opening.

If the scallops are exceptionally fresh, well prepared and in excellent condition they can be used raw for sashimi or simply marinated with an acidic dressing to gently denaturize the flesh.

Scallops can be purchased loose (in their shells) or already shelled and cleaned. The most expensive are diver-caught scallops; these are collected by divers by hand from the sea bed. The other way is by dredging the sea floor with a net, although this can cause damage to the shells.

> **WEB LINK** Use the following link to discover more information regarding diver scallops:
> **http://www.thefishsociety.co.uk**

Razor shell clams

Razor clams are shaped like cut-throat razors. They can be caught by tipping salt onto the sandy shores of a beach: the shells pop out of the ground and are then carefully harvested. Treat in the same way as clams.

> **TASK** Research how razor clams are harvested from the sand and present your findings in a leaflet.

Oysters

There are a variety of oyster species around the globe and therefore they come in a number of shapes and sizes. The best British oysters are known as 'natives' or 'flat'. Other British oysters include rock oysters. Natives are available from September to April, though they are at their best from late October to late February when the sea temperature is colder. Pacific oysters are available all year. Scrub the shells well before opening. To open the shells use an oyster knife because using a normal kitchen knife could be hazardous and it may break easily.

Any oysters that have an unusual smell should be discarded. Native oysters are best eaten raw as soon as possible after capture. Raw oysters are best served with freshly squeezed lemon or shallot vinaigrette. Cooked rock oysters can be served in chowders and stews.

Step-by-step: Preparation of oysters

1. Hold the oyster in a thick cloth to protect the hand from the sharp edges of the oyster shell.

2. Keeping the oyster flat, use an oyster knife and place the blade between the shells by the hinge and using *gentle* force carefully twist the knife to open the shell.

3. Lift the top shell off and sever the muscle. Discard the top shell.
4. Slide the knife carefully under the oyster to free it. Take care not to cut into the oyster or spill any of the liquid inside the shell. Check for any loose shell and discard.

Mussels

These molluscs are often seen attached to rocks and wooden structures around the coastline worldwide and have a distinctive oval blue and black-coloured shell. The vibrant orange-coloured flesh inside is sweet and salty to taste. Mussels should only be collected from unpolluted waters between September and March: they should be left alone during the summer months. Purchasing smaller or medium-sized mussels will help to ensure that they taste sweet and full of flavour. Approximately 450 g should be enough per portion. Mussel beds are situated by estuaries which potentially filters clean water all year round. To prepare mussels it is important that they are scrubbed under cold running water to remove all grit and scrape off any barnacles using a small knife. Any beards should also be removed from the shells.

Cephalopods

Squid

Squid is commonly referred to as 'calamari' and varies in size from small – 7 cm – to larger ones of about 25 cm. Squid is available all year round either fresh or frozen. It freezes very well and preparing squid is relatively straightforward. The ink, found in a small sac from the innards, is used to colour pasta and seafood sauces. There is a transparent flexible cartilage within the squid called the quill, which must be removed. Cooking must be either very quick or slowly braised; otherwise the flesh will become tough.

PREPARATION OF SQUID

- Pull the head and tentacles away from the body (mantle). The eye and ink sac will come away with the tentacles.

- Cut the edible tentacles from the head, cutting just above the eye. Discard the head.

- Open the tentacles and pull out the beak in the centre (its mouth). Discard it and rinse the tentacles under cold running water.

- Remove the transparent quill from the body by pulling it out.

- Clean any excess membranes from inside the body. Rinse the insides under cold running water.

Crustaceans

Crab

There are restrictions to the size of crab that can be sold in the United Kingdom although there are no restrictions on the number, design or size of the traps used to catch them. Live crabs should be handled as little as possible after capture, and the claws may be shed quickly if not killed before cooking. They should be packed, in ventilated boxes, quite close together and preferably with wet seaweed or cloth in the bottom of the box. Live storage is difficult and crabs do not travel well. Where live storage is necessary, they should be tightly packed in baskets in aerated sea water.

Transit time should be as short as possible and preferably overnight, when air temperature is lower.

There are many varieties of crab and many regions throughout the world where crabs are abundant. Europe is well known for the brown crab and the spider crab: in the eastern USA the blue crab is caught. The Dungeness crab is caught on the Pacific coast off the USA.

The soft brown flesh from under the upper shell is strong and full-flavoured, this contrasts with the sweet, delicate white flesh found in the claws and body.

Male crabs often have larger claws and therefore more white flesh. However, females may have 'coral' – a red-coloured roe that is found on the underside of the body.

Brown crab from Europe is available all year, and reaches 20–25 cm across with heavy front claws with almost-black pincers. Its shell is a rusty-red or brown colour.

The Atlantic blue crab grows to 20 cm but is usually sold smaller. It has a blue-brown shell. When newly moulted these crabs are caught with soft shells and are prepared and shallow or deep fried for eating whole. This crab has plenty of white meat. The meat in the shell is also fine and notably different for its pale grey colour.

The spider crab is popular in France and Spain. It is a sweet-flavoured crab that resembles a large spider and has no large claws. One crab should be sufficient per person.

Purchase crabs that feel heavy for their size and smell fresh whether alive or cooked. If there is a hint of ammonia do not buy. Crabs are best bought alive and cooked fresh. There is approximately 115 g of meat per portion; this is about 450 g for a whole crab with the shell intact.

To prepare a cooked crab:

- Lay the crab on its back on a chopping board and remove the legs and claws by firmly twisting and pulling from the body. Lift the triangular flap (called the apron) on the underside of the crab, twist it off and discard.

- Hold the belly of the crab by the eyes and pull downwards, the underside will be prised off in one piece. Remove any white meat from this area using a teaspoon.

- Inside you will see the gills (dead man's fingers) and a sac behind the eyes, discard all of these. Spoon out the meat from the shell and reserve it to serve with the white meat (keep the brown and white meat separate).

- Crack each leg with poultry shears and using a lobster pick, remove the white meat.

- The inside of the claws can be accessed by cracking the shell with the back of a knife or by using lobster crackers and then carefully peeling the shell away to reveal the white meat. Remove any membrane from the meat.

- Clean the main shell and dry before placing all the reserved meat back into the shell.

Langoustine (Dublin Bay prawns)

Langoustine are relatives of lobsters and crabs and live in deep water off the United Kingdom coast. Also known as Norway lobster and scampi, these orange-pink shellfish from the north-east Atlantic and Mediterranean resemble small, slim lobsters. They can be expensive with little meat, but are delicious if freshly caught and cooked. The best specimens can be bought from late spring to late autumn and are cooked in the same way as lobster. Because of their smaller size, they need less cooking. Usually only the tail is sold. In their shells 200 g should be enough per portion; however, removed from their shells, half this amount will be adequate. They are available frozen all year round.

To prepare a cooked langoustine:

- Pull the heads from the bodies (save for stock).

- Snip underneath the belly of the tail with a pair of scissors, taking great care not to pierce the flesh.

- Remove the legs and peel the shells carefully.

- Make an incision along the back of the tail and remove the dark intestinal vein running along the back.

- Rinse under clean water and pat dry.

Prawns

One method used for the transportation of prawns is in plastic tubes. It seems that although the tubes are open-ended, the prawn stays inside of its own accord, as though it were hiding on the sea bed. The tubes are put into the hold of a long-range fish trawler and refrigerated sea water is pumped around the hold.

There are many prawn species and they vary in size from 5–18 cm long. King prawns grow even larger at up to 23 cm. Shrimps are very small and require boiling before serving whole as an appetiser. Prawns come in many colours, from the familiar common pink prawns to the brown-blue tiger prawns.

Prawns are available all year round, though usually frozen in the UK. Fresh raw prawns are the tastiest. They should be firm and springy with bright shells. If they are limp, soft or have an ammonia smell then discard them. Ensure frozen prawns are properly defrosted before using.

Prawns can be prepared the same as langoustines but do not require the scissor cut to peel as the shells are softer.

Lobster

A male lobster is called a cock and a female a hen or chicken. There are two kinds of lobsters, the 'true' lobster (also called American lobster) and the spiny lobster. The true lobster has claws on the first four legs, lacking in the spiny lobster. The spiny lobster has a pair of horns above the eyes, lacking in the true lobster. Spiny lobsters also have two large cream-coloured spots on the top of the second segment of the tail.

Small lobsters, less than 4 cm carapace (carapace length is measured from the rear of the eye socket to the rear of the main body shell), hide in and about sea weeds and rocky habitat that provide enough food and shelter from predators. Adolescent lobsters, 4 cm to 9 cm carapace, are found in coastal habitats and offshore areas. Adult lobsters inhabit deeper waters, but return seasonally to shallow warmer waters. Spiny lobsters inhabit tropical and subtropical waters of the Atlantic Ocean, Caribbean Sea and Gulf of Mexico.

Lobster can have many different colours, including blue-green, blue, red, yellow, red-orange and white. Some lobsters come in two colours, having half of their shell one colour and the other half another.

TEST YOURSELF

1   Name two types of oyster.

2   Name the attachment on the outside of a mussel which must be removed.

3   What is the orange mass on a scallop called?

4   Name two members of the cephalopod family.

5   Which of the shellfish below is not part of the prawn family:

Langoustine, crayfish, razor clam?

6   Which of the shellfish below is not a bivalve:

Whelks, cockles, clams?

7   Name three varieties of crab.

8   What can squid ink be used for?

9   When should native oysters not be eaten?

10   List four gastropods.

Shellfish

Moules mariniére

Ingredients	Makes approximately 4 portions	Makes approximately 10 portions
Mussels, scrubbed, washed and de-bearded	2 kg	5 kg
Butter	50 g	125 g
Sunflower oil	2 tblspn	5 tblspn
Garlic cloves finely chopped	1	3
Shallots finely chopped	2	5
Flat leaf parsley	2 tblspn	5 tblspn
White wine	200 ml	500 ml
Good quality salt	To taste	To taste
White pepper	To taste	To taste

energy	cal	fat	sat fat	carb	sugar	protein	fibre
3046 kJ	725 kcal	31.4 g	10.0 g	20.1 g	2.4 g	84.2 g	0.7 g

METHOD OF WORK

1 To clean the mussels, scrub them under cold, running water, pulling off the gritty beards as you go. Discard any open mussels that do not shut firmly when tapped.

2 Heat the butter and oil in a very large, deep saucepan over a medium heat.

3 Add the garlic and shallots and sweat for about 5 minutes until translucent but not coloured.

4 Stir in the parsley and white wine.

5 Cover the pan, increase the heat to high and bring to the boil.

6 Once the wine is boiling, tip in the mussels, cover the pan and cook for 2–3 minutes. Give the pan a good shake or stir the mussels to make sure they are cooking evenly.

7 Cook the mussels for another minute or two, or until the mussels are open and tender.

8 Discard any mussels that haven't opened during cooking.

9 Use a large slotted spoon to transfer the steamed mussels to deep plates or bowls then ladle over the cooking liquid and serve straight away.

CHEF'S TIP This dish is best served with pieces of baguette or crusty bread to absorb the juices.

SOURCING Mussels can be purchased wild or farmed: rope grown mussels for example are farmed and contain very little or no waste products as they do not touch the sea bed.

WEB LINK Mussels and other shellfish should only be eaten seasonally. Use the following link to discover further details:
http://eattheseasons.co.uk

VIDEO CLIP Preparing mussels.

VIDEO CLIP Moules mariniére.

Deep fried clams *in a peppered crumb with sauce vert*

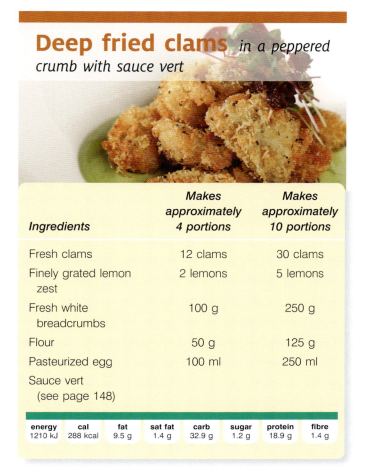

Ingredients	Makes approximately 4 portions	Makes approximately 10 portions
Fresh clams	12 clams	30 clams
Finely grated lemon zest	2 lemons	5 lemons
Fresh white breadcrumbs	100 g	250 g
Flour	50 g	125 g
Pasteurized egg	100 ml	250 ml
Sauce vert (see page 148)		

energy	cal	fat	sat fat	carb	sugar	protein	fibre
1210 kJ	288 kcal	9.5 g	1.4 g	32.9 g	1.2 g	18.9 g	1.4 g

METHOD OF WORK

1 The fresh clams should be washed and scrubbed well and they may require purging if they are very gritty.

2 Open each clam very carefully using a knife to work in between the top and bottom shells. Twist the knife upwards to open the clam.

3 Carefully slide the knife under the clam to separate it from the shell. Remove any dark membrane from the clam.

4 Mix the white breadcrumbs and finely grated lemon zest together.

5 Pass the raw clams through seasoned flour, egg and breadcrumbs with lemon zest mixed in. Repeat this step again to double coat the clam for protection against the hot fat when cooking.

6 Deep fry the clams at 185 °C until golden.

Thai green curry tiger prawns

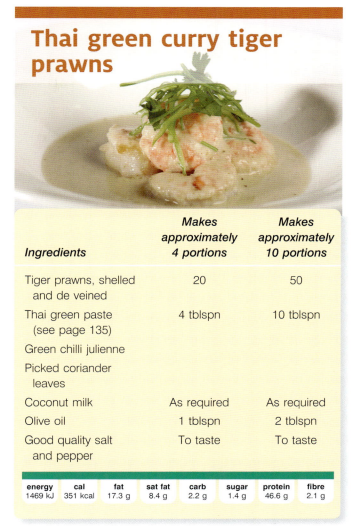

Ingredients	Makes approximately 4 portions	Makes approximately 10 portions
Tiger prawns, shelled and de veined	20	50
Thai green paste (see page 135)	4 tblspn	10 tblspn
Green chilli julienne		
Picked coriander leaves		
Coconut milk	As required	As required
Olive oil	1 tblspn	2 tblspn
Good quality salt and pepper	To taste	To taste

energy	cal	fat	sat fat	carb	sugar	protein	fibre
1469 kJ	351 kcal	17.3 g	8.4 g	2.2 g	1.4 g	46.6 g	2.1 g

METHOD OF WORK

1 In a sauté pan heat the oil then add the tiger prawns and fry for 30 seconds.

2 Add the paste and mix well, add enough coconut milk to produce a sauce consistency.

3 Adjust the seasoning and serve with the chilli and coriander.

CHEF'S TIP Keep leftover prawn, shrimp, crab and lobster shells for making bisques and shellfish stocks. They should be washed and used as quickly as possible.

Scallops served in the shell with vegetable brunoise and lemon oil

Ingredients	Makes approximately 4 portions	Makes approximately 10 portions
Diver scallops in the shell	4	10
Brunoise of vegetables (carrot, shallot, aubergine, courgette, garlic)	200 g	500 g
Lemon oil	1 tblspn	2 tblspn
Olive oil	1 tblspn	2 tblspn
Good quality salt and pepper	To taste	To taste

energy	cal	fat	sat fat	carb	sugar	protein	fibre
704 kJ	169 kcal	12.7 g	1.8 g	3.6 g	1.7 g	10.2 g	1.2 g

METHOD OF WORK

1 Heat the olive oil in a sauté pan then add the brunoise of vegetables and cook quickly for 1 minute.

2 Place the scallop and shell on a baking sheet then drizzle a little lemon oil over the flesh, season and top with the brunoise of vegetables (completely covering the scallop).

3 Place in an oven at 180 °C for 3–5 minutes until the scallop is just cooked but still a little pink in the centre.

4 Remove from the oven and scrape the brunoise off the scallop as shown.

5 Serve with a little more lemon oil and garnish.

VIDEO CLIP Steaming fish.

Langoustines en papilotte

Ingredients	Makes approximately 4 portions	Makes approximately 10 portions
Langoustines	20 in number	50 in number
Carrots cut into julienne	100 g	275 g
Leek cut into julienne	100 g	275 g
Onion cut into julienne	100 g	275 g
Soy sauce	40 ml	90 ml
Sweet chilli sauce	40 ml	90 ml
Coconut milk	50 ml	100 ml
White wine	50 ml	100 ml
Good quality salt	To taste	To taste
Black pepper	To taste	To taste

energy	cal	fat	sat fat	carb	sugar	protein	fibre
764 kJ	182 kcal	3.6 g	2.1 g	6.1 g	5.4 g	29.4 g	2.1 g

METHOD OF WORK

1 Preheat an oven to 190 °C.

2 Slice the carrots, onions and leeks into a julienne and sweat them down in a pan with a little vegetable oil and season well. Leave to one side.

3 Take a sheet of baking parchment and cut into 10 × 10 cm squares, for one portion. Repeat this process depending on the number of portions needed.

4 Place the cooked vegetables, followed by the langoustines onto the parchment.

5 Add a splash of soy sauce, sweet chilli sauce, white wine and coconut milk. Season well and then fold over the baking parchment and fold over the open edges to make a secure seal.

6 Place the papilotte into the pre-heated oven for 6 minutes.

7 Serve by placing the parcels onto serving plates and allow each guest to open their own parcel.

CHEF'S TIP   The recipe explains how to cook shellfish in a parcel. The traditional **en papilotte** method makes use of baking parchment; however, tin foil and banana leaves work well too.

Oysters cooked three ways: deep fried beignet, grilled with a herb crumb and with a champagne jelly

Ingredients	Makes approximately 4 portions	Makes approximately 10 portions
Oysters	12	30
Tempura batter (see page 303)		
Champagne	50 ml	125 ml
Agar agar	1% = 0.5 g	1% = 1.25 g
Salmon caviar	2 tsp	5 tsp
Sauce vert	2 tblspn	5 tblspn
Fresh white breadcrumbs	1 slice	2½ slices
Butter	50 g	125 g
Good quality salt	To taste	To taste
Black pepper	To taste	To taste

energy	cal	fat	sat fat	carb	sugar	protein	fibre
3336 kJ	797 kcal	30.2 g	11.9 g	81.6 g	0.4 g	44.0 g	0.3 g

METHOD OF WORK

1 Shuck or remove the shell from the oysters and brush any residual shell away using a soft pastry brush and cold water.

2 Dissolve the agar agar in the champagne for 2 minutes, heat in a pan until it boils, remove and allow to cool.

3 Pour over one of the oysters per portion; once set garnish with salmon eggs.

4 In a sauté pan melt the butter and add the breadcrumbs, cook until just coloured – light brown, then spoon over one oyster per person and place in the oven at 180 °C for 3 minutes.

5 In the last oyster shell remove the meat and coat in tempura batter then deep fry at 180 °C until coloured: approximately 2 minutes.

6 Meanwhile spoon some sauce vert into the shell and place the oyster on top.

7 Arrange all three oysters on a plate sitting on salt.

Crab and prawn cakes with mango salsa

Ingredients	Makes approximately 4 portions	Makes approximately 10 portions
Cooked prawns	280 g	700 g
White crab meat	280 g	700 g
Mayonnaise	2 tblspn	5 tblspn
White breadcrumbs	200 g	450 g
Fresh chopped dill	3 tblspn	6 tblspn
Grain mustard	1 tblspn	2 tblspn
Finely chopped shallots	50 g	100 g
Flour	60 g	160 g
Pasteurized egg	75 g	200 g
Finely chopped red chilli peppers	½ chilli	1 chilli
Lime juice and zest	1 lime	3 limes
Diced mango	½ mango	1½ mangos
Vinaigrette (see page 149)	20 ml	45 ml
Good quality salt and pepper	To taste	To taste

energy	cal	fat	sat fat	carb	sugar	protein	fibre
2373 kJ	565 kcal	21.3 g	3.0 g	56.3 g	6.3 g	40.3 g	3.9 g

METHOD OF WORK

1 Mix together the cooked prawns, white crab meat, half of the breadcrumbs, chopped shallots, mayonnaise, grain mustard and freshly chopped dill together in a bowl. Season well and cover with plastic film before placing into a refrigerator to chill for 30 minutes.

2 Divide the mix equally with one per portion.

3 Flatten each ball and use a palette knife to form discs of approximately 5 cm in diameter and 1.5 cm thick.

4 Pass through seasoned flour and then into the pasteurized egg before coating in breadcrumbs and placing onto a tray. Cover with plastic film and chill in a refrigerator.

5 Combine the chilli, lime, mango and fresh coriander with the vinaigrette.

6 Deep fry the cakes until golden then serve with the mango salsa and herb oil (see page 151).

CHEF'S TIP An alternative to using white breadcrumbs is polenta, cornmeal or wholemeal breadcrumbs. Care must be taken when frying that the core temperature is sufficiently high. This is the temperature in the centre of the item being cooked. To test the core temperature, a temperature probe is inserted into the centre. The electronic reading then displays the temperature in the centre of the food, telling you if the item has reached a safe temperature to kill bacteria, making the food safe to eat.

Tempura of crayfish with basil mayonnaise

Ingredients	Makes approximately 4 portions	Makes approximately 10 portions
Prepared and cooked crayfish tails	28	40
Tempura flour (see chef's tip)	200 g	350 g
Iced water	75 g	110 g
Sauce vert	100 g	250 g
Basil oil	2 tblspn	4 tblspn
Sea salt	Pinch	Pinch
Deep fried basil leaves	4	10
Red Belgian endive	50 g	125 g
White pepper	To taste	To taste

energy	cal	fat	sat fat	carb	sugar	protein	fibre
1707 kJ	409 kcal	22.4 g	2.8 g	46.9 g	0.4 g	5.5 g	0.8 g

METHOD OF WORK

1 Preheat the deep fryer to 190 °C.

2 Prepare the cooked crayfish tails breaking off the head and gently squeeze the tail to break the shell. Remove the tail by pulling off the sides of the shell. De-vein with a sharp knife as for preparing prawns.

3 Mix together the sauce vert with the basil oil. Season to taste and reserve to one side for service.

4 Mix the tempura flour ingredients together and sieve once. Combine the appropriate amounts with the ice water to form a batter (it should be slightly thinner than a usual batter).

5 Season and lightly flour the crayfish and pass through the tempura batter.

6 Deep fry for at least 2 minutes until a light golden colour has been achieved and that there is a crisp appearance.

7 Arrange the Belgian endive, basil mayonnaise and crayfish on the plate and serve.

CHEF'S TIP To prepare a tempura flour combine the following ingredients together, sieve and store in an airtight container:

- 75 g cornflour
- 375 g soft flour
- 2 tsp baking powder
- 1 tsp sea salt

Lobster thermidor

Ingredients	Makes approximately 4 portions	Makes approximately 10 portions
Lobster 750 g – steamed or poached for 7 minutes	2	5
Butter	25 g	60 g
Finely chopped shallot	1	3
Fish stock	200 ml	500 ml
White wine	50 ml	125 ml
Cream double	100 ml	250 ml
English mustard	1 tblspn	3 tblspn
Finely chopped parsley	1 tblspn	3 tblspn
Grated parmesan	200 g	500 g
Lemon juice	½ lemon	1½ lemons
Good quality salt and white pepper	To taste	To taste

energy	cal	fat	sat fat	carb	sugar	protein	fibre
3310 kJ	791 kcal	40.2 g	22.1 g	2.2 g	2.1 g	103.1 g	0.5 g

4 For the sauce, put the butter in a pan, add the shallots and cook until softened.

5 Add the stock, wine and double cream and bring to the boil.

6 Reduce by half. Add the mustard, parsley and lemon juice and season to taste then combine and place the mixture back into the shell.

7 Sprinkle the lobster with the grated cheese.

8 Place under the salamander for 3 to 4 minutes, until golden brown.

9 Serve with lemon muslin.

CHEF'S TIP   Crustaceans will lose on average between 10 and 15 per cent of their original weight after being boiled. The shells and unused parts (such as the head) can represent as much as 70 per cent of the total weight being discarded. Cooked prawns and shrimps will yield up to 40 per cent edible flesh.

METHOD OF WORK

1 Cut the lobster in half and remove the meat from the claws and tail. Leave to one side.

2 Remove any head matter and set aside.

3 Cut the meat into small pieces and reserve.

Razor clams and chorizo, butter bean and tomato stew

Ingredients	Makes approximately 4 portions	Makes approximately 10 portions
Razor clams	8	20
Vine ripened plum tomatoes	400 g	1 kg
Finely chopped shallots	2	5
Finely chopped garlic	2 cloves	5 cloves
Tinned butter beans	100 g	250 g
Olive oil	50 ml	125 ml
White wine	50 ml	125 ml
Thyme	Sprigs	Sprigs
Good quality salt and white pepper	To taste	To taste

energy	cal	fat	sat fat	carb	sugar	protein	fibre
1502 kJ	364 kcal	33.8 g	16.0 g	6.3 g	4.7 g	6.6 g	2.3 g

METHOD OF WORK

1 For the stew: blanch, peel and deseed the vine ripened tomatoes then cut into concassée.

2 Gently heat the oil, add the garlic, thyme and shallots, cook without colour.

3 Add the concassée and cook very gently for 30 minutes.

4 Season to taste and reserve.

5 Heat a sauté pan then add the butter and then the cleaned razor clams, pour over the wine, cover and cook for 2 minutes.

6 Remove from the heat, open the shells and cut the meat into neat pieces.

7 Add the beans to the stew and heat through.

8 Add the clams and serve: garnish as required.

Guest Chef

Kentish sea bream with courgette ribbons and langoustine and mussel broth

Chef: *Sean Stratton*
Centre: *Mid Kent College, Medway*

The bream is from Whitstable, as is the sea food, and the courgette is from the local farmers' market at Rochester.

Ingredients	Makes 1 portion
Black sea bream	1 fillet
Courgette	1
Fresh langoustine	3
Fresh mussels	3
Fish stock	50 ml
White wine	50 ml
Double cream	50 ml
Chervil for garnish	
Sea salt	To taste
Seasoning	To taste

METHOD OF WORK

1   Reduce the fish stock and white wine by half in a small pan, along with the langoustine shells and heads then pass.

2   Return to a clean pan, add the mussels and langoustines. Cover until the mussels are open and remove mussels and langoustine tails.

3   Add double cream to stock/wine mixture and continue to reduce.

4   Add the courgette ribbons (made by drawing a peeler slowly down the whole length of the courgette) and cook for 45 seconds.

5   Season the bream fillet and pan fry, skin side down first, for about 1–2 minutes each side.

6   Arrange the courgette ribbons in the middle of a pasta bowl and place the mussels and langoustine tails around the bowl.

7   Place the sea bream on top of the courgette ribbons and dress the bowl with reduced sauce (the sauce should just coat the back of a spoon).

8   Garnish with chervil and serve.

Poultry

8

Recipes

CHICKEN AND POUSSIN
Chicken chasseur   314
Chicken fricassée   315
Chicken Madras   315
Chicken wings with pea and mint
   risotto and garlic foam   316
Coq au vin   317
Poached chicken duxelle   318
Roast chicken English style   319
Spatchcock poussin with grain
   mustard compound butter   320

TURKEY
Breaded escalope of turkey with
   chateau potatoes, sherry and morel
   sauce   320
Suprême of turkey wrapped in bacon
   with croquette potatoes   321

DUCK
Confit of duck lyonnaise   322
Pan fried duck breast with sauté
   potatoes and orange sauce   323

ONLINE RECIPES

LEARNER SUPPORT
Preparation of chicken suprême
   for Kiev
Chicken Kiev

NVQ

Unit 2FP4 Prepare poultry for basic dishes

Unit 2FC4 Cook and finish basic poultry dishes

VRQ

Unit 210 Prepare and cook poultry

Introduction

When we refer to poultry we describe birds specifically reared for the table. They include chicken, guinea fowl, turkey, goose and duck.

Chicken

Chicken is the world's most popular meat and until the mid 20th century it was considered to be a luxury meat, on a par with sirloin steak both in terms of quality and cost. This came to an end when intensive rearing methods were developed. Today battery-reared broilers (the industry term for a chicken reared specifically for the table) are the most economical and versatile of all products used in the professional kitchen.

TASK Poultry is thought of as a 'healthy eating option' by many people. Using the internet, research the benefits of having poultry as part of your diet. Make a table showing the benefits and also the disadvantages of poultry as a food, give reasons for the benefits and the disadvantages.

In the UK more than 98 per cent of chickens are battery reared. Because of intensive husbandry, the birds are bred to achieve slaughter weight at six weeks. They are rather tasteless and have a tough texture. For this reason, modern chefs impose flavours upon them.

Free range and especially organic chickens are allowed to forage in the open and have space to develop muscle and a stronger bone structure. They are usually slow-growing breeds that can take around 20 weeks to reach slaughter weight. There are several labelling systems in use for these birds such as soil association and little red tractor. One British company has adopted a system of labelling similar to the French *Label Rouge*. The name is 'label Anglaise', a producer that uses older breeds and free range/organic methods of rearing. The label is featured on menus and assures the guests that the chicken has been well reared and is flavourful.

Corn-fed chickens are fed on a diet of either corn or a proportion of corn. This does not guarantee any kind of quality assurance. The distinctive yellow colouring of the skin is gained by the introduction of a yellow dye into the feed and not by the corn itself. The flavour may sometimes be only marginally better than that of a broiler.

Quality points

When buying chickens we should be able to identify the quality points associated with them:

● Clear skin with no blemishes (the colour varies from breed to breed, but the most common battery reared breeds, the hybrids, Ross and Cobb have a pale creamy colour).

● Flesh should be firm and pliable.

● Not too much fat. Check the abdominal cavity for excess.

● No bruising, blood clots, ammonia sores on the legs or cuts.

● The breastbone should be pliable (this is for younger birds that are destined to be grilled, roasted or sautéed).

Purchase specifications

● For the modern chef it is important to be able to tell your supplier exactly what you require from them.

● If a supplier has an understanding of your requirements, they will be only too happy to oblige.

● Constant communication or dialogue between the chef or the **garde-manger** and the poultry supplier leads to a more harmonious relationship.

CHICKEN WEIGHT SPECIFICATION

TYPE	AVERAGE WEIGHT
Poussin	250–400 g
Spring chicken	1–1.25 kg
Chicken	1–2 kg
Boiling fowl	2–4 kg
Capon (de-sexed cockerels)	2–4 kg

Grades of poultry. Left to Right – Battery chicken, free range, corn-fed

Types of chicken. Top – Capon, boiling fowl, Bottom – Poussin, spring chicken, chicken

Turkey

Turkey

The Aztecs and Mexicans domesticated the turkey and it was introduced to Europe by the Spanish, becoming popular because of its delicate flavour. The term 'turkey' is said to have come from the belief that the Spanish imported them from Turkey. The Spanish referred to them as 'Indian chickens' because even though they were in Mexico they believed they were still in the West Indies.

When the colonists settled in America they relied on turkeys to stave off famine. The turkey is still the festive bird used at Thanksgiving. Turkeys are mainly battery farmed, but it is well worthwhile sourcing and using organic and free range birds should budgets permit.

Turkey is available in a vast array of weights from 4 to 15 kg depending on requirements. In percentage terms, the larger the bird, the greater the yield.

Quality points

- Cock birds have a tendency to be drier and tougher than hens.

- Bronze birds can have residual dark feather stubs: these can be removed with duck tweezers.

- The flesh should be dry to the touch without excess blemishes.

- If the windpipe is still intact, it should be pliable and not rigid.

- The breast should be plump in domesticated birds and slightly leaner in the rarer wild variety.

Duck

Duck is a web-footed waterfowl, originally domesticated by the Chinese about 2000 years ago. It is highly appreciated in Europe for its rich moist meat. Although intensive farming produces 20 million, it is a type of meat that can still be palatable and requires less intervention by the chef to make an acceptable meal. It is worth noting that the type and breed of duck should be taken into account when purchasing for specific reasons, e.g. Barbary ducks yield excellent suprême portions, while Aylesbury ducks are ideal for roasting.

Quality points

When buying duck, check that the birds are:

- pale skinned (except with wild varieties, see game section)
- fresh and pleasant smelling
- moist but not sticky
- free from bruises, feathers and blemishes.

BREEDS

- Aylesbury   a small bird with white feathers and delicate flesh.
- Gressingham   a cross between a domesticated duck and a mallard, a highly prized breed with a low fat content and rich flesh.
- Norfolk   from the county of Norfolk, a domesticated fowl with similar attributes to Aylesbury.
- Barbary   firm, lean flesh with a stronger flavour.
- Nantes   small and slightly fatty with delicate flesh.

Guinea fowl

Originally from West Africa, guinea fowl has been raised for the table for many centuries. It is an excellent alternative to battery-farmed chicken in that the flesh is comparable to organic free range chickens. It can have a tendency to be dry so care must be taken when cooking this bird. All recipes that apply to chicken also apply to guinea fowl.

Goose

This traditional festive bird fell out of favour when turkey became popular, mainly because it has resisted intensive rearing. This makes the cost high in comparison to other poultry.

Goose has a rich dark flesh with a copious covering of fat which means that it will very rarely dry out during cooking. Birds can weigh anything from 2.5 to 12 kg, depending on whether they were used for the production of foie gras or not. Goose should have the same quality points as duck and when not in season can be purchased frozen.

Next in this chapter, various techniques for the preparation of poultry will be demonstrated. It should be noted that the structure of poultry birds is very similar and the techniques used can be transferred between each type.

HEALTH & SAFETY

- Poultry carries a naturally occurring bacteria called salmonella.
- This is present in the birds as well as eggs.
- Pasteurization kills this bacteria which is why some chefs only use pasteurized eggs for cooking with.
- Care must be taken to ensure utensils, equipment and preparation areas are disinfected before and after working with poultry.
- Chilled poultry should remain under 8 °C and above 63 °C once cooked.
- The core temperature should reach 70 °C for two minutes when cooking to ensure bacteria have been reduced to a safe level during cooking.
- Poultry should be stored in no drip containers in the bottom of a fridge. Ideally poultry will have its own fridge space.
- The products should be covered and clearly labelled.
- Poultry is suitable for freezing also so it can be kept at −18 °C for up to three months.

Key preparation techniques for poultry

VIDEO CLIP Preparing poultry.

Step-by-step: Preparation of chicken for sauté

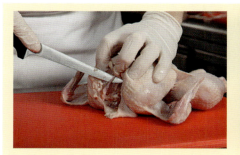

1. Remove wishbone, by scraping the bone then use a knife or fingers to remove it intact.

2. Cut around the top of the wing to sever the connection to the breast; then as shown using the back of the knife make one firm connection to the wing bone – this will cause a clean break.

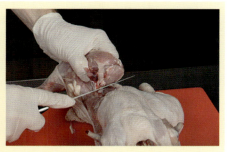

3. Remove the legs by cutting through the skin between the leg and the breast: lifting the leg upwards to dislocate the joint, remove the flesh taking care to remove the oyster in the process.

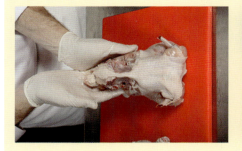

4. Once both legs have been removed the chicken should look like this.

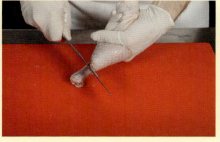

5. Holding the leg firmly as shown cut around the knuckle: this will sever the tendons and make a neater finish.

6. The trimmed leg ready to be separated into two pieces.

CHEF'S TIP Use a sharp heavy knife to remove the knuckle from the leg. This minimizes bone splinters.

VIDEO CLIP Cutting a chicken for saute.

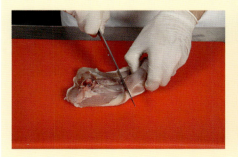

7. Separating the drumstick from the thigh: use a finger to feel where the joint is and then cut in this place: the knife should not make contact with bone.

8. The trimmed and folded thigh on the left and the trimmed drumstick on the right.

9. As a guide the cut to remove the suprêmes should be an equal distance from the side of the bird to the centre as shown: once the flesh is cut downwards the attached bone should come away easily.

10. An example of the remaining breast after both suprêmes have been removed successfully.

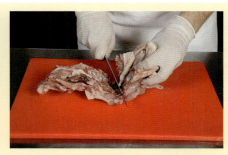

11. Holding onto the breast cut below to separate the carcass from the flesh.

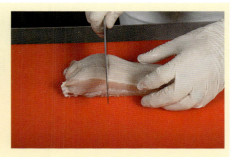

12. Once the carcass has been removed, lay the breast flat and feel for the soft pliable breast bone – this will be slightly raised: cut through the breast as shown to produce two pieces (note they will not be identical in shape but should be in weight).

13. The two pieces of breast – note the bone is still attached to the underside.

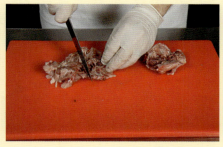

14. Trim the carcass of any excess fat then cut into three even pieces.

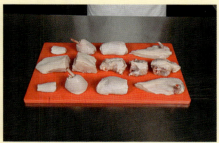

15. The completed chicken cut for sauté.

From top left – Winglet, drumstick, thigh, suprême; Centre from left – Breast x 2, carcass x 3; From bottom left – Winglet, drumstick, thigh, suprême; in total there are 13 pieces of chicken when cut for sauté.

CHEF'S TIP The carcass section of the chicken is used to intensify the sauce's flavour.

WEB LINK Use the following link to investigate how British poultry welfare is safeguarded: http://www.poultry.uk.com

Step-by-step: Preparation of chicken for roasting

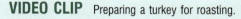 **VIDEO CLIP** Preparing a turkey for roasting.

1. Remove the wishbone and add the stuffing if required, stretching the neck skin as far as possible.

2. Truss the chicken by threading a trussing needle with string and pulling it through the wings after they have been pushed behind the back.

3. Thread the needle through the skin flap of the neck to seal in the stuffing, and then out through the wings again.

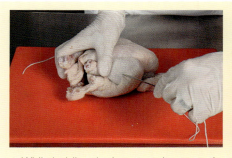

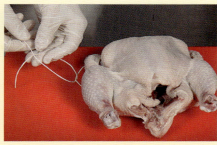

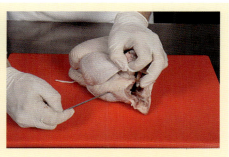

4. While holding the legs together pass the needle through as shown and through the cavity without piercing the breast meat.

5. Taking the two ends of string tie securely to complete the first stage of trussing.

6. Pass the needle and string through the area behind the thigh passing through the cavity.

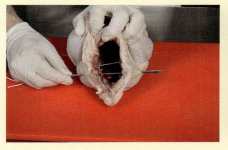

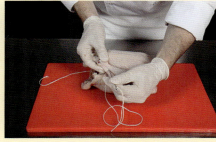

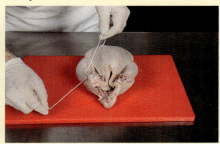

7. This is the cross section showing the needle and string passing though the cavity.

8. Once the needle and string has passed through the bird pierce the tops of the drumsticks (achilles) and through the flap of skin below the breast.

9. Securely tie the two ends of the string: this now completes the trussing of a bird for roasting.

TASK Use the following link to produce a chart which highlights different breeds of chickens which could be used for cooking and egg production: **http://www.poultryandeggs.co.uk**

VIDEO CLIP Trussing a chicken.

TEST YOURSELF

1 Name four types of poultry.

2 How many pieces do you get from a chicken when cut for sauté?

3 What flavoured butter is used for Kiev?

4 What wine is used in coq au vin?

5 What fat is duck confit cooked in?

6 What bacteria is associated with poultry?

7 Name two breeds of duck.

8 What is boiling fowl used for?

9 What bone should be removed to ease carving of poultry?

10 Which region does guinea fowl originate from?

Recipes
Chicken and poussin

Chicken chasseur

Ingredients	4 portions	10 portions
Chickens (1.3–1.6 kg)	8 pieces	20 pieces
Shallots	100 g	300 kg
Tomato concassée	200 g	600 g
Button mushrooms	200 g	600 g
Demi glace	200 ml	600 ml
Oil or butter		
White wine	100 ml	300 ml
Chopped tarragon	1 tsp	1 tblspn
Parmentier potatoes		
Good quality salt and pepper	To taste	To taste

energy	cal	fat	sat fat	carb	sugar	protein	fibre
3443 kJ	826 kcal	48.7 g	8.7 g	20.0 g	4.3 g	73.2 g	4.1 g

METHOD OF WORK

1 Melt the butter in a sauté pan
2 Season and add the chicken in a sequence that takes into account the density of the flesh, e.g. thighs first then drumsticks, breast, suprême and finally the carcass.
3 Sauté until cooked.
4 Remove from the pan and keep hot.

5 Add the shallots and the sliced mushrooms and allow cooking.
6 Add the wine and reduce by half.
7 Add the tomato concassé and demi glace.
8 Correct the seasoning and consistency and serve on a plate or service dish, with appropriate garnish such as parmentier potatoes.

CHEF'S TIP When cooking a chicken dish for sauté the entire cooking method should take place in a sauté pan on top of the stove.

CHEF'S TIP Remember leg meat takes longer to cook than breast meat.
Drumsticks and thighs should be added first.

VIDEO CLIP Saute chicken chasseur.

Chicken fricassée

Ingredients	4 portions	10 portions
Chickens cut for sauté (1.3–1.6 kg)	8 pieces	20 pieces
Button onions cooked	80 g	240 g
Sauté button mushrooms	80 g	240 g
Butter	60 g	180 g
Plain flour	40 g	120 g
Chicken stock	500 ml	150 m
Double cream	100 ml	300 ml
Egg yolks	2	6
Oil or butter		
Good quality salt and pepper	To taste	To taste
Thyme sprigs		

energy	cal	fat	sat fat	carb	sugar	protein	fibre
3939 kJ	948 kcal	69.3 g	23.8 g	9.8 g	1.5 g	71.8 g	1.6 g

METHOD OF WORK

1 Remove the skin from the chicken pieces.
2 Melt the butter in a sauté pan.
3 Season the chicken, sauté the chicken until cooked without colour.
4 Add the flour to make a loose roux.
5 Add the stock, bring to the boil and simmer very gently until cooked.
6 Add the onions and mushrooms.
7 Mix the yolks and cream together, add a little of the sauce to the liaison and then add the liaison back to the sauce. This makes the sauce into a velouté. Do not allow the sauce to reboil.
8 Serve the chicken coated with the sauce and garnished.

Note:

● This dish can be made using 200 g of diced chicken per portion instead of chicken cut for sauté.

● The dish can be served with or without the garnish as shown here.

Chicken Madras

Ingredients	4 portions	10 portions
Diced chicken	600 g	1.5 kg
Oil	50 ml	125 ml
Madras paste (see page 133)	100 g	250 g
Chopped beef tomatoes	200 g	500 g
Fresh chicken stock (see page 114)	100 ml	250 ml
Boiled or braised rice		
Chiffonade of coriander		
Salt		

energy	cal	fat	sat fat	carb	sugar	protein	fibre
2129 kJ	510 kcal	23.6 g	3.8 g	24.7 g	2.5 g	49.0 g	2.2 g

METHOD OF WORK

1 Marinate the chicken in Madras paste for 6 hours or overnight if possible.
2 Heat the oil then fry off the chicken for 2–3 minutes, add the chopped tomatoes and enough stock to moisten.
3 Simmer for 20 minutes, season to taste.
4 Serve with rice and a chiffonade of coriander.

Chicken wings with pea and mint risotto and garlic foam

Ingredients	4 portions	10 portions
Chicken wings	24	60
Blackened cajun seasoning	20 g	50 g
Juice and grated zest of lemon	1	2
Salt		
Oil	20 ml	50 ml
Pea and mint risotto (see page 239)	80 ml	200 ml
Chicken stock	50 ml	125 ml
Milk	50 ml	125 ml
Garlic	1 clove	2 cloves

energy	cal	fat	sat fat	carb	sugar	protein	fibre
2962 kJ	708 kcal	47.2 g	12.8 g	10.4 g	1.5 g	57.2 g	1.0 g

METHOD OF WORK

1   Remove the wing tips from the wings and cut in half at the joint.

2   Place the wings in a bowl and pour on the oil and lemon juice and mix until they are coated.

3   Add the spices, lemon zest and season lightly with salt and mix until all the wings have a light dusting. Increase the amount of cajun spices as necessary.

4   Marinate for 3–4 hours in the lemon juice.

5   Grill until thoroughly cooked.

6   For the foam, heat the stock until boiling then add the garlic and milk, simmer for 10 minutes.

7   With a hand blender pulse the liquid until a foam is formed, spoon off as much as required.

8   Serve accompanied by pea and mint risotto and garlic foam.

HEALTH & SAFETY   Chicken wings can be quite fatty so use long tongs at the grill to prevent burning from flame bursts.

CHEF'S TIP   The wing pieces have had one of the small bones removed to improve presentation.

WEB LINK   The UK is governed by official standards that regulate the breeding, husbandry and slaughter of animals. The site below lists details of these practices.
  Use the link to broaden your knowledge:
http://www.defra.gov.uk/foodfarm/food/industry/sectors/

Coq au vin

Ingredients	4 portions	10 portions
Chickens cut for sauté (1.3–1.6 kg)	8 pieces	20 pieces
Button onions cooked	80 g	200 g
Sauté button mushrooms	80 g	200 g
Lardons	80 g	200 g
Diced shallots	40 g	100 g
Red wine	200 ml	500 ml
Heart shaped croutons cooked in butter until golden brown	4	10
Demi glace	200 ml	500 ml
Oil or butter	50 g	125 g
Good quality salt and pepper	To taste	To taste

energy	cal	fat	sat fat	carb	sugar	protein	fibre
3549 kJ	850 kcal	48.0 g	12.1 g	18.4 g	2.2 g	77.7 g	2.0 g

4 Add the shallots and lardons and continue to cook.

5 Add the wine and reduce by half, then add the demi glace, bring to the boil and simmer very gently.

6 Add the chicken, cover with a lid and cook until finished.

7 Add the mushrooms and button onions.

8 Serve the chicken coated with the sauce and garnished with the croutons and chopped parsley.

CHEF'S TIP Coq au vin was traditionally made using cockerels: however hen chickens are now used as much as cocks.

CHEF'S TIP Beurre manié (see page 109) can be added to thicken the sauce if required.

METHOD OF WORK

1 Melt the butter or oil in a sauté pan.

2 Season the chicken and sauté until almost cooked.

3 Remove from the pan.

Poached chicken duxelle

Ingredients	4 portions	10 portions
Chickens suprême (skinless)	4	10
Diced shallots	100 g	250 g
Button mushrooms	200 g	500 g
Butter	20 g	100 g
Dry white wine	50 ml	125 ml
Chicken stock	100 ml	250 ml
Double cream	100 ml	250 ml
Good quality salt and ground white pepper	To taste	To taste

energy	cal	fat	sat fat	carb	sugar	protein	fibre
2051 kJ	492 kcal	29.2 g	12.6 g	2.0 g	1.8 g	53.3 g	1.4 g

METHOD OF WORK

1   Finely dice the shallots and mushrooms.

2   Cook in the butter until brown and the moisture has evaporated.

3   Add half the wine and continue to cook until it has evaporated. Season and allow to cool. This is the basic preparation called duxelle.

4   Remove the fillet from the suprême and bat out until thin but not broken.

5   Make an incision in the suprême. Stuff with the duxelle and secure with the fillet.

6   Roll the chicken in cling film to form a sausage shape.

7   Pour the stock and the remainder of the wine into a saucepan and reduce.

8   Add the double cream and reduce to a sauce consistency, season to taste.

9   In a pan of boiling water add the chicken and simmer until a core temperature of 70 °C is achieved for 2 minutes.

10   Remove the chicken from the pan and rest for 1 minute, then quickly roll the chicken in a sauté pan of hot butter to colour slightly.

11   Slice the chicken and serve with the sauce and garnish.

VIDEO CLIP   Ballotine of chicken.

Roast chicken English style

Ingredients	4 portions
Spring chicken, 1.3 kg	1
Butter	80 g
Onions	80 g
Fresh breadcrumbs	120 g
Chopped parsley	1 tsp
Chopped thyme	1 tblspn
Good quality salt and milled pepper	
Chicken livers	1
Chicken giblets	1
Carrot, onion, celery, leek	500 g
Chipolatas or sausages	4
Streaky bacon rashers	4
Bread sauce (see page 134)	150 ml
Watercress	I bunch
Brown chicken stock	300 ml

energy	cal	fat	sat fat	carb	sugar	protein	fibre
4584 kJ	1096 kcal	53.8 g	21.7 g	38.0 g	8.3 g	115.2 g	5.7 g

METHOD OF WORK

1 Cut the onion for the stuffing into a fine brunoise and sweat in the butter until cooked.

2 Add to the breadcrumbs along with the parsley and thyme and allow to cool.

3 Crush the livers and add to the stuffing.

4 Stuff and truss the bird as shown in the step-by-step sequence (see pages 312–313).

5 Chop the vegetables into a rough mirepoix and place them in a roasting pan.

6 Place the chicken on the bed of roots: brush with a little oil and put into an oven at 240 °C to caramelize. When this is achieved turn the chicken and caramelize the breast.

7 Turn the heat down to 130 °C and continue to cook until a core temperature of 70 °C is reached for a minimum of 2 minutes and the juices run clear when the thigh is pierced.

8 Remove from the dish: drain any juices from the cavity and allow the chicken to rest in a warm place (above 63 °C).

9 Meanwhile wrap the chipolatas or sausages in streaky bacon and then fry until coloured nicely and cooked all the way through.

10 Place the roasting pan on a high heat and cook until brown and any juices from the chicken have reduced to a thick syrup.

11 Add the stock and boil rapidly until the pan has been completely deglazed.

12 Strain into a clean pan and remove any fat from the gravy. Reduce to the required quantity and adjust the seasoning.

13 Serve the chicken accompanied by roast gravy, bread sauce, chipolatas and bacon roll and watercress.

CHEF'S TIP If the stuffing seems dry it can be moistened with some chicken stock.

In addition game chips can be served as a classical garnish with this dish (see page 439).

Turkey

Spatchcock poussin with grain mustard compound butter

Ingredients	4 portions	10 portions
Poussin prepared for spatchcock (see game prep shots, page 330)	4	10
Grain mustard compound butter	12 slices	30 slices
Good quality salt and ground white pepper	To taste	To taste
Oil		

energy	cal	fat	sat fat	carb	sugar	protein	fibre
1245 kJ	300 kcal	25.6 g	12.4 g	0.4 g	0.3 g	17.3 g	0.4 g

METHOD OF WORK

1 Brush the poussin with a little oil and season well.
2 Place onto a contact grill (char grill) and colour on both sides.
3 Take care not to burn the outside: the poussin should be fully cooked on this surface.
4 Serve with slices of grain mustard compound butter.

CHEF'S TIP Other compound butters also work well with grilled poultry: try and use an alternative (see pages 144–146).

VIDEO CLIP Spatchcock chicken for grilling.

Breaded escalope of turkey with chateau potatoes, sherry and morel sauce

Ingredients	4 portions	10 portions
Turkey escalopes	8 × 75 g	20 × 75 g
Good quality salt and milled pepper	To taste	To taste
Flour		
Egg wash		
Breadcrumbs		
Ivory sauce	100 ml	250 ml
Morels (dried)	16	40
Sherry	100 ml	250 ml
Chateau potatoes	12	30

energy	cal	fat	sat fat	carb	sugar	protein	fibre
2640 kJ	755 kcal	19.6 g	3.6 g	75.0 g	6.3 g	40.7 g	9.5 g

METHOD OF WORK

1 Rehydrate the morels in sherry overnight.
2 Pané the turkey escalopes and pan fry until golden brown.
3 Heat the sauce and then add the morels.
4 Serve with chateau potatoes.

VIDEO CLIP Prepare and cook escalopes of turkey.

Suprême of turkey wrapped in bacon with croquette potatoes

Ingredients	4 portions	10 portions
Turkey suprême	400 g	1 kg
Sliced pancetta	10 rashers	25 rashers
Sausage meat	200 g	500 g
Chestnuts	12	40
Chicken jus (see page 120)	100 ml	250 ml
Croquette potatoes (see page 437)	12	30
Good quality salt and pepper	To taste	To taste

energy	cal	fat	sat fat	carb	sugar	protein	fibre
5239 kJ	1249 kcal	55.0 g	21.1 g	125.3 g	14.2 g	69.7 g	12.7 g

METHOD OF WORK

1 Trim the turkey into neat cylinders, and season well.

2 Lay the pancetta onto cling film overlapping to produce a square.

3 Lay the turkey on top of the pancetta: carefully spoon the sausage meat into position on top of the turkey.

4 Fold over the pancetta and seal with cling film – this technique is the same as for monkfish (see page 289).

5 Place into boiling water and cook until a core temperature of 70 °C is achieved for 2 minutes.

6 Heat the jus and add the chestnuts, allow to simmer for 5 minutes.

7 Remove the turkey from the water and rest for one minute.

8 Remove the cling film and fry the turkey in butter until the bacon becomes crispy.

9 Slice the turkey and serve with croquette potatoes and chestnut jus.

WEB LINK Turkeys can be of average quality and have limited flavour, it is important to use traceable sources and well kept animals. This family run business is famous for its turkeys:
http://www.kelly-turkeys.com

Duck

Confit of duck lyonnaise

Ingredients	4 portions	10 portions
Duck legs	4	10
Rock salt	20 g	100 g
Sugar	10 g	50 g
Star anise	1	2
Orange zest	1	2
Thyme	2 sprigs	5 sprigs
Rosemary	2 sprigs	5 sprigs
Duck fat (sufficient to cover the legs)	500 g	1 kg
Finely sliced onions fried until caramelized	100 g	250 g
Duck jus	100 ml	250 ml
Glazed carrots (see recipe online)		

energy	cal	fat	sat fat	carb	sugar	protein	fibre
1806 kJ	431 kcal	30.2 g	11.5 g	8.9 g	6.3 g	30.3 g	2.6 g

METHOD OF WORK

1   Remove the thighbone from the legs and lightly score the thigh piece.

2   Coat the thighs in salt and then add the remainder of the ingredient and allow to cure in a non metallic container for at least 24 hours and up to 48 hours.

3   At this stage some brine will have formed. Discard this and pat the legs dry with a clean cloth or paper towel.

4   Place the duck fat in a casserole or crock pot and melt.

5   Add the duck legs together with the aromatic ingredients and very gently simmer in the fat for 3–4 hours taking care not to let the fat become so hot that the legs begin to fry.

6   Remove from the heat and cool.

7   Store in a cool larder or refrigerator covered with the fat until required (up to 2 months).

8   Place the trimmed duck confit in a hot oven to become crispy, serve with the onions, jus and carrots.

HEALTH & SAFETY   If the confit is to be stored ensure that it is completely covered and that the utensils are thoroughly sterilized.

CHEF'S TIP   This method of cookery was traditionally used to preserve the geese that were used for foie gras and it was said that the flavour and texture of a confit took six months to mature.

Pan fried duck breast with sauté potatoes and orange sauce

Ingredients	4 portions	10 portions
Duck breasts	4	10
Chopped shallots	80 g	200 g
Oranges (juice and zest)	3	7
Sugar	20 g	50 g
Wine vinegar	20 ml	50 ml
Demi glace (see page 130)	100 ml	250 ml
Sauté potatoes (see page 438)		
Good quality salt and pepper	To taste	To taste

energy	cal	fat	sat fat	carb	sugar	protein	fibre
4825 kJ	1164 kcal	95.8 g	27.1 g	35.6 g	15.5 g	41.2 g	4.3 g

METHOD OF WORK

1   Dust the orange zest with a little sugar and arrange on silicone paper, place under hot lights or a very low oven and allow to dry.

2   Season the suprêmes and pan fry skin-side down over a gentle heat until the skin has rendered most of its fat and has become golden brown.

3   Turn the suprêmes and continue to cook to the desired degree of doneness.

4   Place in a warm place to rest.

5   Make a caramel with the sugar and vinegar. Add the shallots, juice of the oranges and demi glace.

6   Slice the duck and arrange on the sauté potatoes. Finish with the sauce, orange segments and zest.

Guest Chef

Pan roasted chicken suprême on crushed new potatoes, with sautéed wild mushrooms and a tarragon velouté

Chef: *Johannes Keevey*
Centre: *MidKent College, Gillingham*

At MidKent College we only use locally grown, or bred foods. Our chicken comes from farms in the Tonbridge/ Malling areas. Mushrooms are grown locally, and bought from the Rochester Farmers Market, as well as the herbs. There are several potato farms around Medway, so potatoes are easily sourced.

Ingredients	Makes 1 portion
Chicken suprême	1
Freshly chopped parsley	½ tblspn
Butter	50 g
Local wild mushrooms (button, chestnut, shitake, oyster) or just button mushrooms	small selection
Velouté or a white wine, cream reduction	enough to dress the plate
Chopped fresh tarragon	½ tblspn
Salt and cracked pepper	To taste
Olive oil for frying	

METHOD OF WORK

1   Clean the suprême bone, using a boning knife and a red board, and season with salt and pepper.

2   In a hot pan, with a teaspoon of oil, seal the suprême with the flesh side down.

3   Turn the suprême onto the skin side, place in a pre-heated oven (180 °C–200 °C) for about 8–10 minutes or until cooked. Turn over after 7 minutes.

4   Crush the new potatoes in a saucepan and warm with the parsley, 25 g of butter and salt and pepper to taste.

5   Sauté the mushrooms with a little oil, 25 g of butter and salt and pepper.

6   Warm the velouté, with the tarragon.

7   Slice the chicken suprême from the thick end (with the bone on) to the thin end at an angle.

8   Place a pastry cutter in the middle of the plate, and fill with the crushed new potato then remove the cutter.

9   Place the chicken piece with the bone on top of the potatoes, and then the other piece, so as to let it face straight up.

10   Scatter the mushrooms around the plate.

11   With a dessert spoon, neatly pour the sauce around the plate.

Game

Recipes

GAME

Sauté of pigeon   336
Fricassée of rabbit   336
Pot roasted stuffed saddle of rabbit
   with lemon thyme   337
Venison bitok lyonnaise   338
Grilled 'tornedos' of venison   338
Spiced tempura quail breasts with
   chilli dipping jam   339

9

NVQ

Unit 2FPC5 Cook and finish basic game dishes

VRQ

Unit 209 Prepare and cook meat and offal
Unit 210 Prepare and cook poultry

LEARNING OBJECTIVES

The aim of this chapter is to enable the candidate to develop skills and implement knowledge in the preparation and cookery principles of basic game dishes. This will also include materials, ingredients and equipment.

At the end of this chapter you will be able to:

● Identify each variety of both feathered and furred game and their finished dish.

● Understand the use of relative ingredients in game preparation and cookery.

● State the quality points of various game items and dishes.

● Prepare and cook each type of game variety.

● Identify the storage procedures of all types of game, both raw and cooked.

● Have a good knowledge of preparing and cooking a range of basic game-based dishes.

● Be able to cook basic game dishes.

● Be able to finish basic game dishes.

Background

Game is one of the only truly seasonal products in this country, and in the culinary world it remains very much unchanged in seasonality today.

This is because it is very difficult to rear wild animals in farms to the same standard they develop to in the wild. This gives game items their distinct and intense flavour.

The hunting and gathering of wild animals has always been part of human existence, so to know that this continues today makes game items that little bit more special.

The hunting season starts from 12 August each year in the United Kingdom – it is more commonly known as the Glorious Twelfth because this is the start of the grouse shooting season.

The hunting and shooting season varies depending on the type of game you require. The table below indicates approximate hunting times during the year (for Scotland, England and Wales), when the various types of game are in their correct season.

The only exceptions to this rule, due to their breeding habits, are hares and rabbits which can be hunted all year round.

SPECIES	SCOTLAND	ENGLAND AND WALES
FURRED GAME		
Red stag	1 July – 20 October	1 August – 30 April
Red hinds	21 October – 15 February	1 November – 28/29 February
Fallow buck	1 August – 30 April	1 August – 30 April
Fallow doe	21 October – 15 February	1 November – 28/29 February
Roe buck	1 April – 20 October	1 April – 31 October
Roe doe	21 October – 31 March	1 November – 28/29 February
Sika stags	1 August – 30 April	1 August – 30 April
Sika hinds	21 October – 15 February	1 November – 28/29 February
GAME BIRDS		
Grouse	12 August – 10 December	12 August – 10 December
Red grouse	12 August – 10 December	12 August – 10 December
Snipe	12 August – 31 January	12 August – 31 January
Partridge	1 September – 1 February	1 September – 1 February
Wild duck and geese (inland)	1 September – 31 January	1 September – 31 January
Mallard, teal and widgeon	1 September – 31 January	1 September – 31 January
Wild duck and geese (below high water mark)	1 September – 20 February	1 September – 20 February
Woodcock	1 October – 31 January	1 October – 31 January
Pheasant	1 October – 1 February	1 October – 1 February

There are now some very good venison farms, which enable this type of game to be available all year round. The farming of some game items will help create the same natural environment for the animal to exist, and can have higher quality results in respect of good availability and consistency of meat than wild game.

Having set periods to hunt and understanding the seasonality can help maintain wild game numbers and stop over hunting. This reduces the possibility of eliminating certain breeds.

As the season is relatively short for each type of game, this immediately makes these meats more appealing to both chefs and customers alike. Game helps to make menus seem that little bit more interesting. It shows customers that the menu is not just the same all year and that fresh local produce can be a major factor to a strong menu.

As game is generally wild birds and animals, they have very little apparent fat making it a healthy meat to eat, as well as being unique in their flavour. One difficulty with game, however, can be that because they are so active their muscles undertake a lot of work and this may result in tougher-textured meat.

However, the tougher the actual meat the more flavour it has because of the red cells produced in working muscles. This is why venison will have a stronger flavour than beef.

CHEF'S TIP Wrapping game items in bacon, pork fat or pig's caul will help keep them moist as they are very lean and do not have much, if any, fat on them to aid this.

The purpose of hanging game is to give the meat time to relax into a less rigid state. When any muscle is consistently used, the fat marbling is less and muscle fibres and connective tissue become tougher. If the animal or bird is killed while it is in action, the meat will be very firm. Hanging the meat gives it time to drain of the blood, making the muscles relax again. The older the animal is, the longer it will have to be hung so that this slow disintegration process can compose the meat to a softer and more edible texture. Furred game should be hung by its feet with its head to the ground so gravity can naturally cause the blood to flow down towards the head and away from the areas of flesh that will be cooked. Hang birds from neck.

Types of feathered game

Pheasant

Pheasants live around woodland and open farmland, eating all kinds of vegetable matter and insect life. Pheasants are not, as many of us think, a native of the British Isles but were

introduced into this country by the Romans, who even left detailed accounts of rearing methods and cooking recipes.

Many cross-breeds have been released by shooting estates in order to produce larger, higher-flying and faster birds.

Pheasant cock (right) and female (left)

Males, called cocks, have rich chestnut, golden-brown and black markings on their body and tail, with a dark green head and red face wattling. Females are smaller and mottled pale brown and black.

Red-legged partridge

The French, or red-legged partridge, as it is more commonly known, is not native to the British Isles. Its origins are in the semi-arid regions of the Mediterranean. This type of game mainly feeds on vegetable matter and is therefore found in many agricultural areas.

Grey (top) and red-legged (bottom) partridge

Males (cocks) and females (hens) are hard to differentiate as both are grey in colour with a white throat, black and brown flecks and have a red beak and legs. The only real difference is that the males have small spurs and are slightly larger in size.

Grey partridge

The grey partridge is native to the UK. Unfortunately its numbers have been in decline due to changes in farming methods and the wide use of pesticides. Pesticides are killing off insects that are important in the diet of its chicks.

More recently they have started to make a very slow comeback in some areas, owing to the increasing popularity of organic farming. They thrive best in large areas of open agricultural land and during winter months live in large groups called coveys.

CHEF'S TIP If you are finding it hard to pluck feathered game, a useful trick to make this easier is to plunge the bird quickly into boiling water for a few seconds so that the skin loosens. The feathers should then come away without too much effort.

It is hard to differentiate between males and females. Both have an orange/red head and a red/brown heart in the middle of a grey breast: the only real difference is that the males are very slightly larger.

Red grouse

The opening of grouse shooting season in the UK is 12 August (referred to as the Glorious Twelfth). The red grouse is a species unique to the British Isles and is generally found in the uplands of the country, particularly the north of England, Scotland and the northern part of Ireland. Other members of the same family are blackcock, ptarmigan and capercaillie.

Red grouse

Grouse moors must be carefully managed, with the burning away of old heather to give rise to new growth which is a vital food source. Males are a reddish brown colour and

have two scarlet combs which are particularly prominent during springtime courtship. The female, hen bird is duller and without combs. Both sexes have feathered feet.

Snipe

The snipe is one of Britain's most striking game birds, living in areas of moorland fringe – heather moorland and pine tree areas. It is closely related to the woodcock.

snipe

Quail

Quail live on open grassland and cereal fields where they eat seeds and insects. They live solitary lives, coming together only to breed and migrate through southern Europe. It is illegal to hunt wild quail in Britain due to its declining numbers, but farm-bred birds close to the wild variety are available.

Being a small game bird, the combination of its stocky body and long, pointed wings makes it quite distinctive. It has a brown back streaked and barred with buff, while its breast is a warm orange.

Quail, with a quail's egg

Wood pigeon

The wood pigeon is not considered a game bird but more of a pest, so they are in season all year round. The wood pigeon is the UK's largest and most common pigeon.

Farmers are constantly at war with the wood pigeon. Crops, such as cabbages, sprouts, peas and grain, are a staple part of its diet and they contribute towards destroying these.

Wood pigeon

Wood pigeons are easily identifiable birds, grey with a patch of white on the neck and wings (making it clearly visible in flight) and a rosy coloured breast.

Basic game bird preparation

Removal of the wishbone

Once the birds have been plucked and drawn, the wishbone should be removed to facilitate carving (when cooked) or any type of portioning or preparation. The only exceptions to this rule are snipe and woodcock. These two birds can be cooked whole and with the intestines intact, and require no preparation other than plucking and removal of the gizzard.

VIDEO CLIP Removing wishbones in game birds.

HEALTH & SAFETY When preparing birds in feather, it is important to avoid plucking game in a kitchen area. A separate area away from the main preparation areas is therefore essential.
   This will prevent any potential cross contamination problems.

CHEF'S TIP Marinating game items in acidic liquids such as wine or oil-based marinades can help to add flavour as well as tenderizing the meats.

The wishbone is situated at the neck end and you will find that it runs either side of the cavity left by the crop and ends up meeting at the top of the breastbone. Place the tip of your knife on the board and use the blade to scrape along the bone on each side.

HEALTH & SAFETY It is good practice to wear disposable gloves where possible when handling raw meat.

HEALTH & SAFETY When working with raw meat always ensure that it is only out of a refrigerator for a short period of time. If not needed straight away, always refrigerate.

CHEF'S TIP When stuffing game items with a mousse it is easier to use pork or chicken as they have a flavour that can easily be managed much easier with other flavourings.

Removing legs and breasts

The legs on most game birds are very sinewy and tough. Consequently, they require longer cooking methods than the breast. They have a very rich gamey flavour because of this and can be very good for enriching game stock to make a strong flavoured jus. The breast, on the other hand, can be cooked quickly and have only one piece of sinew which runs along the inner fillet. This sinew can be removed carefully if you are to pan fry or grill the breast. Legs and breasts are removed in the same way as chickens (see pages 311–312)

CHEF'S TIP Using a flavoured butter underneath the skin when cooking feathered game can aid flavour and stop the item from drying out.

VIDEO CLIP Removing legs and stuffing.

CHEF'S TIP To add another dimension to roasted dishes, cooking game birds on hay, pine sticks, fennel or liquorice sticks can help enhance flavours even further.

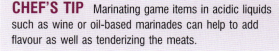

Trussing whole birds for pot roasting or roasting

Trussing is a way of tying game birds and poultry so that they become a tight uniform package. This aids the cooking because the carcass cooks evenly and at the same time. If a bird is not trussed, the legs tend to cook before the breast so that by the time the breast is cooked the legs are dry and inedible. The process of trussing is the same for poultry (see pages 312–313).

Splitting and flattening small game birds for grilling

Small birds can have their backbones removed and be flattened out – spatchcocked – so they can be grilled under a salamander or on a barbeque grill. This works well with partridge, quail, woodcock, snipe and pigeon. With birds that are not drawn, the intestines can be removed after the backbone is cut out, the legs turned around and pushed through an incision cut above the vent. Most game supplied to the catering industry are already drawn through the vent and because of this you will not be able to secure the legs as

mentioned. Below is a step by step way to prepare birds that have been already drawn by securing the legs with a skewer.

> **WEB LINK** It is important to source and select good quality seasonal sustainable game: use this link to research where most of the game is sourced from:
> **http://www.manorfarmgame.co.uk**

Shot damage

Great care needs to be taken when buying game birds. Because of the way birds are shot with shotgun cartridges, some damage is inevitable, but be aware that excessive bruising can ruin the colour of the meat and the flavour of any sauce made from the bones.

Small furred game

Wild rabbit

Rabbits originate from the western Mediterranean and were introduced to Britain by the Normans in the twelfth century to provide meat and fur.

Step-by-step: Making a spatchcock

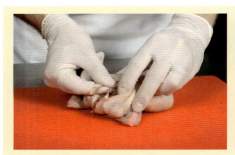

1. Before starting, remove the wishbone.

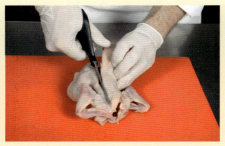

2. Place the poultry scissors into where the crop would be. Cut along the backbone to the vent. Repeat this on the other side and remove the backbone.

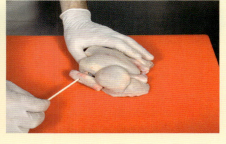

3. Turn the bird over and using the palm of your hand flatten the breast, pulling the legs around to either side of the breast. Push a skewer under the leg bone at the first joint. Go through the breast and out the other side. This will hold the legs and breast together and will allow the bird to cook evenly.

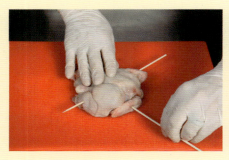

4. Repeat the process on the other side forming a cross pattern.

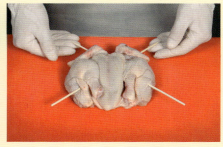

5. The finished spatchcock ready for grilling.

> **VIDEO CLIP** Spatchcock chicken for grilling.

They are now widespread throughout Britain and Ireland and in the UK are considered somewhat of a pest. They eat crops and spoil large areas of pasture land meant for farm animals. However, in the rest of Europe the rabbit is a highly prized game species. Rabbits in southern Europe live on rocky mountainous ground and tend to eat wild thyme which greatly flavours their meat.

Brown hares

These were most probably introduced to the UK, since there is no evidence of their presence in Britain before Roman times and they are now widespread on low ground throughout England.

Brown hares live in very exposed habitats, relying highly on their acute senses and being able to run at speeds of up to 45 mph to evade predators. Hares do not use burrows, but instead make small depressions in the ground among long grass, commonly known as a 'form'.

CHEF'S TIP As game can be very strong in flavour, game stocks or liquors can be too pungent when reduced or used. It is best to have a brown chicken or veal stock to hand as the flavour of these is much more subtle and will dilute the game flavour enough for you to be able to achieve the end result you require.

Preparation of small ground game

Rabbits and hares

Rabbit in fur

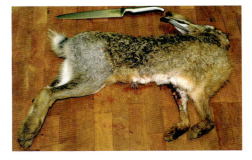

Hare in fur

Difference in size between a rabbit (below) and a hare (top)

In this country we tend to under-use these two wonderful commodities. They are abundant at certain times of year and can be relatively cheap.

The difference between rabbits and hares is obvious, and when they are seen together you are able to see just how much larger a hare is: they can weigh up to 5 kg. The following guidelines concentrate on brown hares, but there is another species, blue or white hares, which come from the highlands of Scotland. These are smaller than brown hares and are not as gastronomically prized as their larger cousins.

1 The rabbit is visibly much smaller than its cousin the hare – see photo above.

2 The hare has a reddish-brown fur which will become flecked with grey as the animal gets older. The rabbit tends to be a light or in some cases dark grey colour.

3 Another distinguishing feature is the ears. The hares' ears are large with black points whereas rabbits' ears are smaller and grey.

4 The meat of rabbits and hare is very different. Hare is very red in colour, not unlike venison. It has a rich flavour and, if roasted, should be served under-done because, like venison, it has very little fat and if over-cooked will dry out. Rabbit has a much lighter colour and flavour and as it is a white meat should not be under cooked. Unlike the hare it should be only just cooked if roasted.

Step-by-step: Jointing small ground game

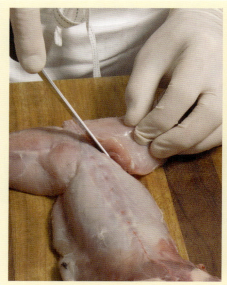

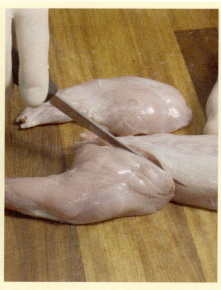

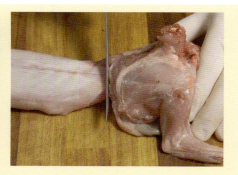

1. Feel for the pelvic bone and make a cut around it leaving the pelvis attached to the saddle.

2. After cutting around the top side of the leg, turn the carcass over and cut at the same angle on the inside of the leg as shown. Once the meat has been cut away, pop the ball and socket joint to release the leg. When cutting around the hip bone stay as close to the bone as you can. You will end up with a 'V' shape at the bottom of the saddle once both legs are removed.

3. Counting from tail to head, find the second rib bone and make a cut between the second and third rib bones outwards, away from the loin, then turn the carcass around and carefully with one sweeping cut, cut through the loin and stop at the backbone. Again do the same on the other side of the carcass and then chop through the backbone.

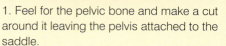

4. After cutting away the first membrane you will see another thicker membrane in place around the loins. To remove this start at one end and using a thin sharp filleting knife place the tip of the knife under the membrane and keeping it as close to its underside as possible. Push the knife up to the top. Once the knife comes out the other end, angle it upwards and cut around the loin and downwards.

5. This picture shows five pieces (one leg is not dissected in half). By cutting the saddle into three pieces the end result would be eight pieces or four good portions. The best end, the neck and the head, should all be added to jugged hare as should the blood.

VIDEO CLIP Skinning and preparing a rabbit.

VIDEO CLIP Dissecting a rabbit.

TASK   Produce a rabbit or hare recipe for each of the following cooking methods:

- sauté
- braised
- roasted
- poached.

Large furred game

Red deer

Our largest deer species, red deer can be up to 1.2 metres in height at the shoulder. In Britain most red deer are found on the open moorlands of the Highlands and Islands of Scotland, although scattered populations are also found in places such as north-west England, East Anglia and Exmoor. Red deer lend themselves well to farming.

During the summer, red deer are dark red or brown with a lighter cream underbelly, inner thighs and rump. In winter the pelage changes to a darker brown or grey. Lowland red deer stags grow larger antlers with more points than highland deer, which tend to stop at 12 points and are known as 'royal stags'.

CHEF'S TIP   Always check the skin or flesh for bruising or redness as this can be missed by the supplier and pellets and shots can still be left in the animal.

Fallow deer

Fallow deer were abundant in prehistoric times but became extinct in Britain during the Ice Age. The Norman nobility reintroduced them to Britain around the end of the eleventh century.

Fallow deer have the widest variation of coat colour or pelage of any wild British deer, ranging from very dark black to white.

The summer coat of the common fallow deer is deep chestnut in colour with white spots, which in winter turns to a dark brown and the spots fade. Fallow bucks' antlers are flattened unlike those of the red deer which are pointed.

WILD BOAR

There is a resurgence in meat from wild boar. They are part of the pig family.

WEB LINK   Find out more about wild boar products at:
http://www.therealboar.co.uk/

SOURCING   Game to eat is an industry leader promoting game within the UK, sourcing sustainable, local quality produce; use the following link to broaden your knowledge:
http://www.gametoeat.co.uk

How to define age in game

Feathered game

There are three main indications as to the age of game birds:

1 *Spurs* – in cock (male) birds the spurs get longer as the bird gets older.

2 *Beaks* – the younger the bird, the more pliable the beak will be.

3 *Feet* – in younger birds with webbed feet the webbing will tear more easily.

QUALITY POINTS

● Age is a very important factor to take into account when considering the quality of game and its suitability for certain dishes and cooking methods.

● Older animals are better suited for braising, stewing and boiling, whereas younger animals lend themselves well to roasting, grilling, pan-frying, pot roasting and griddling.

Game birds should not have any broken limbs or any tears or breaks to the skin and should not be slimy to the touch. They should smell strong in flavour but not be pungent or off-putting. The breast should be prominent and have a good shape and, along with the legs, should not have darkened patches, bruising or major shot damage. These factors can be harder to spot if the birds are in feather, but all animals should be thoroughly inspected before purchasing or receiving.

With most game birds the meat will be dark in colour, but the meat should not be too dark as this could mean there is excess blood in the meat where it may not have been hung properly or can also indicate bruising. Bear in mind the size of the animal you are using as you will not always get a great yield from certain game birds, so check its meat to bone ratio to see if the bird is of good quality.

Furred game: small

There are three main indications of age in small ground game:

1 *Teeth* – in young rabbits and hares the two front teeth should be quite white, clean and not protrude from the mouth.

2 *Feet* – in rabbits and hares the longer the claws are, the older the animal.

3 *Ears* – the ears on young rabbits and hares will tear more easily.

With rabbits, hare, and other small game animals the main things to consider are that when in fur, they should not have excess blood on the fur, should have no tears or breaks in the fur or skin and again should have no major shoot damage or injuries.

The meat on rabbits should be pale pink in colour with no major bruising or dark blood spots. Unlike game birds or hares rabbits should have a fresh smell and not be tacky to the touch.

Furred game: large

Apart from size, there are three further factors to consider when choosing large game.

1 *Time of year* – bucks or stags (male deer) are at their best just before the 'rut' (breeding season) starts as they have built up fat reserves to give them strength and vitality at this time of year. The same applies to does or hinds (female deer) as at this time of year the pickings will have been rich and allowed them to prepare for the winter. This small amount of fat adds to the quality of the meat. The meat in younger animals that have not bred is of much better quality than older ones, although these younger deer do not have the meat yield of older specimens.

2 *Shot damage* – because all game (with the possible exception of some farmed venison) will be killed with a shotgun or rifle, you should look for damage caused by the shot entering the animal. With game shot using a shotgun, the damage can be quite severe if it is shot at close range and these animals should not be accepted. With rifle shot game, look at the entrance and exit wounds: if it has been shot in the wrong place, large areas of the carcass can be lost.

Shot damage

3 The meat itself should be a deep red in colour, like beef or duck. It should smell strong but not off – there is a noticeable difference between the two. Venison only has about 5 per cent fat compared to other meats that average between 18 to 22 per cent and should therefore not have excess fat or marbling.

TASK Research the prices of all the types of game listed in this book to provide four portions. Show your findings in a table, stating the source.

Storage of game

Storage of game animals can be an issue for several reasons. As they are classed as 'wild' the rules enforced by Environmental Health state that unless premises are a learning environment or teaching area, feathered and furred game should not enter a food preparation area.

As noted earlier, game animals should be hung from their feet ideally in an ambient temperature and should not be plucked or drawn. Furthermore, they should also be stored away from prepared meat and poultry items and if possible they should have their own designated area or fridge. Prepared game items that have been de-furred and feathered should be stored with the same general hygiene rules of below 5 °C, labelled and dated.

CHEF'S TIP As game only has a short season, items such as pigeon, venison, pheasant and rabbit can be hot- or cold-smoked very easily to help preserve them. This of course is as well as cooking and settling them in duck or goose fat as for confits or rillettes.

VIDEO CLIP Removing breast from large game birds.

TEST YOURSELF

1 What does the term 'Glorious Twelfth' relate to?

2 What can be wrapped around game to retain moisture?

3 Name four types of feathered game.

4 Name two types of small ground game.

5 What three indicators are used to assess the age of game birds?

6 What three indicators are used to assess the age of small furred game?

7 What three indicators are used to assess the age of large furred game?

8 Which of the following is only in season on the 1st February: snipe, partridge, wild duck?

9 What percentage of fat does venison have?

10 Name three types of deer.

Recipes

Sauté of pigeon *with black pudding, roasted cherry tomato salad and pommes au lard*

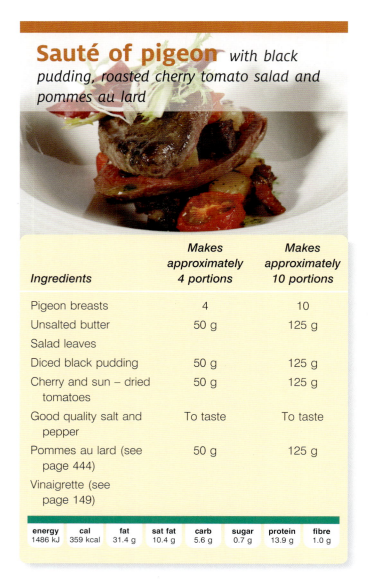

Ingredients	Makes approximately 4 portions	Makes approximately 10 portions
Pigeon breasts	4	10
Unsalted butter	50 g	125 g
Salad leaves		
Diced black pudding	50 g	125 g
Cherry and sun – dried tomatoes	50 g	125 g
Good quality salt and pepper	To taste	To taste
Pommes au lard (see page 444)	50 g	125 g
Vinaigrette (see page 149)		

	energy 1486 kJ	cal 359 kcal	fat 31.4 g	sat fat 10.4 g	carb 5.6 g	sugar 0.7 g	protein 13.9 g	fibre 1.0 g

METHOD OF WORK

1   Fry the black pudding in butter for 2 minutes, then remove, add the pigeon breasts and cook until pink.
2   Heat the pomme au lard and add the tomatoes, spoon over a little vinaigrette.
3   Layer the ingredients neatly in a bowl.
4   At the last minute slice the pigeon and arrange.
5   Garnish with dressed lettuce leaves.

CHEF'S TIP   When sautéing game do not overload the pan as this will reduce the temperature in the pan, stop the game from sealing in its flavour and it will end up stewing.

Fricassée of rabbit *with orange and chives*

Ingredients	Makes approximately 4 portions	Makes approximately 10 portions
Rabbit loin cut into slices	500 g	1500 g
Double cream	500 ml	1 litre
Orange segments, zest and juice	1	3
Chicken stock	100 ml	300 ml
White wine	100 ml	300 ml
Chives, chopped	10 g	25 g
Good quality salt and pepper	To taste	To taste
Carrots and courgettes for garnish		

	energy 3375 kJ	cal 816 kcal	fat 72.5 g	sat fat 44.0 g	carb 7.7 g	sugar 7.5 g	protein 29.8 g	fibre 1.3 g

METHOD OF WORK

1   Season the meat with salt and pepper and sauté quickly in a very hot frying pan until golden. Remove the meat from the pan and keep warm.
2   Deglaze the pan with the white wine and reduce by half, then pour into a saucepan along with the orange zest and juice, and the chicken stock and reduce by a further half.
3   Add the cream followed by the sautéed rabbit and any juice that may be in the bottom of the pan.
4   Continue to simmer gently over a medium heat until the meat is tender and the sauce has thickened.
5   Garnish with vegetables, chopped chives, orange zest and segments.

Pot roasted stuffed saddle of rabbit with lemon thyme

Ingredients	Makes approximately 4 portions	Makes approximately 10 portions
Prepared saddle of rabbit	1	3
Leek	50 g	100 g
Celery	50 g	100 g
Onion	50 g	100 g
Bouquet garni	1	1
Lemon thyme	30 g	50 g
Red wine	200 ml	400 ml
Chicken stock	500 ml	1 ltr
Butter, cold and cut into small pieces	250 g	500 g
Double cream	100 ml	250 ml
Good quality salt and pepper	To taste	To taste
Endive halved and sautéed in butter	2	5
Dauphinoise potatoes (see page 445)	4	10
Minced pork	50 g	125 g
Egg	1	2
Thyme leaves	1 tsp	2 tsp
Diced carrots, blanched	2 tblspn	5 tblspn

energy	cal	fat	sat fat	carb	sugar	protein	fibre
5814 kJ	1407 kcal	122.8 g	75.7 g	36.5 g	5.4 g	31.6 g	7.4 g

METHOD OF WORK

1   Combine the minced pork with the egg, thyme leaves and carrots. Mix well.

2   Open the saddle of rabbit and stuff with the pork mixture.

3   Season the saddle with salt and pepper. In a thick bottomed ceramic casserole dish gently brown the saddle and then remove, placing into a separate dish and keep warm.

4   Add the vegetables, bouquet garni, half the herbs and sweat gently for a few minutes.

5   Make a bed on the bottom of the pan with the white mirepoix and place the saddle on top followed by the rest of the herbs and half of the wine. Brush the saddle with a little melted butter and place a lid on.

6   Place the dish into a hot oven at 200 °C and cook for approximately 15–20 minutes, frequently basting.

7   Once cooked remove the saddle and any liquid left in the pot and allow to rest for 10 minutes.

8   Place the pot over a high heat and colour the vegetables for a few minutes. Add the rest of the wine, any juices taken earlier and reduce by half.

9   Add the stock and reduce by the half. Add the cream and reduce by a further half. Now whisk in the butter until it has amalgamated with the sauce and the sauce has a glossy finish.

10 To serve, carve the loins off the rabbit saddle arrange on the plate with the endive, dauphinoise potatoes and suitable garnish.

Venison bitok lyonnaise

Ingredients	Makes approximately 4 portions	Makes approximately 10 portions
Minced venison	500 g	1300 g
Onion	2 half dice/half sliced	5 half dice/half sliced
Dried mixed herbs	40 g	100 g
Egg yolks	3	6
Dried breadcrumbs	100 g	300 g
Butter	30 g	60 g
Flour	30 g	60 g
Game or beef stock	500 ml	1 ltr
Good quality salt and pepper	To taste	To taste

energy	cal	fat	sat fat	carb	sugar	protein	fibre
1972 kJ	476 kcal	14.3 g	6.5 g	36.2 g	4.8 g	52.4 g	2.6 g

METHOD OF WORK

1   To make the burgers mix the mince, herbs, egg yolks, breadcrumbs and diced onion together, then using your hands and a palette knife shape into burger patties.

2   To produce the lyonnaise sauce: using the butter, sweat the sliced onions for about 15 minutes over a medium heat until golden.

3   Add the flour to the onions and cook the flour out for approximately 2 minutes before slowly adding the stock to form a sauce.

4   Pan fry, grill or bake the patties and serve together with the lyonnaise sauce.

Grilled 'tornedos' of venison *with pan-fried foie gras*

Ingredients	Makes approximately 4 portions	Makes approximately 10 portions
Venison loin steaks	4	10
Foie gras	About 4 slices 50 g	About 10 slices 50 g
Wild mushroom	250 g	750 g
Game or good beef jus	150 ml	500 ml
Madeira	10 ml	50 ml
Good quality salt and pepper	To taste	To taste

energy	cal	fat	sat fat	carb	sugar	protein	fibre
1681 kJ	402 kcal	22.7 g	6.3 g	2.0 g	1.0 g	46.0 g	1.5 g

METHOD OF WORK

1   Sauté the wild mushrooms and flambé with the Madeira until golden and softened. Add to a saucepan with the jus and reduce until thickened.

2   Season the steaks and rub with a little oil, then grill to medium or however liked and allow to rest.

3   Very quickly in a hot pan, fry the foie gras slices until golden on each side.

4   To serve, place the steak onto the plate topped with foie gras, spoon the sauce and mushrooms around.

CHEF'S TIP   Semi freeze the foie gras in a freezer or store in a fridge until the very second it is needed to help keep its shape as it will go very soft quickly which will make it impossible to fry.

This chilling process will help retain the shape and help reduce wastage.

Spiced tempura quail breasts with chilli dipping jam

Ingredients	Makes approximately 4 portions	Makes approximately 10 portions
Quail breast	12	30
Chilli powder	1 tsp	2 tsp
Soft flour	50 g	125 g
Rice flour	50 g	125 g
Corn flour	50 g	125 g
Egg whites	3	6
Iced sparkling water	500 ml	1 ltr
Red chilli	1	2
Honey	30 ml	90 ml
White wine	90 ml	220 ml
Good quality salt and pepper	To taste	To taste
Julienne of vegetables		

energy	cal	fat	sat fat	carb	sugar	protein	fibre
2369 kJ	564 kcal	22.5 g	6.1 g	42.0 g	10.7 g	43.7 g	2.1 g

METHOD OF WORK

To make the batter:

1   In a bowl combine all the flours together with the chilli powder and salt.

2   Whisk in the sparkling water to form a smooth batter.

3   Whisk the egg whites to form stiff peaks and fold into the batter.

To make chilli dipping jam:

4   In a small saucepan sweat the diced red chilli before adding the wine and honey and then reduce until slightly thickened.

To finish:

5   Season the breasts and pass through flour and tempura batter. Deep fry until the batter is crispy and golden.

6   Serve the deep fried tempura coated breasts with julienne of vegetables and chilli dipping jam.

CHEF'S TIP Not only is quail a very delicate tasty bird but they also produce excellent quality eggs.
   Try this dish with the addition of a soft poached quail egg.

Guest Chef

Ingredients — Makes 1 portion

Ingredients	Makes 1 portion
Comice pear, peeled and cored, stalk left on	1
Red wine	100 ml
Sugar	1 tblspn
Cinnamon stick	1
Loin of Brecon venison, trimmed	150 g
Salt and freshly ground black pepper	To taste
Madeira jus	35 ml
Knob of butter	1
Parsnips, peeled	2
Vegetable oil for frying	250 ml
Cream	1 tblspn
Rosemary	1 sprig
Beetroot, cooked	1 medium
Thyme	1 sprig
Vine tomatoes	4
Red potatoes	2

Pan roasted loin of shire venison with poached Penderyn pear, parsnip purée, leek and potato cake with roasted beetroot, vine tomatoes and parsnip crisp

Chef: Tony Burgoyne
Centre: Coleg, Powys Newtown

In this recipe I have used Brecon venison from a local wild game centre.

METHOD OF WORK

1 Place the prepared pear into a pan with red wine, sugar and the cinnamon stick, bring to the boil and simmer until the pear is soft, remove from wine and let it drain, then set aside.

2 Preheat the oven to 200 °C (Gas Mark 6).

3 Season the venison with salt and the freshly ground pepper and rub with the olive oil.

4 Heat an oven proof frying pan until hot, put in the venison and sear briefly.

5 Top the venison with either kitchen foil or butter paper and roast in the oven for 6 mins, turning over halfway through.

6 Foil the beetroot then place in oven and roast.

7 Remove the venison from the pan and allow to rest. Add the Madeira jus and butter to the venison pan to scrape the sediment from the pan.

8 Boil the parsnips until tender: drain.

9 Take one parsnip and cut into slithers lengthways. Heat the oil for deep frying in a deep fat-fryer or wok and deep-fry the parsnips slivers until golden. Remove and drain on kitchen paper.

10 Steam the leeks until tender, season to taste.

11 Blitz the other parsnips until smooth, add the cream and season with salt and freshly ground pepper.

12 Boil and cream the potatoes, add the leeks and season. Make into cakes and sauté until brown on both sides.

13 Roast off vine tomatoes in the oven.

14 Gently warm the Madeira jus.

15 To serve: Place the potato cake onto a plate, arrange the sliced venison in a fan by the cake, fan the pear, add vine tomatoes and parsnip purée.

16 Drizzle the jus around the plate and garnish with the rosemary, thyme and the deep-fried parsnip crisp.

Meat and offal

10

NVQ

Unit 2FC3 Prepare, cook and finish meat dishes

Unit 2FPC6 Preparation and cooking of offal dishes

VRQ

Unit 209 Prepare and cook meat and offal

Recipes

BEEF

Brown beef stew   356

Chilli con carne   357

Steak and kidney pudding   357

Steak and kidney pie   358

Boiled salt beef with carrots and
   dumplings   358

Braised beef in beer   359

Beef stroganoff   359

Stir fried beef with oyster sauce   360

Italian meatballs with pepperonata   361

Yorkshire pudding   362

Roast beef and Yorkshire pudding   362

Beef goulash   363

Mexican beef fajitas   363

Beef bourguignon   364

Grilled steaks and their garnishes   364

LAMB

Pasty   368

Lancashire hotpot   368

Mixed grill   369

Navarin of lamb   369

Roast leg of lamb   370

Shepherd's pie   370

PORK

Roast pork   371

Boiled gammon with parsley
   sauce   371

Toad in the hole   372

Pork cutlets with cranberries   372

VEAL

Escalope of veal cordon bleu   373

Blanquette of veal   373

CALVES' OFFAL

Calve's liver stroganoff   381

Calve's sweetbread fricassee with
   whisky and wholegrain mustard   382

LAMB'S OFFAL

Lamb's liver with balsamic-glazed
    onions and salt-roasted walnuts   383
Lamb sweetbreads pan fried with
    rosemary and lemon butter   384

PORK OFFAL

Marinated pork kidney and chorizo
    skewers   384

CHICKEN OFFAL

Chicken liver stir fry   385

ONLINE RECIPES

LEARNER SUPPORT

Lamb meatballs with spaghetti
Moussaka
Barbecued baby back ribs
Veal saltimbocca with grain
    mustard mash
Lamb cutlets Milanese
Pig liver escalopes stuffed with
    lemon and caper butter
Ox liver and pancetta hotpot

LEARNING OBJECTIVES

The aim of this unit is to enable the candidate to develop skills and implement knowledge in the preparation and cookery principles of basic meat and offal dishes. This will also include materials, ingredients and equipment.

At the end of this chapter you will be able to:

● Demonstrate a range of skills related to the preparation of meat and offal.

● Demonstrate cookery skills using meat or offal as the main ingredient.

● Identify quality points of beef, lamb, pork, various offal items and dishes.

● List health and safety regulations relating to the preparation, cooking and storage of meat, meat dishes, and all types of offal, both raw and cooked.

● Identify the different cuts of meat and relate appropriate cookery methods for them.

● Identify each variety of offal and its finished dish.

● Identify healthy options with the preparation and cookery of meat and offal dishes.

Introduction to meat

Meat for the catering industry is the flesh of any animal reared for the table, mostly beef, pork and lamb.

There have been few societies in history that haven't recorded meat in their diet. In relative terms vegetarianism is a recent phenomena. Meat is a rich source of high-quality protein. Historically it has been an important factor in the nutritional requirements of humans.

What is meat?

Meat has three distinctive parts: muscle, fat and connective tissue.

Muscle

Most of the meat we consume is the muscle of the animal. The fat is usually trimmed to lessen calorific intake and lower the consumption of saturated fats (a major factor in high cholesterol levels).

Muscle fibres are made up of long, thin threads that are not usually visible. In themselves they are not strong enough to do the work, so they are gathered in bundles similar to ropes. A sheath of connective tissue holds the bundles together, adding even greater strength. Muscle fibres split easily along the grain but not across. That is why we carve across the grain with a sharp knife, allowing the customer to easily cut the meat with a dinner knife.

Some muscles do more work than others, making the fibres thicker and requiring them to be cooked for a longer period of time than the more tender and fine-fibred muscles. Leg and neck muscles do most work whereas loin muscles are there mainly to protect the backbone. (See the usage charts and anatomical diagrams, see pages 345, 348, 352 and 354.) Hard-working muscles are more flavourful than the finer textured muscles, so the chef must take this into consideration when deciding upon cooking techniques.

Fat

If you completely remove all traces of fat from meat it is almost impossible to detect the true characteristics of the type of meat that is being eaten. If you add minced pork fat into very lean minced beef it will taste like pork and not beef. The flavour is in the fat and even in our culture of almost zero fat consumption we still need a vestige of fat to add flavour, succulence and necessary nutrition.

Very lean meat dishes usually have added fat, for example by braising beef topside and adding cheese and ham to pork escalope dishes.

There are three types of fat:

1 Subcutaneous: fat that is under the skin and surrounds the muscle.

2 Intermuscular: fat that is in-between muscles.

3 Intramuscular: fat that is inside the muscle (marbling).

Subcutaneous fat

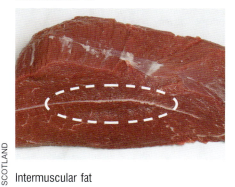

Intermuscular fat

Intramuscular fat (marbling)

IMAGES COURTESY OF QUALITY MEAT SCOTLAND

Connective tissue

There are three types of tissue that can be described as connective tissue:

1 **Collagen**, which converts to gelatine when it is cooked for a long period of time. It is essential when making clarifications for consommés. It is also known as white connective tissue.

2 **Elastin**.

3 **Reticulin**.

Both elastin and reticulin remain tough no matter how long they are cooked.

Meat ageing

The **ageing** of meat is a complex series of chemical processes that alter fats and proteins, develop flavour compounds, and tenderize the meat.

If you cooked the meat of a freshly slaughtered animal it would be tough and flavourless, practically inedible, because muscles tighten after slaughter and do not begin to relax for 24 hours, but then continue to relax for about six days.

Beef should be aged for at least 10 days and up to 42 days, although after 21 days the benefits of continued ageing are negligible. Mutton should be aged for one week. Lamb and pork need little ageing because they are from young animals with little fat and connective tissue.

There are two types of ageing:

1 *Dry ageing* takes place in refrigerators at 1–2 °C with controlled humidity. The meat is usually hung to allow air to circulate. If the meat is hung by the aitch-bone, the resultant stretching of the muscles leads to greater tenderness. This is not a very common practice due to the extra space that is required in the refrigerators.

2 *Wet ageing* takes place in vacuum pouches but has the disadvantages of producing a lower intensity of flavour and increased expense of storage.

Purchasing meat and offal

There are so many benefits to buying meat locally that it seems a terrible shame to do anything else.

Although many people say that they cannot buy meat locally because it is too expensive, this really isn't the case. Of course, if you compare deals on intensively reared animals from the supermarket with the very best organic, free range animals from your local farm shop, the local meat will be far more expensive.

If you take into consideration the superior taste of the local meat, the treatment of the animal, the sustainability and the ecological impact, there really is no competition.

SOURCING 'The traceability of our produce is achieved by a system of labels and barcodes on each carcass, from when it arrives from the abattoir. The coding system, is maintained as it passes through the various stages of processing.'

This is a quote identifying how the traceability system is being used to ensure quality and enhance locally used products.

Use this web link to discover more:
http://www.graigfarm.co.uk

Block scraper, steel butcher's knives, a boning knife and meat bat

Storing meat and offal

Meat should always be covered by plastic wrap when stored in a refrigerator to help prevent oxidation of protein. The temperature should be 1–4 °C and meat should always be used as quickly as possible. Frozen meat should be covered to prevent freezer burn and kept at –18 °C. The thawing of meat should take place in a refrigerator on the bottom shelf in a tray. This will prevent liquid and blood from leaking uncontrollably.

Raw meat should always be stored at the bottom, any cooked food may be stored above if this is the only option available – this will prevent micro biological cross-contamination.

Butcher's saw, chain mail glove and cut proof glove

VIDEO CLIP Organizing a professional butchery department.

VIDEO CLIP Inside Smithfield meat market.

Equipment

When preparing meat all equipment must be cleaned and sprayed with an antibacterial spray after each use. While the meat itself may not be contaminated, it is an ideal medium in which pathogens can multiply. All manufacturer safety guidelines must always be followed. It is recommended that a chain mail or cut-proof glove be worn when cutting meat.

HEALTH & SAFETY A chain mail glove will prevent a trainee from accidentally cutting their hands: this is also true for a more experienced chef/butcher who will be producing large quantities.

Quality

The idea of first and second quality meat is an incorrect assumption. The quality of meat is directly related to the cookery method. If a tender fillet steak is stewed for two hours it will completely disintegrate in the sauce, if chuck beef is used it will be tender and succulent. On the other hand if you grilled the chuck beef it would be almost impossible to chew. Careful consideration should be made when marrying cookery techniques and cuts of meat. Prime cuts of meat are the more tender muscles that lend themselves to dry cookery methods, such as frying and grilling.

Cuts of beef

Beef varies remarkably in taste and quality depending on the age, breed, diet, lifestyle, slaughter and processing of the animal. So it's wise to choose and cook your meat carefully and to tailor the cut you buy to the dish you want to cook. Aberdeen Angus is a well-known good-quality breed of beef, but there are dozens of other breeds native to Britain or established for centuries. Native breeds include the Welsh Black, Highland, Lincoln Red, South Devon, Sussex and Hereford. Rare British breeds cover the Irish Moiled, Beef

Shorthorn, Belted and Black Galloways, Red Poll, White Park, British White, Longhorn, Gloucester and Dexter.

The different cuts of beef that are available are shown below.

Beef hindquarter

BREAKDOWN OF A HINDQUARTER OF BEEF

JOINT	USE	RECIPE EXAMPLES	AVERAGE WEIGHT
1 Fillet	Grilling, roasting, frying	Page 359	3–3.5 kg
2 Sirloin	Grilling, roasting, frying	Page 360	12–14 kg
3 Wing rib	Grilling, roasting, frying	Page 362	3–4 kg
4 Thin flank	Braising, stewing	Page 361	8–10 kg
5 Rump	Frying, roasting, braising		10 kg
6 Topside	Braising, stewing, slow roasting	Page 359	9–10 kg
7 Thick flank	Braising, stewing	Page 356	10–11 kg
8 Silverside	Pickling, boiling	Page 358	12–14 kg
9 Shin	Consommé, braising		6–7 kg
10 Kidney	Pies, puddings	Page 359	1–2 kg
11 Fat (suet)	Suet pastry, rendering	Page 359	5–6 kg

As a guide beef should be cooked:

55°C Rare

63°C Medium rare

68°C Medium

75°C+ Well done

These temperatures are ideal for more tender cuts such as fillet, sirloin, wing rib and rump.

The other cuts require longer cooking to allow the muscles to relax and become softer and more digestible.

BREAKDOWN ON A HINDQUARTER OF BEEF

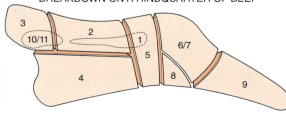

IMAGE COURTESY OF QUALITY MEAT SCOTLAND

QUALITY POINTS

- The muscle should be red with slight marbling.
- The fat should be creamy in colour and brittle.

- There should be a pleasant aroma that shows no signs of rancidity.
- The lean meat should not feel sticky to the touch.

Beef forequarter

Average weight 75–80 kg

BREAKDOWN OF A FOREQUARTER OF BEEF

JOINT	USE	RECIPE EXAMPLE	AVERAGE WEIGHT
1 Fore rib	Roast, grilling, frying	Page 362	6.5 kg
2 Middle rib	Braising, roasting	Page 362	8.5 kg
3 Chuck rib	Stewing, braising	Page 357	13 kg
4 Sticking piece	Stewing, mincing	Page 361	7 kg
5 Plate	Stewing, mincing, boiling		8.5 kg
6 Brisket	Brining, boiling		16 kg
7 Leg of mutton cut	Braising steaks, paupiettes, stew, mince	Page 359	9 kg
8 Shin	Clarification, mince		5 kg

BREAKDOWN ON A FOREQUARTER OF BEEF

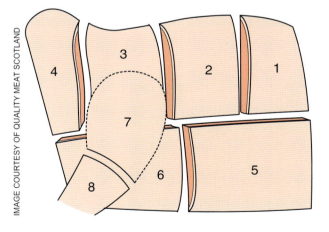

IMAGE COURTESY OF QUALITY MEAT SCOTLAND

CHEF'S TIP LMC refers to the leg of mutton cut of beef. There can be confusion with telesales people and sometimes a leg of mutton will be delivered. Use the term 'LMC beef' to overcome this confusion.

Step-by-step: Preparation of a leg of mutton cut of beef into steaks and carbonnade

1. Cut away the leg of mutton cut (LMC) of all silver gristle and fat.

2. Remove thin muscle.

3. Remove the sinew from the secondary muscle.

4. The main and secondary muscle.

5. Slice the main muscle into steaks.

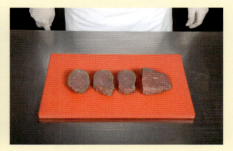

6. The sliced steaks.

7. Slice the secondary muscle into carbonnade.

8. Continue to slice the secondary muscle into carbonnade.

9. Bat out carbonnade between a vacuum pack bag.

10. A carbonnade steak.

Step-by-step: Preparation of paupiettes of beef

1. Arrange the filling (e.g. sausage meat) onto the carbonnade steak as shown.

2. Spread the filling along the length of the steak leaving a gap at the top.

3. Roll the steak up tightly as shown.

4. Once rolled place the steak inside cling film and roll up to produce a sausage shape, twist the ends and tie with a knot to secure: the paupiette can now be steamed until a core temperature of 70 °C for two minutes is achieved.

> **CHEF'S TIP** Once the beef is cooked and rested, remove from the cling film and roll in foaming butter, this will give a golden colour and will add additional flavour.

Veal

Veal is the meat from milk-fed calves that are slaughtered at around four months. The meat is always very pale in colour, but a calf of only two-and-a-half months is highly prized for its white flesh. The meat is usually from the male offspring of dairy cattle, as they would not make high quality beef. There is a growing fondness for 'pink' or 'rose' veal that has had a little time to graze before slaughter, this gives a deeper flavour than the purely milk fed variety.

Almost all the joints of veal are tender and can be cooked in a short time. It is by nature a very lean meat, which lends itself to cream sauces, the addition of cheese and cooking using barriers of flour, eggs or pané.

Quality points

- The fat is white, pleasant to smell and mainly situated around the kidneys.

- The muscles should not feel sticky to the touch.

- The flesh is very lean and a pale pink colour except when a rose colour is specifically ordered.

BREAKDOWN OF A SIDE OF VEAL

JOINT	USE	RECIPE EXAMPLE	AVERAGE WEIGHT
1 Scrag	Stews, mince		1.25 kg
2 Neck	Braising, stew mince		1.5 kg
3 Best end	Roasting, pot roasting, cutlets, frying		1.5 kg
4 Loin	Roast, grilling, frying		1.5 kg
5 Rump	Roast, grilling, frying	Veal saltimbocca with grain mustard mash (online)	1 kg
6 Leg	Pot roast, frying, grilling	Page 373	4 kg
7 Knuckle/ shank	Mince, stew, osso bucco		2 kg
8 Shoulder	Braising, stewing, forcemeats	Page 373	2.5 kg
9 Breast	Stewing, braising		2 kg

BREAKDOWN OF A SIDE OF LAMB/MUTTON

JOINT	USES	RECIPE EXAMPLE	AVERAGE WEIGHT
1 Scrag	Stewing, broths	Moussaka (online)	1 kg
2 Middle neck	Stewing	Lamb meatballs with spaghetti (online)	2 kg
3 Shoulder	Roasting, stewing	Page 368	2 × 2 kg
4 Best end	Roasting, grilling, frying (cutlets, racks)	Lamb cutlets Milanese (online)	2 kg
5 Saddle	Roast, frying, grilling (chops, cannon, filet mignon)		2 kg
6 Rump	Braising, roast		2 kg
7 Breast	Slow roasting, stewing, steaming	Page 368	2 kg
8 Leg	Roasting, frying (steaks), braising (shanks)	Page 370	2 × 2.5 kg

IMAGE COURTESY OF QUALITY MEAT SCOTLAND

BREAKDOWN OF A SIDE OF VEAL

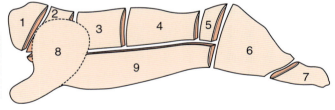

BREAKDOWN OF A SIDE OF LAMB/MUTTON

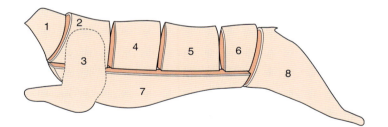

WEB LINK All animals for the professional culinary market, including veal calves, should have a good standard of living and welfare. Use this web link to research what is meant by animal welfare: http://www.meateat.co.uk/why-british-veal-more-ethical-choice.html

Lamb and mutton

Lamb is the meat from farmed sheep less than 12 months old. Over the age of 12 months the meat is technically described as hoggett. Over 24 months it is mutton. The flesh can vary in colour and flavour depending on the breed, feeding regime and age of slaughter.

Quality points

- The lean flesh should be a ruddy red colour.
- The fat should be evenly distributed, dry to the touch and flaky in texture.
- The smell of lamb is pleasing and characteristic to the animal.
- The bones should be porous and have a small degree of blood present.
- It is important to keep lamb cold when cutting the meat as otherwise the fat becomes greasy and knife handles become slippery.

Step-by-step: Preparation of a shoulder of lamb

1. Shoulder of lamb.

2. Trim excess fat.

3. Trim the end of the shank.

4. Scrape the flesh from the bone.

5. Saw the end of the bone.

6. Cut along the shoulder blade.

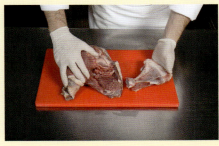

7. Pull out the shoulder blade.

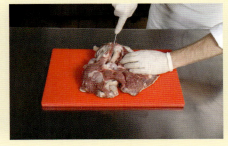

8. Cut along the humerus bone.

9. Remove the humerus bone.

10. Rub the marinade into the flesh of the boned shoulder of lamb.

11. Tie the shoulder of lamb at 2 cm intervals.

12. The completed stuffed and tied shoulder of lamb.

TASK Create a chart with a range of different marinades that can be used for lamb, for example: rosemary, garlic and olive oil or coriander, garlic, ginger, lemon grass and turmeric paste.

VIDEO CLIP Technique producing a leg of lamb for roasting.

Step-by-step: Preparation of a leg of lamb

1. Cut around the knuckle as shown in the middle of the muscle.

2. Use the boning knife to remove all flesh and sinew from the bone.

3. Cut through the bone cleanly using a saw.

4. Carefully remove the aitch bone – the bone is shaped like this:

5. The aitch bone removed.

6. Tie the leg in 2 cm intervals.

Simply follow the outline as indicated. The additional point is situated within the leg out of sight: use the knife to feel this.

7. Score the leg of lamb: creating holes which can be stuffed with aromatics such as rosemary and garlic.

8. The completed stuffed, boned and tied leg of lamb ready for roasting.

Step-by-step: Preparation of a rack of lamb

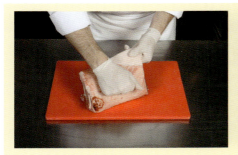

1. Removing the bark from the outside, exposing the fat.

2. Turn the lamb over to expose the bones, using a small saw cut along the back bone.

3. The back bone has been removed exposing the flesh.

4. Score along the top end of the fat down to the bones underneath, approximately one third of the length of the bones.

5. This shows the scored line of fat removed from the bones.

6. Scrape any excess fat or flesh from the bones.

7. Holding the rack firmly peel the fat and sinew backwards away from the bones.

8. Trim the fat and sinew away from the back of the rack of lamb and discard, leaving the bones clean.

9. Laying the rack of lamb fat side down, trim the fat and sinew away from the base.

10. The trimmed flesh is now visible.

11. Tie the rack of lamb between each set of bones.

12. Cut in half to produce a 3–4 bone rack as required.

Pork

Pork is the meat from pigs which are usually slaughtered between 10 and 12 months old. Intensively farmed pigs are usually quite large for their age and the main breeds for this type of farming are Danish Landrace, Belgian Pietrain and Western Whites. However, older breeds are now becoming more popular using less intensive methods of farming, such as Gloucester Old Spot and Tamworth.

BREAKDOWN OF A SIDE OF PORK

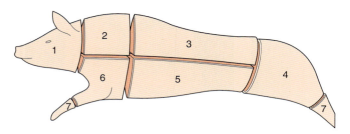

TASK A common phrase is: 'the only thing you cannot eat on a pig is the squeal'.

List the different parts of a pig then create two seasonal dishes for each part.

Try to pay attention to the accompanying ingredients so they are seasonal and sustainable.

WEB LINK Use the following web link for guidance: http://eatseasonably.co.uk

BREAKDOWN OF A SIDE OF PORK

JOINT	USES	RECIPE EXAMPLE	AVERAGE WEIGHT
1 Head	Brawn, stuffing, buffet centre pieces, this is usually boned and pressed by the butcher		4 kg
2 Spare rib	Sausages, stewing	Barbecued baby back ribs (online)	2 kg
3 Loin	Frying (chops), grilling, roasting, sauté	Page 372	5 kg
4 Leg	Roasting, frying, stir-frying, boiling	Page 371	4 kg
5 Belly	Braising, curing, boiling, stuffing, roasting		3 kg
6 Shoulder	Sausages, pies stewing, roasting, pies	Page 372	3 kg
7 Trotters	Boiling, stocks The preparation techniques involve boiling for 4–5 minutes then removing and scraping the hairs off with the back of a knife. The trotters can then be split in half and used as required.		0.5 kg

Step-by-step: Preparation of a rolled belly of pork

1. Belly of pork.

2. Singeing hairs.

3. Uncovering the floating ribs.

4. Removing the floating ribs.

5. Trimmed belly of pork with all bones removed.

6. Rubbing in the marinade.

7. Rolling the marinated belly of pork.

8. The rolled and tied pork belly.

Step-by-step: Preparation of a tenderloin of pork

1. Trim any fat and sinew away from the tenderloin.

2. Trim the sides of the tenderloin to leave a smooth edge.

3. Place the knife under the sinew and lift slightly, run the knife along to remove the sinew without touching the flesh.

4. The tenderloin can be sliced into medallions or into a piece suitable for roasting as shown. the tail piece (top right) can be cut into strips which are used for dishes such as stroganoff.

5. Split the tail end length ways.

6. Cut each piece into neat strips.

7. From left – medallions, roasting piece and strips.

Quality points

- Pork should have pale pink flesh with a fine texture.
- Skin should be free of bristle and not wet to the touch.
- There should be a covering of fat that is not excessive.
- The bones should be small and pink.
- There should not be excessive connective tissue.

Bacon

The meat from the pig to produce bacon is cured in salt brine or smoked. The cured bacon is commonly referred to as green bacon. The flesh should be firm to the touch and a dark pink colour with a slightly creamy fat colour, unless it has been smoked whereby the fat colour will have a light caramel colour to it.

BREAKDOWN OF A SIDE OF BACON

JOINT	USES	RECIPE EXAMPLE	AVERAGE WEIGHT
1 Gammon	Boiling, grilling (gammon steaks)	Page 371	7–8 kg
2 Back	Grilling, frying		9–10 kg
3 Collar	Boiling		4–5 kg
4 Hock	Boiling		4–5 kg
5 Belly	Boiling, grilling		4–5 kg

BREAKDOWN OF A SIDE OF BACON

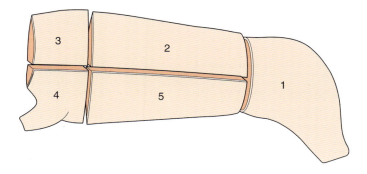

QUALITY POINTS

- The lean muscle should be pink, firm and not sticky to the touch.

- The fat should be white and not excessive.

- The rind must be free from wrinkles and not sticky.

- The bacon in general should not feel wet or sticky to the touch.

TASK There are numerous types of bacon both in relation to the cuts and the techniques used.

Create a chart that shows the different parts of the meat used as well as the techniques used to produce it.

TEST YOURSELF

1 What is the difference between gammon and pork?

2 List the joints of pork suitable for roasting.

3 What can a belly of pork be used for?

4 How many primary cuts are in a side of pork?

5 What are the average weights of pigs' trotters?

6 What are the two methods to produce bacon from pork?

7 List the joints suitable for frying.

8 List two breeds of pig indigenous to the UK.

9 List three quality points when receiving beef.

10 What are the three types of fat called associated with meat.

11 Which of the below converts to gelatine when cooked for long periods:

elastin, collagen, reticulin?

12 What are the two types of ageing called?

13 How many primary cuts are in a side of veal?

14 Which of the following lamb/mutton cuts are not suitable for stewing:

scrag, shoulder, leg?

15 Lamb is farmed from sheep less than how many months old:

10 months, 11 months, 12 months?

Recipes

Beef

Brown beef stew

Ingredients	4 portions	10 portions
Diced chuck beef	600 g	1.5 kg
Carrots	80 g	200 g
Celery	1 stick	2 sticks
Onion	80 g	200 g
Bouquet garni	1 small	1 large
Garlic	1 clove	2–3 cloves
Oil	40 ml	100 ml
Flour	40 g	100 g
Brown beef stock	800 ml	2 ltr
Tomato purée	40 g	100 g
Good quality salt and white pepper	To taste	To taste

energy	cal	fat	sat fat	carb	sugar	protein	fibre
2257 kJ	539 kcal	29.5 g	8.1 g	11.8 g	3.5 g	56.9 g	1.6 g

METHOD OF WORK

1   Remove sinews and excess fat from the beef and cut into 2 cm dice.
2   Peel and chop the carrot, onion, celery and garlic into a large dice.
3   Heat the oil in a pan and sear the meat until brown on all sides.
4   Add the mirepoix and continue to brown.
5   Add the flour and cook for 1–2 minutes, remove from the heat and allow to cool slightly.
6   Add the tomato purée and stock and stir with a wooden spoon or spatula. Ensure that there are no lumps then add the bouquet garni, season and cover with a lid.
7   Simmer gently for 2–2½ hours.
8   Skim any fat from the surface and remove the meat to a clean pan.
9   Pass the sauce onto the meat.
10 Correct the seasoning and serve with turned new potatoes or appropriate garnish.

CHEF'S TIP   The browning of the meat will give additional colour and flavour to the dish. Caution should be take not to burn the meat as this will taint the overall end product.

Chilli con carne

Ingredients	4 portions	10 portions
Chuck beef	600 g	1.5 kg
Onions	80 g	200 g
Chillies	2	5
Garlic cloves	2	5
Canned tomatoes	400 g	1 kg
Canned red kidney beans	200 g	500 g
Brown beef stock (approximately)	200 ml	500 ml
Sugar	½ tsp	2 tsp
Good quality salt and black pepper	To taste	To taste
Oil	40 ml	100 ml

energy	cal	fat	sat fat	carb	sugar	protein	fibre
1560 kJ	372 kcal	18.1 g	3.8 g	12.6 g	4.8 g	39.9 g	2.1 g

METHOD OF WORK

1   Trim the beef of excess fat and connective tissue, cut into large dice and pass through a medium plate of a mincer.

2   Crush the garlic, chop the onion and chillies. Fry the beef in the oil stirring continuously to break it up.

3   Add the onions, garlic and chillies. Continue to cook until they are well sweated.

4   Add the sugar, red kidney beans tomatoes and enough stock to moisten.

5   Bring to the boil and simmer very gently for 1–2 hours. Add more stock when necessary and skim.

6   Serve with plain boiled rice and flour tortillas.

HEALTHY OPTION Instead of frying the beef in oil use the natural fat present in the meat.

   If any excess fat is produced this can be drained off and discarded.

Steak and kidney pudding

Ingredients	4 portions	10 portions
Diced chuck beef	500 g	1.25 kg
Ox kidney	100 g	250 g
Worcestershire sauce	To taste	To taste
Onion (chopped)	1	2–3
Flour	40 g	100 g
Beef stock	160 ml	400 ml
Good quality salt and white pepper	To taste	To taste
Suet paste (see page 471)	300 g	750 g

energy	cal	fat	sat fat	carb	sugar	protein	fibre
2684 kJ	641 kcal	29.1 g	14.6 g	44.5 g	6.4 g	51.0 g	2.4 g

METHOD OF WORK

1   Remove the core from the kidney and dice.

2   Line a greased pudding basin with three quarters of the paste.

3   Mix the remainder of the ingredients and place in the bowl.

4   Roll out the remainder of the paste, moisten the paste in the basin and cover.

5   Cover with a lid of cling film reinforced with tin foil.

6   Steam for 3–4 hours.

7   Allow to rest for 30 minutes in a warm place then turn out onto a serving dish and serve.

CHEF'S TIP Vegetable suet can be used as a substitute for beef suet.

Steak and kidney pie

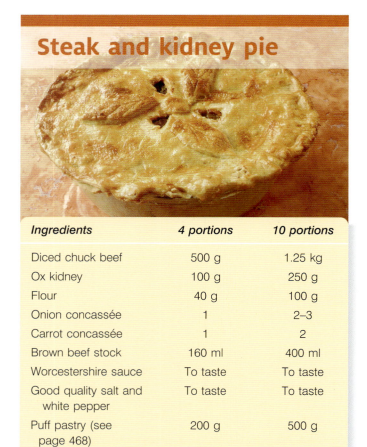

Ingredients	4 portions	10 portions
Diced chuck beef	500 g	1.25 kg
Ox kidney	100 g	250 g
Flour	40 g	100 g
Onion concassée	1	2–3
Carrot concassée	1	2
Brown beef stock	160 ml	400 ml
Worcestershire sauce	To taste	To taste
Good quality salt and white pepper	To taste	To taste
Puff pastry (see page 468)	200 g	500 g

energy	cal	fat	sat fat	carb	sugar	protein	fibre
1883 kJ	448 kcal	27.9 g	6.7 g	26.9 g	3.8 g	51.4 g	2.9 g

METHOD OF WORK

1 Dust the beef with the flour, sear in the oil and allow to cool.
2 Mix with the remainder of the ingredients and place in a pie dish that allows the mixture to come almost to the top.
3 Roll out the pastry and put onto the moistened dish.
4 Allow to rest in the refrigerator for 2–3 hours.
5 Egg wash and place in an oven at 175 °C for 15 minutes until the pastry has begun to colour.
6 Reduce the temperature to 130 °C and continue to cook for a further 2 hours.
7 Clean the rim of the pie dish and serve.

CHEF'S TIP The filling can be precooked and chilled to allow the pies to be cooked in an à la carte situation.

Boiled salt beef with carrots and dumplings

Ingredients	4 portions	10 portions
Salted silverside of beef	800 g	2 kg
Small carrots	8	20
Onions sliced	8	20
Suet paste (see page 471)	40 g	1 kg
Good quality salt and white pepper	To taste	To taste

energy	cal	fat	sat fat	carb	sugar	protein	fibre
2207 kJ	524 kcal	17.7 g	6.7 g	28.3 g	19.4 g	64.9 g	9.4 g

METHOD OF WORK

1 Place the meat in cold water and bring to the boil.
2 Remove to a clean pan and cover with some more clean water.
3 Bring to the boil again and simmer for 1½ hours.
4 Add the carrots and sliced onions then simmer for a further 20 minutes.
5 Divide the suet paste into even pieces and add to the cooking liquor.
6 Simmer for a further 20 minutes.
7 Serve carved onto a plate or service dish garnished with the vegetables and dumplings.

CHEF'S TIP The salt beef can be soaked overnight in cold water to remove excess salt. This cuts down on the cooking time.

Braised beef in beer
and onions (Carbonnade of beef)

Ingredients	4 portions	10 portions
Lean beef (topside or trimmed leg of mutton cut)	600 g	1.5 kg
Sliced onions	300 g	750 g
Brown beef stock	400 ml	2 ltrs
Ale	300 ml	750 ml
Flour	40 g	100 g
Sugar	10 g	25 g
Oil		
Good quality salt and white pepper	To taste	To taste

energy	cal	fat	sat fat	carb	sugar	protein	fibre
1786 kJ	426 kcal	21.6 g	4.5 g	15.8 g	7.2 g	39.7 g	1.5 g

METHOD OF WORK

1 Cut the meat into thin slices and bat out to 2 mm in thickness.
2 Dust the beef in flour and season and beat it in with the back of a knife.
3 Fry quickly in hot fat and place in a casserole.
4 Add the onions to the pan and sauté to a light brown colour.
5 Add to the beef with the beer and stock.
6 Cover and cook in the oven for approximately 1½ hours.
7 Serve with appropriate garnish.

CHEF'S TIP Rump beef or LMC beef are ideal for this dish as they have very little fat and no gristle.

Beef stroganoff

Ingredients	4 portions	10 portions
Beef fillet (tail)	600 g	1.5 kg
Shallots	1	2
Button mushrooms	100 g	250 g
Butter	50 g	125 g
Brandy	20 ml	100 ml
Double cream	150 ml	350 ml
Lemon	½	1½
Good quality salt and white pepper	To taste	To taste
Pilaff rice (see page 228)	4 portions	10 portions
Paprika	To taste	To taste

energy	cal	fat	sat fat	carb	sugar	protein	fibre
3153 kJ	760 kcal	58.2 g	31.7 g	10.9 g	1.8 g	44.6 g	1.4 g

METHOD OF WORK

1 Cut the beef into fingers 4 cm x ½ cm, roll them in paprika.
2 Cut the shallots into a fine brunoise and finely slice the mushrooms.
3 Heat the butter in a sauté pan until foaming but not browning.
4 Add the beef and sauté briskly over a high heat.
5 Add the shallots and mushrooms and continue to cook for 1 min. Season.
6 Add the brandy and set alight. When the flames have gone add the cream.
7 Allow the cream to come to the boil and add the lemon juice.
8 Serve with pilaff rice.

Stir fried beef with oyster sauce

Ingredients	4 portions	10 portions
Oyster sauce marinade		
Soy sauce	1 tblspn	2 tblspn
White wine	2 tsp	2 tblspn
Salt	To taste	To taste
Sugar	1 tsp	1 tblspn
Bicarbonate of soda	¼ tsp	½ tsp
Ground black pepper	¼ tsp	½ tsp
Water	1 tblspn	2 tblspn
Cornflour	2 tsp	2 tblspn
Oil	2 tblspn	4 tblspn
The beef		
Lean beef	400 g	1 kg
Oyster sauce	2 tblspn	4 tblspn
Salt	To taste	To taste
Sugar	1 tsp	1 tblspn
Spring onions	2	4–5

energy	cal	fat	sat fat	carb	sugar	protein	fibre
1242 kJ	297 kcal	16.5 g	4.4 g	8.6 g	4.3 g	28.8 g	0.8 g

METHOD OF WORK

1. Mix all the ingredients for the marinade together.
2. Slice the meat into thin slices and then into ribbons, add to the marinade and marinate for 4–6 hours.
3. Remove from the marinade and **stir fry** in a hot wok for 1 minute.
4. Pour off the oil and add the spring onions, oyster sauce, salt and sugar.
5. Continue to cook for a further 1 minute and serve with braised or boiled rice.

CHEF'S TIP The bicarbonate of soda is used to tenderize the meat, if the meat is left to marinade too long it will become slimy.

Italian meatballs with pepperonata

Ingredients	4 portions	10 portions
Minced beef	400 g	1 kg
Fresh breadcrumbs	50 g	125 g
Finely chopped parma ham	40 g	100 g
Grated parmesan	30 g	75 g
Eggs	2	5
Dried oregano	1 tsp	1 tblspn
Grated nutmeg	Pinch	2 pinches
Smoked paprika	Pinch	2 pinches
Vegetable oil for frying		
Good quality salt and black pepper	To taste	To taste
Pepperonata		
Olive oil	40 ml	100 ml
Sliced onion	80 g	200 g
Sliced red pepper	2	5
Sliced yellow pepper	2	5
Ripe plum tomatoes	4	10
Good quality salt and black pepper	To taste	To taste
Chopped parsley		

energy	cal	fat	sat fat	carb	sugar	protein	fibre
2483 kJ	595 kcal	38.5 g	10.0 g	25.8 g	15.5 g	37.9 g	4.5 g

METHOD OF WORK

1   Place half the breadcrumbs and all the ingredients for the meatballs in a bowl and mix thoroughly.

2   Divide into 16 or 40 equal pieces and shape into smooth balls.

3   Roll the meatballs in the breadcrumbs.

4   Allow to chill for 1–2 hours.

5   Make the pepperonata. Sweat the onion in the oil, add the peppers and continue to cook for 3–4 minutes.

6   Add the spices and herbs and tomatoes.

7   Season, cover with a lid and simmer for 10 minutes.

8   Uncover and reduce until thick.

9   Fry the meat balls in 2 cm of oil, turning frequently until a core temperature of 75 °C has been reached.

10   Serve with the pepperonata.

CHEF'S TIP   Use 50/50 of pork shoulder and chuck beef to get an even more succulent meatball.

SOURCING   It is worthwhile sourcing high quality Hungarian or Polish paprika, as the flavour is much more pungent.

Yorkshire pudding

Ingredients	4 portions	10 portions
Milk	100 ml	250 ml
Eggs	100 ml	250 ml
Flour	100 g	250 g
Good-quality salt and white pepper	To taste	To taste
Oil or beef dripping	100 ml	250 ml

energy	cal	fat	sat fat	carb	sugar	protein	fibre
1490 kJ	359 kcal	28.4 g	2.8 g	20.7 g	1.6 g	6.4 g	0.8 g

METHOD OF WORK

1   Sift the flour and seasoning into a bowl.
2   Combine the eggs and milk.
3   Make a well in the centre of the flour, add the liquids and mix to a light batter.
4   Allow to rest in a refrigerator for at least 1 hour.
5   Pour 25 ml of oil into each of the pudding moulds and place in a hot oven until almost smoking (190 °C).
6   Pour in the batter and place into the oven until well risen and crispy.
7   When the puddings are brown and well risen test by lifting one: if it feels light it is cooked, if not, return to the oven at 130 °C until light and crisp.

CHEF'S TIP   The golden rule for Yorkshire pudding is that the proportions of mixture are the same. It doesn't matter if it is in cups, pints or litres.

Roast beef and Yorkshire pudding

Ingredients	4 portions	10 portions
Sirloin, fillet or rib of beef (allow 150 g per portion off the bone and 200 g on the bone)	800 g	2 kg
Salt and pepper	To taste	To taste
Brown beef stock	160 ml	400 ml
Beef bones	1 kg	2 kg
Watercress	1 bunch	2 bunches
Horseradish sauce	4 portions	10 portions
Yorkshire puddings (see opposite)	4	10

energy	cal	fat	sat fat	carb	sugar	protein	fibre
6851 kJ	1629 kcal	104.2 g	40.6 g	12.5 g	7.4 g	159.6 g	32.4 g

METHOD OF WORK

1   Prepare the beef.
2   Season with salt and pepper.
3   Place the fore rib on the bones in a roasting dish.
4   Place in a hot oven to brown.
5   Turn the heat down to 130 °C and continue to cook until the joint is done as requested. The centre temperature should be:
   55 °C   Rare
   63 °C   Medium rare
   68 °C   Medium
   75 °C+   Well done
6   Remove the meat, cover with tin foil and rest for 20–30 minutes.
7   Pour off the excess fat, remove the bones and place on a hot stove.
8   Allow the sediment to brown taking care not to burn it.
9   Pour on the stock, deglaze the pan and allow to simmer for 10 minutes.
10   Strain into a clean pan, season if necessary and degrease.
11   Carve the meat across the grain accompanied with gravy, horseradish sauce, watercress and Yorkshire puddings.

Beef goulash

Ingredients	4 portions	10 portions
Diced chuck beef	600 g	1.5 kg
Carrots	80 g	200 g
Celery	1 stick	2 sticks
Onion	80 g	200 g
Bouquet garni	1 small	1 large
Garlic	1 clove	2–3 cloves
Oil	40 ml	100 ml
Flour	40 g	100 g
Brown beef stock	800 ml	2 ltr
Tomato purée	40 g	100 g
Paprika	1 tsp	1 tblspn
Gnocchi romaine (see page 206)	4 portions	10 portions
Turned new potatoes		
Good quality salt and white pepper	To taste	To taste

energy	cal	fat	sat fat	carb	sugar	protein	fibre
4994 kJ	1192 kcal	58.4 g	24.0 g	90.3 g	20.4 g	80.9 g	5.2 g

METHOD OF WORK

1   Remove sinews and excess fat from the beef and cut into a 2 cm dice.
2   Peel and chop the carrot, onion, celery and garlic into a large dice.
3   Heat the oil in a pan and sear the meat until brown on all sides.
4   Add the mirepoix and continue to brown.
5   Add the flour and paprika. Cook for 1–2 mins, remove from the heat and allow to cool slightly.
6   Add the tomato purée and stock and stir with a wooden spoon or spatula ensuring that there are no lumps, add the bouquet garni, season and cover with a lid.
7   Simmer gently for 2–2½ hours.
8   Skim any fat from the surface and remove the meat to a clean pan.
9   Pass the sauce onto the meat add the turned new potatoes and allow to cook through.
10   Correct the seasoning and serve accompanied by the gnocchi shaped as required.

Mexican beef fajitas

Ingredients	4 portions	10 portions
Topside beef	400 g	1 kg
Crushed garlic	1 clove	2 cloves
Jalapeno peppers	1	2
Oil	50 ml	125 ml
Dry sherry	40 ml	100 ml
Chilli flakes	1 tsp	1 tblspn
Ground cumin	1 tblspn	2 tblspn
Flour tortilla	4	10
Grated cheese	100 g	250 g
Tomato concassée	100 g	250 g
Shredded iceberg lettuce	100 g	250 g

energy	cal	fat	sat fat	carb	sugar	protein	fibre
1893 kJ	453 kcal	25.5 g	7.8 g	21.4 g	3.2 g	32.9 g	2.4 g

METHOD OF WORK

1   Purée the garlic, jalapenos, chilli flakes, cumin and sherry until smooth.
2   Add the beef, cut into strips, and marinate for 24 hours.
3   Drain the beef and sauté in the oil for 2–3 minutes.
4   Add the marinade and simmer until cooked.
5   Serve in the tortillas with the cheese, lettuce, tomato and salsa verde.

CHEF'S TIP The intensity of this dish relies upon the strength of the chillies. If it is too hot advise your guests to eat some yoghurt to nullify the capsaicin from the chilli.

Beef bourguignon

Ingredients	4 portions	10 portions
Beef	600 g	1.5 kg
Demi glace (see page 130)	400 ml	1 litre
Red wine	200 ml	500 ml
Oil	20 ml	50 ml
Button mushrooms	100 g	250 g
Dry-cured streaky bacon	100 g	250 g
Button onions	100 g	250 g
Good quality salt and white pepper	To taste	To taste
Sugar	Pinch	½ tsp

energy	cal	fat	sat fat	carb	sugar	protein	fibre
2020 kJ	484 kcal	27.9 g	7.1 g	4.2 g	1.7 g	45.7 g	1.3 g

METHOD OF WORK

1   Remove sinews and excess fat from the beef and cut pieces 2 cm × 2 cm × 1 cm.

2   Remove the rind from the bacon and cut into 2 cm dice (lardons).

3   Heat the oil in a pan and sear the meat until brown on all sides.

4   Add the demi glace and red wine and cover with a lid. Simmer gently for approximately 2–2½ hours.

5   Blanch the onions and lardons in boiling water.

6   Fry the bacon (lardons) in a little oil. Add the mushrooms and onions, sprinkle with a pinch of sugar and sauté until cooked, season with salt and pepper.

7   Serve the beef accompanied by the garnish.

Grilled steaks and their garnishes

Ingredients	4 portions	10 portions
Beef steak	4 x 150 g	10 x 150 g
Oil		
Good quality salt and white pepper	To taste	To taste
Straw potatoes (see page 437)	4 portions	10 portions
Named garnish or sauce	4 portions	10 portions

energy	cal	fat	sat fat	carb	sugar	protein	fibre
3026 kJ	721 kcal	31.4 g	15.3 g	65.0 g	5.8 g	45.3 g	5.1 g

METHOD OF WORK

1   Brush the steaks with oil.

2   Place on a hot grill, griddle or frying pan and allow to sear.

3   Turn and cook on the other side until the steak is cooked to the desired degree.

The degree that a steak is cooked to is purely a matter of personal preference, and the opinion of the customer. As a chef you must try to interpret a customer's desires. With experience simply touching a steak can tell you how well it is done.

Types of beefsteak:

● *Fillet steak* Taken from the fillet of beef

● *Tournedos* From the centre of the fillet and can sometimes be barbed with fat bacon.

● *Rump* From the rump of beef. Popular as a grill steak in pubs.

● *Sirloin steak* Cut from a boned sirloin after the rump piece.

● *Minute steak* Cut from the sirloin or rump and batted to ½ cm thickness.

● *Rib eye steak* Taken from a boned-out fore rib of beef or the rib end of a sirloin and usually has the outer fat removed.

● *T-bone* Cut from across the rump end.

Garnishes and named sauces

- *Steak au poivre* Pepper sauce.
- *Chasseur* Chasseur sauce.
- *Champignon* Mushroom sauce.
- *Vin rouge* Red wine sauce.

- *Bordelaise* Red wine sauce and poached bone marrow.
- *Vert pre* Watercress and straw potatoes.
- *Béarnaise* Watercress and béarnaise sauce.
- *Lyonnaise* Served with sauté onions.

Step-by-step: Stages of preparation of sirloin steaks

1. Boneless 2 rib sirloin.

2. Remove the chin.

3. Remove visible gristle and connective tissue.

4. Remove back strap (5 cm wide) and trim the tail (2 cm from the tip of the eye muscle).

5. Trim fat to a maximum depth of 15 mm.

6. Remove 3–4 steaks from the rump end until gristle in the centre of the steak has disappeared.

7. Remainder of the sirloin to be cut into steaks 2 cm thick.

8. Steaks to be of even thickness (not wedge shape).

Steak cuts

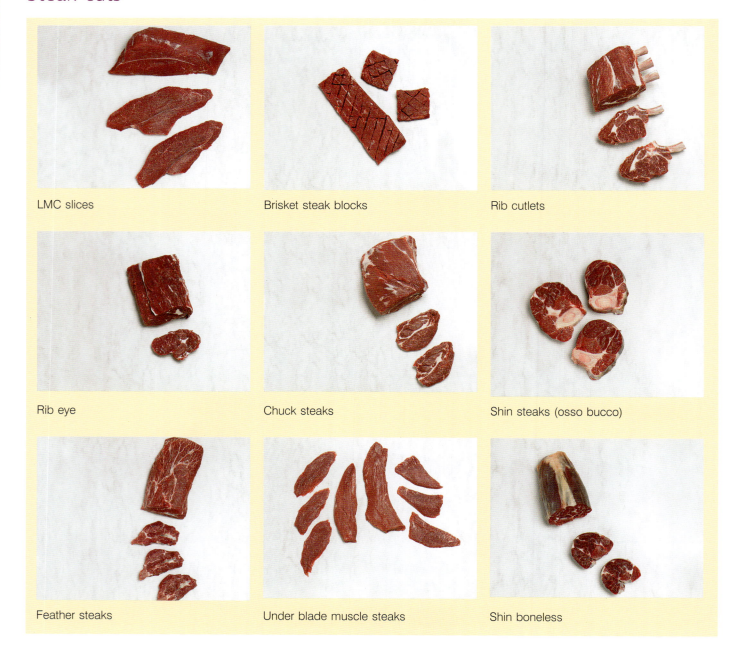

LMC slices

Brisket steak blocks

Rib cutlets

Rib eye

Chuck steaks

Shin steaks (osso bucco)

Feather steaks

Under blade muscle steaks

Shin boneless

Cooking specifications for steak

Blue – core temperature up to 29 °C

Rare – core temperature up to 51 °C

Medium rare – core temperature 57–63 °C

Medium – core temperature 63–68 °C

Medium well – core temperature 70–75 °C

Well done – core temperature 77 °C

ALL IMAGES COURTESY OF QUALITY MEAT SCOTLAND

CHEF'S TIP Cook the steaks from room temperature, this allows the meat to relax quicker and has less blood loss after cooking.

Lamb

Pasty

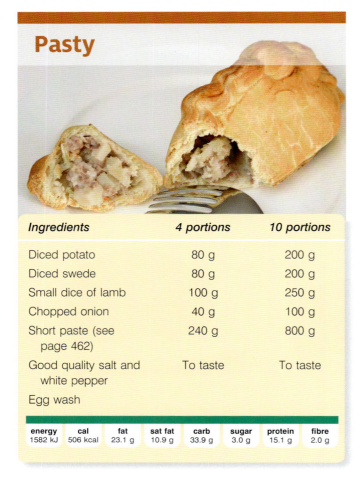

Ingredients	4 portions	10 portions
Diced potato	80 g	200 g
Diced swede	80 g	200 g
Small dice of lamb	100 g	250 g
Chopped onion	40 g	100 g
Short paste (see page 462)	240 g	800 g
Good quality salt and white pepper	To taste	To taste
Egg wash		

energy	cal	fat	sat fat	carb	sugar	protein	fibre
1582 kJ	506 kcal	23.1 g	10.9 g	33.9 g	3.0 g	15.1 g	2.0 g

METHOD OF WORK

1   Divide the pastry and roll out to 15 cm discs.
2   Mix the filling and moisten if necessary.
3   Place the filling on each round.
4   Moisten the edges of each piece of pastry.
5   Fold in half and crimp the edges to resemble a knot.
6   Brush with the egg wash and bake in the oven at 150 °C for approximately 1 hour until cooked through and golden brown.
7   Serve hot or cold.

Note: In 2011 the term 'Cornish pasty' was awarded Protected Geographical Indication (PGI) status by the European Commission. The PGI status means that only Cornish pasties prepared in Cornwall can be called a 'Cornish Pasty'.

Lancashire hotpot

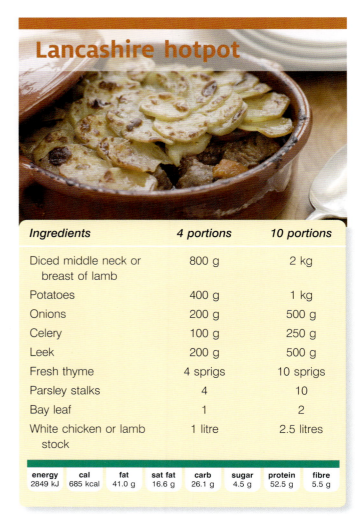

Ingredients	4 portions	10 portions
Diced middle neck or breast of lamb	800 g	2 kg
Potatoes	400 g	1 kg
Onions	200 g	500 g
Celery	100 g	250 g
Leek	200 g	500 g
Fresh thyme	4 sprigs	10 sprigs
Parsley stalks	4	10
Bay leaf	1	2
White chicken or lamb stock	1 litre	2.5 litres

energy	cal	fat	sat fat	carb	sugar	protein	fibre
2849 kJ	685 kcal	41.0 g	16.6 g	26.1 g	4.5 g	52.5 g	5.5 g

METHOD OF WORK

1   Place the diced lamb into a saucepan and fill with cold water. Bring to the boil to blanch the meat and then refresh under cold running water. Heat some fat in a frying pan, season the lamb and fry without letting it colour too much.
2   Slice the potatoes into 2–3 mm slices.
3   Mix the remaining ingredients with the lamb and season.
4   Place one third of the lamb into earthenware dishes.
5   Arrange a layer of potatoes on top of the lamb.
6   Repeat this process twice, finishing with a neat layer of potatoes on top.
7   Brush with melted butter and bake at 150 °C until the meat is tender and there is a light golden brown finish to the potatoes.

CHEF'S TIP Ensure that the lamb is very lean and of the same quality with no fat or gristle.

Mixed grill

Ingredients	4 portions	10 portions
Lamb chops	4	10
Chipolata sausages	4	10
Lambs kidney	4	10
Gammon steak 60–80 g	4	10
Plum tomatoes	2	5
Flat mushrooms	4	10
Minute steak 60–80 g	4	10
Parsley butter (see page 139)		
Straw potatoes (see page 437)	4 portions	10 portions

energy	cal	fat	sat fat	carb	sugar	protein	fibre
4465 kJ	1073 kcal	67.0 g	22.9 g	15.9 g	2.8 g	100.8 g	3.9 g

METHOD OF WORK

1 Prepare the chops.
2 Cut the kidneys in half and remove the core.
3 Brush the meat and vegetables with oil.
4 Grill all the items until cooked and serve with straw potatoes and parsley butter.

Navarin of lamb

Ingredients	4 portions	10 portions
Middle neck of lamb	600 g	1.5 kg
Carrots (turned)	80 g	200 g
Celery	1 stick	2 sticks
Onion	80 g	200 g
Bouquet garni	1 small	1 large
Garlic	1 clove	2–3 cloves
Oil	40 ml	100 ml
Flour	40 g	100 g
Brown stock	800 ml	2 litres
Tomato purée	40 g	100 g
Good quality salt and white pepper	To taste	To taste
Turned new potatoes		

energy	cal	fat	sat fat	carb	sugar	protein	fibre
3094 kJ	743 kcal	50.1 g	17.0 g	26.8 g	4.2 g	46.8 g	2.9 g

METHOD OF WORK

1 Remove sinews and excess fat from the lamb. Cut with a meat saw at the point where the ribs meet the chine bone and cut into uncovered cutlets.
2 Peel and chop the carrot, onion, celery and garlic into a large dice.
3 Heat the oil in a pan and sear the meat until brown on all sides.
4 Add the mirepoix and continue to brown.
5 Add the flour and cook for 1–2 mins, remove from the heat and allow to cool slightly.
6 Add the tomato purée and stock and stir with a wooden spoon or spatula ensuring that there are no lumps. Add the bouquet garni, season and cover with a lid.
7 Simmer gently for 2–2½ hours.
8 Skim any fat from the surface and remove the meat to a clean pan.
9 Pass the sauce onto the meat.
10 Correct the seasoning and serve with turned new potatoes.

Roast leg of lamb

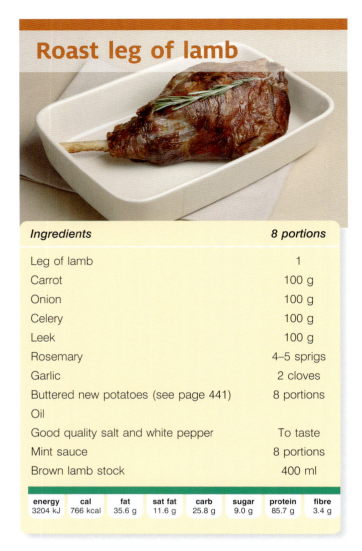

Ingredients	8 portions
Leg of lamb	1
Carrot	100 g
Onion	100 g
Celery	100 g
Leek	100 g
Rosemary	4–5 sprigs
Garlic	2 cloves
Buttered new potatoes (see page 441)	8 portions
Oil	
Good quality salt and white pepper	To taste
Mint sauce	8 portions
Brown lamb stock	400 ml

energy	cal	fat	sat fat	carb	sugar	protein	fibre
3204 kJ	766 kcal	35.6 g	11.6 g	25.8 g	9.0 g	85.7 g	3.4 g

METHOD OF WORK

1 Prepare the leg of lamb as shown in the step-by-step sequences (see page 350).

2 Peel and roughly chop the vegetables and place in a roasting dish with the garlic and rosemary.

3 Rub the lamb with a light coating of oil and season with salt and pepper.

4 Place the lamb on the bed of roots and place in an oven at 260 °C until caramelized. Lower the temperature to 130 °C and allow to cook to the required temperature.

5 Remove from the pan and rest in a warm place for 15–20 minutes.

6 Place the pan on a hot stove and caramelize the vegetables.

7 Add the stock and cook out until the pan is deglazed.

8 Strain the gravy into a clean sauce pan and allow to simmer.

9 Degrease and correct the seasoning.

10 Serve the lamb with the gravy, mint sauce and new potatoes.

Shepherd's pie

Ingredients	4 portions	10 portions
Minced lamb	500 g	1.25 kg
Diced onions	100 g	250 g
Oil	40 ml	100 ml
Demi glace (see page 130)	200 ml	500 ml
Duchesse potatoes (see page 435)	500 g	1.25 kg
Good quality salt and white pepper	To taste	To taste

energy	cal	fat	sat fat	carb	sugar	protein	fibre
2380 kJ	571 kcal	36.2 g	12.8 g	25.7 g	2.1 g	36.6 g	2.7 g

METHOD OF WORK

1 Cook the lamb and onions in the pan until browned and well broken up.

2 Add the demi glace and allow simmering for 30 minutes, correct the seasoning.

3 Place in either individual bowls or earthenware dishes.

4 Pipe the potato on top and bake until golden brown.

5 Garnish as required (such as broccoli, courgettes and carrots).

Pork

Roast pork

Ingredients	4 portions	10 portions
Loin, shoulder, or leg of pork	800 g	2 kg
Apple sauce	4 portions	10 portions
Carrots, onion, leeks, celery (roughly cut – mirepoix)	200 g	500 g
Brown stock	400 ml	1 litre
Vinegar	1 tsp	1 tblspn
Boiled, mashed parsnips finished with butter		
Good quality salt and white pepper	To taste	To taste

energy	cal	fat	sat fat	carb	sugar	protein	fibre
2537 kJ	605 kcal	27.5 g	11.9 g	25.1 g	19.4 g	65.5 g	5.6 g

METHOD OF WORK

1   Prepare the pork for roasting.

2   Place in a hot oven, 260 °C, until brown.

3   Turn down the heat and continue to roast until a core temperature of 75 °C is achieved.

4   Remove from the oven, remove the rind and place it back into a hot oven to crisp up for crackling.

5   Allow the loin to rest in a warm place.

6   Pour off the excess fat from the roasting pan and place it on the stove to caramelize.

7   Deglaze with the stock and boil for a few minutes.

8   Strain the gravy into a clean pan and thicken with a little arrowroot if necessary, correct the seasoning.

9   Serve with apple sauce, gravy, roast potatoes and crackling.

Boiled gammon with parsley sauce

Ingredients	4 portions	10 portions
Boned and rolled gammon (allow 150 g of cooked gammon per portion)	4	10
Parsley sauce (see page 125)	4 portions	10 portions
Turned carrots and courgettes for garnish		

energy	cal	fat	sat fat	carb	sugar	protein	fibre
1749 kJ	419 kcal	25.3 g	9.1 g	10.0 g	6.2 g	38.6 g	1.8 g

METHOD OF WORK

1   Soak the gammon for 24 hours in cold water.

2   Place into a pan and cover with fresh cold water.

3   Bring to the boil and simmer for 3½–4 hours until cooked.

4   Test by pushing a skewer into the thickest part. There should be little resistance when the skewer is withdrawn.

5   Remove the rind and carve into thin slices. Serve coated with parsley sauce.

Toad in the hole

Ingredients	4 portions	10 portions
Pork sausages	8	20
Yorkshire pudding batter	200 ml	500 ml
Oil	20 ml	50 ml

energy	cal	fat	sat fat	carb	sugar	protein	fibre
2316 kJ	558 kcal	44.3 g	10.9 g	21.5 g	2.5 g	19.7 g	1.0 g

METHOD OF WORK

1   Fry the sausages until golden brown.

2   Heat the oil in individual dishes or a roasting pan.

3   Add the sausages and pour over the batter.

4   Place in a hot oven, 220 °C, for 20–30 minutes until the batter has risen and is a golden brown.

5   Serve with onion gravy.

Pork cutlets with cranberries

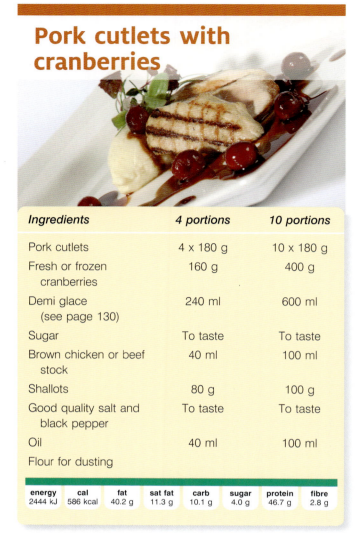

Ingredients	4 portions	10 portions
Pork cutlets	4 x 180 g	10 x 180 g
Fresh or frozen cranberries	160 g	400 g
Demi glace (see page 130)	240 ml	600 ml
Sugar	To taste	To taste
Brown chicken or beef stock	40 ml	100 ml
Shallots	80 g	100 g
Good quality salt and black pepper	To taste	To taste
Oil	40 ml	100 ml
Flour for dusting		

energy	cal	fat	sat fat	carb	sugar	protein	fibre
2444 kJ	586 kcal	40.2 g	11.3 g	10.1 g	4.0 g	46.7 g	2.8 g

METHOD OF WORK

1   Cut the cutlets from a chinned loin of pork.

2   Trim the bones and scrape clean.

3   Peel and cut the shallots into a fine brunoise.

4   Heat the oil in a thick-bottomed frying pan.

5   Season the flour and dust the pork cutlets.

6   Fry the cutlets in the oil until golden brown. Place on a tray and put into oven at 130 °C.

7   Add the shallots to the pan and sweat without letting them colour.

8   Add the cranberries and stock, cover with a lid and cook until the cranberries split.

9   Add the demi glace, bring to the boil, adjust the seasoning and add the sugar as desired.

10 Return the cutlets to the pan and simmer gently until the cutlets are cooked.

11 Serve with creamed potatoes and seasonal vegetables.

Veal

Escalope of veal cordon bleu

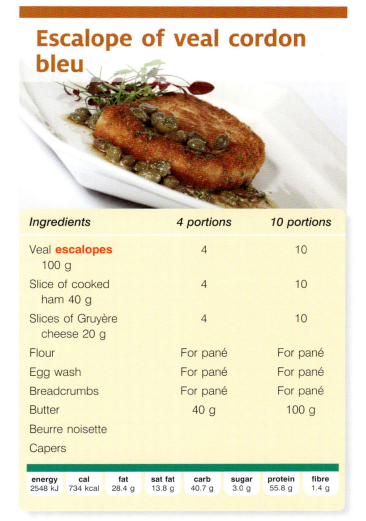

Ingredients	4 portions	10 portions
Veal **escalopes** 100 g	4	10
Slice of cooked ham 40 g	4	10
Slices of Gruyère cheese 20 g	4	10
Flour	For pané	For pané
Egg wash	For pané	For pané
Breadcrumbs	For pané	For pané
Butter	40 g	100 g
Beurre noisette		
Capers		

energy	cal	fat	sat fat	carb	sugar	protein	fibre
2548 kJ	734 kcal	28.4 g	13.8 g	40.7 g	3.0 g	55.8 g	1.4 g

METHOD OF WORK

1 Bat out the escalopes until they are 150 mm round.
2 Place a slice of ham on each escalope.
3 Place a slice of Gruyère cheese on half of each escalope.
4 Fold in half to make a 'D'-shape, season each side with salt and pepper.
5 Pané with flour, egg wash and breadcrumbs, and reshape to a neat oval.
6 Heat the butter in a pan until foaming but not starting to colour.
7 Pan fry the escalopes until golden brown on each side.
8 Serve with beurre noisette and capers.

Blanquette of veal

(with onions and mushrooms *Blanquette de veau à l'ancienne*)

Ingredients	4 portions	10 portions
Diced veal	500 g	1.25 kg
White veal stock	1 litre	2.5 litres
Onion studded with cloves	1	2
Bouquet garni	1 small	1 large
Button onions	20	50
Button mushrooms	20	50
Lemon juice	½	1
Flour (for the roux)	20 g	50 g
Flour	80 g	200 g
Butter (for the roux)	80 g	200 g
Double cream	80 ml	200 ml
Egg yolks	4	10
Sliced bread	4	10
Butter for frying	100 g	250 g

energy	cal	fat	sat fat	carb	sugar	protein	fibre
4838 kJ	1160 kcal	74.4 g	35.8 g	67.2 g	10.8 g	56.9 g	7.6 g

METHOD OF WORK

1 Blanch the veal in boiling water and refresh in cold water.
2 Place the blanched veal into the stock with the bouquet garni and onion clouté and simmer until tender (1–1½ hours).
3 Meanwhile cook the onions and mushrooms in a blanc (water mixed with the lemon juice, flour and seasoning).
4 Make a roux with the flour and butter.
5 Remove the meat from the stock and add the stock to the roux, cook for 20–25 minutes until the flour is cooked.
6 Make a liaison with the cream and yolks. Add a little sauce to the liaison and add this back to the sauce. DO NO ALLOW THE SAUCE TO REBOIL.
7 Meanwhile mix the cooked veal with the garnish and keep hot.
8 Cut the bread into heart-shaped croûtons and cook in clarified butter until a light golden brown.
9 Coat the meat with the sauce and serve.

Introduction to offal

The term offal refers to certain internal organs and other parts of an animal that should not be confused with the flesh (meat) of an animal. Offal has always been considered the cheapest of meat cuts and is known in France and other European countries as the 'fifth quarter'. This name comes from the fact that offal cuts are derived 'outside' of the four quarters of the animal and are removed from the carcass before the animal is broken down into the relative joints.

The reason these items are cheaper is because they are classed as an inferior cut of the animal. Historically these cuts were brought by poor customers and were thought of as a good way of adding flavour to soups and stews for little extra financial outlay. In addition to this, offal has a good nutritional value and was used to provide a cheaper alternative in creating a balanced diet.

In recent times, however, offal has appeared on menus used as a dish on its own or as a garnish. Once again this is partly due to the cost of offal – it is cheaper to purchase – but is also because of its defined and strong flavour. Offal is now used to create interesting dishes in its own right to add variety to modern menus.

Certain items of offal, such as duck or goose liver, can be quite expensive. Usually this is because of the increased labour which is required to prepare such delicacies as foie gras, or due to the fact that certain offal such as lamb sweetbreads can be hard to purchase from suppliers due to seasonality or lack of quality supply.

> **CHEF'S TIP** Once offal has been soaked or prepared, one way to enhance its flavour is to marinate it in herbs, spices and oil.

The variety of organs and tissues that are collectively known as offal generally contain more connective tissue than ordinary meat. Because of this they will benefit from a slow and moist cooking (stewing, braising) to dissolve the collagen. Certain offal such as liver contains relatively little collagen and because this organ experiences very little mechanical strain it is usually a delicate texture. If liver is slightly undercooked it will be tender and moist: if over-cooked it will become dry and crumbly.

Many offal cuts such as hearts and sweetbreads are often trimmed and cleaned before being blanched or covered with cold water and brought slowly to the boil. The blanching process will help to remove any waste materials from the organ and will lessen any strong smells on the meat surface.

More chefs are beginning to understand and realize the flexibility that using offal brings to an individual dish or menu. The more adventurous among us have fashioned reputations for using offal and this is beginning to bring the use of offal back into mainstream cookery.

You will begin to explore some modern ideas of preparing, cooking and presenting offal, but classical methods of preparation should also be understood as a basis for progression.

Basic types of offal

There are two main types of offal: red and white. Red offal consists of liver, kidneys, heart, oxtail, lungs and tongue. White offal consists of sweetbreads, brain, bone marrow, tripe, the head, trotters and stomach. Other parts that have not been mentioned are classed as offal too, such as cheek and pig's ears.

The main offal items that are generally utilized are obtained from pork, beef, ox, calves, lambs, poultry, rabbit and some feathered game such as pheasant. Each type of animal or bird offal will have its own distinct flavours, textures and use. Therefore it is important that chefs have an understanding of the techniques and skills needed to obtain the finest flavours and eating quality from each product.

This chapter will concentrate on three main types of offal used in cooking: kidney, liver and sweetbreads.

Liver

The liver is the largest organ in the body and most of the nutrients that the body absorbs from food will travel here first to be processed for distribution around the body, hence it has a sponge-like texture and is extremely delicate. Generally both the flavour and the texture of liver will become stronger and coarser with age.

> **CHEF'S TIP** To add texture to a shallow-fried dish coat the offal in breadcrumbs, polenta, brioche crumbs or herbed breadcrumbs.

Uses

Liver is one of the most versatile offal categories. It can be used shallow fried on its own, braised, made into pâtés, parfaits, terrines or farces. As liver has little fat (between 4–8 per cent), if it is slightly over-cooked it can become very dry.

Because the texture of liver is delicate it is able to absorb flavours very well. Various herbs such as sage, thyme, rosemary and chives combine well with liver as do shallots, onions or smoked products like pancetta and cured bacon.

Nutritional information

The composition of liver is up to 31 per cent protein. It has many nutrients such as iron and folic acid, a vitamin that is traditionally associated with helping to reduce the risk of heart disease.

Quality points

- When purchasing liver it is essential to check that it has a good even colouration throughout with no discoloured patches on the surface of the liver.

- It should be as fresh as possible and have no unpleasant odour or stickiness.

Kidneys

Kidney has a very distinct but delicate flavour. The function of the kidneys is to purge the body from liquid waste materials, therefore care must be taken to ensure that they are correctly cleaned and prepared before use in cooking. The best way of cleaning kidneys is to soak them in milk as this helps to draw out the impurities and encourage the natural kidney flavour. Kidney has approximately 16–26 per cent protein, and 3–6 per cent fat content.

Veal kidney is the most respected of all the different varieties of kidney as they have a tender and full flavour.

Because they are of such a delicate texture, they can be cooked using dry and quick-cooking methods.

Calf's kidney has a light colour and a delicate flavour similar to that of veal. This is a product that has a diverse appeal because it can be used for a variety of dishes and methods of cookery.

Pork kidney has a smooth, larger appearance than veal kidney, and also has a stronger flavour. The kidney can be quite tough depending on the age of the animal, so quick-cooking methods may not always give the best results. Moist and slow methods such as braising will be best.

Lamb's kidney is tender and light in colour. The kidneys have a subtle flavour and can be cooked by grilling and frying, but also can be cooked using moist methods of cookery such as stewing.

Mutton kidney is darker in colour and has a stronger flavour than lamb's kidney. Ox kidney is thought to be the toughest-textured kidney available. It has a dark colour and strong flavour and is generally used mixed with beef for steak and kidney pudding.

Purchase specifications

For the purchase of kidney the chef should always look at the following factors:

- All kidneys should be as fresh as possible.

- Both ox and lamb's kidney should have a covering of fat to maintain their natural moisture. This should not be removed until just before preparation for cooking.

- The smell of the kidney and fat should not be overpowering. Any trace of an ammonia odour means that the kidney should be discarded.

- Storage temperature can be as low as −1 °C for fresh kidney and should not really be stored for any longer than a maximum of three days.

CHEF'S TIP In longer cooking processes such as braising or stewing, adding the kidney too early can result in them becoming tough through overcooking. It is best to seal the kidneys by shallow frying them separately and adding them towards the end of the cooking process to retain the texture and flavour.

Sweetbreads

Sweetbreads are the soft-textured thymus and pancreas glands of calves and lambs and are a respected food commodity in gastronomic kitchens across the world. Although they are still under-utilized as a product or a dish in their own right, they can generally be found as a component of a dish or as a garnish. They are a light meat that is firm in texture. Veal sweetbreads are considered the best: beef sweetbreads are rather fatty and coarse, but if well prepared, they will taste similar to veal. Sweetbreads contain between 12 and 33 per cent protein content and approximately 3–23 per cent fat (of which most can be removed during the preparation stage).

Sweetbreads require a great deal of preparation before they can be used and cooked as they are a gland from either the throat or heart area and contain certain impurities that need to be removed by soaking and blanching before being pressed. Pressing is not always applicable with sweetbreads, however, as this depends on the cooking process used.

Sweetbreads should be soaked in cold salted water in a refrigerator for approximately four hours and then washed under cold running water to remove all traces of blood and return them to a white colour. When blanching, veal sweetbreads should be blanched for five minutes and lamb sweetbreads for about three minutes; then refreshed immediately in cold water. This will aid the removal of the skin, which can be difficult in its raw state. All fat and gristle should be removed at this stage. Place on a tray between two clean and damp kitchen cloths before setting a lightly weighted tray on top. Leave in a refrigerator for four hours to become firm and slightly pressed.

Storage of offal

When storing any offal it is important to remember that because these are organs and parts of the body they may have blood retained inside them. It is necessary to ensure that offal is stored in deep containers (minimum 8 cm depth) with a filter tray or absorbent paper underneath to soak or easily remove discarded fluids and blood.

Refrigeration temperatures can be adjusted to as low as –1 °C for the storage of fresh offal so that deterioration is slowed. Offal should be regularly checked during storage for signs of decline.

The following information will give a brief summary of the various offal products, detailing their French terminology, how to recognize the item by appearance and how best to prepare the product for cooking.

Offal products

Beef/ox liver

- *French term* – Foie de boeuf.

- *Appearance* – Should be large in size, deep red in colour and will have a strong smell, although not too pungent. The product should look moist but not slimy and have no tearing, cuts or dark spots on the flesh.

- *Preparation* – Care must to be taken not to dissect the liver too much.
  Remove the outer skin membrane with a sharp knife making sure you do not pierce the flesh, at the same time trimming off any excess fat and removing any sinews and tubes.

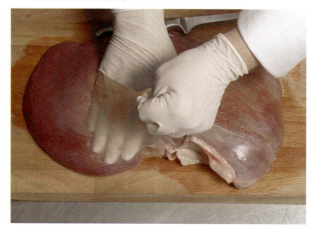

Use the hand to release the membrane

Beef/ox livers can be left whole but this is no longer a general procedure. The preference today is to cut the product into slices or thin strips or dice depending on the dish to be produced. Following this procedure the product can then be stored as mentioned earlier, or utilize the milk soaking process to further remove any impurities.

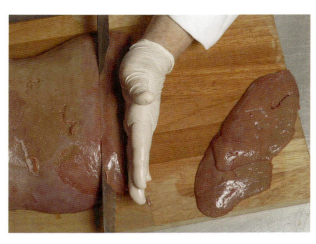

Slicing the ox liver

Beef/ox kidney

- *French term* – Rognon de boeuf.

- *Appearance* – Bright and a deep red, it should not have an overpowering smell and should be evenly coloured with no dull or dark spots on the flesh. It should be moist and not dry, with unbroken skin and without any cuts. If there is any fat around the kidneys, it should be white in colour and not an off-yellow.

Step-by-step: Preparing beef kidney

- *Preparation* – Remove the outer membrane with a sharp knife, making sure you do not pierce the flesh, at the same time trimming off any excess fat and removing any tubes.

- Beef/ox kidney can be left whole or cut in half lengthways, with the cortex and white fat part being removed following which they can then be sliced into bundles and cooked.

- If not being prepared for immediate use, the kidneys should be soaked in milk to remove any impurities.

- These items are generally diced and sliced then placed into pies and puddings.

Pig liver

- *French term* – Foie de porc.

- *Appearance* – A bright red-brown colour, this product will be firmer to the touch and have quite a strong smell. Should be moist but not slimy with no cuts, tearing or dark spots on the surface of the flesh.

- *Procedure* – Remove outer skin with a sharp knife, making sure you do not pierce the flesh. Trim off excess fat if necessary and remove any sinews and tubes.

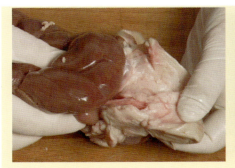

1. Remove the fat and outer skin membrane from the kidney.

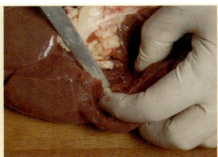

2. Remove the cortex from the kidney.

3. Soaking kidneys in milk.

Step-by-step: Preparing pig's liver

1. Cutting into strips.

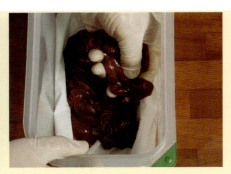

2. Storing in a deep plastic container with absorbent paper underneath.

This product can be left whole or cut into slices, diced or cut into strips depending on the dish.

Following this procedure the product can then be stored as normal meat and poultry would be. If storing in raw state it is best to utilize the milk soaking process.

Pig kidney

Cut the kidneys in half lenghways

Opening the cut kidney into a round shape

- *French term* – Rognon de porc.

- *Appearance* – Red, should not have an overbearing acidic smell. Should be evenly coloured and have no dull or dark spots on its flesh, moist and not dry. The flesh should not be broken or have any cuts and if there is any fat around the kidney it should be white in colour and not off-yellow in appearance.

- *Procedure* – Remove the outer membrane with a sharp knife making sure you do not pierce the flesh. Trim off any excess fat and remove any tubes. The kidney can be left whole or cut in half lengthways and the cortex removed.

    They can also be cut along the thicker edge of the kidney, not cutting all the way through, and opened up into a round shape.

If not being prepared for immediate use, they should be soaked in milk to remove any impurities. These items are generally diced and sliced then placed into pies and puddings.

Lamb/mutton liver

- *French term* – Foie d'agneau.

- *Appearance* – Deep red in colour and should not smell strong. This will be of a medium size compared to veal or ox. It should have a moist texture but not be slimy to the touch. The product should be in one whole piece with no tearing or cuts to the flesh.

- *Procedure* – Remove the outer skin with a sharp knife, making sure you do not pierce the flesh. Trim off any excess fat if necessary and remove any sinews and tubes.

    Can then be left whole or cut into slices, diced or into strips depending on the dish.

    The product can be stored as normal meat and poultry would, but if storing in raw state it is best to utilize the milk soaking process.

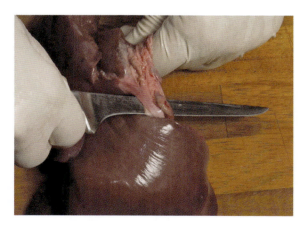

Trim any excess fat from the liver

Cutting the liver into dice

Lamb/mutton kidney

- *French term* – Rognon d'agneau.

- *Appearance* – Pale red, not purple, and should not have an acidic smell. Lamb/mutton kidneys should be evenly coloured and have no dull or dark spots on the flesh, which should also be moist, not dry. The skin should not be broken or have any cuts. If there is any fat around the kidneys it should be white in colour and not an off-yellow.

- *Procedure* – Remove the outer membrane with a sharp knife making sure you do not pierce the flesh. Trim off any excess fat and remove any tubes. Can be left whole or cut in half lengthways and the cortex removed.

  They can be slit along the thicker side, not all the way through, and opened up into a round shape. If not being prepared for immediate use, soak in milk to remove any impurities.

> **VIDEO CLIP** Preparing lamb's kidney.

Lamb sweetbreads

- *French term* – Ris d'agneau.

- *Appearance* – Should be plump and firm to the touch and pale-white in colour. May sometimes be bloody in appearance but this should wash out with soaking and washing. There are two types – thymus and pancreas glands – so the shape will vary. These are from two areas of the animal – the throat, and nearer the heart, which is rounder in shape.

Soak the sweetbreads in water

- *Procedure* – Soak in water to remove blood or impurities and to whiten them in colour. Blanch and refresh in iced water. They can then be trimmed of any sinews or fat.

Press between two clean trays and clean/damp kitchen cloths for approximately four hours in a refrigerator. Use whole or slice for cooking.

Blanching the sweetbreads and refreshing them in cold water

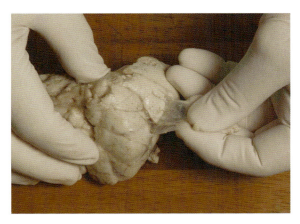

Trim and remove any fat and sinew

Pressing the sweetbreads between two trays

Veal liver

- *French term* – Foie de veau.

- *Appearance* – Should be pale pink or rose red in colour and will be quite large in size. They should be moist but not slimy and have no cuts or blemishes to the flesh.

- *Procedure* – Remove the outer membrane with a sharp knife making sure you do not pierce the flesh. Trim off any excess fat and remove any sinews and tubes. They can be left whole or cut in half lengthways and the cortex removed. Can be slit along the thicker side, not all the way through, and opened up into a round shape. If not being prepared for immediate use, soak in milk to remove any impurities.

Veal kidney

- *French term* – Rognon de veau.

- *Appearance* – Pale red, not purple, and should not have an acidic smell. Evenly coloured with no dull or dark spots on the flesh, which should also be moist and not dry. The skin should not be broken or have any cuts. If there is any fat around the kidneys it should be white in colour and not an off-yellow.

- *Procedure*– Remove the outer membrane with a sharp knife making sure you do not pierce the flesh. Trim off any excess fat and remove any tubes. Can be left whole or cut in half lengthways and the cortex removed. If not being prepared for immediate use, soak in milk to remove any impurities.

Veal sweetbreads

- *French term* – Ris de veau.

- *Appearance* – Plump and firm to the touch, evenly shaped and pale (white) in colour. May sometimes be bloody in appearance but this should wash out with soaking. As with lamb's sweetbreads, there are two types so the shape and size will vary.

- *Procedure* – From two areas of the animal – the throat, and nearer to the heart, which is rounder in shape. Soak in water to remove blood and impurities and to whiten the colour. Blanch and refresh in iced water. They can then be trimmed of any sinews or tubes, and pressed as shown with the lamb's sweetbreads.

Chicken/duck liver

- *French term* – Foie de volaille/foie de caneton.

- *Appearance* – Should be brown- and red-coloured offal, quite pale and reasonably small in size. Due to the delicate nature of the livers, they may sometimes be broken or torn. They will be soft to the touch, should be moist but not slimy and smell fresh and not strong. Any green-coloured residue or flesh should be removed.

- *Procedure* – Remove the gallbladder if attached, taking care that it does not burst or split. Trim any excess yellow-coloured strands. It can then be left whole or cut into small pieces. If not prepared for immediate use, soak in milk to remove any toxins or impurities.

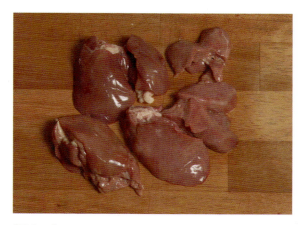

Chicken livers

Recipes
Calves' offal

Calve's liver stroganoff

Ingredients	4 portions	10 portions
Butter	100 g	250 g
Paprika	50 g	100 g
Calves liver, sliced into strips	400 g	1 kg
Onion, sliced	150 g	275 g
Beef or vegetable stock	45 ml	100 ml
Button mushrooms, thinly sliced	200 g	400 g
Soured cream or crème fraîche	250 ml	525 ml
Chopped fresh parsley	2 tblspn	5 tblspn
Good quality salt and white pepper	To taste	To taste

energy	cal	fat	sat fat	carb	sugar	protein	fibre
2542 kJ	615 kcal	52.5 g	24.0 g	6.7 g	5.1 g	27.8 g	6.4 g

METHOD OF WORK

1   In a large bowl season the liver with salt, pepper and paprika making sure it is covered evenly. Lightly flour each slice of liver.

2   Over a high heat sauté the calves' livers in oil until golden in colour then remove from pan.

3   Now add the onions and cook until brown and softened then remove from pan.

4   Deglaze the pan with the beef or vegetable stock to remove the residue from the bottom of the pan and bring to the boil.

5   Sauté the mushrooms and cook until softened, then add the onions, mushrooms and liver can be added back to the pan with the cooking juices.

6   Simmer for a few minutes before adding the parsley and correcting the seasoning. Remove from the heat and cool slightly before stirring in the soured cream or the crème fraîche.

CHEF'S TIP Sour cream and crème fraîche are good alternatives to double cream for flavour and consistency. However, do not boil the cream to avoid the sauce from splitting. Always remove from the heat and cool slightly before adding.

Calves' sweetbread fricassee with whisky and wholegrain mustard

Ingredients	4 portions	10 portions
Calves' sweetbreads soaked in iced water overnight	500 g	1.25 kg
Beef stock	500 ml	1.25 litres
Onion, finely chopped	75 g	200 g
Fresh sage leaves, chopped	10 g	25 g
Whisky	100 ml	200 ml
Double cream	600 ml	1.5 litres
Wholegrain mustard	1 tblspn	2½ tblspn
Butter	50 g	125 g
Garlic, finely chopped	1 clove	3 cloves
Good quality salt and white pepper	To taste	To taste

energy	cal	fat	sat fat	carb	sugar	protein	fibre
4898 kJ	1184 kcal	105.7 g	56.7 g	5.0 g	4.1 g	39.2 g	0.9 g

METHOD OF WORK

1 Rinse the sweetbreads until the water runs clear, drain and pat dry with a clean kitchen cloth.

2 Gently poach the sweetbreads for 3–4 minutes in water before peeling the membrane away, removing any excess fat and slicing into small even pieces.

3 Sweat the chopped onion, sage and finely chopped garlic in the butter until softened.

4 Add the whisky and flambé to remove the alcohol before returning the sweetbreads to the pan and turning over in the cooking liquor for a minute.

5 Add the hot beef stock and reduce gently until only about 100 ml remains.

6 Add the double cream and mustard. Cook out gently for approximately 1 hour or until the sweetbreads are tender. Correct the seasoning and serve with garnish.

Lamb's offal

Lamb's liver with balsamic-glazed onions and salt-roasted walnuts

Ingredients	4 portions	10 portions
Lamb's liver, sliced into 80 g sized pieces	8	20
Flour	4 tblspn	10 tblspn
Mustard powder	1 tsp	3 tsp
Button onions	200 g	500 g
Butter	50 g	125 g
Balsamic vinegar	120 ml	250 ml
Soft brown sugar	2 tblspn	5 tblspn
Walnut halves	100 g	200 g
Good quality salt	1 tblspn	3 tblspn
White pepper	To taste	To taste
Olive oil	30 ml	80 ml

energy	cal	fat	sat fat	carb	sugar	protein	fibre
3373 kJ	811 kcal	56.1 g	17.3 g	22.5 g	10.1 g	54.1 g	2.3 g

METHOD OF WORK

1   Preheat an oven to 170 °C. Blanch the walnuts in boiling water for 3 minutes and leave to dry. Remove the skins of the walnuts.

2   In a sauteuse melt the butter and add the button onions, sauté until lightly coloured and softened before adding the balsamic vinegar and sugar. Allow the contents to caramelize and glaze the onions. Leave to one side keeping them covered and warm.

VIDEO CLIP   Preparing lamb's liver.

3   In a shallow frying pan add the olive oil and heat until almost smoking, add the walnuts and salt and toss for one minute off the heat. Place into the oven for 5 minutes or until lightly coloured, remove from the oven and pan and leave to cool.

4   Mix the flour and mustard powder together in a bowl then coat the slices of liver lightly in the flour mixture. Pat any excess flour off each slice and season well.

5   Shallow fry the liver slices in a frying pan on both sides until light golden brown and medium in cooking degree. Allow to rest for 2 minutes.

6   To serve the lamb's liver place the slices on a bed of the balsamic onions, sprinkle the walnuts around the plate and with any remaining glaze decorate over the liver and around the plate.

TASK   Research the nutritional composition of assorted livers: pay particular attention to iron and vitamins.

Lamb sweetbreads pan fried with rosemary and lemon butter

Ingredients	4 portions	10 portions
Lamb sweetbreads, soaked overnight in iced water	500 g	1.25 kg
Button mushrooms	100 g	250 g
Flour	100 g	250 g
Lamb stock	500 ml	1.25 litres
Butter	200 g	500 g
Lemon	1	2
Fresh rosemary, finely chopped	10 g	25 g
Good quality salt and white pepper	To taste	To taste

energy	cal	fat	sat fat	carb	sugar	protein	fibre
3521 kJ	846 kcal	65.9 g	29.0 g	20.9 g	1.1 g	43.7 g	1.9 g

METHOD OF WORK

1   Soak the sweetbreads for 4 hours, rinse until the water runs clear and drain.

2   In the stock, gently poach the sweetbreads for 3–4 minutes, remove, drain and cool before removing the membrane and fat from the outside of the sweetbreads. Press the sweetbreads between two trays lined with a clean kitchen cloth for 4 hours and leave in a refrigerator.

3   Once pressed, slice, season and pass through the flour. Melt 50 g of the butter and gently shallow fry until golden on both sides, then add the mushrooms.

4   Drain and place on a serving plate.

5   Add the rest of the butter to a hot pan and allow to bubble until a nutty brown colour begins to appear and the bubbles have disappeared. Squeeze in the lemon juice and serve.

VIDEO CLIP Preparing lamb's sweetbread.

Pork offal

Marinated pork kidney and chorizo skewers

Ingredients	4 portions	10 portions
Pork kidney, 2 cm dice	400 g	1 kg
Chorizo, 2 cm dice	200 g	500 g
Wooden skewers	4	10
Olive oil	50 ml	125 ml
Fresh parsley	10 g	25 g
Fresh basil	10 g	25 g
Roasted yellow peppers	50 g	125 g
Diced apples	½	1
Garlic, chopped	1 clove	2 cloves
Fresh coriander	10 g	25 g
Good quality salt and white pepper	To taste	To taste

energy	cal	fat	sat fat	carb	sugar	protein	fibre
1970 kJ	473 kcal	33.6 g	9.6 g	4.4 g	3.8 g	38.7 g	0.9 g

METHOD OF WORK

1   Blend the chopped fresh herbs and garlic with the olive oil to create the marinade.

2   Carefully skin the kidneys, trimming off any excess fat and the cortex, cut into large 2 cm dice, season and coat in the marinade. Leave covered in a refrigerator for a minimum of 30 minutes.

3   Using the skewers, place alternate pieces of the kidney and chorizo onto these ensuring an even portion size between each skewer.

4   Brush the skewers with a little marinade and either grill lightly under a salamander, griddle, bake or shallow fry until cooked.

5   Serve with the apples and roasted yellow peppers.

Chicken offal

Chicken liver stir fry

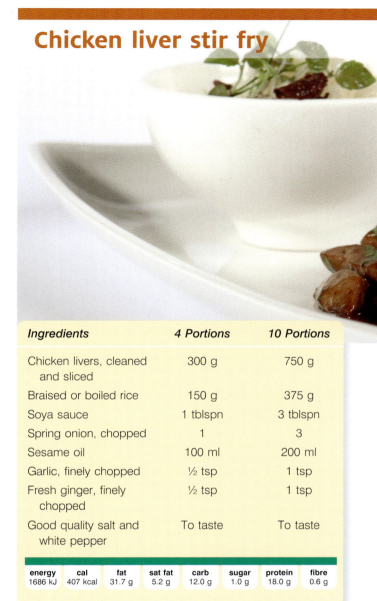

Ingredients	4 Portions	10 Portions
Chicken livers, cleaned and sliced	300 g	750 g
Braised or boiled rice	150 g	375 g
Soya sauce	1 tblspn	3 tblspn
Spring onion, chopped	1	3
Sesame oil	100 ml	200 ml
Garlic, finely chopped	½ tsp	1 tsp
Fresh ginger, finely chopped	½ tsp	1 tsp
Good quality salt and white pepper	To taste	To taste

energy	cal	fat	sat fat	carb	sugar	protein	fibre
1686 kJ	407 kcal	31.7 g	5.2 g	12.0 g	1.0 g	18.0 g	0.6 g

METHOD OF WORK

1 Using a hot wok or shallow pan quickly stir fry the garlic, ginger and livers in the sesame oil.

2 Add the spring onion, soy sauce and correct the seasoning before serving with the rice.

CHEF'S TIP When stir frying use a wooden spoon rather than tossing the pan as this reduces the heat in the pan which is needed for this quick cooking process.

Ingredients   Serves 4–6

For the stuffed pork fillet

Tamworth pork fillet	1 kg
Salt and pepper to season	To taste
Tamworth streaky bacon	250 g
Savoy cabbage leaves blanched and refreshed	150 g
Grated carrot	1 medium
Tinfoil sheets, to roll	2

For the black pudding

Tamworth black pudding	
Oil for frying	

For the Boxty potato

Grated raw potato	300 g
Egg	1
Plain flour	30 g
Butter or dripping, melted	100 g
Salt and pepper	To taste

For the wild bilberry and crab apple jelly

Wild bilberries or blue berries	200 g
Crab apples	500 g
Water	1 litre
Lemon rind and juice	1 lemon and 1 tsp of juice
Orange rind and juice	1 orange
Star anise	1
Cloves	2
Chopped mint leaves	
Sugar	300 g

To garnish

Baby carrots and turnips, washed and peeled	
Candied crab apple slices	

Guest Chef

Stuffed Tamworth pork fillet, black pudding, boxty potato, wild bilberry and crab apple jelly

Chef: *Emmett McCourt*

Centre: *North West Regional College, Londonderry, N. Ireland*

This dish uses the Tamworth pig. It is the closest type of pig to the Irish pig, but rare breed pork can be used. Killing a pig in Ireland was a day of great celebration, all parts of the pig were used in cooking. Wild bilberries and crab apples grow abundantly around the north west of Ireland from July through to September and the boxty potato originates from Ulster County Derry.

METHOD OF WORK

Wild Bilberry and Crab Apple Jelly

1 Wash apples and bilberries, roughly chop apples.
2 Add fruit to deep saucepan with all other ingredients.
3 Cover with water and simmer for 15 mins.
4 Pass through a fine chinoise, leave to drain.
5 Reduce for a further 10 mins, until syrup consistency, pass through muslin cloth.
6 Pour into shot glasses when cooled slightly, chill to set.

Stuffed pork fillet

1 Clean and trim the pork fillet removing the chain and fat.
2 Place the pork fillet lengthways on a chopping board, slice inwards along the fillet to form an escalope shape, be careful not to slice straight through.
3 Cover the fillet with cling film and baton out flat.
4 Lay the fillet flat on two sheets of seasoned tin foil.
5 Layer first with streaky bacon then blanched cabbage leaves and finally with grated carrot, season with salt and pepper.
6 Roll as tightly as possible in tinfoil, turning ends as you go.
7 Place on tray and roast in oven for 40 mins at 180 °C, Gas 6, leave to rest.

Boxty potato

1   Grate potato and drain. Add to a steel bowl with other ingredients' and mix well.

2   Heat a non stick pan, add oil and round steel or square cutter.

3   Add potato mix to cutter, to ½ cm thick, press down while cooking.

4   Cook on both sides for 4 mins until golden brown and cooked through.

To serve

1   Place boxty potato in centre of plate.

2   Place slices of pan-fried black pudding around plate and vegetable garnish. You could also place squares of braised pork belly around the plate, as shown in the photograph.

3   Slice fillet and serve on boxty.

4   Drizzle sauce on and around the pork.

5   Serve with chilled jelly and candied crab apple slices.

Recipes

VEGETABLES

Braised baby gem lettuce   415
Braised cabbage   416
Braised fennel   417
Braised red cabbage   418
Broccoli polonaise   418
Buttered asparagus   419
Buttered Brussels sprouts   419
Artichokes alla Romana   420
Cauliflower mornay   422
Buttered samphire with sesame
   seeds   422
Creamed spinach purée   423
Pumpkin purée   423
Deep fried courgettes   424
Chicory au gratin   424
Stir-fried vegetables   425
Stuffed mushrooms   425
Stuffed aubergines   426
Stuffed tomatoes   427
Broad beans   428
Vichy carrots   428
Peas French style   429
Shallow fried chicory   429
Ratatouille   430
Roast parsnips in honey   431
Swede purée   431
Braised leeks   432

POTATOES

Anna potatoes   433
Mashed potatoes   434
Biarritz potatoes   434
Duchesse potatoes   435
Marquis potatoes   436
Dauphine potatoes   436
Croquette potatoes   437
Straw potatoes   437
Sauté potatoes   438
Sauté potatoes with onions   438
Game chips and gaufrette
   potatoes   439
Boulangère potatoes   440
Chipped potatoes (chips)   440

11

Vegetables, fruits and vegetable protein

NVQ

Unit 2FP7 Prepare vegetables for basic dishes

Unit 2FC7 Cook and finish basic vegetable protein dishes

VRQ

Unit 208 Prepare and cook fruit and vegetables

Pont-neuf potatoes 441

Boiled potatoes 441

Fondant potatoes 442

Matchstick potatoes 443

Mignonette potatoes 443

Château potatoes 444

Pommes au lard 444

Dauphinoise potatoes 445

Delmonico potatoes 446

Parmentier potatoes 446

VEGETABLE PROTEIN

TVP Moussaka 447

Stir-fried tofu with egg noodles 448

Sweet and sour Quorn™ 448

Courgette and seitan fritters 449

Cajun tofu with couscous 450

ONLINE RECIPES

LEARNER SUPPORT

Steamed chicory with bacon
Deep fried onion rings
Baby glazed carrots with thyme
Bavarian braised cabbage
Swiss potato cake
Quorn™ shepherds pie
Quorn™ chilli con carne

LEARNING OBJECTIVES

The aim of this chapter is to enable you to develop knowledge and apply skills in the preparation and cookery principles of vegetables, fruit and vegetable protein. This will also include information on materials, a variety of ingredients and associated equipment.

At the end of this chapter you will be able to:

- Identify each vegetable variety and selected finished dishes.
- Identify the seasons for commonly used fruit and vegetables.
- Understand the use of comparative ingredients in vegetable cookery.
- Recognize the quality points of various vegetable commodities and dishes.
- Prepare, cook, finish and hold each type of vegetable variety.
- Identify the correct tools and equipment to utilize during the preparation and production of vegetables.
- Identify the correct storage procedures for vegetables.
- State the preservation methods for fruit and vegetables.

Introduction

It is believed that the first evidence of farming wheat and barley dates from 8000 BC in the Middle East. The discovery of edible plants was then developed into the farming and crop harvesting trade we recognize today. Lettuce, peas and beans were among the first vegetables farmed in Greece and formed a staple part of the country's diet, they were easy to cultivate and ideal for storing once dried. In Rome lettuce was served both at the beginning and conclusion of meals, and fruit was used as a dessert. Fruits were preserved whole in honey and the Roman gastronome *Apicius* produced a recipe for pickled peaches.

Vegetables on a market stall

On Marco Polo's travels to Eastern Asia he returned to Europe with a variety of aromatic spices, such as cinnamon, cloves and nutmeg. The European appetite for Asian spices was an important aspect in the development of Spain, Portugal, Italy, France, Holland and England into major sea powers. This introduced the exportation of vanilla and chillies from the West Indies and Christopher Columbus returned from his travels with potatoes, squash, tomatoes and peppers. These commodities eventually became staple ingredients in the new cuisines of the old world.

During the seventeenth and eighteenth centuries the cultivation and breeding of plants, fruits and vegetables was of greater significance as cooks began to take a new interest and use them in recipes with greater refinement. Plants, fruits and vegetables were now grown locally in larger quantities and had to be eaten quickly or preserved by drying or pickling. With the industrialization of developed countries in the early nineteenth century supply routes became more reliable and faster (the advance in rail transportation is an example). The introduction of both canning and refrigeration also helped the transportation of supplies.

Today we can purchase exactly what we want, when we want, due to an exceptional world transportation system. This has positive and negative points: fruits and vegetables are now available to purchase nearly all year long because growers are breeding and cultivating fruits and vegetables to withstand the rigours of technical harvesting, transport and storage. They are often harvested while still hard and under-ripe because it can be weeks before they are sold and eaten. These varieties often have a poor flavour value. This situation has stimulated the trend to eat food 'out of season' which can also be extremely expensive due to transportation costs when purchasing from long distance. The flavour and quality of fresh seasonal fruit and vegetables is second to none. Where something comes from is called its **provenance**.

The rediscovery of the traditional system of food production and the enjoyment of consuming locally grown and sold products in the form of farmers markets and farm shops is now on the increase. Organic practices also represent an essential alternative to industrial farming as it encourages attention to the quality and sustainability of agricultural produce once more. Chefs are now becoming more conscious with respect to their locality and the produce and purchase of locally grown commodities. This emphasis is being encouraged by leading associations such as the Academy of Culinary Arts, the Craft Guild of Chefs and the Slow Food Movement who have developed support campaigns to promote this development.

Provenance

The food industry is very interested in provenance or the origin of the ingredients we purchase and eat. Many reasons drive this. Understanding the provenance of food, i.e. how it is produced, transported, and delivered to us, is turned into a competitive advantage by the food industry, since it allows it to demonstrate quality (in taste, in carbon foot print, or in ethics). Regulations, such as the EU Food law, require the traceability of food, feed, food-producing animals and any other substance that will be, made into a food or feed to be known at all stages of production, processing and distribution.

IMAGE COURTESY OF WWW.THINKVEGETABLES.CO.UK

Harvesting vegetables

The importance of vegetables

Vegetables are very important for our nutrition. Experts recommend that we eat at least five portions of fruit or vegetables a day. The nutritional values of vegetables depend on a number of factors, such as the type, size, season, freshness, preparation method and cooking techniques used. With the exception of pulses, vegetables do not contain much protein or fat. Vegetables are a main source of vitamin C, as well as some of the A, B and D group vitamins that are water or fat soluble. The body will be able to produce vitamin A, if vegetables such as carrots, tomatoes and peppers (which contain beta-carotene, an **antioxidant**) are consumed.

The majority of vegetables contain folic acid, iron, magnesium, calcium and potassium as well as other minerals in smaller amounts. Green vegetables are rich in minerals (calcium and iron), vitamin C and beta-carotene.

The human body needs to fight potential infection and tissue damage by forming antioxidants. Although the body does make a few antioxidant molecules of its own, it is important to supplement them by the rich supply found in vegetables. Vegetables with high starch content (potatoes) contain carbohydrates which produce energy as well as fibre.

The vitamin and mineral content in vegetables is at its highest when immediately picked but begins to recede when the produce is exposed to sunlight or left to perish slowly in uncontrolled storage conditions. The majority of the nutrients are found in the skin or the layer just below the skin, so where possible during preparation simply wash the vegetables to achieve the maximum nutritional benefit.

Vitamins B and C are water soluble which means they are lost when exposed to hot water (boiled, stewed or steamed). The smaller cuts of vegetables introduces a greater loss of vitamins and minerals because the surface area becomes larger.

Vitamin C is destroyed by long cooking processes, so where possible attempt to use quick methods of cookery to retain the nutritional value. As the cooking liquor will undoubtedly absorb some vitamins and nutrients it can be used to make sauces, which will return some of the nutrients back to the dish.

Trace compounds called phytochemicals are found in plants, including herbs and spices, and have beneficial effects on health and disease prevention. They have a wide-ranging effect on the avoidance of damage to various body mechanisms, such as the heart, blood, eyes and the prevention of cancer cells. The following table gives a simple guide to which vegetables are high in specific vitamins.

VITAMIN	RECOMMENDED DAILY ALLOWANCE	WHAT IS IT NEEDED FOR?	STRONG SOURCE	USEFUL SOURCE
A Retinol	600 µg/day women 700 µg/day men	Growth, development, healthy skin and eyes. Important for a healthy immune system.	Pak choi, peppers, sweet potato	Pumpkin, Brussels sprouts, red cabbage, carrots, spinach, butternut squash
B1 Thiamine	0.8 mg/day women 1.0 mg/day men	Maintain a healthy nervous system.	Sweetcorn, onions, potatoes	Broad beans, cauliflower, leeks, garlic, swede, parsnips, courgettes, celery
B2 Riboflavin	1.1 mg/day women 1.3 mg/day men	The release of energy from food.		Asparagus, watercress, leeks, mange tout, mushrooms, peppers, tomatoes
B5 Pantothenic acid	None set	Energy production.		Green cabbage, carrots, broad beans, asparagus, broccoli, cauliflower
B6 Pyridoxine	1.2 mg/day women 1.4 mg/day men	Healthy nervous system and production of red blood cells.	Potatoes	Aubergine, peppers, shallots, okra, brown onion, butternut squash
C Ascorbic acid	40 mg/day women 40 mg/day men	Creates collagen – a protein necessary for healthy bones, teeth, gums, blood and all connective tissue. Acts as powerful antioxidant and helps protect against certain types of cancer and coronary heart disease. Has an important role in the healing of wounds.	Cauliflower, spring greens, kale, broccoli, peppers, red cabbage	Swede, spinach, potatoes, mange tout, Savoy cabbage, aubergine, courgette, tomatoes
E Tocopherols	None set	Powerful antioxidant. Helps protect against heart disease and cancer.	Broccoli	
Beta-carotene	None set	The body can convert beta-carotene into vitamin. A but beta-carotene also acts as an antioxidant, protecting cells from damage. Can help to prevent heart disease and certain types of cancer.	Peppers, sweet potato	Spring greens, Brussels sprouts, butternut squash, pumpkin, spinach, carrots, tomatoes
Biotin	None set	Release of energy from foods.		Cauliflower, broccoli, Brussels sprouts, carrots, broad beans
Folate	200 mg/day women 200 mg/day men.	Production of red blood cells and the release of energy from food. Essential during pregnancy for folic acid.	Baby corn, asparagus	Beetroot, kale, leeks, cauliflower, spinach, broccoli, spring greens, aubergine, potatoes, Chinese leaf
B3 Niacin	13 mg/day women 17 mg/day men	Release of energy from food and a healthy nervous system.	Broad beans	Artichokes, watercress, red cabbage, Savoy cabbage, sweet potato, spring greens, leeks, marrow, courgette

WEB LINK The new Fruits & Veggies – More Matters campaign takes the place of the 5 A Day programme. Visit the new **FruitsandVeggiesMatter.gov.uk** website to get tools and information to help you eat more fruits and vegetables each day.

Types of vegetables

Vegetables are classified into the following varieties: roots, bulbs, flower heads, fungi, tubers, leaves, stems and shoots, seeds and pods, vegetable fruits and sea vegetables. In this section we will analyze the vegetable classifications and list possible cooking techniques.

Roots

The root of the plant anchors itself into the ground: the roots absorb water and nutrients from the soil and transport them to the rest of the plant.

QUALITY POINTS FOR PURCHASING

- Generally clean and free from soil.
- Firm, not soft, free from bruising and blemishes, evenly sized and shaped.
- Ensure that the grading of the root vegetable is correct and matches your needs to the menu.

EXAMPLES	PICTURE
Parsnips *(boiled, roasted, creamed, fried, soup)* A common root vegetable, creamy white parsnips have a sweet, nutty and earthy flavour. Before the introduction of potatoes from South America, roast parsnips were the traditional accompaniment to roast beef. In the past they were included in sweet dishes such as cakes and jams before sugar was widely available. When purchasing look for small to medium parsnips with a fresh creamy white appearance. Baby parsnips are also available.	
Turnips *(boiled, buttered, fried, soup)* Turnips have a subtle peppery flavour and a purple or green tinged creamy white skin. Baby turnips have particularly tender flesh with a sweetish, delicate flavour. Choose turnips that have smooth, unblemished skins without bruising and feel heavy for their size. Keep in a cool, dry, dark place for up to 1 week.	
Celeriac *(blanched for salads, boiled, buttered, creamed, roasted or braised)* With the flavour of celery and the appearance of a rough, creamy brown turnip, celeriac is a root vegetable. It has a dense texture similar to turnip or potato when cooked and is also known as turnip-rooted celery. Purchase small to medium firm bulbs that feel heavy for their size, larger bulbs are likely to be woody in texture. If possible choose ones that have a smoother outside to avoid excess wastage when peeling.	
Swede *(boiled, buttered, fried, purée, soup, roast)* With its creamy-purple skin and rounded shape swede is a popular root vegetable. It has an attractive pale orange-yellow coloured flesh with a bittersweet, mustardy flavour. Swedes are the traditional accompaniment to haggis which is eaten in Scotland on Burns night where they are known as 'neeps'. Over-sized swedes tend to be woody and tough so choose smaller swedes, with smooth skin if possible. Avoid any that have damaged or blemished skin.	
Beetroot *(steamed, boiled, shredded, purée, salad, roast, soup)* Related to the sugar beet and also known simply as beet, it is naturally high in sugar and has an earthy, sweet flavour with a hint of smokiness and a velvety smooth texture when cooked. When buying, look for firm, unblemished small to medium-sized beetroot with crisp, fresh looking tops. Beetroot tops can also be eaten. The crinkly green leaves have an attractive red stalk, cook and serve as for spring greens.	
Carrots *(buttered, glace, Vichy, purée, baby, soup)* One of the most versatile, reasonably priced and popular vegetables in the UK, carrots have a sweet flavour, crisp texture and a distinctive orange colour. Baby carrots, which are cooked whole, are especially tender and sweet. Choose carrots that feel firm to the touch, have a smooth skin and a bright colour.	

VIDEO CLIP Covent Garden market.

TASK Check your vegetable order and select five different vegetables on the list. Determine the provenance of each vegetable by researching where it was grown and how many food miles each has taken to reach your kitchen.

QUALITY POINTS FOR PURCHASING

- Cauliflowers should have tight and firm flower heads that are white in colour.
- Other brassicas should also have tight heads and bright colouring.
- They should not feel limp and the stems should be strong.
- Look for flower heads with an even size and without bruising or signs of frost marks.

Brassicas/flower heads

This plant is allowed to develop so the main part of the vegetable emerges and forms a shoot and in some cases a flower head.

EXAMPLES	PICTURE
Cauliflower *(boiled, buttered, stir-fried, gratin, creamed, served with a cheese sauce, garnished à la polonaise)* Cauliflower was first eaten in Europe in the 13th century and was originally from the Middle East. It was originally known as *coleflower*, meaning cabbage flower. With its classic creamy white florets and delicate flavour it is an attractive and popular choice. As well as the familiar white variety, Romanesco cauliflowers are available. These are conical-shaped and pale green in colour. Baby cauliflowers can also be purchased and are ideal size for a single portion. Whatever variety you buy choose a cauliflower that has a clean, firm head with crisp-looking green outer leaves.	
Purple sprouting broccoli *(boiled, buttered, fried, gratin, creamed, served with a cheese sauce, garnished à la polonaise)* Often simply referred to as purple sprouting; this is the original version of broccoli and has long stalks and small purple flower heads. The leaves, heads and stalks are all tender and edible. Look for strong, firm green stalks with tightly packed purplish green heads.	
Calabrese *(boiled, buttered, stir fried)* Also known as broccoli (it is originally from the Calabria region of Italy) calabrese with its tiny bright green buds, is one of the most popular vegetables in the UK. Along with cauliflower and cabbage it is a member of the brassica family. Look for bright green flower heads with firm stalks; avoid yellowing heads or wilting stalks.	
Brussels sprouts *(boiled, sautéed, buttered)* Brussels sprouts are leafy side shoots that have not elongated. They were developed from wild cabbage and are thought to have originated near Brussels in Belgium in the 13th century. Often associated with a traditional Christmas dinner, they are a versatile winter vegetable. They have a distinctive flavour, which can be unpleasant if they are overcooked. Choose small, green sprouts for the best flavour and firm compact ones for a good texture.	
White cabbage *(boiled, braised, stuffed, pickled)* is a leafy main shoot that hasn't elongated. Also known as green cabbage is one of the most popular types of cabbage available because of its flexibility in cuisine. Choose white cabbage that has crisp, bright looking leaves without any holes or discoloured patches. It should be firm and heavy for its size. Keep refrigerated after purchase.	

EXAMPLES	PICTURE
Kale *(boiled, steamed, buttered)* Kale is an attractive looking member of the cabbage family. With its dark green or red frilly leaves and distinctive cabbage and iron flavours it is a popular alternative to cabbage, spring greens or spinach. Look for small bunches of kale with crisp, fresh-looking leaves. Keep refrigerated after purchase.	
Chinese cabbage *(boiled, buttered, stir-fried)* A type of Oriental cabbage, Chinese leaves or Peking cabbage as it is also known is a pale green, closely packed long cabbage with elongated crinkly leaves. It has a subtle cabbage flavour and is used mainly for its crunchy texture rather than its flavour. Chinese leaves have the ability to absorb other flavours and are often combined with rich or strong-tasting foods. Look for firm, compact leaves that feel crisp and fresh. Keep in the fridge for up to 5 days.	
Pak choi *(boiled, buttered, fried)* These leafy greens are a popular Chinese vegetable that are similar to bok choi and spring greens. Pak choi has pretty paddle-shaped dark green crisp and crunchy leaves with a thick creamy stalk and a mild flavour. Choose fresh-looking pak choi with bright green, tender leaves; avoid any that is yellowed or wilting. Keep in the fridge for up to 5 days.	
Spring greens *(boiled, buttered, braised)* Spring greens are actually young, tender cabbage plants and are sold as loose heads of thick green leaves. Spring greens do not have the hard core which is found in the middle of fully-grown cabbages. Keep refrigerated after purchase.	

Tubers

This part of the plant grows beneath the surface from planting to harvesting. The roots feed the plant with water and nutrients.

QUALITY POINTS FOR PURCHASING

- Clean and free from soil.
- Firm and not soft or dried-out skin.
- Even size and shape with no bruising or blemishes.

New potatoes

POTATOES

These vegetables actually merit a subdivision of their own due to their versatility and every day use in modern professional kitchens around the world. The potato is a tuber which means that it grows underground and the stem of the plant stores reserves of food at the tip of the stalk.

Potatoes can be imported from Europe, the Canary Islands, Egypt, North Africa and America. Different varieties have different characteristics which mean that some are more suitable for certain methods of cookery than others. There are thousands of different varieties of potato, but only around 80 types are commercially grown of which approximately 20 are commonly available. Some heritage varieties are becoming easier to purchase. Heritage potatoes are specially grown for their gourmet eating qualities – excellent flavours, textures, colours, shapes, and historical value.

Potatoes generally fall into three main categories:

- New season first earlies (May/June to July)
- New season second earlies (August to September)
- Main season – main crop (September to May).

The difference between the skin finish of the new season and the main crop is that new season potatoes have a loose skin that just needs a gentle wash for preparation before

NEW SEASON 1ST EARLY	NEW SEASON 2ND EARLY	MAIN SEASON
Charlotte (pale skin and yellow flesh, firm, waxy texture and good flavour) *Good for salad potatoes and boiling*	**Saxon** (white skin and flesh, firm and moist texture) *Good for boiling, mashing, baking and chipping*	**Bintje** (white/yellow skin, yellow flesh) *Good for roasting and chipping*
Jersey Royals (kidney-shaped, pale yellow flesh) *Good for boiling and salads*	**Estima** (yellow flesh and pale skin) *Good for boiling, wedges and baking*	**Ratte (Asparges) 1872** (Heritage potato with long tubers with white skin and yellow flesh) *Good for boiling, salads and mashing*
Maris Bard (white flesh, waxy texture) *Good for boiling*	**Carlingford** (tight white flesh with a firm texture) *Good for wedges and boiling*	**Sante** (light yellow skin and flesh, dry and firm texture) *Good for boiling, wedges, chipping and roasting*
Epicure 1897 (Heritage potato with brown skin, deep eyes and white flesh) *Good for boiling and salads*	**Marfona** (light yellow skin and flesh, smooth waxy texture) *Good for boiling, wedges and baking*	**Desirée** (pink skin, soft yellow flesh) *Good for boiling, wedges, baking, chipping, roasting, mashing*
Rocket (white skin and flesh, firm and waxy texture) *Good for boiling*	**Nadine** (cream skin and flesh, firm, waxy texture) *Good for boiling, mashing and roasting*	**King Edward** (creamy-white colour with floury texture) *Good for chipping, roasting and potato Dauphinoise*
Premiere (yellow skin and flesh, firm and slightly dry texture) *Good for boiling and chipping*	**Wilja** (pale yellow skin and flesh, moderately waxy and slightly dry texture) *Good for boiling, chipping, roasting and mashing*	**Maris Piper** (pale skin, creamy white flesh) *Good for boiling, wedges, baking, chipping and roasting*
Sharpe's Express 1900 (Heritage potato with white skin and flesh with a waxy texture) *Good for boiling and salads*	**Rooster** (purple skin and white flesh) *Good for boiling, roasting, chipping and mashing*	**Romano** (red skin, creamy flesh, soft and dry texture) *Good for boiling, baking, roasting and mashing*
	Royal Kidney 1899 (Heritage potato with white skin and flesh, firm waxy flesh) *Good for boiling, steaming and salads*	**Kerr's Pink** (pale-pink skin, creamy flesh) *Good for salad potato, boiling and mashing*
	Maris Peer (cream skin and flesh with a dry, firm waxy texture) *Good for boiling, wedges and chipping*	**Golden Wonder** (pale flesh, medium colour skin) *Good for boiling and roasting*
		Cara (white skin, pale flesh and pink eyes, soft waxy texture) *Good for boiling*
		Edzell Blue 1915 (Heritage potato with a blue/purple skin and a white flesh) *Good for boiling or steaming with the skin on – which turns a creamy colour upon cooking*
		Pentland Dell (oval shape, floury texture) *Good for chipping, baking and mashing*
		Pink Fir Apple 1850 (Heritage potato with a pink skin, yellow flesh) *Good for boiling and sautéing*

cooking. This often means that the skins are usually flaky because the skins have not been fully set.

Fundamentally, there are two main parts of a potato – water and starch. The higher starch content (dry matter) in a potato the more *floury* it is and the more water, the *waxier* in texture. It is important to remember that both behave differently when cooked. To determine which category a potato falls into, the exact percentage of dry matter is measured (the percentage within the potato which is not water). Unwashed potatoes should be stored in a cool, dark, frost-free and dry place for up to 1 month, but not in the refrigerator. Washed potatoes should be stored in a refrigerator for up to 1 week. Potatoes should not be exposed to light as they can turn green and begin sprouting.

CHEF'S TIP **Floury potatoes** have high starch content with a dry and delicate texture. They break up easily when cooked and can absorb a lot of liquid and flavour. The common varieties of floury potatoes are Wilja, Maris Piper, King Edward and Rooster. They are suitable for baking, mashing and chipping and will have a soft, dry texture when cooked.

CHEF'S TIP **Waxy potatoes** have high water content, a dense texture and maintain their shape during cooking. They will not generally absorb much flavour or fat (such as butter). The common varieties of waxy potatoes are Nadine, Charlotte and Estima.

CHEF'S TIP

- Order the best quality potatoes – buying cheap potatoes is a false economy as damaged or green potatoes take far longer to prepare, give greater wastage and are more likely to lead to customer dissatisfaction.
- Check out with your supplier what varieties they have available.
- Order the right variety for your cooking purpose.
- Order the amount you need and in good time to ensure good stock rotation.
- Rotate your stocks every few days.

TASK Why are heritage potatoes becoming more popular with chefs and what do you think the benefits are when placing them on your menu?

SWEET POTATO

Although not related to the ordinary potato, sweet potatoes can be prepared and served in the same way. They have a creamy flesh with a sweet flavour that is similar to squash or roasted chestnuts. There are two main types of sweet potato, red skinned with a white flesh and brown skinned with a bright orangeflesh. Sweet potatoes are a staple food in the West Indies, Africa and Asia and are increasingly popular in Western cuisines. Choose firm sweet potatoes with undamaged skin. Sweet potatoes should be stored in a cool, dark, frost-free and dry place, but not in the refrigerator. Remove sweet potatoes from the plastic bag that they are usually sold in and transfer to a brown paper bag if possible.

Bulbs

These are vegetables with a strong leaf top. They are formed with many layers and are crammed with carbohydrates and water. The lower the temperature these vegetables are grown in the stronger the flavour will be.

QUALITY POINTS FOR PURCHASING

- Skin should not be damaged.
- No bruising or blemishes.
- Fennel should be crisp and firm, leeks should be predominantly clean and free from soil.
- Ensure that the class grading system is correct and you purchase the correct grade to meet your menu requirements.

EXAMPLES	PICTURE

Brown onion *(braised, fried, chopped, sliced)* This is the most widely used onion. With its pungent aroma and strong flavour it is a good all-round onion. Choose firm, blemish-free onions and avoid any that have green shoots. Keep in a cool, dry place for up to 1 month.

Garlic *(peeled, sliced, chopped, fried, marinated, soup)* A member of the onion and leek family, garlic is one of the most commonly used flavouring ingredients worldwide. With its distinctive flavour and aroma it is especially popular in Asian, Oriental and Mediterranean cuisines. Fresh garlic is harvested and dried to produce the bulbs that are available all year round. Garlic bulbs consist of several individual cloves, which are wrapped in fine paper-like skin. When purchasing garlic choose plump succulent bulbs with unblemished skin. Avoid any bulbs that are sprouting. Keep in a cool, dry place.

Red onion *(braised, fried, chopped, sliced)* A sweet and juicy, mild to strong flavoured onion with an attractive dark red-purple flesh, which is flecked with white lines. Choose firm onions with an evenly coloured skin; avoid those with any signs of softness or green shoots. Keep in a cool, dry place for 1–2 weeks.

Spring onion *(braised, fried, chopped, sliced, salads)* With their mild and delicate flavour spring onions, also known as salad onions or scallions, are small, immature onions that have been picked before the bulb has swollen. They have a narrow white bulb and a tender green shoot which is also used in cooking and provides a subtle onion flavour. Look for spring onions with bright, lively looking leaves and firm, clean white bulbs. Spring onions should be stored in the refrigerator for up to 3 days.

Fennel *(boiled, buttered, gratin, serve with cheese sauce and hollandaise)* With its creamy white bulb, pale green stalks and feathery leaves fennel is a pretty vegetable that is packed full of flavour. It has a distinctive aniseed flavour that goes particularly well with fish or chicken dishes. All parts of the vegetable are edible; the bulb and stalk can be sliced and eaten raw or cooked and the fine leaves can be used as a garnish or flavouring for a sauce. Baby fennel is also available and is ideal for cooking whole. Choose small, pale green or white unblemished bulbs as dark green bulbs tend to have a bitter flavour. Keep refrigerated after purchase.

Shallot *(peeled, chopped, sliced)* These onions have a mild, delicate flavour. They grow in a similar way to garlic and when peeled will divide into two or more cloves. There are also *banana shallots* which are slightly larger and have a distinctive longer shape to them. Keep in a cool, dry place for 1–2 weeks.

Leek *(braised, buttered, boiled, gratin)* A versatile vegetable, which is a member of the onion and garlic family. Leeks have a milder, sweeter flavour than onions, although they need to be cooked thoroughly to bring out the sweetness and to avoid an overpowering flavour. Small to medium leeks are the most tender. Choose leeks with firm white bulbs and bright green crisp leaves. Avoid leeks that have had the base of the root removed as they will deteriorate quickly. Keep in the refrigerator, for up to 1 week.

Leaves

These vegetables, as the name suggests, are grown for their leaves.

QUALITY POINTS FOR PURCHASING

- Should be fresh with leaves that are bright and vibrant in colour.

- The leaves should be crisp and not wilted without any bruising or cutting marks on them.

EXAMPLES	PICTURE
Spinach *(boiled, sautéed, creamed, wilted, purée, salad)* With its uniqdue flavour and bright green colour, spinach is a popular, easy-to-prepare and simple-to-cook vegetable. It is especially popular in Italy where Florentine dishes have a high spinach content. It wilts quickly so when purchasing seek crisp, dark green leaves with firm, hard stalks. Avoid spinach that has yellow patches or looks limp. When choosing, buy plenty as it reduces on cooking; 225 g spinach is sufficient for one serving. Keep in the refrigerator for up to 2 days.	
Chicory *(steamed, braised)* Also known as *Witloof* and *Endive*, Chicory is a superbly versatile vegetable. It is available all year round, grown in the UK, in both red and white (yellow-tinged) varieties. A popular misconception about chicory is that it has an inherently bitter flavour. The vegetable has a root that is indeed bitter, and the leaf flavour is affected by direct light – the more light it has and the more colour in the leaves then the stronger the flavour will be. However, in the UK, chicory is grown in dark rooms to ensure a smooth, distinctive flavour without too much bitterness. It has proven pro-biotic properties, promoting good bacteria in the stomach, and contains just 1 calorie per leaf. Store in a refrigerator and most importantly, keep chicory in the dark to avoid it developing a bitter flavour.	
Lettuce *(salad, braised)* Lettuce is most often grown as a leaf vegetable. In many countries, it is typically eaten raw in salads or braised as a vegetable accompaniment. Lettuce is a low calorie food and is a source of vitamin A and folic acid. Some lettuces (especially iceberg) have been specifically bred to remove the bitterness from their leaves. These lettuces have a high water content and so are less nutritionally dense than are the more bitter lettuces and those with darker leaves.	
Watercress *(salad, soups and garnishes)* A dark green leaf with a distinctive peppery and pungent flavour. Watercress can be used as a salad leaf instead of rocket or it can be included in recipes instead of spinach. Look for dark, green, fresh leaves and avoid any that are wilting or yellowing. Watercress is sold in bunches or ready-to-use in bags. Keep in a refrigerator for up to 2 days.	

Seeds and pods

These vegetables are eaten whole or as seeds. They grow from bushes and often hang so they are simple to harvest.

QUALITY POINTS

- Peas and beans should be crisp.

- If purchased in pods, peas should be full and beans not stringy.

- Good, bright colouration and no bruising or damage.

EXAMPLES	PICTURE
Okra *(boiled, buttered, stir-fried, deep fried, sautéed)* Originally from Africa and also very popular in Indian, Caribbean and Middle Eastern cookery, okra are also known as *ladies' fingers*. They are narrow, green-skinned, ribbed pods that contain rows of edible creamy seeds that ooze a glutinous liquid when cooked. They have a mild-bean like flavour when cooked. Look for firm, small green pods (a brownish tinge indicates they are stale) no longer than 8 cm and avoid any that appear shrivelled or feel soft when gently squeezed. Keep in a refrigerator for up to 3 days.	
Sweetcorn *(boiled, buttered, fried, soup, grilled)* Kernels of sweetcorn grow on cobs about 18 cm long and are surrounded by soft pale green leaves known as husks. With its distinctive bright yellow colour and sweet flavour, sweetcorn or corn-on-the-cob, can be served whole or the kernels can be removed. Choose medium-sized cobs with healthy-looking green husks wrapped tightly around them. When the husks are pulled away the kernels should be a pale yellowy white colour (this will brighten during cooking) and plump. Can be stored in a refrigerator for 3–4 days but is best eaten as soon as possible. Store with the husks wrapped around the corn.	
Peas *(boiled, stir-fried, soups, buttered)* Frozen peas are convenient and one of the most popular vegetables, but the flavour of fresh peas is much superior. They have a sweet taste, crisp texture and vivid bright green colour. When purchasing fresh peas in the pod, 1 kg of pods will give 350–450 g of peas. Choose bright green, firm, young pods with a little air-space left between the individual peas. Avoid discoloured or wrinkled pods; overfull pods may contain hard, tough peas so avoid these too. Peas should be eaten as fresh as possible for the very best flavour. Keep fresh peas in the pod, and keep refrigerated after purchase.	
Broad beans *(boiled, buttered)* Broad beans are small oval shaped creamy green beans with a distinctive flavour and a smooth creamy texture. They are available either in the pod or removed from the pod. Choose young small tender plump pods or small beans for the best flavour. Keep refrigerated after purchase.	
Runner beans *(boiled, buttered)* Long, flat green beans that have a coarse textured skin. More mature beans may have a fibrous string running down each side. Wash and top and tail the beans and if necessary remove the string from the side of the bean using a small, sharp knife. Keep refrigerated after purchase.	
Sugar snaps *(boiled, sautéed)* These are small, rounded pods, containing tiny peas. They are similar to mange tout, and the whole pod is eaten, but they are plumper. Sugar snaps have a fresh, sweet flavour and a crunchy texture. Look for bright green, crisp pods, which are full of peas but not bursting at the seams. Keep refrigerated after purchase.	
Mange tout *(boiled, sautéed)* The fine and slender almost translucent pods of mange tout (from the French for 'eat all') contain very young tiny tender peas. The whole mange tout pod is eaten and they have a crisp texture with a flavour similar to peas. Look for bright green, crisp pods. Keep refrigerated after purchase.	

Vegetable fruits

These vegetables usually grow from a stem and have seeds: they can be dry or juicy on the inside.

QUALITY POINTS

- Ripe, firm to the touch and not too soft.
- Good deep colouration without bruising or blemishes.
- Ensure the grading system used is approved and that you purchase the correct graded vegetable to meet the requirements of your menu.

EXAMPLES	PICTURE

Aubergine *(fried, grilled, baked, stuffed)* This dark, glossy purple vegetable is often thought to be native to the Mediterranean but in fact it was originally from Asia. Also known as the *eggplant*, aubergines have a meaty texture and a very subtle, but delicious earthy flavour. Aubergines have the ability to absorb other flavours and are often cooked with a selection of aromatic spices and onions. They are a particularly popular ingredient in Mediterranean and Middle Eastern cookery. When purchasing, look for plump, heavy aubergines with a shiny, unblemished skin. Keep refrigerated after purchase.

Tomato *(grilled, stuffed, blanched, baked)* Ranging in colour from vivid cherry red to bright yellow, in flavour from sweet and juicy to tangy and in size from tiny cherry varieties to plump beefsteak tomatoes, they are a versatile and popular ingredient. All types are now often sold on the vine as well. When buying, choose firm tomatoes with a bright unflawed skin: they should have a subtly sweet aroma. Types of tomatoes widely available include:
Beef tomatoes: The largest of the tomato varieties, these have a sweet dense red flesh. Ideal for stuffing, slicing or cooking with.
Vine ripened tomatoes: These are packed with flavour and mature further and keep better on the vine. With a distinctive tomato aroma they are delicious in salads or try roasted on the vine.
Cherry tomatoes: These are much smaller than other tomato varieties and have a very intense sweet flavour. Delicious as a lunchbox snack, in salads or roasted.
Cherry tomatoes on the vine: The small cherry tomato with a more intense flavour and aroma. Try roasting them on the vine or on the barbecue.
Plum tomatoes: These egg-shaped tomatoes have a meaty flesh and concentrated flavour, which makes them especially well-suited to cooking. They are available in various sizes including baby. Plum tomatoes are the most popular variety for canning. Tomatoes dislike the cold and storing at room temperature maximizes their flavour. Keep in a cool dry place away from sources of heat or sunlight.

Courgette *(stuffed, served à la Provençale, stir-fried, sautéed)* A member of the squash family, the courgette or *zucchini* is a summer squash with tender flesh and seeds and soft edible skin. Courgettes range in size from about 6 to 15 cm, and baby courgettes have the sweeter flavour. As well as the familiar green type, attractive bright yellow courgettes are also available. When purchasing either type, look for small (larger courgettes tend to have tougher skins), firm courgettes with smooth unblemished skins and a bright colour. Courgette flowers can also be eaten; they are a rich yellow colour and can be coated in batter and deep fried or they can be stuffed and steamed or baked. Keep refrigerated after purchase.

Marrow *(stuffed, served à la Provençale, baked, stir-fried)* A member of the squash family, the marrow is a distinctive looking vegetable. Its edible shiny skin can be any shade of green and its flesh is tender with a subtle flavour. When buying marrow choose the smallest one that you can. Over-sized marrows tend to have watery, bitter-tasting flesh. It should be firm and heavy for its size. Keep refrigerated after purchase.

Pepper *(grilled, stuffed, sautéed, soup)* Brightly coloured and sweet flavoured, peppers (also known as bell peppers) are a versatile vegetable that are eaten both raw and cooked and are used in many different cuisines including Chinese, Thai, Mexican, Spanish, Italian and French. A choice of different colours are available all peppers are originally green, and as they ripen and sweeten they turn red, orange or yellow. Peppers are sometimes skinned before using and this can help to enhance their sweet flavour. When buying look for firm textured, bright and shiny peppers, and bear in mind that orange, red and yellow varieties have a sweeter flavour than green peppers. Avoid bruised, wrinkled or blemished peppers as they will be past their best. Keep in a refrigerator for up to 5 days.

EXAMPLES	PICTURE
Pumpkin *(soup, boiled, purée)* Most often associated with lanterns at Halloween, pumpkins have a sweet, honey flavour and they are especially popular in North America. When choosing a pumpkin, it should have a smooth skin and be firm to the touch. Smaller pumpkins contain more flesh and are best for eating. Pumpkin is an excellent source of antioxidant beta-carotene, has useful amounts of vitamins B1, C and E. It is also a good source of the phytochemical lutein.	
Butternut squash *(purée, baked, roast, soup)* A large winter squash, about 15–20 cm long, which is similar in shape to a rounded pear. Butternut squash has a pale brown-orange skin and a deep, orange flesh. The wonderfully moist flesh has a sweet, buttery flavour and a slightly fibrous firm texture. Keep in a cool, dry place for up to 1 month.	
Avocado *(baked, grilled and salads)* Avocados are a commercially valuable fruit and are cultivated in tropical climates throughout the world (and some temperate ones, such as California), producing a green-skinned, pear-shaped fruit that ripens after harvesting. Avocados are high in valuable fats and appear to have a beneficial effect on blood serum levels. About 75 per cent of an avocado's calories come from fat, most of which is monounsaturated fat. Avocados also have 60 per cent more potassium than bananas. A ripe avocado yields to gentle pressure when held in the palm of the hand and squeezed. The flesh is prone to enzymatic browning and turns brown quickly after exposure to air. To prevent this, lime or lemon juice can be added to avocados after they are peeled.	

Stems

These vegetables are rooted and grow out of the ground: they can have leaves too.

QUALITY POINTS

- Generally clean and free of soil.
- Stems should be firm, crisp and free of bruising.
- Bright colouring.

EXAMPLES	PICTURE
Celery *(salads, braised, soup)* A versatile vegetable that is widely used in a variety of recipes. It adds a fresh flavour as well as a distinctive crunchy texture to both cooked dishes and salads. Celery was first introduced to the UK in the 17th century from Italy. The Romans used to wear it as a protection against hangovers! When buying celery look for regular shaped stalks that are not broken or bruised, it should look moist and crisp and be tight and compact. The darker the celery, (it can range from white to darkish green) the stronger its flavour. Over-large heads of celery tend to be stringy and are best avoided. Keep in its plastic sleeve (if provided) in the refrigerator for up to 1 week.	
Asparagus *(tips, hollandaise, buttered, vinaigrette)* Often considered to be a delicacy, with its straight spears and compact tip, asparagus is an attractive, elegant-looking vegetable with a wonderfully subtle flavour. Choose firm, fresh-looking stalks. Asparagus comes in a white or green variety. Wash each stalk and snap or cut off the end if it is woody or tough. Trim the stalks to approximately the same length to ensure even cooking. Tie in bunches of 6–8 stems. Keep in a refrigerator for up to 2 days.	

EXAMPLES	PICTURE

Globe artichoke *(boiled, fried)* An impressive-looking green-purple globe-shaped vegetable covered in layers of leaves, that is actually an edible type of thistle. Globe artichokes require a little effort in preparation and cooking, however the results are well worth it and they are often considered to be a luxury. A hairy choke is surrounded by the inner leaves which are not eaten but are discarded to reveal the deliciously nutty edible part of the artichoke the heart. If the artichokes are young and fresh the stem can also be eaten. Choose artichokes with slightly closed stiff leaves and a short stalk. Keep in a refrigerator for up to 1 week.

Kohlrabi *(salads, boiled and baked)* The taste and texture of kohlrabi are similar to those of a broccoli stem or cabbage heart, but milder and sweeter, with a higher ratio of flesh to skin. Kohlrabi can be eaten raw as well as cooked. There are several varieties commonly available, including White Vienna, Purple Vienna, and Grand Duke. Coloration of the purple types is superficial: the edible parts are all pale yellow. The leafy greens can also be eaten. Keep in a refrigerator for up to a week.

Fungi

Mushrooms/fungi are grown in damp, dark, mossy conditions. They grow well cultivated and in the wild. Wild mushrooms are very delicate and care should be taken when handling and storing them.

QUALITY POINTS

- Clean and free from grit, sand and soil.
- Ensure that wild mushrooms are easily identifiable.
- No blemishes, bruising or early signs of wilting.

HEALTH & SAFETY Care should be taken when harvesting wild mushrooms as some are toxic.

EXAMPLES	PICTURE

Button *(baked, poached, sautéed, grilled)* The most popular type of mushroom available, closed cup or button mushrooms have creamy white caps with pink gills which darken to beige as they grow. Keep in a paper bag in the fridge for up to 3 days. Do not store them in a plastic bag because they will sweat and quickly spoil.

Chestnut *(baked, poached, sautéed, grilled)* Also known as brown cap mushrooms, chestnut mushrooms have a strong taste and look like a darker version of the button mushroom. They have pink to dark brown gills. Keep in a paper bag in the fridge for up to 3 days. Do not store them in a plastic bag because they will sweat and quickly spoil.

Chanterelle *(baked, braised, poached, sautéed)* An apricot-coloured mushroom that has a very distinctive frilly trumpet shapes. Chanterelles have a slightly rubbery texture with a subtle fruity flavour. Chanterelles need to be cleaned carefully as dirt gets stuck under the gills, so they need to be rinsed under running water and then dried on kitchen paper. Keep in a paper bag in the fridge for up to 3 days. Do not store them in a plastic bag because they will sweat and quickly spoil.

EXAMPLES	PICTURE
Shiitake *(grilled, baked, poached, sautéed)* Originally from Japan and Korea shiitake mushrooms have firm caps and a light brown meaty flesh with a distinctive flavour. Look for plump mushrooms with curled under caps Keep in a paper bag in the fridge for up to 3 days. Do not store them in a plastic bag because they will sweat and quickly spoil.	
Oyster *(grilled, sautéed)* With a subtle flavour and chewy texture, oyster mushrooms can be grey, yellow or pink in colour. They are so-called because of their distinctive fan-like shape. Keep in a paper bag in the fridge for up to 3 days. Do not store them in a plastic bag because they will sweat and quickly spoil.	
Cep *(grilled, baked, poached, sautéed)* A meaty, creamy yellow mushroom with a spongy underside rather than gills. Ceps have a strong flavour and a velvety texture. Using a small, sharp knife, scrape the spongy underside away before cooking (it goes soggy) and wash. Keep in a paper bag in the fridge for up to 3 days. Do not store them in a plastic bag because they will sweat and quickly spoil.	
Morels *(sautéed, poached)* Morels are a feature of many cuisines. Their unique flavour is prized by chefs worldwide, with recipes and preparation methods designed to highlight and preserve it. As with most edible fungi, they are best when collected or bought fresh. Morels are not improved by extensive washing or soaking, as it may ruin the delicate flavour and require long cooking times. Due to their natural porosity, morels may contain trace amounts of soil which cannot be washed out. Drying is a popular and effective method of long-term storage for morels, and they are readily available commercially in this form: dried morels can be reconstituted by soaking in warm water or milk. They may also be frozen after steaming or frying.	
Portabello *(baked, roasting and sautéed)* Commonly found in fields and grassy areas after rain from late spring through to autumn worldwide. Portobello mushrooms have a robust meaty texture making them good for roasting, baking and stuffing. They are perfect for barbecuing, too – cook for a few minutes until the juices run, or slice thickly and sauté with onions and garlic.	

SOURCING Food miles contribute approximately 2 per cent of the carbon produced in food production whilst making artificial fertilizer contributes about 30 per cent. Blended fertilizers are better to use but we are running out of the mined ingredients for artificial fertilizer. However, organic and bio-dynamic production use natural methods of soil fertility, which produce better results and are more sustainable.

Sea vegetables

These vegetables are becoming better known and used in modern day cooking. They tend to be purchased dried and require soaking to remove the high salt levels. They are a good source of iron.

QUALITY POINTS

● Samphire should have a strong colour and feel firm without signs of deterioration such as a strong odour and weeping moisture.

EXAMPLES	PICTURE

Arame *(Japanese miso soup and salads)* It is a species of *kelp* best known for its use in Japanese cuisine. It is one of many species of seaweed used in Japanese dishes.
Arame is high in calcium, iodine, iron, magnesium, and vitamin A as well as being a good dietary source for many other minerals. Usually purchased in a dried state, it is reconstituted quickly, taking about five minutes. Arame comes in dark brown strands, has a mild, semi-sweet flavour, and a firm texture. Once reconstituted, it may be served alone or as a garnish. It also may be served among other seaweeds as a mixture or a salad, including marinated dishes.

Kelp *(raw or fried)* There are several Pacific based species of kelp, and it is a very important ingredient in Japanese cuisine. It is used to flavour broths and stews (especially Dashi), as a savoury garnish for rice and other dishes, as a vegetable, and a primary ingredient in popular snacks. Transparent sheets of kelp are used as an edible decorative wrapping for rice and other food.

Nori Sometimes known as laver bread, nori is commonly used as a wrap for sushi. It is also a common garnish or flavouring in noodle preparations and soups.

Wakame *(fried, dried, salted, soups, salads)* It has a subtly sweet flavour and is most often served in soups and salads. Japanese and Korean sea-farmers have grown wakame for centuries and they still are the main producers and eaters. The leaves should be cut into small pieces as they will expand during cooking. In Japan and Europe, wakame is distributed either dried or salted, and used in soups (particularly miso soup), and salads (tofu salad), or often simply as a side dish to tofu and a salad vegetable like cucumber. These dishes are typically dressed with soya sauce and vinegar/rice vinegar.

Hijiki *(simmered with other vegetables)* It is a brown sea vegetable growing wild on rocky coastlines around Japan, Korea, and China. Hijiki is known to be rich in dietary fibre and essential minerals such as calcium, iron and magnesium. The seaweed is boiled and dried to be sold in the form of dried hijiki. Dried processed hijiki turns black. To prepare dried hijiki for cooking, it is first soaked in water then cooked with ingredients like soy sauce and sugar to make a dish. Several government food safety agencies (including the UK's FSA) advise consumers to avoid consumption of hijiki seaweed. Test results have indicated that levels of inorganic arsenic were significantly higher than in other types of seaweed.

Samphire *(boiled, steamed, poached and sautéed)* Due to its high salt content, Samphire must be washed and then cooked without any salt added, in plenty of water. It has a hard stringy core, and after cooking, the edible flesh is pulled off from the core. This flesh, after cooking, resembles seaweed in colour, and the flavour and texture are like young spinach stems or asparagus. Samphire is very often used as an accompaniment to fish or seafood. Purchase bright, fresh looking plants with no signs of wilting. Buy samphire as you need it – it does not keep for long. If you must keep it, tightly wrap and refrigerate for not longer than 3 days.

Agar-agar *(vegetarian alternative to gelatine)* The word 'agar' comes from the Malay word agar-agar (meaning jelly). It is also known as kanten, China grass, or Japanese isinglass. White and semi-translucent, it is sold in packages as washed and dried strips or in powdered form. It can be used to make jellies, puddings, and custards. For making jelly, it is boiled in water until the solids dissolve. Sugar, flavour, colour, fruit or vegetables are then added and the liquid is poured into moulds to be served as desserts.

SEASONAL AVAILABILITY FOR VEGETABLES IN THE UK

VEGETABLES	JAN	FEB	MAR	APR	MAY	JUN	JUL	AUG	SEP	OCT	NOV	DEC
Asparagus					X	X						
Aubergine					X	X	X	X	X			
Broad beans					X	X	X	X	X			
Broccoli	X	X	X					X	X	X	X	X
Brussels Sprouts	X	X	X					X	X	X	X	X
Cabbage					X	X	X	X	X	X		
Carrots						X	X	X	X	X	X	X
Cauliflower	X	X	X				X	X	X	X	X	X
Celery				X	X	X	X					
Courgettes						X	X	X	X			
French beans						X	X					
Leeks	X	X						X	X	X	X	X
Lettuce					X	X	X	X	X	X	X	
Marrows								X	X	X		
New potatoes					X	X	X	X	X	X	X	X
Onions	X	X	X				X	X	X	X	X	X
Parsnips	X	X	X					X	X	X	X	X
Peas						X	X					
Potatoes	X	X	X	X	X			X	X	X	X	X
Pumpkin	X	X	X					X	X	X	X	X
Radish			X	X	X	X	X	X	X	X	X	
Runner beans								X	X	X	X	
Spinach				X	X	X	X	X	X	X		
Spring onions						X	X	X	X	X	X	
Swedes	X	X	X					X	X	X	X	X
Sweetcorn									X	X		
Tomatoes				X	X	X	X	X	X	X		
Turnip	X	X							X	X	X	X
Watercress			X	X	X	X	X	X	X	X	X	

Purchasing specifications

Because vegetables are very delicate and prone to damage during harvesting and transport, care must be taken when purchasing. The quality of fresh vegetables will deteriorate rapidly if they have not been correctly stored prior to purchase. The EU has introduced a vegetable quality grading system to aid purchasing:

- Extra class – Produce of the maximum quality
- Class 1 – Produce of good quality
- Class 2 – Produce of reasonable quality
- Class 3 – Produce of low market quality.

Organic farming is a system of crop farming that uses biological methods of fertilization and pest control. Organic materials, including animal manure, compost, grass turf, and straw are applied to fields to improve soil structure and moisture-holding capacity and to nourish soil life. Soil organisms make nutrients available to plants. Biological pest control is achieved through preventive methods, including diversified farming, crop rotation, the planting of pest-deterrent species, and the use of integrated pest management techniques. Chemical fertilizers and pesticides are not used. They are regarded by supporters of organic methods as harmful to health and the environment. Since organic farming is time-consuming, organically grown produce tends to be expensive.

Storage of vegetables

The different types of vegetable may require separate storage methods depending upon the shape, size and species. Onions, garlic, shallots are stored in a cool environment (10–18 °C) and preferably on their own as the smell can overpower any produce nearby. It is best to leave these products whole as cutting will release the strong odour and they will lose flavour. All root vegetables should be removed from their sacks and stored in plastic bins or containers.

Leeks and other green vegetables are best purchased as required and should be placed in a refrigerator if storage is necessary. In general they will last 2–3 days in good condition then deteriorate quickly after that, turning limp and losing colour. They should also be stored away from tomatoes because tomatoes release small quantities of ethylene gas which causes green vegetables to wilt. If green vegetables are damaged they will soon lose their vitamin C content.

Potatoes should be stored in cool, dark places as sunlight causes rapid deterioration of the skin. They should be kept clear of damp areas as this turns them mouldy. Paper bags or sacks are ideal units to store them in as it allows the potatoes to breathe; polythene simply causes humidity and moisture.

Hard vegetables such as carrots, swedes and parsnips should be kept in cool conditions in a refrigerator and will last for approximately 5–6 days until they begin to soften and the texture breaks down. As a general rule hard vegetables will store for longer periods of time and soft/leafy vegetables for only a day or two.

Fruit vegetables such as tomatoes can be purchased slightly unripe and left to ripen slowly at room temperature in the kitchen. The ethylene gas produced by tomatoes is a ripening agent, placing a ripe tomato with unripe ones in a bag helps to speed the ripening process. Salad vegetables should be placed into plastic containers and stored in a refrigerator.

In an ideal kitchen all the produce would be purchased on a daily basis and used immediately. This would increase the vitamin/nutrient content, flavours and textures and ensure only the freshest ingredients are served to the customer.

Preparing vegetables

Vegetables and potatoes should be washed well in clean water and then peeled as finely as possible to retain as much nutritional value as you can. Sometimes the vegetables or potatoes may require a final wash after peeling. The peelings should be placed into a separate bowl to keep the work surface as hygienic as possible. Keep the workstation tidy at all times, dispose of the waste once each task is completed and sanitize the area thoroughly with hot water and a soft detergent.

VEGETABLE CUTS

Julienne – thin matchstick cuts which measure 2 mm × 2 mm × 4 cm long. Cut the vegetable into 2 cm lengths and then cut the lengths into thin slices. Then cut the slices into thin strips.

Brunoise – 2 mm dice cut from the julienne, cutting the strips into 2 mm dice.

 VIDEO CLIP Cutting vegetables brunoise and julienne.

Gros brunoise – a larger 4 mm × 4 mm dice cut in exactly the same way as brunoise but slightly larger.

Jardinière – batons measuring 4 mm × 4 mm × 1.5 cm long. Cut the vegetables into 1.5 cm lengths and cut the lengths to 4 mm slices. Cut the slices into batons.

Macédoine – 5 mm dice cut from the jardinière batons.

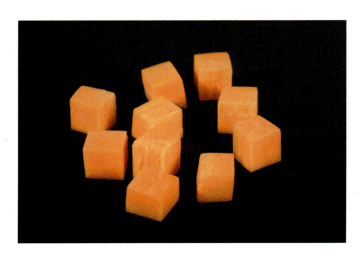

Paysanne – thinly sliced squares, rounds, triangles or rough-sided rounds all 1 cm in diameter. To create an economical cut the shape of the vegetable must dictate the type of shape to cut.

Mirepoix – roughly chopped root vegetables approximately 2 cm × 2 cm.

Sliced onion – first peel the onion and cut in half going across the circular grain. Place the half onion in front of you and slice thinly going with the grain. If the recipe calls for quartered and sliced, simply cut the half onion in half once more going across the grain. Hold the two quarters together in the shape of a half onion and slice going with the grain.

VIDEO CLIP   Finely slicing an onion.

Finely diced onion – follow the steps for sliced onion but instead of slicing with the grain all the way through, slice the onion finely to just before the stem, so that it is still held together by the stem. Now cut into the onion horizontally two or three times up to just before the stem. The greater the number of horizontal cuts, the finer the cubes will be. Finally, cut the onion against the grain, so that it simply falls into fine dice.

VIDEO CLIP   Finely chopping an onion.

Cooking vegetables

There are numerous ways to cook vegetables and the choice depends on the end result that is required.

- The most basic cooking technique is **blanching**. This involves cooking the vegetables in boiling salted water for a very short time, usually no more than a few seconds. They are then plunged into iced water to halt the cooking process immediately. Vegetables are blanched to set the colour, to loosen skin (as for tomato concassée) or to eliminate strong flavours.

- **Parboiling** is to partially cook the vegetable to prepare it for alternative finishing such as deep frying, braising or roasting.

- Cooking **al dente** literally means 'to the tooth' and requires vegetables to be cooked until just firm, crisp and yet tender. This degree of cooking is applied to most green vegetables such as beans, mange tout and sugar snap peas.

● **Fully cooked** means to cook the vegetable until tender and it is normally for root vegetables and potatoes which are usually cooked until fully done.

 VIDEO CLIP Preparing and cooking green vegetables.

Boiling and steaming

As a general indication, vegetables that grow beneath the ground should be placed into cold salted water and brought to the boil. Those vegetables that grow above the ground should be plunged into boiling salted water. This is so that they can be cooked as quickly as possible to retain as much of their flavour, colour and nutrients as possible. The exception to the rule is new potatoes, which should be plunged into boiling salted water. Vegetables grown above the ground should be added to the boiling salted water in small batches to prevent the temperature of the water from dropping too much and therefore prolonging cooking.

All vegetables cooked by boiling can be cooked by steaming. They are prepared in the same way as for boiling, placed into steamer trays and seasoned with salt before

cooking. Steaming vegetables results in a firmer and crisper vegetable because there has been no contact with liquid in the saucepan. In general, you can add seasonings to the steaming liquid, such as lemon zest or fresh herbs, which can impart flavour to the vegetables. White vegetables which discolour once prepared or boiled, such as salsify and Jerusalem artichokes, should be cooked in **au blanc**. Their whiteness can be retained by cooking them in a liquid made up of water, flour, salt and a little lemon juice. Mix the flour with a little water to a smooth paste. Add the remaining water and lemon juice. Season with the salt and bring to the boil while stirring.

Ideally all boiled vegetables should be drained and served immediately. In practice that can generate difficulties, especially where large numbers of customers are served over a long service period. Green vegetables will always discolour quickly and all vegetables will lose flavour if held for too long at hot temperatures. The reheating of boiled vegetables such as French beans, broccoli, peas, asparagus, kale, Brussels sprouts and cauliflower should follow these guidelines:

● As soon as the vegetable is just cooked refresh in iced water as quickly as possible.

● Drain thoroughly, place onto trays and store covered with plastic film in a refrigerator.

● When required for service, using one tray of vegetables at a time, place the required number of portions into a vegetable strainer and plunge into plenty of boiling salted water.

● When the vegetables have just heated through, remove from the boiling water and drain thoroughly before presenting on hot dishes or plates to be served.

This method is economical because any vegetable not used for one service can be utilized for the next.

Baking

Baked potatoes

This is a dry heat method where the vegetable is surrounded by very hot air in an oven chamber. The baking of vegetables will concentrate the natural flavours and will sometimes produce a slight natural caramelization on the skin. Thick-skinned or hard vegetables are most suited to baking, for example potatoes, beetroot, aubergine and tomatoes. Potatoes are often baked in their skins and sometimes wrapped in aluminium foil. The oven temperature is usually around 200 °C and the vegetables should be of an even size.

CHEF'S TIP   Do not pierce beetroot skin before baking as the beetroot will bleed and lose its valuable nutrients and flavour.

Roasting

Roasted vegetables

This is a similar method to baking, utilizing the same heating technique. Normally the vegetables to be roasted will have been washed, peeled and prepared and placed into a roasting tray with a little fat and seasoning. At this stage additional flavours such as herbs, garlic, onions and spices can be added. The oven should be preheated to 200 °C and during the roasting stage natural caramelization will occur to the vegetable. This is to be encouraged to create further colour and flavour enhancements.

CHEF'S TIP   Other vegetables which can be successfully roasted are asparagus, carrots, swede and parsnips.

CHEF'S TIP   Use sunflower, canola, groundnut and olive oil for sautéeing. Butter (either clarified or whole) and goose fat will also add plenty of flavour when shallow frying. When using olive oil for sautéeing, ensure that it does not overheat. Olive oil has a lower smoke point than other oils and will burn easily.

Frying

Shallow frying is a quick method of cookery that uses small amounts of fat. The normal procedure consists of heating butter or oil in a frying pan until it just begins to brown before adding the vegetables, seasoning and cooking until lightly coloured on all sides.

Sautéeing is another alternative and is a similar method of cookery to shallow frying. The difference is that the amount of fat used to sauté is usually less and the vegetables are 'tossed' while cooking is being undertaken. Vegetables suitable for sautéeing include leafy greens, onions, mushrooms and beans. Sometimes both sautéeing and shallow frying is seen as a finishing step for vegetables that are parboiled.

Stir frying vegetables

Stir frying is a traditional Chinese method of cooking and is a variation of sautéeing. The technique consists of prepared vegetables being placed into a little very hot oil in a wok or heavy frying pan with curved sides. The cooking is carried out quickly in as high a heat as possible while continuously stirring or 'tossing' the vegetables. The vegetables are cooked when they are judged to be still slightly crisp and firm. The quality points for a stir fried vegetable are crispness, firmness, the original colour is maintained and a good fresh flavour preserved.

Deep frying has a number of applications for vegetables such as fritters or tempura. With a few exceptions, vegetables should be cut into small pieces or florets, seasoned or marinated in a little flavoured oil or lime juice and fresh herbs and passed through the prepared batter.

CHEF'S TIP   If there is no thermometer to measure the temperature of hot fat to deep fry, heat the oil in a saucepan for eight minutes. Drop a small piece of the vegetable that is going to be deep fried into the hot fat. If it floats to the top, the oil is at the correct temperature. If not, continue heating and testing at one minute intervals.

Deep fry quickly at approximately 185 °C, until golden brown in colour. Other vegetables can be passed through milk and then seasoned flour and deep fried or through seasoned flour and beaten egg before cooking. All deep fried vegetables should be thoroughly drained before serving and should not be covered with a lid as condensation will quickly make the vegetable become soft and soggy.

> **HEALTH & SAFETY** **Hot fat and water do not mix** – the water vaporizes so quickly it explodes!
>
> 1. All operators should know fire drill and how to use the deep fat fryer.
> 2. Only half fill the deep fat fryer with fat (the level is usually marked) and do not overload with the food to be cooked.
> 3. Always drain and dry the food from any excess water before frying to prevent a dangerous splashing reaction from the water and hot oil.
> 4. Always place food in fryer away from you to prevent splashing and burning–do not throw in.
> 5. Always have basket and spider to hand so that food can be removed quickly and safely.
> 6. Take care when moving a free standing fryer – do not carry around the kitchen with hot fat in it.
> 7. Keep your sleeves rolled down and use clean, dry, thick cloths.

> **HEALTH & SAFETY** If a fire occurs in a deep fryer, these are the first two things you would do.
>
> 1. Turn off heat source.
> 2. Cover with lid, fire blanket or damp cloth.

Grilling

Vegetable kebabs

This is a healthy method of cookery because little or no fat is required. Most vegetables are suitable for this method of cookery although some, for example potatoes, fennel and carrots, may need to be parboiled first. Additional flavours can be added in the form of flavoured oils, herbs and spices, and left to marinate prior to grilling. Vegetables can be grilled under a salamander where the position of the rack is important to help ensure even cooking and prevent burning. Alternatively, grilling on a char-grill will produce a direct heat via the hot bars. This will give attractive grilled bar marking on the vegetable surface.

> **CHEF'S TIP** When preparing vegetables for grilling ensure that they are cut into equal-sized pieces so that they cook evenly.

Stewing

Stewed vegetables

Vegetables which have high moisture content such as courgette, aubergine and marrow can be stewed successfully. For this method of cookery the vegetables are simmered in a stock or flavoured liquid for an extended period of time. Stewing can take place in the oven or on the stove top. A well-known stewed vegetable dish is ratatouille.

Braising

This is a similar method of cookery to stewing but it uses less liquid and some of the recipes for braising do not call for sweating or browning any flavouring agents such as garlic before adding the vegetables. Cabbage, endive, leeks and celery are all vegetables that can be braised successfully.

When cooking with potatoes it is important to use the correct variety to give the best results.

Braised vegetables

Preserving

The preserving of vegetables or fruits by sealing in airtight cans or jars is a good way of using up excess stores of seasonal vegetable and fruit items. In preserving, the food is heated – or processed – for a specified time in a closed jar and hermetically sealed with a two-piece cap. Heating the jar expels air and halts decay. As the jar cools, the lid seals onto the rim and creates a vacuum.

Vegetables for preserving fall into two categories: high acid or low acid. High-acid foods, such as tomatoes, are processed using a boiling-water preserving method at a temperature of 100 °C. With this method, packed jars are placed in a rack and lowered into a large pot of boiling water. Boiling-water processing is easiest for the chef to achieve.

Low-acid foods must be preserved with steam-pressure at a temperature of 116 °C. Low-acid foods include green beans, carrots, beetroot, peas and sweetcorn. All canned or bottled foods must be processed for the specific amount of time required in the recipe to ensure a safe product.

Chefs can pickle almost any type of vegetable. It is a simple way to store many crops, from shallots to beetroot and even cabbage and marrow. Some ideas for vegetable pickles are below:

- *Spicy pumpkin chutney* – a pickle made with brown sugar, steamed pumpkin, and red chillies, native to the Caribbean.

- *Sauerkraut* – white cabbage pickled in its own brine, traditionally made in an earthenware jar and served with grilled sausages.

- *Balsamic beets* – baby beetroot pickled in a mixture of distilled and balsamic vinegar, sweetened with a little brown sugar and served with cheeses.

Vegetable protein

Some vegetables, especially légumes, are rich in protein and are used to substitute protein from other sources, such as meat, fish and dairy products or in their own right.

Soya products

The soya bean has been part of the diet of the Chinese for over 4000 years, and part of the Western diet for 60 years. It is believed that the low rates of colon and breast cancer in China and Japan are attributable to the consumption of soya products.

Soya is the most nutritious of the leguminous seeds. High in protein and cholesterol-free, it contains all eight of the essential amino acids that cannot be made in the body. It is exceptionally versatile and is processed into many products.

Various soy products

PREPARING, PORTIONING AND COOKING TOFU

Tofu

The beans are boiled mashed and sieved to make soya milk, which is processed in a similar way to soft cheese. It is pressed and made into several derivatives. Tofu should be kept in a refrigerator for up to one week after purchase. The water should be changed daily and the tofu washed prior to preparation. Tofu does not freeze well as the freezing process changes the texture.

Silken tofu is a good alternative to cream in a vegan diet: it has the same qualities as cream and can be used as a fat-free method of making cream soups, sauces, and desserts.

Firm tofu is the fully pressed version of tofu. It is sold in blocks that can be sliced or diced and used in almost any vegetarian dish. It is quite bland in flavour and benefits from being marinated and sautéed in flavoured oils.

OTHER DERIVATIVES OF SOYA BEANS

TEMPEH

Fermented soya beans, cooked and pressed. It is similar to tofu but has a firmer texture and a slightly nutty flavour. Tempeh can be bought chilled and stored for seven days or frozen and stored up to the use by date.

TVP (TEXTURED VEGETABLE PROTEIN)

Made from processed soya beans, TVP is a dry product that needs rehydrating in hot stock or water. TVP is a meat replacement that can be used in stews or minced meat

dishes. Keep in the dry stores in an airtight container with the use by date on display.

TVP (textured vegetable protein)

Seitan

Seitan is a wheat-based protein which is made with flour that has a high ratio of gluten, by kneading the flour under several changes of water and then boiling the resultant dough. Seitan lacks flavour and benefits from marinating. As it is precooked, all it needs is to be warmed through, so it can be added at the end of the cookery process. Store in the refrigerator for up to seven days.

Mycoprotein (Quorn™)

Quorn™ is made by growing, harvesting and fermenting fungus under controlled conditions. The product is then bound with albumen, textured, flavoured and shaped or sliced to resemble meat. Storage is as per packaging instructions. Quorn™ can be used as either meat substitute or as one of the many convenience products available under the Quorn™ brand name.

TEST YOURSELF

To test your level of knowledge and understanding, answer the following short questions. These will help to prepare you for your summative (final) assessment.

1   Identify two types of the following:

   ● tomatoes_____

   ● artichokes_____

   ● tofu_____

2   Briefly define the following vegetable cuts:

   (a) brunoise _____   (b) julienne_____

   (c) macedoine _____   (d) jardinaire _____

   (e) paysanne _____   (f) mirepoix _____

   (g) chiffonade _____

3   Explain the reason for not storing potatoes in direct sunlight.

4   State two ways of retaining nutrients in potatoes during preparation.

5   State two reasons for green vegetables being cooked in boiling salted water without a lid.

6   When steaming vegetables state two precautions that should be taken.

7   Explain the reasons for removing excess moisture and water from vegetables before deep frying.

8   Quorn™ is produced by fermenting – tofu, fungus, or soya?

9   What does TVP stand for?

10   Soya is high in cholesterol or low in cholesterol?

Recipes

Braised baby gem lettuce *(Laitue braise)*

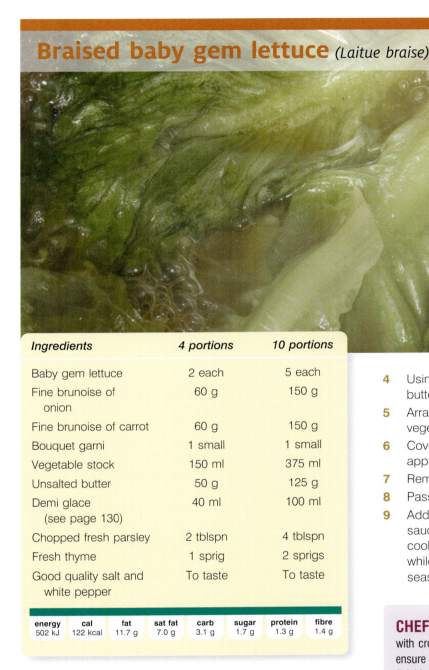

Ingredients	4 portions	10 portions
Baby gem lettuce	2 each	5 each
Fine brunoise of onion	60 g	150 g
Fine brunoise of carrot	60 g	150 g
Bouquet garni	1 small	1 small
Vegetable stock	150 ml	375 ml
Unsalted butter	50 g	125 g
Demi glace (see page 130)	40 ml	100 ml
Chopped fresh parsley	2 tblspn	4 tblspn
Fresh thyme	1 sprig	2 sprigs
Good quality salt and white pepper	To taste	To taste

energy	cal	fat	sat fat	carb	sugar	protein	fibre
502 kJ	122 kcal	11.7 g	7.0 g	3.1 g	1.7 g	1.3 g	1.4 g

METHOD OF WORK

1 Preheat an oven to 180 °C.

2 Remove any outer blemished leaves and wash the lettuce well in plenty of cold running water. Blanch each head of lettuce in boiling salted water for 2 minutes and then refresh immediately in iced water.

3 Drain well and carefully pat the lettuce dry on a clean kitchen cloth. Cut the lettuce in half lengthways.

4 Using a sauteuse lay the onion and carrot on a lightly buttered base.

5 Arrange the lettuce on top, and barely cover with the vegetable stock and add the bouquet garni and thyme.

6 Cover with a cartouche and lid, then braise for approximately 15 minutes.

7 Remove the lettuce and keep warm.

8 Pass the cooking liquor and reduce by half.

9 Add the demi-glace, correcting the consistency of the sauce and then return the lettuce to the pan with the cooking sauce. Coat well by spooning over the sauce while warming through the lettuce and check the seasoning before serving.

CHEF'S TIP The braised lettuce can also be served with croûtons or the demi-glace can be omitted to ensure the dish can be consumed by vegetarians. When finishing the sauce at the end, add a few knobs of unsalted butter to give the sauce a rich glossy appearance and texture.

Braised cabbage (Chou braise)

Ingredients	4 portions	10 portions
Cabbage (Savoy, green or sweetheart)	400 g	1 kg
Brunoise carrot	100 g	250 g
Brunoise onion	100 g	250 g
Vegetable stock	300 ml	750 ml
Bouquet garni	1 small	1 small
Fresh thyme	1 sprig	2 sprigs
Demi glace (see page 130)	100 ml	250 ml
Good quality salt and white pepper	To taste	To taste

energy	cal	fat	sat fat	carb	sugar	protein	fibre
259 kJ	62 kcal	3.4 g	1.0 g	5.9 g	4.3 g	2.5 g	4.1 g

METHOD OF WORK

1 Preheat an oven to 180°C.

2 Remove any blemished outer leaves of the cabbage and wash well. Select clean, unblemished outer leaves and reserve to one side. Cut the cabbage into quarters and remove the stalk. Rewash and drain off the water.

3 Place the cabbage into boiling salted water and blanch for 4 minutes.

4 Remove and refresh the cabbage in iced water and drain well. Place the selected outer leaves into the boiling water for 2 minutes and repeat the process of refreshing in iced water.

5 Reserve the outer leaves leaving one per portion. Place them onto a clean tea towel and dry carefully.

6 Finely slice the remaining cabbage and press dry to remove any excess water.

7 Divide the finely sliced cabbage onto each leaf and season well. Manipulate the clean kitchen cloth to roll the cabbage balls tightly.

8 Using a sauteuse pan, place the brunoise of onion and carrot on the bottom and put the cabbage parcels on top. Pour over the vegetable stock halfway up the side of the cabbage parcels.

9 Add the bouquet garni, fresh thyme and bring to the boil on the stove, cover with a cartouche and a lid then bake for about 45 minutes.

10 Carefully remove the cabbage parcels and pass the liquid, return to a clean saucepan to reduce the quantity by half. Add the demi glace and correct the consistency and seasoning.

11 Return the cabbage to the sauce and use it to glaze the cabbage before serving or serve the sauce separately from the cabbage parcels if required.

CHEF'S TIP The addition of julienne carrot, leek and bacon mixed into the finely sliced cabbage centre will supplement the flavour of the dish. Never add bicarbonate of soda, as some suggest, to the boiling water to help maintain the bright green colour of the vegetable. The soda will soften the leaves, break down the nutrient value of the vegetable and degrade the flavour.

Step-by-step: Braised cabbage

1. Place the finely sliced cabbage onto the dried outer leaves.

2. Form a ball and carefully set the shape.

3. Wrap the clean kitchen cloth tightly around the parcel to help hold the shape, although this is not always necessary provided that a gentle braise is achieved during cooking.

Braised fennel *(Fenouil braise)*

Ingredients	4 portions	10 portions
Fennel bulbs (medium in size)	2 bulbs	5 bulbs
Brunoise onion	100 g	250 g
Brunoise leek	100 g	250 g
Vegetable stock	300 ml	750 ml
Fresh thyme	1 sprig	2 sprigs
Lemon juice	¼ of a lemon	½ of a lemon
Unsalted butter	30 g	70 g
Fresh flat leaf parsley	A few sprigs	A few sprigs
Good quality salt and white pepper	To taste	To taste

energy	cal	fat	sat fat	carb	sugar	protein	fibre
390 kJ	94 kcal	8.0 g	4.3 g	4.2 g	3.1 g	1.8 g	4.1 g

METHOD OF WORK

1 Preheat an oven to 180 °C.
2 Trim any outer stalks that are blemished and remove any fronds (reserve to one side). Wash and trim the green tops back leaving a small amount and remove any stringy or damaged outer layers.
3 Slice the bulbs lengthwise into quarters.
4 Lay the leek and onions into a sauté pan with the already melted butter and place the fennel on top.
5 Barely cover with the stock, season well and add the thyme and lemon juice.
6 Bring to a gentle simmer and then cover with a cartouche and a lid and braise for approximately 20 minutes or until the bulbs are tender.
7 Remove the fennel from the pan and pass the liquor.
8 Season the liquor.
9 Dress the fennel on a serving dish with the cooking liquor chopped fronds of fennel and the coarsely chopped flat leaf parsley.

CHEF'S TIP Combine red and brown onion in this recipe and braise together for a different flavour contrast. To turn this recipe into a gratin, substitute the chicken stock with double cream and sprinkle breadcrumbs and parmesan cheese on top and bake in the oven.

Braised red cabbage
(Chou rouge à la flamande)

Ingredients	4 portions	10 portions
Red cabbage	300 g	750 g
Sliced onions	50 g	125 g
Butter	60 g	150 g
Red wine	80 ml	200 g
Red wine vinegar	60 ml	150 g
Grated Cox's apples	140 g	350 g
Caster sugar	15 g	30 g
Streaky bacon (optional)	50 g	125 g
Good quality salt and white pepper	To taste	To taste

energy	cal	fat	sat fat	carb	sugar	protein	fibre
875 kJ	211 kcal	15.9 g	9.0 g	9.6 g	9.1 g	3.9 g	2.8 g

METHOD OF WORK

1 Preheat an oven to 175 °C.

2 Remove any blemished outer leaves and wash the red cabbage. Cut into quarters and carefully cut out the cabbage stalks.

3 Thinly slice the red cabbage rewash and dry the cabbage. Place into a heavy-based, well buttered, saucepan or casserole dish.

4 Add the wine, vinegar, chopped bacon, sliced onion and butter. Season well.

5 Cover with a cartouche and with a lid then braise in the oven for approximately 50–60 minutes.

6 Add the diced apple and caster sugar: re-cover and continue braising for another 40 minutes.

7 Remove from the oven once tender and cooked, correct the seasoning and serve.

CHEF'S TIP The bacon can be left out of this recipe for vegetarian diets. Sultanas or peeled chestnuts can be supplemented instead to enhance the sweetness if desired.

Broccoli polonaise

Ingredients	4 portions	10 portions
Broccoli	2 medium-sized heads	4 medium-sized heads
Butter	100 g	250 g
Fresh white breadcrumbs	100 g	250 g
Chopped fresh parsley	3 tblspn	6 tblspn
Grated hard-boiled egg	2 eggs	5 eggs
Good quality salt	To taste	To taste

energy	cal	fat	sat fat	carb	sugar	protein	fibre
1444 kJ	347 kcal	24.9 g	14.1 g	21.4 g	2.3 g	10.8 g	5.6 g

METHOD OF WORK

1 Wash the broccoli well and dry. Trim the broccoli heads into 2 cm-sized florets.

2 Rewash and place into plenty of boiling salted water. Simmer until tender but slightly firm.

3 Drain the broccoli well and arrange in a serving dish.

4 Heat the butter in a frying pan and add the breadcrumbs. Fry until golden, add the freshly chopped parsley and grated egg.

5 Spoon over the broccoli and serve.

CHEF'S TIP Care must be taken when cooking the broccoli as over-cooking will render the flowers spongy, broken and without colour. The water must be boiling and salted to cook as quickly as possible to retain the broccoli's green colour. Purple sprouting broccoli can also be cooked and presented in the same way.

Buttered asparagus
(Asperges au beurre)

Ingredients	4 portions	10 portions
Medium asparagus	20 spears	60 spears
Butter	100 g	250 g
Good quality salt and white pepper	To taste	To taste

energy	cal	fat	sat fat	carb	sugar	protein	fibre
876 kJ	212 kcal	21.4 g	13.1 g	1.6 g	1.6 g	3.6 g	1.7 g

METHOD OF WORK

1 Wash the asparagus well to remove any sand and grit.

2 Hold the asparagus spears at the tip and base then snap in half. The hard root end should be discarded or used as flavouring in soups.

3 Remove all the small spurs from the top section of the asparagus with the back of a knife.

4 Thinly peel the base of the halved stem and wash well again.

5 Tie the asparagus in bunches of 3–6 spears and trim the base neatly.

6 Place the bundles carefully into boiling salted water and cook until the tips are just tender.

7 Remove from the water carefully, detach the string, cut in half if required and quickly toss in melted butter in a pan for one minute. Season and serve.

CHEF'S TIP Try to use asparagus when it is in season and therefore at its freshest. The older the asparagus, the woodier the base will be and the edible end will be smaller. Asparagus has quite a short season from the end of April to early June. It is good practice when preparing asparagus to keep the clean stalk ends for asparagus soup.

Buttered Brussels sprouts
(Chou de Bruxelles au beurre)

Ingredients	4 portions	10 portions
Brussels sprouts	400 g	1 kg
Butter	80 g	150 g
Good quality salt and white pepper	To taste	To taste

energy	cal	fat	sat fat	carb	sugar	protein	fibre
766 kJ	184 kcal	17.7 g	10.7 g	3.7 g	3.1 g	3.0 g	2.6 g

METHOD OF WORK

1 Remove the outer leaves, trim the stalks and cut a cross in the base of the stalk so as to help ensure even cooking. Alternatively cut the Brussels sprouts in half. Wash well in cold water.

2 Place into boiling salted water and cook until tender.

3 Remove the Brussels sprouts from the water when cooked and toss in a pan with the butter. Season with salt and pepper and serve.

CHEF'S TIP When boiling vegetables that have bright colours such as beetroot, carrots and turnips, cover the pan during boiling to help retain the acids that help keep the colour. However, with green vegetables such as Brussels sprouts the pan should not be covered, because they will lose their colour quickly.

Artichokes alla Romana *(Carciofi alla Romana)*

Ingredients	4 portions	10 portions
Globe artichokes	4	10
Acidulated water (1 lemon to 500 ml water)	1 litre	2 litres
Lemon juice	1	3
Boiling water	400 ml	1.25 litres
Chopped fresh parsley	3 tblspn	6 tblspn
Chopped fresh mint	6 tblspn	15 tblspn
Finely chopped garlic	2 cloves	5 cloves
Extra virgin olive oil	50 ml	125 ml
Dry white wine	75 ml	150 ml
Good quality salt and white pepper	To taste	To taste

energy	cal	fat	sat fat	carb	sugar	protein	fibre
716 kJ	172 kcal	13.1 g	2.1 g	8.4 g	3.0 g	5.1 g	13.6 g

METHOD OF WORK

1   Cut the stalk of the artichoke off close to the base, or leave approximately 2 cm on for decoration, and remove the bottom layer of leaves.

2   Lay the artichoke on its side and cut through and leave 1½ cm remaining at the base.

3   Using a small, sharp knife, carefully trim all of the leaves leaving a neat circular disc.

4   Scoop out the furry centre using a small spoon. Rub well with half a lemon to help stop any discolouring.

5   Place the trimmed artichoke into acidulated water (use the lemon juice mixed with the water) to prevent discolouration.

6   In a small bowl, combine the chopped parsley, mint, garlic, salt and 1 tablespoon olive oil. In the cavity of the artichoke from which the choke was removed, place 1 teaspoon of the herb mixture. Repeat this procedure with the remaining chokes.

7   Arrange all chokes in a deep pan that keeps them standing up.

8   Add the wine, boiling water, remaining oil and a pinch of salt. Cover and simmer on the top of the stove for 60 minutes.

CHEF'S TIP To prepare a cooking blanc to classically cook the artichokes   This is to prevent discolouration in the vegetable. Mix 10 g flour and 400 ml water together, then add salt and some lemon juice. Bring the liquid to the boil stirring regularly. Place the artichokes into the blanc and simmer until cooked, approximately 20 minutes.

CHEF'S TIP   Globe artichokes can be stuffed with other vegetables or farces and baked.

   To prepare artichokes whole, simply remove the stalk, cut 2 cm from the top and snip the remaining leaves with scissors, they can be cooked in acidic salted water for approximately 20 minutes then refreshed and the centre removed. Then add the farce or prepared vegetables.

Step-by-step: Preparing globe artichokes

1. Remove the outer leaves and discard them.

2. Continue to remove the leaves until all of them have been disconnected.

3. Cut the artichoke across to remove the stem.

4. Trim the outer edges.

5. Cut and discard the centre carefully.

6. Using a spoon scoop out the soft centre scraping away the 'choke' until clean.

Step-by-step: Preparing cauliflower

1. Pull the cauliflower leaves back to expose the vegetable.

2. Cut the leaves from the cauliflower.

3. Cut into florets.

Cauliflower mornay
(Chou-fleur mornay)

Ingredients	4 portions	10 portions
Cauliflower	1½ medium-sized	3 medium-sized
Mornay (cheese) sauce (see page 124)	275 ml	650 ml
Grated cheddar cheese	50 g	125 g
Good quality salt	To taste	To taste

energy	cal	fat	sat fat	carb	sugar	protein	fibre
1143 kJ	274 kcal	17.0 g	9.0 g	13.2 g	8.3 g	17.8 g	5.4 g

METHOD OF WORK

1   Remove the outer leaves, cut the stalks and wash the cauliflower.

2   Break the cauliflower into 3 cm florets.

3   Place into plenty of boiling salted water and cook until tender but slightly firm.

4   Remove from the boiling water and drain well.

5   Arrange in a serving dish.

6   Coat with the hot mornay sauce and top with grated cheese.

7   Place in the oven to gratinate or brown under the salamander.

Buttered samphire with sesame seeds

Ingredients	4 portions	10 portions
Samphire	400 g	1 kg
Unsalted butter	50 g	125 g
Sesame seeds	1 tblspn	2 tblspn
Sesame oil	1 tblspn	2 tblspn
Black pepper	To taste	To taste

energy	cal	fat	sat fat	carb	sugar	protein	fibre
721 kJ	174 kcal	16.8 g	7.4 g	2.2 g	2.0 g	3.7 g	2.0 g

METHOD OF WORK

1   Soak the fresh samphire for five minutes and rinse with clean water to wash out any sand or grit. Discard any wilted stems.

2   Place a pan of salted water onto the stove and bring to the boil.

3   Blanch the samphire in boiling water for 5 minutes and then refresh immediately in iced water.

4   Carefully pull the samphire off each woody stalk and discard the stalks.

5   Heat the butter and a little sesame oil in a wok.

6   Add the samphire and the sesame seeds. Toss in the hot fat for 2 minutes.

7   Season with a little black pepper and serve.

Removing the wooden stalks from the samphire

CHEF'S TIP   Samphire can be quite salty because it grows near the sea shores and in salt water marshes. It must be washed thoroughly to remove salt deposits and any grit or sand.

Creamed spinach purée
(Purée d'epinards à la crème)

Ingredients	4 portions	10 portions
Spinach leaves	1 kg	2.5 kg
Double cream	80 ml	200 ml
Béchamel sauce (see page 123)	40 ml	100 ml
Good quality salt and white pepper	To taste	To taste

energy	cal	fat	sat fat	carb	sugar	protein	fibre
664 kJ	161 kcal	13.6 g	7.5 g	3.6 g	2.9 g	6.2 g	5.1 g

METHOD OF WORK

1. Wash the spinach, pick the stalks from the leaves and discard.
2. Rewash the leaves several times in plenty of cold water and then drain.
3. Blanch in boiling salted water for a few seconds.
4. Remove and refresh in iced water to halt the cooking process immediately.
5. Drain well and squeeze any excess water out of the spinach.
6. Place into a food processor and blend until puréed.
7. Place the spinach into a saucepan with the double cream and béchamel sauce.
8. Simmer, season with salt and pepper and serve.

CHEF'S TIP A spinach purée can be produced without adding cream or béchamel sauce, simply dry the spinach out well in a pan on the stove to remove any excess moisture before blending. This will create a slightly firmer purée.

Pumpkin purée

Ingredients	4 portions	10 portions
Pumpkin	400 g	800 g
Olive oil	drizzle	drizzle
Double cream	100 ml	200 ml
Fresh milk	100 ml	200 ml
Cold unsalted butter in cubes	40 g	80 g
Good quality salt and white pepper	To taste	To taste

energy	cal	fat	sat fat	carb	sugar	protein	fibre
1107 kJ	268 kcal	27.4 g	14.6 g	3.9 g	3.5 g	2.0 g	1.1 g

METHOD OF WORK

1. Preheat an oven to 200°C.
2. Cut the pumpkin into quarters and remove all the seeds. Place onto a baking sheet, drizzle with the olive oil and cover with tin foil. Bake in the oven until the pumpkin flesh is tender.
3. Remove from the oven and scrape the flesh from the skin and place the flesh in a food blender.
4. Pour the cream and milk together in a saucepan and bring to the boil. Add the boiled cream and milk to the pumpkin and blend until smooth.
5. Add the cubes of butter a little at a time, season to taste and check for the required consistency. Reserve to one side for further use.

CHEF'S TIP This purée can be reheated and finished with a hand blender at the last moment if required. The recipe can be used for other squash or root vegetables such as butternut squash, beetroot, carrot and Jerusalem artichoke.

Deep fried courgettes
(Courgettes frites)

Ingredients	4 portions	10 portions
Courgettes	400 g	1 kg
Plain flour	100 g	250 g
Milk	100 ml	250 ml
Good quality salt and white pepper	To taste	To taste

energy	cal	fat	sat fat	carb	sugar	protein	fibre
678 kJ	160 kcal	5.6 g	0.7 g	23.3 g	4.1 g	5.8 g	1.7 g

METHOD OF WORK

1 Remove the stalks and wash the courgettes.
2 Cut into slices on a mandolin to ½ cm thick.
3 Pass the slices through the milk and then through the seasoned flour.
4 Shake off the surplus flour and deep fry at 180 °C until golden in colour.
5 Drain well, season with a little salt and pepper and serve.

CHEF'S TIP A tempura batter can also be used for a light and crisp finish to the dish. Mix this just as you are about to cook. Sift 85 g plain flour and 1 tblspn cornflour with ½ tsp fine sea salt into a large mixing bowl. Whisk in 200 ml ice-cold sparkling mineral water along with a few ice cubes using a whisk, but do not over beat. It will not matter too much about a few small flour lumps. Use this batter immediately. To keep the batter crisp the secret is to not over-mix it, or let it stand; keep the batter ice-cold and the frying oil hot; and do not fry too many pieces at once as this will reduce the temperature of the oil.

Alternative coatings for the courgettes are to simply pass through seasoned flour, through batter or in breadcrumbs to give different textures.

Chicory au gratin (Gratin d'endives)

Ingredients	4 portions	10 portions
Chicory	4 heads	10 heads
Unsalted butter	100 g	225 g
Vegetable stock or white wine	75 ml	300 ml
Double cream	150 ml	350 ml
Gruyere cheese	200 g	500 g
Breadcrumbs	75 g	200 g
Good quality salt and white pepper	To taste	To taste

energy	cal	fat	sat fat	carb	sugar	protein	fibre
2693 kJ	650 kcal	58.2 g	36.1 g	16.6 g	1.6 g	16.9 g	0.8 g

METHOD OF WORK

1 Preheat oven at 200 °C. Wash the chicory and trim and discard any bruised outer leaves.
2 Melt two tablespoons of butter in a sauteuse. Add the prepared chicory to the butter, season with a little salt and pepper. Cook gently on all sides and allow the chicory to take on a little colour.
3 Add a little vegetable stock or white wine as necessary. Cover with a cartouche and a lid and allow braising for 15 to 20 minutes over low heat (12 minutes or so for halves).
4 If necessary, add a little more stock to prevent burning. When they are cooked to a tender texture, there should be a few spoons of remaining liquid to baste them with.
5 Carefully transfer to a baking dish large enough to hold the chicory. Pour over the cream. Mix together the bread crumbs and the cheese and distribute over the chicory.
6 Place in the hot oven for 6–8 minutes and then finish under the salamander until the cheese is bubbly and turns slightly brown.

CHEF'S TIP You can make this dish using béchamel sauce. Just make enough to cover the chicory, and then distribute the cheese and bread crumb mixture. Another variation is to sauté a tablespoon of small diced red and green pepper per chicory. Add this as the chicory is braising.

Stir-fried vegetables

Ingredients	4 portions	10 portions
Sunflower oil	2 tblspn	5 tblspn
Pak choi – shredded	400 g	1 kg
Mushrooms – cut into quarters	200 g	500 g
Onions cut into paysanne	1 medium	3 medium
Ginger (grated fresh root)	15 g	40 g
Green pepper, deseeded and cut into paysanne	1	2
Yellow pepper, deseeded and cut into paysanne	1	2
Carrot cut into paysanne	100 g	250 g
Celery cut into paysanne	100 g	250 g
Soy sauce	30 ml	75 ml
Good quality salt and white pepper	To taste	To taste

energy	cal	fat	sat fat	carb	sugar	protein	fibre
843 kJ	204 kcal	16.3 g	1.7 g	10.1 g	7.9 g	4.5 g	4.2 g

METHOD OF WORK

1 Heat the oil in a wok or high sided sauteuse.
2 Add the carrots, celery and ginger and stir on the heat for two minutes.
3 Add the pak choi and stir for a further minute.
4 Add the remaining vegetables and cooking while stirring for another two minutes.
5 Add the soy sauce and check the seasoning before serving.

CHEF'S TIP Stir-fry vegetables according to density, with the densest vegetables being stir-fried first and for the longest time. Denser vegetables such as broccoli, carrots and aubergine require more cooking time than green leafy vegetables such as pak choi.
  Ensure that all the vegetables are cut or sliced to a similar size to help ensure even and quick cooking.

Stuffed mushrooms
(Champignons farcis)

Ingredients	4 portions	10 portions
Large field mushrooms	400 g	1 kg
Chopped shallots	50 g	110 g
Chopped garlic	2 cloves	4 cloves
Toasted white or wholemeal breadcrumbs	4 tblspn	10 tblspn
Fresh herb leaves for garnish		
Butter	50 g	125 g
Grated Stilton cheese	80 g	200 g
Olive oil	2 tblspn	5 tblspn
Good quality salt and white pepper	To taste	To taste

energy	cal	fat	sat fat	carb	sugar	protein	fibre
1893 kJ	458 kcal	41.3 g	13.6 g	12.8 g	1.1 g	9.4 g	2.7 g

METHOD OF WORK

1 Preheat an oven to 200 °C.
2 Wash the mushrooms, peel the outer skin and remove the stalks. Carefully brush the insides of the mushrooms clean to remove any grit. Finely chop the stalks and reserve to one side for the filling.
3 Place the mushrooms cup side up on a baking tray.
4 Melt the butter in a saucepan and sweat the garlic, onion and chopped mushroom stalks until translucent.
5 Drizzle the mushrooms with a little olive oil and place under a salamander until half cooked.
6 Combine the onion and garlic mixture with the toasted breadcrumbs and grated Stilton cheese.
7 Cover the mushrooms with the stuffing and place into the oven to bake until golden-coloured on the top.
8 Dress with the herb leaves for garnish.

CHEF'S TIP Do not leave the mushrooms to soak in the water when washing because they absorb moisture quickly and become spongy, losing texture and flavour. Always dry them with a clean kitchen towel after washing.

Stuffed aubergines
(Aubergine farcie)

Ingredients	4 portions	10 portions
Aubergines	2	5
Finely chopped shallots	50 g	125 g
Chopped garlic	2 cloves	4 cloves
Butter	100 g	250 g
Fresh wholemeal breadcrumbs	8 tblspn	20 tblspn
Tomato concassée	2 tblspn	5 tblspn
1 cm diced green, yellow and red peppers	½ of each coloured pepper	1½ of each coloured pepper
Grated gruyère cheese	50 g	125 g
Olive oil	4 tblspn	10 tblspn
Fresh basil leaves	To taste	To taste
Good quality salt and white pepper	To taste	To taste

energy	cal	fat	sat fat	carb	sugar	protein	fibre
3092 kJ	744 kcal	70.7 g	21.9 g	19.8 g	7.3 g	8.6 g	5.1 g

METHOD OF WORK

1 Preheat an oven to 170 °C.
2 Remove the green parts of the aubergine and discard. Wash and cut the aubergines in half lengthways. Using a sharp knife score the flesh in a criss-cross fashion without piercing the skin.
3 Drizzle over the olive oil and freshly chopped garlic.
4 Place onto a pan or baking tray and bake in the preheated oven until the flesh is soft.

Score the aubergine, drizzle with oil and rub in the garlic

5 Remove from the oven, and using a spoon carefully hollow out the flesh, leaving the empty skins to one side for later use. Chop the aubergine flesh into smaller pieces.
6 Sauté the chopped shallots and diced peppers in the butter and then add the aubergine.
7 Fold in the breadcrumbs and tomato concassé before seasoning with the salt and pepper. Cook gently until any excess moisture has evaporated. Add the basil leaves.
8 Spoon the mix back into the aubergine skins.
9 Cover with grated Gruyère cheese and gratinate in a hot oven.

CHEF'S TIP Sprinkle salt onto the aubergines after they have been cut in half and leave in a colander for 10 minutes to drain before cooking to remove excess water. Also known as the eggplant, the aubergine has a meaty texture.

TASK Aubergines have the ability to absorb other flavours and are often prepared and cooked with a variety of aromatic spices, herbs and flavourings. They are a particularly popular vegetable in Mediterranean and Middle Eastern cookery. Find out what other dishes aubergines can be used for.

Stuffed tomatoes
(Tomates farcies)

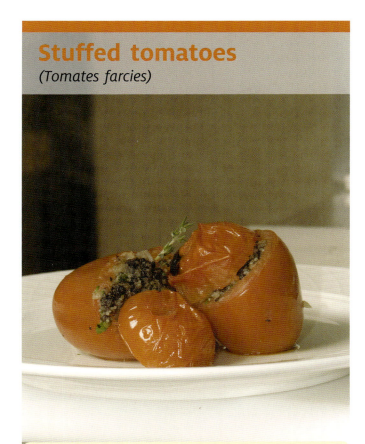

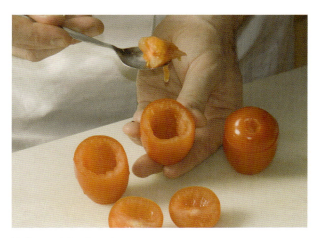

Hollow out the tomatoes

METHOD OF WORK

1 Preheat an oven to 180 °C.
2 Wash and remove the eyes from the tomatoes.
3 Cut off the top quarter from the tomato with a knife.
4 Remove the seeds from the tomatoes carefully with a small spoon. Place the tomatoes onto a greased baking tray. Season inside the tomatoes with salt and pepper.
5 Melt the butter in a sauteuse and sweat the garlic and shallots without letting them colour.
6 Add the breadcrumbs, cooked mushrooms, freshly chopped parsley and seasoning.
7 Fill the tomatoes.
8 Brush with a little melted butter and bake for 5 minutes or until just cooked.

CHEF'S TIP The filling can be enhanced with diced ham, lardons of bacon alternative herbs such as basil and thyme and citrus zests.

Ingredients	4 portions	10 portions
Medium-sized tomatoes	8 each	20 each
Finely chopped shallots	20 g	50 g
Chopped garlic	1 clove	2 cloves
Butter	30 g	75 g
Chopped fresh parsley	3 tblspn	5 tblspn
Fresh white or wholemeal breadcrumbs	30 g	75 g
Chopped sweated button mushrooms	2 tblspn	5 tblspn
Good quality salt and white pepper	To taste	To taste

energy	cal	fat	sat fat	carb	sugar	protein	fibre
525 kJ	126 kcal	8.1 g	5.6 g	11.2 g	5.3 g	2.6 g	3.1 g

Broad beans *(Fèves)*

Ingredients	4 portions	10 portions
Broad beans	1 kg	2.5 kg
Good quality salt and white pepper	To taste	To taste
Butter	50 g	175 g

energy	cal	fat	sat fat	carb	sugar	protein	fibre
894 kJ	213 kcal	12.3 g	6.8 g	14.2 g	2.3 g	12.8 g	16.3 g

METHOD OF WORK

1. Remove the beans from their pods and cook in boiling salted water for 10–15 minutes.
2. Refresh immediately in iced water.
3. Carefully remove the shells from each bean to reveal the bright green, tender bean.
4. To serve: melt some butter in a sauteuse and lightly toss the broad beans in the butter to warm through. Season with salt and pepper before serving.

Vichy carrots *(Carottes Vichy)*

Ingredients	4 portions	10 portions
Carrots	400 g	1 kg
Butter	30 g	70 g
Caster sugar	5 g	10 g
Vichy water (or other mineral water)		
Chopped parsley	1 tblspn	3 tblspn
Good quality salt and white pepper	To taste	To taste

energy	cal	fat	sat fat	carb	sugar	protein	fibre
357 kJ	86 kcal	6.6 g	4.0 g	6.4 g	6.0 g	0.8 g	1.7 g

METHOD OF WORK

1. Select carrots no wider than 2 cm and peel and wash them.
2. Cut into 2 mm slices on a mandolin or cut into baton shapes.
3. Place in a saucepan with a little salt, the sugar and butter. Barely cover with the Vichy or mineral water.
4. Place on the stove to bring to the boil and when the water has completed evaporated, check if the carrots have cooked through. Do not overcook but if they are not fully cooked add a little more water and continue cooking.
5. Toss the carrots over a high heat for a couple of minutes to help accentuate the glaze and serve sprinkled with chopped parsley.

Peas French style *(Petits pois à la Française)*

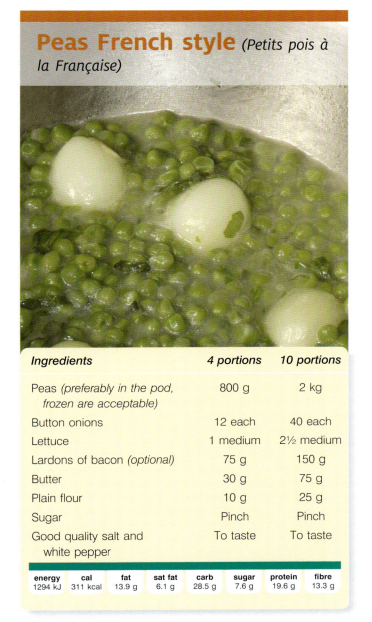

Ingredients	4 portions	10 portions
Peas *(preferably in the pod, frozen are acceptable)*	800 g	2 kg
Button onions	12 each	40 each
Lettuce	1 medium	2½ medium
Lardons of bacon *(optional)*	75 g	150 g
Butter	30 g	75 g
Plain flour	10 g	25 g
Sugar	Pinch	Pinch
Good quality salt and white pepper	To taste	To taste

energy	cal	fat	sat fat	carb	sugar	protein	fibre
1294 kJ	311 kcal	13.9 g	6.1 g	28.5 g	7.6 g	19.6 g	13.3 g

METHOD OF WORK

1 If the peas are fresh, shell and wash in plenty of cold water.
2 Wash and peel the onions.
3 Mix the flour with an equal amount of butter to create the beurre manié.
4 Place the peas, lardons and onions together in a pan with the remaining butter, sugar and salt.
5 Add the water, cover with a tight-fitting lid and cook until tender, approximately 30 minutes.
6 Cut the lettuce into a chiffonade and add to the peas.
7 Drop in small pieces of butter/flour mix and allow the liquid to thicken by stirring carefully.
8 Adjust the seasoning and serve.

CHEF'S TIP Frozen peas are available at all times of the year. If you use them for this recipe, the size and the quality should be considered and the cooking times adjusted.

Shallow fried chicory *(Endive meunière)*

Ingredients	4 portions	10 portions
Chicory	400 g	1 kg
Sugar	½ tsp	1 tsp
Lemon juice	1 lemon	2 lemons
Butter	80 g	200 g
Chopped parsley	2 tblspn	4 tblspn
Good quality salt and white pepper	To taste	To taste

energy	cal	fat	sat fat	carb	sugar	protein	fibre
668 kJ	162 kcal	16.8 g	10.6 g	3.3 g	1.6 g	1.0 g	0.8 g

METHOD OF WORK

1 Preheat an oven to 180 °C.
2 Wash the chicory, trim the stems and discard any brown outer leaves.
3 Place into a buttered ovenproof dish, season and add the sugar.
4 Add half the lemon juice and half the butter.
5 Pour in 2 tblspn of water per portion. Season well.
6 Cover with a cartouche and a lid. Bake at 180 °C for 45 minutes.
7 Once cooked remove from the ovenproof dish. Set aside.
8 Heat the butter in a shallow frying pan until it foams and just turns nut brown. Add the chicory. Fry until light brown colour is obtained on all sides.
9 Squeeze the lemon juice over the chicory and add the freshly chopped parsley.

CHEF'S TIP The chicory could be placed in a sealed vacuum pack bag with butter, lemon, sugar and seasoning, then steamed for 40 minutes to obtain braised chicory. This method retains more nutrients and flavour.

Ratatouille

Ingredients	4 portions	10 portions
Aubergine 1 cm dice	200 g	500 g
Courgettes 1 cm dice	200 g	500 g
Onion 1 cm dice	50 g	125 g
Chopped garlic	3 cloves	6 cloves
1 cm diced green, yellow and red peppers	½ of each coloured pepper	1½ of each coloured pepper
Tomato concassée 1 cm dice	200 g	500 g
Chopped fresh parsley	4 tblspn	6 tblspn
Chopped fresh basil	2 tblspn	4 tblspn
Fresh thyme	1 sprig	2 sprigs
White wine	50 ml	125 ml
Olive oil	4 tblspn	10 tblspn
Good quality salt and white pepper	To taste	To taste

energy	cal	fat	sat fat	carb	sugar	protein	fibre
1528 kJ	367 kcal	34.0 g	5.2 g	10.1 g	8.5 g	4.0 g	4.1 g

METHOD OF WORK

1 Wash the courgettes, aubergines and peppers well.

2 In a heavy-based saucepan heat the olive oil and cook the peeled and finely chopped onions and garlic without letting them colour.

3 Add the various coloured peppers and cook for a few minutes, then add the tomato concassée, mix together and set aside.

4 Heat some more olive oil in a saucepan, add the courgettes and cook for approximately 3 minutes. Remove from the pan and add to the cooked onions and peppers.

5 Add the aubergines to the saucepan with a little extra olive oil and cook again for 3 minutes. Remove from the pan and add to the onions, peppers and courgettes.

6 Pour in the white wine, season well and place back onto the stove to cook for approximately a further 6 minutes covered with a lid.

7 Remove from the heat and fold in the freshly chopped parsley and basil, correct the seasoning and serve.

CHEF'S TIP Ratatouille is a classical Provençale dish. The word is derived from the French word touiller (to mix or stir). Traditionally each vegetable is cooked separately before being combined and then stewed. This dish can be served with lamb, chicken or venison as well as braised fish dishes.

Roast parsnips in honey

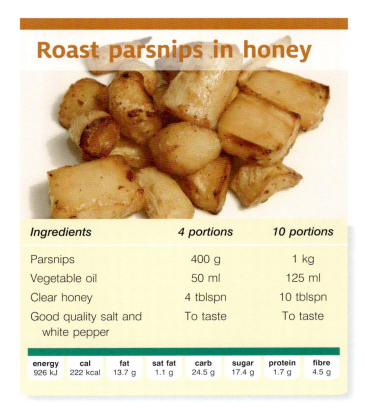

Ingredients	4 portions	10 portions
Parsnips	400 g	1 kg
Vegetable oil	50 ml	125 ml
Clear honey	4 tblspn	10 tblspn
Good quality salt and white pepper	To taste	To taste

energy	cal	fat	sat fat	carb	sugar	protein	fibre
926 kJ	222 kcal	13.7 g	1.1 g	24.5 g	17.4 g	1.7 g	4.5 g

METHOD OF WORK

1   Preheat the oven to 185 °C.
2   Wash, peel and rewash the parsnips.
3   Cut into 4 cm lengths, split in half lengthways and remove the core.
4   Heat the oil in a roasting tray and add the parsnips.
5   Roast in the oven for approximately for 20 minutes.
6   Add the honey and then return to the oven for a further 10 minutes.
7   Season and serve.

CHEF'S TIP Parsnips that are in season and as fresh as possible will be less woody and have a sweeter flavour.

Swede purée *(Rutabaga purée)*

Ingredients	4 portions	10 portions
Swede	400 g	1 kg
Butter	40 g	100 g
Good quality salt and white pepper	To taste	To taste

energy	cal	fat	sat fat	carb	sugar	protein	fibre
353 kJ	86 kcal	8.3 g	5.2 g	2.5 g	2.3 g	0.4 g	1.9 g

METHOD OF WORK

1   Wash, peel and dice the swede.
2   Rewash and place in a steamer until just cooked and tender.
3   Remove and drain if necessary in a colander. Pass through a sieve or blend in a food processor or mouli.
4   Place in a saucepan and dry out over a gentle heat.
5   Add the butter, season and serve.

CHEF'S TIP Celeriac, turnips and parsnips can be used for this recipe also. Puréeing with a mouli or a sieve will remove any fibres from fibrous vegetables, such as swede or celeriac. If using a blender to purée it is best to then pass the mixture through a sieve to remove the fibres.

Braised leeks (Poireau braise)

Ingredients	4 portions	10 portions
Leeks	800 g	2 kg
Sliced carrot	60 g	150 g
Sliced onion	60 g	150 g
Bouquet garni	1 small	1 small
Vegetable stock	150 ml	375 ml
Butter	50 g	125 g
Demi glace (see page 130)	40 ml	100 ml
Good quality salt and white pepper	To taste	To taste

energy	cal	fat	sat fat	carb	sugar	protein	fibre
646 kJ	157 kcal	13.0 g	7.1 g	7.2 g	5.4 g	3.1 g	4.7 g

METHOD OF WORK

1 Preheat an oven to 180 °C.

2 Wash and trim the root from the leeks along with any blemished outer leaves.

3 Cut lengthways and rewash the leeks thoroughly.

4 Fold over in half and tie together. Blanch in boiling salted water until tender.

5 In a pan place the butter, onion, carrot and bouquet garni.

6 Lay the leeks on top and pour in the stock, season well.

7 Cover with a cartouche and lid then braise for 45 minutes.

8 Carefully remove the leeks and snip the string off.

9 Strain the cooking liquid and reduce by a half. Add the demi glace and cook out.

10 Add the leeks and coat well with the cooking sauce, check the seasoning and serve.

CHEF'S TIP The leeks can be cut into large diamonds and cooked slowly in half water and half butter to give a glazed finish.

Potatoes

Anna potatoes *(Pommes Anna)*

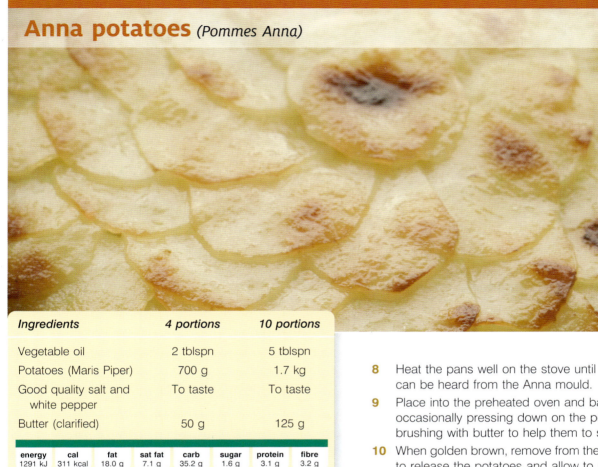

Ingredients	4 portions	10 portions
Vegetable oil	2 tblspn	5 tblspn
Potatoes (Maris Piper)	700 g	1.7 kg
Good quality salt and white pepper	To taste	To taste
Butter (clarified)	50 g	125 g

energy	cal	fat	sat fat	carb	sugar	protein	fibre
1291 kJ	311 kcal	18.0 g	7.1 g	35.2 g	1.6 g	3.1 g	3.2 g

METHOD OF WORK

1   Preheat the oven to 220 °C.

2   Warm the oil and brush the inside of a clean Anna mould.

3   Wash and peel the potatoes, and cut to even cylindrical shapes with a plain cutter or large metal disc cutter.

4   Using a mandolin slice the potatoes into thin 1–2 mm slices.

5   Place a layer of the potato slices in the bottom of the Anna mould, neatly overlapping. Butter and lightly season.

6   Continue to build up each layer in the same way until the mould is almost full.

7   Butter the top layer.

8   Heat the pans well on the stove until a sizzling sound can be heard from the Anna mould.

9   Place into the preheated oven and bake for 1 hour, occasionally pressing down on the potatoes and brushing with butter to help them to stick together.

10   When golden brown, remove from the oven, knock firmly to release the potatoes and allow to rest for 10 minutes.

11   Carefully turn out of the mould and cut into the required portions.

CHEF'S TIP Do not wash the potato slices because the starch on the surfaces will help them to stick together to compact the potatoes together.

CHEF'S TIP Heavy omelette pans can be used instead of Anna moulds. The pans should always be kept clean by wiping with kitchen paper or cloth and coating with a little clean fat.

Mashed potatoes
(Pommes purées)

Ingredients	4 portions	10 portions
Potatoes (King Edward reds if possible)	400 g	1 kg
Butter	40 g	100 g
Milk	50 ml	125 ml
Good quality salt and white pepper	To taste	To taste

energy	cal	fat	sat fat	carb	sugar	protein	fibre
692 kJ	167 kcal	8.5 g	5.4 g	20.7 g	1.5 g	2.2 g	1.8 g

METHOD OF WORK

1 Wash, peel and cut the potatoes into an even size.

2 Rewash, place into a saucepan of cold salted water and bring to the boil.

3 Simmer until the potatoes are cooked. Remove from the heat and drain in a colander.

4 Return to a light heat in the saucepan without the water, cover with a lid and heat for 2 minutes to allow the potatoes to dry out.

5 Pass the potatoes through a mouli, potato ricer or mash by hand.

6 Add the butter and warm milk and mix to the required consistency.

7 Check the seasoning and use as required.

Biarritz potatoes
(Pommes biarritz)

Ingredients	4 portions	10 portions
Mashed potato (see previous recommendation)	600 g	1.5 kg
1 cm diced cooked ham	60 g	150 g
1 cm diced cooked pimento	30 g	75 g
Finely chopped fresh parsley	3 tblspn	7 tblspn
Clarified butter	40 g	100 g
Good quality salt and white pepper	To taste	To taste

energy	cal	fat	sat fat	carb	sugar	protein	fibre
1261 kJ	304 kcal	19.6 g	12.1 g	26.3 g	2.4 g	6.4 g	2.8 g

METHOD OF WORK

1 Take the hot mashed potato and add the ham, pimento and chopped parsley.

2 Ensure the ham and pimento are warm before adding or the final mix will be cold.

3 Mix well and arrange in a serving dish. Dip a palette knife in the clarified butter and make little decorative marks on top of the potatoes.

4 Briefly place under the salamander to raise the final temperature and serve immediately.

CHEF'S TIP Ensure the ham and pimentos are cut neatly and the ham is free from fat and gristle. The mix can be kept warm during service in a bain-marie for up to one hour. Any longer and the pimento begins to bleed into the potato.

Duchesse potatoes *(Pommes duchesse)*

Ingredients	4 portions	10 portions
Mashed potato without the butter or milk	600 g	1.5 kg
Egg yolk	2	5
Butter	30 g	75 g
Whole egg	1	2
Good quality salt and white pepper	To taste	To taste
Grated nutmeg	To taste	To taste

energy	cal	fat	sat fat	carb	sugar	protein	fibre
969 kJ	233 kcal	10.3 g	5.1 g	30.3 g	1.4 g	5.5 g	2.8 g

METHOD OF WORK

1   Wash, peel and rewash the potatoes, cut into even-sized pieces and place into boiling salted water.

2   Simmer gently for approximately 25 minutes until cooked. Drain well and return to the pan, placing on the stove, covered with a lid to dry out for 2 minutes.

3   Pass the potatoes through a potato ricer, mouli or pass through a medium sieve. Place into a clean bowl.

4   Beat in the egg yolk and add the butter. Season well with the salt, pepper and nutmeg.

5   Place the mixture into a piping bag with a large star tube.

6   Lightly butter a baking tray and then pipe neat spiral shapes no bigger than 2 cm wide and 5 cm tall. Allow two per portion.

7   Bake for 2 minutes at 140 °C to give the outside a dry surface.

8   Beat the whole egg and brush over the potato spirals.

9   Return to the oven and bake at 220 °C until golden brown.

CHEF'S TIP Duchesse potato is a basic mixture and is widely used in the preparation of many other potato dishes as well as being used to provide a garnish for fish and meat dishes.

CHEF'S TIP A little potato starch can be added to the mix if the end product is too wet to pipe and hold up, this will stiffen the mixture and the duchesse potatoes will hold up better.

VIDEO CLIP Preparing and cooking duchesse potatoes.

Marquis potatoes
(Pommes marquis)

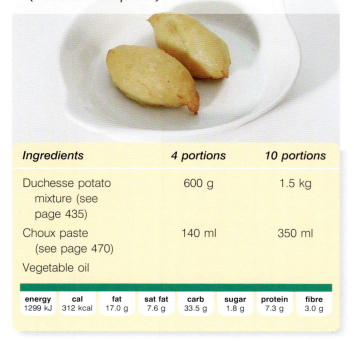

Ingredients	4 portions	10 portions
Duchesse potato mixture (see page 435)	600 g	1.5 kg
Plum tomatoes blanched, peeled, deseeded and neatly diced	6	15
Finely chopped shallots	1 whole	2 whole
Butter	30 g	75 g
Garlic chopped	1 clove	2 cloves
Finely chopped fresh parsley	3 tblspn	8 tblspn
Whole egg	1	2
Good quality salt and white pepper	To taste	To taste

energy	cal	fat	sat fat	carb	sugar	protein	fibre
1351 kJ	325 kcal	17.6 g	10.7 g	34.1 g	7.2 g	8.4 g	5.7 g

METHOD OF WORK

1 Make the duchesse potato mixture on page 435.

2 Place the duchesse mixture into a piping bag with a large star tube.

3 Pipe the potato onto a buttered baking tray into the form of round nests, approximately 5 cm wide by 2.5 cm tall. Allow two per portion.

4 Place into a hot oven for a few minutes to dry the outside of the potato. Brush with the beaten egg and return to the oven to colour golden brown.

5 Sweat the shallots and garlic in the butter and then add the parsley and tomato, season and cool.

6 Spoon the tomato mixture into the centre of the potato and return to the oven to heat through.

CHEF'S TIP Any tomato mixture left can be chilled and reused or added to salads, sauces and used for garnishes.

Dauphine potatoes
(Pommes dauphine)

Ingredients	4 portions	10 portions
Duchesse potato mixture (see page 435)	600 g	1.5 kg
Choux paste (see page 470)	140 ml	350 ml
Vegetable oil		

energy	cal	fat	sat fat	carb	sugar	protein	fibre
1299 kJ	312 kcal	17.0 g	7.6 g	33.5 g	1.8 g	7.3 g	3.0 g

METHOD OF WORK

1 Make the duchesse potatoes as instructed.

2 Mix the duchesse potato mix with the choux paste thoroughly and place in a refrigerator to chill.

3 Mould into quenelle shapes using the vegetable oil if needed to coat the spoons and help release the potato shape (approximately 2 cm wide by 5 cm long).

4 Place onto strips of oiled greaseproof paper and allow three pieces per portion.

5 Holding the paper firmly slide the potatoes into a deep fat fryer and fry at 180 °C until golden, drain and serve.

CHEF'S TIP Ensure the formed shape before cooking is as neat as possible because the frying will exaggerate any imperfections.

Croquette potatoes
(Pommes croquette)

Ingredients	4 portions	10 portions
Duchesse potato mix	600 g	1.5 kg
Flour	100 g	250 g
Whole egg	6	15
White breadcrumbs	200 g	500 g
Good quality salt and white pepper	To taste	To taste

energy	cal	fat	sat fat	carb	sugar	protein	fibre
2453 kJ	583 kcal	18.5 g	7.0 g	86.2 g	3.0 g	22.4 g	4.6 g

METHOD OF WORK

1   Make the duchesse potatoes as instructed (see page 435).

2   Mould the duchesse mixture into 2 cm by 5 cm cylinders, allowing three per portion.

3   Place in a refrigerator to chill for 30 minutes.

4   Pass the potato cylinders through the seasoned flour, beaten egg and then the breadcrumbs.

5   Use a palette knife to remould the cylinders and pack the breadcrumbs in tightly.

6   Place into frying baskets and deep fry at 185 °C until golden brown, drain and serve.

CHEF'S TIP   As an alternative to breadcrumbs, use nibbed almonds instead. Prepare and cook as for this recipe, but with the coating of almonds this dish is named Pommes amandine (almond potatoes).

Straw potatoes *(Pommes pailles)*

Ingredients	4 portions	10 portions
Good frying potatoes (for example King Edward)	200 g	500 g

energy	cal	fat	sat fat	carb	sugar	protein	fibre
319 kJ	77 kcal	3.8 g	0.3 g	10.0 g	0.4 g	0.9 g	0.9 g

METHOD OF WORK

1   Wash, peel and rewash the potatoes.

2   Cut the potatoes into julienne strips about 6 cm long.

3   Wash well and drain, dry thoroughly in a clean kitchen cloth.

4   Deep fry at 180 °C moving constantly to achieve a golden brown colour.

5   Drain well and season with a little salt.

CHEF'S TIP   Straw potatoes are normally used as a garnish for grilled meats such as steaks and lamb chops. They are sometimes used in other dishes such as salads to give an added texture and flavour combination.

Sauté potatoes
(Pommes sautées)

Ingredients	4 portions	10 portions
Potatoes (Maris Piper for example)	600 g	1.5 kg
Vegetable oil	100 ml	250 ml
Butter	50 g	120 g
Good quality salt and white pepper	To taste	To taste
Chopped parsley	3 tblspn	6 tblspn

energy	cal	fat	sat fat	carb	sugar	protein	fibre
1864 kJ	451 kcal	35.6 g	8.4 g	30.5 g	1.6 g	3.0 g	3.1 g

METHOD OF WORK

1 Wash the potatoes well and place onto steaming trays. Steam the potatoes until just cooked (approximately 12 minutes) then cool slightly and peel.

2 Cut into neat slices approximately 3 mm thick.

3 Place the oil in a heavy frying pan and heat the oil. Add the sliced potatoes and gently fry until golden brown in colour. Toss occasionally to ensure that the potatoes are cooked on both sides.

4 Drain in a colander.

5 Heat the frying pan, add the potatoes, season and add the butter. Toss over and add chopped parsley then serve.

CHEF'S TIP   The potatoes can be steamed or boiled in their skins. Always try to select even sizes to facilitate even cooking and uniformity of the end product.

Sauté potatoes with onions
(Pommes lyonnaises)

Ingredients	4 portions	10 portions
Sauté potatoes	600 g	1.5 kg
Sliced onions	200 g	500 g
Butter	50 g	125 g
Good quality salt and white pepper	To taste	To taste
Freshly chopped parsley	3 tblspn	6 tblspn

energy	cal	fat	sat fat	carb	sugar	protein	fibre
2300 kJ	557 kcal	46.1 g	15.0 g	32.8 g	3.2 g	3.7 g	4.2 g

METHOD OF WORK

1 Fry the onions separately in the butter until they begin to caramelize and turn golden brown.

2 Mix with the sauté potatoes, correct the seasoning and serve with some freshly chopped parsley.

CHEF'S TIP   Slowly cooking with butter will give the onions a good flavour but it can be difficult to control the heat process and prevent the butter from burning. Use 50 per cent oil and 50 per cent butter to correct this problem and help raise the smoke point of the fat.

Game chips and gaufrette potatoes *(Pommes chips et pommes gaufrette)*

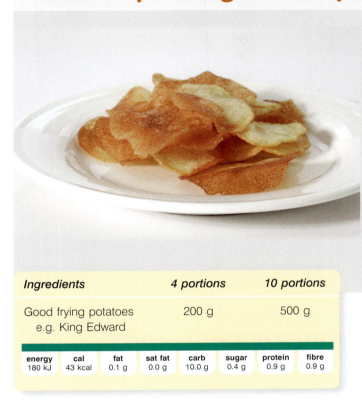

Ingredients	4 portions	10 portions
Good frying potatoes e.g. King Edward	200 g	500 g

energy	cal	fat	sat fat	carb	sugar	protein	fibre
180 kJ	43 kcal	0.1 g	0.0 g	10.0 g	0.4 g	0.9 g	0.9 g

METHOD OF WORK FOR GAME CHIPS

1   Wash, peel and then rewash the potatoes. Trim into a cylindrical shape.

2   Using a mandolin slice the potatoes to 1 mm thick. Wash again in plenty of cold water.

3   Drain and pat dry with a clean kitchen cloth.

4   Place the potatoes into a frying basket and deep fry at 180 °C, moving the potatoes constantly until golden brown in colour.

5   Drain well, season with a little salt and serve as a garnish for roast poultry and game.

METHOD OF WORK FOR GAUFRETTE POTATOES

1   Once the potatoes are peeled, wash and trim into cylindrical shapes using the corrugated blade of the mandolin.

2   Give a half turn to the potato between each slicing action. This will produce a trellis pattern.

3   Cook in the same way as game chips.

CHEF'S TIP Game chips and gaufrette potatoes are used for a garnish and can also be used as part of a canapé service within a cocktail bar setting. They are not served as a potato dish on its own. Care must be taken as they burn very quickly in the hot fat, especially if they are not well dried before placing them in the deep fryer.

Boulangère potatoes
(Pommes boulangère)

Ingredients	4 portions	10 portions
Potatoes (Maris Piper are best)	400 g	1 kg
Finely sliced onions	150 g	375 g
White vegetable or chicken stock	250 ml	625 ml
Butter	50 g	125 g
Chopped fresh parsley (optional)	2 tblspn	4 tblspn
Good quality salt and white pepper	To taste	To taste

energy	cal	fat	sat fat	carb	sugar	protein	fibre
831 kJ	200 kcal	11.6 g	6.9 g	22.1 g	2.3 g	2.4 g	2.8 g

METHOD OF WORK

1 Preheat an oven to 200 °C.
2 Wash, peel and rewash the potatoes.
3 Cut the potatoes into 2 mm thick slices. Reserve the best slices for finishing the dish.
4 Lightly cook the sliced onions without colour in a little butter.
5 Grease a deep baking tray or dish and arrange the potatoes and onions layer by layer, seasoning with salt and paper between each layer of potatoes.
6 Neatly arrange the reserved potato slices on the top.
7 Pour in the stock barely covering the potatoes.
8 Add a few pieces of butter on the top of the potatoes.
9 Place in the oven for approximately 25–30 minutes to achieve a little colour.
10 Lower the heat to 170 °C and press the potatoes down flat occasionally. Continue to cook for approximately 1 hour until the liquid has almost been absorbed. Brush with melted butter and serve with the chopped parsley if desired.

CHEF'S TIP The use of a round cutter to achieve neat discs of potato to layer on top will give the finished dish a neater presentation.

Chipped potatoes (chips)
(Pommes frites)

Ingredients	4 portions	10 portions
Good frying potatoes (for example King Edward, Maris Piper, Cara or Désirée)	600 g	1.5 kg

energy	cal	fat	sat fat	carb	sugar	protein	fibre
540 kJ	129 kcal	0.2 g	0.0 g	30.0 g	1.3 g	2.6 g	2.7 g

METHOD OF WORK

1 Wash, peel and rewash potatoes.
2 Trim the potatoes to give straight sides.
3 Cut into neat batons measuring 5 cm long by 1 cm × 1 cm.
4 Wash well and dry in a clean kitchen cloth.
5 Deep fry at 170 °C to blanch until soft without colour.
6 Drain and place on tray and store in a refrigerator until required.
7 When required, deep fry at 180 °C until golden in colour and crisp.
8 Remove from the fryer, drain and season with salt.

CHEF'S TIP Temperature control is very important when cooking chipped potatoes in a deep fat fryer:

If the oil temperature exceeds 199 °C it will quicken the breakdown of the fat which means that it will need to be changed more often.

Chipped potatoes can be blanched twice, first at 140 °C and then again at 160 °C until they are just lightly coloured. A final cook at 180 °C will ensure a deep golden and crispy outside texture with a fluffy centre.

Cook chipped potatoes in smaller quantities to help the oil maintain and recover to its correct cooking temperature. The potatoes will cook quicker and will not absorb as much fat.

Pont-neuf potatoes
(Pommes pont-neuf)

Ingredients	4 portions	10 portions
Good frying potatoes (for example King Edward)	600 g	1.5 kg

energy	cal	fat	sat fat	carb	sugar	protein	fibre
540 kJ	129 kcal	0.2 g	0.0 g	30.0 g	1.3 g	2.6 g	2.7 g

METHOD OF WORK

1 Prepare as for chips (see page 440).
2 Cut into large batons 6 cm long × 2 cm × 2 cm.
3 Wash and dry in a clean kitchen cloth.
4 Deep fry at 170 °C to blanch until soft without colour.
5 Drain and place on tray and store in a refrigerator until required.
6 When required, deep fry at 180 °C until golden in colour and crisp.
7 Remove from the fryer, drain and season with salt.
8 Pont-neuf potatoes are usually served with grilled steaks as an accompaniment.

CHEF'S TIP Peeled potatoes will blacken when exposed to the air. Cook them immediately if possible; if they have to be kept, cover with cold water.

CHEF'S TIP For service pont-neuf potatoes should be stacked like building blocks onto the service plate. It is thought that the name for this dish may come from the Pont-neuf, the oldest surviving bridge over the river Seine in the centre of Paris.

Boiled potatoes
(Pommes à l'Anglaise)

Ingredients	4 portions	10 portions
New potatoes	600 g	1.5 kg
Good quality salt	To taste	To taste
Butter	To garnish	To garnish

energy	cal	fat	sat fat	carb	sugar	protein	fibre
731 kJ	176 kcal	5.3 g	3.3 g	30.1 g	1.3 g	2.6 g	2.7 g

METHOD OF WORK

1 Wash and trim any blemishes from the new potatoes. Rewash and set aside.
2 Place a saucepan of salted water on the stove and bring to the boil.
3 Carefully add the new potatoes and simmer for 20 minutes until just cooked through.
4 Drain well and serve with a little butter, chopped fresh parsley or fresh mint if required.

Note: if you are using older potatoes these should be placed into *cold* water and brought to the boil.

CHEF'S TIP Blackening after cooking is caused by acid and iron in the potato, or by the water in certain areas. A little lemon juice or vinegar added to the cooking water helps prevent this.

HEALTH & SAFETY Whenever possible, cook potatoes in their skins to preserve the minerals and vitamin C which lay under the skin, peel after boiling if necessary.

Fondant potatoes
(Pommes fondants)

Ingredients	4 portions	10 portions
Potatoes (preferably Maris Piper)	900 g	2 kg
Butter – melted	40 g	75 g
White vegetable or chicken stock	400 ml	1 litre
Good quality salt and white pepper	To taste	To taste

energy	cal	fat	sat fat	carb	sugar	protein	fibre
1195 kJ	287 kcal	10.2 g	5.8 g	45.7 g	2.4 g	4.2 g	4.5 g

METHOD OF WORK

1   Preheat the oven to 200 °C.

2   Wash, peel and rewash the potatoes.

3   Cut each potato into sections and turn the potatoes into barrel shapes with eight sides. Each should measure 5 cm long and at the largest width 2 cm thick. Allow three per portion.

4   Wash the potatoes and pat dry with a clean kitchen cloth.

5   Brush the potatoes with some melted butter and place in a deep baking tray.

6   Add sufficient stock so it reaches halfway up the potatoes.

7   Season and bake until the potato is just cooked and the stock is almost completely reduced. Spoon over the cooking stock occasionally during cooking.

8   Continue brushing with butter to help build up a nice glossy-looking potato dish.

CHEF'S TIP   Fondant potatoes can be cut into squares or rounds and then cooked.

VIDEO CLIP   Preparing and cooking fondant potatoes.

Step-by-step: Turning potatoes into barrel shapes

1. Select, wash, peel and rewash your potatoes.

2. Top and tail the potato cutting carefully to maintain a level edge.

3. Begin turning the potatoes into barrel shapes using a turning knife by cutting around the sides of the potato.

4. Continue cutting around the potato to obtain the barrel shape.

5. Check the shape to see that all sides are equal.

6. The finished turned potato.

Matchstick potatoes
(Pommes allumettes)

Ingredients	4 portions	10 portions
Good frying potatoes (for example King Edward)	400 g	1 kg

energy	cal	fat	sat fat	carb	sugar	protein	fibre
360 kJ	86 kcal	0.1 g	0.0 g	20.0 g	0.9 g	1.7 g	1.8 g

METHOD OF WORK

1   Wash, peel and rewash the potatoes.
2   Trim the potatoes into a rectangular shape with even sides.
3   Cut slices measuring 4 cm × 3 mm.
4   Cut the slices into 3 mm × 3 mm matchsticks 4 cm long.
5   Wash well and then dry with a clean kitchen towel.
6   Deep fry at 180 °C moving them constantly to ensure an even cooking until golden.
7   Remove from the fryer and drain, season with salt and serve.

CHEF'S TIP To help cook the deep fried matchstick potatoes evenly it is worthwhile to cut uniform sizes using a sharp knife. Matchstick potatoes are served in the same way as game chips.

Mignonette potatoes
(Pommes mignonettes)

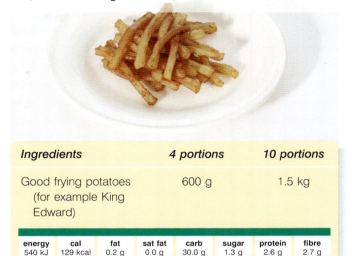

Ingredients	4 portions	10 portions
Good frying potatoes (for example King Edward)	600 g	1.5 kg

energy	cal	fat	sat fat	carb	sugar	protein	fibre
540 kJ	129 kcal	0.2 g	0.0 g	30.0 g	1.3 g	2.6 g	2.7 g

METHOD OF WORK

1   Wash, peel and rewash the potatoes.
2   Trim to give straight sides and cut into batons measuring 4 cm × ½ cm × ½ cm.
3   Rewash, drain and dry in a clean kitchen cloth.
4   Deep fry at 180 °C until golden in colour.
5   Drain well and season with salt.

CHEF'S TIP Mignonette potatoes can be par-cooked until soft at 165 °C before service and when required plunged into a deep fryer at 180 °C to complete the cooking process.

Château potatoes *(Pommes château)*

Ingredients	4 portions	10 portions
Maris Piper or good roasting potatoes	600 g	1.5 kg
Vegetable oil or goose fat	50 ml	125 ml
Good quality salt and white pepper	To taste	To taste

energy	cal	fat	sat fat	carb	sugar	protein	fibre
1004 kJ	242 kcal	12.7 g	0.9 g	30.1 g	1.3 g	2.6 g	2.7 g

METHOD OF WORK

1. Preheat an oven to 200 °C.
2. Wash, peel and rewash the potatoes.
3. Cut into even sections slightly larger than for the fondant potatoes.
4. Trim the potatoes into the same shape as for fondant potatoes; 5 cm in length, allowing 3 pieces per portion.
5. Place the potatoes into a pan of boiling salted water and cook for 3 minutes. Remove and drain in a colander. Dry with a clean kitchen cloth.
6. Heat the oil or goose fat in a roasting tray and then add the potatoes, season with the salt and pepper.
7. Lightly brown the potatoes evenly all over.
8. Place into an oven to roast for 35 minutes or until just cooked and golden in colour. Keep basting the potatoes every few minutes.
9. Drain off the fat and toss the potatoes in a little melted butter and serve.

CHEF'S TIP The potatoes can be cooked in goose fat for a richer flavour. The addition of fresh rosemary adds an extra feature to the dish and overall aroma. Rissolée potatoes are half the size of château, and cooked the same way, but for a shorter period of time because they are smaller. Cocotte potatoes are a quarter of the size of château and cooked for an even shorter period.

Pommes au lard

Ingredients	4 portions	10 portions
Potatoes (Pentland Dell or Maris Piper)	600 g	1.5 kg
Vegetable, peanut or sunflower oil	50 ml	125 ml
Lardons of bacon or pancetta	50 g	125 g
Button onions	50 g	125 g
Good quality salt and white pepper	To taste	To taste

energy	cal	fat	sat fat	carb	sugar	protein	fibre
1166 kJ	281 kcal	15.4 g	1.9 g	30.6 g	1.6 g	5.7 g	2.9 g

METHOD OF WORK

1. Select medium to large potatoes.
2. Wash, peel and rewash the potatoes. Trim on three sides and cut into 1 cm slices.
3. Cut the slices into 1 cm strips.
4. Cut the strips into 1 cm dice.
5. Wash once again and dry well using a clean kitchen cloth.
6. Heat the oil in a shallow pan or sauteuse and add the potatoes. Add the onions and the lardons.
7. Cook until they have developed a golden brown colour all over and that they are tender to the touch.
8. Drain well, season and served sprinkled with an appropriate herb such as parsley.

Dauphinoise potatoes *(Pommes dauphinoise)*

Ingredients	4 portions	10 portions
Potatoes (Pentland Dell or other good baking varieties)	600 g	1.5 kg
Double cream	350 ml	575 ml
Chopped garlic	2 cloves	4 cloves
Grated Gruyère cheese	70 g	175 g
Good quality salt and white pepper	To taste	To taste

energy	cal	fat	sat fat	carb	sugar	protein	fibre
2629 kJ	636 kcal	53.0 g	32.9 g	31.8 g	2.8 g	8.8 g	2.8 g

METHOD OF WORK

1   Preheat an oven to 200 °C.

2   Place the double cream and the chopped garlic into a saucepan and bring to the boil.

3   Remove from the heat and leave to sit for 2 minutes to infuse the garlic flavour.

4   Wash, peel and rewash potatoes.

5   Cut the potatoes into 2 mm slices.

6   Add the potatoes to the cream mixture, season well and place back onto the stove to cook for 3 minutes.

7   Carefully deposit the potatoes and garlic cream into a buttered deep-sided baking tray and sprinkle the cheese on top.

8   Lay a sheet of silicone paper on top of the cheese and then place a weighted baking tray on top of it.

9   Bake for approximately 30 minutes, until the potatoes are cooked.

10   Remove from the oven and cool down. Place into a refrigerator and chill to set the potato mixture.

11   Remove the heavy tray and silicone paper. Cut out the potatoes into the desired portion size.

12   Reheat with a little extra cheese sprinkled on top. Ensure that the potato has heated through completely.

CHEF'S TIP   The chilling of the potato dish allows it to set and makes cutting into portions much easier. However, this can be served straight from the oven if required. Herbs such as fresh tarragon can be added to enhance the flavour.

CHEF'S TIP   The traditional way of serving this dish is with a mixture of eggs, cream and milk poured over the potato slices that have been rubbed with cloves of garlic. An alternative is gratin savoyard which consists of alternating layers of potatoes and beaufort cheese with pieces of butter and covered with a white stock.

Delmonico potatoes
(Pommes delmonico)

Ingredients	4 portions	10 portions
Potatoes (Pentland Dell or Maris Piper)	600 g	1.5 kg
Fresh milk	350 ml	575 ml
Good quality salt and white pepper	To taste	To taste
Melted butter	50 g	125 g
Breadcrumbs	50 g	125 g

energy	cal	fat	sat fat	carb	sugar	protein	fibre
1283 kJ	307 kcal	12.2 g	7.5 g	44.0 g	5.8 g	7.2 g	3.1 g

METHOD OF WORK

1 Wash, peel and rewash the potatoes.
2 Cut into 6 mm dice.
3 Barely cover with milk, season well with salt and pepper and allow to cook in a saucepan for approximately 30 minutes.
4 Place the potatoes and the remaining milk into an earthenware dish, sprinkle the breadcrums and melted butter over the top and brown in a pre-heated oven or under the salamander.
5 Clean around the edges of the dish and serve.

Parmentier potatoes
(Pommes parmentier)

Ingredients	4 portions	10 portions
Potatoes (Pentland Dell or Maris Piper)	600 g	1.5 kg
Vegetable, peanut or sunflower oil	50 ml	125 ml
Good quality salt and white pepper	To taste	To taste

energy	cal	fat	sat fat	carb	sugar	protein	fibre
1004 kJ	242 kcal	12.7 g	0.9 g	30.1 g	1.3 g	2.6 g	2.7 g

METHOD OF WORK

1 Select medium to large potatoes.
2 Wash, peel and rewash the potatoes. Trim on three sides and cut into 1 cm slices.
3 Cut the slices into 1 cm strips.
4 Cut the strips into 1 cm dice.
5 Wash once again and dry well using a clean kitchen cloth.
6 Heat the oil in a shallow pan or sauteuse and add the potatoes. Cook until they have developed a golden brown colour all over and are tender to the touch.
7 Drain well, season and served sprinkled with an appropriate herb such as parsley or rosemary.

VIDEO CLIP Preparing various fried potato dishes.

Vegetable protein

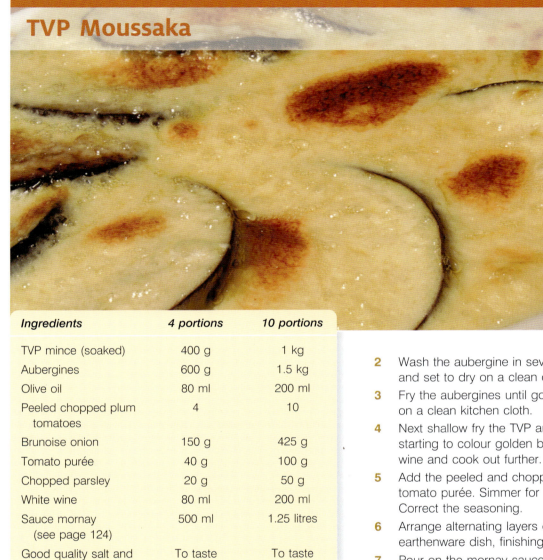

TVP Moussaka

Ingredients	4 portions	10 portions
TVP mince (soaked)	400 g	1 kg
Aubergines	600 g	1.5 kg
Olive oil	80 ml	200 ml
Peeled chopped plum tomatoes	4	10
Brunoise onion	150 g	425 g
Tomato purée	40 g	100 g
Chopped parsley	20 g	50 g
White wine	80 ml	200 ml
Sauce mornay (see page 124)	500 ml	1.25 litres
Good quality salt and milled pepper	To taste	To taste
Baby plum tomatoes	40 g	100 g

energy	cal	fat	sat fat	carb	sugar	protein	fibre
4670 kJ	1120 kcal	93.6 g	21.1 g	35.7 g	20.0 g	32.5 g	13.5 g

METHOD OF WORK

1   Slice the aubergines, sprinkle them with a little salt in a colander and leave for 1 hour to draw out excess moisture.

2   Wash the aubergine in several changes of fresh water and set to dry on a clean cloth.

3   Fry the aubergines until golden brown and set aside on a clean kitchen cloth.

4   Next shallow fry the TVP and onion in a little oil until starting to colour golden brown. Deglaze with the white wine and cook out further.

5   Add the peeled and chopped plum tomatoes and the tomato purée. Simmer for approximately 30 minutes. Correct the seasoning.

6   Arrange alternating layers of TVP and aubergines in an earthenware dish, finishing with a layer of aubergines.

7   Pour on the mornay sauce, and finish with the baby plum tomatoes cut in half. Bake in the oven at 180 °C for 30–35 minutes until the surface is golden brown.

8   Serve hot with green salad.

CHEF'S TIP   Salting the aubergines removes a lot of moisture and bitterness. They will absorb less oil and so be less soggy when cooked.

Stir-fried tofu with egg noodles

Ingredients	4 portions	10 portions
Egg noodles	200 g	500 g
Firm tofu	300 g	750 g
Light soy sauce	60 ml	150 ml
Sherry	40 ml	100 ml
Sliced red and green pepper	½ each	2 each
Sliced red onion	1	2–3
Grated ginger	40 g	100 g
Sliced red chilli	1	2–3
Vegetable stock (see page 114)	200 ml	500 ml
Black bean sauce	40 g	100 g
Corn flour	15 g	35 g
Oil	20 ml	50 ml
Good quality salt and pepper	To taste	To taste

energy	cal	fat	sat fat	carb	sugar	protein	fibre
1442 kJ	345 kcal	19.8 g	1.0 g	19.8 g	7.4 g	20.5 g	3.2 g

METHOD OF WORK

1. Wash the tofu in clean cold water.
2. Dice the tofu into 1 cm cubes and marinate in the soy sauce and sherry for 2–3 hours.
3. Place the noodle in a dish of seasoned boiling water and allow to stand for 5–6 minutes until regenerated and cooked.
4. Stir-fry the onions and peppers for 1 minute. Add the chilli and garlic and continue to cook for a further 1 minute. Add the stock and bring to the boil.
5. Drain the tofu and stir-fry until golden brown.
6. Mix the black bean sauce and cornflour with the marinade and add to the stock to thicken (use more or less cornflour as required).
7. Add the tofu to the sauce and serve with the egg noodles.

Sweet and sour Quorn™

Ingredients	4 portions	10 portions
Diced Quorn™	400 g	1 kg
Sliced green pepper	½	2
Sliced red pepper	½	2
Sliced onion	100 g	250 g
Sliced leek	75 g	150 g
Canned pineapple	200 g can	500 g can
The sauce		
Brown sugar	120 g	300 g
Rice vinegar	120 ml	300 ml
Crushed garlic	1 clove	2–3 cloves
Grated root ginger	40 g	100 g
Tomato ketchup	80 ml	200 ml
Juice from canned pineapples	80 ml	200 ml
Oil for frying		

energy	cal	fat	sat fat	carb	sugar	protein	fibre
2176 kJ	520 kcal	28.6 g	2.4 g	51.6 g	49.2 g	15.9 g	6.7 g

METHOD OF WORK

1. Shallow fry the Quorn™ until golden brown and cooked. Drain onto absorbent paper and keep hot for service.
2. Stir fry the onions, leeks, sliced pineapples and peppers for two minutes. Remove from the wok and put to one side.
3. Mix all the sauce ingredients together and bring to the boil, stir continuously until the sauce thickens and becomes clear. Check seasoning and consistency.
4. Just prior to service; combine the Quorn™, vegetables and sauce together and serve immediately with steamed rice.

Courgette and seitan fritters

Ingredients	4 portions	10 portions
Shredded seitan	200 g	500 g
Grated courgette	300 g	750 g
Grated parmesan	40 g	100 g
Plain flour	50–60 g	125–150 g
Eggs	2	5
Oil for frying		
Good quality salt and milled pepper	To taste	To taste
For the sweet chilli dressing		
Olive oil	20 ml	50 ml
Finely diced onions	40 g	100 g
Chopped garlic	1 clove	2 cloves
Red chillies	2	5
Muscavado sugar	30 g	75 g
Water	20 ml	50 ml
White wine vinegar	10 ml	25 ml

energy	cal	fat	sat fat	carb	sugar	protein	fibre
2384 kJ	573 kcal	42.4 g	5.5 g	27.3 g	11.4 g	23.2 g	4.4 g

METHOD FOR THE DRESSING

1 Sweat the onions, garlic and chilli in the oil for 10–15 minutes, stirring frequently.

2 Add the mixture to a food processor along with the sugar, water and vinegar.

3 Liquidize roughly.

4 Return to the pan and stir over a low heat until the sugar has dissolved.

5 Adjust the seasoning as required.

METHOD FOR THE FRITTERS

1 Grate and season the courgettes with salt and leave in a colander for 10 minutes to allow excess water to be released. Squeeze out the remaining water.

2 Mix the courgettes, seitan, cheese, flour and eggs to make a light paste.

3 Divide the mix and shallow fry the fritters for 3–4 minutes on each side until golden brown and cooked through.

4 Serve with the chilli dressing and garnish.

Cajun tofu with couscous

Ingredients	4 portions	10 portions
Tofu blocks	4 x 100 g	10 x 100 g
Blackened cajun spices	10 g	25 g
Diced onions	80 g	200 g
Chopped red chillies	1	2–3
Crushed garlic	I clove	2–3 cloves
Plum tomato concassée	200 g	500 g
Chopped soft green herbs	1 tblspn	2 tblspn
Couscous	200 g	500 g
Oil	100 ml	250 ml
Good quality salt and pepper	To taste	To taste
Vinegar	20 ml	50 ml
Sugar	20 g	100 g

energy	cal	fat	sat fat	carb	sugar	protein	fibre
2708 kJ	652 kcal	43.8 g	2.8 g	38.9 g	10.6 g	27.8 g	3.5 g

METHOD OF WORK

1   Drain and wash the tofu, brush with oil and season with blackened cajun seasoning. Allow the tofu to marinate in the spices for 1 hour.

2   Heat half the oil in a saucepan, add the onions, garlic and chillies and sweat until tender.

3   Add the vinegar and sugar and allow to reduce to form a gastrique.

4   Add the tomato concassée and remove from the heat.

5   Mix the couscous with a little oil, seasoning and pour over boiling water to just cover: place a sheet of cling film on top and leave for 8 minutes.

6   Use a fork to break up the couscous and mix in the tomato mixture with some fresh herbs.

7   Dice the tofu and then bake the tofu in a hot oven until a core temperature of 75 °C is achieved.

8   Spoon the couscous into a bowl and mix with the tofu before presenting in a bowl-plate.

Guest Chef

Vegetable moussaka

Chef: *Ben Ross*
Centre: *South Downs College*

The goats cheese used in this recipe is produced by Loosehanger Cheeses based in the New Forest, Hampshire. We also use locally produced fruits and vegetables supplied by Hampshire Fayre who are our local suppliers.

Ingredients	Makes 6 portions
Onions	50 g
Garlic	1 clove
Courgettes	200 g
Mushrooms	200 g
Aubergines	200 g
Tomatoes	250 g
Flour (for dusting)	
Oil	60 ml
Butter	20 g
Goats cheese	200 g
Vegetable stock	200 ml

METHOD OF WORK

1　Finely dice the onion and garlic.
2　Cook in the butter without colour.
3　Add the diced courgettes, cook for a few minutes.
4　Add the tomato purée and then the vegetable stock.
5　Allow to simmer until cooked.
6　Correct seasoning and consistency. The mixture should be fairly dry.
7　Slice the aubergine into thin slices, dust with the flour and shallow fry until light brown. Retain to use later.
8　Peel the tomatoes, deseed and dice the flesh into concassée.
9　Place six stainless steel rings onto a tray and layer the cooked vegetables, chopped tomatoes and aubergine into them finely covering the top with a slice of aubergine.
10　Place a thick slice of goats cheese on top and place into a pre-heated oven at 230 °C until golden brown and heated through.
11　Sprinkle with chopped parsley and serve.

Recipes

BASIC RECIPES FOR PASTES

Shortcrust paste 462

Lining paste 463

Pie paste 463

Sweet paste 464

Puff paste recipe with pastry
    margarine 468

Rough puff paste 468

Choux paste 470

Suet paste 471

PASTE BASED RECIPES

French cheese and ham savoury
    flan 472

Dutch apple tart 473

Treacle tart 473

Fresh fruit tart 474

Fig slice 475

Tart tatin 475

French apple flan 476

Egg custard tart 477

Bakewell tart 478

Chocolate tart 478

Gâteau pithivier 479

Palmiers 480

Cheese straws 481

Vol-au-vents 481

Tranche mille feuille 482

Profiteroles with chocolate sauce 484

Coffee and chocolate éclairs 485

Steamed jam roll 486

Spotted dick 486

ONLINE RECIPES

LEARNER SUPPORT

Stilton, asparagus and tomato
    tartlets

Goats cheese and herb filo
    tartlets

Fresh fruit tartlets

Mince pies

Gâteau Paris-Brest

Orange and lime tart

Eccles cakes

Apple and blackberry pie

12 Pastes, tarts and pies

NVQ

Unit 2FPC10 Prepare, cook and finish basic pastry products

VRQ

Unit 213 Produce paste products

Introduction

The pastry department has an important role in the overall operation of a professional kitchen. This specialist area uses techniques that are very different from that of the main kitchen. The correct use of commodities must be understood, from accurate weighing, employing correct mixing methods and baking at the right temperature to utilizing fine presentation and decoration skills. This chapter often refers to pastes and dough as separate items. Dough is a product that is produced using fermentation or chemical aeration as a way of introducing expansion or lightness in a product. Due to the high fat content generally found in pastes they have dense textures. So they will not aerate by using yeast or baking powders, so techniques such as lamination are employed to achieve this.

Among some of the pastes that are described in this chapter are shortcrust (pâte brisée) and sweet paste (pâte sucrée). These are fine, short, crisp and crumbly textured pastes which are used to contain or form a base for fillings, various custards and fruits. Puff paste (pâte feuilletée) has a complex texture of alternate fine layers of paste and fat. During the baking process the paste rises up to form thin, buttery flakes of paste. Choux paste (pâte à choux) is a heavily moisturized and airy paste which puffs up in the oven to form a crisp outer shell and that is hollow inside. It can be piped into different shapes and is usually filled with creams, mousses and custards. Suet paste (pâte à grasse de boeuf) is normally required to produce sweet puddings that can be steamed or baked and is a soft paste using beef or vegetable suet. Although the confections made from this paste can be classed under hot desserts, the paste can also be rolled out to line pudding moulds to contain fillings such as steak and kidney. Therefore it is classified as a paste.

Ingredients used in pastes

An understanding of the variations in the different ingredients will help you to achieve the results you are aiming for.

Flour

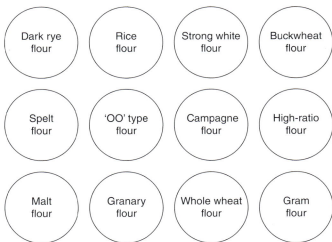

Dark rye flour	Rice flour	Strong white flour	Buckwheat flour
Spelt flour	'OO' type flour	Campagne flour	High-ratio flour
Malt flour	Granary flour	Whole wheat flour	Gram flour

One of the most important factors that influence our choice of flour is the gluten content. Gluten is protein that is present in flour. It provides baked products with strength and structure. The remaining content of flour is made up of starch as the main component, water, sugar and mineral matter (ash). Most of the flour used today is wheat flour although there is a vast array of different types available to use.

> **HEALTH & SAFETY** Coeliac disease is an autoimmune disease. Gluten, which is found in wheat, barley and rye triggers an immune reaction in people with coeliac disease. This means that eating gluten damages the lining of the small intestine. Other parts of the body may be affected. A gluten-free diet is the treatment for coeliac disease. Taking gluten out of the diet allows the gut to heal and symptoms to improve.

> **WEB LINK** For further information on coeliac disease go to http://www.coeliac.org.uk/coeliac-disease

Flour is mostly made up from the endosperm of the wheat grain, which contains starch and protein. Mixing flour with water will eventually turn it into a tacky paste and part of this characteristic is because the gluten content is reacting with the water. The proportion of starch to gluten content will vary in different wheat and those with low gluten content are generally suitable for making pastry.

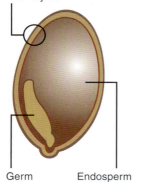

Bran layers

Germ   Endosperm

Whole grain kernel

During the milling process the whole grain is broken so that the bran layers and wheatgerm are removed. However, wholemeal flour uses both these components and they are left in the flour which is considered to have stronger dietary benefits than white flour, as 100 per cent of the grain is used. White flour contains up to 85 per cent of the grain, of which the part of the grain used is only the endosperm. Wheatmeal flour contains up to 95 per cent of the grain while high-ratio flour uses only 40 per cent.

- *Strong flour* is sometimes referred to as bread flour. It has a high gluten content which is developed when moisture is added and it is manipulated into a dough or paste. It is mostly used to produce yeast fermented dough such as bread, buns and croissants, and is also the preferred choice of flour for choux paste and puff paste.

- *Soft flour* is sometimes referred to as cake flour. It contains low gluten content and is more suited to the production of cakes, sponges and short pastes.

- *Medium flour* is generally known as all-purpose flour. It has slightly higher gluten content than soft. It can be used to produce batters for deep frying where crispness is required for fritters and is also used to create some specialized pastes and biscuits.

- *Spelt flour* is the finely milled grain of spelt, an ancient variety of wheat and sub-species of the common wheat. Once widely grown in continental Europe, spelt has enjoyed a revival due to its nutritious qualities and as a result is now grown in Britain. The flour is a pale greyish-yellow, gritty in texture, and has a slightly nutty flavour. Spelt is generally used in bread-making.

- *OO flour* is also known as Italian or dopio zero flour. This flour is traditionally used for making pasta and is made from coarsely ground durum wheat. Italian flour is mixed with water to make robust pasta dough that holds its shape during cooking and will not disintegrate into a starchy paste. In Italy, pasta flour is commonly known as semolina.

- *Wholemeal flour* is made from the whole wheat grain which includes the bran layers and the germ. Generally it is used for bread making, but if the milling process has refined the flour to smaller particles, it can be used as a healthier option to white flours when producing some pastes. This is due to its high fibre content. Normally this type of flour has a shorter shelf life due to the germ still being present in the flour, which contains a small amount of oil content and can turn rancid after a few days' storage.

- *Gram flour* is flour made from ground chickpeas, a légume otherwise known as chana-dal. It is also known as chickpea flour, garbanzo flour, or besan. Used in many countries, it is a staple ingredient in Indian, Pakistani and Bangladeshi cuisines. It contains a high proportion of carbohydrates but no gluten content is apparent. Despite this, in comparison to other flours, it has a relatively high proportion of protein.

- *Buckwheat flour* This is flour milled from buckwheat, a cold climate plant from the same family as rhubarb and sorrel. Buckwheat's pointed, triangular seeds resemble cereal grains, and the fine-textured flour is grey with black speckles. It has a strong, distinctive, slightly sour and nutty taste and is rich in vitamins and minerals and low in calories. It is also gluten-free, so it can be used by those on a special diet.

- *Campagne flour* is a combination of white flour with whole wheat flour or rye flour. Before the advent of roller milling, virtually all wheat was milled by stone grinding. In order to produce lighter bread, the whole wheat flour was sifted using mesh or cloth. This resulted in whiter flour that still retained some of the bran and germ. The addition of rye flour in some recipes probably originates from the presence of rye growing amongst the wheat. All the grain was harvested together, and as much as 10 per cent of it would be rye. Rye flour ferments more quickly than wheat flour and it imparts a distinctive flavour to traditional pains de Campagne.

For further information on flours refer to the next chapter on fermented products.

SOURCING Organic flour is produced from organic grain from local farms, who are certified by The Soil Association. This ensures that the authenticity of the product is maintained from the seed being planted on the farm through to the flour leaving the mill. The crops receive no artificial fertilizers, herbicides, insecticides or pesticides and the grain is cleaned and stored under The Soil Association standards.

Fats and oils

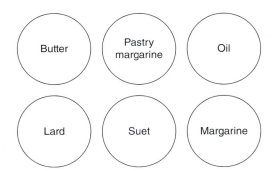

When choosing an appropriate fat to be used for a specific baked product, the plasticity of the fat will be a major determining factor. This refers to the ability of the fat to maintain its shape at room temperature but still have the ability to be manipulated. The melting point of the fat ultimately determines its plasticity. Butter is plastic at a cool room temperature but when refrigerated it is too firm. Vegetable shortening is plastic at both sets of temperatures and is therefore easier to work with than butter. However, the greater plasticity of fat, the less desirable it may be to eat because it will have a higher melting point than human body temperature, which means it will not melt in the mouth.

- *Butter* has excellent creamy qualities, stable texture and the best flavour of all fats. It must be used at cool temperatures to maintain its plasticity. Unsalted butter is often preferred due to its creamier texture and flavour. It will normally have a fat content of up to 86 per cent and melts at between 30 and 35 °C.

- *Margarine is* manufactured from various oils that have been hardened or hydrogenated, and has a similar plasticity and colour to butter. It still contains a similar fat content to butter and is therefore excellent for creaming and using in pastes. Margarine can contain up to 10 per cent butterfat.

- *Pastry margarine* has a firm texture and high melting point. It is used in the production of puff paste. It lacks colour and flavour and therefore has reduced eating qualities. It is sometimes referred to as vegetable shortening.

- *Lard* has very good shortening qualities in pastes such as short savoury. It is a solid fat that is rendered from pork and has a high melting point with no colour.

- *Oils* are perceived to be healthier due to their higher levels of unsaturated fats. They have no creaming ability so they are not a viable alternative to butter when making short pastes. However, they can be used for dough items and strudel paste.

- *Suet* is a hard fat and does not have creaming properties. Traditionally it is used for the production of suet paste and puddings. It should be stored in a refrigerator and in an airtight container.

Solid fats absorb flavours and odours and need to be stored in the refrigerator away from strong-smelling ingredients. They can also be frozen for several weeks if required. Oils can turn rancid more quickly and should always be stored in airtight bottles or containers. If stored in a refrigerator some oils may begin to solidify, so they will need to be brought back to room temperature before using.

The role of fat in making a pastry is to give texture to the final product. Depending on the kind of fat used, the pastry will also have a specific flavour. Chefs use various types of fats, such as vegetable shortening, butter, or lard to make pastry. Though they are all fats, they have major differences. Vegetable shortening is a blend of partially hydrogenated cottonseed and soybean oil with fully hydrogenated cottonseed oil and soybean oil. Hydrogenation makes oil solid at room temperature. The optimum working temperature range of vegetable shortening is 12–30 °C. This means that it can be worked (kneaded or mixed) without getting too soft within this temperature range. The working range for lard is 15–24 °C. Outside of the working range, the fat does not hold its shape and leaks oil.

TASK

Polyunsaturated fats:

- are liquid at room temperatures as well as at cold temperatures
- include the omega-3 group of fatty acids, which are anti-inflammatory and your body can't make. In addition, omega-3 fats are found in very few foods.

Find out what the primary sources of polyunsaturated fats are.

TASK

Saturated fats:

- are usually solid at room temperature and have a high melting point.
- saturated fat raises low-density lipoprotein (LDL or 'bad') cholesterol that increases your risk of coronary heart disease (CHD)
- it is unnecessary to eat saturated fat sources since our bodies can produce all the saturated fat that we need when we consume enough of the good fats.

Find out what the primary sources of saturated fats are.

Sugar is sometimes referred to as sucrose and it plays a very important role in bakery. Besides acting as a sweetener: it provides tenderness to baked products; caramelizes during cooking to impart colour; absorbs moisture from the atmosphere to maintain shelf life and moisture in baked produce, such as pastries and cakes; aids the aeration process during the creaming of fats; and used skilfully it can fashion many different finishes to create confectionery.

Sucrose is extracted from sugar cane or sugar beet where the natural syrup is then processed into a variety of different types of sugar including liquid glucose, molasses and treacle. The majority of the sugar that is used currently is extracted from sugar cane which is grown all over the world. There are a wide range of different cane sugars available, from the popular white granulated to a range of brown sugars, where the variations in flavour, colour and texture depend on their molasses content and degree of refinement. Sugars with high molasses content are darker, stickier and have a stronger flavour.

Sugar

Fresh sugar cane cut and tied for market

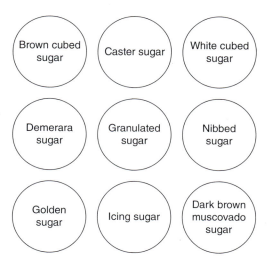

Brown cubed sugar

Caster sugar

White cubed sugar

Demerara sugar

Granulated sugar

Nibbed sugar

Golden sugar

Icing sugar

Dark brown muscovado sugar

Fresh suger beet

- *Cube sugar* is generally regarded as one of the most pure forms of refined white sugars and is traditionally used for boiled sugar items and to make caramel. It is made by pressing the sugar crystals together while they still have some moisture, drying in large blocks before cutting into small cubes and packaging them. Two types of sugar cubes are available – white and demerara.

    To store: Keep in a cool, dry place for up to one year and once opened store in an airtight container to prevent the cubes from disintegrating and turning damp.

- *Granulated sugar* is a coarse-grained sugar and is used as a sweetener and for dissolving in liquid solutions to make jams, compôtes and stewed fruit products. It can also be used to boil and create caramelized finishes to baked items, such as profiteroles dipped in caramel.

    To store: Same as cube sugar.

- *Caster sugar* is a fine-grained sugar and is the most widely used sugar in the kitchen. It is used in the production of pastes and aids the creaming process very well.

    To store: Same as cube sugar.

- *Icing sugar*, otherwise known as confectioner's sugar, is a fine powdered sugar used mainly for the production of icings and glazing. It is produced by grinding white sugar to a very fine powder. Icing sugar is a versatile ingredient in cooking. It is different from other types of sugar in that it dissolves very quickly in cold water. For best results pass through a fine sieve before use.

    To store: Keep in a cool, dry place for up to 6 months, once opened store in an airtight container.

- *Liquid glucose* is sometimes referred to as corn syrup because it is made from corn starch and is a transparent and thick syrup. This is an important addition to the sugar range because it prolongs shelf life in many baked products and also helps to prevent caramelized sugar from returning to its granular form. When used with ice-cream, it adds plasticity and soft texture as well as helping to prevent crystallization.

    To store: Keep a sealed plastic container to prevent drying.

- *Honey* is classified as a natural sugar that has its own distinguishing flavour and can be used in certain recipes as a substitute for sugar. It is the oldest known sugar and is 30 per cent sweeter than sucrose. It will lower freezing points of sorbets and ice-creams but it also has its own distinct flavour, which it will impart to any preparation.

    To store: Same as for liquid glucose.

- *Golden sugar* is a granulated raw cane sugar that is slightly less refined than white. It contains traces of molasses and often tends to have an acidic flavour. It has a fine free flowing texture and a light golden colour. It is different from standard caster sugar because the light presence of molasses adds a delicious flavour, sweetness and aroma, but it can be used in place of standard caster sugar.

    To store: Same as cube sugar.

- *Dark brown muscovado sugar* has a distinctive dark brown colour. This raw cane sugar has a rich flavour and aroma. It contains about 13 per cent molasses and has a soft, fine-grained texture. It is ideal for dark fruit cakes and puddings.

    To store: Same as cube sugar.

- *Nibbed sugar* (also pearl sugar and hail sugar) is a product of refined white sugar. The sugar is very coarse, hard, opaque white, and does not melt at temperatures typically used for baking. The product is usually produced by crushing blocks of white sugar, then sifting to obtain fragments of a specific diameter. It is used to add decoration to baked products.

    To store: Same as cube sugar.

- *Isomalt* is a sweetening agent that has been used by the food manufacturing industry for many years to produce candies and gums. Recently pastry chefs have used this type of sugar as a matter of choice for producing artistic sugar showpieces because it is not as hygroscopic

(material which attracts moisture from the atmosphere) as normal sugar. So it prolongs the shelf life of their decorative work. It has half the sweetness of sucrose.
To store: Keep in an airtight plastic container.

> **HEALTH & SAFETY** A sugar substitute is a food additive that duplicates the effect of sugar in taste, usually the substitute is saccharine or sucralose. Some sugar substitutes are natural and some are synthetic. Those that are not natural are, in general, called artificial sweeteners.

> **WEB LINK** For sugar-free recipe ideas try:
> http://www.sugarfreerecipes.co.uk/

Eggs

Eggs perform a number of functions such as introducing richness, colour, increased structure and moisture to a product. The pastry kitchen will use large quantities of eggs, so it is important to maintain a good stock rotation system. Eggs are used for binding, emulsifying and coating products. They contain both protein and fat. Egg yolks are an important emulsifier used in the kitchen, and the lecithin protein allows it to emulsify or thicken other ingredients such as milk when heated to 82 °C. The albumen, or egg white, contains protein but little or no fat, and can be used in cooking separately from the yolk. Egg whites may be aerated to a light, fluffy consistency and are often used in desserts, such as meringue.

- *Fresh* eggs should be refrigerated before use, although some recipes call for eggs to be used at room temperature. It is important that they are as fresh as possible. They are graded according to size: 1 is the largest and 7 the smallest. A standard size is grade 3 and a general rule is that each egg weighs approximately 50–60 grams.

- *Frozen* eggs are available in 1 kilogram tetra packs of yolks, whites and mixed whole eggs. Once defrosted and opened they should be treated exactly the same as fresh egg.

- *Dried* form is usually albumen and is used to make meringue products and icings. Store in an airtight container and in a cool, dry store room.

> **HEALTH & SAFETY** The risk of an egg being contaminated with salmonella bacteria is very low, about 1 in 20 000 eggs. However, the risk of contracting food-borne illness should always be eliminated. The correct handling of eggs can reduce, and even entirely remove, the risk of contamination e.g. store in a refrigerator and keep dry.

> **WEB LINK** Check the following website for further information on eggs:
> http://www.britegg.co.uk/

Nuts

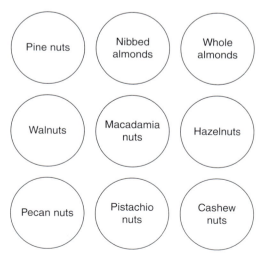

Pine nuts	Nibbed almonds	Whole almonds
Walnuts	Macadamia nuts	Hazelnuts
Pecan nuts	Pistachio nuts	Cashew nuts

Nuts contribute flavour, texture and decorative appeal. They contain proteins, fibre, vitamins and minerals and eaten in moderation can be a healthy addition to any diet, except of course for those people with nut allergies. This is why every product that contains nuts in some form *must* be declared on menus or package labels.

Nuts contain natural oils that impart flavour. However, because of their fat content, they can go rancid quickly and they must be stored in an airtight container in a cool area. Nuts can be frozen successfully and this will prolong their shelf life.

Nuts can generally be purchased whole, halved, chopped or ground. Chestnuts must always be cooked before using and can be used whole, glacé (cooked in a sugar syrup) or puréed. It is important to understand about products derived from nuts so you can be aware of potential nut cross-contamination in the kitchen. Almond paste and marzipan are made from almonds and sugar. They have a paste-like consistency and are used in many cake, torten and tart recipes or used in petit fours. Praline and praline paste consists of caramelized hazelnuts. This product is used mainly as a flavouring or as a decorative item. Gianduja is a similar product to praline but with the addition of milk chocolate and is finely ground to a smooth paste. It is used to flavour desserts and is also used in confectionery. Coconut products such as milk, cream and desiccated nut are used as flavouring or to add texture.

Marzipan is made from almonds

The flavour of most nuts can be enhanced by lightly roasting or toasting. Although this procedure is quite simple, care must be taken because the fat content in nuts can cause them to burn easily. The nuts should be placed onto a baking sheet and placed into a preheated oven at 170 °C. The roasting process should only take approximately ten minutes and should be checked every three minutes or so. There should be a light golden colouration to the nuts before they are ready to be removed from the oven and left to cool to room temperature.

Storing bakery items

Maintaining the quality of ingredients in the pastry kitchen is a concern for all chefs. Many of the commodities used are very prone to contamination and great care needs to be taken to ensure hygienic storage and refrigeration measures are maintained.

- Dairy products and eggs should be stored in air-circulated refrigeration units and kept in clean, covered plastic containers.

- Separate dairy and egg products from other ingredients to avoid cross-contamination. A separate refrigerator is best practice if possible.

- Dry commodities need to be stored in clean, sealed plastic containers on clean shelving in a separate storage room. The room needs to be maintained at a constant cool temperature and should have a dry atmosphere.

- Stock rotation should be employed so that all ingredients are used up and then replenished by a new batch of ingredients. The empty container should be cleaned before replenishing.

- It is not recommended to store baked products for long periods of time in a refrigerator because of starch breakdown and loss of flavour.

- To store baked items for short periods in a refrigerator it is essential that they are wrapped in plastic film or placed into airtight plastic containers. Items that contain large amounts of sugar will take longer to become stale.

- Storing baked products in a freezer is an alternative method that works well. However, the baked item should be completely cool before wrapping tightly in plastic and then aluminium foil. Label and date the item before freezing.

- Good practice is to blast freeze any item for 30 minutes before placing into a holding freezer. This process helps to maintain moisture content in the product and to eliminate potential freezer burn.

TASK State how you would store a baked apple tart for service the next day and the steps you would take to reheat and present it for service.

The use of convenience pastes

The use of convenience pastes helps to ease the production of complex pastes, such as puff paste and filo paste. The products mean that the utilization of human resources, time, cost and standardization of the product is the principal factor for many kitchens. Today's popular use of filo paste is greatly attributed to its success as an easy to use, convenient paste rather than having to spend time making it from fresh.

Most pastes can be purchased as a convenience product in either a frozen or fresh variety. If using frozen paste it is important that the paste is correctly defrosted in a refrigerator in the original packaging it was first purchased in (provided that it is hygienic and unperforated). Otherwise the texture of the paste may be altered significantly enough to render it unusable. The paste should then be used and correctly stored following the same guidelines as fresh paste: wrapped in plastic film, refrigerated and labelled accurately. Care should be taken when storing as the paste will become discoloured with a greyish hue if not correctly wrapped.

Frozen pre-rolled pastry in packaging

Convenience pastry mixes and 'ready-rolled' pastry is available for the chef to save on time and labour costs and some of these products will produce very good results if handled correctly and used imaginatively. There are also a broad range of frozen products available to serve as morning or afternoon tea pastries. These include fruit tarts, pies, pastries and gateaux. The vast majority are ready to be served and simply need de-frosting and sometimes warming or baking with a minimum of finishing required to serve. The use of convenient products such as these, permits the chef or manager to cut costs on labour while enabling the team to concentrate on other areas of the menu.

Short pastes

There is a specific family of tart and pie pastes, each one having its own method of preparation and uses. Four specific pastes will be explained in this section. A good quality short paste should be slightly golden and have an even colour when baked. The texture of the cooked paste should be light and crumbly and not too thick when it has been lined.

1   Shortcrust paste – la pâte brisée

2   Lining paste – la pâte à foncer

3   Sweet paste – la pâte sucrée

4   Pie paste – la pâte à pâté

Raw short paste before rolling out

These pastes all fall under the collective heading of 'les pâtes friable', because all of them are short, crisp and friable (crumbly).

There are two main methods used to obtain this characteristic crispness:

1   **Rubbing-in** (sablage) – the aim of this method is to rub the fat and flour together to prevent the gluten strands from becoming activated, which would result in a tough paste with a hard crust.

2   **Creaming** – in this method the butter is aerated with the sugar before the liquid ingredients are combined and worked to a smooth cream. This mixture contains a large amount of fat, so this method tends not to work the flour too much because the flour is added at the last stage.

It is important to remember that if the liquid ingredients used in a paste are composed of fats (for example eggs, instead of water) there is less chance of the gluten within flour being activated, resulting in a flakier and light-textured paste.

Uses of short pastes

- *La pâte brisée* – savoury crisp items: quiche, tartlets, barquettes, canapés.

- *La pâte à foncer* – sweet and savoury pies and tarts with a wet filling apple, blackberry, savoury custards.

- *La pâte sucrée* – sweet tartlettes, barquettes, flans, pies.

- *La pâte à pâté* – used for pies, pâtés en croûte and raised pies.

HEALTH & SAFETY If the raw paste is kept above refrigeration temperature, production of acids formed by bacteria will cause sourness and make the paste unsuitable for use.

TASK Produce a working list of all the equipment, resources, commodities and machinery needed to produce 250 individual portions of fresh fruit tartlets.

Specialist baking equipment

Bain-marie A French term for a hot water bath. It can be used as a double-boiler with a second bowl placed over a pan of simmering water to create such confections as a sabayon or Swiss meringue. It can also be used as a technique to ensure gentle, even baking for custard-based desserts such as crème caramel or cheesecakes.

Bench and bowl scrapers The bench scraper, sometimes known as a dough scraper, is a small metal rectangular blade attached to a handle. It is used to cut and scale pieces of dough and to clean work surfaces by scraping it against a table top to loosen pieces of paste and dough. A bowl scraper is flexible plastic and is used to scrape around the inside of mixing bowls to use every last piece of the prepared mixture.

Disposable piping bag This is a cone-shaped plastic bag used to pipe various preparations with ease and hygienically. Use the bag only once, fitted with a nylon piping tube.

Sieve A sieve can be a small tool the size of a tea strainer to finish off desserts with a fine dusting of cocoa powder or it can be a large, drum-shaped utensil used to sift flours, ground almonds and icing sugar.

False-bottomed tart tins These tins are usually fluted and are excellent for producing fine short paste tart cases. This is because the base is removable making it easy to de-mould the lined, blind baked pastry case.

Offset palette knife This is a wide, paddle-style knife usually without a sharp blade. There should be a slight bend to the handle to make it easier to use. They are purchased in varying sizes.

Grater Usually made of metal with sharp holes of varying grades. Fruits such as oranges and lemons are rubbed alongside the holes to remove and finely shred the zests. It can also be used to shred chocolate, cheese and vegetables.

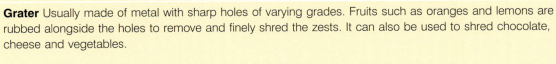

Pastry brush Indispensable in the pastry kitchen, is used to apply glazes to tarts and desserts, egg-washes and butter to various products. It should always be kept very clean as it can be a major cross-contaminator.

Basic recipes for pastes

Shortcrust paste *(Pâte brisée)*

Ingredients	Makes approximately 400 g
Butter or margarine	65 g
Lard or vegetable fat	65 g
Salt	5 g
Soft flour	250 g
Egg (medium sized)	1
Cold water	1 tblspn (approx)

energy	cal	fat	sat fat	carb	sugar	protein	fibre
827 kJ	198 kcal	12.6 g	6.2 g	18.3 g	0.4 g	3.0 g	0.8 g

METHOD OF WORK

1 Sieve the flour onto a clean work surface or into a stainless steel bowl.

2 Cut the butter and lard (at room temperature) into small pieces and rub into the flour with the salt.

3 When the fat has been successfully rubbed into the flour, incorporate the cold liquid and the whole egg.

4 Gently amalgamate the ingredients together, forming a light paste. Do not overwork this paste and adjust with a little additional flour if necessary.

5 Wrap well in polythene or silicone paper and place in a refrigerator for 30 minutes to rest the paste before using.

CHEF'S TIP   The amount of liquid (in this case egg and water) varies according to the type and grade of flour used (fine flour is generally more absorbent), and the temperature that the raw paste is exposed to during production. If the environment is warm the paste may not require as much liquid. This paste will keep well for several days in a refrigerator or for several weeks in a freezer, if wrapped well in plastic film. The egg content can be replaced in this recipe with an additional 4 tbsp of cold water.

SOURCING   The cornerstone of all bakery products is flour. Organic flour is a very desirable product to use. Finding organic flour is easy. However, finding a consistent flour supply at a reasonable price can be difficult. Finding more than one source for every ingredient is an essential aspect of successful organic and conventional baking. Finding multiple sources for all ingredients, despite how minor these ingredients may appear, protects the chef on many levels. For example, multiple suppliers per ingredient ensures that a chef is always protected in case a primary supplier loses his crop, misses a delivery or prices increase drastically.

Lining paste (Pâte à foncer)

Ingredients	Makes approximately 500 g
Soft flour	250 g
Softened butter	125 g
Egg (medium sized)	1
Cold water	40 ml
Salt	5 g
Caster sugar (optional)	20 g

energy	cal	fat	sat fat	carb	sugar	protein	fibre
678 kJ	162 kcal	9.4 g	5.6 g	17.0 g	2.1 g	2.6 g	0.6 g

METHOD OF WORK

1 Sift the flour onto a clean work surface or into a stainless steel bowl.
2 Cut the butter (at room temperature) into small pieces and rub into the flour with the sugar (if using) and the salt.
3 When the butter has been successfully rubbed into the flour, incorporate the cold water and the whole egg.
4 Gently amalgamate the ingredients together, forming a light paste. Do not overwork this paste.
5 Wrap well in polythene or silicone paper and place in a refrigerator for 45 minutes before using.

VIDEO CLIP Short savoury paste.

Pie paste (Pâte à pâté)

Ingredients	Makes approximately 400 g
Soft flour	250 g
Softened butter	140 g
Egg (medium sized)	1
Cold water	50 ml
Salt	5 g

energy	cal	fat	sat fat	carb	sugar	protein	fibre
1364 kJ	327 kcal	20.5 g	12.5 g	30.5 g	0.7 g	5.0 g	1.3 g

METHOD OF WORK

1 Sift the flour into a stainless steel bowl with the salt.
2 Cut the butter (at room temperature) into small pieces and rub into the flour to give a granular texture.
3 Whisk the egg and the water together. When the butter has been successfully rubbed into the flour, incorporate the water and egg mixture into the flour mixture.
4 Gently amalgamate the ingredients together, forming a light paste. Do not overwork this paste.
5 Wrap well in polythene or silicone paper and place in a refrigerator for 60 minutes before using.

SOURCING Salt is a natural mineral made up of white cube-shaped crystals composed of two elements, sodium and chlorine. When chemically united they form the compound sodium chloride. Sodium chloride is readily soluble in water yet insoluble or only slightly soluble in most other liquids. It is translucent, colourless, odourless and has a distinctive and characteristic taste.

Sea salt is the growing choice of people who prefer a more natural flavour.

Sweet paste *(Pâte sucrée)*

Ingredients	Makes approximately 530 g
Soft flour	250 g
Butter or margarine	100 g
Caster sugar	80 g
Salt	5 g
Egg (medium sized)	100 g
Vanilla extract	Optional

energy	cal	fat	sat fat	carb	sugar	protein	fibre
576 kJ	137 kcal	6.4 g	3.7 g	17.8 g	5.9 g	2.4 g	0.5 g

METHOD OF WORK 1

1 Sift the flour onto a clean work surface or into a large stainless steel bowl. Make a well in the centre.

2 Cut the butter (at room temperature) into small pieces and place in the centre of the well with the salt and sugar.

3 Work the butter and sugar with your fingertips until completely creamed together and pale in colour.

4 Slowly incorporate the whole egg, mixing well until the mixture is completely smooth and creamy. At this stage you can add a few drops of vanilla extract to help flavour the paste.

5 Gradually draw the flour into the creamed butter and when all ingredients are thoroughly mixed, lightly work the paste to a smooth texture. Do not overwork the paste at this point.

6 Wrap well in polythene or silicone paper and place in a refrigerator for 60 minutes before using.

METHOD OF WORK 2

1 Sieve the flour and the salt together. Lightly rub in the fat to achieve a sandy texture.

2 Create a well in the centre and add the sugar and the beaten egg.

3 Mix the sugar and the egg until dissolved.

4 Gradually incorporate the flour and fat and carefully mix to a light paste. Allow to rest in polythene or silicone paper and place in a refrigerator for 60 minutes before using.

CHEF'S TIP This paste can be quite fragile when baked, so care must be taken when filling and decorating. The raw paste keeps well for a few days in a refrigerator.

VIDEO CLIP Sweet paste.

Step-by-step: Preparing sweet paste

1. Place the flour onto a clean work surface. Make a well in the centre.

2. Cut the butter (at room temperature) into small pieces and place in the centre of the well with the salt and sugar.

3. Work the butter and sugar with your fingertips until completely creamed together and pale in colour.

4. Slowly incorporate the whole egg, mixing well until the mixture is completely smooth and creamy. Add a few drops of vanilla extract to help flavour the paste.

5. Gradually draw the flour into the creamed butter.

6. Lightly work the paste to a smooth texture, taking care not to overwork the paste at this point.

Notes on lining flans

Roll out the paste evenly, and approximately 4 cm larger than the ring to be lined. Brush any excess flour from the paste. The ring can be brushed with melted clarified butter and the baking sheet should be clean and prepared with baking parchment. The flan should be lined on a lightly floured board or clean work surface and then transferred onto the baking sheet.

Step-by-step: Lining a flan ring with paste

1. Roll the paste up on the rolling pin and carefully lay it out over the prepared flan ring.

2. Using the fingertip gently lift and carefully push the paste into the sides and base of the flan ring, ensure that the paste is neatly pushed into the angle of the flan ring to prevent air pockets from forming under the paste.

3. Using the rolling pin cut away the excess paste from the overlap by rolling it across the top of the flan ring.

4. Carefully thumb the paste in the flan ring to ensure that it is pushed up the side of the ring, so producing an edge all the way around the top. Pinch in from the outside and push in from the inside to produce a decorative edge. Always check at this point that the paste has not cracked or torn in the flan ring.

5. Carefully lift the flan ring with the lined paste onto the prepared baking sheet. To make this easier place the baking sheet as close as possible to the prepared flan ring.

6. To bake blind (cuire à blanc): line the flan by covering the inside with a cartouche of baking parchment (some chefs use a layer of plastic film) and fill with baking beans. Allow to rest if necessary in a refrigerator and bake at the specified oven temperature.

Puff paste: *Pâte à feuilletée*

VIDEO CLIP Lining a tart tin.

QUALITY SPECIFICATION

Puff paste has a specific layered structure consisting of numerous alternating tiers of *détrempe* (the basic paste) and *beurrage* (the butter or fat used). This structure is obtained by rolling and folding the layers over each other in succession. In following this precise technique the chef should always look for certain quality points:

- Puff paste should have a firm consistency and be worked at cool temperatures.
- The basic paste must not become too elastic. It is therefore important not to overwork the ingredients while assembling the détrempe.

- Successful puff paste requires considerable attention to detail when making the basic paste and folding in the fat layers, take time to ensure you get it right.
- The different types of puff paste are all prepared in three stages: basic paste, fat (folding in the butter or shortening) and the turning (rolling out the dough).
  The only exception is the rough puff paste method, in which the butter is mixed in with the basic paste using a slow speed on a mixing machine or carefully by hand.
- Always brush excess flour off the paste before making each turn.

How puff paste rises

Allow the paste to rest for the indicated time. When baking, the heat of the oven melts the butter into the leaves of the basic paste and creates steam from the moisture of the butter. This steam, plus the moisture contained in the basic paste, is released, forcing the leaves to rise one by one. At the same time the starch in the flour will coagulate, strengthening the leaves and helping each to stand separately.

Three basic methods for puff paste

1   *French method*. It is essential to work on marble to keep the paste cold, using the **'envelope'** method to create layers. Fold and give three **'book' turns**, resting approximately 30 minutes between each turn.

2   *English method*. Roll the basic paste to an oblong and place the fat on one-third of it. Fold over and give six single turns, resting for at least 30 minutes between each turn.

3   *Rough or Scottish method*. The fat is incorporated to the basic paste in pieces. Give up to four book turns. This is known as a fast method of making puff paste but is not as precise.

CHEF'S TIP Uses for puff paste

- Vol-au-vents
- Fleurons and various savoury decorations
- Bande aux fruits
- Eccles cakes and banbury buns
- Chaussons aux pommes
- Tart shells for assorted large and individual tarts
- Sausage rolls
- Allumettes
- Pithiviers
- Mille feuille
- Palmiers
- Cream horns

CHEF'S TIP Possible reasons for faults in puff paste:

- Hard – too much water used in the recipe, over-handled or flour insufficiently brushed away during the folding process.
- Shrunken – insufficient resting between turns or over-stretching.
- Soggy – under-baked or oven too cold.
- Uneven rise – uneven distribution of fat, uneven folding and turning, sides and corners not straight or insufficient resting.
- Release of fat during baking – oven too cold, uneven folding and rolling, or paste (détrempe) too soft.

SOURCING   Some chefs prefer to use an extra dry butter for making puff paste. This type of butter is slightly richer in fat content than traditional butter and it has a higher melting point. It brings stronger flavour and a lighter texture to all variations of puff paste. Because of the higher fat content it is slightly easier to use when creating the turns required in the production of puff paste. In France this product is known as *beurre extra-sec*.

Storage

If well wrapped in plastic, puff paste can be stored for 3–4 days in a refrigerator at 5 °C. It is also possible to freeze puff paste, well wrapped in plastic. Once frozen, the paste should be given 24 hours to defrost before use. Regardless of storage location, the paste should rest, in a cold area after the fourth turn. Wait for the paste to reach room temperature before attempting to roll it out. If the paste is too cold when it is rolled out, it may tear and cause butter to run onto the baking sheet in the oven during baking.

Step-by-step: Rolling puff paste with pastry margarine

1. On a lightly floured marble top roll out the paste to form a rectangle.

2. Take a square of pastry margarine which will fit neatly on to one end of the rolled-out paste.

3. Roll out the paste to between 15 and 20 mm thick. It must be four times as long as it is broad and a precise rectangle.

Puff paste recipe with pastry margarine (Pâte feuilletée)

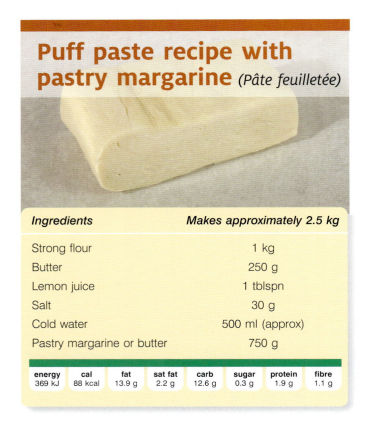

Ingredients	Makes approximately 2.5 kg
Strong flour	1 kg
Butter	250 g
Lemon juice	1 tblspn
Salt	30 g
Cold water	500 ml (approx)
Pastry margarine or butter	750 g

energy	cal	fat	sat fat	carb	sugar	protein	fibre
369 kJ	88 kcal	13.9 g	2.2 g	12.6 g	0.3 g	1.9 g	1.1 g

METHOD OF WORK

1 Sift the flour into a bowl.

2 Combine the salt, lemon juice and water.

3 Rub the butter into the flour.

4 Mix in the liquid to form a firm but elastic paste, depending on the flour used and the product to be made.

5 On a lightly floured marble top roll out the paste to form a rectangle twice as long as broad and about 20 mm thick. (Alternatively a large envelope can be produced using the French method of preparation.)

6 Take a square of pastry margarine (also 20 mm thick) which will fit neatly on to one end of the rolled out paste.

7 Fold the paste back over the fat to enclose it. Seal the edges well.

8 Roll out the paste to between 15–20 mm thick, it must be four times as long as it is broad and a precise rectangle.

9 Give one book turn (double turn). Cover the paste with a sheet of plastic. Rest in a refrigerator for 30 minutes.

10 Repeat steps 8 and 9 three more times before it is ready to use.

VIDEO CLIP Puff paste.

Rough puff paste

Ingredients	Makes approximately 1 kg
Strong flour	500 g
Butter	375 g
Lemon juice	1 tblspn
Salt	5 g
Cold water	300 ml (approx)

energy	cal	fat	sat fat	carb	sugar	protein	fibre
780 kJ	187 kcal	13.1 g	8.2 g	15.8 g	0.4 g	2.5 g	1.3 g

METHOD OF WORK

1 Sift the flour and salt into a stainless steel bowl. Cut the butter, which must be firm and cold, into 2 cm cubes and mix lightly into the flour.

2 Create a bay in the centre of the flour and add the cold water mixed with the lemon juice. Mix to a firm paste.

3 Turn out the paste onto a lightly floured work surface and press the paste with a rolling pin to flatten it out slightly and then roll out to an oblong approximately 60 cm x 20 cm, keeping the sides straight at all times.

4 Fold in three and then roll it out again in the opposite direction from before to the same length and width. Once again fold in three and wrap in polythene before leaving to rest in a refrigerator for 30 minutes. The puff paste has now been given two turns.

5 Repeat the rolling and folding sequence two more times so as to give it six turns. Resting it for 30 minutes between each turn.

6 Use as required and store wrapped in polythene in a refrigerator until needed.

CHEF'S TIP If desired 75 g of the butter content may be rubbed into the flour at stage 1 and the remainder cut into cubes and added as normal. This kind of puff paste can be used for items which do not require a great amount of rise.

Choux paste

The origin of choux paste dates back to the sixteenth century. We can attribute the invention to an Italian pastry chef named Popelini. It was not until the eighteenth century that this paste was perfected. In 1760 it was changed with a basic addition of eggs to create the blown and toasted choux paste. It was Antonin Carême (1784–1837), the famous French chef, who took choux paste and created numerous classical gâteaux and cakes which we now know as French classical pastries. such as choux buns and éclairs.

> ### CHEF'S TIP
> **Possible reasons for faults in choux paste**
>
> - Greasy and heavy-textured – basic mixture before the eggs have been added was overcooked.
> - Lack of aeration – flour insufficiently cooked, oven too cold, paste under-baked or not enough eggs added.

The technique of producing choux paste

During the first part of the production the chef is looking to cook out the mix of water, fat, flour, sugar and salt. This will change the structure of the starch found in flour to a thick paste.

The second phase is the *re-moisturization* of the paste with the addition of eggs in order to obtain a paste of piping consistency. During baking the moisture will play an important role in developing steam and providing the raising agent for the paste.

While baking the choux paste, the heat from the oven will convert the moisture from the paste into steam. The eggs and starch found within the paste begin to coagulate, forming an outside layer which will retain the steam inside. The steam will try to escape and in doing so will push and bring about the inflation of the paste which continues to coagulate and will become solid when the paste has cooked. All of this contributes to the choux paste's final appearance.

VIDEO CLIP Preparing choux paste.

Step-by-step: Producing choux paste

1. Cut the butter into small cubes and melt them in the water on the stove.

2. Remove from the heat and add the flour.

3. Return to the heat and while constantly stirring cook out the flour, water and butter mixture.

4. When the mixture is cooked out it will start to come away from the sides of the pan and form a starchy mass, this is sometimes referred to as a panada.

5. After the cooked out panada has cooled a little start adding the eggs a little at a time and beating the mixture to incorporate the egg.

6. The mixture is at the correct consistency when it drops from a spoon under its own weight and has a glossy finish to it.

Choux paste *(Pâte à choux)*

Ingredients	20 éclairs or 40 profiteroles
Water	150 ml
Butter	60 g
Strong white flour (sieved)	90 g
Sugar	5 g
Salt	5 g
Whole eggs	3

energy	cal	fat	sat fat	carb	sugar	protein	fibre
205 kJ	49 kcal	3.3 g	1.8 g	3.7 g	0.3 g	1.5 g	0.3 g

CHEF'S TIP Uses of choux paste

- Cream buns
- Profiteroles
- Choux paste fritters (beignets)
- Éclairs.

METHOD OF WORK

1 Place the water and fat into a saucepan and bring to the boil.

2 Take off the heat and stir in the sieved flour.

3 Return to the heat and cook out, continuously stirring until it leaves the sides of the pan clean.

4 Allow the paste to cool until it can be touched by the fingers and feel warm on contact.

5 Beat in the eggs a little at a time, making sure that they are well incorporated to produce a 'dropping' consistency.

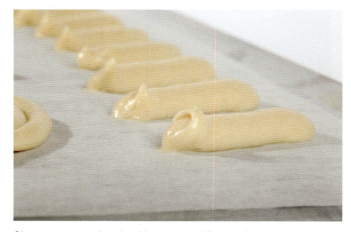

Choux paste can be piped into many different shapes, including fingers to make éclairs

Suet paste

Suet paste can be cooked by boiling, steaming or baking. It is used for plain puddings that are made of fruits such as apples, gooseberries, blackberries and for dumplings. If correctly produced, it will form a light and soft cooked paste, and the suet will not be evident.

The suet must not be melted before it is used but cut or minced as fine as possible and mixed cold with the flour. If using the suet paste for making dumplings to serve with a stew or boiled mutton, the dough must be rolled out thick, and cut out using pastry cutters to the size required.

A survey of period cookbooks confirms that this particular paste was used to create roly-poly and the spotted dick pudding popular in Victorian times. It was most often served up as a sweet dish, but savoury recipes exist as well. It was also referred to in novels by Charles Dickens and Beatrix Potter.

The first printed evidence of the phrase 'spotted dick', as it relates to food, is attributed to Alexis Soyer, the chef of London's illustrious Reform Club, 1849.

CHEF'S TIP Possible reasons for faults in suet paste:

- Heavy and soggy – too low cooking temperature, leakage in the cartouche or silicone wrapping or too much liquid added.
- Hard texture – over-handling or over-cooking.

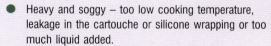

Suet paste *(Pâte à grasse de bœuf)*

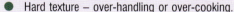

Ingredients	Makes approximately 500 g
Soft flour	250 g
Baking powder	5 g
Beef suet	150 g
Good quality salt	3 g
Cold water	125 ml
Caster sugar (optional)	25 g

energy	cal	fat	sat fat	carb	sugar	protein	fibre
1527 kJ	366 kcal	22.2 g	12.6 g	38.1 g	5.0 g	3.9 g	1.4 g

METHOD OF WORK

1 Sift together the flour, baking powder and salt into a stainless steel bowl. Add the suet and mix in lightly.

2 If using sugar as part of the recipe add to the water to dissolve. Make a well in the centre of the flour mixture and add the sugar solution.

3 Mix lightly together to form a firm paste. Rest for 5 minutes in the bowl covered with plastic film before using.

CHEF'S TIP Vegetable suet can replace the beef variety if vegetarian products are to be made using this paste. The beef suet is found from around the kidney area of the carcass and is chopped and dried with a little additional flour.

Paste Based Recipes

French cheese and ham savoury flan (Quiche Lorraine)

Ingredients	4 portions	10 portions
Puff or shortcrust paste	100 g	250 g
Lardons of bacon (smoked or unsmoked)	75 g	150 g
Gruyère cheese	50 g	120 g
Medium size egg, beaten	1	2
Milk	65 ml	150 ml
Crème Fraîche	60 ml	150 ml
Cayenne pepper and good quality sea salt		

energy	cal	fat	sat fat	carb	sugar	protein	fibre
1003 kJ	241 kcal	24.2 g	10.1 g	8.7 g	1.3 g	11.5 g	0.7 g

METHOD OF WORK

1 Lightly grease a flan ring or individual tartlet rings and roll out your selected paste to line inside. Pre-heat an oven to 200 °C.

2 Cover the lined paste with a cartouche of baking parchment, fill with baking beans and bake in the oven approximately 8 minutes to set the paste. Remove the cartouche and beans and bake for another 4 minutes until the paste is pale golden. If you notice any small holes or cracks, patch up with paste trimmings and bake for a little longer.

To prepare the filling

1 Heat a small frying pan, and add the lardons of bacon, frying for a couple of minutes without adding any additional oil. Drain off any liquid or fat that escapes, then continue cooking until the lardons just start to colour, but do not crisp. Remove and drain on clean kitchen paper towels. Cut three quarters of the cheese into small dice and finely grate the rest. Scatter the diced cheese and fried lardons over the base of the blind baked pastry case.

2 Using a spoon beat the crème fraîche to slacken it and slowly beat in the milk. Mix in the beaten eggs. Season with a little salt and the Cayenne pepper. Pour the filling into the pastry case all the way to the top of the pastry.

3 Lower the temperature of the oven to 190 °C. Scatter the grated cheese over the top and carefully place back into the oven. Bake for about 20 minutes, or until golden and softly set (the centre should not feel too firm). Remove from the oven and let the quiche settle for 5 minutes, and then remove from the flan ring. Serve warm or cold.

CHEF'S TIP This recipe can be varied with the addition of some chopped cooked onions, chopped fresh sage and parsley. Ham can be substituted for lardons of bacon and different cheeses can also be used to create an alternative flavour combination.

Dutch apple tart

Ingredients	8 portions (1 × 20 cm tart)	16 portions (2 × 20 cm tarts)
Lining paste (see page 463)	175 g	350 g
Filling		
Cooking apples peeled and cored	1 kg	2 kg
Demerara sugar	125 g	250 g
Sultanas	100 g	200 g
Powdered cinnamon	3 tsp	6 tsp
Zest of lemon	1 lemon	2 lemons
Icing sugar	70 g	140 g
Crème chantilly to serve	200 g	400 g

energy	cal	fat	sat fat	carb	sugar	protein	fibre
1505 kJ	357 kcal	14.9 g	9.1 g	55.5 g	47.1 g	2.8 g	3.6 g

METHOD OF WORK

1 Preheat the oven to 220 °C.
2 Prepare and rest the lining paste in the refrigerator for 20 minutes.
3 Line a flan ring with the paste leaving the remaining paste rolled out and cut into strips to create a lattice for the top of the tart.
4 Peel, core and slice the apples; mix with the sugar, sultanas, cinnamon and grated lemon zest. Place this filling into the lined pastry case; layer the lattice over the top.
5 Egg-wash the lattice and bake for 15 minutes. Reduce the temperature of the oven to 180 °C and complete the baking process for a further 25 minutes.
6 Remove from the oven and dust with icing sugar if preferred.
7 Serve warm with crème Chantilly.

Treacle tart

Ingredients	4 portions	10 portions
Sweet paste (see page 464)	200 g	500 g
Treacle filling		
Golden syrup	300 g	640 g
Unsalted butter	50 g	125 g
Double cream	100 ml	275 ml
Fresh eggs	2	4
Lemon juice and zest	½ lemon	1 lemon
Breadcrumbs	80 g	200 g

energy	cal	fat	sat fat	carb	sugar	protein	fibre
3193 kJ	762 kcal	35.7 g	20.9 g	101.7 g	65.6 g	9.5 g	1.3 g

METHOD OF WORK

1 Preheat the oven to 200 °C.
2 Gently heat the golden syrup in a saucepan until melting point. Remove from the heat and stir in the butter.
3 Beat in the eggs, cream, lemon zest and juice. Reserve to one side.
4 Line a large tart ring or individual rings as required with the sweet paste and then pour the filling into the pastry case.
5 Bake for approximately 30 minutes.
6 Leave to cool and rest for 10 minutes before removing from the case and cutting.
7 Serve slightly warm.

Fresh fruit tart

Ingredients	4 portions	10 portions
Sweet paste (see page 464)	200 g	500 g
Crème pâtissière filling		
Fresh milk	250 g	450 g
Caster sugar	60 g	120 g
Good quality salt	2 g	3 g
Cornflour	20 g	40 g
Custard powder	5 g	10 g
Egg yolks	2	4
Whole eggs	½	1
Vanilla extract	5 g	10 g
Unsalted butter	20 g	30 g
Fruit decoration		
As required (but can include strawberries, kiwi, star fruit, fresh cherries, peaches, raspberries and banana)	Approximately 75 g per portion	Approximately 75 g per portion
Apricot glaze		
Apricot jam	75 g	150 g
Water	20–30 g	30–50 g
Kirsch (optional)	5 g	15 g

energy	cal	fat	sat fat	carb	sugar	protein	fibre
1914 kJ	455 kcal	17.6 g	9.5 g	67.3 g	44.7 g	8.5 g	1.7 g

METHOD OF WORK

1 Preheat the oven to 200 °C.
2 Carefully line the sweet paste into the tart ring.
3 Place a cartouche of baking beans on top and bake blind for 20 minutes.
4 Remove the pastry case from the oven and remove the baking beans.
5 Brush the inside of the pastry case with egg-wash.
6 Return to the oven for approximately 5 minutes.

7 Remove from the oven. Leave to cool and rest for 5 minutes before removing from the tart ring.
8 Cool to room temperature.

METHOD OF WORK–CRÈME PÂTISSIÈRE

1 Reserve 50 g of milk to one side and bring the remaining milk to the boil in a saucepan.
2 In a separate bowl mix together the sugar, cornflour, custard powder, salt, 50 g milk and vanilla. Add the eggs to this preparation and mix well with a whisk.
3 Add some of the hot milk to the egg mixture, constantly stirring.
4 Pour the warm egg preparation into the remaining milk, whisking continuously.
5 Return the saucepan to a low heat and continue to cook while stirring all the time, taking care not to burn the bottom.
6 When the crème has thickened and the flavour of raw starch has been cooked out, remove from the heat.
7 Beat in the diced butter and then pour the crème onto a baking sheet lined with plastic film, cover the top with another layer of plastic film and cool.

TO ASSEMBLE THE TART

1 Pipe the crème pâtissière into the pastry case to approximately halfway up.
2 Prepare the fresh fruits by washing, drying and removing any pips and seeds where possible.
3 Arrange the fruit in a decorative manner.
4 Place the apricot jam and water together in a saucepan and bring to the boil, stirring constantly. Add the Kirsch for flavour if required.
5 Pass the glaze through a sieve and bring back to the boil. Carefully brush the glaze onto the fruit immediately.

CHEF'S TIP Once this tart has been prepared and presented it should be served as quickly as possible. If refrigerated, the pastry will begin to absorb the moisture from the filling and the fruit and eventually begin to collapse.

CHEF'S TIP Certain fresh fruits can be served in barquette moulds (boat shaped). The preparation is the same as for a fruit tart.

VIDEO CLIP Blind baking and finishing a fresh fruit tart.

Fig slice *(Bande aux figues)*

Ingredients	10 portions
Sweet paste or puff paste	225 g
Fresh figs	400 g
Crème pâtissière (see page 474)	250 ml
Glaze (see page 474)	

energy	cal	fat	sat fat	carb	sugar	protein	fibre
956 kJ	226 kcal	5.9 g	3.1 g	42.0 g	33.3 g	3.4 g	1.8 g

METHOD OF WORK

1   Roll out the sweet paste and place it in a tranche mould and bake blind as for recipe 14. Allow to cool when it has baked through and has reached a golden colour.

2   If using puff paste; roll out the paste 3 mm thick in a strip 12 cm wide. Place onto a greased baking sheet and moisten the two edges with egg-wash.

3   Place two strips of puff paste 2 cm wide along each edge. Seal firmly and mark decoratively with the back of a knife. Prick the base of the slice with a fork. Bake blind.

4   Pipe the crème pâtissière into the cooled base and then dress the washed and sliced figs neatly in overlapping layers. Coat with the glaze to finish and then serve.

CHEF'S TIP   Instead of using figs, other prepared fruit can be used or mixed fruits to create vibrant colours, textures and flavours.

Tart tatin

Ingredients	8 portions
Dessert apples such as Braeburn	12 medium-sized
Lemon juice	1 lemon
Unsalted butter	240 g
Granulated sugar	400 g
Puff paste or trimmings (see page 468)	500 g
Flour for dusting	50 g

energy	cal	fat	sat fat	carb	sugar	protein	fibre
2834 kJ	673 kcal	45.8 g	19.0 g	101.8 g	78.6 g	4.6 g	6.4 g

METHOD OF WORK

1   Preheat the oven to 220 °C.

2   Peel, core and halve the apples, slice them 3 cm thick and sprinkle with lemon juice and reserve to one side.

3   Evenly grease the base of the pan or mould with butter.

4   Cover the bottom of the pan with sugar and arrange the apples, rounded side down packed tightly together in a crescent shape on the bottom of the pan.

5   On a lightly floured surface roll out the puff paste.

6   Lay the pastry over the apples, allowing an overlap of 2 cm.

7   Tuck in the pastry at the edge of the pan and trim off the excess with a knife.

8   Leave to rest in a cool place for about 20 minutes.

9   Set the pan over a fierce heat for 10–15 minutes, until the butter and sugar are bubbling.

10   Bake in the preheated oven for 20 minutes.

11   Serve turned out onto a plate accompanied with a caramel ice cream or crème Chantilly if desired.

French apple flan (tarte aux pommes)

Ingredients	4 portions	10 portions
Sweet paste (see page 464)	100 g	250 g
Crème pâtissière (see page 474)	250 ml	630 ml
Cooking apples such as Bramley	400 g	1 kg
Caster sugar	50 g	130 g
Apricot glaze (see page 474)	3 tblspn	7 tblspn

energy 1333 kJ	cal 316 kcal	fat 8.9 g	sat fat 4.4 g	carb 56.2 g	sugar 45.1 g	protein 5.1 g	fibre 2.2 g

METHOD OF WORK

1   Line a flan ring with the sweet paste and pierce the base several times with a fork.

2   Pipe a layer of crème pâtissière onto the base of the flan.

3   Peel, quarter and wash the apples. Slice thinly and begin to lay carefully on the crème, overlapping each slice.

4   Sprinkle a little sugar on the top of the flan and bake in a preheated oven at 220 °C for approximately 30 minutes.

5   When the flan has baked and the apples resemble a golden colour, remove from the oven to cool on a wire rack for five minutes.

6   Remove the ring and carefully brush with the hot apricot glaze.

Step-by-step: French apple flan

1. Pipe the crème pâtissière carefully into the flan base.

2. Slice the apples thinly to prepare the decoration of the flan.

3. Assemble the apple slices on top of the flan.

4. Complete the assembly steadily overlapping each slice into the centre of the flan, maintaining a rose pattern as you continue.

5. The baked French apple flan.

6. Finish by brushing on the hot apricot glaze.

Egg custard tart

Ingredients	10 portions
Sweet paste (see page 464)	250 g
Egg yolks	4
Whole fresh egg (medium sized)	3
Caster sugar	80 g
Single cream	500 ml
Vanilla pod	1
Cinnamon sticks	2
Fresh bay leaf	½ a leaf
Freshly grated nutmeg	
Egg-wash	

energy	cal	fat	sat fat	carb	sugar	protein	fibre
1149 kJ	326 kcal	18.5 g	10.1 g	23.3 g	14.3 g	7.3 g	0.4 g

METHOD OF WORK

1 Line a flan ring with the sweet paste and bake blind with a cartouche and baking beans in a preheated oven at 180 °C.

2 When the paste has begun to turn a golden colour remove the cartouche and the baking beans. Brush a little egg wash into the base of the pastry and return to the oven for another 3 minutes.

3 Turn the oven down to 130 °C and remove the pastry case.

4 Make the custard filling by warming the single cream with the cinnamon sticks, split vanilla pod, bay leaf and a little grated nutmeg to infuse the flavour. Whisk together the egg yolks, whole eggs and sugar and add the cream and mix well. Strain this mixture through a fine sieve.

5 Fill the pastry case to just below the top of the pastry. Place it carefully in the centre of the oven and bake for approximately 30–40 minutes.

6 When the custard has just set remove from the oven and sprinkle some more grated nutmeg on the surface. Allow to cool to room temperature before serving.

Bakewell tart

Ingredients	10 portions
Sweet paste (see page 464)	250 g
Raspberry jam	50 g
Apricot glaze	50 g
Frangipane	
Butter	100 g
Ground almonds	75 g
Caster sugar	100 g
Whole eggs (medium sized)	2
Soft flour	25 g
Almond flavour (optional)	
Flaked almonds	40 g

energy	cal	fat	sat fat	carb	sugar	protein	fibre
1384 kJ	331 kcal	20.4 g	8.7 g	32.4 g	21.8 g	5.8 g	1.5 g

METHOD OF WORK

1 Line a fluted or plain flan ring with sweet paste at about 3 mm thick and prick the base lightly with a fork to help prevent the paste from lifting during the baking process.

2 Preheat an oven to 180 °C.

3 Spread the raspberry jam over the base of the lined flan ring.

4 To produce the frangipane: Cream the butter and the sugar together. Gradually beat in the eggs and almond flavour. Mix in the ground almonds and flour.

5 Pipe the frangipane onto the jam ensuring an even distribution of the almond mixture.

6 Bake in the oven for 15 minutes and then add the flaked almonds on top. Return to the oven for another 20 minutes or until baked.

7 Remove from the oven and immediately brush the hot apricot glaze over the top of the tart.

8 Leave to cool and then mix the icing sugar with a few drops of water to create a thin water icing and brush this over the top of the tart. Serve.

CHEF'S TIP A lattice topping made from surplus sweet paste can be applied before baking and brushed with egg wash to give a golden colour.

Chocolate tart

Ingredients	10 portions
Sweet paste (see page 464)	250 g
Dark chocolate at 70%	500 g
Whole eggs (medium size)	3
Fresh milk	200 ml
Double cream	350 ml
Vanilla flavour	
Unsalted butter	30 g

energy	cal	fat	sat fat	carb	sugar	protein	fibre
2516 kJ	607 kcal	50.0 g	16.5 g	29.8 g	5.8 g	9.6 g	0.4 g

METHOD OF WORK

1 Line a flan ring with the sweet paste to 2 mm thick and bake blind at 180 °C.

2 Melt the chocolate in a microwave or over a bain-marie.

3 Mix together the milk and the cream and bring to the boil.

4 Pour onto the eggs and whisk together. Pour onto the chocolate and stir in with the vanilla.

5 Slowly stir the pieces of butter into the chocolate mixture without incorporating any air into the mix.

6 Pour the chocolate mixture into the blind baked pastry case and drop the oven temperature to 150 °C.

7 Place the tart into the oven for approximately 25 minutes or until the chocolate mixture has just set. Remove from the oven and place on a wire rack to cool to room temperature. Serve with some crème Chantilly.

Gâteau pithivier

Ingredients	8 portions	16 portions
Puff paste (see page 468)	500 g	1 kg
Almond essence or dark rum	To taste	To taste
Unsalted butter	125 g	250 g
Tant pour tant (equal quantities of sieved icing sugar and ground almonds)	250 g	500 g
Soft white flour	25 g	50 g
Eggs (medium sized)	2	4
Egg yolk lightly beaten with a little milk for egg-wash	1	2
Icing sugar, for dusting	30 g	60 g

energy	cal	fat	sat fat	carb	sugar	protein	fibre
1907 kJ	457 kcal	44.3 g	12.7 g	42.6 g	21.3 g	8.5 g	3.0 g

METHOD OF WORK

1 Work the butter with a beater until very soft.

2 Gradually add the tant pour tant and the flour.

3 Slowly add the eggs, beating between each addition.

4 The mixture should be light. Stir in the almond flavour or dark rum according to your taste.

5 Cut the puff paste into two parts, one slightly larger than the other.

6 Roll out the smaller piece of dough until you have a circle of about 28 cm in diameter.

7 Place on a baking sheet lined with silicone paper and use the larger piece of dough to roll out the top. Make it slightly bigger and 1 mm thicker.

8 Pipe the almond preparation into the centre of the pastry base, and then spread it with a palette knife to within 3–4 cm of the edge.

9 Glaze the exposed edge with egg wash.

10 Place the second circle on top and press the edges of the two circles firmly together so that they are well sealed. Chill for 30 minutes.

11 Press down a 24 cm flan ring over the pithivier and with a sharp knife, trim the overhanging dough into a scalloped shape border. Glaze with egg wash and rest in a refrigerator for 20 minutes.

12 Mark the traditional pithivier rosette on top with a sharp knife.

13 Preheat the oven to 240 °C. Bake the pithivier for 10 minutes, and then lower the oven temperature to 220 °C. Cook for a further 25 minutes.

14 Sprinkle the pithivier with the icing sugar and bake for a final 5 minutes to give a sugar glaze.

15 Serve warm with crème Chantilly or sauce Anglaise.

Step-by-step: Preparing the pithivier

1. Place the second circle on top and press the edges of the two circles firmly together so that they are well sealed. Chill for 30 minutes.

2. Glaze with egg wash and rest in a refrigerator for 20 minutes.

3. Mark the traditional pithivier rosette on top with a sharp knife.

Palmiers

Ingredients	20 portions	40 portions
Puff paste (see page 468)	500 g	1 kg
Caster sugar (to dust the surface)	50 g	100 g
Caster sugar	60 g	120 g

energy	cal	fat	sat fat	carb	sugar	protein	fibre
314 kJ	74 kcal	8.3 g	1.3 g	13.3 g	5.9 g	1.2 g	0.6 g

METHOD OF WORK

1 Sprinkle the work surface with caster sugar and roll out the puff paste to a rectangle 20 cm wide and 3 mm thick.

2 Lightly mark a centre line along the length of rolled out paste and brush with a little water. Sprinkle with the second quantity of caster sugar.

3 Fold each side into three towards the centre leaving a gap down the centre of approximately 1 cm and then fold one side onto the other.

4 Flatten slightly to seal together, and then cut the strip into 1 cm slices. Dip the cut edges into caster sugar and place onto a baking sheet lined with silicone baking parchment. Space each palmier about 8 cm apart from each other.

5 Allow to rest in a refrigerator for approximately 30 minutes.

6 Preheat an oven to 220 °C and place the baking sheet into the oven to bake the palmiers for 10 minutes until lightly caramelized.

7 Turn over with a small palette knife and bake for a further few minutes to obtain a golden brown colour.

8 Place on a wire rack to cool before serving.

CHEF'S TIP Palmiers are used as petit fours but can also be used as an accompaniment for desserts or afternoon tea.

Cheese straws *(Paillettes au fromage)*

Ingredients	60 straws	120 straws
Puff paste (see page 468)	300 g	600 g
Grated cheese such as cheddar	30 g	60 g
Grated parmesan cheese	40 g	80 g
Cayenne pepper		
Poppy seeds (optional)		
Egg wash		

energy	cal	fat	sat fat	carb	sugar	protein	fibre
71 kJ	25 kcal	2.2 g	0.6 g	1.7 g	0.2 g	0.8 g	0.2 g

METHOD OF WORK

1   Preheat an oven to 230 °C.
2   Roll out the puff paste in a 60 × 30 cm rectangle.
3   Brush this paste with some egg wash and then sprinkle with the two grated cheeses, cayenne pepper and the poppy seeds if using.
4   Lightly roll into the surface and then cut into strips 1 cm wide and approximately 30 cm long.
5   Twist each strip several times and fix on a baking tray that has been greased and slightly dampened with a little water.
6   Allow to rest in a refrigerator for 30 minutes and then bake in the preheated oven until golden brown in colour.
7   Trim the ends and cut into approximately 10 cm lengths while still warm and serve.

Vol-au-vents

Ingredients	10 cases	20 cases
Puff paste (see page 468)	650 g	1.3 Kg
Egg wash		

energy	cal	fat	sat fat	carb	sugar	protein	fibre
589 kJ	191 kcal	22.4 g	3.7 g	20.2 g	1.0 g	4.0 g	1.7 g

METHOD OF WORK

1   Preheat an oven to 210 °C.
2   Roll out the puff paste to 8 mm thick and cut into rounds with a 8 cm diameter plain cutter.
3   Place upside down on a greased and dampened baking sheet.
4   Dip a 6 cm diameter plain cutter into hot oil and cut evenly, half way through each round of paste.
5   Brush these discs with some egg wash and leave to rest in a refrigerator for 30 minutes.
6   Bake in the preheated oven until golden brown in colour (approximately 20 minutes).
7   Remove from the oven and allow to cool on a wire rack. Remove the centres carefully with a small knife and reserve for use as the lids for each vol-au-vent. Empty the case of any soft paste.

CHEF'S TIP You can prepare bouchées in the same way as vol-au-vents, rolling out the paste 4 mm thick and cutting out with a 5 cm fluted cutter. Use a 4 cm plain cutter to cut half way through each round.

Tranche mille feuille *(Pastry cream slice)*

Ingredients	8 slices
Puff paste (see page 468)	250 g
Crème pâtissière	250 ml
Unsalted butter	100 g
Apricot or strawberry jam	100 g
Fondant	200 g
Melted dark chocolate	50 g

energy	cal	fat	sat fat	carb	sugar	protein	fibre
1536 kJ	366 kcal	25.6 g	9.1 g	50.2 g	37.4 g	4.0 g	1.0 g

METHOD OF WORK

1   Pin out the puff paste to 60 cm × 30 cm and place onto a baking sheet lined with baking parchment. Place another sheet of baking parchment on top and lay another baking sheet on top to weight the paste down.

2   Preheat an oven to 220 °C.

3   Bake in the oven until the paste has been evenly cooked, remove and cool on a wire rack.

4   While still slightly warm, cut three even sized rectangles using a ruler to measure the cutting accurately.

5   Beat the crème pâtissière in a bowl and slowly add the small cubes of unsalted butter. By adding the butter, this will help to set the crème a little more making it easier to pipe and hold its shape when cutting.

6   Warm the chosen jam and spread this onto the first layer of baked puff paste. Pipe the crème pâtissière on top of the first layer.

7   Place the second strip on top and pipe the remaining crème pâtissière on top.

8   Warm the fondant to 36 °C and correct the consistency with a little stock syrup if necessary – note: do not heat the fondant more than this temperature otherwise the shiny glaze appearance will be lost.

9   Brush a layer of apricot jam onto the top layer and then quickly spread the fondant over covering the whole layer with an even coating.

10   Immediately pipe the chocolate lengthwise in lines approximately 1 cm apart from each other.

11   Working quickly with the back of a sharp knife, wiping it after every stroke, mark across the slice at 2 cm intervals.

12   Reverse the marking by now creating the mark in the opposite direction to finish the feathering decoration sequence.

13   Allow to set and place the top layer on top of the other two layered puff paste tranches. Place in a refrigerator to totally set before trimming the edges of the mille feuille and cutting even portions with a sharp knife dipped into hot water and wiped clean after every cut.

CHEF'S TIP   The puff paste can be flavoured with chocolate by substituting 75 g of flour for cocoa powder and then flavouring the crème pâtissière with grated orange zest and Grand marnier to create a variation on the classic mille feuille.

Step-by-step: Producing a tranche mille feuille

1. Cut three layers from the baked puff paste using a sharp serrated knife.

2. Piping the crème pâtissière onto the puff paste slices.

3. Warm the fondant and adjust to the correct consistency before pouring the fondant onto the top puff paste slice that has been brushed with apricot glaze.

4. Working quickly, pipe the melted chocolate in lines along the length of the puff paste tranche.

5. Using the back of a small knife mark across the chocolate piping wiping the blade after each stroke of the knife.

6. Mark across the chocolate piping in the opposite direction to finish the feathering effect on the fondant.

Profiteroles with chocolate sauce (Profiteroles au chocolat)

Ingredients	10 portions
Choux paste (see page 470)	
Egg wash	
Chocolate sauce	
Dark chocolate (60%)	250 g
Water	350 ml
Caster sugar	60 g
Double cream	50 ml
Filling	
Crème Chantilly	500 ml

energy	cal	fat	sat fat	carb	sugar	protein	fibre
1983 kJ	529 kcal	40.8 g	17.8 g	23.7 g	9.2 g	7.4 g	0.6 g

METHOD OF WORK

1   Make the choux paste and place into a piping bag with a 1 cm plain tube. Pipe out small balls of the paste approximately the size of a 50 pence piece, onto a lightly greased baking sheet.

2   Brush each profiterole with some egg wash and bake at 200 °C until fully cooked and golden in colour, cooling on a wire rack.

3   Meanwhile make the chocolate sauce by chopping the chocolate into small pieces. Bring to the boil the water and sugar, simmer for 2 minutes before stirring in the chocolate off the heat to melt.

4   Bring the chocolate mixture back to a simmering point and continue simmering for 15 minutes, stirring all the time. Add the cream, mix in quickly and pass the sauce through a fine chinois. Reserve warm for service.

5   Make the crème Chantilly and pierce the bottoms of the profiteroles with a small knife. Pipe the crème Chantilly into each profiterole to completely fill them.

6   Serve five profiteroles per portion with the warm chocolate sauce.

CHEF'S TIP The chocolate sauce can be served either warm or cold. It can also be served separately, in which case the profiteroles should be dusted with icing sugar for decoration. This chocolate sauce recipe can have additional flavours added to it such as coffee, rum or orange zest.

Coffee and chocolate éclairs
(Éclairs au café et chocolat)

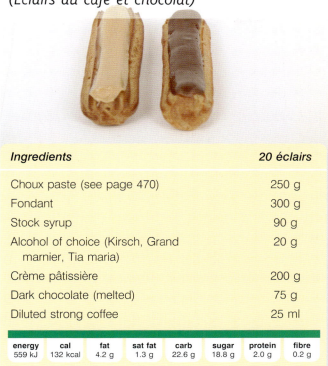

Ingredients	20 éclairs
Choux paste (see page 470)	250 g
Fondant	300 g
Stock syrup	90 g
Alcohol of choice (Kirsch, Grand marnier, Tia maria)	20 g
Crème pâtissière	200 g
Dark chocolate (melted)	75 g
Diluted strong coffee	25 ml

energy	cal	fat	sat fat	carb	sugar	protein	fibre
559 kJ	132 kcal	4.2 g	1.3 g	22.6 g	18.8 g	2.0 g	0.2 g

METHOD OF WORK

1 Preheat an oven to 220 °C.

2 Place the prepared choux paste into a piping bag and using a 1 cm plain tube pipe out 10 cm lengths on a silicone baking mat or a lightly greased and floured baking sheet.

3 Brush the choux with egg wash and bake in the preheated oven for approximately 30 minutes until crisp and light brown in colour.

4 Place on a wire rack and allow them to cool down.

5 Take the crème pâtissière and divide it into enough separate bowls to create as many different flavours as required (in this case one for chocolate and one for coffee).

6 Flavour the crème pâtissière by adding some melted chocolate into one and the diluted coffee into the other. Flavoured alcohols can be added to enhance the flavour if required.

7 Pierce the end of each éclair with a knife. Place the flavoured crème pâtissière into different piping bags, fitted with a small plain tube and fully fill each éclair.

8 Prepare the fondant by warming in a double boiler to a temperature no higher than 36 °C. Add a little stock syrup to create the correct consistency and flavour/colour the fondant as required (in this case one bowl of chocolate and one bowl of coffee).

9 Carefully dip the tops of the éclairs into the correct coloured and flavoured fondant and remove any surplus with a clean finger. Leave to set and serve for afternoon tea.

CHEF'S TIP To ensure that each éclair is piped to the same size, mark two tramlines down the baking sheet as a guide for the correct size and portion control.

Step-by-step: Preparing éclairs

1. Pipe out 10 cm lengths on a silicone baking mat/parchment or a lightly buttered and floured baking sheet.

2. The finished piped éclairs ready to be baked.

Steamed jam roll

Ingredients	4 portions	8 portions
Suet paste (see page 471)	200 g	425 g
Raspberry or strawberry jam	125 g	270 g
Fresh or frozen raspberries or strawberries	200 g	400 g
Fresh custard sauce	200 g	500 g

energy	cal	fat	sat fat	carb	sugar	protein	fibre
1484 kJ	353 kcal	13.6 g	7.7 g	54.7 g	32.2 g	5.2 g	2.4 g

METHOD OF WORK

1   Set the steamer to 118 °C.

2   Roll out the suet paste, using a little flour to dust, to a rectangle shape (3 cm × 16 cm).

3   Warm the jam in a saucepan and then spread over the suet paste leaving 1 cm clear on each edge.

4   Wash and chop the berries and liberally cover the jam surface of the paste.

5   Fold over the two short sides by 1 cm and then begin to roll the paste from the top downwards.

6   Moisten the bottom edge with milk or water to help secure a seal.

7   Wrap in double muslin cloth. Tie both ends well.

8   Place in the steamer to cook for 1½ hours.

9   Carefully turn out of the cloth when cooked and serve accompanied with the custard sauce.

Spotted dick

Ingredients	4 portions	8 portions
Suet paste (see page 471)	200 g	425 g
Mixed spice	5 g	8 g
Demerara sugar	100 g	200 g
Currants	100 g	200 g
Sultanas	50 g	100 g
Butter	100 g	200 g
Custard sauce to serve		

energy	cal	fat	sat fat	carb	sugar	protein	fibre
2397 kJ	574 kcal	34.2 g	20.6 g	65.5 g	57.1 g	4.2 g	1.6 g

METHOD OF WORK

1   Set the steamer to 118 °C.

2   Roll out the suet paste, using a little flour to dust, to a rectangle shape (3 cm × 16 cm).

3   Mix together the currants, sultanas, ¾ of the butter and ¾ of the sugar with the mixed spice. Spread onto the suet paste leaving 1 cm clear on each edge.

4   Fold over the two short sides by 1 cm and then begin to roll the paste from the top downwards. It can be used as a double-boiler with a second bowl placed over the a pan of simmering water to create such confections as a sabayon or Swiss meringue.

5   Moisten the bottom edge with milk or water to help secure a seal.

6   Wrap in double muslin cloth. Tie both ends well.

7   Place in the steamer to cook for 1½ hours.

8   Carefully turn out of the cloth when cooked and slice. Place the slices onto a baking sheet and place small pieces of the remaining butter on top and sprinkle with the remaining sugar. Place under a hot salamander to glaze each slice and then serve accompanied with custard sauce.

TEST YOURSELF

You have now learned about the use of the different types of pastes and how to produce a variety of pastry products. These utilize a range of commodities and preparation techniques.

1 Explain the difference between and oil and a fat.

_____

_____

_____

_____

_____

2 State the reason why weighing and measuring is so important to pastry production.

_____

_____

_____

_____

_____

3 In which paste can icing sugar be used instead of caster sugar?

_____

_____

_____

_____

4 Name the preparation method used for pâte sucrée.

_____

_____

_____

_____

_____

5 Identify the difference between a profiterole and an éclair.

_____

_____

_____

6 Describe the storage procedure for storing raw puff paste.

_____

_____

_____

_____

_____

7 State the reason wholemeal flour is perceived as healthier that white flour.

_____

_____

_____

_____

_____

8 Explain the method used to produce choux paste.

_____

_____

_____

_____

_____

9 State the main difference between puff paste and rough puff paste.

_____

_____

_____

_____

10 State the different pastes that you would use to make the following items:

- profiteroles
- quiche Lorraine
- tart tatin
- tranche mille feuille.

Guest Chef

Rhubarb and sour cream royal tart

Chef: *Huw Southcott*
Centre: *Leeds City College*

Early, forced (grown in the dark) rhubarb is mainly produced in the famous 'rhubarb triangle'. This used to extend from Wakefield to Leeds and Bradford, but is now concentrated between Wakefield, Morley and Rothwell. It covers 23 km^2.

Ingredients	Makes 1 × 28 cm flan ring
For sweet pastry	
Flour	225 g
Butter	110 g
Egg yolks	2
Caster sugar	25 g
Salt	½ tsp
Water	1 tblspn
For the filling	
Frozen or fresh rhubarb (diced)	200 g
For the sour cream royal	
Egg white	2
Caster sugar	35 g
Egg yolks	2
Caster sugar	35 g
Sour cream	85 g
Custard powder	20 g
Plain flour	40 g
Melted butter	15 g
Apricot jam	25 g

METHOD OF WORK
To make the pastry

1 Sieve the flour, sugar and salt together into a bowl.
2 Cut the fat into 1.5 cm cubes and rub lightly into flour, lifting the mixture to add air, until the mixture resembles breadcrumbs.
3 Make a well in the middle of the mixture and stir in the beaten egg yolks and water using a knife, until a soft but not sticky pastry is formed.
4 Cover tightly and allow to rest in a fridge for 15–30 minutes.
5 Roll out to the required thickness. At this stage the pastry may be frozen if required.
6 Bake in a preheated oven at between 190 °C and 220 °C depending on thickness and use.

To make the sour cream royal

1 Whisk the egg yolks and 35 g sugar together until light and fluffy.
2 Whisk together the egg whites and 35 g sugar together until a meringue is formed and firm peaks are achieved.
3 Sieve together the flour, sugar and custard powder.
4 Fold the sour cream into the egg yolk and sugar and then fold in the flour, sugar and custard powder.
5 Fold in the butter and egg whites.

To bring together

1 Roll out the pastry and cut out a disk of pastry the size of the flan ring and fully bake in an oven at 180 °C.
2 Place the flan ring over the pastry and evenly scatter the rhubarb over the cooked pastry.
3 Pour over the sour cream royal mixture and bake in an oven at 160 °C for 15–18 mins or until the mixture has set and a golden colour is achieved.
4 While still hot brush with apricot jam and allow to cool.

Breads and dough

Recipes

Basic white bread rolls and loaves   498
Basic wholemeal bread   499
Country bread   500
Tarragon bread   501
Fougasse   502
Soda bread   502
Garlic and herb rolls   503
Onion and rosemary bread   504
Sun-dried tomato bread   505
Ciabatta   505
French baguette   506
German rye bread   507
Olive bread   508
Pitta bread   509
Pizza dough   510
Naan bread   511
Bagels   512
Focaccia   513
Basic bun dough   514
Rum babas   517
Doughnuts   518

ONLINE RECIPES

LEARNER SUPPORT
Gruyère bread with caraway seeds
Chappatis

NVQ

Unit 2FPC9 Prepare, cook and finish basic bread and dough products

VRQ

Unit 216 Produce fermented dough products

Introduction

Bread is the most important food in Europe, America, and North Africa. Now bread is mostly made from wheat flour but it can be made from flour of other cereals such as rye, barley or maize. The dough is cultured with yeast and allowed to rise before being baked in an oven.

There is evidence that bread was being made 30 000 years ago, but about 10 000 years ago, with the start of agriculture, cereal grains became the main ingredient of bread. Yeast spores are in the air and on the grains of cereals, so any dough will become leavened if left out. Early bread makers used the foam off the top of fermenting beer or a paste made from grape juice and flour to make their bread rise.

To make good quality dough products it is important to appreciate the functions of the basic components (flour, salt, water, sugar and yeast), how they can be controlled and the appropriate methods of making the dough for different types of bread and dough products.

The use of liquids in bread making

Mineral water, fresh milk and milk powder

Water

Water is essential in bread making to hydrate the insoluble wheat proteins that form gluten. It will also dissolve salt, sugar and other soluble proteins to help form elastic and soft dough. Water has a noticeable effect on the speed of fermentation – soft-textured dough ferments quicker than a hard and tight dough. The water content will vary according to the absorption rate of different flours. Water is the second most important ingredient in bread making after flour, and it will also create the humid environment necessary for the development of bread during fermentation.

Milk

Like water, milk contributes by adding moisture to dough. Its fat content makes it an important agent in helping to achieve a soft texture to the finished product. It also plays a minor role in colouring the product during the baking process and this is primarily due to its sugar content (lactose). Whole or skimmed milk powder is the form of milk most widely used in baking. Lactic acid in fresh milk can break down the gluten content over time and can create a sour taste in the finished product.

CHEF'S TIP Insoluble wheat proteins are those that do not dissolve in a liquid such as water. However, the water softens them to help develop the gluten strands needed in the production of bread.

The role of dry ingredients in bread making

Salt

Good bread and dough products require salt to offset blandness and introduce the flavours present in the dough. It is also necessary because it helps to stabilize the gluten, retain moisture and control the fermenting yeast which affects the final crumb texture and crust colour. Salt can benefit the production of dough and bread significantly by slowing down the action of yeast and helping to retain moisture in the dough.

Obviously the salt content will help improve the flavour of all fermented products, and its inclusion also has an influence on the storage life of bread because it helps to delay the drying-out process. When the salt content is added to the dough it can also influence the overall crumb colour. Salt added at the end of the kneading process will achieve a whitening of the crumb after baking.

Granulated table salt, rock salt, sea salt flakes, and smoked salt

Yeast activity is slowed down by too much salt being added and excessive amounts will stop fermentation completely. With the yeast activity decreased, the gluten tightens, resulting in a smaller volume and heavy dough.

The use of flour in bakery

There are two basic types of flour for bread making; wholemeal and strong white flour. Wholemeal flour contains whole wheat grain with nothing added or taken away during processing. Strong white flour has higher protein content and therefore more gluten than soft flour. Wholemeal flours tend to have a greater water absorption rate than white flours so the dough can be stickier when processing. Extra enzymes found in the bran coating will help to speed up the dough ripening, so the dough temperature for wholemeal bread should be made a little cooler to slow down fermentation. Because the physical and chemical changes in the dough are more rapid, wholemeal dough needs a shorter fermentation time.

Selection of flours used in bakery

When selecting flour to use for bread making you should always choose the best quality possible. It is important to be aware of its chemical and physical composition and also to bear in mind other criteria.

- **Colour** – to form a clear idea of the colour of the flour it is best to press a small quantity under a sheet of glass. This can be done with more than one flour at a time. This method not only facilitates a comparison of the whiteness of different flours but also allows for an inspection of impurities. The flour should have a regular consistency and not contain any specs of dust, dirt or infestations.

- **Texture** – the texture and size of the grains play an important role in kneading and also determine the speed at which the dough rises. The finer the grain the longer the fermentation process can take.

- **Rising ability and elasticity** – several factors determine the rising ability and elasticity of flour. The greatest is the quantity of protein available in flour. The higher the amount of protein content the more water will be absorbed, which also means a greater elasticity, strength and ability of the flour to expand under fermentation and baking.

- **Moisture content** – the moisture content of flour must not exceed 16 per cent or the flour will have a shorter shelf life and lower yield. Generally moisture content of flour is about 12 per cent.

- **Absorption ability** – this is a measure of the amount of water that can be absorbed by a given quantity of flour. In bread making, it is usually preferable to have flour that can absorb a large amount of water.

Over 25 different varieties of wheat are grown in the United Kingdom. Local millers will carefully select from these, and a small amount of imported wheat, those varieties with the characteristics to produce specific flour. By blending wheat and extracting flours at different stages in the milling process, a mill will typically produce as many as 60 different flours. However, in Britain, whatever the baking characteristics of flour, most fall into one of the following main categories:

- *Wholemeal* – 100 per cent extraction, made from the whole wheat grain with nothing added or taken away.

- *Brown* – usually contains about 85 per cent of the original grain. Some bran and germ have been removed.

- *White* – usually 75 per cent of the wheat grain. Most of the bran and the wheat germ have been removed before milling.

- *Wheat germ* – white or brown flour with at least 10 per cent added wheat germ.

- *Malted wheatgrain* – brown or wholemeal flour with added malted grains.

- *Stoneground* – wholemeal flour ground in the traditional way, between two rotating stones.

GLUTEN

Gluten, which is found in flour, helps to trap the gas generated by the fermentation process and holds it in the dough structure. When coagulated in baking it becomes the framework of the loaf and stops it collapsing. There are five wheat proteins: albumin, globulin, proteose, gliadin and glutenin. The first three, which account for 1–2 per cent of the flour, are water soluble and provide the necessary nitrogenous yeast food during fermentation. The last two, which are not water soluble, together form gluten. Gliadin gives dough elasticity, glutenin gives stability.

Gluten is conditioned by many factors including the amount of yeast and how active it is, the amount of salt and water there is in the dough, fermentation time, dough temperature, acidity of the dough and manipulation or kneading. The approximate protein value in various flours can differ depending on the manufacturer's specifications, but as a general rule they follow the pattern listed in the table. Some people are allergic or intolerant to gluten, see Chapter 16 for more about this.

FLOUR	PERCENTAGE OF GLUTEN
Strong white flour	12–17
Medium flour	11
Soft flour	8–9
Cake flour	7
Type 55 (blended)	9–10
Wholemeal flour	11–15

Given good materials and the correct balance of ingredients, nothing contributes more to successful bread making than kneading, mixing, fermentation and **knocking back**. Correct mixing gives the gluten the ability to absorb the maximum amount of water and become thoroughly hydrated.

Yeast

Yeast is a living organism capable of feeding and reproducing itself when placed in suitable surroundings. It is a fungus that changes sugar into carbon dioxide, alcohol and other by products. The gas is caught up in the gluten network that aerates the dough. Existing as a single cell it is invisible to the naked eye but easily discernible under a microscope.

Dried yeast, fresh block yeast and fermenting yeast

The second function of yeast, equally vital to producing good quality bread, is to assist in the ripening or mellowing of the gluten in the dough, so that when the item is baked, the gluten is in a condition which gives evenness to the expanding dough.

For fermentation to occur, yeast needs a source of glucose. Simple sugars and carbohydrates are converted to glucose by enzymes found naturally in the flour.

VIDEO CLIP Using dried yeast.

YEAST ACTIVITY TEMPERATURES	
1–4 °C	Yeast remains dormant
10 °C	Yeast cells slowly begin activity
16–21 °C	Yeast cells become more active
21–27 °C	Optimum fermentation range
50 °C	Reduction in yeast activity
60 °C	Yeast is killed

Fresh yeast must be in good condition to work efficiently. It should be cool to the touch and a creamy colour. Small quantities can be kept pressed into a stone jar at 4 °C. If it is dark, soft and has an unpleasant smell then it should not be used. It should never be mixed directly with dry salt or sugar or dispersed in a strong solution of either, which will kill the yeast.

CHEF'S TIP To convert a recipe using fresh yeast to dry yeast, use half of the stated amount of dried yeast.

Enriching ingredients

Bread is sometimes enriched with fat, milk, eggs or spices to increase the food value, add to the flavour, produce a softer crumb and retard staling. Salt may have to be reduced when using salted butter or margarine, which contains approximately 2 per cent salt. Fermentation is slower in enriched dough, so the dough should be kept a little softer.

Sugar is another ingredient that requires careful usage in the presence of yeast. It should be used sparingly and should never come into direct contact with yeast because the yeast will break down chemically and become inactive.

Honey, milk, spices, treacle, egg, butter and sugar

Terms used in bakery

Before finding out about the process of bread-making, it will help to understand the terms:

- *Kneading or working the dough* – After the ingredients have been mixed together it requires **'kneading'** or 'working'. This is to essentially stretch the dough to develop the gluten structure. Hand kneading should be gentle but thorough in technique.

- *Ferment* – The term 'levain' is also used here and means a mixture of ingredients (usually flour, water and yeast) that is left in a plastic container with a lid and left at room

temperature for at least six hours. Added to bread dough this can increase flavour and lightens the finished bread texture.

- *BFT (bulk fermentation time)* – This term is used to explain the amount of time required for the first **prove** of the dough to create the fermentation of the dough.

- *Knocking back* – This is the gentle kneading of the dough after the first prove.

- *Resting the dough* – The dough should be covered with a clean tea towel or plastic sheet for a short period of time. This relaxes the gluten and makes it easier to manipulate into shapes.

- *Scaling* – Pieces of dough are weighed on a scale to help establish portion control and size. Some establishments use a 'dough divider' for this process for the quick dividing of a large piece of dough into small rolls.

- *Shaping* – In France this is known as *la tourne* which means to form elongated loaves. In the strictest sense of the term it means to create the final shape of the bread.

Bread loaves being proved for a final time

The dough being gently kneaded after proving

Moulding the dough by hand into rolls

- *Final prove* – The final fermentation process of the finished and shaped dough to increase the volume. This improves the resulting texture of the bread.

- *Baking* – The dough is now ready for baking. Care must be taken in identifying the correct oven temperature.

- *Steam injecting* – Steam can be introduced into the oven chamber by adding a pan of water into the oven with the dough in the first five to ten minutes to help create a 'hard crust' to bread.

- *Crumb* – This refers to the texture of the baked bread on the inside of the product. An open texture means that large irregular holes (such as ciabatta bread) are produced. A closed texture means that a uniformity of smaller pockets is present (such as Swiss buns or white sandwich bread).

- *Scoring or marking* – Some breads require a scored finish to help identify them or to create an additional

finish. This is where a loaf or roll can be slashed with a sharp implement such as a small knife or razor. The cuts are shallow.

- *The Maillard reaction* – When the oven temperature reaches up to between 150 and 260 °C, the moisture on the surface of the dough combines with the broken down starch and proteins within the flour. It forms a crisp golden brown crust with complex 'burnt' caramel flavours. This chemical reaction is known as the Maillard reaction after the scientist who first observed it.

The Maillard reaction

- *Cooling* – The bread is removed from the oven and allowed to cool on large wire racks. These cooling racks allow maximum air circulation which aids the evaporation of any excess moisture.

Bread cooling on a wire rack

- *Storing* – The successful storage of yeast breads and products is very important in maintaining the quality of the finished item. Usually bread should be consumed within the day of its production. However, to store bread for a longer period of time it should be completely wrapped in plastic and placed in a refrigerator or an airtight container. Alternatively a freezer can be used to increase the storage time.

CHEF'S TIP   When shaping the dough handle it as little as possible. Over-handling develops the gluten further, making the dough harder to shape.

Closed (left) and open-textured (right)

Bread-making methods

Bulk fermented dough (straight dough)

This is the process bakers use to make bread. Flour and salt are blended together with water and yeast. These are mixed to form a smooth, clear dough. The dough is then covered to prevent it drying out and a skin forming; it is given a 'bulk fermentation time' (BFT), when all the ingredients mix together and ferment. The dough is knocked back (de-gassed) after the BFT and kneaded to encourage continued yeast activity, develop the gluten in the flour and promote an even dough texture.

Knocking the dough back after the BFT

The dough is rested for a few minutes, covered as always, and is then scaled off to produce various breads. The total BFT can vary from 1 to 12 hours depending on the recipe, so it is best to follow the recipe given.

The effect of temperature on fermented dough

It is important to maintain the ideal dough temperature to control the speed of fermentation. Fermentation will begin as soon as the ingredients have been mixed together and kneaded, indeed even the kneading process can increase the temperature of dough. The best temperature for fermentation of dough is between 25 and 29 °C. Above 32 °C, the fermentation process becomes more rapid but the dough structure will get progressively weaker, so care must be taken to slow this process down. At less than 24 °C the fermentation process will be much slower. This is not necessarily critical because gradually the dough will develop greater flavour and a better overall structure to the texture. Without understanding this, it is easy to be tempted to ferment yeast at too high a temperature. This can cause the skinning of the dough and the encouragement of other undesirable characteristics such as lack of flavour in the finished product.

Ferment and dough

This process is intended for heavily enriched dough to allow yeast to become accustomed to high levels of fat and sugar, which slow yeast activity.

In the first stage the ferment (yeast) is blended to a thin batter and fermented with about 20 per cent of the recipe's flour and all of the water. Fermentation time depends on the yeast content, but it is ready when it drops back (the ferment rises so much that it cannot support its own bulk and drops back). It is best fermented in a prover or similar atmosphere and needs to be sufficiently warm after dropping back to maintain the correct dough temperature.

The ferment is then blended with the remaining flour, salt, fat and milk powder to form the dough. It is then bulk fermented for about the same time as the ferment and then scaled off. This method is sometimes known as a 'flying ferment'.

Baking

All fermented goods require a hot oven 200–235 °C. Goods rich in sugar and fat require a lower temperature. Foods lean in sugar and fat require the higher temperature. For best baking conditions some steam should be present in the oven. A full oven should produce sufficient steam (generated by the goods themselves) otherwise moisture needs to be injected into the oven area. This is to create a slightly humid atmosphere and prevent the skin of the goods setting until they have had a chance to expand. The steam will also help to create a moist eating product.

CHEF'S TIP To check if a loaf is correctly baked turn it out and tap the bottom of the bread. It should sound hollow if it is baked properly.

Faults found in bread

During the process of proving, an under-ripe dough describes dough that has not been proved long enough. Over-ripe dough is where the dough has been over proved. The common indicators below represent how to identify these two descriptions.

Under-ripeness

1 High crust colour.

2 Small volume of buns and rolls.

3 Poor shapes, split at the sides or top.

4 Tough, close-textured crumb.

Showing over-ripe (left) and under-ripe (right) bread rolls

Under-ripeness is caused by insufficient fermentation, and may be due to:

- insufficient yeast
- too cool a dough temperature
- too much sugar, salt, spice, fat or enriching ingredients
- yeast coming into contact with salt at the mixing stage
- insufficient BFT
- insufficient final prove.

Over-ripeness

1 Anaemic colour crust.

2 Flat shape, no stability.

3 Loose, woolly crumb.

Over-ripeness is caused by too much fermentation and may be due to:

- excessive amount of yeast
- too high a dough temperature
- omission of salt or sugar
- too prolonged dough time (final prove)
- too prolonged BFT.

Specialist baking equipment

The preparation of equipment when baking bread and dough products is very important. For example, having the oven preheated to the correct temperature is essential so that the product commences cooking as soon as it is placed into the oven. Failure to do this may have a damaging effect on the finished product.

Weighing scales It is of the utmost importance that all ingredients are weighed and measured accurately. One set of measurement should be used (e.g. grams and kilograms). Ensure that scales have been calibrated so that they measure weight correctly.

Wire cooling rack When hot-baked fermented items such as bread, buns and rolls are taken from the oven, it is essential to place them directly onto cooling racks so that the cool air can circulate around each product.

Electric mixer with dough hook and beater attachment The dough hook is used for yeast dough to stimulate the kneading process. It is used to thoroughly mix ingredients and to encourage the development of gluten.

Rolling pin Wooden rolling pins should be stored correctly after cleaning to prevent the wood from distorting. However, polyethylene rolling pins are widely available, keep their shape better and are easier to sanitize.

Baking sheets Some baking sheets are non-stick and some are aluminium-based. The sheets should always be kept clean and dry, ready for use

Silicone baking mat These mats offer excellent, non-stick baking surfaces. They are reusable, flexible sheets that can withstand extreme temperatures.

Silicone paper This is baking parchment that has been treated with silicone to prevent foods from sticking to it. It will not burn in a hot oven and can be used to protect food when baking and to create piping cones.

Metal pastry scraper Sometimes referred to as a 'bench scraper'. It is used to cut and scale pieces of dough and to clean work surfaces by scraping it against a table to loosen pieces of dough or flour.

HEALTH & SAFETY It is important to ensure that when kneading and mixing dough, all the tools, equipment and work surfaces are exceptionally clean. Bacteria will multiply extremely quickly under the same conditions that we need to promote fermentation, so strict attention to hygienic practices are essential.

Storage of bread

Bread is best consumed the day it is baked. However, there are ways to keep your bread fresh if it is stored correctly.

- The moister the bread, the longer it will keep.
- Keep soft-crusted breads in a plastic bag or airtight container.
- Store crispy-crusted bread in paper.
- Keep the bread in a cool dry place, such as a bread container.
- Keep freshly baked bread at room temperature in the open until it has cooled. Otherwise the mould development in the bread will be accelerated.
- Do not store bread in the refrigerator. This will dry it out and it will become stale faster.

- Freeze your bread to keep it for several months. Keep the bread wrapped tightly in plastic and place in the freezer.
- Any bread can be freshened by quickly dipping it in cold water, draining, and heating it in the oven.

Different types of breads have different shelf lives. Keep this in mind when storing your bread:

- 1 day – French and Italian breads
- 2–3 days – sourdoughs, white and wholemeal breads
- 3–5 days – rye breads.

Once a bread has gone stale there are still options for use. The uses for stale bread are varied and the following ideas are just two examples of recipes to make use of your leftover bread.

- Croutons – Cut stale slices of bread half an inch thick. Trim off crusts (which may be set aside and used for puddings), butter the slices, and cut into half-inch cubes. Place in a shallow pan and brown in a hot oven, turning them so that they do not burn. Serve with soup.
- Bread and butter pudding.

Recipes

Basic white bread rolls and loaves

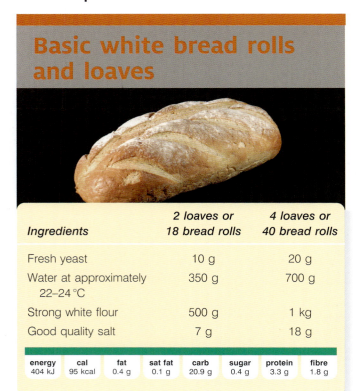

Ingredients	2 loaves or 18 bread rolls	4 loaves or 40 bread rolls
Fresh yeast	10 g	20 g
Water at approximately 22–24°C	350 g	700 g
Strong white flour	500 g	1 kg
Good quality salt	7 g	18 g

energy	cal	fat	sat fat	carb	sugar	protein	fibre
404 kJ	95 kcal	0.4 g	0.1 g	20.9 g	0.4 g	3.3 g	1.8 g

METHOD OF WORK

1 Preheat the oven to 220°C.

2 In a bowl, mix together the water and the fresh yeast. Ensure that the yeast has completely dissolved in the water.

3 Combine the flour and salt and add to the yeast liquid. Mix well.

4 Create soft, slightly sticky dough, resisting the temptation to add any more flour that might dry out the dough.

5 Scrape any excess ingredients and dough off the sides of the bowl and **knead** together. Leave the dough to rest for about 10 minutes.

6 Place the dough into a stainless steel bowl, cover with a damp clean kitchen cloth or plastic film and place in a prover or warm place for the bulk fermentation. The BFT should be approximately 30–45 minutes.

7 Carefully knock back the dough and knead lightly by folding the dough over itself. Leave to rest for a further 10 minutes.

8 Prepare a baking sheet by lightly greasing it. Divide the dough into two or four equal pieces (depending on the quantity of the recipe used) and shape each piece into balls (*boules*). Leave them to rest under cover for a few minutes before carefully rolling them out with the palm of your hand to an elongated oval shape. Place them side-by-side onto the baking sheet. Alternatively for the bread rolls scale off the dough at 45 g each to shape into smaller balls for bread rolls and then shape them accordingly before setting onto the baking sheet.

9 Place into a prover to double in size. The prover should be set to approximately 30–36°C.

10 Dust some flour onto the top of the loaf and score each loaf with a sharp blade. Finish the bread rolls with seeds, egg wash or flour and place into the preheated oven. After 15 minutes reduce the heat of the oven to 190°C and bake for a further 25 minutes for the loaf or a further 15 minutes for the bread rolls.

11 Remove from the oven when baked and leave to cool on a wire rack.

CHEF'S TIP Instead of using flour to dust the top decorate using a range of different seeds such as sesame, poppy, sunflower or caraway.

VIDEO CLIP Basic bread dough.

VIDEO CLIP Preparing various bread loaves and rolls.

Basic wholemeal bread

Ingredients	1 loaf or 18 bread rolls	2 loaves or 40 bread rolls
Fresh yeast	10 g	20 g
Water at approximately 22–24 °C	350 g	700 g
Strong wholemeal flour	300 g	600 g
Strong white flour	200 g	400 g
Good quality salt	7 g	18 g

energy	cal	fat	sat fat	carb	sugar	protein	fibre
382 kJ	90 kcal	0.5 g	0.1 g	19.0 g	0.5 g	3.5 g	2.2 g

METHOD OF WORK

1   Preheat the oven to 250 °C.

2   In a bowl, mix together the water and the fresh yeast.

3   Ensure that the yeast has completely dissolved in the water.

4   Combine the wholemeal and white flour and salt and add to the yeast liquid. Mix well.

5   Create soft, slightly sticky dough, resisting the temptation to add more flour.

6   Scrape any excess ingredients and dough off the sides of the bowl and knead together. Leave the dough to rest for about 10 minutes.

7   Place the dough into a stainless steel bowl and place in a prover or warm place for the bulk fermentation. The BFT should be approximately 25 minutes.

8   Carefully knock back the dough and knead lightly by folding the dough over itself. At this stage it is important not to overwork the dough. Leave to rest for a further 10 minutes.

9   Prepare a baking sheet by lightly greasing it. Divide the dough into two or four equal pieces (depending on the quantity of the recipe used) and shape each piece into balls (*boules*). Leave them to rest under cover for a few minutes before carefully rolling them out with the palm of your hand to an elongated oval shape. Place them side-by-side onto the baking sheet. Alternatively for the bread rolls scale off the dough at 45 g each to shape into smaller balls for bread rolls and then shape them accordingly before setting onto the baking sheet.

10   Place into a prover to double in size. The prover should be set to approximately 30–36 °C.

11   Score each loaf with a sharp blade. Finish the bread rolls with grains or cereal and place into the preheated oven. After 15 minutes reduce the heat of the oven to 190 °C and bake for a further 25 minutes for the loaf or a further 15 minutes for the bread rolls.

12   Remove from the oven when baked and leave to cool on a wire rack.

CHEF'S TIP   For heavier textured dough replace 200 g of the white flour with wholemeal flour. This will give a stronger flavoured bread but the method of production will have to change to a ferment and dough method.

Take half of the yeast and 250 g each of the flour and water to make a 'poolish' (ferment). Leave covered for up to four hours before mixing in with the rest of the ingredients.

Country bread *(Pain de campagne)*

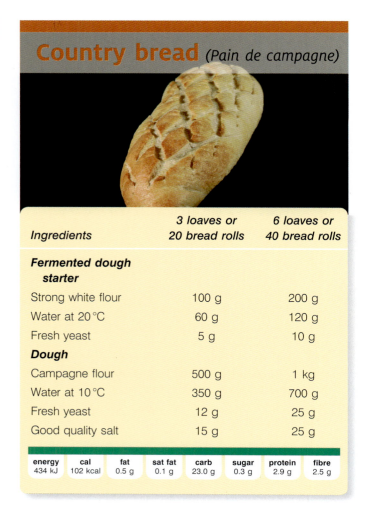

Ingredients	3 loaves or 20 bread rolls	6 loaves or 40 bread rolls
Fermented dough starter		
Strong white flour	100 g	200 g
Water at 20 °C	60 g	120 g
Fresh yeast	5 g	10 g
Dough		
Campagne flour	500 g	1 kg
Water at 10 °C	350 g	700 g
Fresh yeast	12 g	25 g
Good quality salt	15 g	25 g

energy	cal	fat	sat fat	carb	sugar	protein	fibre
434 kJ	102 kcal	0.5 g	0.1 g	23.0 g	0.3 g	2.9 g	2.5 g

METHOD OF WORK

1 Preheat the oven to 250 °C.

2 To make the fermented dough starter, mix the flour and water together with the yeast and gently knead for 10 minutes.

3 Place the ferment into a bowl and cover it with a clean cloth or lid. Rest the ferment at room temperature for at least 3 hours.

4 Knock back the ferment, replace in a bowl and repeat the fermentation process for a further 3 hours.

5 To make the country bread: using a stainless steel bowl, mix together the water and the fresh yeast. Ensure that the yeast has completely dissolved in the water.

6 Combine the campagne flour and salt and add to the yeast liquid. Mix well.

7 Create a soft, slightly sticky dough, resisting the temptation to add more flour. Add the ferment starter dough and mix well.

8 Scrape any excess ingredients and dough off the sides of the bowl and knead together. Leave the dough to rest for about 10 minutes.

9 Place the dough into a bowl and place in a prover or warm place for the bulk fermentation. The BFT should be approximately 60 minutes.

10 Carefully knock back the dough and knead lightly by folding the dough over itself. Leave to rest for a further 10 minutes.

11 Cut the dough into equal pieces according to the recipe used and shape each piece into balls (*boules*). Let the dough rest for 2 minutes before manipulating further into baton shapes. Place onto a baking tray on top of a clean tea cloth, separate with a fold in the cloth to prevent from sticking to each other. Alternatively, scale off the dough at 45 g each to shape into smaller balls for bread rolls.

12 Place into a prover to double in size.

13 Dust some flour onto a baking tray and carefully transfer the proved loaves onto the tray. Score the top of the loaf or each bread roll with a sharp blade for decoration.

14 Place into the preheated oven with a small tray of water to help inject steam into the oven chamber.

15 Bake the rolls for approximately 10–15 minutes and the loaves for at least 25–30 minutes.

16 Remove from the oven when baked and leave to cool on a wire rack.

CHEF'S TIP Hold the blade of the sharp knife flat against the surface of the bread at a 30° angle. Ensure that cuts are not too deep.

Tarragon bread

Ingredients	15 bread rolls	30 bread rolls
Strong white flour	450 g	900 g
Good quality salt	10 g	15 g
Fresh yeast	15 g	25 g
Water at 16 °C	250 g	500 g
Fresh tarragon	4 large sprigs	8 large sprigs
Cracked black pepper	To taste	To taste
Rock salt	To taste	To taste

energy	cal	fat	sat fat	carb	sugar	protein	fibre
444 kJ	104 kcal	0.5 g	0.1 g	22.9 g	0.4 g	3.7 g	2.1 g

Take some fine tarragon leaves and brush onto the tops of each roll with a little water

METHOD OF WORK

1 Preheat the oven to 240 °C.

2 In a bowl, mix together the water and the fresh yeast. Ensure that the yeast has completely dissolved in the water.

3 Combine the flour and salt and add to the yeast liquid. Mix well.

4 Create soft, slightly sticky dough, resisting the temptation to add more flour.

5 Scrape any excess ingredients and dough off the sides of the bowl and knead together. Leave the dough to rest for about 10 minutes.

6 Place the dough into a stainless steel bowl and place in a prover or warm place for the bulk fermentation. The BFT should be approximately 30 minutes.

7 Carefully knock back the dough and knead lightly by folding the dough over itself, this time adding the chopped fresh tarragon and ground black pepper to taste. Leave to rest for a further 10 minutes.

8 Scale off the dough at 45 g each to shape into smaller balls for bread rolls. Take some fine tarragon leaves and brush onto the tops of each roll with a little water.

9 Set onto a baking tray and sprinkle a little cracked black pepper and rock salt on top and place into a prover to double in size.

10 Dust with a little flour and place into the preheated oven. After 15 minutes reduce the heat of the oven to 190 °C and bake for a further 10 minutes.

11 Remove from the oven when baked and leave to cool on a wire rack.

CHEF'S TIP Spray a little clean, cold water onto your work surface to allow the dough to stick slightly to the work surface, which will help with better shaping.

Fougasse

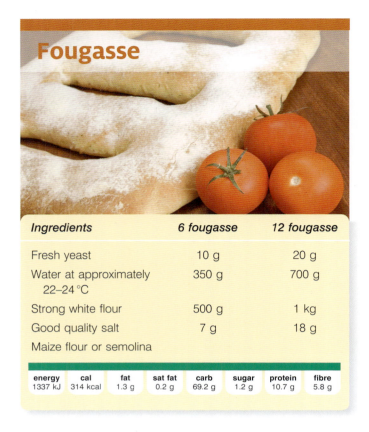

Ingredients	6 fougasse	12 fougasse
Fresh yeast	10 g	20 g
Water at approximately 22–24 °C	350 g	700 g
Strong white flour	500 g	1 kg
Good quality salt	7 g	18 g
Maize flour or semolina		

energy	cal	fat	sat fat	carb	sugar	protein	fibre
1337 kJ	314 kcal	1.3 g	0.2 g	69.2 g	1.2 g	10.7 g	5.8 g

METHOD OF WORK

1   Make the bread dough in the same way as recipe for basic white bread rolls and loaves.

2   Using the maize flour dust the surface that you will be preparing the fougasse on.

3   Cut the dough into the required number of pieces and flatten out one piece at a time using your hand to stretch the dough.

4   Make a large diagonal cut across the centre, but not cutting to the edges of the dough. Make three smaller cuts fanning out either side of the diagonal large cut.

5   Using your fingers gently pull open the cuts to reveal holes. Leave to rest on a floured baking sheet for a few minutes.

6   Upturn a baking sheet and place onto the bottom of the oven set at 250 °C. Slide the fougasse onto the upturned baking sheet and quickly spray a little water before closing the oven door.

7   Turn down the heat to 230 °C and bake the bread for 10–12 minutes until golden brown.

CHEF'S TIP As a variation add some halved, stoned olives, roasted peppers and roasted red onion slices with a little fresh rosemary into each fougasse before baking.

Soda bread

Ingredients	1 loaf or 18 rolls	2 loaves or 40 rolls
Soft wholemeal flour	150 g	350 g
Soft white flour	180 g	400 g
Good quality salt	4 g	10 g
Bicarbonate of soda	4 g	10 g
Baking powder	5 g	15 g
Buttermilk	290 g	600 g

energy	cal	fat	sat fat	carb	sugar	protein	fibre
281 kJ	66 kcal	0.4 g	0.1 g	13.5 g	1.1 g	2.6 g	1.1 g

METHOD OF WORK

1   Preheat the oven to 200 °C.

2   Sieve all the dry ingredients together and create a well in the centre of the bowl.

3   Pour in the buttermilk and mix lightly to form a soft and sticky dough. Rest for 5 minutes covered by a clean cloth.

4   Knead lightly and rest again.

5   Scale the dough off at 200 g and shape each piece into a ball. Rest once more for 5 minutes.

6   Flatten each ball slightly and cut a cross on top without cutting all of the way through the dough. Rest the dough for 20 minutes before baking in the oven for approximately 25 minutes.

7   Remove from the oven when baked and leave to cool on a wire rack.

CHEF'S TIP Soda bread tends to go stale very quickly. It should be used and eaten on the same day to maintain a good quality product.

Garlic and herb rolls

Ingredients	15 bread rolls	30 bread rolls
Strong white flour	450 g	900 g
Good quality salt	10 g	15 g
Fresh yeast	15 g	25 g
Water at 16 °C	250 g	500 g
Fresh garlic, finely chopped	4 cloves	8 cloves
Fresh herbs (parsley, sage and thyme)	4 tblspn	8 tblspn
Cracked black pepper	To taste	To taste
Rock salt	To taste	To taste

energy	cal	fat	sat fat	carb	sugar	protein	fibre
456 kJ	107 kcal	0.5 g	0.1 g	23.4 g	0.5 g	3.8 g	2.3 g

METHOD OF WORK

1 Preheat the oven to 240 °C.

2 In a bowl, mix together the water and the fresh yeast. Ensure that the yeast has completely dissolved in the water.

3 Combine the flour and salt and add to the yeast liquid. Mix well.

4 Create soft, slightly sticky dough, resisting the temptation to add more flour.

5 Scrape any excess ingredients and dough off the sides of the bowl and knead together. Leave the dough to rest for about 10 minutes.

6 Place the dough into a stainless steel bowl and place in a prover or warm place for the bulk fermentation. The BFT should be approximately 30 minutes.

7 Sweat the chopped garlic in a little olive oil and set aside to cool down.

8 Carefully knock back the dough and knead lightly by folding the dough over itself, this time adding two-thirds of chopped fresh herbs, garlic and ground black pepper to taste. Leave to rest for a further 10 minutes.

9 Scale off the dough at 45 g each to shape into smaller balls for bread rolls. Take the remaining herbs and garlic, mix together and place onto the tops of each roll.

10 Set onto a baking tray and sprinkle a little cracked black pepper and rock salt on top and place into a prover to double in size.

11 Dust with a little flour if required, and place into the preheated oven. After 15 minutes reduce the heat of the oven to 190 °C and bake for a further 10 minutes.

12 Remove from the oven when baked and leave to cool on a wire rack.

Onion and rosemary bread

Ingredients	3 loaves or 20 bread rolls	6 loaves or 40 bread rolls
Fermented dough starter		
Strong white flour	100 g	200 g
Water at 20 °C	60 g	120 g
Fresh yeast	5 g	10 g
Dough		
Wholemeal flour	500 g	1 kg
Water at 10 °C	350 g	700 g
Fresh yeast	12 g	25 g
Good quality salt	15 g	25 g
Fresh rosemary	A few sprigs	A few sprigs
Sliced onion	2 medium onions	4 medium onions

energy	cal	fat	sat fat	carb	sugar	protein	fibre
420 kJ	99 kcal	0.7 g	0.1 g	20.5 g	1.1 g	4.0 g	2.9 g

METHOD OF WORK

1   Preheat the oven to 250 °C.

2   To make the fermented dough starter, mix the flour and water together with the yeast and gently knead for 10 minutes.

3   Place the ferment into a bowl and cover it with a clean cloth or lid. Rest the ferment at room temperature for at least 3 hours.

4   Knock back the ferment, replace in a bowl and repeat the fermentation process for a further 3 hours.

5   To make the bread, using a stainless steel bowl, mix together the water and the fresh yeast. Ensure that the yeast has completely dissolved in the water.

6   Combine the wholemeal flour and salt and add to the yeast liquid. Mix well.

7   Create a soft, slightly sticky dough, resisting the temptation to add more flour. Add the ferment starter dough and mix well.

8   Scrape any excess ingredients and dough off the sides of the bowl and knead together. Leave the dough to rest for about 10 minutes.

9   Place the dough into a bowl and place in a prover or warm place for the bulk fermentation. The BFT should be approximately 60 minutes.

10   Sweat the sliced onions without any colour and set aside to cool down. Remove the rosemary leaves from the branch, wash and set aside.

11   Carefully knock back the dough and knead lightly by folding the dough over itself. Leave to rest for a further 10 minutes.

12   Cut the dough into equal pieces according to the recipe used and shape each piece into balls adding some of the onion and rosemary for flavour (*boules*). Let the dough rest for 2 minutes before manipulating further into baton shapes. Place onto a baking tray on top of a clean tea cloth, separate with a fold in the cloth to prevent from sticking to each other. Alternatively, scale off the dough at 45 g each to shape into smaller balls for bread rolls again using the cooked onion and fresh rosemary. Always leave some onions and rosemary to place on top of the bread for decoration.

13   Place some onion and rosemary on top and put into a prover to double in size.

14   Dust some flour onto a baking tray and carefully transfer the proved loaves onto the tray.

15   Place into the preheated oven with a small tray of water to help inject steam into the oven chamber.

16   Bake the rolls for approximately 10–15 minutes and the loaves for at least 25–30 minutes.

17   Remove from the oven when baked and leave to cool on a wire rack.

Sun-dried tomato bread

Ingredients	2 loaves	4 loaves
Sun-dried tomatoes, chopped	110 g	220 g
Water at 36 °C	300 ml	600 ml
White strong flour	200 g	400 g
Wholemeal flour	300 g	600 g
Good quality salt	10 g	15 g
Skimmed milk powder	12 g	24 g
Olive oil	12 g	24 g
Fresh yeast	20 g	40 g
Caster sugar	10 g	15 g

energy	cal	fat	sat fat	carb	sugar	protein	fibre
621 kJ	147 kcal	4.9 g	0.7 g	22.8 g	1.8 g	4.5 g	3.0 g

METHOD OF WORK

1 Preheat the oven to 200 °C.

2 Soak the sun-dried tomatoes in boiled water for 20 minutes.

3 Mix together the white and wholemeal flour with the milk powder, salt and sugar.

4 Dissolve the yeast in the water, add the olive oil and mix into the dry ingredients.

5 Mix well to form a smooth and elastic dough.

6 Cover the dough and allow to prove for 40 minutes.

7 Knock back carefully, drain the sun-dried tomatoes and dry them on some clean kitchen paper before chopping and adding to the dough. Leave to rest, covered for 30 minutes.

8 Divide the dough into 450 g pieces of dough and mould into ball shapes. Rest for another 10 minutes keeping the dough covered at all times to prevent a dry skin from forming.

9 Carefully roll out the balls with your hands to form baton shapes and place onto a baking sheet that has been greased.

10 Prove once more at approximately 38 °C until the dough has almost doubled in size and place into the preheated oven to bake for 25 minutes or until the bread is golden and well cooked in the centre. Tap the base of the loaf and listen for a hollow sound to see if it is cooked all the way through.

11 Leave to cool down on wire racks before slicing and serving.

Ciabatta

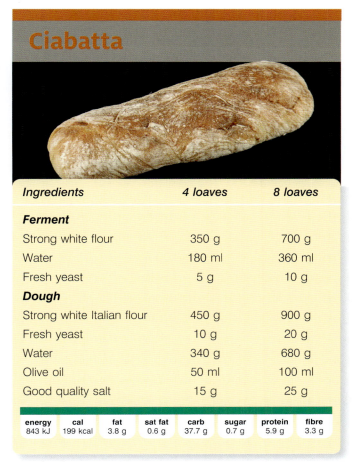

Ingredients	4 loaves	8 loaves
Ferment		
Strong white flour	350 g	700 g
Water	180 ml	360 ml
Fresh yeast	5 g	10 g
Dough		
Strong white Italian flour	450 g	900 g
Fresh yeast	10 g	20 g
Water	340 g	680 g
Olive oil	50 ml	100 ml
Good quality salt	15 g	25 g

energy	cal	fat	sat fat	carb	sugar	protein	fibre
843 kJ	199 kcal	3.8 g	0.6 g	37.7 g	0.7 g	5.9 g	3.3 g

METHOD OF WORK

1 To prepare the ferment 24 hours in advance mix the ingredients for the ferment together for about 5 minutes until you create a dough. Place the dough into a bowl, cover loosely with plastic film and a clean kitchen cloth and leave to rest in a draught free cupboard for between 18–24 hours.

2 Preheat the oven to 220 °C.

3 To make the dough place the flour in a mixing bowl and rub in the fresh yeast. Place the ferment into the bowl and add the water, oil and salt, mixing well to combine everything.

4 Turn the dough out onto a work surface and gently knead the dough for 5 minutes, stretching and pulling to develop the gluten.

5 Place into a lightly oiled bowl and leave to rest for 1½ hours covered with plastic film.

6 Flour the work surface with semolina or maize flour and turn out the dough onto it. Divide the dough into equal pieces depending on the recipe, gently press each piece down and fold into three by folding each side into the centre and then folding in half lengthways.

7 Place the ciabatta dough onto a greased baking sheet, cover with plastic film and leave to prove for 45 minutes.

8 Spray the inside of the oven with a little water to create some steam and quickly place the ciabatta into the oven to bake for 20 minutes until light and golden brown.

9 Cool on a wire rack.

French baguette

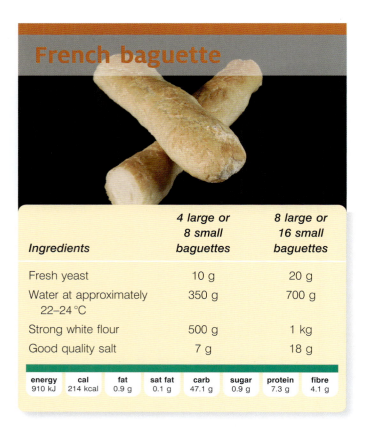

Ingredients	4 large or 8 small baguettes	8 large or 16 small baguettes
Fresh yeast	10 g	20 g
Water at approximately 22–24 °C	350 g	700 g
Strong white flour	500 g	1 kg
Good quality salt	7 g	18 g

energy	cal	fat	sat fat	carb	sugar	protein	fibre
910 kJ	214 kcal	0.9 g	0.1 g	47.1 g	0.9 g	7.3 g	4.1 g

METHOD OF WORK

1 Preheat the oven to 220 °C.

2 In a bowl, mix together the water and the fresh yeast. Ensure that the yeast has completely dissolved in the water.

3 Combine the flour and salt and add to the yeast liquid. Mix well.

4 Create soft, slightly sticky dough, resisting the temptation to add any more flour that might dry out the dough.

5 Scrape any excess ingredients and dough off the sides of the bowl and knead together. Leave the dough to rest for about 10 minutes.

6 Place the dough into a stainless steel bowl, cover with a damp clean kitchen cloth or plastic film and place in a prover or warm place for the bulk fermentation. The BFT should be approximately 30–45 minutes.

7 Carefully knock back the dough and knead lightly by folding the dough over itself. Leave to rest for a further 10 minutes.

8 Line a baking sheet with a lightly floured clean kitchen cloth. Turn out the dough onto a floured work surface and cut the dough into the required amount of pieces as per the recipe quantity. Roll each piece into a ball and rest, covered with a cloth for five minutes.

9 To shape the baguettes repeat this process with each ball, following the sequence: flatten the dough ball with your hand into an oval shape; fold one side over to the middle of the oval; press it down and bring the other side over to the middle and press down again.

10 Fold this in half, lengthways and roll out with your hands to create a long log shape. Place each baguette onto the floured cloth.

11 Lay the baguettes next to each other, making a pleat in the towel between each baguette to prevent them from touching and sticking to each other as they rise.

12 Place into a prover to double in size. The prover should be set to approximately 30–36 °C.

13 Place a baking stone or upturned heavy baking sheet into your oven and then using a sharp small blade make up to seven diagonal cuts across the top of the baguettes. Carefully place the baguettes onto the oven baking stone surface or upturned baking sheet and quickly spray the inside of the oven chamber with water to create steam which will help to create a crust to the baguettes. Bake for approximately 12 minutes or until they are golden brown in colour.

14 Remove from the oven when baked and leave to cool on a wire rack.

CHEF'S TIP In France each baguette should weigh 320 g and there should be seven diagonal cuts on each bread. Artisan boulangers (bakers) usually add their own signature or style to their baguettes so that everyone recognizes their work when customers purchase them.

German rye bread *(Roggenbrot)*

Ingredients	Makes 2 loaves	Makes 4 loaves
Fresh yeast	20 g	40 g
Water at approximately 22–24 °C	280 g	560 g
Dark rye flour (plus extra for dusting)	400 g	800 g
White strong flour	100 g	200 g
Skimmed milk powder	15 g	30 g
Malt extract or black treacle	20 g	40 g
Butter	15 g	30 g
Good quality salt	15 g	25 g
Caraway seeds	20 g	40 g

energy	cal	fat	sat fat	carb	sugar	protein	fibre
524 kJ	123 kcal	1.6 g	0.6 g	25.1 g	0.6 g	4.0 g	4.4 g

METHOD OF WORK

1 Place 250 g of the rye flour and the yeast in a large mixing bowl. Add 180 ml of the water and mix it thoroughly to make a thick ferment.

2 Set the ferment aside to rest for 2 hours or until it has risen and then fallen back.

3 Add the remaining flours, remaining water, salt, malt/treacle, butter, milk powder and caraway seeds and mix together to produce an elastic and smooth rye dough.

4 Dust the inside of rye loaf baskets with a little additional rye flour. Divide the dough according to how many loaves you will be producing and shape into balls.

5 Place into the prepared baskets and set aside to prove for 2 hours.

6 Preheat the oven to 220 °C and prepare a baking sheet lined with baking parchment or just lightly greased.

7 Tip the risen rye dough balls gently onto the prepared baking sheet. Dust lightly with rye flour and bake for 30 minutes.

CHEF'S TIP Rye bread is made with flour produced from the rye grain. It can be light or dark in colour, depending on the type of flour used and the addition of colouring agents. It is typically denser than bread made from wheat flour. It is higher in fibre than many common types of bread and is often stronger in flavour.

Since rye gluten is not particularly strong we can add strong white flour to the recipe to help with the structure of the bread. Pure rye bread however contains only rye flour. German-style pumpernickel is a dark, dense and close-textured loaf, and is made from crushed or ground whole rye grains, baked for long periods at low temperatures in a covered tin. Rye and wheat flours are often used to produce a rye bread which has a lighter texture, colour and flavour than Pumpernickel. 'Light' or 'dark' rye flour can be used to make rye bread; the flour is classified according to the amount of bran left in the flour after milling. Dark treacle or molasses are used for colouring and caraway seeds are often added to rye bread to increase flavour.

Olive bread

Ingredients	2 loaves	4 loaves
Black olives, chopped	150 g	300 g
Water at 36 °C	300 ml	600 ml
White strong flour	200 g	400 g
Wholemeal flour	300 g	600 g
Good quality salt	10 g	15 g
Skimmed milk powder	10 g	20 g
Olive oil	15 g	30 g
Fresh yeast	20 g	40 g
Caster sugar	5 g	10 g

energy	cal	fat	sat fat	carb	sugar	protein	fibre
526 kJ	124 kcal	2.5 g	0.4 g	22.7 g	1.2 g	4.3 g	2.9 g

METHOD OF WORK

1   Preheat the oven to 220 °C.

2   Mix together the white and wholemeal flour with the milk powder, salt and sugar.

3   Dissolve the yeast in the water, add the olive oil and mix into the dry ingredients.

4   Mix well to form a smooth and elastic dough.

5   Cover the dough and allow to prove for 40 minutes at 32 °C.

6   Knock back carefully and add the chopped black olives to the dough. Leave to rest, covered for 30 minutes.

7   Divide the dough into 450 g pieces of dough and mould into ball shapes. Rest for another 10 minutes keeping the dough covered at all times to prevent a dry skin from forming.

8   Carefully roll out the balls with your hands to form baton shapes and place onto a baking sheet that has been greased.

9   Prove once more at approximately 38 °C until the dough has almost doubled in size and quickly score the tops of the loaves three times diagonally with a small sharp blade.

10   Place into the preheated oven to bake for 25 minutes or until the bread is golden and well cooked in the centre. Tap the base of the loaf and listen for a hollow sound to see if it is cooked all the way through.

11   Leave to cool down on wire racks before slicing and serving.

Pitta bread

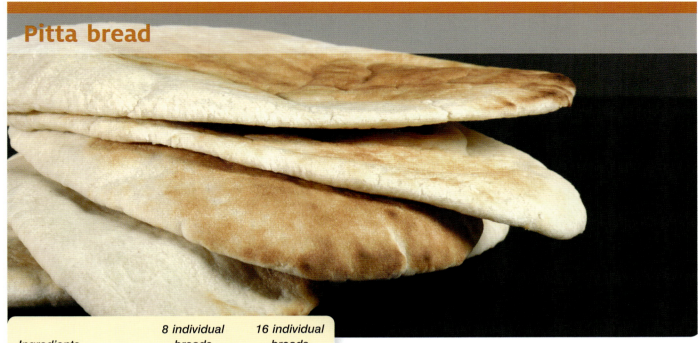

Ingredients	8 individual breads	16 individual breads
Ferment starter		
Fresh yeast	4 g	8 g
Water at 24 °C	125 g	250 g
Strong white flour	100 g	200 g
Dough		
Water at 22 °C	180 g	350 g
Soft white flour	200 g	400 g
Strong white flour	250 g	500 g
Caster sugar	25 g	40 g
Good quality salt	5 g	10 g

energy	cal	fat	sat fat	carb	sugar	protein	fibre
1049 kJ	247 kcal	0.9 g	0.1 g	54.5 g	4.2 g	7.4 g	3.6 g

METHOD OF WORK

1 Preheat the oven to 250 °C.

2 Create a ferment by mixing together the yeast and the first water in a bowl and adding the flour. Mix to a smooth batter.

3 Cover and leave in a warm place to ferment for approximately 1½ hours.

4 To make the dough, mix the second water with the ferment. Then add all of the remaining ingredients. Mix to a soft and sticky dough, cover and rest for 10 minutes.

5 Knead the dough and then leave it to rest for 30 minutes. Repeat this process one further time.

6 Place a clean baking tray into the oven to heat up. On a lightly floured surface scale off the dough at 100 g each. Shape each piece into a ball and leave to rest, covered with a clean cloth for about 15 minutes.

7 Roll out each ball into an oblong about 5–6 mm thick.

8 Carefully pick up the individual pitta dough pieces and place onto the hot baking sheet. Bake for 5 minutes without too much colour. Remove from the oven and repeat the process until every piece has been baked.

9 Leave to cool on a wire rack before using.

CHEF'S TIP   Ensure that the oven is at the correct temperature for this recipe. It should be very hot. Also that the baking sheet has had plenty of time to reach the required temperature prior to baking.

Pizza dough

Ingredients	Makes 450 g	Makes 900 g
Water at 22 °C	150 g	300 g
Fresh yeast	4 g	10 g
Caster sugar	5 g	10 g
Olive oil	25 g (plus a little extra for kneading)	60 g (plus a little extra for kneading)
00 grade Italian flour	160 g	320 g
Strong white flour	110 g	220 g
Good quality salt	5 g	10 g

energy	cal	fat	sat fat	carb	sugar	protein	fibre
640 kJ	152 kcal	4.2 g	0.6 g	26.6 g	1.2 g	3.5 g	1.5 g

METHOD OF WORK

1   Mix yeast and the water and then add the sugar and the olive oil.

2   Sieve the flours together and add the salt. Add the yeast liquid and mix together into a soft mass. Scrape any excess ingredients and dough off the sides of the bowl and knead together. Leave the dough to rest for about 10 minutes.

3   Lightly knead the dough and leave to prove at room temperature with a clean cloth covering it for about 1 hour.

4   Divide the dough into 200 g balls and roll out each piece into a thin circle. Cover with a cloth and leave to rest for 10 minutes.

5   Preheat the oven to 220 °C and lightly brush a baking tray with olive oil. Sprinkle with some polenta.

6   Roll the discs of dough thinner and carefully place each disc onto the prepared baking tray. Brush the dough with olive oil and dust lightly with sea salt.

7   At this stage you can begin to add any type of topping required.

8   Place in the oven for approximately 12–15 minutes depending on how much topping you use. The edges of the pizza should be just crisp to the touch when finished.

Brush the dough with olive oil and dust lightly with sea salt

CHEF'S TIP   Different types of pizza topping can be added to the basic tomato base:

- Calzone – mozzarella, prosciutto cotto (or salami), ricotta, olive oil, grated parmesan or pecorino cheese. The unique aspect of calzone is that it is a folded pizza.
- Napoletana – tomato concassée, garlic, oregano, drizzle of olive oil.
- Quattro stagioni – ham, mushrooms, artichoke hearts and olives.

Naan bread

Ingredients	4 breads	8 breads
Water at 22 °C	150 g	300 g
Fresh yeast	5 g	10 g
Soft white flour	250 g	500 g
Plain yoghurt	50 g	100 g
Good quality salt	3 g	6 g
Baking powder	½ tsp	1 tsp
Sunflower oil		
Chopped fresh coriander (optional)		

energy	cal	fat	sat fat	carb	sugar	protein	fibre
1163 kJ	276 kcal	7.0 g	1.6 g	46.4 g	1.4 g	6.7 g	2.0 g

METHOD OF WORK

1   Mix the water and the yeast together and add half of the flour. Mix well and cover the bowl and leave to ferment in a prover for 30 minutes.

2   Stir in the yoghurt, remaining flour, salt and baking powder. Mix well to a dough and finally brush some of the sunflower oil over the dough to help prevent skinning. Cover and leave to rest for 15 minutes.

3   Repeat the process of light kneading and resting once more.

4   Divide the dough into equal pieces and knead each piece lightly on an oiled surface. Dust with flour and leave to rest for 5 minutes.

5   Heat a wok over a moderate heat.

6   Taking one piece of dough at a time, roll out into a pear shape using a little more flour if necessary. You should aim to pin the dough out to 3 mm thick.

7   When the wok is very hot, brush the surface of the naan bread with some sunflower oil and sprinkle with the coriander if desired. Place a lid on the wok and pin out the next piece of dough, leaving the first to rest briefly.

8   The naan is ready to cook when there is further evidence of fermentation beginning to start: small pockets of air should be forming just underneath the surface of the bread.

9   Place the bread carefully into the wok and cook on one side until it has slightly browned. Flip it over and apply the same cooking process for a further minute.

10   When the naan is cooked on both sides carefully remove from the wok. Keep the naan breads wrapped in a clean cloth in a warm oven, these should be served to the customer within 3–4 minutes of cooking.

Place the bread carefully into the wok and cook on one side until it has browned slightly

CHEF'S TIP   If you cannot use a wok, a non-stick frying pan will make a good replacement. The use of a lid is essential to help maintain the heat of the pan.

Bagels

Ingredients	6 bagels	12 bagels
Water	60 ml	130 ml
Fresh milk	125 ml	245 ml
Fresh yeast	6 g	12 g
Strong white flour	225 g	450 g
Good quality salt	3 g	6 g
Egg wash	½ tsp	1 tsp
Sesame seeds	1 tblspn	2 tblspn
Caster sugar	1 tblspn	2 tblspn

energy	cal	fat	sat fat	carb	sugar	protein	fibre
691 kJ	164 kcal	2.4 g	0.5 g	31.9 g	4.2 g	5.6 g	2.7 g

METHOD OF WORK

1 Preheat an oven to 210 °C.

2 Warm the water and milk to 36 °C and dissolve the yeast into it. Leave to stand in a warm place for 10 minutes.

3 Add the flour, sugar and salt and mix to form a smooth and elastic dough.

4 Turn out the dough onto a lightly floured surface and continue to knead for a further 10 minutes. Place the dough into an oiled bowl and place into a prover for 1 hour to prove or double in size.

5 Turn the dough out onto a lightly flour work surface and divide the dough according to how many bagels your recipe states and knead each one into a ball.

6 Create a hole in the centre of each ball by placing a small rolling pin in the centre and carefully rotating the ball until a smooth hole appears without breaking the ring.

7 Place the bagels onto a greased baking sheet and prove once again until they have doubled in size.

8 Heat a large pan of boiling water and reduce it to a rolling simmer. Drop each bagel into the water individually preventing them from touching each other. Turn the bagels over after 1 minute.

9 Remove from the water and drain well before carefully placing them onto a greased baking sheet. Brush each bagel with egg wash and sprinkle the tops with the sesame seeds and bake in the preheated oven for approximately 20 minutes.

10 Cool on a wire rack.

Focaccia

Ingredients	6 portions	12 portions
Fresh yeast	25 g	45 g
Water at 28 °C	300 ml	600 ml
Caster sugar	5 g	10 g
Strong white flour	450 g	900 g
Good quality salt	1 tsp	2 tsp
Olive oil	50 ml	100 ml
Course sea salt, fresh rosemary, sliced onions and additional olive oil for the topping		

energy	cal	fat	sat fat	carb	sugar	protein	fibre
1554 kJ	369 kcal	12.8 g	1.9 g	57.9 g	2.1 g	9.2 g	5.4 g

METHOD OF WORK

1 Mix the yeast and water together, and add the sugar and about 2 tablespoons of the flour.

2 Place this ferment in a warm area to activate for about 30 minutes, or until the yeast mixture is rising and looks as though it is about to collapse.

3 Place the remaining flour on to a clean worktop and make a well in the centre. Pour in the yeast mixture and knead it into the flour, adding a little more warm water if required. Add the salt and oil and knead well for 10 minutes.

4 Transfer the soft, elastic and shiny dough to a large floured bowl. Oil a piece of plastic film and place it oil-side down over the dough. Set aside in the prover or a warm place for about 2 hours or until the bread has doubled in size.

5 Preheat the oven to 220 °C.

6 Pull the dough apart into sections of about 400 g each. Shape into rough boules and flatten them between the palms of your hands. Lay them onto a well oiled baking sheet scattered with coarse semolina or polenta to help cause air pockets to form under the dough. Leave to rest again covered with some plastic film for another hour.

7 Force small indentations into the surface of the focaccia with your fingertips, then generously scatter with more olive oil, water, fresh rosemary and salt crystals and bake for about 10 to 12 minutes, or until the top is golden and crisp and the focaccia moves freely on the baking sheet.

8 Slide off the baking sheet onto a wire rack to cool slightly before serving warm.

Basic bun dough

Ingredients	14 individual buns	30 individual buns
Strong white flour	475 g	950 g
Good quality salt	5 g	10 g
Caster sugar	65 g	130 g
Milk powder	10 g	20 g
Butter	40 g	80 g
Whole egg	½ beaten egg	1 egg
Fresh yeast	25 g	50 g
Water	250 ml	500 ml

energy	cal	fat	sat fat	carb	sugar	protein	fibre
683 kJ	161 kcal	3.0 g	1.6 g	30.8 g	5.7 g	4.6 g	2.3 g

METHOD OF WORK

1   Preheat the oven to 220 °C.

2   In a bowl, mix together the water and the fresh yeast. Ensure that the yeast has completely dissolved in the water.

3   Combine the sieved flour, sugar and salt and rub in the butter.

4   Add the yeast liquid and the beaten egg. Mix well. If using a mechanical mixing machine, use the dough hook and set on second speed for 5 minutes.

5   Create a soft dough resisting the temptation to add more flour.

6   Scrape any excess ingredients and dough off the sides of the bowl and knead together. Leave the dough to rest for about 10 minutes.

7   Place the dough into a stainless steel bowl and place in a prover or warm place for the bulk fermentation. The BFT should be approximately 45 minutes.

8   Carefully knock back the dough and knead lightly by folding the dough over itself. Leave to rest for a further 10 minutes.

9   Scale off the bun dough into 45 g balls and leave to rest under a sheet of plastic to prevent from skinning. Mould each bun dough ball into small, neat round buns and place onto a baking sheet.

10   Set onto a baking tray and place into a prover to double in size.

11   Place into the preheated oven. After 15 minutes reduce the heat of the oven to 190 °C and bake for a further 20 minutes.

12   Remove from the oven when baked and leave to cool on a wire rack.

CHEF'S TIP   Some buns will need to be glazed immediately after they are removed from the oven, but traditionally Devonshire splits do not need to be. Ensure they are cooled quickly on a wire rack to prevent the bases from becoming moist and eventually soggy.

Bun glaze

Some bun recipes demand to be glazed immediately after they are removed from the oven. A milk and sugar glaze is normally used, or another syrup.

- 500 g sugar
- 500 g water
- 2 leaves gelatine.

Bring the sugar and water to the boil and soften the gelatine in cold water. Add the gelatine to the sugar solution and pass through a chinois.

Bun varieties

DEVONSHIRE SPLITS

Mould into balls, prove to double size. Bake at 232 °C. Cool on a wire rack. Cut a slit three-quarters through the top at an angle. Pipe in a bulb of strawberry or raspberry jam. Follow with a bulb of whipped fresh cream. Dust with icing sugar.

SWISS BUNS

Scale and mould the pieces into balls. Rest for 10 minutes. Elongate the pieces to form fingers. Place on a baking tray, prove, and bake at 232 °C for about 12 minutes. Cool and dip into fondant or water icing which may be flavoured or coloured.

CURRANT BUNS

Carefully mix 75–100 g currants into the bun dough recipe so that no bruising occurs and proceed as for Devonshire splits. When baked glaze immediately.

TEA CAKES

Scale and mould as for currant buns. Allow 15 minutes recovery and then pin out to 6 mm thick to an oval or round shape. Set onto a silicone baking tray and lightly dock each one. Bake at 226 °C.

CHELSEA BUNS

Roll out basic dough to cover an area of 38 cm × 60 cm. Mix 75 g brown sugar and 5 g mixed spice together, spread this mixture over the dough and sprinkle over with currants. Roll up Swiss roll fashion. Brush the surface with melted butter. Cut into equal slices. Place flat side down onto a square, high-sided baking tray with the pieces almost touching. Prove and bake at 226 °C for 15 minutes. When baked brush with a syrup and dust with caster or nibbed sugar.

Video Clip Preparing Chelsea buns.

BATH BUNS

Mix dried fruit and sugar nibs into the basic dough with a little beaten egg. Divide into the appropriate number of buns on a baking sheet lined with a silicone mat, in a rough shape. Prove and sprinkle the tops with nibbed sugar. Bake at 226 °C for about 15 minutes. Glaze and then cool.

HOT CROSS BUNS

Add 50–75 g currants or sultanas and 5 g bun spice to the basic recipe. Place crosses on top of each fruited and spiced bun after the proof. Pipe a thin paste using a plain number 3 tube. Spice may be added in liquid form or as ground spice.

Bun cross paste

- 500 g soft flour
- 550 g water
- 110 g shortening
- 4 g baking powder
- 55 g milk powder
- 4 g salt

Mix all ingredients together to form a smooth paste.

BELGIAN BUN, ALSO KNOWN AS VIENNA BUN

Proceed as for Chelsea buns but replace the mixed spice with either cinnamon or ginger. Prove and bake as for Chelsea buns, glaze with white fondant and decorate with a glacé cherry.

Rum babas

Ingredients	8 individual baba	20 individual baba
Strong white flour	200 g	500 g
Fresh yeast	5 g	12 g
Fresh milk	125 ml	300 ml
Eggs (medium sized)	2	5
Softened butter	50 g	125 g
Caster sugar	10 g	20 g
Good quality salt	3 g	5 g
Soaking syrup for babas		
Caster sugar	200 g	400 g
Zest and juice of lemon	1 lemon	2 lemons
Zest and juice of orange	1 orange	2 oranges
Water	600 ml	1.2 litres
Coriander seeds	7	14
Vanilla pod	1	2
Cinnamon stick	1	2
Bay leaf	1	2

energy	cal	fat	sat fat	carb	sugar	protein	fibre
1137 kJ	269 kcal	7.1 g	3.9 g	49.1 g	30.2 g	5.3 g	2.1 g

METHOD OF WORK

Rum babas

1 Sieve the flour into a bowl and create a well in the middle. Mix together the yeast with half of the fresh milk before adding to the well in the flour.

2 Sprinkle a little flour from the sides of the well on top of the yeast mixture, cover with a clean kitchen cloth and leave in a warm place to begin fermentation.

3 Beat the eggs together with the sugar and salt and add the remaining milk and add to the ferment. Mix well to form a dough. Turn out of the bowl and knead for 5 minutes.

4 Replace the dough back into the bowl and slowly begin to knead in the butter in small pieces (at this stage the use of a mechanical mixing machine helps).

5 When all the butter has been successfully incorporated into the dough, cover with some plastic film and prove until it doubles in size.

6 Grease the dariole moulds to bake the babas in and knock back the dough with a spoon before half filling each mould and placing into a prover to prove for another 30 minutes. Preheat an oven to 220 °C.

7 Bake the babas in the oven for approximately 25 minutes and turn out of the moulds as soon as they have been taken out of the oven and cool on a wire rack. When cool, store in an airtight container and keep dry.

8 Place all the ingredients together in a large saucepan and slowly bring to the boil.

9 Simmer for 3 minutes and then pass through a strainer.

10 Ensuring that the syrup is very hot, place each baba into the syrup, one at a time to soak.

11 Remove and brush with a hot apricot glaze.

To serve

The babas can be served slightly warm with the rum added at the last moment into the baba and served with crème Chantilly. Alternatively a crème mousseline can be piped inside an incision made lengthways to the baba and again the rum is to be added at the last moment.

Doughnuts *(Boules de Berlin)*

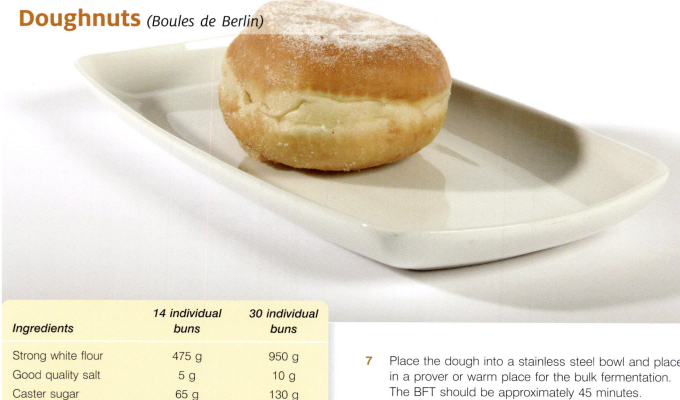

Ingredients	14 individual buns	30 individual buns
Strong white flour	475 g	950 g
Good quality salt	5 g	10 g
Caster sugar	65 g	130 g
Milk powder	10 g	20 g
Butter	40 g	80 g
Whole egg	½ beaten egg	1 egg
Fresh yeast	25 g	50 g
Water	250 ml	500 ml

energy	cal	fat	sat fat	carb	sugar	protein	fibre
683 kJ	161 kcal	3.0 g	1.6 g	30.8 g	5.7 g	4.6 g	2.3 g

METHOD OF WORK

1 Preheat the oven to 220 °C if required, or preheat a deep fat fryer to 185 °C.

2 In a bowl, mix together the water and the fresh yeast. Ensure that the yeast has completely dissolved in the water.

3 Combine the sieved flour, sugar and salt and rub in the butter.

4 Add the yeast liquid and the beaten egg. Mix well. If using a mechanical mixing machine, use the dough hook and set on second speed for 5 minutes.

5 Create a soft dough, resisting the temptation to add more flour.

6 Scrape any excess ingredients and dough off the sides of the bowl and knead together. Leave the dough to rest for about 10 minutes.

7 Place the dough into a stainless steel bowl and place in a prover or warm place for the bulk fermentation. The BFT should be approximately 45 minutes.

8 Carefully knock back the dough and knead lightly by folding the dough over itself. Leave to rest for a further 10 minutes.

9 Scale off the bun dough into 45 g balls and leave to rest under a sheet of plastic to prevent from skinning. Mould each bun dough ball into small, neat round buns and place onto a baking sheet.

10 If deep frying doughnuts the fat should be clean. When cooking they will need to be turned over as the doughnuts will float.

CHEF'S TIP The use of silicone mats on which to bake buns is recommended where there is fruit and sugar which may make the buns stick to the tray and eventually burn.

HEALTH & SAFETY Care must be taken when using a deep fat fryer. Ensure the correct temperature is maintained, because too low an oil temperature will saturate the doughnut, resulting in a product that is heavy in fat.

Varieties of doughnut

RINGS

Roll out the dough to 12 mm thick and cut out rings using two cutters of different dimensions to create a ring. Deep fry and drain before rolling in cinnamon sugar.

JAM DOUGHNUTS

Create a ball with the dough and press a floured thumb into each. Pipe a little jam into each hole and mould carefully to seal the hole. Prove on an oiled tray and deep fry, drain and finish with a little cinnamon sugar.

FINGERS

After moulding to a ball, rest for 10 minutes. Roll out to the form of a finger shape. Cook by deep frying, drain and cool. Split down the centre and pipe a small amount of jam and then fill with cream. Dust with icing sugar. Alternatively, after draining on clean kitchen paper, roll the fingers in cinnamon sugar.

TEST YOURSELF

To test your level of knowledge and understanding, answer the following short questions. These will help to prepare you for your summative (final) assessment.

1 Explain the importance of selecting the correct type, quality, quantity of ingredients when meeting dish requirements.

2 State the quality points to look for when producing basic white bread dough.

3 State two reasons you would need to use a thermometer in the production of bread.

4 Briefly describe the fermentation process.

5 State how a bread roll is tested in order to see if it is correctly baked.

6 Briefly describe the difference between a BFT and a ferment.

7 Give three different enriching ingredients.

8 What influence does salt have on the fermentation process?

9 State the difference between a strong and soft flour.

10 Why can water be sprayed into an oven chamber as bread is just beginning to bake?

Guest Chef

Pot roasted Welsh loin of lamb with carrot and laverbread mousse, and bubble and squeak

Chef: *Dr Shyam Patiar*
Centre: *Llandrillo College, North Wales*
(Coleg LLandrillo Cymru)

Good food in any form stems from top quality natural produce combined with first-class cookery skills and Wales has both. Lamb, leeks, and that healthy and extraordinary seaweed, laverbread, among so many other locally produced ingredients, many of them organic combine to make this dish.

Ingredients	4 portions
Pot roasted loin of lamb	
Welsh loin of lamb (on the bone)	2 x 500 g
Butter	100 g
Onions	250 g
Carrots	150 g
Celery	125 g
Leeks	25 g
Shallots, finely chopped	100 g
Carmarthen ham, finely chopped	100 g
Mushrooms, finely chopped	100 g
Caerphilly cheese	100 g
Welsh sea salt and black pepper	To taste
Garlic	4 cloves
Welsh honey	2 tblspn
Celtic whiskey	100 ml
Can-y-Delyn liqueur	100 ml
Carrot and laverbread mousse	
Carrots	350 g
Green cardamoms	4
Milk	500 ml
Butter	50 g
Eggs	3
Double cream	250 ml
Salt and white pepper	To taste
Laverbread	50 g
Leeks	25 g
Bubble and squeak	
Potatoes	500 g
Spring green cabbage	125 g
Leeks	75 g
Salt and white pepper	To taste
Nutmeg	To taste
Garlic	1 clove

METHOD OF WORK

Pot roast loin of lamb

1. Bone and prepare the loins of lamb. Stuff with the mixture of finely chopped shallots, garlic, mushrooms, Carmarthen ham and Caerphilly cheese and roll them.
2. Season the lamb and seal on top of the stove.
3. Prepare matignon of vegetables – onions, carrots, celery and leeks.
4. Sweat vegetables in butter on top of the stove.
5. Add crushed garlic.
6. Place sealed lamb on the matignon.
7. Cover with a lid and pot roast in the oven. When almost cooked take off lid, baste with Welsh honey and colour the lamb, keeping it pink inside.
8. Carve the loins of lamb and serve four slices per portion.
9. Season with Welsh sea salt and freshly ground black pepper.
10. Sauté the vegetables in a casserole dish on top of the stove.
11. Drain the fat and add the estouffade (brown lamb stock).
12. Lightly thicken the sauce with fécule.
13. Strain and finish it with Celtic whiskey and Can-y-Delyn liqueur.

Carrot and laverbread mousse

1 Wash, peel and grate the carrots.
2 Cook the carrots in milk with green cardamom.
3 Season with salt and white pepper.
4 Make a fine purée of carrots and mix with the mixture of thick double cream, one whole egg and two egg yolks.
5 Place this mixture in buttered dariole moulds.
6 Stir the laverbread into each mould.
7 Cover with buttered greaseproof paper and poach them in the oven until firm.
8 Demould the mousse and garnish with blanched strips of the green part of the leeks.

Bubble and squeak

1 Wash, peel and boil the potatoes.
2 Wash and boil the spring cabbage retaining its green colour.
3 Wash and shred the leeks.
4 Mix all the cooked vegetables.
5 Season with salt, white pepper, grated nutmeg and touch of crushed garlic.
6 Place the potato mixture in 3 inch or 8 cm mould and cook in the oven until golden brown.

Recipes

HOT DESSERTS

Sticky toffee pudding with toffee
   sauce   532

Steamed lemon sponge pudding
   with lemon sauce   533

Steamed walnut sponge pudding
   with maple syrup   534

Steamed chocolate sponge pudding
   with chocolate sauce   535

Steamed treacle pudding   536

Chocolate fondant   537

Banana fritter with almond
   ice cream   538

Bread and butter pudding   539

Dark chocolate brownie with a vanilla
   ice cream   540

Vanilla pudding soufflé   541

Beignets soufflés   542

Crêpes   542

Crêpe parisienne with strawberry
   compôte   543

Crêpes normande   544

Vanilla rice pudding with rhubarb
   compôte   544

Apple charlotte   545

Vanilla soufflé   546

Chocolate soufflé   547

Baked Alaska with kirsch   548

Cabinet pudding   549

**SAUCES AND DECORATIONS
FOR DESSERTS**

Crème anglaise and derivatives   550

Custard sauce   551

Stock syrup   551

Fruit coulis   552

Crème pâtissière   552

Crème Chantilly   553

Dark chocolate sauce   553

Butterscotch sauce   554

Caramel sauce   554

Chocolate ganache   555

Fruit crisps   555

Bubble sugar   556

Preserved vanilla sticks   556

14 Desserts

NVQ

Unit 2FPC14 Prepare, cook and finish basic hot and
cold desserts

VRQ

Unit 213 Prepare and cook desserts and puddings

Chocolate acetate motifs   557

Chocolate shavings   558

Caramel and almond swirls   559

Pistachio caramel clusters   560

Caramel springs   560

COLD DESSERTS

White chocolate and mandarin
mousse cake   562

Petit pot of chocolate with a banana
smoothie   563

Crème caramel with caramelized
sultanas and mandarins   564

Vanilla panna cotta with a macédoine
of fruit   565

Lemon crème brûlée with
biscotti   566

Caramel mousse   567

Strawberry bavarois   569

Vanilla bavarois   570

Chocolate bavarois   571

Chocolate mousse   572

Summer fruit pudding   573

Piña colada soup with a vanilla rice
condé   574

Meringue nest with vanilla ice
cream   575

Floating islands with passion fruit 576

Italian meringue   577

Trifle   578

Vanilla ice cream   579

Assorted ice cream flavours   580

Strawberry ice cream   581

Banana sorbet   582

Poached pears with cinnamon and
cider   583

Rhubarb and ginger fool   583

Peach melba   584

ONLINE RECIPES

LEARNER SUPPORT

Steamed white chocolate and
banana sponge pudding

Apple fritters with caramel sauce

Baked apple

Crêpes suzette

Passion fruit soufflé

Christmas pudding

Tiramisu

Chocolate mousse delice

LEARNING OBJECTIVES

The aim of this chapter is to enable the candidate to develop techniques and implement knowledge in the principles of producing a range of hot and cold desserts and puddings. This will also include the understanding of materials, ingredients and equipment.

At the end of this chapter you will be able to:

● **Identify each type of dessert and pudding.**

● **Understand the use of relative ingredients in the production of desserts.**

● **State the quality points of various dessert dishes.**

● **Understand the different techniques required to prepare and cook each type of dessert.**

● **Identify the storage techniques and procedures of desserts.**

● **Identify the correct tools and equipment used.**

● **Identify the modern and classical presentation skills required for a range of hot and cold desserts.**

● **Identify ingredients in desserts and puddings that may cause allergic reactions (see Chapter 16).**

Introduction

Desserts are usually sweet and therefore contain sugar. Although honey was the first naturally sweet substance recorded, sugar was first thought to have been discovered in India in around 1200 BC. Sugar cane, which is a giant grass, is native to India. According to legend, the ancestors of Buddha came from the land of sugar, or Gur, a name then given to Bengal. The export of sugar cane began to spread through the Middle East, from India towards Europe. In a syrup form, it was considered as the most expensive spice commodity and was used in medicine by the Egyptians even before the Greeks and Romans. Until modern times, sugar was an expensive medicine to Europeans, or a luxury reserved for the rich and powerful.

With the cultivation of fruits, nuts and spices, such as cinnamon, cooks began to experiment with sweet confections. These were often used to help portray great wealth during a banquet. Initially sweets, vegetables, meat and fish dishes were served all together on one table.

In the seventeenth century, desserts had become one of the main spectacles of a dinner and ornate designs were presented to allow the chef to demonstrate their skills.

The 'king of chefs', Antonin Carême, was born into a poor family in 1784. He attained an apprenticeship in a pâtissèrie and eventually worked for Talleyrand, George IV, Tsar Alexander I and the Baron de Rothschild. Throughout his career he dedicated his skills to the art of the pâtissière and generally changed the way menus and food were served. By the time of Carême, desserts were large, elaborate set pieces, often fashioned in great detail. Although Carême took this art form on to greater heights, the idea of the dessert essentially as the last course of a meal was born. Nowadays it is usually the dessert course that most people remember first from their dining experience. The word is founded from *desservir* which means 'to remove that which has been served'. Also at the end of the eighteenth century ice creams were being introduced and were usually served frozen into various forms using copper moulds.

In modern times the dessert has become far less elaborate and today's chef has to comprehend and take advantage of many new flavours and ideas. The introduction of a new, healthier lifestyle means that chefs have to produce lighter and sometimes more diet-conscious sweets, confections and desserts.

The specialized nature of the pastry section often means that it tends to operate separately from the main kitchen. The techniques used are very different from those of the main kitchen and they must be understood comprehensively and followed exactly to produce satisfactory results.

SOURCING   With added interest in producing food locally there is a great **provenance** to honey, it is a very place-specific product. Bees fly no more than three miles from their hive so it is absolutely local food. The geographic region in which a honey is produced also influences a honey's essence. Soil and climate are the most effective elements of provenance. An in land clover honey may differ noticeably from coastal clover honey because these regions' climates and soils are dissimilar.

Another effect of provenance on honey is related to the floral diversity of the region. Some regions contain vast areas of just one floral species, and from this species honeybees produce mono-floral honeys. It is more frequently the case, however, that honeybees collect nectar from numerous flora over a given period of time.

The careful reading of a recipe

Reading a recipe carefully is the first skill of a successful pastry chef. Although this sounds tedious, many chefs tend to scan the recipe too quickly and do not pick up on distinctive points or ingredients. If read without consideration the recipe will not have the correct result.

Another reason to read each recipe carefully is so that the chef can identify the technique and methods used to produce the dessert and how long it will take. Also, it allows the chef to envisage when each stage will occur and ultimately what the final presentation will look like.

Some recipes may need to be calculated to yield a greater portion size. In order to increase the yield of a dessert it is not necessarily the case that you should multiply

the ingredients because the recipe may eventually become unbalanced. The first step is to identify the percentage value for each ingredient, so when the measurement of the ingredient is increased it maintains the percentage ratio of the original dessert recipe.

A system of increasing the correct portion yield from a base recipe that involves percentages to express the formula used has been developed. This approach identifies the exact increase for each ingredient to meet the portion yield without throwing the recipe out of balance. The example below illustrates how to use the formula effectively.

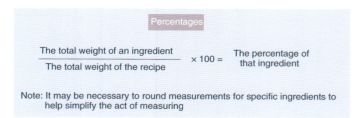

Percentages

$$\frac{\text{The total weight of an ingredient}}{\text{The total weight of the recipe}} \times 100 = \text{The percentage of that ingredient}$$

Note: It may be necessary to round measurements for specific ingredients to help simplify the act of measuring

Using this formula to identify each ingredient in terms of percentage rather than metric weight will ensure that calculations are more accurate when increasing or decreasing a recipe.

TASK   Below are the ingredients for chocolate pudding. Calculate the percentage of each ingredient and then extend the recipe for 10 covers.

Ingredients	4 portions
Melted dark chocolate	45 g
Cocoa powder	60 g
Unsalted butter	100 g
Caster sugar	125 g
Whole eggs	2
Egg yolk	1
Self-raising flour	200 g
Fresh milk	1–2 drops if needed

Select another dessert recipe from this chapter and calculate the percentage of each ingredient and then extend the recipe for 125 covers.

Storage concerns for ingredients used to make desserts

Maintaining the quality of ingredients for desserts is a major concern for all chefs. The commodities used are prone to rapid disintegration, with fresh fruits and dairy products causing particular concern with their shelf life. Care needs to be taken to ensure hygienic storage and refrigeration measures are maintained.

- *Dairy products* and eggs should be stored in air-circulated refrigeration units and kept in clean, covered plastic containers. Separate dairy and egg products from other ingredients to avoid cross contamination. Using a separate refrigerator to store these items is best practice if at all possible.

- *Fruit* should be removed from the boxes and trays that they were used to journey in as these can be contaminated or contain fruit flies and other insects. The fruit should be stored in clean, plastic trays in refrigerated conditions. Any bruised or damaged fruit should be removed. Bananas should not be stored in a refrigerator because the skin will discolour quickly.

- *Dry commodities* need to be stored in clean, sealed plastic containers on clean shelving in a separate storage room. The room needs to be maintained at a constant cool temperature and should have a dry atmosphere.

- *Stock rotation* should be employed so that all ingredients are used up and then replenished by a new batch of ingredients. The empty container should be cleaned before replenishing. This is called the 'first in first out' method. It is not recommended to store finished

desserts for long periods of time in a refrigerator because of starch break-down and loss of colour and flavour over a relatively short period of time. To store desserts for short periods in a refrigerator it is essential that they are covered in plastic film or placed into airtight plastic containers. Items that contain large amounts of sugar will attract moisture which may deteriorate the dessert quicker.

- *Storing prepared desserts* in a freezer is an alternative method that works exceptionally well. However, the dessert should have completely cooled to 5 °C or below before placing into plastic boxes. Label and date the item before freezing.

HEALTH & SAFETY It is good practice to blast freeze any item for 30 minutes before placing into a holding freezer. This process helps to maintain moisture content in the product and to eliminate potential freezer burn.

Specialist dessert equipment

Graters and micrograters

This is usually in the form of a small rectangular strip or metal box with sharp holes of varying sizes. This is used to grate the zest of citrus fruits such as lemons and oranges. It can also be used to grate chocolate for decorative purposes.

Stainless steel moulds

These come in different shapes and sizes and are used to mould mousses, bavarois, crèmes and sponges. Care must be taken when storing large quantities of moulds as they can be quite heavy and will easily bend out of shape. A cheaper alternative to purchasing expensive stainless steel round moulds is to purchase plastic piping from a local DIY store and cut the mould to size.

Ramekin dishes

A **ramekin** is a small baking dish usually made of ceramic or heat-resistant glass to bake soufflés, cakes and custards. These come in varying sizes.

Plastic sauce bottles

These are used to pipe sauces onto plates to create intricate designs for the presentation of desserts. They can be warmed up to maintain a hot sauce such as crème anglaise or used for cold fruit coulis.

Ice cream machine

This is a specialist machine which should always be sterilized before and after use. A good machine will produce a litre of ice cream within a matter of minutes. It has a churning mechanism within a freezing unit so that the mixture can be constantly churned as it sets and eventually freezes. This action will help reduce coarse ice crystals forming within the mixture.

Sugar thermometers

These are used to measure temperatures accurately for cooking jams, preserves and sugar. They should be cleaned and sterilized after every use. Care should be taken not to plunge the thermometer into cold water after having measured very high sugar temperatures as this may cause a breakage. Digital thermometers are just as effective but are more expensive to purchase.

Copper sugar boiler

These pans are used solely for the cooking of sugar-based confections and syrups. Copper has a good transference of heat but they should be kept scrupulously clean and free of oils and fats. Cleaning with hot water and a mild detergent, followed by a second clean of vinegar and salt and then a rinse with cold water, will obtain the best results.

Dariole moulds

These can be purchased in aluminium or stainless steel and are used primarily for the cooking of puddings and pudding soufflés.

TASK Complete a chart like the one below describing how to use, clean and maintain the following items of equipment and the safety considerations associated with them.

	CLEANING	STERILIZING	STORING	SAFETY PROCEDURES
Silicone baking mats				
Nylon piping bags				
Ice cream machine				

The use of fruit in desserts

Fruits have always been available to the chef in great variety and abundance. They were the world's first convenience food and although the early Greek and Roman writers include them as components of meat and fish dishes, traditionally fruits bring a meal to its conclusion.

Fruit provides a ready source of energy because it is rich in sugar (fructose), minerals and vitamins. It is also a good source of dietary fibre, both in the edible skin and in the water-soluble fibre called pectin found in certain fruits such as apples and quinces. Almost all fruit has a low calorie count.

Purchasing and storage of fruit

- Above all, fruit should look fresh and appetising. Fresh fruit should be plump and firm, this is a sign of good moisture content, and be without bruising and wrinkles. Soft fruits, such as berries, should look dry on the outside and full. Avoid those with signs of mould or moisture, including any leakage in the packaging. Whether the fruit skins are edible or inedible, always make sure that they are not bruised, split or broken or have signs of insect damage.

- Citrus fruit will keep well for a couple of weeks if necessary, but the skins will begin to toughen, dry out and wrinkle and they will lose some of their essential oils which help flavour many desserts. If the citrus fruit is purchased for its zest, then it must be used within a couple of days. Pineapples and melons are best eaten just chilled at 5 °C; however, this causes a slight problem in storage because their scent is so penetrating that they must be well wrapped, or they will pass on their flavours to other refrigerated foods stored nearby.

● Odour is a good indication of ripeness. Fruit, such as melon, should smell fragrant. Although they will keep quite well for a week or so, they will not ripen if bought under ripe. Hard fruit such as apples and pears, as long as they are purchased unblemished, will keep for a few weeks in the refrigerator. Any fruit stored at room temperature will ripen and deteriorate quicker than if stored in a cool place, because the water content gradually evaporates and with it the sweet moisture within the fruit. Some fruits are best purchased for immediate use. All the soft berry fruits come into this category. All fruits should be carefully washed before cooking and eating.

CHEF'S TIP Many fruits will ripen successfully in storage, but it is always best to buy fruit on a daily basis to ensure freshness. However, bananas are often sold immaculately pale yellow and tinged with green. These need to be ripened to a warm yellow and slightly marked with small brown streaks.

SOURCING Many varieties of fresh fruit are available all year in almost every part of Europe, because of excellent transportation and storage facilities. For the greatest nutritional value and flavour, however, choose fruits at the peak of their freshness.

Also, between 20 and 30 per cent of the global warming caused by human activity is contributed by our food and agriculture systems. Buying more sustainable ingredients is not just the right thing to do ethically – it makes good business sense because more customers are demanding that sustainable and seasonal foods are used.

Fruits and their seasonal availability

It is important that we should recognize seasonality as much as possible and buy our commodities according to seasonal availability. If a fruit is available throughout the year it is generally recognized that it is purchased overseas.

TASK Find out the types of fruit that are available in November and in April from your suppliers and where they originate from. Make a list of the miles the fruit will have travelled to reach the table.

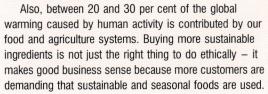

However, purchasing fruit within season and locally will help to ensure freshness because the storage time before purchase has been minimal. The travelling expense and carbon footprint is kept to minimum because it is locally grown, which might also help lower the price of the fruit. The list below is a general guide to the seasonal availability of fruit.

NAME OF FRUIT	SEASON
Apple (*pomme*)	All of the year
Apricot (*abricot*)	May – September
Blackberry (*mûre*)	May – September
Cherry (*cerise*)	May – July
Clementine (*clémentine*)	All of the year
Cranberry (*airelle rouge*)	November – January
Damson (*prune de damas*)	September – October
Fig (*figue*)	July – September
Gooseberry (*groiselle à macquereau*)	June – July
Greengage (*Reine-Claude*)	August – September
Grapefruit (*pamplemousse*)	All of the year
Grapes (*raisin*)	All of the year
Lemon (*citron*)	All of the year
Melon (*melon*)	May – October
Nectarine (*brugnon*)	June – September
Peach (*pêche*)	June – September
Pear (*poire*)	All of the year (best in Autumn – Winter)
Plum (*prune*)	July – October
Pineapple (*ananas*)	All of the year
Raspberry (*framboise*)	June – October
Rhubarb (*rhubarbe*)	January – July
Strawberry (*fraise*)	June – September

The preservation of fruit

● *Drying* Apples, pears, apricots, peaches, bananas and figs can be dried. Plums when dried are called prunes, and currants, sultanas and raisins are produced by drying grapes. Also, fruit crisps can be produced by macerating thinly sliced fruits such as pineapple for a few minutes and then drying out in a low-heated oven.

● *Canning* Almost all fruits may be canned. Apples are packed in water and known as 'solid packed apples'. Other fruits are canned in light syrup.

● *Bottling* This is used domestically, but very little fruit is commercially preserved in this way. Cherries are bottled in maraschino liqueur.

● *Candied* Orange and lemon peels are candied. Other fruits with a strong flavour, such as pineapple, are preserved in this way. The fruit is covered in hot syrup, which is increased in sugar content from day to day until the fruit is saturated in very heavy syrup. It is then allowed to dry slowly until it is no longer sticky and moist.

DIFFERENT CATEGORIES OF FRUITS

STONE FRUITS	HARD FRUITS	SOFT FRUITS	CITRUS FRUITS	TROPICAL FRUITS
Apricots	Apples	Bilberries	Clementine	Bananas
Cherries	Crab apples	Blackberries	Grapefruit	Cape gooseberries
Damsons	Pears	Blackcurrants	Kumquats	Carambola (star fruit)
Greengages		Blueberries	Lemons	Dates
Nectarines		Gooseberries	Mandarins	Figs
Peaches		Loganberries	Limes	Granadillas
Plums		Raspberries	Oranges	Guavas
		Redcurrants	Tangerines	Kiwi fruit
		Strawberries	Blood orange	Lychees
		Tayberries	Satsuma	Mangoes
		White currants		Passion fruit
				Papaya (pawpaw)
				Pineapples
				Sharon fruit
				Tamarillo

Other fruits: cranberries, grapes, melons, rhubarb.

- *Glacé* The fruit is first candied and then dipped in fresh syrup to give a clear finish. This method is applied to cherries.

- *Crystallized* After the fruit has been candied it is left in fresh syrup for 24 hours and then allowed to dry very slowly until crystals form on the surface of the fruit.

- *Jam* Some stone and all soft fruits can be used to make jam. The fruits are boiled with sugar and pectin may be added to help set the mixture.

- *Jelly* Jellies are produced from fruit juice and can be set with either gelatine or pectin.

- *Quick freezing* Strawberries, raspberries, loganberries, apples, blackberries, gooseberries, grapefruit and plums are frozen and must be kept below zero and preferably at −18°C.

- *Cold storage* Apples are stored at temperatures between 1 and 4°C, depending on the variety of apple. This suppresses the ripening of the fruit.

- *Gas storage* Fruit can be kept in a sealed storage room where the atmosphere is controlled. The amount of air is limited, the oxygen content of the air is decreased and the carbon dioxide increased which controls the respiration rate of the fruit and preserves it for longer.

Milk and milk-based products for desserts

Milk has been an important source of food for thousands of years and is highly regarded for its versatility. Milk contains fat, protein, carbohydrates in the form of natural milk sugar (lactose), calcium, phosphorus, sodium and potassium. Vitamins A, C, D and the B vitamins riboflavin, thiamine and B12 are also present.

The milk that is generally used in the pastry kitchen is obtained from four main sources: cow, goat, soya and ewe's milk. Primarily milk is used as a moisturizing agent as it is 87 per cent water. It is also used as an enriching agent depending on the amount used and whether it is full cream, half cream (semi-skimmed) or skimmed.

Pasteurized milk

Much of fresh cow's milk is pasteurized to destroy pathogenic bacteria found in fresh milk. There are two ways of pasteurizing milk.

1   Heat the milk to a temperature of 145°F and maintain this temperature for 30 seconds and then cool it rapidly.

2   Heat the milk to 162°F for 15 seconds and cool it rapidly.

This general purpose milk contains about 4 per cent fat and keeps for four to five days in a refrigerator.

Homogenized milk

This is treated so that the cream content is dispersed throughout the milk. It has the same fat content as pasteurized milk and can be used in all recipes requiring milk.

Semi-skimmed milk

With a fat content of 1.5–1.8 per cent, this tastes less rich than full cream milk, but is fine to use for most recipes.

Skimmed milk

This milk has a fat content of no more than 0.3 per cent which makes it ideal for anyone wishing to cut down on their fat intake. Since most of the fat has been removed, many of the natural soluble vitamins will also be lost, although the other nutrient values will still remain. The milk looks thinner and is less fatty tasting.

Channel Islands and Jersey milk

This is produced from Jersey and Guernsey cows, and is normally quite yellow in colour as it has a high fat content of about 4–8 per cent.

Buttermilk

A liquid by product of butter making, **buttermilk** is a thin and unstable liquid which is left after the fat from the cream has coagulated to form butter.

UHT milk

Ultra-Heat Treated or long-life milk can be kept for several months without refrigeration but once it has been opened it should be treated as normal fresh milk. The fat is evenly distributed during this process and it is therefore a stable milk to cook with.

Soya milk

Soya milk retains most of the high nutritional value of the soya bean. It can be used in cooking although it can curdle if mixed with certain hot liquids. Soya milk is an acceptable alternative to milk in the diet of those who are lactose intolerant.

The contamination of milk products

In general milk keeps less well than other foods. Contamination can occur with the use of unclean equipment and unhygienic procedures at the initial stage in the dairy or during transit and in the course of improper storage. Fresh milk should be purchased daily and stored:

● in the container in which it is delivered

● in a refrigerator at below 5 °C

● away from strong odours such as onion and fish.

Cream and yoghurt

Cream is derived from milk and is essentially the butterfat content that is separated from the milk. It will pass through the same pasteurization or sterilization process as milk and should be treated, transported and stored in the same manner as fresh milk.

UHT – ultra heat treated

This process is applied to single, whipping and double creams. The cream is homogenized and heated to 132 °C and cooled very quickly where it is packed into foil-lined and sealed containers. The shelf life of this product is far longer than fresh cream.

Single cream

This has a low fat content of 18 per cent, which makes it unsuitable for **whipping**. However, it can be used to enrich soups, sauces or for serving as an accompaniment for desserts or coffee. It is also available in UHT form. This cream can be infused with other flavours when it is hot or cold. If a cold infusion is taking place (such as vanilla added to the cream) it is best left for a minimum of 12 hours.

Whipping cream

Because its fat content is 35 per cent, whipping cream is ideal for aeration with a wire balloon whisk. Once aerated it can be used as a decoration medium, or folded into bavarois and mousse preparations to lighten the texture. This cream is also suitable for serving in the same way as single cream and is also available in UHT form. For whipping cream to achieve a good aeration it must be aerated or whipped at 4 °C.

Double cream

The fat content of double cream is 48 per cent, which will add richness of texture and flavour to a wide range of dishes. Although it can be aerated, care should be taken not to over-whip the cream so that it becomes grainy and starts to separate. This can happen quite quickly due to the greater fat content.

Clotted cream

This is the richest of all creams and has a yellow shade of colour which denotes the high fat content. It contains 55 per cent fat and is very thick in texture. This cream is traditionally manufactured from the English counties of Devon, Cornwall and Somerset. Generally it is used as an accompaniment for desserts and especially with the afternoon tea service of warm scones and fruit preserve.

Crème fraîche

This cream is treated with a bacterial culture to create a slightly acidic flavour. It has a similar consistency to that of double cream although it has a 35 per cent fat content.

Soured cream

This is a commercially prepared cream which has a similar fat content to single cream. It is made from homogenized cream with a bacterial culture added to create a slightly sour flavour. This can be used to enrich soups and sauces or used as an accompaniment to many dishes.

Yoghurt

This product has had two types of active bacteria added to create the thick textured and acidic flavour we associate with yoghurts today. The nutritional qualities of yoghurt vary greatly according to whether it has been produced with whole or skimmed milk and whether it has had cream, sugar or fruit added to it. There may be preservatives or starches added so it is always best to check the labelling on the packaging before purchase. The storage of yoghurt is the same as for fresh milk and cream.

The process of heat treating dairy products

There are different methods of processing available to preserve milk and dairy products but heat treatment is still considered as a better alternative. The process of pasteurization was named after Louis Pasteur who discovered that spoilage organisms could be inactivated in wine by applying heat at temperatures below its boiling point. The process was later applied to milk and remains the most important operation in the processing of milk.

There are three types of pasteurization used today:

- high temperature/short time (HTST)
- ultra-high temperature (UHT)
- low temperature/long time (LTLT).

There are fundamentally two methods for the HTST type of pasteurization in use: batch and continuous flow. In the batch process, a large quantity of milk is held in a heated vat at 65 °C for 30 minutes, followed by rapid cooling to 4 °C. In the continuous flow process also known as HTST, milk is forced through pipes heated on the outside by hot water to the same temperature profile as mentioned earlier.

LTLT pasteurization is a heat treatment that was originally a batch process in which the milk was heated to 63 °C in open vats and held at that temperature for 30 minutes. This method is called as the 'low temperature long time (LTLT)' method. Currently milk is usually heat treated in continuous processes (such as HTST pasteurization and UHT treatment) where bulk milk can be processed in a short span of time.

Ultra-High Temperature processing, or Ultra-Heat Treatment (both abbreviated to UHT), is the sterilization of food by heating it for a short time, around 1–2 seconds, at a temperature exceeding 135 °C, which is the temperature required to kill spores in milk. The most common UHT product is milk, but the process is also used for fruit juices, cream, yoghurt and wine. UHT milk was invented in the 1960s, and became generally available for consumption in 1970s.

High heat during the UHT process can cause **Maillard** browning and change the taste and smell of dairy products. UHT milk has a typical shelf life of six to nine months, until opened.

HEALTH & SAFETY

The importance of calcium

Calcium is a mineral that helps build strong bones and teeth, regulates muscle contraction (including the heart-beat) and makes sure the blood is clotting normally. Milk and dairy products have long been held as an important source of calcium. Other sources of calcium include:

- fish (for example sardines)
- dried fruit
- sesame seeds
- almonds
- soya
- dark green leafy vegetables.

Similarly, sufficient exercise is another vital factor in maintaining healthy bone structure and density. Concerns have been voiced that a lack of exercise in growing children will have a detrimental effect on their bones.

Hot and cold desserts

Hot desserts play an important part in the construction of a menu, varying the selection of desserts available. Also, rather obviously, they give a change of temperature to the normal cold dessert that is pleasant, especially during the autumn/winter months. With this temperature change an alteration in the texture of the dessert emerges. The balance of hot desserts to cold desserts on a menu is important and the time of year should influence how many hot desserts should be present. Chefs now use combinations of hot elements and cold elements to produce one dessert (e.g. hot apple pie served with vanilla ice cream) and this has been taken further with the development of desserts that are served warm such as chocolate tart.

DERIVATIVES OF SOME CLASSICAL 'ENTREMENTS CHAUDS'

Beignets	Beignets soufflé, Beignets de pommes
Charlottes	Apple charlotte, timbale d'Aremberg
Croquettes	Croquette de fruits, croquette de riz
Croutes	Croute aux fruits, croute joinville
Crêpes	Crêpe Normande, crêpe Suzette
Dumplings	Apple dumplings
Fruit desserts	Abricots Condé, bananes Bourdaloue
Omelettes	Omelette à la confiture, omelette mousseline
Pannequets	Pannequets à la confiture, pannequets à la Lyonnaise
Fruit pies and tarts	Apple pie (tarte aux pommes)
Puddings	Cabinet pudding, queen's pudding
Soufflés	Soufflé au chocolat, soufflé au Grand Marnier
Strüdel	Apfelstrüdel, kirschenstrüdel
Various hot desserts	Clafoutis, kesari bhata (sweet rice Indian style)

TEST YOURSELF

To test your level of knowledge and understanding, answer the following short questions. These will help to prepare you for your summative (final) assessment.

1 State two processes in the pastry kitchen, which are most likely to kill food poisoning bacteria.

2 Explain the reasons for sterilizing the ice cream machine before and after use.

3 Describe how hot desserts can be modified to take account of healthy eating trends.

4 Name three desserts that can be produced from eggs, milk, cream and sugar.

5 State the reason that diary products are pasteurized when making an ice cream.

6 Why is gelatine used in specific desserts and how should the leaf gelatine be used?

7 How can ice creams be modified to produce healthy options?

8 Plan and state the recipes for three desserts suitable for a luncheon buffet to celebrate a summer wedding.

9 At what temperature should you store ice cream?

10 What temperature should sugar be cooked to in the production of Italian meringue?

Hot desserts

Sticky toffee pudding with toffee sauce

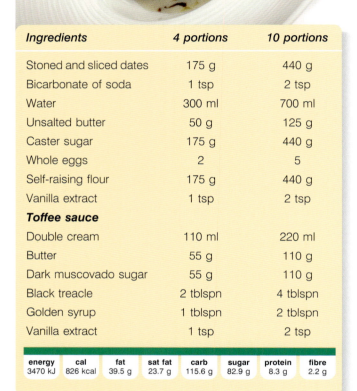

Ingredients	4 portions	10 portions
Stoned and sliced dates	175 g	440 g
Bicarbonate of soda	1 tsp	2 tsp
Water	300 ml	700 ml
Unsalted butter	50 g	125 g
Caster sugar	175 g	440 g
Whole eggs	2	5
Self-raising flour	175 g	440 g
Vanilla extract	1 tsp	2 tsp
Toffee sauce		
Double cream	110 ml	220 ml
Butter	55 g	110 g
Dark muscovado sugar	55 g	110 g
Black treacle	2 tblspn	4 tblspn
Golden syrup	1 tblspn	2 tblspn
Vanilla extract	1 tsp	2 tsp

energy	cal	fat	sat fat	carb	sugar	protein	fibre
3470 kJ	826 kcal	39.5 g	23.7 g	115.6 g	82.9 g	8.3 g	2.2 g

METHOD OF WORK

1   Preheat the oven to 180 °C and butter individual pudding moulds with some clarified butter.

2   Bring the water to the boil and add the dates. Boil the dates for 5 minutes before adding the bicarbonate of soda.

3   Cream (see below) the butter and the caster sugar together until light. Beat the whole eggs and slowly add to the creamed butter and sugar.

4   Drain the dates and mix into the egg and butter preparation, combining the flour and the vanilla into the preparation at the last moment and folding in gently.

5   Pour the mixture into the prepared pudding moulds, place into a bain-marie and bake in the oven for approximately 30–40 minutes. Each pudding should be slightly firm and have a spring to the texture when touched.

6   To make the toffee sauce: place all the ingredients into a heavy based saucepan and slowly bring to the boil while constantly stirring. Continue heating and stirring until the required consistency to the sauce has been achieved.

7   Serve with a combination of crème anglaise (see page 550) and the toffee sauce.

> **CHEF'S TIP**   Although they can be slightly expensive, Medjool dates from Egypt are best suited for this recipe because they are large and have a sweet, dense flesh.

Step-by-step: Preparing a pudding mix

1. Beat the unsalted butter and sugar together until the mixture is a pale colour and has a fluffy texture

2. Beat in one egg at a time

3. Add the flour and mix carefully

Steamed lemon sponge pudding with lemon sauce

Ingredients	4 portions	10 portions
Finely grated lemon zest and juice	2 lemons	5 lemons
Unsalted butter	100 g	250 g
Caster sugar	125 g	300 g
Whole eggs	2	5
Egg yolk	1	3
Self-raising flour	200 g	500 g
Fresh milk	1–2 drops if needed	4–5 drops if needed
Lemon sauce		
Lemons	2	4
Water	500 ml	1 litre
Caster sugar	125 g	250 g
Cornflour	30 g	60 g
Lemon curd	2 tblspn	4 tblspn

energy	cal	fat	sat fat	carb	sugar	protein	fibre
2940 kJ	697 kcal	25.4 g	14.4 g	115.9 g	70.1 g	8.5 g	2.0 g

METHOD OF WORK

1   Preheat the steamer to 118 °C and lightly grease and flour each individual pudding mould. Cut small discs of silicone paper the circumference of the top of each pudding mould and brush one side with some melted butter.

2   Beat the unsalted butter and sugar together until the mixture is light in colour and has a fluffy texture. Add the finely grated lemon zest. This stage is important to help ensure a successful preparation to combine the eggs, so you should ensure that the butter and sugar mixture is light and soft.

3   Beat in one egg at a time; ensure that each egg has been completely mixed into the butter and sugar preparation before adding another to prevent the mixture from separating.

4   Add the flour and mix carefully, also adding the lemon juice at this point.

5   Check the consistency of the mixture. If the mixture is slightly heavy mix in a few drops of milk to ensure the correct 'dropping' consistency is obtained.

6   Spoon or pipe the mixture into the moulds up to three-quarters' full. Cover the moulds with the buttered silicone paper discs.

7   Place onto a tray and steam for approximately 45 minutes.

8   To make the lemon sauce: remove the zest from one lemon with a peeler and leave to one side. With the other lemons finely grate the zest into the quantity of water and squeeze all the juice from each lemon into the water too. Bring water and lemon to the boil with the sugar.

9   Dilute the cornflour with a little cold water and mix into the boiling liquid stirring all the time with a spoon. Add the lemon curd, re-boil and then pass through a fine chinois. Cut the peeled lemon zest into a very fine julienne, blanch well in boiling water and add to the sauce.

10 Remove the puddings from the steamer and de-mould.

11 Place the pudding onto a plate and spoon over the lemon sauce.

CHEF'S TIP Alternative flavour combinations can be used for this recipe such as orange marmalade, chocolate, treacle or apricot. If making larger sized puddings the steaming time will need to be increased to approximately 1 hour and 25 minutes.

SOURCING Purchasing small lemons will not give the optimal amount of freshly squeezed lemon juice. Instead, purchase large lemons which feel heavy as this is an indication the lemon is ripe and full of juice. Around 50 varieties of lemon exist in the world today and can be divided into the categories acidic and sweet.

VIDEO CLIP Steamed sponge pudding.

Steamed walnut sponge pudding with maple syrup

Ingredients	4 portions	10 portions
Walnuts (chopped)	75 g	200 g
Walnuts (halves)	16	40
Unsalted butter	100 g	250 g
Caster sugar	125 g	300 g
Whole eggs	2	5
Egg yolk	1	3
Self-raising flour	200 g	500 g
Fresh milk	1–2 drops if needed	4–5 drops if needed
Maple syrup	75 ml	175 ml

energy	cal	fat	sat fat	carb	sugar	protein	fibre
3391 kJ	812 kcal	48.9 g	16.8 g	84.5 g	45.7 g	13.5 g	2.8 g

METHOD OF WORK

1   Preheat the steamer to 118 °C and lightly grease and flour each individual pudding mould. Cut small discs of silicone paper the circumference of the top of each pudding mould and brush one side with some melted butter.

2   Place the chopped walnuts onto a baking tray and toast under a salamander for a few minutes. Leave to cool and then blend to a course powder in a food blender.

3   Beat the unsalted butter and sugar together until the mixture is light in colour and has a fluffy texture. Add the blended walnuts. This stage is important to help ensure a successful preparation to combine the eggs, so you should ensure that the butter and sugar mixture is light and soft.

4   Beat in one egg at a time: ensure that each egg has been completely mixed into the butter and sugar preparation before adding another to prevent the mixture from separating.

5   Add the flour and mix carefully, also adding a little maple syrup to taste at this point.

6   Check the consistency of the mixture. If the mixture is slightly heavy mix in a few drops of milk to ensure the correct 'dropping' consistency is obtained.

7   Spoon or pipe the mixture into the moulds up to three-quarters' full. Cover the moulds with the buttered silicone paper discs.

8   Place onto a tray and steam for approximately 45 minutes.

9   Poach the walnut halves in a little milk for 4 minutes and leave to one side.

10 Remove the puddings from the steamer and de-mould.

11 Place the pudding onto a plate and set four poached walnut halves on top of the pudding, warm the remaining maple syrup and drizzle over the top of each pudding. Serve with crème anglaise.

Steamed chocolate sponge pudding with chocolate sauce

Ingredients	4 portions	10 portions
Melted dark chocolate	45 g	90 g
Cocoa powder	60 g	120 g
Unsalted butter	100 g	250 g
Caster sugar	125 g	300 g
Whole eggs	2	5
Egg yolk	1	3
Self-raising flour	200 g	500 g
Fresh milk	1–2 drops if needed	4–5 drops if needed
Chocolate sauce		
Milk (1)		100 ml
Cocoa powder		80 g
Cornflour		50 g
Single cream		300 ml
Milk (2)		400 ml
Icing sugar		120 g
Dark chocolate (60%)		60 g

energy	cal	fat	sat fat	carb	sugar	protein	fibre
4806 kJ	1146 kcal	60.9 g	29.2 g	133.5 g	72.3 g	24.3 g	11.4 g

METHOD OF WORK

1 Preheat the steamer to 118 °C and lightly grease and flour each individual pudding mould. Cut small discs of silicone paper the circumference of the top of each pudding mould and brush one side with some melted butter.

2 Sieve the cocoa powder and flour together.

3 Beat the unsalted butter and sugar together until the mixture is light in colour and has a fluffy texture. This stage is important to help ensure a successful preparation to combine the eggs, so you should ensure that the butter and sugar mixture is light and soft.

4 Beat in one egg at a time; ensure that each egg has been completely mixed into the butter and sugar preparation before adding another to prevent the mixture from separating.

5 Add the sieved cocoa powder and flour and mix carefully, also adding the melted chocolate at this point.

6 Check the consistency of the mixture. If the mixture is slightly heavy mix in a few drops of milk to ensure the correct 'dropping' consistency is obtained.

7 Spoon or pipe the mixture into the moulds up to three-quarters' full. Cover the moulds with the buttered silicone paper discs.

8 Place onto a tray and steam for approximately 45 minutes.

9 To make the chocolate sauce: mix together the milk, coca powder and cornflour in a basin. Bring the single cream to the boil with the icing sugar and the second quantity of milk. Pour onto the diluted cocoa powder mixture and whisk thoroughly. Return to a saucepan and bring back to the boil, stirring constantly. Pass through a fine chinois and then stir in the chocolate at the last moment.

10 Remove the puddings from the steamer and de-mould.

11 Place the pudding onto a plate and serve the warm chocolate sauce over the top of each pudding.

Steamed treacle pudding

Ingredients	4 portions	10 portions
Soft flour	120 g	275 g
Baking powder	5 g	10 g
Salt	3 g	6 g
White breadcrumbs	120 g	275 g
Suet	120 g	275 g
Caster sugar	70 g	150 g
Eggs (medium)	1	2
Milk	90 ml	200 ml
Butter	15 g	25 g
Golden syrup	100 g	250 g
Zest of lemon	¼ lemon	1 lemon
Vanilla extract	1 tsp	3 tsp

energy	cal	fat	sat fat	carb	sugar	protein	fibre
2801 kJ	668 kcal	31.7 g	17.6 g	89.0 g	39.6 g	8.8 g	1.8 g

METHOD OF WORK

1   Preheat the steamer to 118 °C and lightly grease and flour each individual pudding mould. Cut small discs of silicone paper the circumference of the top of each pudding mould and brush one side with some melted butter.

2   Sieve the soft flour, baking powder and salt together, twice.

3   Add the breadcrumbs, zest of lemon and suet to the flour and mix before making a well in the centre.

4   Beat the eggs, vanilla and the milk together and pour into the well and gently mix until a light dropping consistency has been reached.

5   Check the consistency of the mixture. If the mixture is slightly heavy mix in a few drops of milk to ensure the correct 'dropping' consistency is obtained.

6   Pour the golden syrup into the bottoms of the prepared moulds and divide the mixture to spoon on top up to three-quarters' full.

7   Cover the moulds with the buttered silicone paper discs.

8   Place onto a tray and steam for approximately 60 minutes.

9   Remove the puddings from the steamer and de-mould.

10   Place the puddings onto service plates and serve with a custard sauce, ice cream or crème anglaise.

CHEF'S TIP Alternative flavours and finishes can be added to this recipe by using jam or marmalade instead of golden syrup. Alternatively some sultanas, diced apple, raisins and mixed spices can also be added.

Chocolate fondant *(Moelleux au chocolat)*

Ingredients	4 portions	10 portions
Cocoa powder	15 g	40 g
Caster sugar	15 g	40 g
Dark chocolate (60%)	80 g	200 g
Butter	80 g	200 g
Eggs (medium)	2	5
Egg yolk	1	3
Icing sugar	45 g	100 g
Arrowroot	15 g	35 g
Butter for greasing the moulds		

energy	cal	fat	sat fat	carb	sugar	protein	fibre
1722 kJ	414 kcal	32.1 g	13.3 g	26.1 g	15.8 g	6.5 g	1.2 g

METHOD OF WORK

1 Grease the insides of the stainless steel ring moulds, 5 cm in diameter and 6 cm deep with a little butter.

2 Mix together the cocoa powder and caster sugar until well combined. Dust the insides of the ring moulds with this mixture and shake off any excess. Place the moulds onto a baking sheet lined with silicone paper.

3 Melt the chocolate and the butter in a bowl over a saucepan of just simmering water.

4 Whisk together the eggs and egg yolk in a separate bowl until pale and aerated. Gradually sift the icing sugar into the aerated eggs, whisking continuously.

5 Whisking further, continue until the egg mixture has doubled in volume.

6 Sift in the arrowroot and whisk again. Fold in the melted chocolate mixture very carefully so as not to lose too much aeration.

7 Fill each of the prepared moulds with the chocolate mixture and set the oven to preheat at 210 °C. Place the chocolate fondant in a refrigerator for at least 30 minutes to chill.

8 Bake in the oven for up to 7 minutes. Remove from the oven and leave to rest for a further 5 minutes before turning out of the moulds onto a serving plate, dust with icing sugar and serve with a vanilla or almond ice cream (see page 580).

Banana fritter with almond ice cream

Ingredients	4 portions	10 portions
Sweet cider	300 g	750 g
Soft white flour (sieved)	100 g	250 g
Caster sugar	25 g	60 g
Bananas, peeled and cut in half	2	5
Almond ice cream (see page 580)	4 balls	10 balls
Toasted flaked almonds	40 g	100 g
Fresh mint garnish	4 plûches	10 plûches
Strawberry coulis (see page 552)	50 ml	100 ml

energy	cal	fat	sat fat	carb	sugar	protein	fibre
3819 kJ	914 kcal	51.5 g	22.3 g	92.0 g	70.6 g	18.4 g	4.4 g

METHOD OF WORK

1   Preheat the deep fat fryer to 180 °C.

2   Mix the cider, flour and sugar together and leave to rest for approximately half an hour at room temperature. Ensure that there are no lumps of raw flour in the mixture.

3   Prepare the bananas by cutting them in half, and lightly flour each piece.

4   Dip each piece into the batter and transfer into the deep fat fryer. Fry for about 4 minutes until a pale golden colour has been obtained. The fritters will rise to the surface when they are cooked.

5   Carefully remove and drain the fritters, placing them onto absorbent kitchen paper and keeping them warm for service.

6   Cook the remaining fruit in batches following the same procedure.

7   To serve, place one banana fritter onto a plate and decorate with the strawberry coulis. Place a ball of almond ice cream for each portion. Decorate with the mint and the toasted almonds.

CHEF'S TIP Pears, apricots, apples, pineapples and peaches can be deep fried and served in the same way. A combination of fruit sauces or coulis can be served to complement the dish.

HEALTH & SAFETY Carefully dip the fritters into the deep fat fryer before letting go at the last moment. This method will prevent the hot fat from splashing up and potentially burning.

Bread and butter pudding

Ingredients	4 portions	10 portions
Medium-sliced white bread or brioche	10 slices	25 slices
Unsalted butter	50 g	125 g
Egg yolks	6	14
Whole egg	1	3
Caster sugar	130 g	260 g
Vanilla pod or extract	1	3
Fresh milk	250 ml	600 ml
Double cream	250 ml	600 ml
Sultanas	25 g	60 g
Raisins	25 g	60 g
Icing sugar for glazing	60 g	150 g

energy	cal	fat	sat fat	carb	sugar	protein	fibre
4088 kJ	977 kcal	55.7 g	31.0 g	108.8 g	65.8 g	17.1 g	2.8 g

METHOD OF WORK

1   Preheat the oven to 180 °C.

2   Remove the crusts from the bread or brioche if required and melt the unsalted butter. Brush the butter onto each slice of bread. Use any remaining butter to lightly grease the sides of the baking dish used to bake the pudding in.

3   Split the vanilla pod in half and add to the milk and cream combination, slowly bring to the boil.

4   Whisk the egg yolks, whole egg and caster sugar together in a bowl.

5   Pour the boiled milk and cream onto the egg preparation and stir well to form a light custard.

6   Arrange the bread in layers in the baking dish sprinkling the sultanas and raisins between each layer. Finish with a final layer of bread.

7   Pour the custard mixture over the bread through a chinois to strain the vanilla pod. Leave the custard to soak into the bread for approximately 20 minutes.

8   Place the dish into a bain-marie and bake in the preheated oven for approximately 25 minutes or until the pudding begins to set.

9   Remove from the oven, dredge the top with icing sugar and glaze under a hot salamander or coat with a hot apricot glaze. Clean the edges of the dish and serve immediately.

CHEF'S TIP   To add flavour to the sultanas and raisins, macerate in dark rum or brandy for 12 hours prior to using.

CHEF'S TIP   Using brioche instead of bread is a modern twist on the traditional bread and butter pudding. The richness of the brioche, which has been enriched with additional butter and eggs, will add colour, texture and flavour to the pudding.

Dark chocolate brownie with a vanilla ice cream

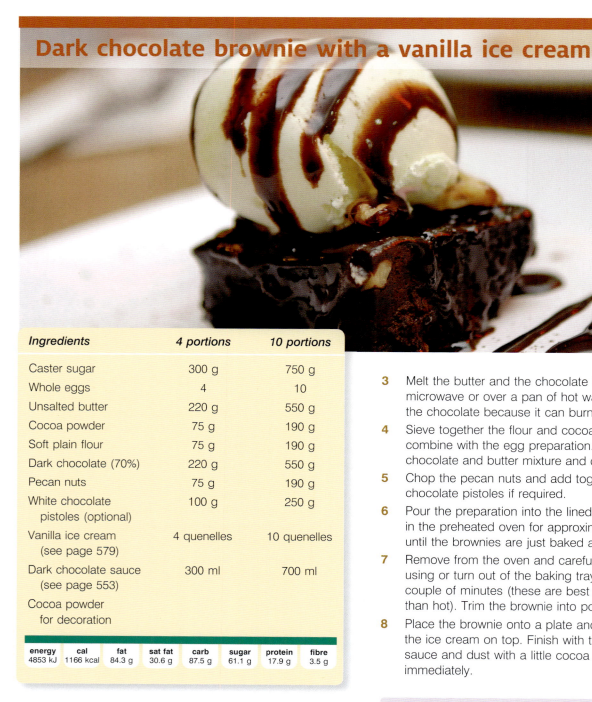

Ingredients	4 portions	10 portions
Caster sugar	300 g	750 g
Whole eggs	4	10
Unsalted butter	220 g	550 g
Cocoa powder	75 g	190 g
Soft plain flour	75 g	190 g
Dark chocolate (70%)	220 g	550 g
Pecan nuts	75 g	190 g
White chocolate pistoles (optional)	100 g	250 g
Vanilla ice cream (see page 579)	4 quenelles	10 quenelles
Dark chocolate sauce (see page 553)	300 ml	700 ml
Cocoa powder for decoration		

energy	cal	fat	sat fat	carb	sugar	protein	fibre
4853 kJ	1166 kcal	84.3 g	30.6 g	87.5 g	61.1 g	17.9 g	3.5 g

METHOD OF WORK

1 Preheat the oven to 180 °C, lightly butter a high sided baking tin and line with silicone paper (or use individual stainless steel rings). Set on a silicone lined baking sheet ready for use.

2 Using a whisk beat together the caster sugar and eggs to create a light aerated foam.

3 Melt the butter and the chocolate together either in a microwave or over a pan of hot water. Do not overheat the chocolate because it can burn easily.

4 Sieve together the flour and cocoa powder and combine with the egg preparation. Add the melted chocolate and butter mixture and carefully mix together.

5 Chop the pecan nuts and add together with the white chocolate pistoles if required.

6 Pour the preparation into the lined mould and bake in the preheated oven for approximately 25 minutes or until the brownies are just baked and set.

7 Remove from the oven and carefully remove the rings if using or turn out of the baking tray. Leave to set for a couple of minutes (these are best served warm rather than hot). Trim the brownie into portions.

8 Place the brownie onto a plate and place a quenelle of the ice cream on top. Finish with the warm chocolate sauce and dust with a little cocoa powder. Serve immediately.

CHEF'S TIP If the white chocolate pistoles are not available you can chop up white chocolate into 1 cm chunks instead. It is important that you try to use a chocolate that has a minimum of 70 per cent cocoa content as this will have a stronger, almost bitter flavour that will balance with the high sugar content in this dessert.

Vanilla pudding soufflé *(Pouding soufflé vanille)*

Ingredients	4 portions	10 portions
Unsalted butter	50 g	120 g
Caster sugar	50 g	120 g
Soft white flour	50 g	120 g
Fresh milk	190 ml	400 ml
Vanilla pod	1	2
Egg yolks	2	5
Egg whites	2	5
Vanilla crème anglaise (see page 550)	400 ml	900 ml

energy	cal	fat	sat fat	carb	sugar	protein	fibre
1620 kJ	387 kcal	21.4 g	11.0 g	39.7 g	30.6 g	11.0 g	0.4 g

METHOD OF WORK

1 Preheat the oven to 150 °C and lightly butter and sugar each individual dariole mould.

2 Cream together the butter and sugar and slowly combine the flour into the mixture. This is sometimes referred to as a panada.

3 Split the vanilla pod and place into a saucepan with the milk, bring to the boil.

4 Add the boiled milk to the panada and return to the stove. Cook out the mixture, stirring all the time until the mixture leaves the sides of the saucepan.

5 Remove the vanilla pod, wash and dry it then cut fine julienne strips with a sharp knife. Dust each pod with icing sugar and place onto a silicone baking mat. Place into the oven to further dry out each strip of vanilla to a crisp. This should take approximately 20 minutes.

6 After the panada has cooled, gradually add the egg yolks.

7 Whisk the egg whites to a peak with a pinch of salt and sugar to help stabilize the aeration.

8 Carefully fold in the egg whites one-third at a time.

9 Deposit the mixture into the prepared dariole moulds, place into a bain-marie and bake in the preheated oven for approximately 30 minutes.

10 Remove from the oven when cooked and de-mould each pudding to serve.

11 Place the pudding onto a plate with two dried vanilla strands behind the pudding and serve immediately the warm crème anglaise around it.

CHEF'S TIP Derivatives for this basic recipe are:

- Pudding soufflé Saxon: mix the vanilla pudding recipe with grated zest of lemon and finish as the vanilla recipe.
- Pudding soufflé Rothschild: vanilla pudding recipe mixed with candied fruits and square-cut lady finger biscuits soaked in curaçao and served with a kirsch flavoured apricot sauce.
- Pudding soufflé Suchard: substitute cocoa powder for some of the flour and addition of some melted chocolate to the panada. Serve with a chocolate sauce.

Beignets soufflés (Soufflé fritters)

Ingredients	4 portions	10 portions
Choux paste (see page 470)	350 ml	750 ml
Powdered cinnamon	5 g	10 g
Caster sugar	100 g	240 g
Apricot sauce		
Apricot jam	250 g	500 g
Water	50 ml	100 ml
Kirsch	12 ml	25 ml

energy	cal	fat	sat fat	carb	sugar	protein	fibre
1991 kJ	471 kcal	12.7 g	6.8 g	86.6 g	73.2 g	6.2 g	2.7 g

METHOD OF WORK

1 Using two dessert spoons, mould quenelles of the choux paste and put into a deep fat fryer set at a minimum of 150 °C.

2 Allow to fry until golden brown and cooked, this can take up to 10 minutes. Turn the beignets over from time to time to ensure even cooking.

3 Remove from the hot fat and drain well on a kitchen paper towel. Immediately place them into a tray with the caster sugar and cinnamon powder that has been mixed together well.

4 To make the apricot sauce: place the apricot jam in a saucepan with the water and slowly bring to the boil. Allow to simmer for 5 minutes. Pass through a fine strainer and add the kirsch just before serving.

5 Serve the beignets on a dish paper on a flat dish accompanied by a sauceboat of the apricot sauce.

CHEF'S TIP There are classical variations of this recipe such as Beignets soufflés Parisienne which has the beignets filled with rum flavoured crème pâtissière and dusted with icing sugar and Beignets soufflés Dijonaise which has the beignets filled with a blackcurrant jam and served with crème anglaise.

Crêpes

Ingredients	4 portions	10 portions
Soft white flour (sieved)	120 g	250 g
Caster sugar	10 g	30 g
Good quality salt	3 g	5 g
Whole eggs	2	4
Fresh full fat milk	400 ml	700 ml
Melted butter	30 g	60 g

energy	cal	fat	sat fat	carb	sugar	protein	fibre
1125 kJ	269 kcal	13.0 g	7.2 g	29.0 g	7.6 g	9.2 g	0.9 g

METHOD OF WORK

1 Combine the flour, salt and sugar and slowly beat in the eggs.

2 Stir in one-third of the milk and beat to a smooth paste.

3 Add the rest of the milk and melted butter and leave to rest in a refrigerator for one hour before using.

4 Stir the batter, and pass through a fine strainer.

5 Add a little sunflower or vegetable oil to a dry and cleaned crêpe pan and heat on the stove.

6 Pour a little of the batter into the crêpe pan so that it just covers the base and is as thin as you can possibly make it. Cook for approximately 1½ minutes on each side with a little colour.

7 Place each cooked crêpe in between small sheets of silicone paper to retain the soft texture and keep warm until needed.

CHEF'S TIP Ideally crêpes are best when they are freshly made and served immediately, but they can be satisfactorily made in bulk by placing them on top of one another separated by a small sheet of baking parchment or silicone paper. They should be covered to prevent drying out and kept slightly warm.

Crêpe parisienne with strawberry compôte
(Crêpes Parisienne avec compôte de fraises)

Ingredients	4 portions	10 portions
Fresh strawberries	450 g	1 kg
Caster sugar	150 g	350 g
Lemon juice	¼ lemon	½ lemon
Water	75 ml	150 ml
Crêpes (see page 542)	4 large or 8 small	10 large or 20 small
Brandy	25 ml	50 ml
Vanilla macaroons	10 small	25 small

energy	cal	fat	sat fat	carb	sugar	protein	fibre
4134 kJ	982 kcal	34.3 g	8.9 g	149.8 g	126.8 g	22.5 g	5.4 g

METHOD OF WORK

To prepare the crêpes

1 Prepare the crêpe mixture as stated in the recipe (page 542). Stir the batter, adding the brandy at the same time and pass through a fine chinois.

2 Add a little sunflower or vegetable oil to a crêpe pan and heat. Chop the vanilla macaroons into small pieces (leave aside one macaroon per portion for decoration).

3 Ladle a little of the batter into the crêpe pan, sprinkle over the small pieces of macaroons. Cook for approximately one and a half minutes on each side with a little colour.

4 Place each cooked crêpe in between small sheets of silicone paper to retain the soft texture and keep warm until needed.

5 To prepare the strawberry compôte, wash and hull the strawberries, cutting any large ones to maintain a uniform size. Add the strawberries to a saucepan with all the other ingredients. Begin to cook slowly until the strawberries are cooked but still hold their shape. Reserve to one side to keep warm.

6 Using two small or one large crêpe per portion, spoon some of the strawberry compote into the middle of each and gently roll into a cigar shape or cornet shape.

7 Serve immediately by dusting each crêpe with icing sugar and place into the centre of a plate with any remaining liquor from the compôte. You can also add a serving of crème Chantilly to accompany alongside the remaining vanilla macaroons for decoration.

CHEF'S TIP Use a good crêpe pan with a heavy base to help ensure even cooking of the crêpe. If it is a new pan then you will need to 'season' it before using by washing and drying it first before placing onto a low heat for about five minutes. Wipe some vegetable oil into the pan using a kitchen cloth and let it cool down before wiping out the oil with a clean cloth. Now you can reheat the pan and use as required.

Crêpes normande (Crêpes with apple)

Ingredients	4 portions	10 portions
Apples	200 g	450 g
Caster sugar	75 g	120 g
Butter	25 g	50 g
Cinnamon powder	1 g	3 g
Crêpes (see page 542)	8 small crêpes	20 small crêpes

energy	cal	fat	sat fat	carb	sugar	protein	fibre
1699 kJ	405 kcal	18.1 g	10.4 g	53.0 g	31.7 g	9.3 g	1.8 g

METHOD OF WORK

1 Make the crêpes as described in recipe.

2 Wash and core the apples, leave the peel on if preferred and slice the apples thinly.

3 Melt the butter in a sauteuse and when hot, add the apple, cinnamon powder and sugar.

4 Cook quickly and when the apple is cooked remove the apple and set to one side. Continue cooking with the rest of the sauce and fold the warm crêpes in quarters arranging on a service plate.

5 When the sauce has started to caramelize a little, add the apples back to the sauce to warm through and then spoon over the top of the crêpes and serve.

Vanilla rice pudding with rhubarb compôte

Ingredients	4 portions	10 portions
Rice pudding		
Fresh full fat milk	500 ml	1.25 litres
Caster sugar	60 g	150 g
Vanilla pod	1	2
Short grain pudding rice	50 g	125 g
Salted butter	25 g	60 g
Double cream	50 ml	125 ml
Egg yolk (optional)	1	2
Rhubarb compôte		
Fresh rhubarb	450 g	1 kg
Caster sugar	150 g	350 g
Orange zest	¼ orange	½ orange

energy	cal	fat	sat fat	carb	sugar	protein	fibre
1903 kJ	453 kcal	18.2 g	11.0 g	69.1 g	61.8 g	6.7 g	1.6 g

METHOD OF WORK

1 For the rhubarb compôte, wash, trim and slice the rhubarb. Place all the compôte ingredients into a saucepan; slowly stew until the rhubarb has cooked.

2 Remove from the heat, reserve and keep warm.

3 For the vanilla rice pudding, wash the rice in salted water and drain. Bring the milk to the boil and then add the rice, sugar and split vanilla pod.

4 Simmer gently, stirring frequently until the rice is cooked and the liquid has thickened.

5 Remove the vanilla pod. Stir in the butter and cream to correct the consistency.

6 Serve with the warm rhubarb compôte.

CHEF'S TIP When cooking the rice pudding stir frequently to prevent the bottom of the pan from burning.

Apple charlotte *(Charlotte aux pommes)*

Ingredients	4 portions	10 portions
Dessert apples	960 g	2.4 kg
Sliced white bread, slightly stale	450 g	1.1 kg
Caster sugar	180 g	350 g
Melted butter	240 g	500 g
Grated lemon zest	1 lemon	2 lemons
Whole clove	1	2
Crème anglaise to accompany (see page 550)	300 ml	700 ml

energy	cal	fat	sat fat	carb	sugar	protein	fibre
4454 kJ	1062 kcal	57.0 g	34.0 g	132.2 g	84.1 g	13.6 g	6.7 g

METHOD OF WORK

1 Preheat an oven to 220 °C.

2 Wash, peel and core the apples. Cut into fairly thick slices and place into a saucepan with the sugar, one-quarter of the butter, the finely grated zest of lemon and the clove.

3 Do not add any water, gently stew the apples until they are just cooked and still maintain their shape.

4 Take the slices of bread and remove the crusts. Cut out discs (one to fit the top and bottom of the pudding mould). Cut the remaining bread slices into strips up to 25 mm wide.

5 Melt the remaining butter, brush one side of a disc and place into the bottom of a pudding mould. Brush the strips in the same way and place them vertically around the sides of the mould, overlapping without leaving any gaps. Press gently to the sides.

6 Remove the clove from the apple preparation and fill the centre of the mould with the cooked apple.

7 Cover with a disc of bread on top and press down firmly. Place into the preheated oven to bake for approximately 30 minutes, until the bread lining is golden coloured and crisp.

8 Allow to cool slightly before turning out onto a plate and serving with a warm crème anglaise.

CHEF'S TIP Using dessert apples such as Braeburn will produce a more stable cooked apple than using traditional cooking apples. If the apples used are full of water and the apple preparation is slightly thin, it may be stiffened by adding breadcrumbs to the mixture.

CHEF'S TIP Use wholemeal bread instead of white to increase the fibre content of this dessert.

Cut into fairly thick slices and place into a saucepan with the sugar, one quarter of the butter, the finely grated zest of the lemon and the clove.

Vanilla soufflé *(Soufflé a la vanille)*

Ingredients	4 portions	10 portions
Melted butter (for the moulds)	25 g	80 g
Caster sugar (for the moulds)	50 g	120 g
Fresh milk	125 ml	300 ml
Vanilla pod	1 pod	2 pods
Egg yolks	4	10
Egg whites	4	10
Salt	Small pinch	Small pinch
Strong flour	10 g	25 g
Caster sugar	50 g	125 g
Icing sugar for dusting		

energy	cal	fat	sat fat	carb	sugar	protein	fibre
1052 kJ	250 kcal	10.9 g	5.1 g	32.3 g	30.4 g	7.8 g	0.2 g

METHOD OF WORK

1 Lightly brush the inside of the ramekin dishes with melted butter using upward strokes. Apply a coating of caster sugar on top of the butter and shake out the excess sugar.

2 Bring the milk to the boil with the vanilla pod that has been split lengthways and had the seeds scraped out into the milk.

3 Mix half of the egg yolks with the strong flour and caster sugar to a smooth consistency in a mixing bowl.

4 Add the boiled vanilla milk to the mixture; stir well until the mixture is completely incorporated.

5 Return the mixture to a clean saucepan and set over a gentle heat to cook out while continuously stirring with a wooden spoon. Mix thoroughly. Preheat an oven to 220 °C.

6 Aerate the egg whites with a small pinch of salt and just before serving carefully fold the egg whites into the vanilla preparation. Mix the egg whites into the preparation in three stages to help the consistency of the soufflé mixture to remain light and airy.

7 Spoon the mixture into the prepared ramekin dishes, level with the top of the dish. Smooth off the top with a palette knife and run your thumb around the edge of the dish to help to facilitate the rising of the soufflé when it is in the oven.

8 Place the soufflés onto a baking sheet and position the tray into the centre of the oven. The baking time should be between 15 and 20 minutes depending on the size of the soufflé.

9 Remove carefully from the oven, dust quickly with icing sugar and serve immediately.

CHEF'S TIP   A hot soufflé must not be allowed to stand once it has been removed from the oven because it will eventually sink. It is important to send the soufflé to the customer as quickly as possible. The use of a pinch of dried egg white can be added to the fresh egg white to help strengthen and stabilize the aeration process.

CHEF'S TIP   Soufflé puddings are different to normal soufflés because they have a stronger consistency and are able to stand for a while in a bain-marie prior to service without collapsing. They are always turned out of their moulds for service as opposed to a normal soufflé which is always served in a mould or dish that it has been cooked in.

Chocolate soufflé *(Soufflé au chocolat)*

Ingredients	4 portions	10 portions
Melted butter (for the moulds)	25 g	80 g
Cocoa powder (for the moulds)	50 g	120 g
Fresh milk	125 ml	300 ml
Dark chocolate, grated (60%)	40 g	100 g
Egg yolks	4	10
Egg whites	5	11
Salt	Small pinch	Small pinch
Strong flour	10 g	25 g
Caster sugar	50 g	125 g
Cocoa powder for dusting		

energy	cal	fat	sat fat	carb	sugar	protein	fibre
1227 kJ	294 kcal	18.3 g	6.8 g	21.2 g	14.7 g	12.2 g	4.0 g

METHOD OF WORK

1 Lightly brush the inside of the ramekin dishes with melted butter using upward strokes. Apply a coating of cocoa powder on top of the butter and shake out the excess powder.

2 Bring the milk to the boil and add the grated chocolate.

3 Mix half of the egg yolks with the strong flour and caster sugar to a smooth consistency in a mixing bowl.

4 Add the boiled chocolate milk to the mixture; stir well until the mixture is completely incorporated.

5 Return the mixture to a clean saucepan and set over a gentle heat to cook out while continuously stirring with a wooden spoon. Mix thoroughly. Preheat an oven to 220 °C.

6 Aerate the egg whites with a small pinch of salt and just before serving carefully fold the egg whites into the chocolate preparation. Mix the egg whites into the preparation in three stages to help the consistency of the soufflé mixture to remain light and airy.

7 Spoon the mixture into the prepared ramekin dishes, level with the top of the dish. Smooth off the top with a palette knife and run your thumb around the edge of the dish to help to facilitate the rising of the soufflé when it is in the oven.

8 Place the soufflés onto a baking sheet and position the tray into the centre of the oven. The baking time should be between 15 and 20 minutes depending on the size of the soufflé.

9 Remove carefully from the oven, dust quickly with cocoa powder and serve immediately.

Baked Alaska with kirsch *(Omelette en surprise Norvégienne)*

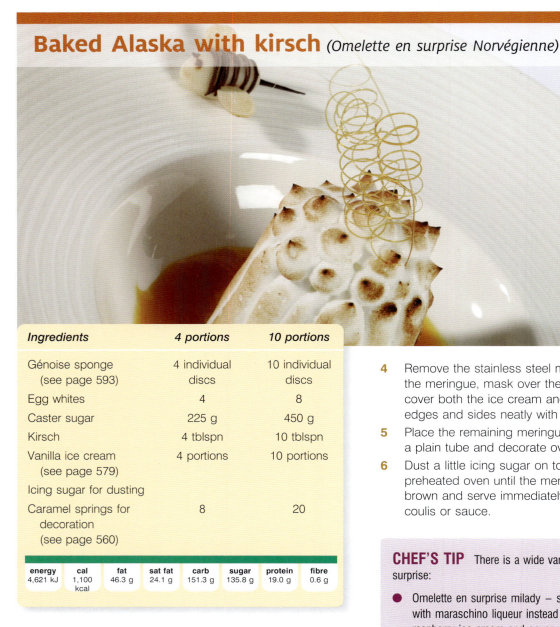

Ingredients	4 portions	10 portions
Génoise sponge (see page 593)	4 individual discs	10 individual discs
Egg whites	4	8
Caster sugar	225 g	450 g
Kirsch	4 tblspn	10 tblspn
Vanilla ice cream (see page 579)	4 portions	10 portions
Icing sugar for dusting		
Caramel springs for decoration (see page 560)	8	20

energy	cal	fat	sat fat	carb	sugar	protein	fibre
4,621 kJ	1,100 kcal	46.3 g	24.1 g	151.3 g	135.8 g	19.0 g	0.6 g

METHOD OF WORK

1 Arrange the Génoise sponge discs onto an ovenproof dish or baking sheet.

2 Sprinkle the kirsch over the Génoise and mould the ice cream into stainless steel rings and place on top of the sponge discs. Set in a freezer until required.

3 Place the egg whites into a clean mixing bowl, add a pinch of salt and whisk to a stiff peak. Whisk in half the caster sugar keeping the meringue stiff and then fold in the remaining sugar. Preheat an oven to 230 °C.

4 Remove the stainless steel mould and then using ¾ of the meringue, mask over the ice cream to completely cover both the ice cream and the sponge. Smooth the edges and sides neatly with a palette knife.

5 Place the remaining meringue into a piping bag with a plain tube and decorate over.

6 Dust a little icing sugar on top and place into the preheated oven until the meringue has coloured golden brown and serve immediately with an appropriate fruit coulis or sauce.

CHEF'S TIP   There is a wide variety of omelettes en surprise:

- Omelette en surprise milady – sprinkle the génoise with maraschino liqueur instead of kirsch, use raspberry ice cream and cover with poached peach halves.
- Omelette en surprise milord – which is the same as Norvégienne, but with poached halves of pears covering the vanilla ice cream.
- Omelette en surprise bresilienne – which uses coffee ice cream and dark rum.

Cabinet pudding

Ingredients	4 portions	10 portions
Sponge fingers or brioche	100 g	250 g
Kirsch	10 ml	30 ml
Glacé cherries, chopped	30 g	75 g
Sultanas	20 g	40 g
Currants	20 g	40 g
Butter (for lining)	10 g	25 g
Caster sugar (for lining)	10 g	25 g
Fresh milk	400 ml	1 litre
Vanilla pod or extract	1 pod	2 pods
Eggs (medium sized)	3	6
Caster sugar	40 g	100 g

energy	cal	fat	sat fat	carb	sugar	protein	fibre
1213 kJ	287 kcal	9.0 g	3.9 g	42.2 g	40.2 g	10.4 g	0.5 g

4 Pass the custard through a fine strainer and fill the moulds almost to the top. Preheat an oven to 170 °C.

5 Place the moulds into a deep baking tray and half fill the tray with warm water. Put into the preheated oven and cook for approximately 30 minutes.

6 When cooked, leave to set for three minutes before de-moulding onto a serving plate and serve with crème anglaise or a hot apricot sauce.

CHEF'S TIP Diplomat pudding is the same recipe as cabinet pudding but it is served cold with either an apricot, redcurrant, raspberry or vanilla sauce.

METHOD OF WORK

1 Cut the sponge fingers or brioche into 5 mm cubes and mix with the fruits and macerate with the kirsch.

2 Butter and sugar the dariole moulds and place an equal quantity of the fruit and sponge in each.

3 Place the milk and vanilla in a saucepan and warm. Mix the eggs and sugar in a bowl and add the milk while still mixing.

Sauces and decorations for desserts

Crème anglaise and derivatives *(English custard sauce)*

Left – Crème angalise, Right – Chocolate sauce

Ingredients	4 portions	10 portions
Full fat fresh milk	500 ml	1.25 litres
Egg yolks	6	15
Caster sugar	75 g	150 g
Vanilla pod	1	2

energy	cal	fat	sat fat	carb	sugar	protein	fibre
1017 kJ	243 kcal	12.7 g	5.4 g	25.4 g	25.3 g	8.2 g	0.0 g

METHOD OF WORK

1   Place the milk into a heavy-bottomed saucepan with one tablespoon of the sugar (this will help to prevent the milk from boiling over).

2   Split the vanilla pod in half lengthways and scrape the seeds from within the pod into the milk. Add the vanilla pod too. Slowly bring the milk to the boil.

3   Meanwhile, using a whisk beat the egg yolks and caster sugar together in a large bowl until pale in colour.

4   At boiling point, remove from the heat and carefully pour it onto the egg yolk mixture, stirring constantly.

5   Return this mixture to the saucepan and cook on a low heat, stirring continuously with a wooden spoon until the sauce thickens enough to coat the back of the spoon. Draw a finger down the back of the spoon to see if an impression has been formed.

6   Alternatively, use a thermometer and ensure that the sauce has been cooked to 85 °C.

7   Remove the saucepan from the heat and strain through a fine strainer into a chilled bowl to prevent the sauce from cooking further and thus overcooking the eggs. Chill until required or serve warm.

CHEF'S TIP If the crème is heated over 86 °C it will begin to curdle the egg content and the emulsion of fat (egg yolk) and water (milk) will be broken down. One way of reversing this is to immediately pour the hot curdled mixture into a food blender and blend for 60 seconds. Then pass the crème through a fine strainer.

CHEF'S TIP Crème anglaise is used to accompany hot desserts as a hot custard sauce or cold desserts as a cold sauce. It is a versatile basic preparation that is used to produce a variety of desserts such as ice cream, bavarois and some mousses. Various flavours can be added to this crème as shown below:

White chocolate Add 50 g of good white chocolate to the milk of the four-portion recipe.

Mint Infuse a few mint leaves in the milk and finely chop some fresh mint to add the sauce at the last moment just before serving.

Coffee Add a dessert spoon of granulated coffee to the milk as it has been brought to the boil. Adjust for flavour and add more if requiring a stronger flavour.

Lavender Infuse some lavender seeds of clean flowers in the milk before passing through a fine strainer.

Orange Add the finely grated zest of 1 orange to the milk. Finish with a little Grand Marnier to add flavour.

Brandy Add a little brandy after cooking to flavour the sauce and serve with Christmas pudding.

At boiling point, remove the milk from the heat and carefully pour it onto the egg yolk mixture.

Draw a finger down the back of the spoon to see if an impression has been formed.

Custard sauce

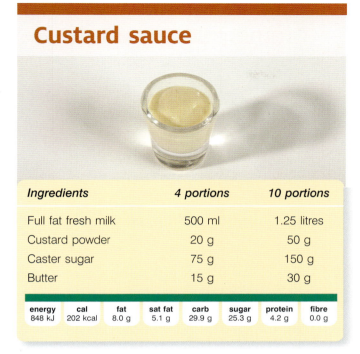

Ingredients	4 portions	10 portions
Full fat fresh milk	500 ml	1.25 litres
Custard powder	20 g	50 g
Caster sugar	75 g	150 g
Butter	15 g	30 g

energy	cal	fat	sat fat	carb	sugar	protein	fibre
848 kJ	202 kcal	8.0 g	5.1 g	29.9 g	25.3 g	4.2 g	0.0 g

METHOD OF WORK

1 Dilute the custard powder with a little of the milk.

2 Bring the remaining milk to the boil with the caster sugar.

3 Pour a little of the boiled milk onto the diluted custard powder and mix well before adding this back to the boiled milk.

4 Bring back to the boil while constantly boiling. Add the butter at the last moment and pass through a fine strainer before serving.

Stock syrup

Left – Spiced stock syrup, Right – Unflavoured stock syrup

Ingredients	750 ml	1½ litres
Granulated sugar	500 g	1 kg
Water	500 g	1 kg
Liquid glucose	50 g	100 g
Cinnamon, star anise, bay-leaf, ginger and cloves can also be added to create a spiced stock syrup		

energy	cal	fat	sat fat	carb	sugar	protein	fibre
363 kJ	85 kcal	0.0 g	0.0 g	22.7 g	21.8 g	0.0 g	0.0 g

METHOD OF WORK

1 Place the sugar and water into a heavy-based saucepan and heat slowly until the sugar has dissolved.

2 Bring the liquid to the boil and add the glucose at boiling point. Boil for a further 4 minutes and remove from the heat.

3 Cool the liquid and pour into a sterilized plastic container with a tight-fitting lid. This syrup will keep for up to 3 weeks in a refrigerator.

HEALTH & SAFETY The use of liquid glucose will help to prolong the shelf life of the stock syrup because it helps to prohibit re-crystallization of the sugar. The use of honey can help to prevent re-crystallization but it will also add flavour and colour to the stock syrup.

CHEF'S TIP It is easier to make plain stock syrup for use in the kitchen as this recipe can always have flavours such as lemon, coffee, alcohol, cinnamon and orange added as you require. For less intense stock syrup, decrease the sugar content by half. This can be used for moistening fresh fruit salads and poaching soft fruits such as strawberries, raspberries and blackberries.

Fruit coulis

Coulis from left to right; mango, raspberry, kiwi, blackcurrant

Ingredients	750 ml	1½ litres
Fruit purée or fresh fruit	800 g	1.7 kg
Stock syrup (see page 551)	200 ml	425 ml
Lemon juice	1 lemon	2 lemons

energy	cal	fat	sat fat	carb	sugar	protein	fibre
202 kJ	47 kcal	0.1 g	0.0 g	11.8 g	11.5 g	0.6 g	0.9 g

METHOD OF WORK

1   Carefully wash the whole fruit if using fresh fruit and place into a food blender with the strained lemon juice and blend to a purée. Alternatively, if using a convenience fruit purée add this to the food blender.

2   Add the stock syrup. Blend the fruit mixture for approximately a minute until a smooth purée has been obtained.

3   Pass the purée through a fine chinois or muslin cloth and correct the consistency by adding more stock syrup or fruit purée.

4   The coulis is now ready for use and will keep for up to 3–4 days in a refrigerator.

CHEF'S TIP   You can replace the use of stock syrup for pure apple juice to create a healthy alternative to using refined sugar. However, this will have an effect on the overall flavour combination of the coulis. Using this uncooked recipe will maintain the qualities and basic vitamin content of the fresh fruit used.

Crème pâtissière *(Pastry cream)*

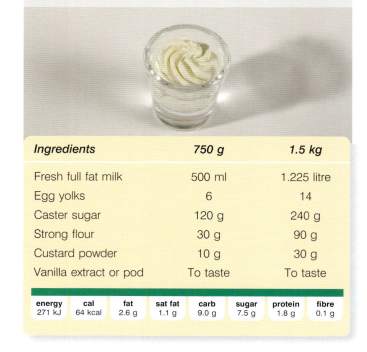

Ingredients	750 g	1.5 kg
Fresh full fat milk	500 ml	1.225 litre
Egg yolks	6	14
Caster sugar	120 g	240 g
Strong flour	30 g	90 g
Custard powder	10 g	30 g
Vanilla extract or pod	To taste	To taste

energy	cal	fat	sat fat	carb	sugar	protein	fibre
271 kJ	64 kcal	2.6 g	1.1 g	9.0 g	7.5 g	1.8 g	0.1 g

METHOD OF WORK

1   Place the egg yolks and two-thirds of the sugar into a bowl and beat using a whisk until the mixture is pale in colour.

2   Sieve the flour and custard powder together and add to the egg yolk mixture.

3   Combine the milk and the remaining sugar with the vanilla extract and slowly bring to the boil.

4   Carefully pour the hot milk onto the egg yolk preparation and stir in well. Return to the pan and cook over a gentle heat, stirring continuously.

5   Cook out the crème until it thickens and it has lost its raw flour taste. Pour it into a chilled bowl or tray and dust the top with icing sugar to prevent it from forming a skin on the top. As it cools, cover with plastic film.

6   Store in a refrigerator for further use. If stored in the correct environment it will keep for up to 4 days.

CHEF'S TIP   Classical derivatives of crème pâtissière are:

- Crème chiboust – with the addition of an equal quantity of Italian meringue.
- Crème mousseline – with the addition of unsalted butter at room temperature.
- Crème diplomat – with the addition of an equal quantity of freshly whipped cream.

Crème Chantilly

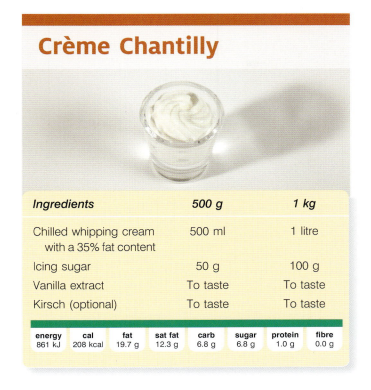

Ingredients	500 g	1 kg
Chilled whipping cream with a 35% fat content	500 ml	1 litre
Icing sugar	50 g	100 g
Vanilla extract	To taste	To taste
Kirsch (optional)	To taste	To taste

energy	cal	fat	sat fat	carb	sugar	protein	fibre
861 kJ	208 kcal	19.7 g	12.3 g	6.8 g	6.8 g	1.0 g	0.0 g

METHOD OF WORK

1 Ensure that the whipping cream, mixing bowl and whisk is well chilled (it is advisable to place the equipment in a refrigerator 30 minutes before use to help stabilize the aeration procedure).

2 Place the cream, sugar and flavourings into the bowl and slowly aerate until a dropping or piping consistency has been obtained.

3 Use the crème Chantilly as soon as it is made; however, it can be kept in an airtight container in a refrigerator for up to 12 hours.

CHEF'S TIP Crème Chantilly is used predominantly as an accompaniment to meringues, bavarois, ice creams and various desserts. Although the name is derived from the château of Chantilly, where the reputation of the fine cuisine of Chef Vatel in the seventeenth century enjoyed adulation, none of the preparations named after it were actually created there.

Dark chocolate sauce (Sauce au chocolat)

Ingredients	600 g	1.2 kg
Fresh full fat milk	250 g	500 g
Dark chocolate (50% minimum cocoa)	300 g	600 g
Whipping cream	125 g	250 g
Unsalted butter	30 g	60 g
Icing sugar	50 g	100 g

energy	cal	fat	sat fat	carb	sugar	protein	fibre
475 kJ	115 kcal	9.1 g	2.2 g	6.7 g	2.8 g	1.7 g	0.0 g

METHOD OF WORK

1 Chop the chocolate into small pieces and place into a heavy-bottomed saucepan with the milk and the cream.

2 Slowly bring the liquid to the boil, stirring occasionally to prevent burning.

3 Remove from the heat and stir in the icing sugar and the butter. Pass through a fine sieve into a bowl and cool immediately.

CHEF'S TIP Cool the chocolate sauce down to 4 °C within one hour of production. Place it into an airtight plastic container and refrigerate. This sauce will keep for up to 3 days if correctly stored. To help maintain its liquid consistency during storage a little (up to 50 g) glucose can be added to the milk before boiling.

Butterscotch sauce

Ingredients	600 g	1.2 kg
Unsalted butter	100 g	200 g
Caster sugar	125 g	250 g
Demerara sugar	125 g	250 g
Golden syrup	100 g	200 g
Double cream	400 ml	1 litre

energy	cal	fat	sat fat	carb	sugar	protein	fibre
700 kJ	168 kcal	12.4 g	7.7 g	14.6 g	14.3 g	0.3 g	0.0 g

METHOD OF WORK

1   Melt the butter in a heavy-bottomed saucepan.

2   Add the caster sugar, demerara sugar and golden syrup and slowly bring to the boil. Stir occasionally.

3   Simmer the sugar solution until an amber colour has been obtained, this should take approximately 4 to 5 minutes.

4   Remove from the heat and very carefully add the double cream.

5   Stir well and place back onto a medium flame to bring back to the boil.

6   Simmer for 3 minutes then pass through a fine sieve into a bowl and cool immediately.

CHEF'S TIP   This butterscotch sauce can be used for the sticky toffee pudding recipe. It can also be used hot or cold as a sauce to accompany many desserts and ice creams. To check the consistency simply add a little more cream if too thick or heat the sauce and reduce a little if it is too thin.

HEALTH & SAFETY   When adding the double cream to the boiling sugar great care must be taken. Remove the pan from the heat and add a small stream of cream to start with as the molten sugar will bubble. Stir the rest in with a wooden spoon as this will help to arrest the temperature of the sugar.

Caramel sauce *(Sauce au caramel)*

Ingredients	4 portions	10 portions
Granulated sugar	50 g	100 g
Water	25 ml	60 ml
Liquid glucose	20 g	40 g
Double cream	250 ml	500 ml
Vanilla extract		

energy	cal	fat	sat fat	carb	sugar	protein	fibre
1559 kJ	377 kcal	33.6 g	20.9 g	18.5 g	16.3 g	1.0 g	0.0 g

METHOD OF WORK

1   Dissolve the sugar in a saucepan with the water over a low heat before then turning up the heat and bringing to the boil.

2   Add the glucose at boiling point and wash down the sides of the saucepan with a clean pastry brush dipped in cold water to help prevent sugar crystals from forming.

3   Cook until the sugar turns a deep amber colour. Immediately remove from the heat and carefully add the cream.

4   Set the saucepan back onto the stove and bring back to the boil while constantly stirring. Simmer for two minutes.

5   Pass through a fine strainer and use or store as required.

Chocolate ganache

Ingredients	350 g	700 g
Double cream	150 ml	300 ml
Liquid glucose	20 g	40 g
Dark chocolate (minimum 60%)	300 g	600 g
Vanilla pod or extract	½ pod	1 pod
Unsalted butter (optional)	30 g	75 g

energy	cal	fat	sat fat	carb	sugar	protein	fibre
1614 kJ	390 kcal	34.2 g	9.4 g	16.2 g	1.5 g	4.5 g	0.0 g

METHOD OF WORK

1 Cut the chocolate into small pieces.

2 Bring the cream to the boil with the vanilla and the glucose in a saucepan.

3 Place the dark chocolate into a bowl and create a well in the centre, slowly pour in the boiled cream together with the vanilla.

4 Whisk the chocolate into the cream until the chocolate has melted and has emulsified with the cream to form a stable mixture.

5 Finally remove the vanilla pod and beat in the unsalted butter if required.

CHEF'S TIP This ganache recipe is used for fillings, gateaux, torten and desserts and is able to take additional flavourings such as orange, lime, coffee and praline.

Fruit crisps

Ingredients	20–30 crisps
Stock syrup (see page 551)	200 ml
Fruit of choice; apples, strawberries, peeled pineapple, pears, oranges, lemons or mangoes	
Lemon juice	½ lemon

energy	cal	fat	sat fat	carb	sugar	protein	fibre
115 kJ	27 kcal	0.0 g	0.0 g	7.1 g	6.9 g	0.0 g	0.2 g

METHOD OF WORK

1 Preheat the oven to below 100 °C.

2 Carefully select the chosen fruit and ensure there are no blemishes or bruising to the flesh. With the exception of mango and pineapple, there is no need to peel the fruit.

3 Slice the fruit very thinly on a mandolin and sprinkle lemon juice over it as quickly as possible.

4 Place the fruit slices to soak in a shallow tray of the stock syrup for approximately ½ a minute before shaking off the excess syrup and carefully placing the slices onto a baking sheet lined with a silicone baking mat.

5 Place into the oven with the door left slightly open.

6 Always check the fruit slices and turn each one over after approximately 1 hour. Leave in the oven for a further hour. The slices are ready when they begin to feel firm, they will become completely crisp once the fruit has cooled.

7 Place in an airtight container for storage. These fruit slices can last for up to one week if they have been properly dried out.

Bubble sugar

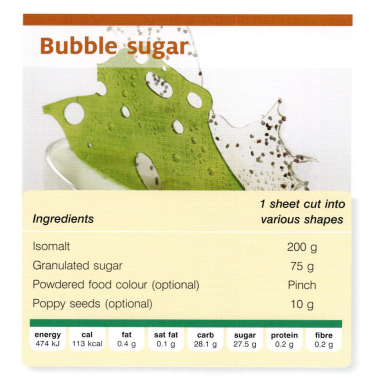

Ingredients	1 sheet cut into various shapes
Isomalt	200 g
Granulated sugar	75 g
Powdered food colour (optional)	Pinch
Poppy seeds (optional)	10 g

energy	cal	fat	sat fat	carb	sugar	protein	fibre
474 kJ	113 kcal	0.4 g	0.1 g	28.1 g	27.5 g	0.2 g	0.2 g

METHOD OF WORK

1   Lay a silicone baking mat onto a baking sheet and preheat the oven to 220 °C.

2   Place the isomalt and sugar into a plastic cup with a tight-fitting lid and add the powdered colour. Shake well to disperse the colour throughout the isomalt.

3   Sprinkle the isomalt over the silicone baking mat and place another silicone mat on top. Place in the oven to melt the Isomalt crystals.

4   Peel back the top silicone mat to check that the isomalt has melted (it should have melted and bubbled after nearly 10 minutes in the hot oven). Remove from the oven and leave to set. While the bubble sugar is still plastic, cut off small pieces and leave to harden in a cool, dry place.

5   Place in an airtight container for storage in a cold, dry area and use as required.

CHEF'S TIP   Another variation is to remove the food colouring and add the poppy seeds to give a speckled effect. Other seeds and edible flower petals such as lavender or herbs such as mint can be used too.

Preserved vanilla sticks

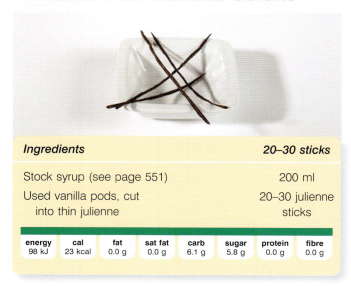

Ingredients	20–30 sticks
Stock syrup (see page 551)	200 ml
Used vanilla pods, cut into thin julienne	20–30 julienne sticks

energy	cal	fat	sat fat	carb	sugar	protein	fibre
98 kJ	23 kcal	0.0 g	0.0 g	6.1 g	5.8 g	0.0 g	0.0 g

METHOD OF WORK

1   Preheat the oven to below 100 °C.

2   Carefully clean, dry and cut the vanilla pods into very thin julienne sticks.

3   Place the vanilla sticks to soak in a shallow tray of the stock syrup for approximately 30 seconds before shaking off the excess syrup and carefully placing the slices onto a baking sheet lined with a silicone baking mat.

4   Place in the oven with the door left slightly open.

5   Always check the vanilla sticks and turn each one over after approximately 20 minutes. Leave in the oven for a further hour. The vanilla sticks are ready when they begin to feel firm, they will become completely crisp once they have cooled.

6   Place in an airtight container for storage. These vanilla sticks can last for up to one week if they have been properly dried out.

WEB LINK   For further information on vanilla see **http://www.uni-graz.at/~katzer/engl /Vani_pla.html**

CHEF'S TIP   This is a resourceful way to employ vanilla pods once you have previously used them to flavour a preparation, sauce or dessert. An alternative use for used vanilla pods is to put them in a jar of caster sugar so that the still fragrant pod will transfer the vanilla scent to the sugar – thus creating vanilla sugar.

Chocolate acetate motifs

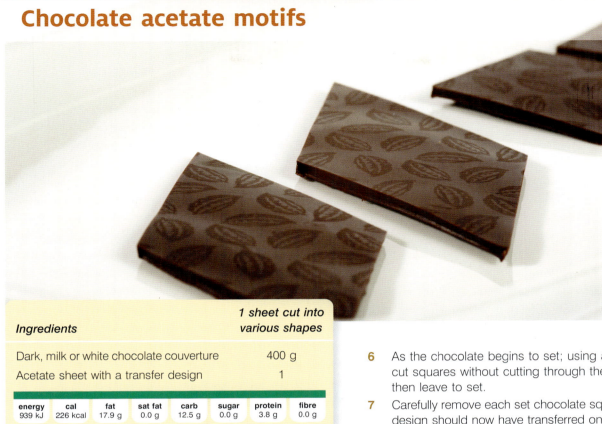

Ingredients	1 sheet cut into various shapes
Dark, milk or white chocolate couverture	400 g
Acetate sheet with a transfer design	1

energy	cal	fat	sat fat	carb	sugar	protein	fibre
939 kJ	226 kcal	17.9 g	0.0 g	12.5 g	0.0 g	3.8 g	0.0 g

METHOD OF WORK

1   Place the chopped couverture chocolate into a clean, dry plastic bowl and place into a microwave oven.

2   On the highest setting, heat the chocolate for 10 seconds only, remove from the microwave oven and stir with a clean plastic spoon.

3   Place back into the microwave and repeat this process until the chocolate begins to melt (never heat for more than 10 seconds otherwise the chocolate will overheat and can burn very easily).

4   When the majority of the chocolate is melted but there are still a few pieces left un-melted, continue stirring without heating in the microwave until the residual heat melts the remaining pieces.

5   Lay the acetate transfer side up and carefully spread the melted chocolate over it. Keep the chocolate quite thin and leave to cool down.

6   As the chocolate begins to set; using a sharp knife cut squares without cutting through the acetate and then leave to set.

7   Carefully remove each set chocolate square. The acetate design should now have transferred onto the chocolate.

8   Place in an airtight container for storage and use as required.

CHEF'S TIP   Using a microwave oven to melt chocolate is a quick way of ensuring that 'tempering' occurs without having to resort to alternative methods. Always ensure that the temperature of the chocolate does not exceed 37 °C and that the remaining pieces of chocolate melt slowly before using.

WEB LINK   For further information on purchasing chocolate acetate sheets contact
http://www.squires-shop.com

Chocolate shavings

Ingredients

Dark, milk or white chocolate couverture in block form	5 kg block

energy	cal	fat	sat fat	carb	sugar	protein	fibre
587 kJ	142 kcal	11.2 g	0.0 g	7.8 g	0.0 g	2.4 g	0.0 g

METHOD OF WORK

1   Two persons are required to create these simple shavings.

2   The first person firmly holds the chocolate block in place, keeping it steady all the time.

3   The second person holds a flexible knife and scrapes the side of the chocolate block back and forth to produce fine shavings of chocolate.

4   Place in an airtight container for storage in a freezer or a cold dry place and use as required.

CHEF'S TIP   Great care should be taken when using this technique. Sometimes it is safer to hold the block of chocolate with thick cloth to obtain a stronger grip and protect the hands. Alternatively if only one chef is able to carry out this task, use a vegetable peeler to run up and down the side of the chocolate rather than a knife.

Step-by-step: Making chocolate acetate motifs

1. Lay the acetate transfer side up and carefully spread the melted chocolate over it.

2. As the chocolate begins to set, using a sharp knife, cut squares without cutting through the acetate, then leave to set.

3. Carefully remove each set chocolate square. The acetate design should now have transferred onto the chocolate.

WEB LINK   For further information on chocolate see
www.barry-callebaut.com

Caramel and almond swirls

Ingredients	20
Granulated sugar	250 g
Water	100 g
Liquid glucose	50 g
Flaked almonds	100 g
Vegetable oil	50 ml

energy	cal	fat	sat fat	carb	sugar	protein	fibre
463 kJ	110 kcal	5.3 g	0.4 g	15.6 g	14.3 g	1.1 g	0.4 g

METHOD OF WORK

1 Lay a silicone baking mat onto a marble slab or stainless steel work surface. Alternatively, if a silicone baking mat is not available, wipe the vegetable oil onto a clean marble surface.

2 Place the sugar and the water into a heavy-based clean saucepan and leave to soak for five minutes.

3 Place the pan onto a medium heat and bring the sugar to the boil. Add the liquid glucose after the sugar has been boiling for 1 minute.

4 Meanwhile, place the flaked almonds onto a baking sheet and toast under a hot salamander until golden in colour. Reserve to one side to cool down.

5 Continue to boil the sugar until a light caramel colour has been achieved. Keep cleaning the inside of the saucepan walls with clean, cold water using a clean pastry brush. This will help to prevent sugar crystals from forming.

6 Remove the saucepan from the heat and arrest the cooking by plunging the pan into cold water for 10 seconds. Let the caramel stand for 2 minutes before using.

7 Sprinkle the flaked almonds over the prepared marble or silicone baking mat.

8 Dip a dessert spoon into the caramel and let a steady, thin stream of hot caramel fall from the spoon. Using this technique draw individual spirals of the streaming caramel onto the flaked almonds and leave to set. Carefully remove from the work surface as the caramel and almond swirls will be quite delicate.

9 Place in an airtight container for storage in a cold, dry area and use as required.

Carefully remove from the work surface

Pistachio caramel clusters

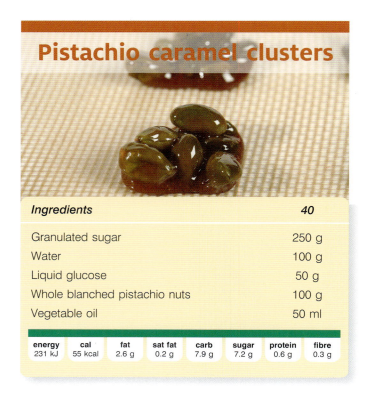

Ingredients	40
Granulated sugar	250 g
Water	100 g
Liquid glucose	50 g
Whole blanched pistachio nuts	100 g
Vegetable oil	50 ml

energy	cal	fat	sat fat	carb	sugar	protein	fibre
231 kJ	55 kcal	2.6 g	0.2 g	7.9 g	7.2 g	0.6 g	0.3 g

METHOD OF WORK

1 Lay a silicone baking mat onto a marble slab or stainless steel work surface. Alternatively, if a silicone baking mat is not available, wipe the vegetable oil onto a clean marble surface.

2 Place the sugar and the water into a heavy-based clean saucepan and leave to soak for five minutes.

3 Place the pan onto a medium heat and bring the sugar to the boil. Add the liquid glucose after the sugar has been boiling for 1 minute.

4 Meanwhile, place the whole blanched pistachio nuts onto a baking sheet and toast under a hot salamander until slightly golden in colour. Reserve to one side and cool down the pistachios.

5 Continue to boil the sugar until a light caramel colour has been achieved. Keep cleaning the inside of the saucepan walls with clean, cold water using a clean pastry brush. This will help to prevent sugar crystals from forming.

6 Remove the saucepan from the heat and arrest the cooking by plunging the pan into cold water for 10 seconds. Let the caramel stand for 2 minutes before using.

7 Place the pistachio nuts into the caramel.

8 Dip a dessert spoon into the caramel and spoon out the pistachio nuts covered in the caramel and place them in small clusters of about five or six nuts onto the prepared surface. Carefully remove from the work surface as the caramel and pistachio clusters will be quite delicate.

9 Place in an airtight container for storage in a cold, dry area and use as required.

Caramel springs

Ingredients	30
Granulated sugar	250 g
Water	100 g
Liquid glucose	50 g
Vegetable oil	25 ml

energy	cal	fat	sat fat	carb	sugar	protein	fibre
193 kJ	46 kcal	0.8 g	0.1 g	10.2 g	9.4 g	0.0 g	0.0 g

METHOD OF WORK

1 Lay a silicone baking mat onto a marble slab or stainless steel work surface. Alternatively, if a silicone baking mat is not available, wipe the vegetable oil onto a clean marble surface.

2 Place the sugar and the water into a heavy-based clean saucepan and leave to soak for five minutes.

3 Place the pan onto a medium heat and bring the sugar to the boil. Add the liquid glucose after the sugar has been boiling for 1 minute.

4 Meanwhile, lightly oil a round-bladed sharpening steel.

5 Continue to boil the sugar until a light caramel colour has been achieved. Keep cleaning the inside of the saucepan walls with clean, cold water using a clean pastry brush. This will help to prevent sugar crystals from forming.

6 Remove the saucepan from the heat and arrest the cooking by plunging the pan into cold water for 10 seconds. Let the caramel stand for 2 minutes before using.

7 Wait for the caramel to slightly thicken and cool.

8 Dip a dessert spoon into the caramel and place the spoon at the neck of the sharpening steel and encircle the steel with a line of caramel streaming from the spoon. The spring will form and set quite quickly. Carefully remove from the sharpening steel as the caramel springs will be very delicate.

9 Place in an airtight container for storage in a cold, dry area and use as required.

Introduction to cold desserts

In the majority of dessert menus and sweet trolleys cold desserts play a very significant role. We should not undermine the stature of hot desserts, tarts and various yeast-based desserts that have an important part to play in the constitution of a dessert menu. However, especially with the advent of modern cuisine, cold desserts are more popular with customers and often dominate most of today's dessert menus.

Advantages of using cold desserts

There are many advantages in the use of cold desserts, which will effect the chef's decision when planning a menu.

1   Colour – A variety of colours can be used to create a decorative dessert. For instance the utilization of the natural colour of fresh fruit without cooking, which can break down the fruit and lose the colour.

2   A large variety of different desserts – There is a huge range of different cold desserts to choose from and from different ethnic cultures and social and religious festivals. Therefore the chef is easily able to create a balanced menu.

3   Ease of storage – Most cold desserts are easily stored for two days either in the refrigerator at below 5 °C or frozen at below –18 °C for longer periods.

4   Ease of service – They can be served quickly, efficiently and decoratively with the use of refrigeration and a good mise-en-place system.

5   Use of seasons – An effective use of seasonal dishes can inspire any menu and can be cost-effective, especially if the ingredients have been purchased locally.

6   Creativity – A good pastry chef is able to use a cold dessert as a decorative medium to create a different way of presenting classical and modern cold desserts. It also gives the chef a chance to create different desserts using alternative flavours, texture and colour combinations to tempt customers.

Classical derivatives of cold desserts

The list below is a breakdown of different types of cold desserts:

1 Ices	Sorbets, coupes, sundaes, biscuit glacé
2 Fruit desserts	Compotes, coupes, macédoine de fruit
3 Rice dishes	Riz a l'Impératrice, condé
4 Crèmes	Brulée, caramel, régence
5 Creams	Vanilla bavarois, blancmange
6 Jellies	Gelée citron, gelée aux liqueurs
7 Charlottes	Russe, royale
8 Mousses	Mousse au chocolat
9 Soufflés	Soufflé froid au citron, soufflé glacé au fraise
10 Trifles	Sherry, ratafia, strawberry, tipsy cake
11 Timbales	Bananes suédoise, palermitaine
12 Miscellaneous	Oeufs à la neige, iles flottante

Cold desserts

White chocolate and mandarin mousse cake

Ingredients	4 individual	10 individual
Mandarin jelly		
Mandarin purée	125 g	250 g
Gelatine leaves	1½	2¼
Icing sugar	20 g	45 g
White chocolate mousse		
White chocolate	120 g	250 g
Whipping cream	45 g	125 g
Egg yolks	2	5
Icing sugar	40 g	80 g
Gelatine leaves	3	6
Whipped cream	200 g	450 g
Mandarin syrup		
Mandarin purée	30 g	60 g
Stock syrup (see page 551)	75 ml	120 ml
To decorate		
1 cm square of vanilla Genoese sponge	4	10
Dark chocolate acetate decoration pieces	4	10
Fresh mandarin segments	8	20
White chocolate melted at 30 °C	300 g	600 g
Cocoa butter melted at 32 °C	300 g	600 g

energy	cal	fat	sat fat	carb	sugar	protein	fibre
7,758 kJ	1,866 kcal	142.4 g	82.5 g	134.8 g	119.0 g	18.5 g	0.9 g

METHOD OF WORK

1 To make mandarin jelly, mix the mandarin purée and icing sugar together. Soften the gelatine in cold water and squeeze to remove any excess water before adding to the purée and pouring into a saucepan. Slowly warm all of the ingredients together so that the gelatine melts. Pour the mixture into 20 mm square moulds, place in the refrigerator to set.

2 To make mandarin syrup, mix together the second amount of mandarin purée and the stock syrup; set aside.

3 To make white chocolate mousse, carefully warm the cream and white chocolate together over a bain-marie of hot water, stirring constantly. Always maintain the melted chocolate/cream mixture at a temperature no higher than 35 °C before combining with other ingredients. Whisk the egg yolk and sugar over the bain-marie in a separate bowl until it begins to thicken (do not over-cook the egg), remove from the heat and continue to beat with a whisk until cool. Soften the gelatine in cold water and squeeze to remove any excess water before adding to a separate bowl and placing over the simmering bain-marie water to gently melt. Immediately add the egg yolk mixture and stir in well. Add to the melted white chocolate, combine all ingredients well, leave to cool for a few minutes before slowly folding in the whipped cream carefully. Ensure that the whipped cream has been aerated to soft peaks before incorporating into the mousse ingredients.

4 Prepare the flexipan square mousse moulds and pipe the chocolate mousse into the bottom, ensuring that the mousse is pushed into the corners. Brush some of the mandarin syrup over each vanilla Genoese disc and reserve. Remove the set jelly from each mould and position in the centre of the white chocolate mousse. Pipe the remaining mousse to completely fill the mould and place the Genoese on top to cap off the dessert. Using a palette knife, smooth the top to create a level finish. Immediately place in the freezer to set and partially freeze.

5 To finish, combine the white chocolate and cocoa butter together, mix well and pour into the chamber of an electric spray gun. Remove the mousse cakes from the freezer and carefully de-mould. Place onto a wire rack and carefully glaze each individual mousse cake with the chocolate by spraying the entire mousse cake while they are still frozen. Leave to set in a refrigerator and to regulate the temperature of the centre of the mousse cake before serving.

6 Serve by dressing each dessert with the chocolate acetate pieces, mandarin segments and dress onto a plate with some mandarin coulis to accompany.

Petit pot of chocolate with a banana smoothie

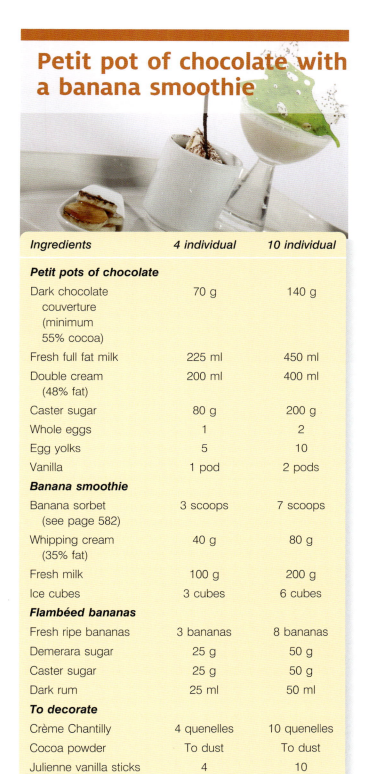

Ingredients	4 individual	10 individual
Petit pots of chocolate		
Dark chocolate couverture (minimum 55% cocoa)	70 g	140 g
Fresh full fat milk	225 ml	450 ml
Double cream (48% fat)	200 ml	400 ml
Caster sugar	80 g	200 g
Whole eggs	1	2
Egg yolks	5	10
Vanilla	1 pod	2 pods
Banana smoothie		
Banana sorbet (see page 582)	3 scoops	7 scoops
Whipping cream (35% fat)	40 g	80 g
Fresh milk	100 g	200 g
Ice cubes	3 cubes	6 cubes
Flambéed bananas		
Fresh ripe bananas	3 bananas	8 bananas
Demerara sugar	25 g	50 g
Caster sugar	25 g	50 g
Dark rum	25 ml	50 ml
To decorate		
Crème Chantilly	4 quenelles	10 quenelles
Cocoa powder	To dust	To dust
Julienne vanilla sticks	4	10
Clear and green bubble sugar	4 pieces	10 pieces

energy	cal	fat	sat fat	carb	sugar	protein	fibre
5049 kJ	1209 kcal	70.0 g	35.8 g	134.0 g	123.4 g	13.9 g	2.3 g

METHOD OF WORK

1   Preheat the oven to 165 °C.

2   To make the chocolate pots, place the chopped chocolate, milk, cream and sugar into a saucepan. Split the vanilla pod in half and scrape the seeds out into the milk, bring slowly to the boil. Ensure that the chocolate has completely melted. Beat together the egg yolks and whole eggs and carefully pour the hot liquid onto them, mixing continuously. Do not over whisk as this creates too much froth (aeration). Pass the mixture through a fine chinois into the dishes and place into a bain-marie. Bake for approximately 25 minutes or until each pot of chocolate sets. Chill as quickly as possible and reserve in a refrigerator.

3   To prepare the banana flambé, slice the bananas to approximately 5 mm thick. Heat a pan over a medium flame and add the two sugars. As they begin to caramelize add the sliced banana and turn over carefully to ensure even cooking and colour. Finally add the dark rum and flambé to cook out the alcohol content. Transfer the banana to a clean bowl and reserve at room temperature.

4   To make the smoothie, place the banana sorbet, cream, milk and ice cubes into a blender and blend to a thick texture. Pour into chilled shot glasses and reserve in a refrigerator.

5   To present, place a quenelle of crème Chantilly on top of the chocolate pot and lightly dust with cocoa powder, finish with a vanilla stick. Set onto a serving plate and place the shot glass of banana smoothie next to it with the bubble sugar. Finally spoon some banana flambé onto a presentation spoon and serve.

CHEF'S TIP The petit pot of chocolate is a classical dessert that is a set cream. It is partly derived from the crème brûlée but is not finished with caramelized sugar. To prevent the bain-marie water from boiling and therefore overcooking the chocolate pots, a sheet of card can be placed to cover the bottom of the bain-marie and the pots placed on top with the water. The card will suppress the water temperature and prevent it from boiling while in the oven.

Crème caramel with caramelized sultanas and mandarins

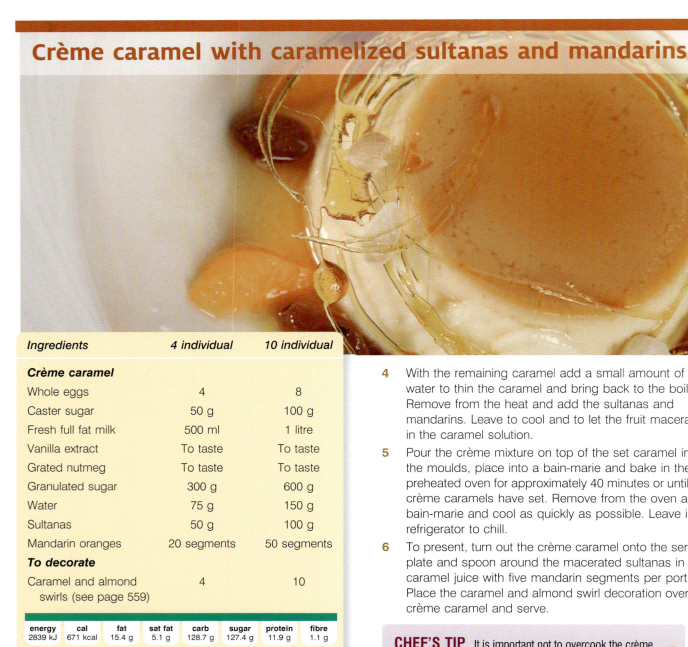

Ingredients	4 individual	10 individual
Crème caramel		
Whole eggs	4	8
Caster sugar	50 g	100 g
Fresh full fat milk	500 ml	1 litre
Vanilla extract	To taste	To taste
Grated nutmeg	To taste	To taste
Granulated sugar	300 g	600 g
Water	75 g	150 g
Sultanas	50 g	100 g
Mandarin oranges	20 segments	50 segments
To decorate		
Caramel and almond swirls (see page 559)	4	10

energy	cal	fat	sat fat	carb	sugar	protein	fibre
2839 kJ	671 kcal	15.4 g	5.1 g	128.7 g	127.4 g	11.9 g	1.1 g

METHOD OF WORK

1   Preheat the oven to 160 °C.

2   To prepare the crème caramel, place the milk, vanilla and nutmeg into a saucepan and warm the milk. Mix the eggs and caster sugar together and add the warmed milk. Pass through a fine sieve into a measuring jug and set aside.

3   Place the granulated sugar into a scrupulously clean saucepan and add the water. Leave to soak for a few minutes before bringing to the boil and cooking to a light, amber caramel. Immediately arrest the cooking process by plunging the pan into a bowl of cold water for 10 seconds. Pour a small amount of the caramel into the bottom of individual moulds.

4   With the remaining caramel add a small amount of water to thin the caramel and bring back to the boil. Remove from the heat and add the sultanas and mandarins. Leave to cool and to let the fruit macerate in the caramel solution.

5   Pour the crème mixture on top of the set caramel in the moulds, place into a bain-marie and bake in the preheated oven for approximately 40 minutes or until the crème caramels have set. Remove from the oven and bain-marie and cool as quickly as possible. Leave in a refrigerator to chill.

6   To present, turn out the crème caramel onto the service plate and spoon around the macerated sultanas in the caramel juice with five mandarin segments per portion. Place the caramel and almond swirl decoration over the crème caramel and serve.

CHEF'S TIP   It is important not to overcook the crème caramels otherwise small air pockets will set in the crème and create a scrambled texture to the finished dessert.

CHEF'S TIP   Traditionally, crème caramels are served on their own without any accompaniments. However, on this occasion the matching of the fruits macerated in the remaining caramel adds colour, flavour, texture and balance to the dessert.

TASK   There are a number of classical derivatives that are produced from a basic egg custard base from this recipe. Can you name two of them and provide brief descriptions and recipes?

Vanilla panna cotta with a macédoine of fruit

Ingredients	4 individual	10 individual
Panna cotta		
Double cream (48% fat)	750 ml	1.5 litres
Caster sugar	130 g	275 g
Vanilla	1 pod	2 pods
Milk	4 tblspn	9 tblspn
Gelatine leaves	3 leaves	6 leaves
Fruit macédoine		
Orange	1	2
Redcurrants	20	60
Strawberries	75 g	250 g
Raspberries	50 g	100 g
Blackberries	12	30
Blackcurrants	36	90
Stock syrup (see page 551)	100 ml	200 ml
Fresh mint	A few leaves	A few leaves
To decorate		
Preserved vanilla sticks	4	10

energy	cal	fat	sat fat	carb	sugar	protein	fibre
4996 kJ	1204 kcal	101.2 g	62.8 g	72.5 g	71.2 g	5.6 g	2.3 g

METHOD OF WORK

1   To prepare the panna cotta, slice the vanilla pods lengthways and scrape out the seeds into a saucepan with the double cream, the remaining vanilla and the caster sugar. Soften the leaves of gelatine in the cold milk. Slowly bring the cream to the boil and then set to simmer so that the liquid reduces by one-third. Remove from the heat and add the milk-softened gelatine leaves, stirring constantly. Pass through a fine sieve into a measuring jug and set aside. Always retain the vanilla pods to wash, dry out and preserve for vanilla sticks. Pour the panna cotta preparation into moulds and leave to set in a refrigerator for at least 4 hours.

2   Slightly warm the stock syrup on the stove but do not bring to the boil. Meanwhile finely slice the fresh mint into a chiffonade and then add to the warm syrup to infuse. Set aside to cool down and then place into a refrigerator to chill.

3   For the fruit carefully wash all fruits before preparing. Ensure all fruits have their pips removed and the oranges are cut into segments. All the fruit should be cut into similar sizes.

4   Place the fruit onto a clean tray, cover with plastic film and refrigerate before service. Try to leave the preparation of the fruit until the last moment to help retain the freshness and moisture content of the fruit.

5   To present, turn out the panna cotta by dipping the mould into hot water for 10 seconds and carefully removing from the mould. Place the panna cotta in the centre of the plate. Arrange the macédoine of fruit around the panna cotta and spoon a little of the mint syrup over the fruit. Decorate with the preserved vanilla sticks and serve.

CHEF'S TIP Alternatives to the macédoine of fruits are:

Salade d'oranges – peeled sliced oranges macerated in grand marnier and sugar.

Salade Maltaise – peeled, segments of oranges, pink grapefruit and mandarins macerated in an orange syrup.

Salade Normande – macédoine of dessert apples (such as Pippin or Braeburn), macerated with sugar and calvados.

Salade à la créole – macédoine of bananas, pineapple, orange segements and mango macerated with rum and sugar.

Lemon crème brûlée with biscotti

Ingredients	4 individual	10 individual
Crème brûlée		
Double cream (48% fat)	500 ml	1 litre
Caster sugar	80 g	150 g
Egg yolks	140 g	280 g
Lemon zest	1 lemon	4 lemons
Biscotti		
Butter	60 g	125 g
Caster sugar	100 g	225 g
Whole eggs	1	2
Aniseed	To taste	To taste
Lemon zest	¼ lemon	½ lemon
Soft white flour	425 g	850 g
Good quality salt	3 g	6 g
Baking powder	4 g	8 g
Flaked almonds	50 g	90 g
To decorate		
Demerara sugar	50 g	120 g
Icing sugar for dusting	40 g	80 g

energy	cal	fat	sat fat	carb	sugar	protein	fibre
6566 kJ	1574 kcal	99.7 g	53.7 g	151.8 g	74.8 g	21.9 g	4.3 g

METHOD OF WORK

1   Preheat the oven to 150 °C.

2   To prepare the crème brûlée, wash the lemons well and finely grate the zest into a saucepan with the double cream. Slowly bring to the boil. Meanwhile combine the egg yolks and the caster sugar and beat with a whisk to a pale colour. Pour the boiled cream onto the egg yolk mixture and combine all the ingredients before carefully pouring into individual ramekin dishes.

3   Line a deep baking tray with double kitchen paper and place the ramekins on top. Pour in enough hot water to reach three-quarters up the side of the dishes. Place this bain-marie into the oven and cook for approximately 30 minutes or until the crème brûlées have just set.

4   Remove each ramekin dish from the bain-marie and cool to room temperature before chilling in a refrigerator for at least 2 hours.

5   For the biscotti, preheat the oven to 180 °C. Cream together the butter and sugar until this mixture is light and fluffy. Sieve the flour, baking powder and salt together before slowly adding the eggs to the creamed butter. Finely grate the lemon and add to the mixture with the aniseed. Fold in the sieved ingredients and combine the almonds. Leave the paste to rest for five minutes. Mould into log shapes and place onto a baking sheet lined with silicone paper and baking for 20 minutes.

6   Remove from the oven to cool for a few minutes before slicing the biscotti into pieces 5 mm thick while still warm. Place the slices facedown onto the baking sheet and place back into the oven to bake for an additional 8 minutes, flip over the biscotti and repeat the process until a golden colour has been achieved.

7   Cool on a wire rack and store in an airtight container.

8   To present, preheat a salamander and sprinkle the demerara sugar on top of each crème brûlée. Caramelize under the hot salamander ensuring an even heat distribution to create a complete caramelized sugar crust. Leave to cool down and set. Place the crème brûlée onto a dessert plate with two biscotti slices next to it. Serve immediately.

CHEF'S TIP Demerara sugar is untreated cane sugar and its melting point is lower than caster sugar, so it will caramelize more easily. The salamander will need to be preheated to create a very strong heat to caramelize the sugar very quickly. If the heat is not hot enough it will slowly cook the top of the crème brûlée. Sometimes the use of a dessert blowtorch can give a better result.

Caramel mousse

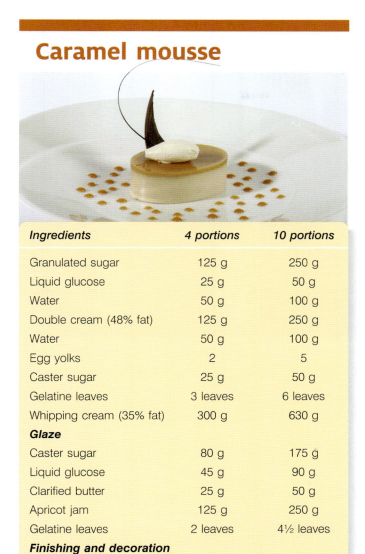

Ingredients	4 portions	10 portions
Granulated sugar	125 g	250 g
Liquid glucose	25 g	50 g
Water	50 g	100 g
Double cream (48% fat)	125 g	250 g
Water	50 g	100 g
Egg yolks	2	5
Caster sugar	25 g	50 g
Gelatine leaves	3 leaves	6 leaves
Whipping cream (35% fat)	300 g	630 g
Glaze		
Caster sugar	80 g	175 g
Liquid glucose	45 g	90 g
Clarified butter	25 g	50 g
Apricot jam	125 g	250 g
Gelatine leaves	2 leaves	4½ leaves
Finishing and decoration		
Vanilla sponge swiss roll sheet (see page 596)	4 small discs	10 small discs
Crème Chantilly	150 g	300 g
Dark chocolate motif	4	10

energy	cal	fat	sat fat	carb	sugar	protein	fibre
5,264 kJ	1,259 kcal	77.4 g	45.2 g	136.7 g	113.8 g	11.5 g	0.8 g

METHOD OF WORK

1 Place the granulated sugar and water into a heavy-bottomed pan and bring to the boil. Add the liquid glucose and boil to an amber, caramel colour.

2 Remove the pan from the heat and leave to settle for 2 minutes before adding the second amount of water and then the double cream very carefully. Place back on the heat and bring to the boil, stirring constantly to melt the caramel into the cream.

3 Blend together the egg yolks and the caster sugar; beat with a whisk until a pale colour has been achieved. Soften the gelatine leaves in cold water.

4 Add the boiled caramel cream to the egg yolks and mix well before returning to the pan and placing over a medium heat. Stirring constantly with a wooden spoon, cook the caramel cream until it begins to coat the back of the spoon.

5 Remove from the heat and add the softened gelatine. Continue stirring for a few more moments before passing the liquid through a sieve into a chilled bowl. Continue to cool down the liquid and then place into a refrigerator to half set.

6 Aerate the whipping cream to form soft peaks.

7 Set the disc of sponge in the base of individual moulds ensuring that the disc is at least 10 mm smaller than the mould.

8 When the caramel cream is half set, carefully fold in the whipped cream and then transfer the mousse into each mould. Place in a refrigerator to set.

9 To make the glaze, soften the gelatine leaves in cold water and place the sugar and the glucose together in a heavy-bottomed saucepan. Slowly heat the glucose and sugar over a medium heat to create a dry caramel. When the correct amber-caramel colour has been achieved, add the melted clarified butter and apricot jam. Mix these ingredients together well and finally add the gelatine leaves. Pass through a chinois into a bowl to cool down.

10 When the glaze has cooled and the mousse is set, spread a little of the caramel glaze on top of each mousse using a small palette knife. Sometimes it is easier to warm the mousse ring carefully to release the mousse from the mould and push the mould up by 2 mm and hold it in place with a plastic scraper before then applying the glaze. Using this method will give a level finish to the top of the mousse.

11 Place into a refrigerator to set for 1 hour.

12 To serve, remove the mould and place a small quenelle of crème Chantilly on top with the chocolate motif for decoration. An apricot coulis could accompany this dessert.

Step-by-step: Preparing a caramel mousse base

1. Add the liquid glucose to the boiling sugar and cook to an amber caramel colour.

2. Remove the pan from the heat before adding the second amount of water, and then the double cream, very carefully stirring with a clean spoon or heat resistant rubber spatula.

3. Soften the gelatine leaves in cold water.

The finished caramel mousse base

CHEF'S TIP   Whipped cream is a delicate and unstable foam. When aerating whipping cream ensure that the bowl being used is chilled and so is the cream. This will help to ensure aeration. If the cream becomes over-whipped when combining the cream with the caramel cream preparation the mousse will split and the texture will be heavy and grainy.

Strawberry bavarois *(Bavarois aux fraises)*

Ingredients	4 portions	10 portions
Fresh strawberries	200 g	550 g
Egg yolks	2	5
Gelatine leaves	3 leaves	6 leaves
Fresh full fat milk	180 ml	400 ml
Caster sugar	50 g	120 g
Whipping cream (35%)	250 ml	600 ml
To decorate		
Vanilla sponge discs	4	10
Fresh mint	4 plûches	10 plûches
Fresh strawberries	2	5
Strawberry coulis	200 ml	600 ml
Crème Chantilly	150 g	400 g
Clear bubble sugar	4 pieces	10 pieces

energy	cal	fat	sat fat	carb	sugar	protein	fibre
3,812 kJ	912 kcal	51.2 g	29.6 g	104.6 g	89.0 g	13.1 g	3.2 g

METHOD OF WORK

1 Soak the leaf gelatine in cold water.

2 Beat the egg yolks and caster sugar until pale in colour.

3 Meanwhile, bring the milk to the boil in a saucepan. Pour onto the egg yolk mixture and combine.

4 Pour back into the saucepan and place on a medium heat. Stirring constantly with a spoon, cook out the crème until the sauce coats the back of the spoon. Remove from the heat, add the softened gelatine and dissolve in the crème. Pass through a fine sieve into a chilled bowl.

5 Wash, hull and place the strawberries into a food processor and blend into a purée. Add this purée to the base preparation and place into a refrigerator to chill and half set.

6 Aerate the whipping cream and carefully fold into the base preparation.

7 Place the discs of vanilla sponge in the bottom of each individual mould. Equally divide the bavarois preparation between the moulds and set in a refrigerator for 1 hour.

8 To serve, de-mould the strawberry bavarois and place onto a dessert plate accompanied by a quenelle of crème Chantilly, half a strawberry and fresh mint dusted with icing sugar. Serve with the strawberry coulis.

CHEF'S TIP   When cooking out the egg yolks and milk it is important not to let this mixture boil. Overheating will allow the egg protein to scramble.

Vanilla bavarois *(Bavarois à la vanille)*

Ingredients	4 portions	10 portions
Vanilla pod	1 pod	2 pods
Egg yolks	60 g	120 g
Gelatine leaves	3 leaves	6 leaves
Fresh full fat milk	240 ml	500 ml
Caster sugar	50 g	125 g
Whipping cream (35%)	240 ml	500 ml
To decorate		
Melted chocolate	100 g	200 g
Caramel spring	4 springs	10 springs
Vanilla stick	4 sticks	10 sticks
Clear bubble sugar	4	10

energy	cal	fat	sat fat	carb	sugar	protein	fibre
2883 kJ	692 kcal	43.0 g	17.7 g	70.4 g	60.9 g	8.8 g	0.2 g

METHOD OF WORK

1   Soak the leaf gelatine in cold water.

2   Beat the egg yolks and caster sugar until pale in colour.

3   Meanwhile, bring the milk to the boil in a saucepan. Pour onto the egg yolk mixture and combine.

4   Pour back into the saucepan and place on a medium heat. Stirring constantly with a spoon, cook out the crème until the sauce coats the back of the spoon. Remove from the heat, add the softened gelatine and dissolve in the crème. Pass through a fine sieve into a chilled bowl.

5   Place into a refrigerator to chill and half set.

6   Aerate the whipping cream and carefully fold into the base preparation.

7   Equally divide the bavarois preparation between the moulds and set in a refrigerator for 1 hour.

8   To serve, carefully de-mould the vanilla bavarois and place onto a dessert plate brushed with the melted dark chocolate. Decorate with a caramel spring, bubble sugar and the preserved vanilla stick.

CHEF'S TIP   Additional flavours can be included to the basic vanilla bavarois recipes as below:

1   Coconut bavarois: replace half the milk with coconut milk and add a little coconut cream for flavour.

2   Coffee bavarois: add essence, extract or instant coffee to the basic recipe.

3   Orange bavarois: add orange flavour or colour alongside some finely grated orange zest to the basic recipe. Decorate with orange segments and a little crème Chantilly.

VIDEO CLIP   Vanilla bavarois.

Chocolate bavarois (*Bavarois au chocolat*)

Ingredients	4 portions	10 portions
Dark chocolate, chopped (60%)	60 g	120 g
Egg yolks	60 g	120 g
Gelatine leaves	3 leaves	6 leaves
Fresh full fat milk	240 ml	500 ml
Caster sugar	50 g	125 g
Whipping cream (35%)	240 ml	500 ml
To decorate		
Melted chocolate	100 g	200 g
Pear coulis	100 g	200 g
Pear crisp	4	10

energy	cal	fat	sat fat	carb	sugar	protein	fibre
2611 kJ	628 kcal	48.4 g	17.6 g	39.6 g	26.9 g	10.2 g	0.6 g

4   Pour back into the saucepan and place on a medium heat. Stirring constantly with a spoon, cook out the crème until the sauce coats the back of the spoon. Add the chopped chocolate and stir until it has melted into the crème. Remove from the heat, add the softened gelatine and dissolve in the crème. Pass through a fine sieve into a chilled bowl.

5   Place into a refrigerator to chill and half set.

6   Aerate the whipping cream and carefully fold into the base preparation.

7   Equally divide the bavarois preparation between the moulds and set in a refrigerator for 1 hour.

8   To serve, carefully de-mould the chocolate bavarois and place onto a dessert plate brushed with the melted dark chocolate. Decorate with a pear crisp and pipe some pear coulis in a decorative form onto the plate.

METHOD OF WORK

1   Soak the leaf gelatine in cold water.

2   Beat the egg yolks and caster sugar until pale in colour.

3   Meanwhile, bring the milk to the boil in a saucepan. Pour onto the egg yolk mixture and combine.

Chocolate mousse

Ingredients	4 portions	10 portions
Dark chocolate (60% minimum cocoa)	120 g	260 g
Unsalted butter	20 g	50 g
Egg yolks	4	10
Egg whites	4	10
Caster sugar	75 g	170 g
To decorate		
Chocolate shavings (see page 558)	50 g	75 g
Crème Chantilly (optional)	150 g	400 g

energy	cal	fat	sat fat	carb	sugar	protein	fibre
4,509 kJ	1,084 kcal	81.0 g	22.6 g	68.7 g	25.8 g	21.6 g	0.6 g

METHOD OF WORK

1. Chop the chocolate up into small pieces and place into a glass bowl with the unsalted butter. Cover the bowl tightly with plastic film and melt in a bain-marie of hot water or use a microwave oven and melt in ten second bursts.

2. Aerate the egg whites with one-quarter of the caster sugar to soft peaks.

3. Beat the egg yolks with the three-quarters of the caster sugar until they are pale in colour. Combine the melted chocolate to the egg yolks and mix well.

4. Lightly fold in the whipped egg whites to the chocolate mixture and place into a piping bag with a plain tube.

5. Pipe the chocolate mousse into a serving glass and refrigerate until required.

6. To serve, arrange some chocolate shavings on top of each mousse with a little crème Chantilly.

CHEF'S TIP There are many additions that can be made to enhance this basic recipe.

- Chocolate and orange – add finely grated zest of orange to the chocolate and 25 ml of Grand Marnier to the egg yolks for 4 portions.
- Chocolate and brandy – add 25 ml brandy to the egg yolks for 4 portions.
- Chocolate and whisky – add 25 ml whisky to the egg yolks for 4 portions.
- Chocolate and praline – add 25 g praline paste to the melted chocolate for 4 portions.

CHEF'S TIP The mousse has three main aspects to its composition:

1. Always maintain the melted chocolate/cream mixture at a temperature no higher than 35 °C before combining with other ingredients.

2. When beating the egg yolk and sugar during the cooking process over a bain-marie, a whisk should always be used. Also, when cooling down a whisk must be employed to aid any aeration.

3. Ensure that the whipped cream has been aerated to soft peaks before incorporating into the mousse ingredients.

Summer fruit pudding

Ingredients	4 portions	10 portions
Strawberries	100 g	250 g
Raspberries	100 g	250 g
Redcurrants	100 g	250 g
Blackcurrants	50 g	150 g
Blackberries	100 g	250 g
Caster sugar	150 g	350 g
Sliced white bread	240 g	600 g
To decorate		
Fresh mint	4 plûches	10 plûches
Crème Chantilly	150 g	400 g
Fresh raspberries	4	10
Icing sugar for dusting	50 g	75 g

energy	cal	fat	sat fat	carb	sugar	protein	fibre
2114 kJ	501 kcal	15.9 g	9.5 g	88.1 g	61.6 g	6.9 g	5.1 g

METHOD OF WORK

1   Ensure all the fruits are ripe and carefully wash and hull where necessary.

2   Place all the fruits and sugar together into a large saucepan and slowly stew over a medium heat. Continue cooking while retaining the shape of the fruit. Overcooking will result in the fruit turning into a purée.

3   Remove from the heat and leave to cool down.

4   Using individual pudding moulds cut the crusts of the bread and trim slices to fit around the sides of the moulds and discs for the top and bottom. Line the bottom of the mould by dipping one side of the bread disc into the fruit stew and placing it downside in the bottom of the mould.

5   Repeat this process to line the sides of the mould before filling the mould with the cooked fruit. Cover with one further disc of bread and press down firmly.

6   Place a sheet of plastic film over the top of the moulded pudding and place a flat baking sheet on top, weighed down to compress the pudding to help set it. Place in a refrigerator for a minimum of 12 hours to set and for the bread to soak the juices of the fruit and change colour.

7   De-mould the summer pudding and place onto a dessert plate accompanied by a quenelle of crème Chantilly, fresh raspberry and fresh mint. Dust with a little icing sugar to finish.

CHEF'S TIP   If there is some stewed fruit remaining after making the summer puddings, it can be puréed and mixed with a little stock syrup to create an accompanying sauce to serve alongside the pudding.

Piña colada soup with a vanilla rice condé
(Soupe de piña colada, riz condé)

Ingredients	4 portions	10 portions
Piña colada soup		
Fresh medium-sized pineapple	1	2½
Coconut milk	550 g	1.2 kg
Icing sugar	100 g	240 g
White rum	50 g	120 g
Condé		
Fresh full fat milk	400 ml	900 ml
Caster sugar	45 g	90 g
Short grain pudding rice	50 g	120 g
Gelatine leaves	1 leaf	2 leaves
Whipping cream	140 ml	300 ml
Vanilla pod	1 pod	2 pods
Pineapple	4 small thin slices	10 small thin slices
To decorate		
Fresh mint	4 plûches	10 plûches
Preserved vanilla sticks	8	20
Bubble sugar	4	10

energy	cal	fat	sat fat	carb	sugar	protein	fibre
4,776 kJ	1,133 kcal	43.4 g	30.4 g	179.4 g	173.6 g	9.8 g	12.5 g

METHOD OF WORK

1 For the condé, split the vanilla pod in half lengthways and scrape the seeds into a saucepan with the milk. Wash the pudding rice in slightly salted water while bringing the milk to the boil.

2 Add the rice and gently simmer for approximately 25 minutes, stirring occasionally. Soften the gelatine leaves in cold water.

3 Once the rice has cooked and the milk has reduced and thickened, remove from the heat. Add the sugar and gelatine. Allow to cool and then chill in a refrigerator.

4 Aerate the whipping cream using a balloon whisk and gently fold into the rice preparation. Transfer into individual pudding moulds to set.

5 Soak the sliced pineapple in the stock syrup for 2 minutes before placing onto a silicone baking mat and drying for 1 hour in a preheated oven at 120 °C, turning over after 30 minutes.

6 For the soup, trim and core the pineapple before cutting into small chunks. Place into a food processor with the coconut milk, sugar and rum and blend to a purée. Pour into a bowl and reserve in the refrigerator until required.

7 To serve, de-mould the condé into the centre of a soup bowl. Blend the chilled soup once again using a hand-held blender and pour around the condé. Decorate with the vanilla sticks, pineapple crisp and fresh mint. Serve.

CHEF'S TIP Traditionally a rice condé is presented with fresh fruit decorated on top and glazed with an apricot glaze. This recipe has modernized the presentation and there is also a reduction in the gelatine content to make a lighter dessert.

Meringue nest with vanilla ice cream *(Vacherin glacée au vanille)*

Ingredients	4 portions	10 portions
Egg whites	6	12
Caster sugar	230 g	460 g
Vanilla extract or pods	1 pod	2 pods
Poppy seeds for decoration		
To decorate		
Vanilla ice cream (see page 579)	4 scoops	10 scoops
Crème Chantilly	150 g	380 g
Strawberry coulis (see page 552)	150 ml	400 ml

energy	cal	fat	sat fat	carb	sugar	protein	fibre
2939 kJ	700 kcal	33.7 g	19.6 g	93.2 g	92.7 g	11.8 g	1.1 g

METHOD OF WORK

1 Preheat the oven to 120 °C.
2 Place the egg whites into a large bowl and using a balloon whisk create a foam that begins to soft peak. Now begin to gradually add the sugar and the vanilla at the very last moment (if using vanilla pods scrape the seeds out and mix with the sugar first).
3 Continue whisking until egg whites have all the sugar incorporated and they show signs of stiffening and holding their own peaks. Other points to look for are that the meringue should be glossy and smooth.

4 Placing the meringue into a piping bag with a star tube, pipe a small individual disc approximately 60 mm in diameter onto a silicone baking mat on a double baking sheet. On the edges of the disc pipe a circle to create a collar. Pipe one more circle on the crown to raise the height of the collar without it collapsing. If desired sprinkle with a few poppy seeds.
5 With any remaining meringue, transfer to another piping bag with a small plain tube and pipe straight tubes up to 16 cm long onto a baking sheet lined with silicone paper. Sprinkle the ends with poppy seeds.
6 Place the baking sheets into the oven and then turn off. Leave the oven door slightly open and let the meringue shells dry for at least 8 hours and the meringue straws for about 2 hours.
7 When dried out, leave to cool on a wire rack for a further hour before serving. The centre of the meringue should not be soft and uncooked.
8 To serve, place the meringue nest in the centre of the plate and position the ice cream of your choice inside it. Decorate with piped crème Chantilly, the meringue straws, preserved vanilla sticks and finish with the fruit coulis presented on the plate.

> **CHEF'S TIP** To test if the meringue is at the correct consistency to pipe, place a fingertip into the meringue and pull it out. If the meringue creates a stiff, long, spiked 'fingernail' then it is ready to be piped.

> **HEALTH & SAFETY** Salmonella is a bacteria often associated with eggs. Precautions should be taken when using fresh eggs, such as ensuring that the shell is clean. Salmonella is destroyed at 71 °C but egg whites coagulate at between 61 and 65 °C. The addition of other ingredients to meringue, like sugar forces the temperature for coagulation higher so that the meringue will coagulate at a similar temperature to that for destroying bacteria.

Step-by-step: Meringue base

1. Place the egg whites into a large bowl and using a balloon whisk create a foam that begins to soft peak.

2. Gradually add the sugar and the vanilla.

3. Continue whisking until the egg whites have all of the sugar incorporated and show signs of stiffening and holding their own peaks.

Floating islands with passion fruit

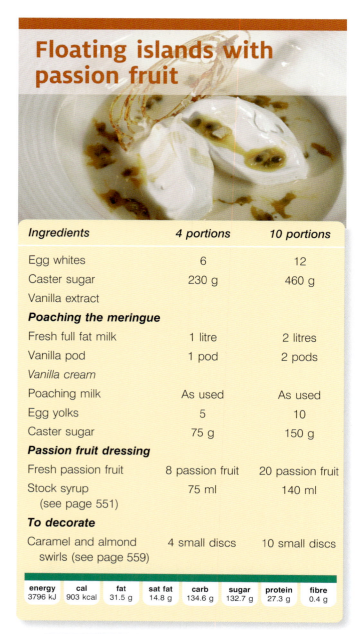

Ingredients	4 portions	10 portions
Egg whites	6	12
Caster sugar	230 g	460 g
Vanilla extract		
Poaching the meringue		
Fresh full fat milk	1 litre	2 litres
Vanilla pod	1 pod	2 pods
Vanilla cream		
Poaching milk	As used	As used
Egg yolks	5	10
Caster sugar	75 g	150 g
Passion fruit dressing		
Fresh passion fruit	8 passion fruit	20 passion fruit
Stock syrup (see page 551)	75 ml	140 ml
To decorate		
Caramel and almond swirls (see page 559)	4 small discs	10 small discs

energy 3796 kJ	cal 903 kcal	fat 31.5 g	sat fat 14.8 g	carb 134.6 g	sugar 132.7 g	protein 27.3 g	fibre 0.4 g

METHOD OF WORK

1   Split the vanilla pods lengthways and place into a large shallow pan with the fresh milk. Bring to the boil and reduce to a simmering point.

2   Using an electric mixing machine with a whisk attachment beat the egg whites to soft peaks before slowly raining in the caster sugar and adding the vanilla extract. Beat until a firm stiff meringue has been achieved.

3   Make three quenelles of meringue per portion and place into the simmering milk to poach for two minutes. Turn the quenelles over and poach for a further two minutes.

4   Removed with a slotted spoon and leave to drain on a small tray with kitchen paper. Continue to poach the meringue until you have the required set portions.

5   Cool the quenelles and refrigerate until service.

6   Pass the milk through a chinois. At this point the milk should have been reduced by half and there should be approximately 500 ml remaining.

7   Whisk the egg yolks with the caster sugar to begin preparing the vanilla sauce. Add the remaining poaching milk and continuously stir over a medium heat until it begins to coat the back of a spoon.

8   Remove from the heat and continue stirring to dissipate the residual heat. Cool down before placing into the refrigerator to chill.

9   To make the passion fruit dressing, remove the flesh from inside the passion fruit and mix together with the stock syrup. Discard the passion fruit shells and reserve the dressing for service.

10 To serve, place some of the vanilla cream into dessert bowls and position the poached meringues to float on top. Drizzle the passion fruit dressing over the meringues and finish with a caramel and almond swirl.

CHEF'S TIP When poaching the meringue it is important not to let the milk boil. The excessive heat will cause the meringue to 'soufflé' and eventually when cooling down it will drop and begin to weep excess moisture.

CHEF'S TIP The poached meringue should always be turned over and should be firm to the touch when testing for cooking. This dessert can also be served warm during the winter months with hot caramel spooned over the meringue just before service.

Make 3 quenelles of meringue per portion and place into the simmering milk to poach for two minutes

Italian meringue

Ingredients	50 small piped meringues
Egg whites	150 g
Caster sugar	300 g
Water	90 g
Cream of tartar	pinch

energy	cal	fat	sat fat	carb	sugar	protein	fibre
106 kJ	25 kcal	0.0 g	0.0 g	6.3 g	6.3 g	0.3 g	0.0 g

Step-by-step: Italian meringue

1. Place the sugar, water and cream of tartar in a saucepan and carefully bring to the boil and heat to 118 °C.

2. Meanwhile aerate the egg whites to a stiff peak.

3. Keeping the egg whites whisking, add the boiled syrup in a steady stream.

4. Continue whisking until the meringue is firm.

5. When the meringue is cool remove from the machine and check the consistency to form stiff peaks.

6. The finished meringue holding its own shape.

CHEF'S TIP This meringue is partially cooked and is used in the making of goods which are decorated with meringue flashed in the oven, for example baked Alaska. It can also be used for piping shapes since it is more stable than a normal cold meringue.

Trifle

Ingredients	4 portions	10 portions
Jelly		
Sweet white wine	200 ml	430 ml
Water	200 ml	400 ml
Sugar	120 g	200 g
Gelatine leaves	3 leaves	6 leaves
Syllabub		
Sweet sherry	150 ml	300 ml
Caster sugar	50 g	100 g
Lemon zest and juice	1 lemon	2 lemons
Double cream	300 ml	600 ml
Cognac	1 tblspn	3 tblspn
Assembly		
Vanilla custard sauce	250 g	500 g
Sponge fingers	4	10
Strawberries	75 g	140 g
Raspberries	50 g (4 left whole)	100 g (10 left whole)
Caramel and almond swirl	4	10

energy	cal	fat	sat fat	carb	sugar	protein	fibre
3745 kJ	896 kcal	47.2 g	25.9 g	94.1 g	85.0 g	8.1 g	1.3 g

METHOD OF WORK

1   To make the jelly: bring the wine and the water to the boil and soak the gelatine. Add the gelatine, pass through a fine strainer and allow to cool.

2   For the syllabub: bring the sherry to the boil and allow to cool, add the zest and juice of the lemon and stand to infuse for 2 hours. Half whip the cream and strain the sherry juice into the cream with the sugar and aerate to a dropping consistency.

3   To assemble: cut the sponge fingers into small pieces and mixed with the raspberries and quartered strawberries. Place into the bottom of each glass. Pour on the white wine jelly to cover and leave to set in a refrigerator.

4   Pipe the vanilla custard on top of the set jelly and place back in the refrigerator to set again for another 30 minutes.

5   Pipe on the syllabub to fill the glasses and smooth the top with a palette knife. Decorate with the remaining raspberries and caramel and almond swirls.

CHEF'S TIP   Traditionally jelly was not used in a classic trifle, only recently has it been added and accepted as a staple part of the trifle structure. Usually preserved or fresh fruit was used instead.

Vanilla ice cream *(Crème glacée à la vanille)*

Ingredients	4 portions	10 portions
Double cream (48% fat)	200 ml	400 ml
Full fat fresh milk	300 ml	600 ml
Egg yolks	6	12
Caster sugar	100 g	200 g
Milk powder	25 g	50 g
Vanilla	1 pod	2 pods

energy	cal	fat	sat fat	carb	sugar	protein	fibre
2101 kJ	506 kcal	37.6 g	20.8 g	33.8 g	33.7 g	9.6 g	0.0 g

METHOD OF WORK

1 Using a whisk, beat together the egg yolks, caster sugar and the milk powder until a pale colour has been obtained.

2 Place the milk and cream in a heavy-bottomed saucepan, split the vanilla pod and scrape the seeds into the milk. Add the vanilla pod, bring to the liquid to the boil and simmer for approximately three minutes to help infuse the flavour.

3 Pour the milk onto the egg mixture whisking continuously and return the mixture to the saucepan on a medium heat.

4 Constantly stir the crème with a wooden spoon until it begins to coat the back of the spoon.

5 Pass immediately through a fine sieve into a chilled bowl and continue stirring for another five minutes to release the residual heat from the crème.

6 Place the crème to mature in a refrigerator (stored away from strong smelling ingredients) for 2 hours before pouring into an ice cream machine and churning to produce the ice cream.

7 Place sterilized container into the freezer for an hour before churning the crème and use this as the container to immediately decant the ice cream into. This will help to prevent the ice cream from melting when removed from the machine.

8 Store the ice cream in an airtight container at −18 °C or below.
Alternative flavours can be added to the ice cream.

CHEF'S TIP   When freezing ice cream the principle is to form very small ice crystals that are encased in a fine film of fat. The aeration of the mixture during the freezing stage is an important process to the overall texture of ice cream. Therefore a rich protein content (in the form of eggs, milk powder, milk and cream) is important within the recipe. Proteins will help to achieve greater aeration in this process and thus a lighter and creamier texture will be achieved. It is also important that a good ice cream machine is used that will churn the mixture quickly and help to aerate the protein and reduce the size of the ice crystals.

HEALTH & SAFETY   Always ensure that all utensils and equipment have been sterilized when producing ice cream. The storage of ice cream is of utmost importance and the following rules should be adhered to:

- Use an airtight container to store ice cream.
- Maintain the freezer temperature at no higher than −18 °C.
- Never re-freeze ice cream after it has been defrosted.

Assorted ice cream flavours

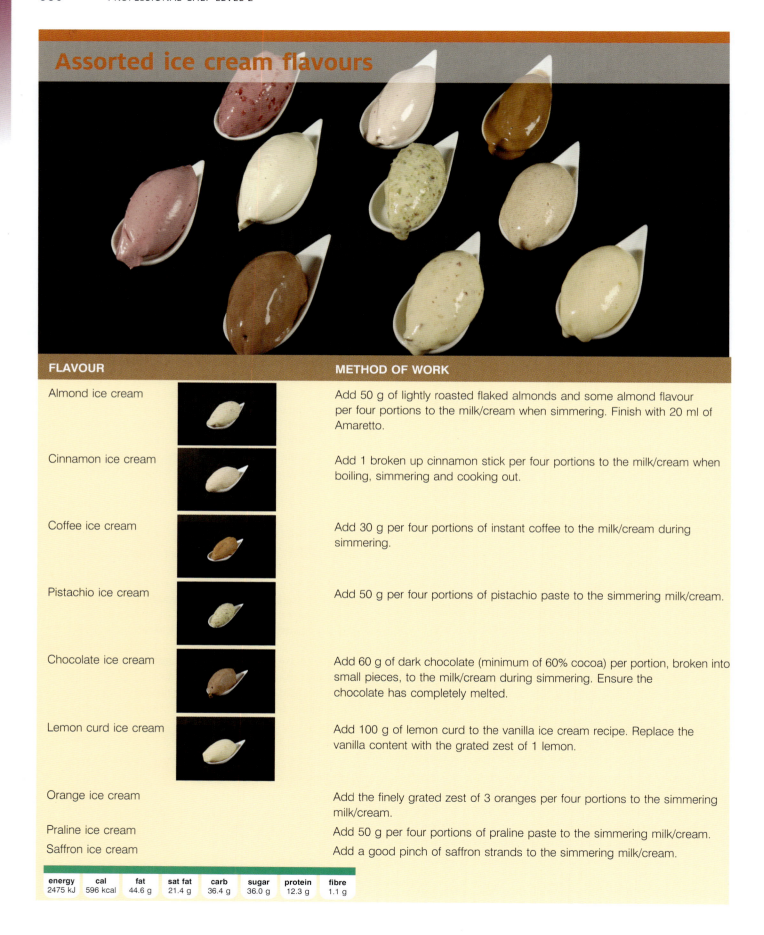

FLAVOUR		METHOD OF WORK
Almond ice cream		Add 50 g of lightly roasted flaked almonds and some almond flavour per four portions to the milk/cream when simmering. Finish with 20 ml of Amaretto.
Cinnamon ice cream		Add 1 broken up cinnamon stick per four portions to the milk/cream when boiling, simmering and cooking out.
Coffee ice cream		Add 30 g per four portions of instant coffee to the milk/cream during simmering.
Pistachio ice cream		Add 50 g per four portions of pistachio paste to the simmering milk/cream.
Chocolate ice cream		Add 60 g of dark chocolate (minimum of 60% cocoa) per portion, broken into small pieces, to the milk/cream during simmering. Ensure the chocolate has completely melted.
Lemon curd ice cream		Add 100 g of lemon curd to the vanilla ice cream recipe. Replace the vanilla content with the grated zest of 1 lemon.
Orange ice cream		Add the finely grated zest of 3 oranges per four portions to the simmering milk/cream.
Praline ice cream		Add 50 g per four portions of praline paste to the simmering milk/cream.
Saffron ice cream		Add a good pinch of saffron strands to the simmering milk/cream.

energy	cal	fat	sat fat	carb	sugar	protein	fibre
2475 kJ	596 kcal	44.6 g	21.4 g	36.4 g	36.0 g	12.3 g	1.1 g

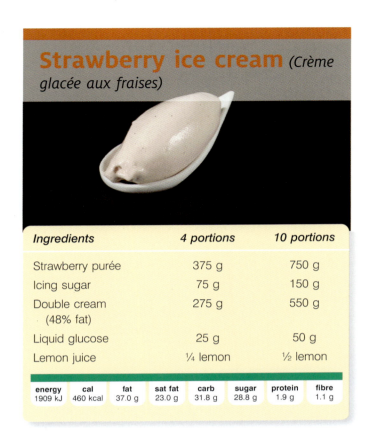

Strawberry ice cream *(Crème glacée aux fraises)*

Ingredients	4 portions	10 portions
Strawberry purée	375 g	750 g
Icing sugar	75 g	150 g
Double cream (48% fat)	275 g	550 g
Liquid glucose	25 g	50 g
Lemon juice	¼ lemon	½ lemon

energy	cal	fat	sat fat	carb	sugar	protein	fibre
1909 kJ	460 kcal	37.0 g	23.0 g	31.8 g	28.8 g	1.9 g	1.1 g

METHOD OF WORK

1. Place the cream, icing sugar and liquid glucose into a heavy-bottomed saucepan and bring to the boil.

2. Meanwhile either wash, hull and purée the required amount of fresh strawberries or alternatively use a good quality fruit purée. Add the lemon juice to the purée.

3. When the cream has boiled, cool for five minutes before combining with the strawberry purée. Pass through a chinois and pour into the ice cream machine and churn.

4. Place a sterilized container into the freezer for an hour before churning the crème and use this as the container into which to immediately decant the ice cream. This will help to prevent the ice cream from melting when removed from the machine.

5. Store the ice cream in an airtight container at −18°C or below.

CHEF'S TIP Always ensure that the fruit is perfectly ripe to obtain the best flavour and colour to the ice cream. The use of lemon juice in this recipe will enhance the fruit flavour and the acid present will help to maintain the colour. Strawberries contain high quantities of vitamin C when at the peak of their season.

ALTERNATIVE FLAVOURS THAT CAN BE ADDED TO THIS RECIPE

FLAVOUR		METHOD OF WORK
Raspberry ice cream		Replace the quantity of fruit purée with a raspberry purée.
Blackcurrant ice cream		Replace the quantity of fruit purée with blackcurrant purée.
Banana ice cream		Replace the quantity of fruit purée with a banana purée. Finish with 20 ml of dark rum.
Mango ice cream		Replace the quantity of fruit purée with a mango purée.
Passion fruit ice cream		Replace the quantity of fruit purée with fresh passion fruit with the seeds removed.
Peach ice cream		Replace the quantity of fruit purée with a peach purée. Finish with 20 ml of peach schnapps.

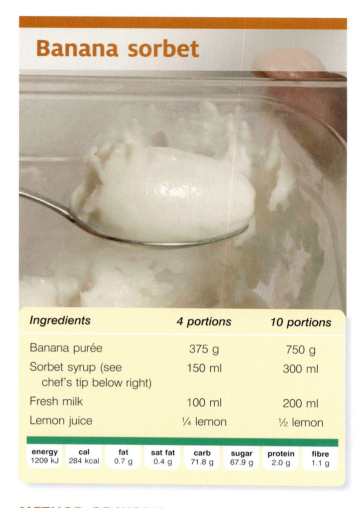

Banana sorbet

Ingredients	4 portions	10 portions
Banana purée	375 g	750 g
Sorbet syrup (see chef's tip below right)	150 ml	300 ml
Fresh milk	100 ml	200 ml
Lemon juice	¼ lemon	½ lemon

energy	cal	fat	sat fat	carb	sugar	protein	fibre
1209 kJ	284 kcal	0.7 g	0.4 g	71.8 g	67.9 g	2.0 g	1.1 g

METHOD OF WORK

1 Place the **sorbet** syrup and fresh milk into a saucepan and bring to the boil.

2 Meanwhile peel and slice the ripest possible bananas, removing any bruises or discolouration, and purée in a food processor with the lemon juice.

3 When the milk and stock syrup has boiled, remove from the heat and stir in the banana purée. Cool for five minutes before blending once again in the food processor. Pass through a chinois and chill in a refrigerator.

4 Pour the mixture into the ice cream machine and churn to freeze. The sorbet should have a firm consistency.

5 Place a sterilized container into the freezer for an hour before churning the crème and use this as the container to immediately decant the sorbet into. This will help to prevent the sorbet from melting when removed from the machine.

6 Store the sorbet in an airtight container at −18°C or below.

ALTERNATIVE FLAVOURS THAT CAN BE ADDED TO THIS RECIPE

FLAVOUR	METHOD OF WORK
Apricot sorbet	Replace the quantity of fruit purée with apricot purée. Replace the milk content with sorbet syrup.
Mango sorbet	Replace the quantity of fruit purée with a mango purée. Also replace the milk content with sorbet syrup.
Melon sorbet	Replace the quantity of fruit purée with fresh melon flesh with the seeds removed. Replace the milk content with sorbet syrup.
Strawberry sorbet	Replace the quantity of fruit purée with a strawberry purée. Replace the milk content with sorbet syrup.
Raspberry sorbet	Replace the quantity of fruit purée with a raspberry purée. Replace the milk content with sorbet syrup.

CHEF'S TIP   The use of the right density of sorbet syrup is very important to help the sorbet freeze to the correct consistency. The recipe given here should be used for all further sorbet recipes.

750 g granulated sugar
650 ml water
70 g glucose syrup

Bring all the ingredients to the boil in a saucepan and simmer for 3 minutes. Strain through a chinois and use only when completely cold. This syrup should keep in an airtight container in a refrigerator for up to 2 weeks.

Poached pears with cinnamon and cider

Ingredients	4 portions	10 portions
Pears	450 g	960 g
Water	150 ml	300 ml
Cinnamon powder	15 g	25 g
Cider	150 ml	300 ml
Caster sugar	120 g	240 g
Lemon juice	1 lemon	2 lemons

energy	cal	fat	sat fat	carb	sugar	protein	fibre
837 kJ	197 kcal	0.4 g	0.0 g	47.1 g	46.2 g	0.5 g	4.6 g

METHOD OF WORK

1 Bring to the boil the water, cider, sugar, cinnamon and lemon juice. Boil for three minutes.

2 Wash, peel, halve and remove the core of the pears.

3 Place the pears into a shallow dish with the syrup, so that it just covers the pears.

4 Cover with a sheet of greaseproof paper.

5 Poach gently on a low heat until the fruit is soft. Leave to cool in its own liquor.

6 Serve as required.

CHEF'S TIP This method can be used for other fruits such as peaches, apples, nectarines and rhubarb. Soft fruits such as strawberries and raspberries will not require so much cooking and usually just the pouring of the hot syrup and leaving cool will be enough to poach them.

Rhubarb and ginger fool

Ingredients	4 portions	10 portions
Rhubarb	490 g	960 g
Caster sugar (1)	110 g	240 g
Water	70 ml	150 ml
Fresh milk	280 ml	600 ml
Caster sugar (2)	25 g	60 g
Cornflour	25 g	60 g
Compôte of rhubarb, chilled (see page 544)	100 g	200 g

energy	cal	fat	sat fat	carb	sugar	protein	fibre
873 kJ	205 kcal	1.4 g	0.8 g	47.5 g	41.7 g	3.7 g	1.9 g

METHOD OF WORK

1 Cook the rhubarb, water and first quantity of sugar to a pulp and pass it through a sieve to form a purée.

2 Add a little fresh milk to the cornflour and the sugar, boil the remainder of the milk.

3 Pour the boiling milk on to the diluted cornflour and stir well.

4 Return the mixture to the saucepan and, on a low heat, stir until it comes to the boil.

5 Mix this with the rhubarb purée.

6 Cool for a while and spoon it in to serving glasses alternating with layers of the chilled rhubarb compôte. Place in a refrigerator and allow to set.

7 Top with some more rhubarb compôte and serve with a shortbread biscuit.

Peach melba

Ingredients	4 portions	10 portions
Poached peaches	450 g	960 g
Melba sauce		
Raspberry jam	240 g	480 g
Water	25 ml	50 ml
Raspberry purée	50 ml	100 ml
Assembly		
Vanilla ice cream (see page 579)	200 g	600 g
Crème Chantilly	100 g	200 g
Biscuit cup, tuille or wafer	4	10

energy	cal	fat	sat fat	carb	sugar	protein	fibre
2349 kJ	558 kcal	20.7 g	11.9 g	93.1 g	86.5 g	5.4 g	3.7 g

METHOD OF WORK

1 For the melba sauce: place the raspberry purée and jam in a saucepan with the water. Boil for three minutes.

2 Pass through a fine strainer, cool for service.

3 Place a biscuit cup on the base of a coupe or serving plate and place a ball of the vanilla ice cream in the centre.

4 Dress half a poached peach over the ice cream and decorate with some piped crème Chantilly and the melba sauce.

5 Finish as required and serve immediately.

Guest Chef

Orange marmalade pudding soufflé with clotted cream and Cointreau custard

Chef: *Ian Corkhill*   **Centre:** *St Helens, Lancs*

This recipe uses locally made marmalade.

Ingredients	Serves 4
Marmalade	2 tblspn
Eggs	8
Caster sugar	100 g
Whipping cream	250 ml
Cointreau	1 measure
Clotted cream	100 g
Fresh mint	4 sprigs
Strong flour	50 g
Butter	50 g
Milk	250 ml
Oranges	2

METHOD OF WORK

1   Finely grate zest of the oranges, add to milk and warm.

2   Melt butter in a pan, add flour, and slowly incorporate milk, making a thick béchamel. Allow to cool.

3   Separate eggs, reserve whites and beat yolks into the above mix.

4   Segment the oranges and reserve.

5   Place the cream in a pan and warm slightly, while the cream is warming, whisk the egg yolks and sugar until thick and white, add the warm cream and return to a clean pan. Cook slowly until thick. Add the Cointreau, allow to cool, refrigerate.

6   Whisk the egg white to stiff peaks and fold into cooled béchamel

7   Place into buttered and sugared dariole moulds, bake in a pre-heated oven 200 °C for 15 minutes.

8   Melt marmalade with a little white wine and pass through a fine strainer. Keep warm.

9   To assemble the dish: Turn out soufflé into the middle of the dish, arrange three orange segments around the soufflé, in between place a spoonfull of custard. Place clotted cream at side of soufflé and finish with a sprig of mint.

Recipes

SPONGES AND CAKES

Genoese sponge   593

Sponge fingers (separated egg
   sponge method)   594

Chocolate Genoese sponge   595

Swiss roll   596

Cat's tongue biscuits   597

Lemon loaf cake   597

Banana bread   598

Coffee gâteau   599

Chantilly gâteau   600

Scones and derivatives   601

Victorian fruit cake   602

Strawberry gâteau with
   fresh cream   603

Victoria sandwich   603

Shortbread biscuits   604

Tuiles   604

Lemon madeleines   605

Macaroons   605

ICINGS, CREAMS, GLAZES AND COVERINGS

Basic buttercream   607

French buttercream   608

Fruit gelatine-based glaze   609

Caramel fudge icing   609

Chocolate glaze   610

ONLINE RECIPES

LEARNER SUPPORT

Apricot financier
Carrot and walnut cake
Himmelsbrot
Fondant icing
Royal icing
Water icing

15 Cakes, biscuits and sponges

NVQ

Unit 2FPC11 Prepare, cook and finish basic cakes, sponges and scones

VRQ

Unit 215 Produce biscuit, cake and sponge products

The role of cakes and pastries in afternoon tea

Afternoon tea or high tea differs from country to country and from establishment to establishment. In the UK, however, it is generally accepted that afternoon tea service commences at 4.00 p.m. and will usually offer a range of different types of teas (Darjeeling and Assam for instance), a good selection of sandwiches and assorted small cakes and pastries. In England, and particularly Devon and Cornwall, the highlight of afternoon tea is the service of warm scones, fruit preserves and clotted cream. This traditional regional delight will now be found in one form or another on most afternoon tea menus.

Initially, afternoon tea was introduced by the upper classes as a way of filling in the gap between luncheon and dinner. Now, however, it is a chance for most high-class establishments to show the skills of their chefs and most importantly the skills of the pastry chef. The idea is to produce small, light and well-presented cakes and pastries that will create a positive lasting memory on the palate of the customer.

It is important that each pastry or cake is not too complicated to produce. There should be a good variety of flavours and textures within the menu. Also, of course, freshness, appearance and attention to detail (e.g. pâté sucrée should be light, crisp and thin) should be closely monitored.

Introduction

Cakes are associated with many celebrations across the world. Birthdays, anniversaries, engagements, weddings and religious festivals are just some examples. The cake varieties are endless and can be in the form of light, aerated sponges to heavy and rich confections. These cakes and sponges can be prepared in a variety of ways. However the actual basic mixing methods are few and once mastered the chef can create limitless types of cakes and sponges.

This chapter discusses the different types of cakes, biscuits and sponges. It is important to be aware of which categories these confections fall into for the purpose of production.

CAKE	SPONGE	BISCUIT
Cup cakes	Genoese	Viennese biscuits
Scones	Swiss roll	Cookies
Wedding cakes	Chocolate	Macaroons
Dundee	Victoria	Langue du chat
Madeira	Plain sponge	Biscuit à la cuillère
Financiers	Othellos	
Madeleines		

Afternoon tea at the Ritz Hotel

Cake preparation methods

To help determine the method of preparation required for each recipe, cakes and sponges can fall broadly into two separate categories – cakes high in fat and cakes low in fat.

Cakes that have a high quantity of fat rely on fats to keep the gluten development minimal in order to produce a tender product. These types of cakes have a longer shelf life because of the high fat content, which slows down the staling process. They also tend to be richer and have higher moisture content. The basic preparation methods employed are shown in the table.

SUGAR BATTER METHOD (SOMETIMES KNOWN AS CREAMING)	FLOUR BATTER METHOD (SOMETIMES KNOWN AS THE TWO-STAGE METHOD)	ONE STAGE METHOD
1 Cream together the fat and sugar until light and fluffy.	Whisk the sugar and egg content to form an aeration.	Blend all the dry ingredients together.
2 Carefully add the egg content, one at a time.	Cream the fat with an equal proportion of flour.	Combine all liquid ingredients together.
3 Add the flour and other dry ingredients, alternating with wet ingredients if there are any to add.	Carefully combine the aerated egg into the creamed fat in four stages.	Carefully incorporate the wet ingredients to the dry ingredients.
4 Combine any fruits, nuts or other ingredients. Ensure even distribution of all ingredients.	Combine the remaining flour, other dry ingredients and any fruits or nuts.	Mix any other ingredients such as fruit to the batter.

Cakes that are low in fat require alternative ingredients to help tenderize the texture. These types of cake tend to have a high sugar content to assist this process. Usually the method employed is to aerate the egg content with the sugar to produce light, airy foams. This will produce a cake/sponge that is drier but flexible and does not crumble as easily as those cakes high in fat. These cakes are used to produce gâteaux and torten and can be used in desserts such as Charlottes.

The basic preparation methods employed are usually as shown in the table below.

GENOESE METHOD (SOMETIMES KNOWN AS A WHOLE EGG FOAM)	SEPARATED EGG METHOD	AERATED EGG WHITE METHOD
1 Whole eggs and warmed sugar are whisked to a foam.	Egg yolks and a percentage of the sugar are beaten.	Dry ingredients with a percentage of the sugar are combined.
2 Sieved dry ingredients are carefully folded in.	Egg whites and the remaining sugar are aerated.	Egg yolks and other liquids and flavours are added.
3 Melted butter can be added at the end.	Egg whites are folded into the yolk mixture alternately with the dry ingredients.	Egg whites are aerated with remaining sugar and folded into the batter.

Sponges

Air becomes incorporated in the form of bubbles when eggs are beaten or whisked. The protein albumen, which is present in the white of an egg, has the ability to trap air. In sponge making the eggs are whisked with the sugar until light and thick, and the flour is then folded in carefully. This helps to strengthen the structure of the albumen.

To aid this process all utensils and mixing bowls should be perfectly clean and free from any fat. The presence of fat will break down the initial structure of albumen trying to 'envelope' the air during mechanical aeration. In order to achieve the maximum aeration of the eggs, best results are achieved by whisking the eggs and sugar over a bain-marie of hot water. The temperature should be around 32 °C and not too hot as this would cook the eggs. Alternatively the sugar can be placed onto a baking sheet and warmed in an oven prior to whisking with the eggs.

Whisk until the mixture becomes thick and light. It should be thick enough to leave the mark of the whisk for a few seconds after it has been removed, otherwise known as the 'ribbon stage'. For best results always bake at between 182 and 204 °C.

The use of baking powder

Baking powder is made as follows:

- 2 parts cream of tartar (acid)
- 1 part bicarbonate of soda (alkali).

Baking powder is a raising agent that is commonly used in cake-making, it is a dry chemical used to increase the volume and lighten the texture of baked goods such as muffins, cakes, scones. The powder is activated when liquid is added, producing carbon dioxide and forming bubbles that cause the mixture to expand. For this reason, it is important to get your cake mixture into the oven quickly once the 'wet' ingredients have been added to the 'dry' ingredients.

Self-raising flour is made from plain flour combined with a small amount of baking powder.

WEB LINK For further information on the history of baking powder and how it is produced check out **http://www.enotes.com/how-products-encyclopedia/baking-powder**

Baking

The aim when baking cakes and sponges is to cook them as quickly as possible without imparting too much colour to the crust. Various factors will affect the baking of cakes and adjustments will need to be made to the overall baking temperature to compensate for this.

Richness of the recipe

If the content of sugar is high within a recipe, over-cooking and too high a temperature will caramelize the colour of the cake or sponge quickly before it is thoroughly baked. The oven temperature must be cool to medium to prevent this happening.

Size of the cake or sponge

The smaller the size of the cake or sponge to be baked the quicker it will cook. Larger cakes will require a lower temperature because they will remain in the oven for a longer period of time.

Shape of the cake or sponge

An appreciation of the shape of the cake or sponge to be baked is important. A large quantity of Genoese sponge can be baked rapidly in large, thin sheets as opposed to 20 cm cake rings. This is because of the depth of the mixture to be baked. A deeper depth should have a cooler oven temperature to facilitate the correct cooking of the item.

> **CHEF'S TIP** How to tell when a cake is baked? There are three basic ways of revealing when a cake is correctly cooked.
>
> - The cake contracts from the side of the baking tin.
> - The cake springs back when it is gently pressed with a finger.
> - A skewer or small knife is inserted gently into the centre of the cake and is removed to reveal an implement free of crumbs and clean of the mixture.

Humidity

The oven chamber should create a humid environment in order to achieve a level top to a cake and to help with consistent and thorough baking. Sometimes a pan of boiled water added to the oven chamber will help create a humid atmosphere.

Addition of other ingredients

Certain additions such as honey, glucose or inverted sugars can increase the overall colour of the finished cake because these are sugar-based ingredients. The baking temperature therefore needs to be lowered. A large amount of preserved or dried fruit will increase the heaviness of a cake and the temperature of the oven needs to be reduced, so too will decorative items such as sugar and almonds sprinkled on the top of a cake.

Basic faults in cake production

Cake sinking in the middle:

- Undercooked.
- Knocked heavily prior to being cooked in the oven.
- Too much liquid added to the recipe.
- Too much baking powder used.
- Too much sugar used (coupled with a dark crust colour).

Fruit sinking in cakes:

- Too much sugar used.
- Fruit was too large and still wet.
- Baking temperature too low.

- Too much baking powder used.
- Cake mixture is too light to hold the fruit.

Small volume and heavy texture of finished cake:

- Insufficient aeration caused by either a lack of baking powder or lack of aeration in the egg content.
- Lack of sugar used in the recipe.

Peaked top to the cake:

- Over-mixed cake mixture.
- Flour used was too strong.
- Oven is too hot and dry.

Please note that some cake recipes require a peaked top as part of their overall presentation: it is not necessarily a fault.

Storing cakes, sponges and biscuits

Maintaining the quality of cakes, sponges and biscuits during storage is a significant issue. Staling and moisture absorption are aspects that need to be considered. Staling refers to a loss of moisture from baked products, such as cakes, biscuits, sponges and yeast goods. This results in a dry, hard and firmer-textured product. Sometimes this is associated with lack of flavour or even rancid taste.

Moisture absorption occurs when moisture from the atmosphere is absorbed into the baked product. The outside crust will become soft in certain baked products, such as heavy cakes and yeast goods. Below are a number of steps that need to be taken to help ensure the correct storage procedures are maintained to guarantee a longer shelf life of baked products such as cakes, sponges and biscuits.

- Dry commodities need to be stored in clean, sealed plastic containers on clean shelving in a separate storage room. The room needs to be maintained at a constant cool temperature and should have a dry atmosphere.
- Stock rotation should be employed so that all ingredients are used up and then replenished by a new batch of ingredients. The empty container should be cleaned before replenishing. It is not recommended to store baked items for long periods of time in a refrigerator because of starch breakdown and eventual loss of colour and flavour.
- To store baked products for short periods in a refrigerator it is essential that they are covered in plastic film or placed into airtight plastic containers. Items that contain large amounts of sugar will attract moisture, which may have an adverse effect on flavour and texture.
- Storing baked products in a freezer is a method that works exceptionally well. The baked product should be completely cooled before wrapping in airtight plastic wrapping and then in aluminium foil. Place this into a plastic bag, sucking out as much air from the packaging as possible. Label and date the item before freezing. Good practice is to blast freeze any item for 30 minutes before placing into a holding freezer. This process helps to maintain moisture content in the product and helps to eliminate potential freezer burn.

TASK Consider how you might store a freshly baked rich fruit cake that will need to be decorated with marzipan and fondant icing in four weeks time?

SPECIALIST BAKING EQUIPMENT

PICTURE	DESCRIPTION
	An electric mixer is an invaluable piece of equipment used in the bakery or pastry kitchens. Most mixers are planetary mixers and can be either tabletop or the larger floor-standing versions. The one feature that all these mixers have is that the mixing bowl remains fixed in one position while the mixing tool fits into an attachment arm that rotates 360° to reach all the areas inside the mixing bowl. Attachments can be whisks, beaters and dough hooks with different speeds able to be implemented to mix diverse preparations.
	Stainless steel cake rings have no top or bottom. They come in various sizes and can be used to bake in or to mould up layers of sponge bases with fillings that need to set into a specific shape. Some of these rings are expandable to create differing size requirements.
	Muffin tins and individual cake tins come in varying sizes according to their traditional shape. The tins require careful cleaning and drying without scratching the moulded impressions.
	Silicone baking moulds with non-stick, flexible surfaces have revolutionized baking for the chef. They withstand very hot temperatures and are moulded into separate shapes. They require no greasing or flouring and only need to be wiped clean with a damp cloth.
	A springform baking tin is a round tin with a removable base. It usually has high sides for baking all types of sponges and cakes and the sides of the tin can be detached for ease of removing baked products.

TASK Select three items of equipment from the above list and provide a cleaning schedule for each of them.

WEB LINK For further information on health and safety check the following website:
http://www.hse.gov.uk/legislation/

HEALTH & SAFETY TIP When using any electrical equipment, such as an electric food mixer, you should always take care and follow the guidelines below:

- Do not wear loose clothing or jewellery that could get caught in the machinery.
- Before you assemble the machine for use, clean or take apart electrical equipment:
  - Turn off the appliance.
  - Turn off the circuit breaker or wall switch or unplug from the electrical outlet.
- Keep your hands and utensils away from the mixer bowl and blades when operating.
- Always follow the cleaning and usage procedures for your equipment.

Recipes

Genoese sponge (Génoise)

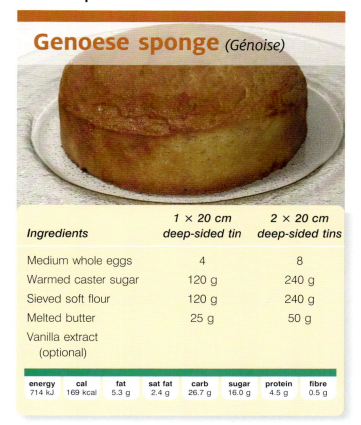

Ingredients	1 × 20 cm deep-sided tin	2 × 20 cm deep-sided tins
Medium whole eggs	4	8
Warmed caster sugar	120 g	240 g
Sieved soft flour	120 g	240 g
Melted butter	25 g	50 g
Vanilla extract (optional)		

energy	cal	fat	sat fat	carb	sugar	protein	fibre
714 kJ	169 kcal	5.3 g	2.4 g	26.7 g	16.0 g	4.5 g	0.5 g

METHOD OF WORK

1 Preheat the oven to 180 °C.

2 Whisk the sugar and eggs together, first to dissolve the sugar and then to form a stiff, light sabayon.

3 After whisking, the foam should be at the classic 'ribbon' stage. Rain the flour into the egg/sugar foam and incorporate the flour by hand.

4 When the flour is almost completely folded in, pour in the butter (this must not be hot). Scoop the Genoese mixture into the prepared tins (greased with butter and floured or lined with silicone paper) to about three-quarters full.

5 Place in the oven and bake for about 30 minutes. The time may vary by a few minutes either way according to the quantity, the tin thickness and the oven.

6 There are two tests to check whether the sponge is baked. First, press the surface in the centre and it should spring back. Second, the sponge should start to shrink from the edges.

7 Turn out onto either a cooling wire rack or silicone paper sprinkled with a little semolina.

CHEF'S TIP Caster sugar is standard for Genoese. It helps to warm the sugar through, either in the oven or in the microwave when using small quantities. About 40 °C is an adequate temperature. Too much sugar added to the mixture will result in a tougher texture and darker sponge colour.

Rain the flour into the egg/sugar foam

Incorporate the flour by hand

When the flour is almost completely folded in, pour in the butter

Sponge fingers (separated egg sponge method)
(Biscuit à la cuillère)

Ingredients	400 g	800 g
Fresh whole eggs	4	8
Caster sugar	110 g	220 g
Sieved soft flour	100 g	200 g
Vanilla extract		
Icing sugar	50 g	100 g

energy	cal	fat	sat fat	carb	sugar	protein	fibre
89 kJ	21 kcal	0.4 g	0.1 g	4.0 g	2.8 g	0.6 g	0.1 g

METHOD OF WORK

1 Preheat the oven to 220 °C.
2 Carefully separate the egg yolks from the whites and place into separate mixing bowls.
3 Beat the egg yolks with two-thirds of the caster sugar to a soft ribbon consistency.
4 Aerate the egg whites until soft peaks have been developed adding the remaining sugar and continuing to beat until the egg whites have held the sugar and the peaks have become firmer.
5 Fold one-third of the egg whites into the egg yolks using a spatula.
6 Fold in the remaining egg whites and carefully fold them into the mixture.

7 Before the egg whites and yolks have been completely combined, rain the flour into the egg/sugar foam and incorporate the flour until the mixture has become smooth.
8 Using a piping bag with a 15 mm plain tube, pipe the mixture as quickly as possible onto a baking sheet lined with silicone paper or a silicone baking mat. Pipe 10 cm long fingers for each biscuit.
9 Lightly dust them with icing sugar, leave to rest for 3 minutes and then dust with icing sugar again.
10 Place in the oven and bake for about 8 minutes. The time may vary by 2 minutes either way according to the quantity and the oven.
11 Lift the biscuits off the baking sheet onto a cooling wire rack.

CHEF'S TIP   Many chefs turn out the baked sponge onto silicone paper sprinkled with sugar. This increases the overall sweetness of the sponge as the sugar clings to it when cooling down. Using semolina is better because it has no sweetness or flavour value and will easily brush off the cooled sponge.

Chocolate Genoese sponge

(Génoise au chocolat)

Ingredients	1 × 20 cm deep-sided tin	2 × 20 cm deep-sided tins
Medium whole eggs	4	8
Warmed caster sugar	120 g	240 g
Sieved soft flour	85 g	165 g
Cocoa powder	35 g	75 g
Melted butter	25 g	50 g

energy	cal	fat	sat fat	carb	sugar	protein	fibre
705 kJ	167 kcal	6.2 g	3.0 g	24.0 g	15.9 g	4.9 g	1.6 g

METHOD OF WORK

1 Preheat the oven to 180 °C.

2 Whisk the sugar and eggs together, first to dissolve the sugar and then to form a stiff, creamy sabayon.

3 After whisking the foam should be at the classic 'ribbon' stage.

4 Sieve the cocoa powder and flour together and carefully rain into the egg/sugar foam and incorporate the flour/cocoa by hand.

5 When the flour/cocoa is almost completely folded in, pour in the butter (this must not be hot). Scoop the Genoese mixture into the prepared tins (greased with butter and floured or lined with silicone paper) to about three-quarters full.

6 Place in the oven and bake for about 30 minutes. The time may vary by five minutes either way according to the quantity, the tin thickness and the oven.

7 There are two tests to check whether the sponge is baked. First, press the surface in the centre and it should spring back. Second, the sponge should start to shrink from the edges.

8 Turn out onto either a cooling wire rack or silicone paper sprinkled with a little semolina.

CHEF'S TIP This recipe can also be used as a basis for various gâteaux and desserts. Simply spread the mixture onto prepared baking sheets and bake for 6 minutes and cool in the same way as for Genoese. Cut out into required shapes as appropriate. Wrap individually in plastic film and store in a refrigerator for a day prior to use.

To check whether the sponge i.s baked, first, press the surface in the centre and it should spring back

Second, the sponge should start to shrink from the edges of the tin when it is cooked

Swiss roll *(Biscuit roulade)*

Ingredients	400 g	800 g
Fresh whole eggs	4	8
Caster sugar	110 g	220 g
Sieved soft flour	80 g	160 g
Potato flour	40 g	80 g

energy	cal	fat	sat fat	carb	sugar	protein	fibre
789 kJ	186 kcal	3.6 g	1.0 g	34.0 g	19.6 g	5.9 g	0.4 g

METHOD OF WORK

1   Preheat the oven to 200 °C.

2   Carefully separate the egg yolks from the whites and place into separate mixing bowls.

3   Beat the egg yolks with two-thirds of the caster sugar to a soft ribbon consistency.

4   Aerate the egg whites until soft peaks have developed, adding the remaining sugar and continuing to beat until the egg whites have held the sugar and the peaks have become firmer.

5   Fold one-third of the egg whites into the egg yolks using a spatula.

6   Add the remaining egg whites and carefully fold them into the mixture.

7   Before the egg whites and yolks have been completely combined, sieve the potato starch and flour together and carefully incorporate into the egg/sugar foam until the mixture has become smooth.

8   Spread the mixture onto a silicone paper lined baking sheet.

9   Place in the oven and bake for about 8 minutes. The time may vary by 2 minutes either way according to the quantity and the oven.

10   Carefully remove the sponge from the baking sheet and place onto silicone paper, lightly sprinkled with semolina. Carefully peel off the silicone paper, gently roll up and allow to cool.

11   After cooling unroll and fill with the required filling such as jam or crème Chantilly, trim the edges and roll up, shaping back into a Swiss roll.

CHEF'S TIP A chocolate version can be produced by substituting 25 g of the potato flour for cocoa powder.

Carefully incorporate the flour into the egg/sugar foam until the mixture has become smooth

Spread the mixture onto a silicone paper-lined baking sheet

Peel off the silicone paper, gently roll up and allow to cool

Cat's tongue biscuits
(Langue du chat)

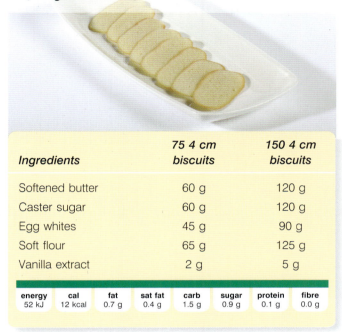

Ingredients	75 4 cm biscuits	150 4 cm biscuits
Softened butter	60 g	120 g
Caster sugar	60 g	120 g
Egg whites	45 g	90 g
Soft flour	65 g	125 g
Vanilla extract	2 g	5 g

energy	cal	fat	sat fat	carb	sugar	protein	fibre
52 kJ	12 kcal	0.7 g	0.4 g	1.5 g	0.9 g	0.1 g	0.0 g

METHOD OF WORK

1 Preheat the oven to 220 °C.

2 Beat together the softened butter and the caster sugar until light in colour and fluffy in texture.

3 Gradually incorporate the egg whites to soften the mixture and then add the vanilla and the flour. Beat to a paste consistency.

4 Place the mixture into a piping bag with a 6 mm plain tube. Pipe the mixture into 4 cm fingers onto a lightly greased baking sheet. Allow sufficient space between each piped finger as the mixture will spread initially when baking.

5 Place in the oven and bake until the edges of each biscuit have a light golden colour.

6 Carefully remove the langues du chat from the baking sheet while still hot and place onto a wire cooling rack.

7 After cooling, store in an airtight container prior to using.

CHEF'S TIP These biscuits are used for decorating various gâteaux, desserts, cakes and torten. They can accompany ice cream dishes, sweet dessert wines or they can be made into petit fours:

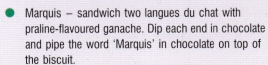

- Marquis – sandwich two langues du chat with praline-flavoured ganache. Dip each end in chocolate and pipe the word 'Marquis' in chocolate on top of the biscuit.
- Copeaux – Pipe the langues up to 8 cm in length. When baked, immediately curl around a dowel to create a curl.

Lemon loaf cake (Gâteau au citron)

Ingredients	1 large loaf tin	2 large loaf tins
Whole eggs	125 g	250 g
Caster sugar	175 g	350 g
Salt	3 g	5 g
Double cream	75 g	150 g
Soft flour	135 g	270 g
Baking powder	3 g	5 g
Finely grated lemon zest	2 lemons	3 lemons
Melted, clarified butter	50 g	100 g
Apricot glaze (see page 474)	50 g	100 g
Lemon water icing (see recipe online)	40 g	80 g

energy	cal	fat	sat fat	carb	sugar	protein	fibre
1243 kJ	296 kcal	12.1 g	6.9 g	44.7 g	32.3 g	3.8 g	0.6 g

METHOD OF WORK

1 Preheat the oven to 180 °C.

2 Mix together the eggs, caster sugar, salt and double cream. Ensure that all the ingredients have been thoroughly mixed.

3 Add the sieved baking powder and flour, and the lemon zest with the clarified butter at the end. Beat all the ingredients together until a smooth paste has been obtained.

4 Line a loaf tin with double thickness silicone paper and distribute the mixture into the tin, evening it out with a scraper.

5 Place in the oven and bake for approximately 50 minutes, checking every so often to ensure even cooking and that the crust is not colouring too quickly.

6 When baked, remove the cakes from their moulds while still hot and place onto a wire cooling rack.

7 Brush immediately with hot apricot glaze (see page 474) and then with the lemon water icing.

8 After cooling, store in an airtight container prior to using.

Banana bread

Ingredients	2 medium loaf tin	4 medium loaf tins
Unsalted butter	140 g	280 g
Icing sugar	220 g	440 g
Salt	2 g	4 g
Eggs	2	4
Walnuts	50 g	100 g
Banana purée	300 g	600 g
Raisins	100 g	200 g
Soft flour	280 g	560 g
Baking powder	10 g	20 g
Nutmeg	2 g	4 g
Apricot glaze (see page 474)	50 g	100 g

energy	cal	fat	sat fat	carb	sugar	protein	fibre
1063 kJ	253 kcal	10.3 g	5.1 g	38.1 g	24.7 g	3.3 g	1.0 g

METHOD OF WORK

1 Preheat the oven to 170 °C.

2 Beat together the butter, icing sugar and the salt. Ensure that all three ingredients have been thoroughly beaten so that they are light and fluffy.

3 Add the eggs one at a time, and mix into the creamed butter.

4 Add the sieved baking powder and flour, then the banana purée with the nuts, raisins and nutmeg. Beat all the ingredients together until a smooth paste has been obtained.

5 Line a loaf tin with double thickness silicone paper and distribute the mixture into the loaf tins.

6 Place in the oven and bake for approximately 60 minutes, checking every so often to ensure even cooking and that the crust is not colouring too quickly.

7 When baked, remove the cakes from their moulds while still hot and place onto a wire cooling rack.

8 Brush immediately with hot apricot glaze.

9 After cooling, store in an airtight container prior to using.

Line a loaf tin with double thickness of silicone paper and distribute the mixture into the tin

Coffee gâteau *(Gâteau mocha)*

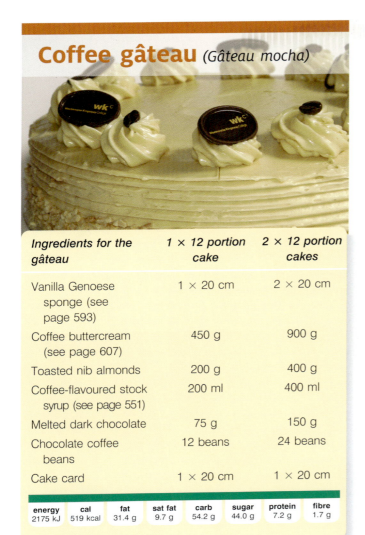

Ingredients for the gâteau	1 × 12 portion cake	2 × 12 portion cakes
Vanilla Genoese sponge (see page 593)	1 × 20 cm	2 × 20 cm
Coffee buttercream (see page 607)	450 g	900 g
Toasted nib almonds	200 g	400 g
Coffee-flavoured stock syrup (see page 551)	200 ml	400 ml
Melted dark chocolate	75 g	150 g
Chocolate coffee beans	12 beans	24 beans
Cake card	1 × 20 cm	1 × 20 cm

energy	cal	fat	sat fat	carb	sugar	protein	fibre
2175 kJ	519 kcal	31.4 g	9.7 g	54.2 g	44.0 g	7.2 g	1.7 g

METHOD OF WORK

1 Carefully slice the sponge into three equal discs. Brush each disc well with the coffee-flavoured stock syrup.

2 Place the top sponge disc onto the cake card and spread with some of the coffee-flavoured buttercream. Place another disc on top and repeat the process, position the final disc on top.

3 Coat the top and the sides of the cake evenly and smoothly with the buttercream.

4 Using a comb scraper, run the scraper around the side of the cake to create even grooves in a decorative effect.

5 Carefully cover the bottom of the sides of the cake with the toasted nib almonds, 1 cm high.

6 Using the melted dark chocolate in a small silicone paper piping bag, create small chocolate motifs onto silicone paper or an acetate sheet. Leave to set in a cool place for a few minutes.

7 Using a 6 mm star piping tube, pipe rosettes of the remaining buttercream to display the portion control of each cake (12 rosettes per cake). Carefully arrange a chocolate motif on each rosette with a coffee bean.

8 With the remaining chocolate pipe the word *Mocha* on the centre of the gâteau and place onto a suitable display dish for service.

Brush each disc well with the coffee-flavoured stock syrup

Run the scraper around the side of the cake to create even grooves in a decorative effect

Chantilly gâteau (Gâteau Chantilly)

Ingredients	1 × 8 portion cake	2 × 8 portion cakes
Vanilla Genoese sponge (see page 593)	1 × 20 cm sponge	2 × 20 cm sponges
Crème Chantilly (see page 553)	450 g	900 g
Langue du chat biscuits	25	50
Kirsch-flavoured stock syrup (see page 551)	200 ml	400 ml
Langue du chat discs or pre-made small macaroons	12	24
Cake card	1 × 20 cm	2 × 20 cm

energy	cal	fat	sat fat	carb	sugar	protein	fibre
2806 kJ	668 kcal	45.9 g	17.1 g	91.8 g	61.8 g	10.8 g	1.0 g

METHOD OF WORK

1 Carefully slice the sponge into three equal discs. Brush each disc well with the Kirsch-flavoured stock syrup.
2 Place the top sponge disc onto the cake card and spread with some of the Chantilly cream. Place another disc on top and repeat the process, position the final disc on top.
3 Coat the top and the sides of the cake evenly and smoothly with the Chantilly cream.
4 Using a comb scraper, run the scraper around the side of the cake to create even grooves in a decorative effect.
5 Trim the bottoms and sides of each langue du chat biscuit and arrange neatly around the sides of the gâteau so that they reach half way up the side.
6 Using a 6 mm star piping tube, pipe rosettes of the remaining Chantilly cream to display the portion control of each cake (eight rosettes per cake). Carefully arrange a half macaroon or langue du chat disc on each rosette.
7 Place onto a suitable display dish for service.

CHEF'S TIP There are many different types of classical fresh cream-based gâteau that can be produced for afternoon tea service or for a simple dessert.

Carefully slice the sponge into three equal discs. Brush each disc well with the Kirsch-flavoured stock syrup

Trim the bottoms and sides of each langue du chat biscuit and arrange neatly around the sides of the gâteau so that they cover the sides of the gateau

Scones and derivatives

Ingredients	15 5 cm scones	25 5 cm scones
Medium flour	225 g	450 g
Baking powder	15 g	30 g
Caster sugar	40 g	65 g
Butter	50 g	100 g
Salt	2 g	4 g
Milk powder	5 g	10 g
Fresh full fat milk	150 ml	275 ml

energy	cal	fat	sat fat	carb	sugar	protein	fibre
404 kJ	96 kcal	3.3 g	2.0 g	15.5 g	3.7 g	1.9 g	0.5 g

METHOD OF WORK

1 Preheat the oven to 200 °C.

2 Sieve the flour, milk powder, salt and sugar together.

3 Rub the butter into the dry ingredients until an even consistency resembling ground almonds has been obtained.

4 Make a well in the centre of the mixture and add the milk.

5 Carefully mix lightly to a smooth paste.

6 Leave the scone paste to rest for 10 minutes in a bowl covered with plastic film.

7 Now roll the paste out to approximately 15 mm thick and cut out with a plain 5 cm round pastry cutter. Place onto a baking sheet lined with a silicone baking mat or a lightly greased baking sheet.

8 Place the scones into a refrigerator to rest for a further 10 minutes, covered with plastic film.

9 Remove the plastic film and carefully brush each scone with egg wash.

10 Bake in the oven for approximately 15 minutes or until they are well-risen with a golden colour.

11 Remove the scones from the baking sheet onto a wire cooling rack.

12 Serve the scones warm with butter, strawberry jam and clotted cream.

CHEF'S TIP Varieties of scones include:

Fruit scones: add 90 g of sultanas per 225 g of flour and add the fruit at the same time the liquid is added to prevent the fruit from breaking up.

Oatmeal scones: replace half the flour with oatmeal.

Coconut scones: add 25 g desiccated coconut to the flour. After egg washing the top of the scone, dip half of the scone into desiccated coconut for decoration before baking.

Victorian fruit cake

Ingredients	1 × 20 cm deep Round cake	2 × 20 cm deep round cake
Butter	225 g	450 g
Soft brown sugar	225 g	450 g
Whole eggs	4	8
Soft flour	210 g	420 g
Baking powder	15 g	30 g
Raisins	225 g	450 g
Sultanas	225 g	450 g
Glacé cherries	100 g	200 g
Mixed spice	5 g	10 g
Brandy (optional)	10 ml	20 ml
Orange zest and juice	1 orange	2 oranges

energy	cal	fat	sat fat	carb	sugar	protein	fibre
1781 kJ	424 kcal	17.5 g	10.4 g	65.1 g	51.9 g	5.0 g	1.6 g

METHOD OF WORK

1 Preheat the oven to 150 °C.
2 Lightly grease and line a 20 cm deep round cake tin with double silicone paper.
3 Place all the raisins and sultanas together and wash in clean, cold water. Drain and add the glacé cherries, brandy and orange zest and juice. Leave this to soak for 2 hours.
4 Beat together the butter and the soft brown sugar until light and slowly add the eggs, one at a time, clearing the mixture before adding further eggs.

5 Sieve the flour, baking powder and the mixed spice together and incorporate into the sugar batter.
6 Combine all the fruit and juices into the mixture and mix together carefully, taking care not to break the fruit.
7 Place the mixture into the prepared baking tin, level the top with a scraper and place in the oven to bake for approximately 2 hours.
8 Halfway through the baking process it is advisable to place a sheet of silicone paper on top of the cake to prevent over-colouring.
9 When cooked the cake should be firm to the touch, and a skewer or knife inserted into the centre should come out clean.
10 Remove from the oven to cool down still in its tin for 30 minutes, then turn out and cool completely on a wire cooling rack.
11 When cooled, brush the top of the cake with an apricot glaze and either decorate with marzipan or glacé fruits or serve it as it is.

CHEF'S TIP If stored in an airtight container and left in a cool, dry and dark place, this cake will last for several days.

Strawberry gâteau with fresh cream

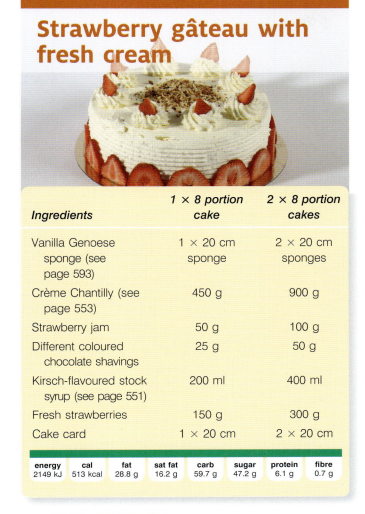

Ingredients	1 × 8 portion cake	2 × 8 portion cakes
Vanilla Genoese sponge (see page 593)	1 × 20 cm sponge	2 × 20 cm sponges
Crème Chantilly (see page 553)	450 g	900 g
Strawberry jam	50 g	100 g
Different coloured chocolate shavings	25 g	50 g
Kirsch-flavoured stock syrup (see page 551)	200 ml	400 ml
Fresh strawberries	150 g	300 g
Cake card	1 × 20 cm	2 × 20 cm

energy	cal	fat	sat fat	carb	sugar	protein	fibre
2149 kJ	513 kcal	28.8 g	16.2 g	59.7 g	47.2 g	6.1 g	0.7 g

METHOD OF WORK

1 Carefully slice the sponge into three equal discs. Brush each disc well with the Kirsch-flavoured stock syrup.

2 Place the top sponge disc onto the cake card and spread with the strawberry jam and then some of the Chantilly cream. Scatter a few sliced strawberries on top. Place another disc on top and repeat the process, position the final disc on top.

3 Coat the top and the sides of the cake evenly and smoothly with the Chantilly cream.

4 Using a comb scraper, run the scraper around the side of the cake to create even grooves in a decorative effect.

5 Slice and trim the bottoms and sides of each remaining strawberry and arrange neatly around the sides of the gâteau so that they reach half way up the side.

6 Using a 6 mm star piping tube, pipe rosettes of the remaining Chantilly cream to display the portion control of each cake (8 rosettes per cake). Carefully arrange a quartered strawberry on each rosette. Sprinkle a little of the chocolate in the centre.

7 Place onto a suitable display dish for service.

Victoria sandwich

Ingredients	1 × 8 portion sandwich	2 × 8 portion sandwich
Butter	100 g	250 g
Caster sugar	100 g	250 g
Eggs (medium sized)	2	5
Vanilla extract		
Soft flour	100 g	250 g
Baking powder	5 g	12 g
Strawberry or raspberry jam	50 g	100 g
Buttercream	75 g	150 g

energy	cal	fat	sat fat	carb	sugar	protein	fibre
1124 kJ	268 kcal	14.3 g	8.5 g	33.5 g	24.2 g	2.9 g	0.5 g

METHOD OF WORK

1 Pre-heat the oven to 180 °C.

2 Cream together the butter and caster sugar until aerated, light and fluffy in texture.

3 Gradually incorporate the beaten eggs and the vanilla extract.

4 Sieve together the soft flour and baking powder twice and mix into the fat and egg mixture.

5 Divide between two 18 cm greased and floured sponge sandwich tins.

6 Place in the oven to bake for between 15 and 20 minutes.

7 Turn out onto a wire rack to cool.

8 Spread one half with the jam and the other half with the beaten buttercream and sandwich the two halves carefully together.

9 Dust with icing sugar and serve.

Shortbread biscuits

Ingredients	makes 16 biscuits	makes 32 biscuits
Soft flour	100 g	200 g
Rice flour	100 g	200 g
Butter	100 g	200 g
Caster sugar	100 g	200 g
Egg (medium sized)	1	2
Vanilla extract		

energy	cal	fat	sat fat	carb	sugar	protein	fibre
502 kJ	120 kcal	5.6 g	3.4 g	16.2 g	6.7 g	1.4 g	0.3 g

METHOD OF WORK

1 Sieve the flour and the rice flour into a basin.
2 Rub in the butter until the texture resembles breadcrumbs and carefully mix in the sugar.
3 Bind the mixture to a stiff paste with the beaten egg and add the vanilla extract at the same time. Knead carefully but do not overwork the paste.
4 Roll out to 5 mm using some extra caster sugar. Prick the tops with a fork and cut neatly into finger shapes with a sharp knife, cutting to 8 cm in length and 3 cm width. Preheat an oven to 190 °C.
5 Place the shortbread onto a baking sheet lined with baking parchment and bake in the oven until just cooked with as little colour as possible.
6 Remove from the oven and cool on a wire rack.

Tuiles

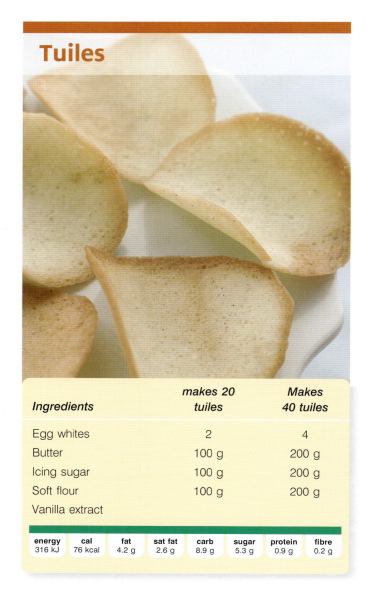

Ingredients	makes 20 tuiles	Makes 40 tuiles
Egg whites	2	4
Butter	100 g	200 g
Icing sugar	100 g	200 g
Soft flour	100 g	200 g
Vanilla extract		

energy	cal	fat	sat fat	carb	sugar	protein	fibre
316 kJ	76 kcal	4.2 g	2.6 g	8.9 g	5.3 g	0.9 g	0.2 g

METHOD OF WORK

1 Beat together the butter and the icing sugar until soft and creamy.
2 Add the egg whites and flour with the vanilla extract.
3 Beat thoroughly and then rest in a refrigerator for 45 minutes.
4 Preheat an oven to 200 °C.
5 Place a teaspoon full of the mixture onto a greased baking sheet and spread with a palette knife, allowing room for the mixture to spread further during baking.
6 Bake until the edges of the tuiles have started to turn golden.
7 Quickly remove each tuile from the oven and while they are still hot drape over a rolling pin to create the classic tuile shape.
8 Leave to cool and store in an airtight container.

Lemon madeleines

Ingredients	8 madeleines	20 madeleines
Unsalted butter	80 g	160 g
Whole eggs	2	4
Caster sugar	80 g	160 g
Ground almonds	40 g	80 g
White soft flour	80 g	160 g
Grated zest of lemon	1 lemon	2 lemons
Icing sugar	50 g	100 g

energy	cal	fat	sat fat	carb	sugar	protein	fibre
923 kJ	221 kcal	12.4 g	5.8 g	24.8 g	17.4 g	3.6 g	0.7 g

METHOD OF WORK

1 Melt the butter in a pan and slowly cook it until a light nut-brown colour has been achieved (do not let the butter burn).

2 Leave the butter to cool for a few minutes and then carefully drain off the fat leaving the residue behind.

3 Whisk the eggs and sugar together using an electric mixing machine. Aerate to soft peaks. Combine the flour, lemon zest and ground almonds together before gradually folding into the egg mixture.

4 Carefully add the melted butter to the mixture and leave to stand for an hour.

5 Lightly grease and flour a madeleine tin (enough for two madeleines per portion) and spoon the mixture into the prepared tin.

6 Bake for approximately 9 minutes until the tops are springy to the touch.

7 Keep in the tins for a couple of minutes to cool slightly and then remove onto a wire rack, dust with icing sugar and reserve warm for service.

Macaroons

Ingredients	8 macaroons	50 macaroons
Ground almonds	125 g	250 g
Icing sugar	225 g	450 g
Egg whites	4	8
Salt	Pinch	Pinch
Colouring		
Flavouring		

energy	cal	fat	sat fat	carb	sugar	protein	fibre
898 kJ	213 kcal	8.7 g	0.7 g	30.6 g	29.9 g	5.1 g	1.3 g

METHOD OF WORK

1 Mix the ground almonds with the icing sugar and pass through a sieve twice.

2 Take half of the egg whites and lightly beat before adding to the ground almond mixture.

3 Aerate the remaining egg whites to peaks with the pinch of salt.

4 Carefully fold into the almond mixture, colour and flavour appropriately.

5 Place this mixture into a piping bag with a 5 mm plain tube fitted and pipe onto a double baking sheet lined with silicone paper small bulbs of the macaroon paste about the size of a 10 p coin. Preheat the oven to 180 °C.

6 Stand for 15 minutes at room temperature.

7 Bake for 10 to 12 minutes in a preheated oven with the door slightly ajar.

8 Place on a wire rack when cooked to cool down and then sandwich together with an appropriate filling.

Assembling and decorating gâteaux

The difference between gâteaux and torten is very fine and, in some cases, it is impossible to tell one from the other. Each term means a large decorated cake. The name 'gâteau' is the French term and the word 'torte' is German. The definition that a torte should be divided into portions within the decoration is the accepted British interpretation, but if classical cakes such as Sacher torte are being sold as a whole it is best to retain the descriptive name of the torte.

Except for specialities, the make-up of most gâteaux is similar to torten. It usually consists of an enriched sponge or Genoese, sandwiched with buttercream, fresh cream, ganache, curd, jam, with or without fruit, liqueur, chocolate, nuts, etc. Buttercream, fresh cream or fondant can be then used to cover the sponge and suitably decorated. Gâteaux may be named according to the type of flavours and mixings used.

Step-by-step: Procedure for assembling a gâteau

1. Trim the edges of the sponge as required.

2. Unless specified the sponge should always be cut into three equal layers and if the sponge used is fairly dry, such as a Genoese, then each layer should be brushed with a flavoured stock syrup appropriate to the main flavour of the gâteau.

3. Apply the filling using a piping bag to help achieve a uniform layer.

4. Continue by placing the second sponge disc on top and repeating the process until the third and final layer is placed on top (note that the top sponge layer is usually the bottom of the initial sponge because the shape is more defined).

5. Finish the top of the gâteau with a clean palette knife. The gâteau is now ready for decorating. The finished result should be similar to the above.

6. Pipe small chocolate motifs onto silicone paper or an acetate sheet to use for decoration.

Icings, creams, glazes and coverings

There are a variety of icings, creams, glazes and coverings that the chef can use to coat and decorate any gâteau or cake. They have numerous advantages in their use because they contribute flavour, colour and texture to the finish. However, they will also improve the appearance greatly if they are carefully applied and the gâteau or cake will have its storage life improved because the coating will form a protective sheet around the sponge.

There are six distinct types of coatings, shown in the table.

ICINGS	CREAMS	BUTTERCREAMS	GLAZES	PASTES	FUDGE ICINGS
Fondant	Chantilly	Basic	Gelatine-based	Marzipan	Caramel
Royal	Whipped cream	French	Pectin-based	Cover	White
Water icing		Italian	Jam-based		Chocolate
			Chocolate		

Recipes

Basic buttercream

Ingredients	250 g	500 g
Unsalted butter	70 g	125 g
Shortening	45 g	70 g
Icing sugar	125 g	250 g
Lemon juice	1 g	2 g
Vanilla extract	2 g	4 g
Warm water	15 g	30 g

energy	cal	fat	sat fat	carb	sugar	protein	fibre
599 kJ	143 kcal	10.3 g	4.8 g	13.2 g	13.0 g	0.0 g	0.0 g

METHOD OF WORK

1   Using a machine with a beater/paddle attachment, cream together the butter, shortening and sugar.
2   Add the lemon juice and vanilla and continue beating the mixture until it is light and fluffy in texture.
3   Finally, slowly add the warm water while beating. This will develop a slightly softer texture.

CHEF'S TIP Egg whites may be added instead of the water to give a slightly lighter texture to the buttercream, egg yolks can be added to give a somewhat richer buttercream.

French buttercream

Ingredients	250 g	500 g
Caster sugar	125 g	250 g
Water	40 g	60 ml
Egg yolks	45 g	90 g
Softened, unsalted butter	150 g	300 g
Vanilla extract	2 g	4 g

energy	cal	fat	sat fat	carb	sugar	protein	fibre
734 kJ	177 kcal	13.7 g	8.2 g	13.2 g	13.2 g	0.8 g	0.0 g

METHOD OF WORK

1 Combine the sugar and the water in a clean, heavy-based saucepan (preferably copper). Let the sugar dissolve for a few minutes before bringing to the boil.

2 Continue to boil while constantly monitoring the temperature using a sugar thermometer. The sugar solution should eventually reach 115 °C before removing it from the heat.

3 While the sugar is boiling, using a mixing machine with a whisk attachment, beat the egg yolks at a fast speed for two minutes.

4 After the sugar has reached the correct temperature, slowly pour a thread of the hot liquid into the egg yolks while whipping the yolks on a medium speed.

5 Continue to add all of the sugar solution and continue to whip the yolks until the mixture is completely cooled and the yolks are pale and thickened.

6 Whisk in the butter, a little at a time on the machine. Finally beat in the vanilla. If the buttercream is too soft, place it in a refrigerator to firm it up.

CHEF'S TIP   Various flavours can be added to this recipe at the time when the vanilla is added.
Chocolate: add 100 g melted chocolate per 300 g butter
Praline: add 75 g per 300 g butter
Coffee: add coffee extract, chicory or diluted strong instant coffee to taste
Orange: add 3 finely grated zests of orange to 300 g butter
Spirits or liqueurs: add according to taste, for example Kirsch, rum, brandy or Grand Marnier.

CHEF'S TIP   Buttercream can be stored covered in a refrigerator for several days. However, it should always be used at room temperature so that the correct consistency is obtained.
   Before using, remove the buttercream from the refrigerator at least 1 hour ahead of the time and wait until it reaches room temperature. If it needs to be warmed quickly, beat the buttercream over a bowl of warm water to prevent curdling.

CHEF'S TIP   There are many different types of buttercream-based gâteaux that can be produced for afternoon tea service or for a simple buffet for example gâteau Nelusko and gâteau Mexicain.

Fruit gelatine-based glaze

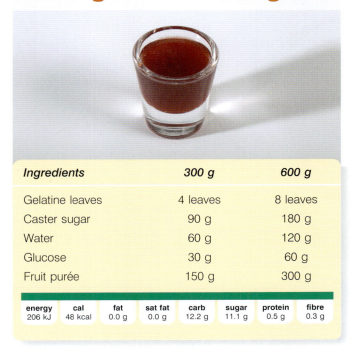

Ingredients	300 g	600 g
Gelatine leaves	4 leaves	8 leaves
Caster sugar	90 g	180 g
Water	60 g	120 g
Glucose	30 g	60 g
Fruit purée	150 g	300 g

energy	cal	fat	sat fat	carb	sugar	protein	fibre
206 kJ	48 kcal	0.0 g	0.0 g	12.2 g	11.1 g	0.5 g	0.3 g

METHOD OF WORK

1 Soften the gelatine leaves in cold water.

2 Place the sugar, water and glucose into a saucepan and heat until the sugar has dissolved. Remove from the heat and stir in the softened gelatine.

3 Add the fruit purée and mix well.

4 Strain the mixture through a chinois or fine strainer.

5 Pour over the top of a cake or dessert and quickly spread to the edges with a palette knife. One 300 g batch will make enough for a large 20 cm cake.

CHEF'S TIP Nearly all types of fruit purée can be used for this recipe. Pineapple and kiwi fruit are the exceptions because they produce an enzyme that breaks down the structure of gelatine.

Caramel fudge icing

Ingredients	500 g	1 kg
Demerara sugar	450 g	750 g
Double cream	180 g	360 g
Unsalted butter	100 g	200 g
Salt	1 g	2 g
Vanilla extract	3 g	5 g

energy	cal	fat	sat fat	carb	sugar	protein	fibre
717 kJ	171 kcal	8.9 g	5.6 g	23.7 g	23.7 g	0.3 g	0.0 g

METHOD OF WORK

1 Combine the demerara sugar and cream in a saucepan. Bring to the boil and continue cooking until a temperature of 115 °C has been reached.

2 Pour the mixture into a bowl of a mixing machine and let it cool down by mixing slowly with the beater/paddle attachment.

3 Slowly add the butter and salt and continue to mix at a slow speed until cool.

4 Add the vanilla and beat the icing until it is smooth and creamy in texture.

5 If necessary the consistency can be further adjusted with hot water.

CHEF'S TIP Stock syrup is equal amounts of sugar and water boiled together and simmered for three minutes. When passed and cooled this can be flavoured with alcohols, such as kirsch and rum or with spices, such as cinnamon, and other ingredients, such as coffee.

Chocolate glaze

Ingredients	600 g	1.2 kg
Fresh milk	100 g	210 g
Double cream	75 g	150 g
Caster sugar	50 g	100 g
Water	50 g	100 g
Glucose	50 g	100 g
Chopped dark chocolate	375 g	750 g

energy	cal	fat	sat fat	carb	sugar	protein	fibre
602 kJ	145 kcal	10.5 g	1.3 g	10.9 g	3.9 g	2.0 g	0.0 g

METHOD OF WORK

1 Place the sugar, milk, cream, water and glucose into a saucepan and heat until the sugar has dissolved. Bring to the boil and remove from the heat.
2 Add the dark chocolate and mix well.
3 Strain the mixture through a chinois or fine strainer.
4 Pour over the top of a cake or dessert and quickly spread to the edges with a palette knife. 1.2 kg is enough to coat 4 × 20 cm cakes.

TEST YOURSELF

To test your level of knowledge and understanding, answer the following short questions. These will help to prepare you for your summative (final) assessment.

1 Explain two ways of telling that butter is rancid.

2 Explain how the creaming method differs from the whisking method.

3 Explain why the presence of grease can destroy the aeration process of a Genoese sponge.

4 Give examples of cakes or sponges that use the following preparation techniques:
   a. Creaming
   b. Addition of melted butter
   c. Folding
   d. Aeration
   e. Separation of eggs.

5 When baking cakes, identify what may happen if they are moved or knocked while in the oven.

6 State what will happen to the finished cake with the following deficiencies:
   a. too much baking powder
   b. too much sugar
   c. too much liquid.

7 Name two different ways of incorporating fat to flour.

8 How does the sugar batter method differ from the flour batter method?

9 State three storage concerns when storing a freshly baked sponge for use the next day.

10 What are the two main components of baking powder and what is the purpose of adding baking powder?

Guest Chef

Glamorgan lamb with Welsh eggs

Chef: *Kevin Fairlie*   ***Centre:*** *Barry College*

The Welsh mountain sheep used in this recipe are local to Glamorgan and are lean with a good flavour.

Ingredients	makes 4 portions
Lamb cutlets, trimmed	8
Good quality lamb mince	480 g
Salt and milled black pepper	To taste
Cayenne pepper	To taste
Quails eggs	4
White breadcrumbs	250 g
Eggs, beaten	4
Mint leaves, blanched	4
Plain flour for coating	150 g
Redcurrants for garnish (if available)	

METHOD OF WORK

1 Bring a pan of water to the boil: prick the top of the quail's eggs with the point of a small knife. Boil for 4 minutes then plunge eggs into ice cold water as soon as they are cooked.

2 While eggs are cooling, season the minced lamb with salt, a small pinch of cayenne pepper and milled black pepper, check the seasoning by frying a small amount for tasting.

3 Shell the eggs and wrap each one in 40 g (a small ball) of minced lamb. The easiest way to do this is to flatten a ball of mince into the palm of your hand and then lay a mint leaf on top of the mince. Place a quail's egg on top of the mint leaf and close the mince around all to form a ball. This process can be aided by the use of a little water on the hand to prevent the meat sticking and also aids the rolling process.

4 Roll the lamb coated eggs in the flour, gently tapping off any excess, then roll in to the beaten eggs (egg wash), then finally in to the breadcrumbs. Repeat the final two processes rolling the ball in to the egg and breadcrumb again to 'double crumb', this provides an improved seal for cooking.

> **CHEF'S TIP** Sometimes the flavour of mint in the mince can be enhanced by the addition of a little mint sauce or jelly.
>

5 Deep fry the 'Welsh eggs' for 5–6 minutes until they turn golden, carefully test the meat to ensure it is cooked. Turn the Welsh eggs out on to absorbent paper to drain.

6 Take the trimmed lamb cutlets, brush with oil and season with good quality salt and milled black pepper. Pre-heat the grill bars and place the lamb cutlets on them.
Cook for approximately 3 minutes, turn and complete cooking until correct degree of cooking is achieved.

7 To serve the dish: Place the lamb cutlets in the centre of the plate (cutlet frills are optional). Cut the Welsh egg in half, use fresh mint and or fresh redcurrants 'en branch' to garnish the plate. Can also be served with sauce Robert.

Healthy foods and special diets

NVQ

Unit 2FPC13 Prepare, cook and finish healthier dishes

VRQ

Unit 204 Healthier foods and special diets

16

Current government guidelines for healthy eating

A balanced diet is one that is made up of a variety of foods in the correct proportions. This ensures your body obtains enough of what is required and is in no way deficient in proteins and vitamins. In fact, recommendations on diet are now laid out, not just to prevent deficiency, but to actively promote optimal health.

Nutritional requirements vary depending on a person's age, sex and overall level of fitness, and with this in mind the Department of Health have set guidelines accordingly. Most of us recognize the term RDA (recommended daily allowance). RDAs have been revised and are now set as Drives (dietary reference values), which are tailored to specific population groups. However, between the ages of 19 and 50 your nutritional requirements do not change a great deal.

For the average adult, it is recommended that approximately 50 per cent of our energy should be provided by carbohydrates, 35 per cent from fats and 15 per cent from protein. For most, putting this into practice will mean making sure that they eat a variety of different foods, with emphasis on foods rich in starch and fibre and smaller proportions of fats and sugars. Also, actively trying to eat more fruit and vegetables is always important as they contain many of the wide range of vitamins and minerals the body needs. The Government gives recommendations for suitable carbohydrates, fats and proteins that they believe contribute towards a healthy and balanced diet and further detail the benefits that these products provide as follows.

Carbohydrates

Carbohydrate-rich foods should make up about a third of the food we eat. With the introduction of diets, such as low carbohydrate regimes, people generally now seem to be eating less of these and often mistake starchy foods as being fattening, but they actually contain less than half the calories of fat unless the food item has fats added for cooking or serving.

Starchy foods are rich in insoluble fibre and contain valuable nutrients, which form part of a healthy diet. Examples of healthy carbohydrate sources are all varieties of bread, potatoes, plantain, yam, sweet potato, wholegrain breakfast cereals, couscous, and bulgur wheat. We need carbohydrates for energy levels and the three main types of carbohydrates are sugar, starch and fibre.

SUGAR

These are the simplest form of carbohydrates and there are several types of sugar including:

● Glucose – found in the blood of animals and in fruit and honey.

● Fructose – found in fruit, honey and cane sugar.

● Sucrose – found in sugar beet and cane sugar.

● Lactose – found in dairy products, such as milk and cream.

● Maltose – found in cereals and grains.

STARCHES

Starches break down into sugars and are present in many different foods such as:

- Pasta.
- Cereals.
- Biscuits and cakes (flour).
- Bread.
- Wholegrains such as barley and rice.
- Powdered grains such as arrowroot, flour and cornflour.
- Vegetables such as potatoes, parsnips and beans.
- Unripe fruits.

FIBRE

Fibre is important because it cannot be fully digested and does not supply energy to the body. It is essential for a balanced diet because:

- It helps to remove waste and toxins from the body.
- It helps to control the digestion and processing of nutrients.
- It adds bulk to diets helping the body not to feel hungry.

Fibre is found in fruits, vegetables, pulses and wholemeal foods such as pasta, breads and rice.

SOURCING Wholefoods are foods that are processed or refined as little as possible before they are eaten. They do not have ingredients added to them, such as sugar or salt. Examples of wholefoods are fruit and vegetables, unpolished grains, unprocessed poultry, meat and fish.

TASK
Find out:

- What wholefoods you use in your establishment.
- Using the internet discover more about why they are thought to be more healthy.
- The difference between wholefoods and organic foods.

Fats

Selection of fats and oils

It is important to have a little fat in our diet because fat helps the body absorb certain vitamins. It is a good source of energy and a source of the essential fatty acids that the body cannot make itself. Fats form an insulating layer under the skin and this helps to protect the vital organs and to maintain a balanced body temperature.

Fat contains a lot of energy, which may not all be used by the body. So eating more fatty food often means increasing body weight. To maintain a healthy and fitting weight, fatty foods should only occasionally be consumed and lower fat alternatives should be used wherever possible. A further recommendation is to increase the intake of omega 3 fatty acids, which are found in foods such as oily fish.

Saturated fat in too higher quantities can increase the amount of cholesterol in the blood, which increases the possibility of developing heart disease. Examples of products that are high in saturated fat include:

- Fatty cuts of meat and meat products such as sausages and pies.
- Butter, ghee and lard.
- Cream, soured cream, crème fraîche and ice cream.
- Cheese, particularly hard cheese.

- Pastries.

- Cakes and biscuits.

- Some savoury snacks.

- Some sweet snacks and chocolate.

- Coconut oil, coconut cream and palm oil.

Most people in the UK eat too much saturated fat – about 20 per cent more than the recommended maximum amount.

- The average man should have no more than 30 g saturated fat a day.

- The average woman should have no more than 20 g saturated fat a day.

Children should have less saturated fat than adults. But remember that a low-fat diet is not suitable for children under five.

Trans-fatty acids imitate the effects of saturated fats on our health, with some evidence suggesting that they may actually even be worse. Scientific evidence suggests trans fatty acids (TFAs) raise LDL cholesterol (bad cholesterol) in the blood and lower HDL cholesterol (good cholesterol), thereby increasing the risk of coronary heart disease. TFAs are found naturally at very low levels in foods such as butter, cheese, milk, beef and lamb. TFAs are also produced as a by product of a process called 'hydrogenation'. This process hardens oils, which makes products containing them last longer, helps them keep their flavour and improves the way they feel in the mouth.

SOURCING Packaged foods should have labels that tell you how much trans fatty acid the product contains. However, some countries do not have this legislation, but you can still work it out. Add up the percentage of saturated, polyunsaturated and monounsaturated fats. If the number is less than the 'Total fats' shown on the label, the unaccounted is trans fat.

Fried foods from some fast food chains are cooked in TFAs, using the Internet try and find out which ones, so you can source a healthier option.

Unsaturated fats can provide a healthy choice as they can essentially reduce cholesterol levels and provide us with the vital fatty acids that the body needs. They include the unsaturated fats found in oily fish, which may further help to prevent heart disease. Products such as oily fish, avocados, nuts and seeds, sunflower oil, rapeseed oil, olive oil/spread and vegetable oils all contain unsaturated fats.

Protein

A selection of foods that contain protein

Protein is contained within most of the main food groups and includes eggs, fish, meats, beans, milk and dairy. Following the recommendations for a healthy and balanced diet, these products should be consumed daily, but in small amounts and via a healthier lower-fat alternative where possible. When using foods that contain protein in dishes as part of a healthy diet, we must consider issues such as seasoning and accompanying sauces, which can transform a food that contains many benefits into a potentially unhealthy option.

We need protein to grow and repair the human tissue. The lifespan of the cells in our bodies varies from a week to a few months. As cells die they need to be replaced and protein is needed to help repair and grow new ones. Protein is made up of chemicals known as amino acids and some of these are essential to the body.

The nutritional value of a protein food can be judged by its ability to provide both the quantity and number of essential amino acids needed by the body. Different food sources contain different groups of proteins, which are made up of different arrangements and amounts of amino acids. In general, proteins from animal sources are of greater nutritional value because they usually contain all the essential amino acids. Proteins from plant sources, such as cereals and vegetables, may be deficient in one or other of the essential amino acids. For example, the proteins obtained from wheat lack adequate quantities of one essential amino acid, and those from beans are deficient in another.

Because the deficiency is different in each food, when they are eaten together they complement each other and the mixture is of higher nutritional value than the separate foods, and is as good as animal protein. It is important, particularly for strict vegetarians who do not consume dairy or egg products, that a variety of different types of protein foods are eaten.

DAILY CALORIE GUIDELINES COVERING ALL AGE GROUPS

AGE IN YEARS	MALE KCALS	FEMALE KCALS
1–3	1230	1165
4–6	1715	1545
7–10	1970	1740
11–14	2220	1845
15–18	2755	2110
19–49	2550	1940
50–59	2550	1900
60–64	2380	1900
65–74	2330	1900

TASK You are looking after a child that is overweight and has been advised to reduce their calorie intake to 1500 calories per day. Suggest a menu for a two days, which will satisfy hunger, is nutritionally balanced, is appealing and in total is less than 1500 calories per day.

WEB LINK Explore this site to find out more about recommendations for healthy eating.
http://www.eatwell.gov.uk/

Preserving nutritional value of food when cooking

The high temperatures used in the cooking process destroys enzymes and vitamins. Cooking also prompts chemical changes in food that produce harmful substances. Heterocyclic amines, for instance, are cancer-causing chemicals created in meat from the reaction of amino acids (the building blocks of protein) and creatine (a chemical present in muscles) at high cooking temperatures.

The importance of raw foods, which hold the greatest nutritional potential and should be included in the diet every day. But cooked foods are an undeniable part of our culinary tradition and heritage. They may also have certain nutritional advantages of their own. The anticarcinogenic carotenoid *lycopene* found in tomatoes, for instance, becomes more bioavailable when heated in cooking or for canning. No one can deny the healing effect that a warm cup of broth or bowl of soup brings to a chilled or tired body.

The key to healthy cooking, then, is to use methods that minimize nutrient loss and maintain the natural state of each food as much as possible.

Cooking in parchment paper is a technique borrowed from French cuisine (the French call it *en papillote* – 'in curl paper'), which permits the cooking of foods while retaining juices. Wash and chop foods and place on a dampened sheet of parchment. Fold the corners of the paper around the food and tie together with a cotton string. Insert the pouch into a pot filled with about five centimetres of gently

CHART OF RECOMMENDED DAILY AMOUNTS

FOOD GROUP	DAILY PORTIONS	WHAT IS ONE PORTION?
Bread, cereal, rice, pasta and potatoes	5–14 portions	1 slice wholemeal bread 1 small egg-sized potato 3 tblspn breakfast cereal 2 heaped tblspn cooked pasta or rice
Vegetables	2–3 as part of the minimum 5 a day	1 medium-sized mixed salad 3–4 tblspn cooked vegetables 150 ml vegetable juice
Fruit	2–3 as part of the minimum 5 a day	1 medium fresh fruit e.g. orange, apple 2 satsumas or kiwi fruit 7 strawberries 150 ml fruit juice
Milk, yoghurt and cheese, dairy	2–3 portions	200 ml semi-skimmed milk 150 g low fat yoghurt 125 g cottage cheese 20–30 g cheese
Meat, poultry, fish, pulses, nuts, seeds and eggs	2–3 portions	85–100 g cooked poultry, fish or lean red meat 3–4 tblspn cooked dried beans 2 tblspn peanut butter 3 tblspn nuts or seeds

boiling water, cover and simmer at low-to-medium temperature.

Steaming is a popular and quick method for cooking vegetables. For best results, bring the steaming water to a boil, place chopped vegetables in the steamer, and close the lid tightly to limit air exposure. Reduce the temperature to low. Do not over steam: remove vegetables when they turn a bright colour and are tender but still crisp. Preserve the steaming water, in which nutrients are dissolved, for use in stews, soups, or sauces: it may be frozen if not used immediately.

WHAT HAPPENS IF YOU DON'T HAVE ENOUGH OF A PARTICULAR NUTRIENT?

NUTRIENT UNDERSUPPLIED	CONSEQUENCES WITH REGARD TO HEALTH
Protein	Water retention, muscle wastage, ulcers, hair loss
Carbohydrate	Weight loss, lack of energy, low immune system
Fat	Weight loss, lack of energy, low immune system
Dietary fibre	Constipation, bowel disorders, bowel cancer
Vitamin A	Potential blindness, hydration problems
Vitamin B1	Nervous disorders
Vitamin B2	Growth, irritable skin, cracks in skin
Vitamin B6	Sickness and depression, eczema, irritability
Vitamin B12	Mental problems, anaemia, blood disorders
Vitamin C	Scurvy, depression, fatigue, blood loss, bruising
Vitamin D	Rickets
Niacin	Cuts in the skin, mental problems, depression, diarrhoea
Iron	Fatigue, lack of strength, lack of energy
Calcium	Rickets
Trace elements	Associated with poor health and development

WHAT HAPPENS IF YOU HAVE TOO MUCH OF A PARTICULAR NUTRIENT?

NUTRIENT OVERSUPPLIED	CONSEQUENCES WITH REGARD TO HEALTH
Carbohydrate	Tooth decay caused by eating sugar
	Overweight
	Diabetes caused by eating too many sugary foods over a long time
Fat	Overweight
	Heart disease, heart attack, high blood pressure, angina, all are linked to a diet high in fat, particularly saturated (animal) fats
Salt (sodium chloride)	High blood pressure and heart problems

Diets, food trends, healthy eating and intolerances

Most diets will follow a set format, creating a balance between the main food groups. However, due to people's concerns regarding weight loss, certain diets will focus only on selective food groups rather than encompassing all of them, therefore usually creating dramatic results but only in the short term. This can prove challenging for any chef who is asked to provide a specific dish that needs to be created by following rules specific to the customer's diet. More importantly, in order to create such dishes, key ingredients, flavours and textures often have to be sacrificed and therefore the overall quality of the dish can be compromised.

A healthy diet is one which is balanced and takes into consideration all the main food groups, balancing these with quality ingredients, variation and all in moderate proportions as referred to in the nutritional tables in this chapter. Along with regular exercise and a sensible lifestyle, keeping fit and healthy is quite simply down to common sense and taking the time to cater for these factors on a daily basis, therefore making it part of your lifestyle as a whole.

Allergies and intolerances

Food intolerance and food allergy are both types of food sensitivity.

For a food allergy, the immune system reacts to a particular food, believing it is not safe, and in severe circumstances this can cause a life-threatening reaction. Theoretically any food can cause an allergy, there are actually only eight main foods, named by the Food Standards Agency, that are held responsible for approximately 90 per cent of allergic reactions to food in the UK. These are milk, eggs, peanuts (groundnuts), nuts (including Brazil nuts, hazelnuts, almonds and walnuts), fish, shellfish (including mussels, crab and shrimps), soya and wheat.

In the case of *food intolerances*, this does not involve the immune system and is generally not life-threatening. However, eating food to which someone is intolerant can make people ill or may affect their long-term health.

The substance in food that causes an allergic reaction in some people is called an allergen. Allergens are normally proteins, and there is usually more than one kind of allergen in each food substance.

Most allergic reactions to food are mild, but sometimes they can be very serious. If someone has a food allergy they can react to just a tiny amount of the food they are sensitive to.

With strict food labelling guidelines now in place, it is much easier to identify ingredients contained in the products that you are purchasing and to find suitable alternatives for allergy or intolerance sufferers.

MILK ALLERGY AND INTOLERANCE

Milk is one of the most regularly experienced food allergies and intolerances, usually occurring in young children. Cow's milk is the most common cause. Sheep's milk and goat's milk cannot be used as substitutes for allergies or in the case of lactose intolerance as they have a very similar protein structure to that of cow's milk.

Soya milk is now commonly used as a substitute, but it is recommended that the person with an allergy consults medical advice before trying any alternatives as these may also contain vitamins or proteins that could affect the health.

EGGS

As with milk, the basis of eggs causing allergic reactions is the protein; in this case the three proteins that are present in the egg white – ovomucoid, ovalbumin and conalbumin. In a

few cases, egg allergy can cause **anaphylaxis**. The cooking of eggs can destroy some of these allergens but not all, which means that if some people are allergic to certain proteins but not others, they will only react to raw eggs.

WEB LINK Go to the following weblink to find out about the symptoms and how to provide emergency treatment for anaphylaxis:
http://www.nhs.uk/conditions/Anaphylaxis

PEANUTS AND NUTS

Peanuts, hazelnuts, pecans, walnuts, almonds, Brazil nuts and cashew nuts are most likely to cause allergic reactions.

Those who suffer with nut allergies must carefully consider all foods that they consume, as a large number of foods are made using nut oils or will have been produced in a factory where nuts have been or are present and could possibly contaminate other foods.

Peanuts can cause the most severe of allergic reactions and anaphylaxis, and is highly transferable to sufferers. For example, just the smell of peanuts can cause a reaction.

All of these nuts, on rare occasions, are capable of causing anaphylaxis in people who are allergic.

FISH AND SHELLFISH

Those that are allergic to fish or shellfish will usually experience an allergy to all types as they contain very similar allergens and can often cause severe reactions, including anaphylaxis. In the case of shellfish, even the vapours when cooking can cause a reaction.

SOYA

This product is commonly used as a substitute for other allergen products or to cater for those with religious or special dietary requirements, i.e. vegans. Soya very rarely causes severe reactions, but it should be noted that many products including bakery goods, sweets, drinks, breakfast cereals, ice cream, margarine, pasta and processed meats can contain soya.

WHEAT

The main allergen in wheat is the protein called gliadin, which is found in gluten and because of this it is common for those that suffer with a wheat allergy to be recommended that they eat a gluten-free diet. Wheat allergy and coeliac disease are completely different conditions. Coeliac disease develops through an intolerance to gluten. So foods that are labelled as being 'gluten-free' may not necessarily be suitable for those who suffer with a wheat allergy.

HEALTH & SAFETY Make sure that all dishes that contain any of the eight allergens listed are clearly labelled in the menu.

Special dietary requirements

Often there are medical, religious or ethical reasons for people choosing a particular special diet, which will dictate the foods that they can and cannot eat. A few examples of special diets are given below.

Kosher food – religious

Within Jewish law certain foods are prohibited. Animals that can be eaten must have cloven hooves and chew their cud, like cows and goats, but animals such as pigs and horses are excluded. Fish that have fins or scales are permitted, but catfish and shellfish are not.

Land animals have to be sacrificed before being eaten and the laws of kashrut dictate how they must be killed and prepared according to strict procedures. There are no rules to follow in the killing or preparing of fish. In order to be confirmed as kosher meat, they must be slaughtered with one stroke of a sharp, clean knife across the throat, which is supposedly painless, and this cut is performed only by a

Jewish butcher, or *shohet*, under the supervision of a rabbi. After slaughtering the animal the blood must be drained from the meat, which is usually done by soaking and salting. The body must then be inspected closely for any deformities or illnesses, which if found would render it non-kosher. Animals which have died a natural death may not be eaten.

Islamic food – religious

Within the Islamic religion certain foods are prohibited. Examples include pork and its by products (such as gelatine), blood, and the flesh of animals that have died without being ritually slaughtered and fully bled.

Some Muslims will not eat the animal's meat if they are uncertain as to how an animal has been slaughtered as they place particular importance on the animal having been slaughtered in a humane fashion, with the remembrance of God and gratefulness for the sacrifice of the animal's life. If this cannot be ascertained, then the meat will not be considered Halaal, and is rendered inedible. Islam also places importance on the animal having been bled properly, as otherwise it would not be considered healthy to eat.

Vegetarianism

Vegetarians will not eat any form of meat, whether this is meat, game, poultry, fish or shellfish, although some forms of vegetarianism may consume the latter two. They do, however, consume the by products from animals, such as milk, eggs and other dairy products.

Generally, vegetarians do not agree with the killing of animals for human consumption, believing this to be cruel and distressing to the animal and completely unnecessary, maintaining that the natural produce of 'the soil' i.e. fruit, vegetables, nuts and seeds, and the natural by-produce of animals (which is not seen to distress or harm the animal in any way) can provide all necessary dietary requirements.

Meat, game, poultry, fish and shellfish all form part of the main food groups and provide important proteins, vitamins and minerals. A vegetarian's diet must consist of alternative foods that will compensate for the lack of protein and vitamins associated with meat and fish products.

Foods such as eggs and dairy products will contain reasonable amounts of alternative proteins, calcium and vitamins which, in controlled amounts, can contribute towards providing a healthy diet. Furthermore, nuts and seeds, pulses, soya, quorn and tofu or mycoprotein products can also help provide a balanced and healthy diet. It is usually recommended that vegetarians take some form of vitamin and mineral supplements in addition to their diet. They are then able to replace any that are only present in very small amounts or not at all not in the foods that they can eat.

Vegan

Vegans are much stricter than vegetarians and will not eat any form of animal or their by-produce, or even wear items of clothing or accessories such as leather shoes.

As a vegan's diet consists of so few of the main food group and is therefore lacking in essential proteins, calcium, vitamins and minerals, it should be substituted by alternative means, i.e. tablets and supplements. However, with dramatic improvements and advancement in scientific knowledge, alternative products are now being created and are more readily available that can help contribute towards a healthy balanced diet, i.e. derivatives, genetically engineered foods and chemical substitutes.

Gluten-free

Gluten-free (free of wheat, barley or rye) diets will apply to those that have intolerance or an allergy to the proteins found in flour gluten and in some cases, to those suffering from coeliac disease. Natural alternatives to wheat flour, barley and rye include rice flour, tapioca flour, potato flour, cornflour, cornmeal, soya flour, gram flour and buckwheat flour. There are a number of others but these are the most widely available.

Some coeliacs may be able to tolerate a small quantity of pure oats but others may not, and there is a great deal of uncertainty as to whether oats are suitable or not for those with this condition. The difficulty with oats is obtaining a pure or unrefined product that is completely free from contamination by wheat either in the field or in the milling process.

There are many pre-prepared foods that may unknowingly contain gluten and should therefore be avoided at all costs. These include items such as stock cubes, baking powder, packet suet, mustard powder, ready grated cheese, soy sauce and some processed meats.

When cooking food for a gluten-free diet, you should ensure, for example, that items are not cooked in fat that has been used to cook products containing gluten, otherwise contamination will occur.

Lactose-free

Lactose is a sugar found within dairy products and therefore appears in a vast number of pre-prepared food products, specifically processed foods.

Lactose-free products are free of unfermented and untreated milk and milk products. Alternatives include such items as rice milk, soya milk and the more recently available 'lactose-free' milk, which can also be used in powder form. Cream alternatives are also available.

Food labelling needs to be carefully checked when purchasing or using items, as a higher percentage of commonly used foods will contain lactose in one shape or form, i.e. milk powder in bread products, breaded or battered coatings on foods and butter in pastry products and sauces.

TASK Look through the recipes in this book and suggest two that would be suitable for a person following these diets:

- vegan
- lactose-free
- gluten-free
- Kosher
- Islamic.

TASK There are two types of diabetes, find out about the differences using the internet.

Type 2 is controlled by diet. Suggest a menu for a day that would be suitable for someone with type 2 diabetes.

Diet trends – weight loss or general health

Diet trends are very common, with people in general being far more aware of healthy eating and conscious of their body weight.

When planning a menu, consideration should be taken so that certain dishes or items will fit the criteria required to match these trends. Diet trends usually vary in levels of certain items contained within foods that should be consumed, such as low salt or sugar, high or low protein and high or low carbohydrates, depending on what the individual diet dictates. The easiest way to cater for this is to cover the main food groups as widely as possible within the remit of a menu.

Illness and diabetes

People who are ill need balanced meals with plenty of the nutrients they need to aid recovery. Good nutritional food is a strong part of the healing process.

CHEF'S TIP People who are ill need to have appetizing meals served to them to tempt them to eat. Here are some tips:

- Small portions.
- No strong flavours.
- Attractive presentation.
- Cook and present foods that stimulate good memories, i.e. childhood desserts.
- Serve on white crockery to highlight vibrant colours from the ingredients.

However, because everything that is eaten is broken down into sugars in our body and some foods are broken down at different speeds. People who suffer from diabetes need to fully understand and monitor their food intake at all times to control their blood sugar levels.

Although a balanced diet is important the details will vary depending on each individual and their level of physical activity and the type of diabetes that they have.

Healthy eating tips

The two keys to a healthy diet are eating the right amount of food for how active you are and eating a range of foods to make sure you are getting a balanced diet.

A healthy balanced diet contains a variety of types of food, including lots of fruit, vegetables and starchy foods, such as wholemeal bread and wholegrain cereals; and some protein-rich foods such as meat, fish, eggs and lentils; and some milk and dairy foods.

Base meals and menus on starchy foods

Starchy foods such as bread, cereals, rice, pasta and potatoes are a very important part of a healthy diet. Try to choose wholegrain varieties of starchy foods whenever you can.

Starchy foods should make up about a third of the food we eat. They are a good source of energy and the main source of a range of nutrients in our diet. As well as starch, these foods contain fibre, calcium, iron and B vitamins. Wholegrain foods contain more fibre and other nutrients than white or refined starchy foods. Wholegrain foods include:

- Wholemeal and wholegrain bread, pitta and chapati.
- Wholewheat pasta and brown rice.
- Wholegrain breakfast cereals.

Eat lots of fruit and vegetables

Most people recognize that we should be eating more fruit and vegetables. Try to eat at least five portions of a variety of fruit and vegetables every day.

For example, you could have:

- A glass of juice and a sliced banana with your cereal at breakfast.
- A side salad at lunch.
- A pear as an afternoon snack.
- A portion of peas or other vegetables with your evening meal.

You can choose from fresh, frozen, tinned, dried or juiced, but remember potatoes count as a starchy food, not as portions of fruit and vegetable.

Eat plenty of fish

Most of us should be eating more fish – including a portion of oily fish each week. It is an excellent source of protein and contains many vitamins and minerals. Aim for at least two portions of fish a week, including a portion of oily fish. You can choose from fresh, frozen or canned – but remember that canned and smoked fish can be high in salt.

Some fish are called oily fish because they are rich in certain types of fats, called omega 3 fatty acids, which can help prevent heart disease.

Cut down on saturated fat and sugar

Fats

To stay healthy we need some fat in our diets. What is important is the kind of fat we are eating. There are two main types of fat:

- Saturated fat – having too much can increase the amount of cholesterol in the blood, which increases the chance of developing heart disease.

- Unsaturated fat – having unsaturated fat instead of saturated fat lowers blood cholesterol.

Try to cut down on food that is high in saturated fat and have foods that are rich in unsaturated fat instead, such as vegetable oils (including sunflower, rapeseed and olive oil), oily fish, avocados, nuts and seeds.

Sugar

Most people in the UK are eating too much sugar. We should all be trying to eat fewer foods containing added sugar, such as sweets, cakes and biscuits, and drinking fewer sugary soft and fizzy drinks.

Having sugary foods and drinks too often can cause tooth decay, especially if you have them between meals. Many foods that contain added sugar can also be high in calories so cutting down could help you control your weight.

Try to eat less salt – no more than 6 g a day

In the UK, 85 per cent of men and 69 per cent of women eat too much salt. Adults – and children over 11 – should have no more than 6 g salt a day. Younger children should have even less.

Three-quarters (75 per cent) of the salt we eat is already in the food we buy, such as breakfast cereals, soups, sauces and ready meals. So you could easily be eating too much salt without realizing it. Eating too much salt can raise your blood pressure. And people with high blood pressure are three times more likely to develop heart disease or have a stroke than people with normal blood pressure.

Get active and try to be a healthy weight

It is not a good idea to be either underweight or overweight. Being overweight can lead to health conditions such as heart disease, high blood pressure or diabetes. Being underweight could also affect your health.

Drink plenty of water

We should be drinking about six to eight glasses (1.2 litres) of water, or other fluids, every day to stop us getting dehydrated. When the weather is warm or when we get active, our bodies need more than this. But avoid drinking soft and fizzy drinks that are high in added sugar.

Eat breakfast

Breakfast can help give us the energy we need to face the day, as well as some of the vitamins and minerals we need for good health. Some people skip breakfast because they think it will help them lose weight. But missing meals doesn't help us lose weight and it isn't good for us, because we can miss out on essential nutrients.

There is some evidence to suggest that eating breakfast can actually help people control their weight.

TEST YOURSELF

To test your level of knowledge and understanding, answer the following short questions. These will help to prepare you for your summative (final) assessment.

1 Name two ways of choosing quality ingredients when writing a menu.

2 Give two alternatives to using sugar in cooking.

3 State an alternative name that can be given to salt when shown on the nutritional labelling of products.

4 Give two examples of healthier ways of making hot sauces that would otherwise use cream as a base.

5 Steaming is a healthy cooking method, but one where you must take the necessary safety precautions. Explain how this cooking method can be carried out in a safe manner.

6 State what is meant by the term special diets?

7 What are the best cooking methods for a healthy menu?

8 What is an omega 3 fat?

9 How would you make roast potatoes more healthy?

10 How could you increase fibre in a diet for a patient in hospital?

Guest Chef

Spiced rock salmon (huss, smooth hound or dog fish)

Chef: *Simon Martin*
Centre: *Highbury College, Hampshire*

This dish uses a sustainable fish from the south coast and reflects the spices and tastes of the south coast docks that have influenced our regional cookery over the past few hundred years. Huss, rock salmon, smooth hound or dog fish, as its locally known in the Solent areas, is an under-used fish with a semi-firm texture and takes well to spices.

Ingredients	Serves 4
Cold pressed rapeseed oil or olive oil	2 tblspn
Large onions or shallots, peeled and chopped finely	2
Crushed garlic	3 cloves
Finely grated galangal or ginger	40 g
Small red chilli, chopped (with seeds) or dried crushed chilli	1 chopped or ½ tsp dried
Fennel seeds	1 tsp
Cumin seeds	1 tsp
Tomato purée	2 tsp
Clear honey	1 tblspn
Brown sugar	1½ tsp
Worcestershire sauce	1½ tsp
Brown sauce (HP/Daddies™ type)	1 tblspn
Tomato sauce (bottled sort e.g. Heinz™/Daddies™)	1 tblspn
Limes, juice and zest	2
Salt and black pepper	To taste
Rock salmon (no skin or bone in, Darnes are best)	4 pieces, 120 g each

METHOD OF WORK

1 Heat the oil in a pan.
2 Cook the shallots, garlic, ginger, chilli, fennel and cumin for 2–3 minutes.
3 Add all the ingredients apart from the fish and mix well.
4 Add 100 ml water, season lightly. Blend until smooth, chill.
5 Cover the fish in the marinade and marinade for a minimum of 3 hours.
6 Pre-heat the oven 200 °C.
7 Lay the rock salmon in a roasting tray on silicone paper.
8 Spoon some marinade over the fish.
9 Cook for 15–20 minutes or until done, basting all the time with the sauce.
10 When ready rest for 2 minutes then serve with an Asian salad or braised rice infused with fennel seeds.

Glossary of terms

00 flour Speciality flour used in pasta making as it has a high gluten content.

à la (French) The style of, such as: à la française (the style of the French).

à la bourgeoisie (French) The style of the family (family style).

à la broche (French) Cooked on a skewer.

à la carte (French) Items on the menu that are priced individually and cooked to order.

à la florentine (French) 'In the style of Florence'. Generally refers to dishes served on a bed of spinach and gratinated with sauce Mornay.

à la française In a French style.

à la Grecque (French) In the Greek style.

à la minute (French) Cook food at the last minute.

à la portugaise In the Portuguese style, cooked with tomatoes, oil and herbs.

à la provençal (French) Dishes prepared with garlic and olive oil.

à la russe (French) In the Russian style.

à point (French) Food cooked just to the perfect point of doneness, when cooking beefsteaks 'à point' means that a steak is cooked medium.

abats (French) Offal.

acetic acid A natural organic acid present in vinegar.

acidulate To give a dish or liquid a slightly acidic, tart or piquant taste by adding some lemon juice, vinegar, fruit juice. Also, one can acidulate fresh cream by adding lemon juice to get sour cream.

acidulated water Water to which a mild acid, usually lemon juice or vinegar, has been added to prevent sliced fruits (especially apples and pears) and peeled or cut up vegetables (i.e. artichokes and salsify) from turning dark during preparation.

additives, food Substances added to food to maintain or improve nutritional food quality and freshness or to make food more tasty. Additives are strictly regulated. Manufacturers must prove the additives they add to food are safe.

ageing A term used to describe the holding of meats at a temperature of 1–4 °C for a period of time to break down the tough connective tissues through the action of enzymes, thus increasing tenderness.

agneau (French) Lamb.

al dente Italian for 'to the tooth'. It refers to the firm but tender consistency of a perfectly cooked piece of pasta.

albumen The protein portion of the egg white, comprising about 70 per cent of the egg. Albumen is also found in animal blood, milk, plants and seeds.

aloyau de boeuf (French) Sirloin of beef.

amandine (French) Prepared with or garnished with almonds.

ambient temperature Room temperature.

amuse bouche (French) This is a pre-starter or 'mouth pleaser' given as an opening for the coming menu.

anaphylaxsis A severe allergic reaction which can be fatal.

anglaise (French) English style.

antioxidants Substances that inhibit the oxidation of meat, vegetables and fruit. They help prevent food from becoming rancid or discoloured.

appareil (French) A mixture of different ingredients to be used in a recipe.

aromates (French) A mixture of herbs and spices to increase or bring out flavours in a dish.

ascorbic acid Vitamin C.

aspic Clear savoury jelly.

au blanc (French) Meaning 'in white'. Foods, usually meats, that are not coloured during cooking.

au bleu (French) 1. A term for the cooking method for Trout: 'Truite au bleu'. The fish is taken from a fish tank, killed, gutted, trussed and slid into boiling court bouillon. The fish skin is not washed. This gives a characteristic silver blue finish to the finished dish. 2. A steak cooked very rare.

au four (French) Baked in the oven.

au gratin (French) Food topped with a sauce and cheese or breadcrumbs, then baked or glazed under a salamander.

au jus (French) Served with natural juices.

au lait (French) With milk.

au naturel (French) Food that is simply cooked with little or no interference in its natural appearance or flavour.

au vin blanc (French) Cooked with white wine.

bacteria Micro-organisms that may cause food poisoning.

baguette (French) A French bread that is formed into a long, narrow cylindrical loaf. It usually has a crisp brown crust and a light, chewy interior.

bain marie (French) Water bath used to cook or store food.

bake To cook in an enclosed oven.

bard To wrap meat, poultry or game with bacon or pork fat. The bard will render during cooking and impart succulence and flavour.

barquette (French) Boat-shaped pastry case or mould.

baste To pour drippings, fat, or stock over food while cooking.

beard The common name for the hair-like filaments that shellfish, such as oysters and mussels use to attach themselves to rocks. They must be trimmed before the shellfish are prepared.

beat To introduce air into a mixture using a utensil, such as a wooden spoon, fork or whisk, in order to achieve a lighter texture.

beurre fondue (French) Melted butter.

beurre manié (French) A raw mixture of one part flour and two parts butter in equal quantities used as a thickening agent.

beurre noir (French) Black butter (can be served with skate wings and brains).

beurre noisette (French) Nut-brown butter served with fish meunière.

blanch To place foods in boiling water or oil briefly either to partially cook them or to aid in the removal of the skin (i.e. nuts, tomatoes). Blanching also removes the bitterness from citrus zests.

blend To mix together ingredients, usually of different consistencies, to a smooth and even texture, utilizing a utensil, such as a wooden spoon or blender.

blind bake To bake pastry without the filling. Metal weights or dried beans are usually used to keep the pastry from rising.

blinis Pancakes made from buckwheat flour and yeast.

boil rapidly Food is submerged into boiling liquid over a high heat and the bubbling state is maintained throughout the required cooking period. This method is also used to reduce sauces by boiling off the liquid and reducing it to a concentrated state.

boil To bring a liquid to boiling temperature and to maintain it throughout the cooking time.

bouchee (French) A small puff pastry case with high sides and a hollow middle.

bouillon (French) 1. Any broth made by cooking vegetables, poultry, meat or fish in water. The strained liquid is the bouillon, which can form the base for soups and sauces. 2. A salt paste used as a stock.

bouquet garni (French) Faggot of herbs and aromatic vegetables, usually parsley, thyme, bay leaf, carrot, leek and celery. Tied together and usually dangled into a stockpot on a string. These herb bundles give the stew, soup or stock an aromatic seasoning. The bouquet garni is removed before serving.

braise Cooking method where food (usually meat) is first browned in oil and then cooked slowly in a liquid (wine, stock or water).

bresaola Beef cured in a wine rich brine. It is then air dried and sliced very thinly for service.

brine Strong solution of water and salt used for pickling or preserving foods.

broil American term for browning under the grill.

brunoise 1 mm dice.

buffet A meal where guests serve themselves from a variety of dishes set out on a table or sideboard.

butterfly To cut food (usually meat or seafood) leaving one side attached and to open it out like the wings of a butterfly.

buttermilk Milk product that is left after the fat is removed from milk to make butter.

calorie Unit of heat; 1 calorie = 4.184 joules (J). The heat required to raise 1 gram of water 1 degree centigrade.

canapé A base of bread, pastry or porcelain onto which savoury food is place as a pre-dinner snack or as a course at the end of a meal prior to dessert.

caramelize To allow the surface sugars of food to brown, giving a characteristic nutty flavour and caramel aroma.

Caroline A savoury mini éclair that can be served hot or cold with a filling on buffets.

carpaccio Originally, paper-thin slices of raw beef with a creamy sauce, invented at Harry's Bar in Venice. In recent years, the term has come to describe very thinly sliced vegetables, raw or smoked meats, and fish.

carte du jour (French) Menu of the day.

cartouche (French) A circle of greaseproof or silicone paper used to prevent dishes from forming a skin or losing moisture.

carving Term used for slicing or cutting items, usually for customers or in front of customers.

casing A synthetic or natural membrane (usually pig or sheep intestines) used to encase food such as sausages.

casserole To cook in a covered dish in the oven in liquid such as stock or wine.

cassoulet A classic French dish from the Languedoc region, consisting of white beans and various meats (such as sausages, pork and preserved duck or goose).

caul Also known as crepinette (lamb) or crepin (pork) it is a thin, fatty membrane that lines the stomach cavity of pigs or sheep. It resembles a lacy net and is used to wrap and protect foods such as pâtés, ballotines etc. The fatty membrane melts during cooking. It should be soaked in slightly salted water before use.

chapelure (French) Dried fresh breadcrumbs.

charcuterie (French) Cured or smoked meat items.

chaud (French) Hot.

chaud-froid A dish that is prepared hot but served cold.

chef (French) A culinary expert. From French for the 'chief' of the kitchen.

chef de partie (French) 'Chief of the section' a chef who leads a team of assistants in a section.

chemiser (French) To line or coat a mould with a substance (either sweet or savoury).

chiffonade (French) 'Made from rags'. In cooking it refers to a small chopped pile of thin strips of an ingredient. Usually it is raw, but sometimes sautéed.

chine Usually refers to the removal of the backbone on a cut of meat, such as a rack of pork.

chinois A metal conical strainer.

clamart Any dish that either contains peas or pea purée.

clarified butter Clarified by bringing to the boil until it foams and then skimming the solids from the top or straining through muslin before use.

clarify To clear a cloudy liquid by removing the sediment.

clouté (French) An onion studded with cloves and bay leaf.

coagulate To solidify protein with heat.

coat the spoon When a substance is rendered thin/thick enough so that when a wooden or metal spoon is inserted into it and taken out, the substance leaves a thin film 'coating the spoon'.

coat To cover with a thin film of liquid, usually a sauce.

cocotte A fireproof dish usually made from porcelain.

coddling Cooking just below the boiling point, for example coddled eggs.

collagen White connective tissue that gelatinizes with long slow cookery.

collop Small thin slices of meat, poultry, fish but mainly referred to as slices across the tail of lobster.

commis chef de partie (French) A qualified chef who is an assistant to a chef de partie.

compote Stewed fruit.

compound salad   Salad with more than one ingredient.

concassée a cuit   A cooked small dice of peeled tomatoes.

concassée   Coarsely chopped, e.g. tomato concassé.

confit   A method of preserving meat (usually goose, duck or pork) whereby it is lightly cured and slowly cooked in its own fat. The cooked meat is then packed into a crockpot and covered with its cooking fat, which acts as a seal and preservative. Confit can be stored in a refrigerator for up to 6 months.

consommé   (French) Clear soup.

coquille   (French) Shell.

cordon   A dish that is surrounded by a thin line of sauce.

Cordon Bleu   (French) 'Blue ribbon'. A term used to describe high quality household cookery.

correct   Adjust the seasoning and consistency of a soup or sauce.

coulis   (French) Fine purée of fruit.

court bouillon   (French) A cooking liquor made by cooking mirepoix in water for about 30 minutes then adding wine, lemon juice or vinegar. The broth is allowed to cool before the vegetables are removed.

couverture   (French) A type of chocolate used for the preparation of cakes, confectionery and a variety of desserts; containing at least 35 per cent cocoa butter and a maximum of 50 per cent sugar.

cream   The process where sugar and softened butter are beaten together with a wooden spoon, until the mixture is light, pale and well blended. This process may also be carried out with a hand-held mixer or in a food processor.

crécy   Any dish that contains carrots.

crêpe   (French) Pancake.

crimp   To seal the edges or two layers of dough using the fingertips or a fork.

cross-contamination   The transfer of pathogen from contaminated food to uncontaminated food.

croute   (French) A bread or pastry base that is used to hold sweet or savoury items.

croûtons   (French) Shaped bread that is fried or toasted to accompany soups, entrées or as a base for canapés.

crudités   (French) Raw vegetables, served with a dip.

curdle   The state of a liquid or food, such as eggs, to divide into liquid and solids, usually due to excessive heat or the addition of an acid such as lemon juice.

curing   The preservation of food items using acidic liquids, salt or marinating.

cut in   To incorporate fat into a dry ingredient, such as flour, by using a knife and making cutting movements in order to break the fat down.

cutlet   A cut of lamb or veal from the loin with the rib bone attached.

dariole   Small mould used to cook individual portions of food, e.g. summer pudding.

darne   A cut of round fish on the bone.

daube   A slow-cooked stew, usually of beef in stock with vegetables and herbs. Traditionally cooked in a sealed daubiere.

debone   Remove bones from meat, fish or poultry.

deep fry   The process of cooking food by immersion in hot fat or oil in a deep pan or electric fryer to give a crisp, golden coating.

deglaze   To add liquid such as wine, stock or water to the bottom of a pan to dissolve the caramelized drippings so that they may be added to a sauce, for added flavour.

degrease   Skim the fat from food e.g. stock.

demi glace   (French) A thick, intensely flavoured, glossy brown sauce that is served with meat.

desalting   The removal of salt from foods. Food is soaked in cold water or washed under running water to dissolve the salt. Some foods such as salt cod require long, overnight soaking.

detrempe   (French) A mixture of flour and water for making a dough or a puff paste.

diced   Cut into cubes.

disgorge   To soak meat, poultry, game or offal in cold water to remove impurities.

doria   Food cooked with or garnished with cucumbers.

dorure   (French) Glazing with an egg mixture on raw pastries and dough before baking to produce an attractive coloured finish.

dredging   To coat with dry ingredients such as flour or breadcrumbs.

drizzle   To drip a liquid substance, such as a sauce or dressing, over food.

drying off   The removal of excess moisture from foods during cooking. Not to be confused with drying or reducing. An example of drying off is when potatoes are placed over a low heat after having been drained in order to dry them off before mashing.

dusting   To sprinkle with sugar or flour.

duxelle   (French) Minced mushrooms and shallots cooked until dry.

ecossaise   (French) Scottish.

eggwash   Beaten egg used to coat food as a glaze or are as a binding agent.

elastin   Yellow connective tissue that doesn't break down during cooking.

emincé   (French) Cut fine, or sliced thin.

emulsify   The blending of two liquids that wouldn't naturally combine into each other without agitation. The classic examples are oil and water, French dressing and mayonnaise.

en croute   (French) Cooked in pastry e.g. Beef Wellington.

en papilotte   (French) Cooked in a folded greaseproof bag.

enrober   (French) To completely cover a food item with a liquid.

entrecote   (French) A steak cut from the boned sirloin.

entrée   (French) Main course of meat or poultry that is not baked or roasted.

escalope   (French) Refers to a thinly sliced, boneless, round cut of meat that is batted until very thin.

espagnole   Basic brown sauce.

farce   (French) Forcemeat or stuffing.

farci   (French) Stuffed.

flake   To separate segments naturally e.g. cooked fish into slivers.

flambé   (French) Ignite alcohol on a dish e.g. Crepe suzette or Christmas pudding.

fleurons   (French) Crescent-shaped puff pastry used to garnish fish dishes.

flute/fluting   Used in pastry or biscuit making as a decoration. Pies and tarts are fluted around the edge by pinching the pastry between the forefinger and thumb to create v-shaped grooves.

fold in   To gently combine lighter mixtures with heavier ones usually using a metal spoon or spatula in a cutting or slicing 'J' movement whilst slightly lifting the utensil.

forcemeat   Ground meat or meats, mixed with seasonings used for stuffing.

freezer burn   Food that is left uncovered in the freezer desiccates and becomes unusable.

fricassée   (French) A white stew where the meat or poultry is cooked in the sauce.

fritture   (French) Deep fat fryer.

froid   (French) Cold.

fromage   (French) Cheese.

fumé   (French) Smoked.

game   Name given to wild feathered and furred animals hunted in certain seasons.

garde manger   (French) The person in charge of the cold meat department.

garnish   To decorate. Also referring to the food used to decorate.

gastrique   A reduced mixture of vinegar and sugar used in the preparation of sauces and dishes with a high degree of acidity. For example tomato sauce.

gastronorm   Plastic storage containers used by the catering industry. They come in standard sizes.

glaze   To give a food a shiny appearance by coating it with a sauce or similar substance such as aspic, sweet glazes or boiled apricot jam.

goujons   Goujons are small strips cut from a fillet of flat fish, often panéd or dipped in batter, and then deep fried.

gourmet   (French) Food connoisseur.

grate   To reduce a food to very small particles by rubbing it against a sharp, rough surface, usually a grater or zester.

grease   To cover the inside surface of a dish or pan with a layer of fat, such as butter or margarine or oil using a brush or kitchen paper.

grill   1. To cook foods with radiated heat 2. A true grill is cooking equipment that radiates heat from below, e.g. barbecue.

gross brunoise   (French) 1 cm square dice.

hacher   (French) To cut very finely (often with a mincing machine).

hanging   Hanging meat from a hook at a controlled temperature to facilitate ageing (see *ageing*).

hors d'oeuvre   (French) Small dishes served as the first course of the meal.

infusion   Liquid derived from steeping herbs, spices, etc.

jardiniere   Batons of vegetables.

julienne   (French) A cut of meat, poultry, or vegetables, which has the same dimensions as a match.

jus   (French) 'Juice'. Usually refers to the natural juice from meat.

jus lié   (French) Thickened gravy.

knead   A rhythmic action in dough making whereby one end of the dough is secured by the heel of one hand and stretched away then pulled back over the top. In bread making, two hands are used.

knocking back   To release pockets of gas in fermented dough before shaping and proving.

lait   (French) Milk.

larding   Larding fat cut into strips inserted into meat with a special needle. Used to add flavour and moisture to meat.

lardons   Bacon that is cut into small dice.

légumes   (French) Dried beans, peas, lentils etc.

liaison   A binding agent made up of egg yolks and cream, used for enriching soups and sauces.

lyonnaise   (French) Refers to dishes accompanied by sauted onions.

macédoine   (French) A neat dice of mainly vegetables which measure ½ cm square.

macerate   To soak a fruit in a liqueur or wine. This softens the fruit whilst releasing its juices and absorbing the macerating liquid's flavours.

marinade   A mixture of wet or dry ingredients used to flavour or tenderize food prior to cooking.

marinate   To let food stand in a mixture called a marinade (such as a liquid, dry cure, or a paste) before cooking. Some marinades add flavour. Others that contain acids, enzymes or fruits such as lemon, wine, vinegar, yoghurt or mangos, papaya or kiwi fruits help to tenderize.

melba toast   Thin triangular pieces of crisp toast classically served with pâté.

menthe   (French) Mint.

minced   Ground, or chopped, usually refers to meat fish, or poultry.

mirepoix   (French) A mixture of diced aromatic vegetables e.g. carrots, onions, celery and leek.

mise en place   (French) Basic preparation prior to cooking.

monosodium glutamate   A flavour enhancer which is a type of salt.

monte au beurre   (French) Addition of butter to create an emulsion of cooking liquor and butter.

mousse   A sweet or savoury preparation that has a very light consistency.

nape   (French) To cover an item with either a hot or cold sauce.

navarin   (French) A brown stew of mutton or lamb.

noir   (French) Black.

noisette   (French) A cut from a boned loin of lamb.

nouilles   (French) Noodles.

nutrients   The essential parts of food that are vital to health.

oeuf   (French) Egg.

offal   The name given to the edible internal organs of an animal.

open sandwich   A sandwich that only has a base of various varieties of bread.

palatable   Pleasant to the taste and edible.

panache   A selection of vegetables.

panada   A paste of various bases, either bread, flour or potato, used to thicken or bind products.

pané   (French) Passed through seasoned flour, beaten egg and then breadcrumbs.

pané à la francaise   (French) Passed through seasoned milk and seasoned flour. Used as a coating for fried foods.

pané anglaise   A coating of flour, eggwash and breadcrumbs.

papillote   (French) Cooked in foil or parchment paper to seal in flavour, then served and cut open at table.

parboiling   To cook by boiling partially for a short period of time.

parfait   (French) 'Perfect'. A smooth pâté or iced dessert which can be sliced leaving an even and consistent appearance.

pass   Push liquids or solids through a sieve.

pâté   (French) 'Paste'. 1. Pâté refers to either a smooth or coarse product made from meat, poultry, fish, vegetable, offal or game that has been blended and cooked with cream, butter and eggs. 2. Pâté is different base pastry products, sweet, short, lining, puff, choux.

pathogen   Micro-organisms that can cause disease.

paupiette   (French) Rolled or stuffed fillet of flat fish.

pavé   (French) A square or diamond-shaped piece of meat, poultry or fish but can also refer to pastry or cakes.

paysanne (French) Vegetables cut into thin slices.

pesto Rustic Italian dressing made with basil, garlic, olive oil and pine nuts.

petit (French) Small.

petit pois (French) Small peas.

pipe To shape or decorate food using a forcing bag or utensil fitted with a plain or decorated nozzle.

piquante A dish or sauce that is sharp to the taste.

pluche Small tips of salad leaves or herbs as a garnish.

poach To cook food in hot liquid over a gentle heat with the liquid slightly below boiling point.

pressing To apply pressure to items to help shape or remove excess moisture, e.g. terrines to help them keep an even layering or sweatbreads to remove excess liquid.

prove To allow yeast dough to rise.

purée (French) A smooth paste of a particular ingredient or a soup that is passed through a sieve.

quenelle (French) A poached dumpling, mousseline or cream presented in an oval shape. Classically made of veal or chicken.

ragout (French) A stew of meat or vegetables.

ramekin Individual or small ceramic round baking dish.

rasher Thin slice of bacon.

rechauffer (French) Reheat food for service.

reduce To concentrate the flavour of a liquid by boiling away the water content.

refresh To plunge food into, or run under, cold or iced water after blanching to prevent further cooking.

reticulin A structural protein resembling elastin.

roast To cook food in an oven or on a spit over a fire with the aid of fat.

roux (French) Fat and flour cooked to white, blond and brown colours used to thicken sauces and soups.

rubbing in The incorporation of fat into flour. Butter is softened and cubed then gently rubbed between the thumb and forefinger, lifting the mixing at the same time, until the fat is fully incorporated and the mixture resembles fine breadcrumbs in appearance.

salad tiède (French) A salad with the addition of warm or hot ingredients.

salamander A small contact grill and poker used to brown or gratin foods or a term to describe an overhead grill.

salami A charcuterie product made of ground pork or beef originating in Italy.

sauté (French) Cook quickly in shallow fat.

savouries A small after meal dish or item as an alternative to a dessert or cheese.

savoury sorbet A flavoured water ice using savoury ingredients such as tomatoes.

scald To heat a liquid, usually milk, until it is almost boiling at which point very small bubbles begin to form around the edge of the pan.

score To make shallow incisions with a small knife.

seal Caramelize the outer surface of meat.

sear To brown the surface of food in fat over a high heat before finishing cooking by another method, in order to add flavour.

season to taste Usually refers to adding extra salt and pepper.

sec (French) Meaning dry.

shallow fry To cook in oil or fat that covers the base of a shallow pan.

shred To tear or cut into food into thin strips.

sift To pass a dry ingredient, such as flour, through a sieve to ensure it is lump free.

simmer To maintain the temperature of a liquid at just below boiling.

simple salad A salad with only one ingredient, e.g. tomato salad.

skim To remove impurities from the surface of a liquid, such as stock, during or after cooking.

skin (to) The removal of skin from meat, fish, poultry, fruit, nuts and vegetables.

slice To cut food, such as bread, meat, fish or vegetables, into flat pieces or varying thickness.

smoking Hot or cold method of curing and flavouring food using wood, herbs or spices.

soaking To immerse in a liquid to rehydrate or moisten a product.

sorbet A smooth frozen ice made with flavoured liquid-based ingredients such as fruit.

sous chef (French) 'Under chief'. Second to the head chef.

steam The cooking of food in steam, over rapidly boiling water or other liquid. The food is usually suspended above such liquid by means of a trivet or steaming basket, although in the case of puddings, the basin actually sits in the water.

steep To soak food in a liquid such as alcohol or syrup until saturated.

stir fry To fry small pieces of food quickly in a large frying pan or wok, over a high heat, using very little fat and constantly moving the food around the pan throughout cooking, keeping them in contact with the hot wok.

stock A cooked flavoured liquid that is used as a cooking liquor or base for a sauce.

sweat To cook gently in a little fat without colour.

table d'hote (French) Set menu at a set price.

terrine A dish used to cook and present pâté.

timbale A small high-sided mould.

tronçon (French) A cut of flat fish on the bone.

truss To tie up meat or poultry with string before cooking.

vegan Someone who will not eat any animal product.

vegetarian Someone who doesn't eat meat or fish but will eat animal products such as milk, eggs and cheese.

velouté (French) A sauce made with stock and a blond roux, finished with a liaison of cream and egg yolks.

viande (French) Meat.

whip To beat an item, such as cream or egg whites, to incorporate air.

whisk To beat air into a mixture until soft and aerated.

zester A hand-held tool with small, sharp-edged holes at the end of it, which cuts orange, lemon or grapefruit peel into fine shreds.

Index

accidents 44
action plans 28–9
agar-agar 404
aïlo 140
al dente 224, 408
allergens 56
allergies and intolerances 617–19
   eggs 618
   fish and shellfish 619
   milk 618
   peanuts and nuts 618
   soya 619
   wheat 619
almond ice cream with banana
   fritter 538
American salads 78
anaphylaxis 618
anchovy
   compound butter 138
   sauce 124
Anna potatoes (pommes Anna)
   433
appearance 51–2
apple charlotte (Charlotte aux
   pommes) 545
apple sauce 140
arame 404
armed forces 8
arson 50
artichokes alla Romana (carciofi
   alla Romana) 420–1
asparagus 401
   buttered buttered (asperges
     au beurre) 419
assault 50
au blanc 409
aubergine 400
aubergines, stuffed (aubergine
   farcie) 426
aurore sauce 126
avocado 401
   and sun blushed tomato
     bruschetta 93

bacillus cereus 56
bacon 354
   breakdown of side of bacon
     354
   quality points 355
bagels 512
bain marie 461

baked Alaska with kirsch (omelette
   en surprise Norvègienne)
   548
baked whiting with herb crust and
   cream sauce 277
bakery terms 493–4
   baking 494
   BFT (bulk fermentation time)
     493
   cooling 494
   crumb 494
   ferment 493
   final prove 494
   kneading 493
   knocking back 493
   Maillard reaction 494
   prove 493
   resting the dough 493
   scaling 493
   scoring or marking 494
   shaping (la tourne) 493
   storing 494
bakewell tart 478
baking equipment 496–7
   baking sheets 497
   electric mixer with dough hook
     and beater attachment
     496, 592
   metal pastry scraper 497
   muffin tins 592
   rolling pin 497
   silicone baking mat 497
   silicone baking moulds 592
   springform baking tin 592
   stainless steel cake rings 592
   weighing scales 496
   wire cooling rack 496
baking powder 589
balsamic beets 412
balsamic split vinaigrette 149
banana bread 598
banana fritter with almond ice
   cream 538
barley 195
basic stocks 104–8
basil oil 150
Bath buns 516
Bath chap terrine 102
beans 187
Béarnaise sauce 136
béchamel sauce 123

beef
   boiled salt beef with carrots
     and dumplings 358
   bourguignon 364
   braised in beer and onions
     (carbonnade of beef)
     359
   brown stew 356
   brown stock 116
   chilli con carne 357
   consommé 170
   cooking specifications for
     steak 367
   cuts 344–5
   forequarter 345
   goulash 363
   grilled steaks with garnishes
     364–7
   hindquarter 345
   Italian meatballs with
     pepperonata 361
   jus 120
   Mexican fajitas 363
   paupiettes 347
   preparation 346–7
   preparation of sirloin steaks
     365
   quality points 345
   roast with Yorkshire pudding
     362
   steak cuts 366
   steak and kidney pie 358
   steak and kidney pudding 357
   steaks and carbonnade 346
   stir fried with oyster sauce 360
   stroganoff 359
   teriyaki 93
   white stock 115
beetroot 392
beignets soufflés (soufflé fritters)
   542
Belgian bun (Vienna bun) 516
bench and bowl scrapers 461
beurre manié 109
Biarritz potatoes (pommes biarritz)
   434
biscuits see cakes, biscuits and
   sponges
bisque 154
black butter 137
   with skate and capers 290

black eyed peas and red lentil
   curry 189
blanching 408
blanquette of veal 373
blinis, wholegrain and dill with
   smoked salmon, crème
   fraîche, bitter leaves and
   salmon caviar 201
boiled
   eggs 247
   gammon with parsley sauce
     371
   potatoes (pommes à
     l'Anglaise) 441
   salt beef with carrots and
     dumplings 358
borlotti beans with steamed lemon
   rice 190
bouillabaisse Marseille 288
bouillon 108
Boulangère potatoes (pommes
   boulangère) 440
bouquet garni 104
braised
   baby gem lettuce (laitue
     braise) 415
   beef in beer and onions
     (carbonnade of beef)
     359
   cabbage (chou braise) 416–17
   fennel (fenouil braise) 417
   Herdwick lamb shank with
     carlings, bacon and
     rosemary, finished
     with lemon, garlic and
     parsley crust 242
   leeks (poireau braise) 432
   red cabbage (chou rouge
     à la flamande) 418
brassicas/flower heads 393
   brussels sprouts 393
   calabrese 393
   cauliflower 393
   Chinese cabbage 394
   kale 394
   pak choi 394
   purple sprouting broccoli 393
   spring greens 394
   white cabbage 393
bread and butter pudding 539
bread sauce 13

bread-making methods
baking 495
bulk fermentd dough (straight dough) 495
faults 496
ferment and dough 495
over-ripeness 496
temperature 495
under-ripeness 496
breadcrumbs/rice 109
breaded escalope of turkey with chateau potatoes, sherry and morel sauce 320
breads and dough 490–519
bagels 512
bakery terms 493–4
baking 495
basic white rolls and loaves 498
basic wholemeal 499
ciabatta 505
country (pain de compagne) 500
dry ingredients 491–3
enriching ingredients 493
equipment 496–7
faults 496
flour 491–2
focaccia 513
fougasse 502
French baguette 506
garlic and herb rolls 503
German rye (roggenbrot) 507
introduction 490
liquids used 490
methods 495
naan 511
olive 508
onion and rosemary 504
pitta 509
pizza dough 510
salt 491
soda 502
storage 497
sun-dried tomato bread 505
tarragon 501
yeast 492–3
breakfast buffet 77
broad bean bruschetta with tomato and oregano 190
broad beans (fèves) 399, 428
broccoli polonaise 418
broths see soups
brown beef stew 356
brown chicken stock (fond brun de volaille) 116
brown hares 331
brown onion 397
brown onion sauce 129
brown sauce (espagnole) 129
brown veal/beef/lamb/game stock (fond brun de veau, estouffade, fond brund de mouton, fond brun de gibier) 116
brunoise 155, 407
brussels sprouts 393

buttered (chou de Bruxelles au beurre) 419
bubble and squeak 521
bubble sugar 556
buck (Welsh) rarebit 99
buckwheat 195–6
buffets
breakfast 77
finger 77
fork 77
full cold 76–7
speciality 77
bulbs 396
brown onion 397
fennel 397
garlic 397
leek 397
red onion 397
shallot 397
spring onion 397
bulgur wheat
aubergine and roasted vegetable cannelloni on tomato and basil with pesto 204
tian of Moroccan spiced quinoa and chick peas with roasted peppers, wild rocket and spiced chutney 204
bun
basic dough 514
Bath 516
Belgian (Vienna) 516
Chelsea 516
currant 515
Devonshire splits 515
glaze 515
hot cross 516
Swiss 515
tea cakes 515
burglary 50
Burgoyne, Tony (guest chef recipe) 340
butter (monte au beurre) 109, 111, 455
butter sauces
Béarnaise 136
black 137
hollandaise 136
melted (beurre fondu) 137
nut brown (beurre noisette) 137
buttered asparagus (asperges au beurre) 419
buttered Brussels sprouts (chou de Bruxelles au beurre) 419
butternut squash 401
and coriander soup 157
ravioli with thyme, tomato and red onion butter sauce 215
butterscotch sauce 554

cabbage
braised (chou braise) 416–17

braised red cabbage (chou rouge à la flamande) 418
cabinet pudding 549
Café de Paris compound butter 138
cajun tofu with couscous 450
cake preparation methods 588
addition of ingredients 590
aerated egg white method 588
flour batter (two-stage) method 588
genoese (whole egg foam) method 588
humidity 590
one-stage method 588
separated egg method 588
sugar batter (creaming) 588
cakes, biscuits and sponges 587–605
assembling and decorating gâteaux 606
baking 589–90
banana bread 598
cake preparation methods 588
cat's tongue (langue du chat) 597
chantilly gâteau (gâteau chantilly) 599
chocolate Genoese (Gènoise au chocolat) 595
coffee gâteau (gâteau mocha) 599
equipment 592
faults in production 590–1
fingers (biscuit à la cuillière) 594
Genoese (Génoese) 593
icings, creams, glazes and coverings 607
introduction 587
lemon loaf (gâteau au citron) 597
lemon madeleines 605
macaroons 605
richness of recipe 589
role in afternoon tea 587
shortbread 604
size 590
sponges 589
storing 591
strawberry gâteau with fresh cream 603
Swiss roll (biscuit roulade) 596
tuilles 604
Victoria sandwich 603
Victorian fruit cake 602
calabrese 393
calories 616
calve's liver stroganoff 381
calves' sweetbread fricassee with whisky and wholegrain mustard 382
camembert, with garlic ciabatta and red onion marmalade 94
campylobacter 56

cannelloni
aubergine and roasted vegetable on tomato and basil bulgur wheat with pesto 204
crab and coconut with lobster bisque 216
caper sauce 127
caramel
and almond swirls 559
fudge icing 609
mousse 567–8
pistachio clusters 560
sauce (sauce au caramel) 554
springs 560
carbohydrates 613–14
Carème, Antonin 523–4
carrot/s 392
and laverbread mousse 521
Vichy (carottes Vichy) 428
cartouche 110
casinos 9
cassoulet 191
cat's tongue biscuits (langue du chat) 597
cauliflower 393
cauliflower mornay (chou fleur mornay) 422
caviar 71
celeriac 392
celery 401
cephalopods 295
chantilly gâteau (gâteau chantilly) 599
charcuterie 72
chasseur sauce 130
château potatoes (pommes château) 444
cheese straws 481
Chelsea buns 516
chick peas
falafel and sweet potato with mint and lime dip 194
stew with red onion and chilli peppers 192
tian of Moroccan spiced quinoa and bulgur wheat with roasted peppers, wild rocket and spiced chutney 204
chicken
Asian stock 117
broth 168
brown stock (fond brun de volaille) 116
chasseur 314
coq au vin 317
cream of chicken soup (crème de volaille) 165
fricassée 315
jus 120
Madras 315
noodle soup with spiced dumplings 176

pan roasted suprême on crushed new potatoes, with sautéed wild mushrooms and a tarragon velouté 324
poached 318
roast (English style) 319
and roasted red pepper terrine 90
spatchcock poussin with grain mustard compound butter 320
and sweetcorn chowder 166
Thai soup 181
white stock (fond blanc de volaille) 114
wings with pea and mint risotto and garlic foam 316
chicken liver
  parfait 91
  stir fry 385
chickens 245–6, 308–9
  barn system 245
  battery 308
  corn-fed 308
  free range 245, 308
  label Anglaise 308
  Label Rouge 308
  laying cages 245
  organic system 245–6
  preparation techniques 311–13
  purchase specifications 308
  quality points 308
  roasting 312–13
  sauté 311–12
  weight specification 308
chicory 398
  au gratin (gratin d'endives) 424
  shallow fried (endive meunière) 429
chilli con carne 357
chilli oil 150
chilli peppers, chickpea stew with red onion 192
Chinese cabbage 393
Chinese crab cakes with mango and lime salsa 231
chinois 105
chipped potatoes (chips) (pommes frites) 440
chocolate
  acetate motifs 557
  bavarois (bavarois au chocolat) 571
  brownie with vanilla ice cream 540
  fondant (moelleux au chocolat) 537
  ganache 555
  Genoese sponge (Génoise au chocolat) 595
  glaze 610
  mousse 572
  petit pot of chocolate with a banana smoothie 563
  sauce 553

shavings 558
soufflé (soufflé au chocolat) 547
sponge pudding with chocolate sauce 535
tart 478
white chocolate and mandarin mousse cake 562
chorizo oil 150
choux paste (pâte a choux) 469, 470
chowder 154
ciabatta 505
citrus fruit 526
clam chowder 167
clams 293
  deep fried in peppered crumb with sauce vert 299
clarified 107
cleaning products
  detergents 62
  disinfectants 62
  heat 62
  sanitizers 62
clostridium perfringens 56
clothing
  accommodation 54–5
  aprons 52
  changing facilities 54–5
  chef jacket 51
  chef's hats (toques) 52
  footwear 52
  necktie 51–2
  protective 58
  trousers 51
cock a leekie soup 177
cockles 294
coffee and chocolate éclairs (éclairs au café et chocolat) 485
coffee gâteau (gâteau mocha) 599
cold sauces 112
collagen 343
communication skills 31–2
companies 3
  limited liability businesses 3
  private 3
  public limited companies (plc) 3
compound butter
  anchovy 138
  Café de Paris 138
  garlic 138
  herb 139
  lobster 139
  mustard 139
  parsley, cayenne and lemon juice 139
  shrimp 139
compound salads 78
concassée 156
confit of duck lyonnaise 322
consommé see soups
contract food service 6–8
  armed forces 8
  corporate hospitality 6–7
  healthcare and hospitals 7

kitchen organization 16–17
menus 22
outside and event catering 6
prison catering 8
residential schools 8
school meals and education sector 7–8
Control of Substances Hazardous to Health (COSHH) Regulations (1999) 42–3
convenience pastes 460
coq au vin 317
Corkhill, Ian (guest chef recipe) 565
corn/maize 196
cornbread 199
cost control 24–7
  fundamentals 25–7
  gross profit 24
  ingredients 25–7
  kitchen waste 25
  net profit 24
  portion control 25
  stock take 25
  supplier 27
  theft 25
courgette/s 400
  deep fried (courgettes frites) 424
  and seitan fritters 449
court bouillon 270
couscous
  with cajun tofu 450
  mint, garlic, olives, tomatoes and cucumber with grilled halloumi cheese 205
crab 295–6
  bisque (bisque de crebbe) 173
  and coconut cannelloni with lobster bisque 216
  and prawn cakes with mango salsa 302
crayfish tempura with basil mayonnaise 303
cream of chicken soup (crème de volaille) 165
cream sauce 124
cream soup 153
cream of spinach soup (crème d'epinard) 166
cream and yoghurt 529–30
  clotted cream 530
  crème fraîche 530
  double cream 529
  single cream 529
  soured cream 530
  UHT 529
  whipping cream 529
  yoghurt 530, see also milk
creamed spinach purée (purée d'epinards à la crème) 423
crème anglaise and derivatives (English custard sauce) 550
crème brûlée with biscotti 566

crème caramel with caramelized sultanas and mandarins 564
crème chantilly 553
crème pâtissière (pastry cream) 474, 552
crêpe Parisienne with strawberry compôte (crêpes Parisienne avec compôte de fraises) 543
crêpes 542
crêpes normande (crêpes with apple) 544
croquette potatoes (pommes croquette) 437
cross-cut filleting of fish 264
croûtes de flûte (toasted flutes) 155
croutons 155, 497
crudités 73
cruise ships 11
crustaceans
  crab 295–6
  langoustine (Dublin Bay prawns) 296
  lobster 297
  prawns 296
Cullen skink 183
currant buns 515
curriculum vitae (CV) 32–3
  education and qualifications 33–4
  exhibitions, awards, prizes, achievements 34
  interests or achievements 34
  key skills 34
  languages 34
  personal details 33
  personal profile 34
  references 34
  work history 34
curried millet and spinach cake, pimento and leek with poached egg and minted yoghurt 202
curry
  black eyed peas and red lentil 189
  Madras sauce 133
  oil 151
  Thai green paste 135
custard sauce 551

dairy products
  heat treating 530
  storage 525, see also butter; cream and yoghurt; milk
dariole moulds 526
dark chocolate brownie with vanilla ice cream 540
dark chocolate sauce 553
darne of salmon 268
Dauphine potatoes (pommes dauphine) 436
Dauphinoise potatoes (pommes dauphinoise) 445

deep fried
    clams in peppered crumb with
        sauce vert 299
    courgettes (courgettes frites)
        424
    haddock and thick cut chips
        278
deglazing 105
délice of sole 266
Delmonico potatoes (pommes
    delmonico) 446
demi glace sauce 130
dessert decorations
    bubble sugar 556
    caramel and almond swirls 559
    caramel springs 560
    chocolate acetate motifs 557
    chocolate shavings 558
    fruit crisps 555
    pistachio caramel clusters 560
    preserved vanilla sticks 556
dessert equipment 525–6
    copper sugar boiler 526
    dariole moulds 526
    ice cream machine 526
    plastic sauce bottles 525
    ramekin dishes 525
    stainless steel moulds 525
    sugar thermometer 526
desserts 523–85
    advantages of cold desserts
        561
    classical derivatives 561
    cream and yoghurt 529–30
    equipment 525–6
    fruit preservation 527–8
    fruit purchase and storage
        526–7
    fruit usage 526–8
    fruits and seasonality 527
    heat treating dairy products
        530
    hot and cold 531
    ingredients storage 524–5
    introduction 523–4
    milk products 528–9
    recipe reading 524
desserts (cold)
    assorted ice cream flavours
        580
    banana sorbet 582
    caramel mousse 567–8
    chocolate bavarois (bavarois
        au chocolat) 571
    chocolate mousse 572
    crème brûlée with biscotti 566
    crème caramel with
        caramelized sultanas
        and mandarins 564
    floating islands with passion
        fruit 576
    Italian meringue 577
    marmalade pudding soufflé
        with clotted cream and
        Cointreau custard 585
    meringue nest with vanilla ice
        cream (vacherin glacée
        au vanille) 575

peach melba 584
petit pot of chocolate with a
    banana smoothie 563
Piña colada soup with vanilla
    rice condé (soupe de
    Piña colada, riz
    condé) 574
poached pears with cinnamon
    and cider 583
rhubarb and ginger fool 583
strawberry bavarois (bavarois
    aux fraises) 569
strawberry ice cream (crème
    glacée aux fraises) 581
summer fruit pudding 573
trifle 578
vanilla bavarois (bavarois à la
    vanille) 570
vanilla ice cream 579
vanilla panna cotta with
    macédoine of fruit 565
white chocolate and mandarin
    mousse cake 562
desserts (hot)
    apple charlotte 545
    baked Alaska with kirsch (om-
        elette en surprise Nor-
        végienne) 548
    banana fritter with almond ice
        cream 538
    beignets soufflés 542
    bread and butter pudding 539
    cabinet pudding 549
    chocolate fondant (moelleux
        au chocolat) 537
    chocolate soufflé 547
    crêpe parisienne with
        strawberry compôte
        543
    crêpes 542
    crêpes normande (crêpes with
        apple) 544
    dark chocolate brownie with
        vanilla ice cream 540
    steamed chocolate sponge
        pudding with chocolate
        sauce 535
    steamed lemon sponge
        pudding with lemon
        sauce 533
    steamed treacle pudding 536
    steamed walnut sponge
        pudding with maple
        syrup 534
    sticky toffee pudding with
        toffee sauce 532
    vanilla pudding soufflé 541
    vanilla rice pudding with
        rhubarb compôte 544
    vanilla soufflé 546
devilled sauce 132
Devonshire splits 515
diabetes and diet 621
diet trends 621
doughnuts (boules de Berlin) 518
    fingers 519
    jam 519
    rings 519

Dover sole 265
    grilled with parsley butter 273
drinking water 54
dry commodity storage 525
Duchesse potatoes (pommes
    duchesse) 435
duck 309
    confit lyonnaise 322
    pan fried breast with sauté
        potatoes and orange
        sauce 323
    potted duck confit 92
    quality points 310
Dutch apple tart 473

E coli 56
éclairs, coffee and chocolate
    (éclairs au café et chocolat)
    485
egg yolks and cream (liaison)
    111–12
egg/s 244–55, 458
    allergy 618
    boiled 247
    cooking and holding
        temperatures 246
    custard tart 477
    dried 458
    en cocotte 247
    en cocotte Alsace style 248
    en cocotte with asparagus 248
    en cocotte with chicken 249
    fresh 245, 458
    fried 250
    frozen 458
    hens 245–6
    nutritional information 244
    omelette 250
    omelette with cheese 251
    omelette with tomato 251
    poached 252
    poached benedict 252
    poached dauphinoise 253
    poached florentine 253
    products 246
    purchasing 245–6
    quality 245
    sauce 124
    scrambled 254
    scrambled with herbs 254
    scrambled with smoked
        salmon 255
    sizes 244
    Spanish (tortilla) 255
    sur le plat 249
    types 244–5
    white (albumen) 246
    yolk 246
elastin 343
Electricity at Work Regulations
    (1989) 44–5
employment 12–15
    job interviews 13–14
    job offer 14–15
    job roles 12
    rights and responsibilities
        12–13
    staffing structures 12

entremets chauds 531
escalope of veal cordon bleu 373
espagnole 108
estouffade 108

Fairlie, Kevin (guest chef recipe)
    611
falafel, sweet potato and chick
    pea with lime and mint dip
    194
fallow deer 333
farfalle with pancetta and oyster
    mushrooms 217
fats and oils 455–6
    butter 455
    lard 455
    margarine 455
    oils 455
    pastry margarine 455
    polyunsaturated 456
    saturated 456, 614–15
    suet 455
    trans-fatty acids 615
    unsaturated 615, see also oil,
        flavoured
feathered game
    defining age 334
    preparation 329–30
    removal of wishbone 329
    removing legs and breasts
        329
    shot damage 330
    splitting and flattening for
        grilling 330
    trussing whole birds for pot
        roasting or roasting 330
    types 327–9
fécule 108
fennel 397
    braised (fenouil braise) 417
fibre 614
fig slice (bande aux figues) 475
fillet of plaice en tresse (plait) 264
finger buffet 77
fire
    extinguisher 47–8
    precautions 46–7
    risk assessment 48–9
Fire Precautions (Workplace)
    Regulations (1997) 47
first aid 49
    burns and scalds 49–50
    cuts 49
first in first out method 66
fish 258–90
    allergy 619
    appearance 259
    Asian stock 117
    baked whiting with herb crust
        and cream sauce 277
    bouillabaisse Marseille 288
    deep fried haddock and thick
        cut chips 278
    ethical fishing 260
    eyes 259
    filleting 262–4
    flesh 259
    gills 259

goujons of lemon sole with lemon in muslin and aioli 276
gravadlax 96
grilled Dover sole with parsley butter 273
grilled sea bream with modern minted pea velouté 280
halibut with lobster mousse, pappardelle, English asparagus and sauce vin blanc 275
hot smoked jasmine and green tea salmon with ribbons of vegetables 283
introduction 258–9
Kentish sea bream with courgette ribbons and langoustine and mussel broth 306
monkfish wrapped in pancetta with salsa 289
nutrition 260
pan fried red mullet with ratatouille and sauce vierge 290
pan fried salmon with asparagus, broad beans, Biarritz potatoes and chive cream sauce 284
paupiettes of lemon sole with baby leek confit and sauce Duglère 274
pie 279
poached trout with carrots and shallots 287
quality points 259
roasted pollack with vegetable julienne and mouclade 281
salmon fish cakes with pea shoots and tartar sauce 285
scales 259
seafood terrine 96
seasonality 261
sesame tuna with hoi sin and pak choi 286
skate with capers and black butter 290
skin 259
smell 259
smoked and cured 72
smoked mackerel with pickled cucumber 97
smoked salmon with classic garnish 97
spiced rock salmon (huss, smooth hound or dog fish) 623
steamed pollack marquise potato, bacon lardons, curly kale and dill cream sauce 282
stock (fumet de poisson) 113
storing and preserving 269–70
yields 259–60

fish cooking methods 270–2
baking 270
boiling 270
deep frying 272
grilling 271
poaching 270
roasting 272
shallow frying 271
stewing 271
fish curing 269–70
canning 270
ceviche 269
escabeche 269
pickling 269
salting 269–70
smoking 270
fish fillet
butterfly 269
cross-cut 264
round fish 262
single filleting flat fish 263
fish preparation 262–9
flat white fish 263–6
oily fish 267–9
round white fish 262–3
floating islands with passion fruit 576
flour 453–4
absorption ability 491
bakery usage 491
brown 492
buckwheat 454
campagne 455
colour 491
gram 454
malted wheatgrain 492
medium 454
moisture content 491
OO (Italian or dopio zero) 454
rising ability and elasticity 491
soft 454
spelt 454
stoneground 492
strong 454
texture 491
wheat germ 492
white 492
wholemeal 454, 492
focaccia 513
fondant potatoes (pommes fondants) 442
food contamination
allergens 56
animals 55
chemicals 56
food handling 55
food preparation 55
food storage 55
heating food 56
food labelling 66–7
food poisoning 56
food safety
deliveries and storage 65–8
enforcement and serving of notices 67–8
hazard analysis critical control points (HACCP) 63

legislation 67
temperature control 64–5
foreign (miscellaneous) soup 154
fork buffet 77
fougasse bread 502
franchises 3–4
fraud 50
French
apple flan (tarte aux pommes) 476
baguette 506
buttercream 608
cheese and ham savoury flan (Quiche Lorraine) 472
onion soup (soupe é l'oignon) 177
fricassée of rabbit with orange and chives 336
fruit 72
coulis 552
crisps 555
gelatine-based glaze 609
odour 527
panna cotta with macédoine of fruit 565
platter 84
purchasing 526–7
seasonality 527
storage 525, 526–7
summer fruit pudding 573
tart 474
tropical platter 89
fruit preserving 527–8
bottling 527
candied 527
canning 527
cold storage 528
crystallized 528
drying 527
gas storage 528
glacé 528
jam 528
quick freezing 528
fungi 402
button 402
cep 403
chanterelle 402
chestnut 402
morels 403
oyster 403
portabello 403
shiitake 403
furred game
defining age 334–5
jointing 332
preparation 331–2
types 330–1, 333
fusilli arrabiatta 217

game 326–40
defining age 334–5
feathered 327–30
fricassée of rabbit with orange and chives 336
grilled 'tornedos' of venison with pan fried foie gras 338
hanging 327

hunting and shooting seasons 326–7
large furred game 333
pan roasted loin of shire venison with poached Penderyn pear, parsnip purée, leak and potato cake with roasted beetroot, vine tomatoes and parsnip crisp 340
pot roasted rabbit stuffed saddle with lemon thyme 337
sauté of pigeon with black pudding, roasted cherry tomato salad and pommes au lard 336
small furred 330–1
small ground game 331–2
spiced tempura quail breasts with chilli dipping jam 339
stock 115
storage 335
venison bitok lyonnaise 338
game chips and gaufrette potatoes (pommes chips et pommes gaufrette) 439
gammon boiled with parsley sauce 371
garlic 397
compound butter 138
and herb rolls 503
oil 151
gastropod shellfish
clams 293
cockles 294
mussels 295
oysters 294
razor shell clams 294
scallops 294
whelks 293
winkles 293
gteau pithivier 479
Gazpacho soup 178
Genoese chocolate sponge (Génoise au chocolat) 595
Genoese sponge (Génoese) 593
German rye (roggenbrot) bread 507
Glamorgan lamb with Welsh eggs 611
glaze 107–8
chocolate 610
fruit gelatine-based 609
globe artichoke 402
preparation 421
gluten 453–4, 492
gluten-free food 620
goods received checklist 66
goose 310
goujons of flat fish 265
goujons of lemon sole with lemon in muslin and aioli 276
goulash 363
grains 195–206
average cooking times 198
barley 195

grains (continued)
  buckwheat 195–6
  corn/maize 196
  millet 196
  oats 196
  preparation 197
  quinoa 197
  rye 197
  storage 197
  wheat (bulgur, semolina, coucous) 196
grater 461
gravy see jus
green pea soup (potage saint germain) 164
grey partridge 328
gribiche sauce 141
grilled
  sea bream with modern minted peas velouté 280
  steaks with garnishes 364–7
  'tornedos' of venison with pan fried foie gras 338
gros brunoise 407
grouse, red 328
guacamole 141
guinea fowl 310

haddock, deep fried with thick cut chips 278
halibut with lobster mousse, pappardelle, English asparagus and sauce vin blanc 275
halloumi
  couscous, mint, garlic, olives, tomatoes and cucumber 205
  and grilled vegetables 95
hares, brown 331
Hazard Analysis Critical Control Points (HACCP) 62–3
hazards and risks 43–8
health and safety 41–3
Health and Safety at Work Act (1974) 41
Health and Safety (Information for Employees) Regulations (1989) 42
healthy diet 621–2
  base meals and menus on starchy foods 621
  cut down on saturated fat and sugar 622
  drink plenty of water 622
  eat breakfast 622
  eat less salt 622
  eat lots of fruit and vegetables 621
  eat plenty of fish 622
  get active and maintain healthy weight 622
healthy foods 613–22
  calorie guidelines 616
  carbohydrates 613
  daily amounts 616
  diets, food trends, intolerances 617–19

fats 614–15
  government guidelines 613–16
  nutrients 617
  preserving nutritional value when cooking 616–17
  protein 615
  special dietary requirements 619–21
  tips 621–2
hens see chickens
herbs 73
  compound butter 139
  oil 151
hijiki 404
Hollandaise sauce 136
honey 457
  and mustard dressing 141
  provenance 524
hors d'oeuvres, appetisers and starters 70–1
  single 71
  varieties 71
hospitality industry 2–3
  business demand 5
  international perspective 4
  products and services 5
  scope of business operations 3–4
  types of establishment 6–11
  UK 4–5
hospitals 7, 16, 21
hot cross buns 516
hot sauces 108
hot smoked jasmine and green tea salmon with ribbons of vegetables 283
hotels 8–9, 16
houmous 142
hygiene, personal see personal hygiene
hygiene, work area see work area hygiene

ice cream
  assorted flavours 580
  banana sorbet 582
  strawberry (crème glacée aux fraises) 581
  vanilla (crème glacée à la vanille) 579
ice cream machine 526
icing, caramel fudge 609
illness and diet 621
in-flight catering 10
independent businesses 4
interview 35
  current issues 35
  evaluating 36
  golden rules 36
  making a good impression 35
  types of questions 35
  what employers like/don't like to see 36
Islamic food 620
isomalt 457–8
Italian meatballs with pepperonata 361

Italian meringue 577
Italian sauce 132
ivory sauce 127

jam roll, steamed 486
jambalaya 234
jardinière 407
job application
  appearance and style 33
  covering letter 34–5
  curriculum vitae (cv) 32–4
julienne 155, 407
jus 104
  aged balsamic 119
  beef 120
  chicken 120
  lamb 122
  lié (thickened gravy) 121
  red wine 122
  rôti (roast gravy) 121
  venison 123

kale 393
kedgeree 235
Keevey, Johannes (guest chef recipe) 324
Keir, David (guest chef recipe) 183
kelp 404
Kentish sea bream with courgette ribbons and langoustine and mussel broth 306
kidney, marinated pork kidney and chorizo skewers 384
kitchen design
  cooking area 19–20
  preparation zone 19
  service counter 20–1
  storage area 19
kitchen hierarchy 17–18
  chef de partie 18
  commis chef 18
  head chef (chef de cuisine) 17
  head pastry chef (chef pâtissier) 18
  second chef (sous chef) 17
kitchen organization 16
  contract catering services 16
  cost controls 25–7
  healthcare homes 16
  hospitals 16
  hotels 16
  restaurants 16
  school meals 16–17
knicking back 492
kohlrabi 402
Kosher food 619–20

lactose-free food 620
lamb and mutton
  biryani 236
  braised Herdwick lamb shank with carlings, bacon and rosemary, finished with lemon, garlic and parsley crust 242
  breakdown of side of lamb/mutton 348

brown stock 116
  Glamorgan lamb with Welsh eggs 611
  jus 122
  lamb's liver with balsamic-glazed onions and salt-roasted walnuts 383
  Lancashire hotpot 368
  mixed grill 269
  navarin of 2369
  pasty 368
  pot roasted Welsh loin with carrot and laverbread mousse, and bubble and squeak 520
  preparation of leg 350
  preparation of rack of lamb 351
  preparation of shoulder 349
  quality points 348
  roast leg 370
  shepherd's pie 370
  sweetbreads pan fried with rosemary and lemon butter 384
  white stock 115
Lancashire hotpot 368
langoustine (Dublin Bay prawns) 296
langoustines en papilotte 300
lard 455
lasagne 219
leaves 398
  chicory 398
  lettuce 398
  spinach 398
  watercress 398
leek/s 397
  braised (poireau braise) 432
  and mushroom pearl barley risotto, parmesan crisps and black truffle oil 200
lemon
  loaf cake (gâteau au citron) 597
  madeleines 605
  oil 151
  sponge pudding with lemon sauce 533
lemon sole
  goujons with lemon in muslin and aioli 276
  paupiettes with baby leek confit and sauce Duglère 274
lentils 186
lettuce 398
  braised baby gem (laitue braise) 415
liaison 111
lighting 54
lime and mint dip with sweet potato and chick pea falafel 194

linguine with smoked salmon, cucumber ribbons and crème fraîche 214
lining flans 465–6
liquid glucose (corn syrup) 457
listeria 56
liver, lamb's with balsamic-glazed onions and salt-roasted walnuts 383
lobster 297
    thermidor 304
lobster bisque (bisque de homard) 174
    with crab and coconut cannelloni 216
lobster mousse with halibut, pappardelle, English asparagus and sauce vin blanc 275
Lucas, Scott (guest chef recipe) 102

macaroni with blue cheese and leeks 220
macaroons 605
McCourt, Emmett (guest chef recipe) 386–7
macédoine 407
Madeira/sherry/port wine/red wine sauce 131
Madras curry sauce 133
mange tout 399
mango and lime salsa 143
Manual Handling Operations Regulations (1992) 45–6
margarine 455
marinated pork kidney and chorizo skewers 384
Marquis potatoes (pommes marquise) 436
marrow 400
matchstick potatoes (pommes allumettes) 443
mayonnaise and Marie Rose sauce 144
meat 342–77
    ageing 343
    bacon 354–5
    beef 344–7
    connective tissue 343
    equipment 344
    fat 343
    garnishes and named sauces 365
    introduction 342
    lamb and mutton 348–51
    muscle 342–3
    pork 352–4
    purchasing 343–4
    quality 344
    storing 344
    veal 347–8, see also beef; lamb and mutton; pork; veal
melted butter (beurre fondu) 137
menus
    à la carte 21
    afternoon tea 22

availability of commodities 23
    balanced 23
    breakfast 22
    competition 23
    contract catering 22
    cyclic 23–4
    dessert 23
    equipment and space available 23
    factors to consider 23
    function 23
    healthcare 21
    hospital 21
    planning 21–4
    pricing policy 23
    school 22
    seasonality 23
    table d'hôte 21
    type of customer 23
    type of establishment 23
meringue
    Italian 577
    nest with vanilla ice cream (vacherin glacée au vanille) 575
Mexican beef fajitas 363
micro herbs 73
mignonette potatoes (pommes mignonnettes) 443
milk 490, 528–9
    allergy and intolerance 618
    buttermilk 529
    Channel Island and Jersey 529
    contamination 529
    homogenized 529
    pasteurized 528–9
    semi-skimmed 529
    soya 529
    UHT 529, see also cream and yoghurt
mille feuille 482–3
millet 196
minestrone soup 179
mint and lime dip with sweet potato and chick pea falafel 194
mint raita 145
mirepoix 408
mixed grill 369
monkfish wrapped in pancetta with salsa 289
mornay sauce 124
moules marinière 298
moussaka
    TVP 447
    vegetable 451
mousses 74
mozzarella and red onion tartlet 94
mushroom/s
    sauce 128
    soup (purée de champignon) 158
    stuffed (champignons farcis) 425
    velouté 163
mushy peas 193

mussels 295
mustard
    compound butter 139
    sauce 125
mutton broth 168
mycoprotein (quorn™) 413

naan bread 511
navarin of lamb 369
nori 404
norovirus 56
nut brown butter (beurre noisette) 137
nuts 458–9

oats 196
offal
    calves' 381–2
    chicken 91
    chicken/duck liver (foie de volaille/foie de caneton) 380
    lamb 383–4
    lamb sweetbreads (ris d'agneau) 379
    lamb/mutton kidney (rognon d'agneau) 379
    lamb/mutton liver (foie d'agneau) 378
    pig kidney (rognon de porc) 378
    pork 384
    purchasing 343–4
    storing 344
    veal kidney (rognon de veau) 380
    veal liver (foie de veau) 380
    veal sweetbreads (ris de veau) 380
offset palette knife 461
oil, flavoured
    basil 150
    chilli 150
    chorizo 150
    curry 151
    garlic 151
    herb 151
    lemon 151
    roasted hazelnut 152
    sun-dried tomato 152
    vanilla 152
    walnut 152, see also fats and oils
okra 399
olive bread 508
onions
    brown 397
    finely diced 408
    red 397
    and rosemary bread 504
    sauce (soubise) 125
    sliced 408
    spring 397
orange marmalade pudding soufflé with clotted cream and Cointreau custard 585
oysters (huîtres) 71–2, 294

deep fried beignet, grilled with herb crumb and champagne jelly 301

paella 238
pak choi 393
palmiers 480
pan fried
    duck breast with sauté potatoes and orange sauce 323
    red mullet with ratatouille and sauce vierge 290
    salmon with asparagus, broad beans, Biarritz potatoes and chive cream sauce 284
papaya and black bean salsa 142
parboiling 408
parfaits 74
Parmentier potatoes (pommes parmentier) 446
parmesan and thyme polenta with Mediterranean vegetables with pesto dressing 203
parsley, cayenne and lemon juice (maitre d'hôtel compound butter) 139
parsley sauce 125
parsnips 392
    roasted in honey 431
partnerships 3
partridge 327–8
pasta 207–22
    butternut squash ravioli with thyme, tomato and red onion butter sauce 215
    cooking, holding and storage 212–13
    crab and coconut cannelloni with lobster bisque 216
    egg dough 214
    equipment and tools 208–9
    farfalle with pancetta and oyster mushrooms 217
    fresh or dried 210
    fusilli arrabiatta 217
    gnocchi parisienne (choux paste-based) 218
    gnocchi piedmontaise (potato-based) 218
    lasagne 219
    linguine with smoked salmon, cucumber ribbons and crème fraîche 214
    macaroni with blue cheese and leeks 220
    polenta gnocchi romaine with parmesan crisp and basil oil 206
    quality points 212
    rolling 208
    spaghetti bolognaise 221
    stir fried tofu with egg noodles 488
    stuffed 210–11

pasta (continued)
    tortellini filled with ratatouille
        on wilted spinach with
        tomato coulis 222
pasta preparation and cooking 212
    baking 212
    blanching 212
    boiling 212
    combination cooking 212
    mixing 212
    straining 212
pastes, tarts and pies 453–86
    bakewell 478
    chocolate 478
    convenience pastes 460
    Dutch apple 473
    egg custard 477
    eggs 458
    fats and oils 455–6
    flour 453–5
    fresh fruit 474
    ingredients 453–9
    introduction 453
    nuts 458–9
    rhubarb and sour cream royal
        tart 488
    short pastes 460–1
    specialist baking equipment
        461
    storing 459
    sugar 456–8
    tart tins 461
    Tatin 475
    treacle 473
pastry
    brush 461
    choux 469
    cream slice (tranche mille
        feuille) 482–3
    puff (pâte à feuilletée) 468
    shortcrust 462–3
    suet (pâte à grasse de boeuf)
        471
    sweet 464–6
pasty, lamb 368
pâtés 74
Patiar, Dr Shyam (guest chef
    recipe) 520–1
paupiettes
    of beef 347
    of lemon sole with baby leek
        confit and sauce
        Duglère 274
    of sole 265–6
paysanne 156, 408
peach melba 584
peanuts and nuts allergy 618
peas 187, 399
    French style (petits pois à la
        Française) 429
    green pea soup 164
    mushy 193
    stuffed plum tomatoes with
        rice 193
    velouté 163
pepper 400
peppercorn sauce 13
personal health 54–5

personal hygiene 53
    cuts, boils and septic wounds
        57
    feet 53
    hair 53, 57
    hand washing 57
    hands 53
    jewellery and cosmetics 58
    mouth and teeth 53
    protective clothing 58
    smoking 53–4, 58
    tasting food while cooking 57
pest control 62
pesto 145
    sun-dried tomato 145
pheasant 327
pickled cucumber with smoked
    mackerel 97
pickled ginger salsa 143
pies see pastes, tarts and pies
pigeon sautéed with black
        pudding, roasted cherry
        tomato salad and pommes
        au lard 336
Piña colada soup with vanilla rice
        condé (soupe de Piña
        colada, riz condé) 574
pistachio caramel clusters 560
pitta bread 509
pizza dough 510
poached
    chicken duxelle 318
    pears with cinnamon and cider
        583
    trout with carrots and shallots
        287
polenta
    gnocchi romaine, parmesan
        crips and basil oil 206
    parmesan and thyme with
        Mediterranean
        vegetables and pesto
        dressing 203
pollack
    roasted with vegetable julienne
        and mouclade 281
    steamed with marquise potato,
        bacon lardons, curly
        kale and dill cream
        sauce 282
pommes au lard 444
pommes frites (chipped potatoes)
    440
Pont-neufs potatoes (pommes
    pont-neuf) 441
pork 352
    boiled gammon with parsley
        sauce 371
    breakdown of side of pork 352
    cutlets with cranberries 372
    marinated pork kidney and
        chorizo skewers 384
    preparation of rolled belly 353
    preparation of tenderloin
        353–4
    quality points 354
    roast 371
    satay 92

    stuffed Tamworth pork fillet,
        black pudding, boxty
        potato, wild bilberry and
        crab apple jelly 386–7
    toad in the hole 372
Portugaise 73
pot roasted stuffed saddle of
    rabbit with lemon thyme
    337
pot-au-feu 153
potage paysanne 164
potatoes 393
    Anna (pommes Anna) 433
    Biarritz (pommes biarritz) 434
    Bintje 395
    boiled (pommes à l'Anglaise)
        441
    Boulangère (pommes
        boulangère) 440
    Cara 395
    Carlingford 395
    Charlotte 395
    château (pommes château)
        444
    chipped (chips) (pommes
        frites) 440
    crocquette (pommes
        croquette) 437
    Dauphine (pommes dauphine)
        436
    Dauphinoise (pommes
        dauphinoise) 445
    Delmonico (pommes delmoni-
        co) 446
    Desirée 395
    Duchesse (pommes duch-
        esse) 435
    Edzell Blue 395
    Epicure 395
    Estima 395
    floury 396
    fondant (pommes fondants)
        442
    game (pommes chips et
        pommes gaufrette)
        439
    gaufrette 439
    Golden Wonder 395
    Jersey royals 395
    Kerr's pink 395
    King Edward 395
    Marfona 395
    Maris Bard 395
    Maris Peer 395
    Maris Piper 395
    Marquis (pommes marquise)
        436
    mashed (pommes purées) 434
    matchstick (pommes allum-
        ettes) 443
    mignonette (pommes
        mignonettes) 443
    Nadine 395
    Parmentier (pommes
        parmentier) 446
    Pentland Dell 395
    Pink Fir Apple 1850, 395
    pommes au lard 444

    Pont-neuf (pommes pont-neuf)
        441
    Premiere 395
    Ratte (asparges) 1872 395
    Rocket 395
    Romano 395
    Rooster 395
    Royal kidney 1899 395
    Sante 395
    sauté with onions (pommes
        lyonnaises) 438
    sauté (pommes sautées) 438
    Saxon 395
    seasonal 395
    Sharpe's express 395
    soup (purée parmentier) 159
    straw (pommes pailles) 437
    waxy 396
    Wilja 395
potted duck confit 92
poultry 308–23
    chicken 308–9
    duck 309–10
    goose 310
    guinea fowl 310
    health and safety 310
    preparation techniques
        311–13
    turkey 309
poussin see chicken
powdered starch thickening
    agents 111
prawn bisque (bisque de
    crevettes) 175
prawn and crab cakes with mango
    salsa 302
prawns 296
pre-prepared stocks 108
preserved vanilla sticks 556
prisons 8
private members' clubs 9
professional associations 15
professional presentation 28
profiteroles with chocolate sauce
    (profiteroles au chocolat)
    484
protein 615
public houses, bars, clubs 10
puff paste (pâte à feuilletée) 466
    English method 467
    French method 467
    rises 467
    rolling 467
    rough or Scottish method 467
    storage 467
puff pastry (pâte à feuilletée)
    with pastry margerine 468
    rough 468
pulses 185–6
    origins 186
    preparation 186
    soaking and cooking times
        187–8
    storage 186
pumpkin 401
pumpkin purée 423
purée soup 153
purple sprouting broccoli 393

quail 328
    egg with smoked haddock on
        parsley mash with
        caper and lemon sauce
        256
    spiced tempura breasts with
        chilli dipping jam 339
Quiche Lorraine 472
quinoa 197
quinoa, spiced tian with bulgur
    wheat, chick peas, roasted
    peppers, wild rocket and
    spiced chutney 204
quorn™ 413
quorn™ sweet and sour 448

rabbit
    fricassée with orange and
        chives 336
    pot roasted stuffed saddle with
        lemon thyme 337
    wild 330–1
rail travel 11
ramekin dishes 525
ratatouille 430
    pan fried red mullet and sauce
        vierge 290
    tortellini on wilted spinach with
        tomato coulis 222
ravioli 211
raw tomato coulis 146
razor clams and chorizo, butter
    bean and tomato stew 305
razor shell clams 294
recipes, reading carefully 524
red
    cabbage, braised (chou rouge
        à la flamande) 418
    deer 333
    grouse 328
    lentil and black eyed peas
        curry 189
    lentil soup 160
    mullet, pan fried with ratatouille
        and sauce vierge 290
red onion 397
    and chilli peppers with
        chickpea stew 192
    marmalade with baked cam-
        embert with garlic
        ciabatta 94
    tartlet and mozzarella 94
red wine jus 122
red-legged partridge 327–8
reducing 106–7
Reform sauce 131
remoulade sauce 146
Reporting of Injuries, Diseases
    and Dangerous Occur-
    rences Regulations (RID-
    DOR) (1996) 41
restaurants 9–10, 16
restoratifs 153
reticulin 343
rhubarb and ginger fool 583
rhubarb and sour cream royal tart
    488
rice 223–41

braised with lemon and
    mustard seed 229
braised (pilaff) 228
chilli bean with sour cream
    230
Chinese crab cakes with
    mango and lime salsa
    231
deep fried balls 232
egg-fried with ham, prawns
    and vegetables 233
jambalaya 234
kedgeree 235
lamb biryani 236
lemon grass rissotto cakes
    with burnt chilli and
    crème fraîche 237
paella 238
pesto with sun-dried tomatoes
    229
preparation and cooking
    226–7
products 225–6
risotto 230
steamed basmati 228
steamed lemon rice with
    borlotti beans 190
storage 227
structure 223
stuffed plum tomatoes and
    peas 193
teriyaki beef with wild rice filo
    parcels with pickled
    cucumber 240
tiger prawn and coconut rice
    241
types 223–5
rice preparation and cooking
    226–7
braised 227
plain boiled 227
stewing 227
stir frying 227
storage 227
texture 227
rice products
    cooked 226
    ground rice 225
    liquid 226
    noodles 226
    rice flour 225
    rice paper 226
rice types
    American 225
    aromatics 224
    basmati 224
    brown long grain (wholegrain)
        224
    easy-cook long grain white
        (parboiled/converted/
        pre-fluffed) 224
    japonica 225
    jasmine (Thai fragrant rice) 225
    long grain white 224
    long grain/all purpose 223–4
    speciality 224
    wild 225
risotto 230

chicken wings with pea and
    mint risotto and garlic
    foam 316
deep fried balls 232
leek and mushroom pearl
    barley with parmesan
    crisps and black truffle
    oil 200
lemon grass cakes with burnt
    chilli and crème fraîche
    237
pea and mint with goat's
    cheese 239
roast
    beef and Yorkshire pudding
        362
    chicken English style 319
    leg of lamb 370
    pork 371
roasted
    bell pepper sauce 133
    hazelnut oil 152
    Mediterranean vegetable soup
        180
    peppers with tian of Moroccan
        spiced quinoa, bulgur
        wheat and chick peas
        with wild rocket and
        spiced chutney 204
    pollack with vegetable julienne
        and mouclade 281
robbery 50
Robert sauce 132
root vegetables 392
    beetroot 392
    carrots 392
    celeriac 392
    parsnips 392
    swede 392
    turnips 392
rosemary and onion bread 504
Ross, Ben (guest chef recipe) 451
roux 108–9
rum babas 517
runner beans 399
rye 197

salads 77–8
    à la grecque 80
    American 78
    avocado and sun blushed
        tomato and bruschetta
        93
    beetroot 80
    Caesar 81
    chicory and orange 81
    coleslaw 83
    compound 78
    cooked served cold 78
    coronation chicken 82
    couscous 82
    French 83
    French bean 83
    fruit platter 84
    green 84
    mixed 85
    mixed bean 85
    Moroccan bulgur wheat 86

Niçoise 86
    potato 87
    Russian 87
    simple 78
    tiède 78
    tomato, basil and mozzarella
        88
    tomato, cucumber and herb
        vinaigrette 88
    tropical fruit platter 89
    Waldorf 89
salmon
    darne of 268
    fish cakes with pea shoots and
        tartar sauce 285
    hot smoked jasmine and green
        tea salmon with ribbons
        of vegetables 283
    pan fried with asparagus,
        broad beans, Biarritz
        potatoes and chive
        cream sauce 284
    suprême 267
salmonella 56
salsa
    mango and lime 143
    papaya and black bean 142
    pickled ginger 143
    tomato, shallot and cucumber
        144
salsa verde 147
salt 491
samphire 404
samphire, buttered with sesame
    seeds 422
sandwiches
    bacon, lettuce and tomato
        (BLT) 98
    bookmaker 98
    closed 74–5
    club 100
    croque monsieur 100
    open or Scandinavian 74
    pumpernickel and smoked
        salmon 99
    varieties 75–6
sanitary conveniences 54
sauces
    cold 112
    hot 106
    thickened 106–12
sauces (savoury)
    aïli 140
    anchovy 124
    apple 140
    aurore 126
    Béarnaise 136
    béchamel 123
    black butter 137
    bread 134
    brown (espagnole) 129
    brown onion 129
    butter 136–7
    caper 127
    chasseur 130
    cream 124
    demi glace 130
    devilled 132

sauces (savoury) (continued)
egg 124
gribiche 141
guacamole 141
Hollandaise 136
honey and mustard dressing 141
houmous 142
Italian 132
ivory 127
Madeira/sherry/port wine/red wine 131
Madras curry 133
mayonnaise and Marie Rose 144
melted butter 137
mint raita 145
mornay 124
mushroom 128
mustard 125
nut brown butter 137
onion (soubise) 125
parsley 125
peppercorn 134
pesto 145
plum tomato coulis 134
raw tomato coulis 146
Reform 131
remoulade 146
roasted bell pepper 133
Robert 132
salsa 142–4
salse verde 147
sun-dried tomato pesto 145
suprême 128
tapenade 147
tartare 148
Thai dressing 148
Thai green curry paste 135
thousand island 146
tomato 135
velouté 126
vert (sauce verte) 148
vinaigrette 149
sauces (sweet)
butterscotch 554
caramel 554
chocolate ganache 555
crème anglaise and derivatives (English custard sauce) 550
crème chantilly 553
crème pâtissière (pastry cream) 552
custard 551
dark chocolate 553
fruit coulis 552
stock syrup 551
sauerkraut 412
sauté of pigeon with black pudding, roasted cherry tomato salad and pommes au lard 336
sauté potatoes (pommes sautées) 438
with onions (pommes lyonnaises) 438
scallops 294

served in the shell with vegetable brunoise and lemon oil 300
schools 7–8, 16–17, 22
scones 601
Scotch broth 169
scrambled eggs 254
with herbs 254
with smoked salmon 255
sea bream
grilled with modern minted pea velouté 280
Kentish, with courgette ribbons and langoustine and mussel broth 306
sea ferries 11
sea vegetables 403
agar-agar 404
arame 404
hijiki 404
kelp 404
nori 404
samphire 404
wakame 404
security 50–1
seeds and pods 398
broad beans 399
mange tout 399
okra 399
peas 399
runner beans 399
sugar snaps 399
sweetcorn 399
seitan 413
and courgette fritters 449
self-employed 3
sesame tuna with hoi sin and pak choi 286
shallot 397
shellfish 291–305
allergy 292, 619
bisque 173–5
bivalve 293–5
cephalopods 295
crab and prawn cakes with mango salsa 302
crayfish cocktail 95
crustaceans 291, 295–7
deep fried clams in peppered crumb with sauce vert 299
gastropod 293
langoustines en papilotte 300
lobster compound butter 139
lobster thermidor 304
molluscs 291
moules marinière 298
oysters cooked three ways 301
quality points 291
razor clams and chorizo, butter bean and tomato stew 305
scallops served in the shell with vegetable brunoise and lemon oil 300
seasonality 291
shrimp compound butter 139

tempura of crayfish with basil mayonnaise 303
Thai green curry tiger prawns 299
transportation and storage 292
shepherd's pie 370
shigella 56
short pastes 460–1
creaming 460
la pâte à foncer 461
la pâte à pâté 461
la pâte brisée 461
la pâte sucrée 461
lining (pâte à foncer) 463
pie (pâte à pâte) 463
rubbing-in (sablage) 460
shortcrust pastry (pâte brisée) 462
sweet (pte sucrée) 464
uses 461
shortbread biscuits 604
sieve 461
sippets 155
skate with capers and black butter 290
skimming 105
small-to medium-sized business enterprises (SMEs) 4
smoked haddock on parsley mash with quail's egg, caper and lemon sauce 256
smoked mackerel with pickled cucumber 97
smoked salmon
with classic garnish 97
with linguine, cucumber ribbons and crème fraîche 214
and pumpernickel sandwich 99
with scrambled eggs 255
wholegrain and dill blinis with crème fraîche, bitter leaves and salmon caviar 201
smoking 53–4, 58
snipe 328
soda bread 502
sole
délice of 266
paupiettes 265–6
sole proprietorship 3
soups
beef consommé 170
bisque 154
broth 153
butternut squash and coriander 157
chicken broth 168
chicken noodle with spiced dumplings 176
chicken and sweetcorn chowder 166
chowder 154
clam chowder 167
classification 153–4
cock a leekie 177

consommé 153–4
crab bisque (bisque de crebbe) 173
cream 153
cream of chicken (crème de volaille) 165
cream of spinach (crème de d'epinard) 166
Cullen skink 183
foreign 154
French onion (soupe à l'oignon) 177
garnishes and accompaniments 155–6
Gazpacho 178
green pea (potage saint germain) 164
history 153
ingredients 154–5
lobster bisque (bisque de homard) 174
minestrone 179
mushroom (purée de champignon) 158
mutton broth 168
potage paysanne 164
potato (purée parmentier) 159
prawn bisque (bisque de crevettes) 175
proprietorship, consommé 153–4
purée 153
red lentil 160
roasted mediterranean vegetable 180
Scotch broth 169
serving temperatures and quantities 156
Thai chicken 181
tomato and basil 161
tools and equipment 154
vegetable (purée de légumes) 162
velouté 153
vichyssoise 182
Southcott, Huw (guest chef recipe) 488
soya products 412–13
allergy 619
spaghetti bolognaise 221
Spanish omelette (tortilla) 255
spatchcock poussin with grain mustard compound butter 320
speciality buffet 77
spiced rock salmon (huss, smooth hound or dog fish) 623
spiced tempura quail breasts with chilli dipping jam 339
spicy pumpkin chutney 412
spinach 398
spinach cake with curried millet, pimento and leek, poached egg and minted yoghurt 202

spinach purée, creamed (purée d'epinards à la crème) 423
spinach soup (crème d'epinard) 166
sponges see cakes, biscuits and sponges
spotted dick 486
spring greens 393
spring onion 397
squid 295
staff 12
    management 12
    operational 12
    supervisory 12
staphylococcus aureus 56
starches 614
starters
    avocado salad and sun blushed tomato bruschetta 93
    baked camambert with garlic ciabatta and red onion marmalade 94
    chicken liver parfait 91
    chicken and roasted red pepper terrine 90
    crayfish cocktail 95
    gravadlax 96
    halloumi and grilled vegetables 95
    mozzarella and red onion tartlet 94
    pork satay 92
    potted duck confit 92
    seafood terrine 98
    smoked mackerel with pickled cucumber 97
    smoked salmon with classic garnish 97
    teriyaki beef 93
steak
    cooking specifications 367
    cuts 366
    garnishes and sauces 365
    and kidney pie 358
    and kidney pudding 357
    preparation of sirloin 365
steamed
    chocolate sponge pudding with chocolate sauce 535
    jam roll pudding 486
    lemon rice with borlotti beans 190
    lemon sponge pudding with lemon sauce 533
    pollack, marquise potato, bacon lardons, curly kale and dill cream sauce 282
    spotted dick pudding 486
    treacle pudding 536
    walnut sponge pudding with maple syrup 534
stems 401
    asparagus 401
    celery 401

globe artichoke 402
kohlrabi 402
sticky toffee pudding with toffee sauce 532
stir fried
    beef with oyster sauce 360
    chicken liver 385
    tofu with egg noodles 448
    vegetables 425
stock
    Asian chicken 117
    Asian fish 117
    Asian vegetable 118
    basic 104–8
    brown chicken (fond brun de volaille) 116
    brown veal/beef/lamb/game stock (fond brun de veau, estouffade, fond brun de mouton, fond brun de gibier) 116
    deglazing 105
    finishing and storage 107
    fish 113
    glazes 107–8
    oriental master stock 118
    points to consider 108
    pre-prepared 108
    quality 107
    reducing 106–7
    skimming 105
    straining and passing 105
    syrup 551
    vegetable 114
    white chicken 114
    white veal/beef/lamb/game (fond blanc de veau, boeuf, mutton, gibier) 115
stock rotation 525
storage
    area 19
    bakery items 458–9, 494, 497
    cakes, sponges and biscuits 591
    dessert ingredients 524–5
    fish 269
    food 55
    food safety 65–8
    fruit 528
    game 335
    grains 197
    pasta 212–13
    procedures 79
    puff paste (pâte à feuilletée) 467
    pulses 186
    rice 227
    stock 107
    vegetables 406
straining and passing 105
Stratton, Sean (guest chef recipe) 306
straw potatoes (pommes pailles) 437
strawberry
    bavarois (bavarois aux fraises) 569

crêpe Parisienne with strawberry compôte (crêpes Parisienne avec compôte de fraises) 543
    gâteau with fresh cream 603
    ice cream (crème glacée aux fraises) 581
stroganoff
    beef 359
    calve's liver 381
stuffed
    aubergines (aubergine farcie) 426
    mushrooms (champignons farcis) 425
    plum tomatoes with rice and peas 193
    tomatoes (tomates farcies) 427
suet 455
suet paste (pâte à grasse de boeuf) 471
sugar 456–8, 613
    caster 457
    copper boiler 526
    cube 457
    dark brown muscovado 457
    golden 457
    granulated 457
    honey 457
    icing 457
    isomalt 457–8
    liquid glucose (corn syrup) 457
    nibbed 457
    thermometer 526
sugar snaps 399
summer fruit pudding 573
sun-dried tomato
    bread 505
    oil 152
    pesto 145
suprême
    of salmon 267
    sauce 128
    of turkey wrapped in bacon with crocquette potatoes 321
    of white round fish 263
swede 392
swede purée (rutabaga purée) 431
sweet paste preparation 465
sweet potato 396
    and chick pea falafel with mint and lime dip 194
sweet and sour quorn™ 448
sweetbreads
    calves' fricassee with whisky and wholegrain mustard 382
    pan fried lamb's with rosemary and lemon butter 384
sweetcorn 399
Swiss buns 515
Swiss roll (biscuit roulade) 596

tapenade 147
tarragon bread 501
tartare sauce 148
tarts see pastes, tarts and pies
tea cakes 515
tempeh 413
temperature control 64
    chilling 64
    cooking and reheating 64–5
    cooling of foods 65
    hot holding 64
tempura of crayfish with basil mayonnaise 303
teriyaki beef 93
    with wild rice filo parcels with pickled cucumber 240
terrine 73–4
    Bath chap 102
    chicken and roasted red pepper 90
terrorism 50
Thai chicken soup 181
Thai dressing 148
Thai green curry
    paste 135
    tiger prawns 299
theft 50
Thorpe, Steve (guest chef recipe) 256
thousand island sauce 146
tiger prawns
    and coconut rice 241
    with Thai green curry 299
toad in the hole 372
tofu 413
    cajun with couscous 450
    stir fried with egg noodles 488
tomato/es 400
    aubergine and roasted vegetable cannelloni on basil bulgur wheat with pesto 204
    avocado and bruschetta salad 93
    basil and mozzarella salad 88
    and basil soup 161
    broad bean bruschetta and oregano 190
    couscous, mint, garlic, olives and cucumber with grilled halloumi cheese 204
    cucumber and herb vinaigrette 88
    plum tomato coulis 13
    raw tomato coulis 146
    sauce 135
    shallot and cucumber salsa 144
    stuffed plum tomatoes with rice and peas 193
    stuffed (tomates farcies) 427
    sun-dried tomato bread 505
    sun-dried tomato oil 152
    sun-dried tomato pesto 145
    vinaigrette 149
tools and equipment
    baking 461, 496–7

tools and equipment (*continued*)
  breads and dough 496–7
  cakes, biscuits and sponges 592
  chopping and blending 154
  cold food preparation 78–9
  desserts 525–6
  gathering 30
  identifying 29
  meat 344
  pasta making 208–9
  preparing 30
  soup making 154
tortellinis 210–11
training 15
  college based 15
  e-learning 15
  on the job 15
  training providers 15
  work placement 15
tranche mille feuille (pastry cream slice) 482–3
treacle pudding 536
treacle tart 473
trifle 578
trout poached with carrots and shallots 287
tubers 394
  potatoes 394–6
  sweet potato 396
tuilles 604
tuna with sesame, hoi sin and pak choi 286
turkey 309
  breaded escalope with chateau potatoes, sherry and morel sauce 320
  quality points 309
  suprême, wrapped in bacon with crocquette potatoes 321
turnips 392
TVP moussaka 447
TVP (textured vegetable protein) 413

vagrancy 50
vandalism 50
vanilla
  bavarois (bavarois à la vanille) 570
  ice cream (crème glacée à la vanille) 579
  ice cream with dark chocolate brownie 540
  meringue nest with vanilla ice cream (vacherin glacée au vanille) 575
  oil 152
  panna cotta with macédoine of fruit 565
  Piña colada soup with vanilla rice condé (soupe de Piña colada, riz condé) 574
  pudding soufflé 541

rice pudding with rhubarb compôte 544
soufflé (soufflé à la vanille) 546
vanilla sticks, preserved 556
veal 347
  blanquette 373
  breakdown of side of veal 348
  brown stock 116
  escalope cordon bleu 373
  quality points 347
  white stock 115
vegan 620
vegetable cooking
  al dente 408
  baking 409–10
  blanching 408
  boiling and steaming 409
  braising 411
  frying 410–11
  fully cooked 409
  grilling 411
  parboiling 408
  preserving 412
  roasting 410
  stewing 411
vegetable cuts
  brunoise 407
  finely diced onion 408
  gros brunoise 407
  jardinière 407
  julienne 407
  macédoine 407
  mirepoix 408
  paysanne 408
  sliced onion 408
vegetable fruits 400
  aubergine 400
  avocado 401
  butternut squash 401
  courgette 400
  marrow 400
  pepper 400
  pumpkin 401
  tomato 400
vegetable garnishes 155–6
vegetable pickles
  balsamic beets 412
  sauerkraut 412
  spicy pumpkin chutney 412
vegetable protein 412
  mycoprotein (quorn™) 413
  seitan 413
  soya products 412–13
vegetable/s 72–3
  brassicas/flower heads 393
  bubble and squeak 521
  bulbs 396–7
  cooking 408–12
  fungi 402–3
  introduction 389–90
  leaves 398
  moussaka 451
  nutritional importance 390–1
  preparation 406–8
  protein 412–13
  provenance 390

purchasing specifications 405–6
  roots 392
  sea 403–4
  seasonality 405
  seeds and pods 398–9
  soup (purée de légumes) 162, 180
  stems 401–2
  stir fry 425
  stock (fond de légumes) 114, 118
  storage 406
  tubers 394–6
  types 392–404
  vegetable fruits 400–1, *see also* asparagus, aubergine, broccoli, Brussels sprouts, cabbage, carrots, cauliflower, chicory, courgettes, artichoke, leeks, lettuce, mushrooms, onion, parsnips, peas, potatoes, tomatoes, red cabbage, samphire, spinach, swede,
vegetarianism 620
velouté 108
  mushroom 163
  pea 163
  sauce 126
  soup 153
venison
  bitok lyonnaise 338
  grilled 'tornedos' with pan fried foie gras 338
  jus 123
  pan roasted loin with poached Penderyn pear, parsnip purée, leak and potato cake with roasted beetroot, vine tomatoes and parsnip crisp 340
ventilation 54
vert sauce (sauce verte) 148
Vichy carrots (carottes Vichy) 428
vichyssoise 182
Victoria sandwich 603
Victorian fruit cake 602
vinaigrette 149
  balsamic split 149
  emulsified (French) 149
  tomato 149
visitor attractions 10
vitamins 390–1
  A (retinol) 391
  B1 (thiamine) 391
  B2 (riboflavin) 391
  B3 (niacin) 391
  B5 (pantothenic acid) 391
  B6 (pyridoxine) 391
  beta-carotene 391
  biotin 391
  C (ascorbic acid) 391

E (tocopherols) 391
  folate 391
vol-au-vents 481

wakame 404
Waldorf salad 89
walnut oil 152
walnut sponge pudding with maple syrup 534
warning signs 46
washing facilities 54
water 490
watercress 398
Welsh (buck) rarebit 99
wheat 196
  allergy 619
  bulgur 196
  couscous 196
  semolina 196
whelks 293
white cabbage 393
white chicken stock (fond blac de volaille) 114
white veal/beef/lamb/game stock (fond blanc de veau, boeuf, mutton, gibier) 115
whiting, baked with herb crust and cream sauce 277
wild boar 333
wild rabbit 330–1
winkles 293
wood pigeon 328–9
work area hygiene 58
  cleaning and maintaining equipment 59–60
  cleaning products 62
  controlling cross contamination 59
  kitchen cloths 61
  knives, spoons and other utensils 61–2
  pest control 62
  reporting of maintenance issues 59
  worktops and chopping boards 60–1
Working Time Directive (1998) 15
Workplace Exposure Limits (WEL) 43
Workplace (Health, Safety and Welfare) Regulations (1992) 42
workplace skills 27–32
  action plans 28–9
  colleagues and customers 30–1
  communication 31–2
  development 36–8
  measuring ingredients accurately 30
  practising good sanitation 30
  reading recipe carefully 29
  tools and equipment 29–30

yeast 492–3
yoghurt *see* cream and yoghurt
Yorkshire pudding 362